C000149952

THE BREEDON BOOK OF

PREMIERSHIP RECORDS

THE BREEDON BOOK OF

PREMIERSHIP RECORDS

The first comprehensive month-by-month review of every Premiership season since its inception, with results, player's records, pictures, league tables, transfers and statistics.

Brian Beard

books
PUBLISHING

First published in Great Britain in 2004 by
The Breedon Books Publishing Company Limited
Breedon House, 3 The Parker Centre,
Derby, DE21 4SZ.

© Brian Beard, 2004

All Rights Reserved. No part of this publication may be reproduced, stored in a retrieval system, or transmitted in any form, or by any means, electronic, mechanical, photocopying, recording or otherwise without the prior permission in writing of the copyright holders, nor be otherwise circulated in any form or binding or cover other than in which it is published and without a similar condition being imposed on the subsequent publisher.

Dedication

I would like to dedicate this book to my father, Gerald, my mother, Vera and my sister, Lorraine. I think they would be as proud of it as I am.

Acknowledgements

Bozenka, Ben and Sam, for their support and understanding during a frenetic six months.
Martin Tyler, for his support and contribution of a superb foreword.
John Richardson (*Sunday Express*), for his objective and expert assistance.
Research for the book has been made considerably easier thanks to the excellent Rothmans and Sky Sports Football Year Books, among other publications. I have also accessed countless helpful Internet sites.
Steve and Susan, they know who they are, for their faith in the project.

Publisher's acknowledgements

The publishers would like to thank Tony Brown, of soccerdata.com, for providing the tables and statistics used in this book.
All photographs © EMPICS.

ISBN 1 85983 419 1

Printed and bound by Scotprint, Gateside Commerce Park, Haddington, East Lothian, Scotland.

Contents

Foreword

Martin Tyler
Senior Football Commentator, Sky Sports

THE DATE – 16 August 1992. The place – the City Ground, home of Nottingham Forest FC. The scene – a group of television professionals who specialise in football collectively holding their breath as the opening titles rolled for Sky Sports' first live transmission of Premier League football: Brian Clough's Forest against Liverpool under the management of Graeme Souness.

If you remember it well the chances are that you have seen those formative moments on one of our nostalgia shows in the intervening years. The viewing figure on that actual day was far shy of the millions who tune in now. Richard Keys cut a dash in jackets of bold colours. Andy Gray was an ex-player by only a couple of years. The scorer of the only goal, Teddy Sheringham, was still hitting the target on the last day of the 12th Premiership campaign in May 2004 – although that very first Premier League weekend produced what turned out to be his only goal in the new league for the East Midlands club.

It was the start of a great adventure, the forging of a new partnership between the game's administrators and a television broadcaster.

I am delighted to say that the fortunes of both parties and that unique relationship have gone from strength to strength. There will always be those who debate the relative technical merits of the best domestic football in Italy and Spain, and even Germany, compared to the English product. I have never doubted that football in this country offers the best value for money, both for paying customers at the grounds and for television subscribers. The huge amount of worldwide sales of Premiership matches also supports this belief.

The ability to scour the world for the best talent available has been the major change since the new format was introduced. The Premiership winners nowadays would give any top international side a good game because they are now international sides themselves at club level.

The game is even more athletic than it used to be, though I still subscribe to the old saying that the criteria by which to judge a footballer should be 'can he play?' not just 'can he run?' Most Premiership performers can do both, extremely well. Painstakingly I prepare pages of notes for each commentary but rarely do I have time to peek at them during a match. You look away from the breathtakingly quick action at your peril.

Over the dozen Premiership years covered by this book which Brian Beard has so diligently researched Sky Sports has shown 738 matches live. Live football in this type of deal has supported the industry so much that at the League's request a fresh television package means even more games on your screens.

I have been lucky to have broadcast many enthralling contests but the one which has always stood out for me was the 4–3 in April 1996 between Liverpool and Newcastle. It had all the qualities which hook the millions of addicts to this glorious game, a rollercoaster ride of an evening that even had Kevin Keegan, the losing manager in a title chase that night as well as the loser of an extraordinary match, proclaiming that he had been thrilled to be involved.

I have been thrilled to be involved as one of the bridges between the Premier League grounds, (and by the way how they have improved as well) and you, the Premier League fans.

The last 12 years have flashed by at such a rate that it is a pleasure to take a look back in a more leisurely fashion by perusing the pages ahead.

Section 1
Season Reviews

Introduction

WHAT BEGAN as a labour of love soon evolved into a labour of Hercules, although cleaning the Augean stables would have been child's play compared to sussing out weekly and monthly movements in the Premier League tables over 12 seasons. I soon realised all those references to the fictitious essay title 'God, discuss' weren't as fanciful as I once thought and were, indeed, highly appropriate in this particular undertaking.

The work involved in tracking and logging the changes at both ends of the Premier League table at least had me yearning for the very tome I was trying to compile, thus justifying the exercise.

My task was made easier, and I use the word 'easier' in a relative context, by Rothmans, now Sky Sports Football Year Book, and the wonder that is the world wide web. Not to mention a dozen years of yellowing newspaper cuttings gathering dust in the attic, hundreds of old football magazines, and piles of programmes from 20 years of match coverage as a journalist, that encompassed many of the games contained within this book.

Hopefully the following pages will satisfy, and bring pleasure to, Premiership followers, from stattos to those who like a good football read.

Putting this record together brought me copious amounts of pleasure and satisfaction, especially now it`s done. Here's to the next 12 years.

Brian Beard, August 2004.

Preparing for the Premiership – summer 1992

Liverpool sign David James from Watford and the club also sack Phil Thompson from his post as reserve team coach.

Don Howe resigns as Coventry manager and is succeeded by the man who was joint manager along with him, Bobby Gould.

For the forthcoming season Premier League referees will be men in green instead of men in black and three substitutes will be permitted, one a goalkeeper, for Premiership matches. The half-time interval is to be 15 minutes.

Middlesbrough winger Stuart Ripley joins Blackburn for £1.3 million and Arsenal pay Brondby £1.1 million for John Jensen. Harry Redknapp joins his former teammate, Billy Bonds, as assistant manager at West Ham.

All Premier League and Football League managers are invited to a seminar to discuss interpretations of the new FIFA ruling concerning the back pass rule.

David Rocastle leaves Arsenal for Leeds for £2 million and referees reject BSkyB's plans to have them wired so they can announce their decisions.

Alan Shearer sets a new British record when he moves from Southampton to Blackburn for £3.6 million while Liverpool pay £2.3 million for Spurs midfielder Paul Stewart.

The Football Association are to introduce compulsory random drug-testing, starting season 1993–94.

Eric Cantona scores a hat-trick as Leeds United beat Liverpool 4–3 in the Charity Shield and Chelsea pay a club-record £2.1 million for Norwich striker Robert Fleck.

Danish international, Jon Jensen, joins Arsenal before the inaugural Premiership season kicks off.

Eric Cantona (Leeds) scores the third goal against Liverpool in the 1992 Charity Shield match.

August

Saturday 15 August	
Arsenal v. Norwich City	2-4
Chelsea v. Oldham Athletic	1-1
Coventry City v. Middlesbrough	2-1
Crystal Palace v. Blackburn Rovers	3-3
Everton v. Sheffield Wed.	1-1
Ipswich Town v. Aston Villa	1-1
Leeds United v. Wimbledon	2-1
Sheffield United v. Manchester United	2-1
Southampton v. Tottenham Hotspur	0-0
Sunday 16 August	
Nottingham Forest v. Liverpool	1-0
Monday 17 August	
Manchester City v. Queen's Park R.	1-1
Tuesday 18 August	
Blackburn Rovers v. Arsenal	1-0
Wimbledon v. Ipswich Town	0-1
Wednesday 19 August	
Aston Villa v. Leeds United	1-1
Liverpool v. Sheffield United	2-1
Manchester United v. Everton	0-3
Middlesbrough v. Manchester City	2-0
Norwich City v. Chelsea	2-1
Oldham Athletic v. Crystal Palace	1-1
Queen's Park R. v. Southampton	3-1
Sheffield Wed. v. Nottingham Forest	2-0
Tottenham Hotspur v. Coventry City	0-2
Saturday 22 August	
Aston Villa v. Southampton	1-1
Blackburn Rovers v. Manchester City	1-0
Manchester United v. Ipswich Town	1-1
Middlesbrough v. Leeds United	4-1
Norwich City v. Everton	1-1
Oldham Athletic v. Nottingham Forest	5-3
Queen's Park R. v. Sheffield United	3-2
Sheffield Wed. v. Chelsea	3-3
Tottenham Hotspur v. Crystal Palace	2-2
Wimbledon v. Coventry City	1-2
Sunday 23 August	
Liverpool v. Arsenal	0-2
Monday 24 August	
Southampton v. Manchester United	0-1
Tuesday 25 August	
Crystal Palace v. Sheffield Wed.	1-1
Everton v. Aston Villa	1-0
Ipswich Town v. Liverpool	2-2
Leeds United v. Tottenham Hotspur	5-0
Sheffield United v. Wimbledon	2-2
Wednesday 26 August	
Arsenal v. Oldham Athletic	2-0
Chelsea v. Blackburn Rovers	0-0
Coventry City v. Queen's Park R.	0-1
Manchester City v. Norwich City	3-1
Saturday 29 August	
Arsenal v. Sheffield Wed.	2-1
Chelsea v. Queen's Park R.	1-0
Coventry City v. Blackburn Rovers	0-2
Crystal Palace v. Norwich City	1-2
Everton v. Wimbledon	0-0
Leeds United v. Liverpool	2-2
Manchester City v. Oldham Athletic	3-3
Nottingham Forest v. Manchester United	0-2
Sheffield United v. Aston Villa	0-2
Southampton v. Middlesbrough	2-1
Sunday 30 August	
Ipswich Town v. Tottenham Hotspur	1-1
Monday 31 August	
Norwich City v. Nottingham Forest	3-1

		P	W	D	L	F	A	Pts
1	Norwich City	6	4	1	1	13	9	13
2	Blackburn Rovers	5	3	2	0	7	3	11
3	Queen's Park R.	5	3	1	1	8	5	10
4	Everton	5	2	3	0	6	2	9
5	Arsenal	5	3	0	2	8	6	9
6	Coventry City	5	3	0	2	6	5	9
7	Leeds United	5	2	2	1	11	8	8
8	Ipswich Town	5	1	4	0	6	5	7
9	Manchester United	5	2	1	2	5	6	7
10	Middlesbrough	4	2	0	2	8	5	6
11	Sheffield Wed.	5	1	3	1	8	7	6
12	Aston Villa	5	1	3	1	5	4	6
13	Oldham Athletic	5	1	3	1	10	10	6
14	Chelsea	5	1	3	1	6	6	6
15	Manchester City	5	1	2	2	7	8	5
16	Liverpool	5	1	2	2	6	8	5
17	Southampton	5	1	2	2	4	6	5
18	Crystal Palace	5	0	4	1	8	9	4
19	Sheffield United	5	1	1	3	7	10	4
20	Nottingham Forest	5	1	0	4	5	12	3
21	Tottenham Hotspur	5	0	3	2	3	10	3
22	Wimbledon	5	0	2	3	4	7	2

Sheffield United's Brian Deane scores the first goal in the Premiership.

THE NEW FA Premier League kicks off with a surprise home defeat for title favourites Arsenal, after they lead 2–0, but it's Brian Deane who makes history by netting the first-ever Premiership goal, after five minutes, when Sheffield United open up with a win over Manchester United. Teddy Sheringham snatches his own slice of Premiership history when, in the very first BSkyB televised game, he scores the goal that beats Liverpool, and the first evening game, on Sky, sees a draw between Manchester City and QPR. Alan Shearer scores Blackburn's first Premiership goal to beat Arsenal but then Norwich go top on goal difference from Coventry, as the only teams with a 100 percent record after two games.

Manchester United's new £1 million arrival from Cambridge United, Dion Dublin, gets his first goal for the club to secure a first win of the campaign and the other Manchester club set a new British record for a full-back when they pay Wimbledon £2.5 million for Terry Phelan.

Leeds, with the help of the first Premiership hat-trick from Eric Cantona, swamp Spurs to go third. The Football Association charge Gordon Durie with misconduct after he feigns injury in an attempt to get an opponent sent off, in the first case of its kind. But his three-match suspension is overturned on appeal. QPR go top when an Andy Impey goal gives them the points at previous leaders Coventry and Spurs sign Teddy Sheringham from Forest for £2.1 million.

Coventry lose again at home and unbeaten Blackburn go top as a consequence of the win in which Alan Shearer gets a fourth goal of the season with his first penalty, because QPR go down at Chelsea. A Jason Cundy goal earns Spurs a draw at Ipswich and takes them off the bottom. Nottingham Forest's fourth consecutive defeat, to Norwich, drops them to 20th as Brian Clough endures the worst start to a season in his career. But the Canaries are singing because they go top as a consequence.

Jason Cundy's goal lifts Tottenham off the bottom.

Tuesday 1 September

Liverpool v. Southampton	1-1
Middlesbrough v. Ipswich Town	2-2
Oldham Athletic v. Leeds United	2-2
Wimbledon v. Manchester City	0-1

Wednesday 2 September

Aston Villa v. Chelsea	1-3
Manchester United v. Crystal Palace	1-0
Queen's Park R. v. Arsenal	0-0
Sheffield Wed. v. Coventry City	1-2
Tottenham Hotspur v. Sheffield United	2-0

Saturday 5 September

Aston Villa v. Crystal Palace	3-0
Blackburn Rovers v. Nottingham Forest	4-1
Liverpool v. Chelsea	2-1
Middlesbrough v. Sheffield United	2-0
Norwich City v. Southampton	1-0
Oldham Athletic v. Coventry City	0-1
Queen's Park R. v. Ipswich Town	0-0
Sheffield Wed. v. Manchester City	0-3
Tottenham Hotspur v. Everton	2-1
Wimbledon v. Arsenal	3-2

Sunday 6 September

Manchester United v. Leeds United	2-0

Saturday 12 September

Arsenal v. Blackburn Rovers	0-1
Chelsea v. Norwich City	2-3
Crystal Palace v. Oldham Athletic	2-2
Everton v. Manchester United	0-2
Ipswich Town v. Wimbledon	2-1
Manchester City v. Middlesbrough	0-1
Nottingham Forest v. Sheffield Wed.	1-2
Sheffield United v. Liverpool	1-0
Southampton v. Queen's Park R.	1-2

Sunday 13 September

Leeds United v. Aston Villa	1-1

Monday 14 September

Coventry City v. Tottenham Hotspur	1-0

Tuesday 15 September

Blackburn Rovers v. Everton	2-3

Saturday 19 September

Aston Villa v. Liverpool	4-2
Everton v. Crystal Palace	0-2
Norwich City v. Sheffield Wed.	1-0
Oldham Athletic v. Ipswich Town	4-2
Queen's Park R. v. Middlesbrough	3-3
Sheffield United v. Arsenal	1-1
Southampton v. Leeds United	1-1
Tottenham Hotspur v. Manchester United	1-1
Wimbledon v. Blackburn Rovers	1-1

Sunday 20 September

Manchester City v. Chelsea	0-1

Monday 21 September

Nottingham Forest v. Coventry City	1-1

Saturday 26 September

Blackburn Rovers v. Oldham Athletic	2-0
Chelsea v. Nottingham Forest	0-0
Coventry City v. Norwich City	1-1
Crystal Palace v. Southampton	1-2
Ipswich Town v. Sheffield United	0-0
Leeds United v. Everton	2-0
Liverpool v. Wimbledon	2-3
Manchester United v. Queen's Park R.	0-0
Middlesbrough v. Aston Villa	2-3

Sunday 27 September

Sheffield Wed. v. Tottenham Hotspur	2-0

Monday 28 September

Arsenal v. Manchester City	1-0

		P	W	D	L	F	A	Pts
1	Norwich City	10	7	2	1	19	12	23
2	Blackburn Rovers	10	6	3	1	17	8	21
3	Coventry City	10	6	2	2	12	8	20
4	Manchester United	10	5	3	2	11	7	18
5	Queen's Park R.	10	4	5	1	13	9	17
6	Aston Villa	10	4	4	2	17	12	16
7	Middlesbrough	9	4	2	3	18	13	14
8	Leeds United	10	3	5	2	17	14	14
9	Arsenal	10	4	2	4	12	11	14
10	Chelsea	10	3	4	3	13	12	13
11	Ipswich Town	10	2	7	1	12	12	13
12	Sheffield Wed.	10	3	3	4	13	14	12
13	Everton	10	3	3	4	10	12	12
14	Manchester City	10	3	2	5	11	11	11
15	Oldham Athletic	10	2	5	3	18	19	11
16	Southampton	10	2	4	4	9	12	10
17	Tottenham Hotspur	10	2	4	4	8	15	10
18	Wimbledon	10	2	3	5	12	15	9
19	Liverpool	10	2	3	5	13	18	9
20	Sheffield United	10	2	3	5	9	15	9
21	Crystal Palace	10	1	5	4	13	17	8
22	Nottingham Forest	9	1	2	6	8	19	5

A COUPLE of firsts come at the beginning of the month as Liverpool celebrate the opening of their new Centenary Stand with a draw against Southampton. Former Chelsea legend Kerry Dixon claims his first goal for the Saints and ex-Southampton defender Mark Wright nets his first league goal for Liverpool. But there is heartache for Manchester United's Dion Dublin. Just over a week after scoring his first goal for the club he breaks his leg against Crystal Palace.

In the match between last year's winners of the old Football League First Division, Leeds United, and Manchester United, the latter emerge as victors thanks to goals from Steve Bruce and Andrei Kanchelskis.

Mark Robins takes his total to six goals in six games as his brace is at the heart of Norwich's comeback from 2–0 down to beat Chelsea, and the Canaries go two points clear at the top of the table. Blackburn secure second place with victory at Arsenal but at the foot of the table the warning signs get clearer for Nottingham Forest, who lose their opening two games of the month and extend their winless run to six as they hit the foot of the table.

Leeds maintain their unbeaten home record but it takes a late Steve Hodge goal to deny Aston Villa a second away win of the campaign. Coventry complete an early season double over Spurs and it's all down to John Williams. The burly striker got both goals in last month's win at White Hart Lane and completes his 'hat-trick' with the only goal at Highfield Road to take City second.

Norwich maintain the unfancied clubs' domination of the top of the table when they go four points clear by beating Sheffield Wednesday and that position is strengthened when second-placed Coventry are held by Nottingham Forest to arrest a run of six consecutive defeats. Forest then hold Chelsea but remain bottom. The Sky Blues hold the league leaders and Blackburn beat Oldham to move above Coventry, just two points behind the Canaries.

At the other end of the table second from bottom Wimbledon shock Liverpool at Anfield and move up to 17th. Sheffield United drop to 19th despite holding Arsenal and end the month 20th despite a draw at Ipswich five days later. Southampton, who were 20th after their draw with Leeds, end September in 16th place following their victory at Crystal Palace, who occupy the second from bottom slot going into the third month of the inaugural Premiership campaign.

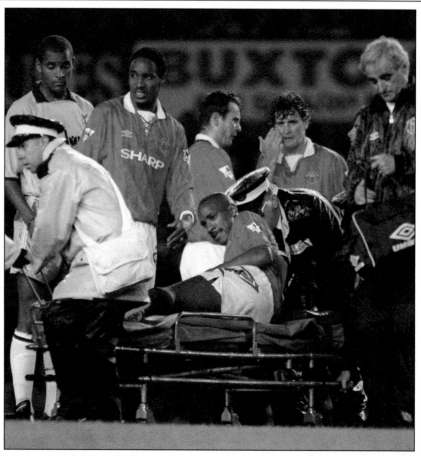

Manchester United's Dion Dublin (centre) is helped on to a stretcher after breaking his leg.

Saturday 3 October	
Arsenal v. Chelsea	2-1
Blackburn Rovers v. Norwich City	7-1
Coventry City v. Crystal Palace	2-2
Ipswich Town v. Leeds United	4-2
Liverpool v. Sheffield Wed.	1-0
Manchester City v. Nottingham Forest	2-2
Middlesbrough v. Manchester United	1-1
Queen's Park R. v. Tottenham Hotspur	4-1
Sheffield United v. Southampton	2-0
Wimbledon v. Aston Villa	2-3
Sunday 4 October	
Oldham Athletic v. Everton	1-0
Saturday 17 October	
Chelsea v. Ipswich Town	2-1
Crystal Palace v. Manchester City	0-0
Everton v. Coventry City	1-1
Leeds United v. Sheffield United	3-1
Norwich City v. Queen's Park R.	2-1
Nottingham Forest v. Arsenal	0-1
Sheffield Wed. v. Oldham Athletic	2-1
Southampton v. Wimbledon	2-2
Tottenham Hotspur v. Middlesbrough	2-2
Sunday 18 October	
Manchester United v. Liverpool	2-2
Monday 19 October	
Aston Villa v. Blackburn Rovers	0-0
Wednesday 21 October	
Nottingham Forest v. Middlesbrough	1-0
Saturday 24 October	
Arsenal v. Everton	2-0
Blackburn Rovers v. Manchester United	0-0
Coventry City v. Chelsea	1-2
Ipswich Town v. Crystal Palace	2-2
Manchester City v. Southampton	1-0
Middlesbrough v. Sheffield Wed.	1-1
Oldham Athletic v. Aston Villa	1-1
Queen's Park R. v. Leeds United	2-1
Sheffield United v. Nottingham Forest	0-0
Sunday 25 October	
Liverpool v. Norwich City	4-1
Wimbledon v. Tottenham Hotspur	1-1
Saturday 31 October	
Chelsea v. Sheffield United	1-2
Everton v. Manchester City	1-3
Leeds United v. Coventry City	2-2
Manchester United v. Wimbledon	0-1
Norwich City v. Middlesbrough	1-1
Nottingham Forest v. Ipswich Town	0-1
Sheffield Wed. v. Blackburn Rovers	0-0
Southampton v. Oldham Athletic	1-0
Tottenham Hotspur v. Liverpool	2-0

		P	W	D	L	F	A	Pts
1	Blackburn Rovers	14	7	6	1	24	9	27
2	Norwich City	14	8	3	3	24	25	27
3	Queen's Park R.	13	6	5	2	20	13	23
4	Arsenal	13	7	2	4	17	12	23
5	Coventry City	14	6	5	3	18	15	23
6	Aston Villa	13	5	6	2	21	15	21
7	Manchester United	14	5	6	3	14	11	21
8	Ipswich Town	14	4	8	2	20	18	20
9	Manchester City	14	5	4	5	17	14	19
10	Chelsea	14	5	4	5	19	18	19
11	Middlesbrough	14	4	6	4	23	19	18
12	Leeds United	14	4	6	4	25	23	18
13	Sheffield Wed.	14	4	5	5	16	17	17
14	Liverpool	14	4	4	6	20	23	16
15	Sheffield United	14	4	4	6	14	19	16
16	Oldham Athletic	14	3	6	5	21	23	15
17	Tottenham Hotspur	14	3	6	5	14	22	15
18	Wimbledon	14	3	5	6	18	21	14
19	Southampton	14	3	5	6	12	17	14
20	Everton	14	3	4	7	12	19	13
21	Crystal Palace	13	1	8	4	17	21	11
22	Nottingham Forest	14	2	4	8	11	23	10

Liverpool's Ian Rush celebrates his record goal.

LEAGUE-LEADERS Norwich are thrashed at Blackburn and US international Roy Wegerle gets two, his first goals of the season, as Rovers take over at the top. A fortnight later, after the internationals, Norwich recover top spot by beating QPR. Ian Rush beats Roger Hunt's Liverpool scoring record when he scores his 287th goal, away against Manchester United, but a pair of late Mark Hughes goals earn United a draw.

Alex Ferguson's team then draw at Ewood Park but Blackburn still go top and

Norwich are unable to close the gap as they are swamped at Liverpool and the month ends poorly for the Canaries, who then draw with Middlesbrough.

Ironically, at the foot of the table, Nottingham Forest's only win in October is against 'Boro and a Hallowe'en defeat by Ipswich leaves Brian Clough's team floundering in 22nd place. Crystal Palace, despite three draws, end the month in 21st place, and Everton slump to 20th following their defeats by Arsenal and Manchester City. Southampton are 19th

despite claiming their only win of the month, against Oldham.

There's a little financial jousting off the field as the FA Premier League decides to contest a writ for more than £2 million against chief executive Rick Parry by the Swiss Bank Corporation, who are claiming commission that is owed for the BSkyB television contract.

Blackburn Rovers and Norwich maintain their places at the top of the table with draws at Sheffield Wednesday and home to Middlesbrough respectively.

November

Sunday 1 November		
Aston Villa v. Queen's Park R.	2-0	
Monday 2 November		
Crystal Palace v. Arsenal	1-2	
Saturday 7 November		
Arsenal v. Coventry City	3-0	
Aston Villa v. Manchester United	1-0	
Blackburn Rovers v. Tottenham Hotspur	0-2	
Chelsea v. Crystal Palace	3-1	
Ipswich Town v. Southampton	0-0	
Liverpool v. Middlesbrough	4-1	
Manchester City v. Leeds United	4-0	
Nottingham Forest v. Everton	0-1	
Wimbledon v. Queen's Park R.	0-2	
Sunday 8 November		
Sheffield United v. Sheffield Wed.	1-1	
Monday 9 November		
Oldham Athletic v. Norwich City	2-3	
Saturday 21 November		
Coventry City v. Manchester City	2-3	
Crystal Palace v. Nottingham Forest	1-1	
Everton v. Chelsea	0-1	
Leeds United v. Arsenal	3-0	
Manchester United v. Oldham Athletic	3-0	
Middlesbrough v. Wimbledon	2-0	
Norwich City v. Sheffield United	2-1	
Sheffield Wed. v. Ipswich Town	1-1	
Tottenham Hotspur v. Aston Villa	0-0	
Sunday 22 November		
Southampton v. Blackburn Rovers	1-1	
Monday 23 November		
Queen's Park R. v. Liverpool	0-1	
Saturday 28 November		
Arsenal v. Manchester United	0-1	
Aston Villa v. Norwich City	2-3	
Blackburn Rovers v. Queen's Park R.	1-0	
Ipswich Town v. Everton	1-0	
Liverpool v. Crystal Palace	5-0	
Manchester City v. Tottenham Hotspur	0-1	
Nottingham Forest v. Southampton	1-2	
Oldham Athletic v. Middlesbrough	4-1	
Sheffield United v. Coventry City	1-1	
Wimbledon v. Sheffield Wed.	1-1	
Sunday 29 November		
Chelsea v. Leeds United	1-0	

		P	W	D	L	F	A	Pts
1	Norwich City	17	11	3	3	32	30	36
2	Blackburn Rovers	17	8	7	2	26	12	31
3	Arsenal	17	9	2	6	22	17	29
4	Aston Villa	17	7	7	3	26	18	28
5	Chelsea	17	8	4	5	24	19	28
6	Manchester United	17	7	6	4	18	12	27
7	Queen's Park R.	17	7	5	5	22	17	26
8	Manchester City	17	7	4	6	24	17	25
9	Liverpool	17	7	4	6	30	24	25
10	Ipswich Town	17	5	10	2	22	19	25
11	Coventry City	17	6	6	5	21	22	24
12	Tottenham Hotspur	17	5	7	5	17	22	22
13	Leeds United	17	5	6	6	28	28	21
14	Middlesbrough	17	5	6	6	27	27	21
15	Sheffield Wed.	17	4	8	5	19	20	20
16	Southampton	17	4	7	6	15	19	19
17	Oldham Athletic	17	4	6	7	27	30	18
18	Sheffield United	17	4	6	7	17	23	18
19	Everton	17	4	4	9	13	21	16
20	Wimbledon	17	3	6	8	19	26	15
21	Crystal Palace	17	1	9	7	20	32	12
22	Nottingham Forest	17	2	5	10	13	27	11

Wimbledon's Vinnie Jones shows off his tattoo.

ARSENAL go top when victories over Crystal Palace and Coventry extend their winning run to six and Ian Wright scores for the third consecutive game. Blackburn lose pole position because of a home defeat to Spurs and Liverpool's mid-table win over Middlesbrough is notable for Ian Rush's 200th league goal. But Arsenal's tenure at the top is short-lived as Norwich reclaim the pinnacle on the back of a Mark Robins hat-trick that downs Oldham: Robins completes his triple in the final minute. Norwich are top with a zero goal difference: 27 scored, 27 conceded.

As Premiership football takes a break for the World Cup qualifiers, Vinnie Jones finds himself £20,000 lighter as the FA impose a record fine for bringing the game into disrepute for his video compilation *Soccer's Hard Men.* Jones also receives a six-month suspension, suspended for six months.

Norwich go four points clear at the top by beating Sheffield United and Arsenal's winning streak is ended by defeat at Leeds. Good news for Liverpool is the return of John Barnes, after a six-month absence, and he stars in the win at QPR that moves them up the table. Off the field the news is made with Alex Ferguson's surprise £1.2 million swoop for Eric Cantona in an attempt to kick-start United's title hopes – they languish in eighth place. The signing is pivotal in the fortunes of both teams as Leeds struggle for the duration of the campaign while United's season just gets better. Norwich just get on with the job and with four months of the season gone show no signs of weakening. The Canaries end the month five points clear after their fifth away win, at Villa. It's Villa's first defeat in 13 games and everyone starts to take the Canaries' title potential seriously.

Alan Shearer's 13th goal of the season, to beat QPR, sees Blackburn second, while Arsenal's defeat by Manchester United drops the Gunners to third.

At the foot of the Premiership table Crystal Palace's single point from this month's games, in a draw with Forest, means they enter December still in 21st place. Forest stay bottom while Wimbledon, who also manage just a single November point, are 20th.

December

Saturday 5 December

Coventry City v. Ipswich Town	2-2
Crystal Palace v. Sheffield United	2-0
Leeds United v. Nottingham Forest	1-4
Middlesbrough v. Blackburn Rovers	3-2
Norwich City v. Wimbledon	2-1
Queen's Park R. v. Oldham Athletic	3-2
Sheffield Wed. v. Aston Villa	1-2
Southampton v. Arsenal	2-0
Tottenham Hotspur v. Chelsea	1-2

Sunday 6 December

Manchester United v. Manchester City	2-1

Monday 7 December

Everton v. Liverpool	2-1

Friday 11 December

Middlesbrough v. Chelsea	0-0

Saturday 12 December

Aston Villa v. Nottingham Forest	2-1
Ipswich Town v. Manchester City	3-1
Leeds United v. Sheffield Wed.	3-1
Manchester United v. Norwich City	1-0
Queen's Park R. v. Crystal Palace	1-3
Sheffield United v. Everton	1-0
Southampton v. Coventry City	2-2
Tottenham Hotspur v. Arsenal	1-0
Wimbledon v. Oldham Athletic	5-2

Sunday 13 December

Liverpool v. Blackburn Rovers	2-1

Saturday 19 December

Arsenal v. Middlesbrough	1-1
Blackburn Rovers v. Sheffield United	1-0
Chelsea v. Manchester United	1-1
Coventry City v. Liverpool	5-1
Everton v. Southampton	2-1
Manchester City v. Aston Villa	1-1
Oldham Athletic v. Tottenham Hotspur	2-1
Sheffield Wed. v. Queen's Park R.	1-0

Sunday 20 December

Crystal Palace v. Leeds United	1-0
Nottingham Forest v. Wimbledon	1-1

Monday 21 December

Norwich City v. Ipswich Town	0-2

Saturday 26 December

Arsenal v. Ipswich Town	0-0
Blackburn Rovers v. Leeds United	3-1
Chelsea v. Southampton	1-1
Coventry City v. Aston Villa	3-0
Crystal Palace v. Wimbledon	2-0
Everton v. Middlesbrough	2-2
Manchester City v. Sheffield United	2-0
Norwich City v. Tottenham Hotspur	0-0
Sheffield Wed. v. Manchester United	3-3

Monday 28 December

Aston Villa v. Arsenal	1-0
Ipswich Town v. Blackburn Rovers	2-1
Leeds United v. Norwich City	0-0
Liverpool v. Manchester City	1-1
Manchester United v. Coventry City	5-0
Middlesbrough v. Crystal Palace	0-1
Queen's Park R. v. Everton	4-2
Southampton v. Sheffield Wed.	1-2
Tottenham Hotspur v. Nottingham Forest	2-1
Wimbledon v. Chelsea	0-0

		P	W	D	L	F	A	Pts
1	Norwich City	22	12	5	5	34	34	41
2	Manchester United	22	10	8	4	30	17	38
3	Aston Villa	22	10	8	4	32	24	38
4	Blackburn Rovers	22	10	7	5	34	20	37
5	Ipswich Town	22	8	12	2	31	23	36
6	Chelsea	22	9	8	5	28	22	35
7	Queen's Park R.	21	9	5	7	30	25	32
8	Coventry City	22	8	8	6	33	32	32
9	Arsenal	22	9	4	9	23	22	31
10	Manchester City	22	8	6	8	30	24	30
11	Liverpool	21	8	5	8	35	33	29
12	Tottenham Hotspur	22	7	8	7	22	27	29
13	Middlesbrough	22	6	9	7	33	33	27
14	Sheffield Wed.	22	6	9	7	27	29	27
15	Crystal Palace	22	6	9	7	29	33	27
16	Leeds United	22	6	7	9	33	37	25
17	Southampton	22	5	9	8	22	26	24
18	Everton	22	6	5	11	21	30	23
19	Oldham Athletic	20	5	6	9	33	39	21
20	Sheffield United	21	5	6	10	18	28	21
21	Wimbledon	22	4	8	10	26	33	20
22	Nottingham Forest	21	3	6	12	20	33	15

Roy Keane gets on the scoresheet as Forest crush Leeds.

NORWICH continue to lord it over the elite when they go eight points clear by coming from a goal down to beat Wimbledon in the last 13 minutes. Blackburn slip up and lose at Middlesbrough to a John Hendrie hat-trick. At the other end of the table there are a couple of firsts when Nottingham Forest claim their first win in six games by beating Leeds United, that club's first home defeat since 13 April 1991.

Manchester United move into gear, and third place, when they prevent Norwich from extending their winning sequence to five with Mark Hughes scoring the only goal of the game, but City stay top. Blackburn lose a second game in a row, for the first time in the campaign, when they lose at Liverpool.

The FA Premier League announces a three-year £3 million deal with Lucozade Sport and Liverpool could have done with an energy infusion as they crash to their worst defeat since 1976, at Coventry, where Scousers Micky Quinn and Brian Borrows do the damage with two goals each. To make matters worse for the Anfield team, Jamie Redknapp is sent off.

East Anglian neighbours Ipswich end Norwich's unbeaten home record and move into sixth place as a consequence. Although the Canaries remain top there is a note of caution, as far as championship potential is concerned, as once again the goal tables show parity: 34 scored but 34 conceded.

Manchester United move from fourth to second after the Christmas programme sees them pick up two away draws before ending the year with a thrashing of Coventry City in which Eric Cantona scores his first penalty for United, who are now just three points behind Norwich, who

draw with Leeds. Defeat at Ipswich, who drop to fifth, sees Blackburn end the year down in fourth place. A first goal in eight games for Dean Saunders, a penalty, beats Arsenal and Aston Villa move into third place, where they see in the New Year.

Down in the basement Oldham beat Spurs to move out of the relegation zone but are soon leapfrogged by Everton, who draw against 'Boro but crash to QPR. Crystal Palace, who began the month in 21st place, end the year with an astonishing run of five consecutive wins to reach 15th.

But there is no respite for Nottingham Forest, who end 1992 in 22nd place after their defeat at Spurs means they enter the New Year with just three league wins. Wimbledon's record isn't much better, though one more win than Forest means they are one place above Brian Clough's side.

Saturday 9 January	
Arsenal v. Sheffield United	1-1
Blackburn Rovers v. Wimbledon	0-0
Chelsea v. Manchester City	2-4
Coventry City v. Nottingham Forest	0-1
Crystal Palace v. Everton	0-2
Ipswich Town v. Oldham Athletic	1-2
Leeds United v. Southampton	2-1
Liverpool v. Aston Villa	1-2
Manchester United v. Tottenham Hotspur	4-1
Middlesbrough v. Queen's Park R.	0-1
Sunday 10 January	
Sheffield Wed. v. Norwich City	1-0
Saturday 16 January	
Everton v. Leeds United	2-0
Manchester City v. Arsenal	0-1
Norwich City v. Coventry City	1-1
Nottingham Forest v. Chelsea	3-0
Oldham Athletic v. Blackburn Rovers	0-1
Sheffield United v. Ipswich Town	3-0
Southampton v. Crystal Palace	1-0
Tottenham Hotspur v. Sheffield Wed.	0-2
Wimbledon v. Liverpool	2-0
Sunday 17 January	
Aston Villa v. Middlesbrough	5-1
Monday 18 January	
Queen's Park R. v. Manchester United	1-3
Saturday 23 January	
Coventry City v. Oldham Athletic	3-0
Tuesday 26 January	
Blackburn Rovers v. Coventry City	2-5
Middlesbrough v. Southampton	2-1
Oldham Athletic v. Manchester City	0-1
Wimbledon v. Everton	1-3
Wednesday 27 January	
Aston Villa v. Sheffield United	3-1
Manchester United v. Nottingham Forest	2-0
Norwich City v. Crystal Palace	4-2
Queen's Park R. v. Chelsea	1-1
Tottenham Hotspur v. Ipswich Town	0-2
Saturday 30 January	
Chelsea v. Sheffield Wed.	0-2
Coventry City v. Wimbledon	0-2
Crystal Palace v. Tottenham Hotspur	1-3
Everton v. Norwich City	0-1
Ipswich Town v. Manchester United	2-1
Leeds United v. Middlesbrough	3-0
Manchester City v. Blackburn Rovers	3-2
Nottingham Forest v. Oldham Athletic	2-0
Sheffield United v. Queen's Park R.	1-2
Southampton v. Aston Villa	2-0
Sunday 31 January	
Arsenal v. Liverpool	0-1

		P	W	D	L	F	A	Pts
1	Norwich City	26	14	6	6	40	38	48
2	Manchester United	26	13	8	5	40	21	47
3	Aston Villa	26	13	8	5	42	29	47
4	Ipswich Town	26	10	12	4	36	29	42
5	Blackburn Rovers	26	11	8	7	39	28	41
6	Manchester City	26	11	6	9	38	29	39
7	Queen's Park R.	25	11	6	8	35	30	39
8	Coventry City	27	10	9	8	42	38	39
9	Sheffield Wed.	25	9	9	7	32	29	36
10	Chelsea	26	9	9	8	31	32	36
11	Arsenal	25	10	5	10	25	24	35
12	Liverpool	24	9	5	10	37	37	32
13	Everton	26	9	5	12	28	32	32
14	Tottenham Hotspur	26	8	8	10	26	36	32
15	Leeds United	25	8	7	10	38	40	31
16	Southampton	26	7	9	10	27	30	30
17	Middlesbrough	26	7	9	10	36	43	30
18	Wimbledon	26	6	9	11	31	36	27
19	Crystal Palace	26	6	9	11	32	43	27
20	Sheffield United	25	6	7	12	24	34	25
21	Nottingham Forest	25	6	6	13	26	35	24
22	Oldham Athletic	25	6	6	13	35	47	24

AFTER cup action the Premiership teams return to the pursuit of league points and Eric Cantona scores Manchester United's first goal of the year as they hit the top of the table for the first time in the campaign, on goal difference, by beating Spurs. Norwich go down to Sheffield Wednesday and lose ground, while Aston Villa split the two and move second with a win at Liverpool and, having read the script, Dean Saunders nets the winner against his old club.

Crystal Palace lose all their games this month and are just above the relegation zone, while Nottingham Forest beat Coventry and Chelsea to move off the bottom for the first time since August. They are replaced by Oldham, who lose four in a row, the last of which is a reverse at the City Ground in the fifth and final game of the month. Norwich reclaim top spot, despite being held by Coventry, but are soon replaced by Aston Villa, who thrash Middlesbrough. However, Manchester United become the third table-toppers in three days when they go into pole position following their win over QPR.

Brian Deane follows up his cup hat-trick with a Premiership treble that sinks Ipswich, taking his tally, in five days, to six goals. Blackburn suffer their heaviest defeat to date when they are crushed at home by Coventry, and miss the chance of going top as Rovers' defender Colin Hendry scores for each side. It gets worse as the Ewood Park outfit drop to fifth, where they end the month, when the next game is also lost. There are no such slip-ups for the top three: Manchester United, Aston Villa and Norwich all, in perfect symmetry, register home wins by two-goal margins.

Wimbledon improve their position by ending the month out of the relegation zone, courtesy of a win at Coventry, but there are worried frowns at Sheffield United as successive defeats by Aston Villa and QPR pull the Blades into the bottom three.

Norwich fly back to the top of the table when their victory at Everton sees them profit from defeats of Manchester United and Aston Villa, by Ipswich and Southampton respectively, and in mid-table Liverpool end their seven-game run without a win against Arsenal. John Barnes is the match-winner with a penalty while the Gunners miss from the spot for the fourth time this season, and Nigel Winterburn is sent off.

Colin Hendry, Blackburn Rovers' defensive rock.

February

Tuesday 2 February		
Blackburn Rovers v. Crystal Palace		1-2
Saturday 6 February		
Aston Villa v. Ipswich Town		2-0
Liverpool v. Nottingham Forest		0-0
Manchester United v. Sheffield United		2-1
Middlesbrough v. Coventry City		0-2
Oldham Athletic v. Chelsea		3-1
Queen's Park R. v. Manchester City		1-1
Sheffield Wed. v. Everton		3-1
Wimbledon v. Leeds United		1-0
Sunday 7 February		
Tottenham Hotspur v. Southampton		4-2
Monday 8 February		
Leeds United v. Manchester United		0-0
Tuesday 9 February		
Ipswich Town v. Queen's Park R.		1-1
Sheffield United v. Middlesbrough		2-0
Wednesday 10 February		
Arsenal v. Wimbledon		0-1
Chelsea v. Liverpool		0-0
Crystal Palace v. Aston Villa		1-0
Everton v. Tottenham Hotspur		1-2
Southampton v. Norwich City		3-0
Saturday 13 February		
Chelsea v. Aston Villa		0-1
Leeds United v. Oldham Athletic		2-0
Southampton v. Liverpool		2-1
Saturday 20 February		
Aston Villa v. Everton		2-1
Liverpool v. Ipswich Town		0-0
Manchester United v. Southampton		2-1
Middlesbrough v. Nottingham Forest		1-2
Norwich City v. Manchester City		2-1
Oldham Athletic v. Arsenal		0-1
Queen's Park R. v. Coventry City		2-0
Sheffield Wed. v. Crystal Palace		2-1
Tottenham Hotspur v. Leeds United		4-0
Wimbledon v. Sheffield United		2-0
Sunday 21 February		
Blackburn Rovers v. Chelsea		2-0
Monday 22 February		
Sheffield United v. Oldham Athletic		2-0
Tuesday 23 February		
Manchester City v. Sheffield Wed.		1-2
Wednesday 24 February		
Arsenal v. Leeds United		0-0
Nottingham Forest v. Queen's Park R.		1-0
Saturday 27 February		
Aston Villa v. Wimbledon		1-0
Crystal Palace v. Coventry City		0-0
Everton v. Oldham Athletic		2-2
Leeds United v. Ipswich Town		1-0
Manchester United v. Middlesbrough		3-0
Nottingham Forest v. Manchester City		0-2
Sheffield Wed. v. Liverpool		1-1
Southampton v. Sheffield United		3-2
Tottenham Hotspur v. Queen's Park R.		3-2
Sunday 28 February		
Norwich City v. Blackburn Rovers		0-0

	P	W	D	L	F	A	Pts
1 Aston Villa	31	17	8	6	48	31	59
2 Manchester United	30	16	9	5	47	23	57
3 Norwich City	29	15	7	7	42	42	52
4 Sheffield Wed.	29	12	10	7	40	33	46
5 Blackburn Rovers	29	12	9	8	42	30	45
6 Queen's Park R.	30	12	8	10	41	36	44
7 Ipswich Town	30	10	14	6	37	33	44
8 Tottenham Hotspur	30	12	8	10	39	41	44
9 Manchester City	30	12	7	11	43	34	43
10 Coventry City	30	11	10	9	44	40	43
11 Arsenal	28	11	6	11	26	25	39
12 Southampton	31	10	9	12	38	39	39
13 Leeds United	31	10	9	12	41	45	39
14 Chelsea	30	9	10	11	32	38	37
15 Liverpool	29	9	9	11	39	40	36
16 Wimbledon	30	9	9	12	35	37	36
17 Crystal Palace	30	8	10	12	36	46	34
18 Everton	30	9	6	15	33	41	33
19 Nottingham Forest	29	8	7	14	29	38	31
20 Sheffield United	30	8	7	15	31	41	31
21 Middlesbrough	30	7	9	14	37	52	30
22 Oldham Athletic	30	7	7	16	40	55	28

Sheffield Wednesday defender Paul Warhurst enjoys his scoring run as an emergency striker.

SEVEN YEARS after losing Martin Keown to Aston Villa for a £200,000 fee that was decided by tribunal, Arsenal pay 10 times that amount to bring the defender back to Highbury from Everton. On the field there's an important result, affecting both ends of the table, when Crystal Palace ease their relegation worries, and badly jolt Blackburn's title aspirations, by winning at Ewood Park.

Manchester United and Aston Villa then take the advantage and move top of the table, with wins over Sheffield Wednesday and Ipswich respectively, as Norwich are without a game. Leeds drop to within four points of the relegation zone with their eighth away defeat in a row, to Wimbledon, who move up to 17th as a consequence. Manchester United then pull clear, by a point, when they are held at Elland Road by Leeds. Home fans give Eric Cantona a hostile reception on his return.

Nottingham Forest continue their push away from the foot of the table and, after their well-won point at Liverpool, consecutive wins over Middlesbrough and QPR take them to the heady heights of 19th. Oldham drop to bottom after they lose three in a row but the biggest shock is for Middlesbrough. After being mid-table before Christmas, they lose all their games in February and drop to 21st after defeat number five, to Manchester United. 'Boro never recover and stay in the relegation zone.

After the internationals and cup competition the Premiership resumes and Aston Villa maintain pole position with three consecutive wins to enter March as league leaders. Successive home wins for Manchester United keep them second, although a Ryan Giggs brace is required to turn a 1–0 deficit to Southampton, after five minutes, into three points, while Norwich's four-point return for February means they have to be content with third.

In the basement Sheffield United only manage two wins in the month but they are against fellow strugglers Oldham and Middlesbrough and the Blades sense survival. Meanwhile, across the city, Wednesday rack up their eighth consecutive victory to go fourth and Paul Warhurst, pushed up front as an emergency striker, scores for the seventh consecutive game.

Arsenal skipper Tony Adams receives 29 stitches in a head wound after he falls down the stairs and is doubtful for the next league game. The stairs apparently recovered without treatment!

Monday 1 March
Chelsea v. Arsenal	1-0

Tuesday 2 March
Ipswich Town v. Middlesbrough	0-1
Sheffield United v. Tottenham Hotspur	6-0

Wednesday 3 March
Coventry City v. Sheffield Wed.	1-0
Everton v. Blackburn Rovers	2-1
Norwich City v. Arsenal	1-1
Nottingham Forest v. Crystal Palace	1-1

Saturday 6 March
Liverpool v. Manchester United	1-2
Queen's Park R. v. Norwich City	3-1
Wimbledon v. Southampton	1-2

Sunday 7 March
Coventry City v. Everton	0-1

Tuesday 9 March
Blackburn Rovers v. Southampton	0-0
Oldham Athletic v. Manchester United	1-0
Wimbledon v. Middlesbrough	2-0

Wednesday 10 March
Aston Villa v. Tottenham Hotspur	0-0
Chelsea v. Everton	2-1
Ipswich Town v. Sheffield Wed.	0-1
Liverpool v. Queen's Park R.	1-0
Manchester City v. Coventry City	1-0
Sheffield United v. Norwich City	0-1

Saturday 13 March
Coventry City v. Arsenal	0-2
Everton v. Nottingham Forest	3-0
Leeds United v. Manchester City	1-0
Middlesbrough v. Liverpool	1-2
Norwich City v. Oldham Athletic	1-0
Queen's Park R. v. Wimbledon	1-2
Southampton v. Ipswich Town	4-3

Sunday 14 March
Manchester United v. Aston Villa	1-1

Monday 15 March
Crystal Palace v. Chelsea	1-1

Wednesday 17 March
Nottingham Forest v. Norwich City	0-3

Saturday 20 March
Arsenal v. Southampton	4-3
Aston Villa v. Sheffield Wed.	2-0
Blackburn Rovers v. Middlesbrough	1-1
Chelsea v. Tottenham Hotspur	1-1
Ipswich Town v. Coventry City	0-0
Liverpool v. Everton	1-0
Manchester City v. Manchester United	1-1
Oldham Athletic v. Queen's Park R.	2-2
Sheffield United v. Crystal Palace	0-1
Wimbledon v. Norwich City	3-0

Sunday 21 March
Nottingham Forest v. Leeds United	1-1

Monday 22 March
Middlesbrough v. Oldham Athletic	2-3

Tuesday 23 March
Crystal Palace v. Liverpool	1-1

Wednesday 24 March
Coventry City v. Sheffield United	1-3
Everton v. Ipswich Town	3-0
Leeds United v. Chelsea	1-1
Manchester United v. Arsenal	0-0
Norwich City v. Aston Villa	1-0
Queen's Park R. v. Blackburn Rovers	0-3
Sheffield Wed. v. Wimbledon	1-1
Southampton v. Nottingham Forest	1-2
Tottenham Hotspur v. Manchester City	3-1

	P	W	D	L	F	A	Pts
1 Norwich City	36	19	8	9	50	49	65
2 Aston Villa	35	18	10	7	51	33	64
3 Manchester United	35	17	12	6	51	27	63
4 Blackburn Rovers	33	13	11	9	47	33	50
5 Sheffield Wed.	33	13	11	9	42	37	50
6 Tottenham Hotspur	34	13	10	11	43	49	49
7 Queen's Park R.	35	13	9	13	47	45	48
8 Manchester City	34	13	8	13	46	39	47
9 Arsenal	33	13	8	12	33	30	47
10 Coventry City	36	12	11	13	46	47	47
11 Wimbledon	35	12	10	13	44	41	46
12 Liverpool	34	12	10	12	45	44	46
13 Southampton	36	12	10	14	48	49	46
14 Chelsea	35	11	13	11	38	42	46
15 Everton	36	13	6	17	43	45	45
16 Ipswich Town	35	10	15	10	40	42	45
17 Leeds United	34	11	11	12	44	47	44
18 Crystal Palace	34	9	13	12	40	49	40
19 Sheffield United	34	10	7	17	40	44	37
20 Nottingham Forest	34	9	9	16	33	47	36
21 Oldham Athletic	34	9	8	17	46	60	35
22 Middlesbrough	35	8	10	17	42	60	34

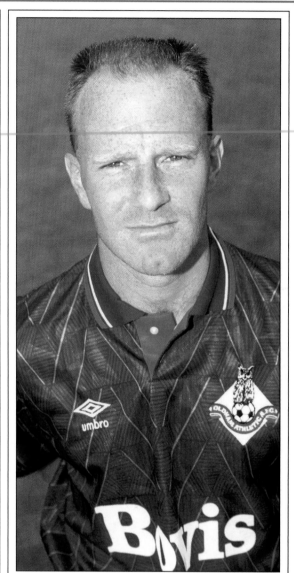

Andy Ritchie, Oldham Athletic.

THE MONTH starts with good wins for two of the bottom clubs as Sheffield United thrash Spurs and Middlesbrough take the points at Ipswich. Tottenham's defeat is their worst for 15 years and ends their six-game winning streak. Norwich lose ground when they are held at Carrow Road by Arsenal and Manchester United move a point clear of Aston Villa at the top following their victory at Anfield. Liverpool are now, astonishingly, a mere three points above the drop zone. Norwich look virtually out of the title race when they lose at QPR.

At the other end of the table Middlesbrough fail to capitalise on their win at Portman Road and follow up by losing to Wimbledon and Liverpool, although a point at Blackburn arrests the slide. Nottingham Forest slip into the bottom two when they lose two consecutive games in 3–0 defeats but Crystal Palace follow up their draws with Forest and Chelsea by beating fellow-strugglers Sheffield United and look likely to avoid relegation.

Oldham stun Manchester United with a Neil Adams winner at Boundary Park, but they remain bottom. Aston Villa, now just a point adrift of top spot, have a game in hand, but they lose that advantage when held by Spurs. Norwich improve on recent form by beating Sheffield United and follow up with successive victories over strugglers Oldham and Nottingham Forest.

Manchester United, obviously stung by the Oldham defeat, draw three consecutive games and slip to second while Aston Villa, who take a point at Old Trafford in the first of United's run of drawn games, take over as leaders following their win over Sheffield Wednesday. Norwich put themselves back in the title race when they follow up their win at Bramall Lane with two more victories, their win at the City Ground keeping Forest in the bottom three. Middlesbrough are just one place better off when they are beaten by Wimbledon and Liverpool and Oldham complete the relegation-threatened trio, despite ending the month with a victory at Ayresome Park.

Sheffield Wednesday's rise up the Premiership, into fourth place, is recognised by an England call-up for Paul Warhurst. The defender, who has been playing as an emergency striker, has scored 12 goals in 12 games but injury prevents him from being capped.

Norwich's recent revival hits the skids with defeat by Wimbledon, and Aston Villa and United leapfrog the Canaries. Just as it looks like a two-horse title race City end the month with a home win over Villa.

At the other end of the table Crystal Palace lift themselves out of the drop zone with a win over Sheffield United, a position they managed to maintain by holding Liverpool.

Matt Le Tissier's only career penalty miss comes in Southampton's game against Forest. Mark Crossley saves the spot-kick and Forest win the game 2–1.

April

Saturday 3 April	
Blackburn Rovers v. Liverpool	4-1
Chelsea v. Middlesbrough	4-0
Coventry City v. Southampton	2-0
Crystal Palace v. Queen's Park R.	1-1
Manchester City v. Ipswich Town	3-1
Oldham Athletic v. Wimbledon	6-2
Sunday 4 April	
Nottingham Forest v. Aston Villa	0-1
Monday 5 April	
Norwich City v. Manchester United	1-3
Tuesday 6 April	
Ipswich Town v. Chelsea	1-1
Middlesbrough v. Arsenal	1-0
Sheffield United v. Leeds United	2-1
Wednesday 7 April	
Nottingham Forest v. Blackburn Rovers	1-3
Oldham Athletic v. Sheffield Wed.	1-1
Friday 9 April	
Sheffield United v. Manchester City	1-1
Tottenham Hotspur v. Norwich City	5-1
Wimbledon v. Crystal Palace	4-0
Saturday 10 April	
Aston Villa v. Coventry City	0-0
Ipswich Town v. Arsenal	1-2
Leeds United v. Blackburn Rovers	5-2
Liverpool v. Oldham Athletic	1-0
Manchester United v. Sheffield Wed.	2-1
Middlesbrough v. Everton	1-2
Queen's Park R. v. Nottingham Forest	4-3
Southampton v. Chelsea	1-0
Monday 12 April	
Arsenal v. Aston Villa	0-1
Blackburn Rovers v. Ipswich Town	2-1
Chelsea v. Wimbledon	4-2
Coventry City v. Manchester United	0-1
Crystal Palace v. Middlesbrough	4-1
Everton v. Queen's Park R.	3-5
Manchester City v. Liverpool	1-1
Nottingham Forest v. Tottenham Hotspur	2-1
Sheffield Wed. v. Southampton	5-2
Tuesday 13 April	
Oldham Athletic v. Sheffield United	1-1
Wednesday 14 April	
Norwich City v. Leeds United	4-2
Saturday 17 April	
Leeds United v. Crystal Palace	0-0
Liverpool v. Coventry City	4-0
Manchester United v. Chelsea	3-0
Sheffield United v. Blackburn Rovers	1-3
Southampton v. Everton	0-0
Tottenham Hotspur v. Oldham Athletic	4-1
Wimbledon v. Nottingham Forest	1-0
Sunday 18 April	
Aston Villa v. Manchester City	3-1
Monday 19 April	
Ipswich Town v. Norwich City	3-1
Tuesday 20 April	
Middlesbrough v. Tottenham Hotspur	3-0
Wednesday 21 April	
Arsenal v. Nottingham Forest	1-1
Blackburn Rovers v. Aston Villa	3-0
Crystal Palace v. Manchester United	0-2
Liverpool v. Leeds United	2-0
Manchester City v. Wimbledon	1-1
Sheffield Wed. v. Sheffield United	1-1

		P	W	D	L	F	A	Pts
1	Manchester United	40	22	12	6	62	29	78
2	Aston Villa	40	21	11	8	56	37	74
3	Norwich City	40	20	8	12	57	62	68
4	Blackburn Rovers	39	18	11	10	64	42	65
5	Liverpool	39	15	11	13	54	49	56
6	Sheffield Wed.	37	14	13	10	50	43	55
7	Queen's Park R.	38	15	10	13	57	52	55
8	Tottenham Hotspur	38	15	10	13	53	56	55
9	Manchester City	39	14	11	14	53	46	53
10	Wimbledon	40	14	11	15	54	52	53
11	Chelsea	40	13	14	13	47	49	53
12	Arsenal	37	14	9	14	36	34	51
13	Coventry City	40	13	12	15	48	52	51
14	Southampton	40	13	11	16	51	56	50
15	Everton	39	14	7	18	48	51	49
16	Ipswich Town	40	11	16	13	47	51	49
17	Leeds United	39	12	12	15	52	57	48
18	Crystal Palace	39	10	15	14	45	57	45
19	Sheffield United	39	11	10	18	46	51	43
20	Oldham Athletic	39	10	10	19	55	69	40
21	Nottingham Forest	40	10	10	20	40	58	40
22	Middlesbrough	40	10	10	20	48	70	40

Steve Bruce's brace snatches victory from the jaws of defeat against Sheffield Wednesday.

THE FA warns it may take action against players and clubs for misconduct for excessive goal celebrations, even if the referee does not.

On the field there's plenty of excitement, particularly around the relegation zone. Oldham crush mid-table Wimbledon and move out of the drop zone but Middlesbrough are swamped by Chelsea. Forest are just one place above them as their home defeat by Villa takes Ron Atkinson's team back to the top. Twenty-four hours later Eric Cantona and Ryan Giggs are the inspiration behind the win, at Carrow Road, that takes United over the Canaries into second spot, just a point adrift of Villa.

Middlesbrough haul themselves off the bottom with a John Hendrie goal that beats Arsenal, while Nottingham Forest's cause isn't helped by news that Stuart Pearce will miss the remainder of the campaign due to a groin injury. Forest then look doomed after losing to Blackburn to remain 22nd.

Significant results at both ends of the Premiership come as Norwich see their title aspirations shattered with a thrashing at Spurs while Wimbledon's crushing of Selhurst Park landlords Crystal Palace puts the Eagles' Premiership future in doubt.

Manchester United are 1–0 down at home to Sheffield Wednesday until two late Steve Bruce headers earn them a dramatic victory and a one-point lead over second-placed Villa, thanks to Coventry claiming a draw at Villa Park.

Nottingham Forest score three at QPR, but lose to a Les Ferdinand hat-trick. Ferdinand repeats the feat in Rangers' next game, at Everton, and QPR go fifth. It's a high-scoring Easter Monday in the Premiership with the nine fixtures generating a total of 36 goals, the QPR win at Everton featuring eight. But Manchester United's narrow win over Coventry keeps them top with Villa's victory at Highbury, with Tony Daley's first goal for more than a year, keeping them in touch.

There's some movement at the foot of the table where Forest move off the bottom by beating Spurs and Palace give themselves hope with victory over Middlesbrough.

Chris Sutton hits his first hat-trick of the season for Norwich, but the faintest of title hopes finally disappears when neighbours Ipswich complete the league double with victory at Portman Road. 'Boro keep survival hopes alive by beating the inconsistent Spurs.

Manchester United open up a four-point lead over Aston Villa with their victory over Chelsea, while the bottom three, Oldham, Forest and Sheffield United, all lose to give a certain finality to the relegation zone.

Villa cut United's lead to a single point by beating Manchester City, and there are just three games left in a two-horse race. But the next fixtures bring massive results that virtually decide the title. While Manchester United win away at Crystal Palace, Aston Villa crash at Blackburn to fall four points adrift, with two games left.

With relegation now almost a mathematical certainty for Nottingham Forest, Brian Clough announces his decision to retire at the end of the season, after spending 18 of his 29 years in management at the City Ground.

May

Saturday 1 May

Chelsea v. Coventry City	2-1
Crystal Palace v. Ipswich Town	3-1
Everton v. Arsenal	0-0
Leeds United v. Queen's Park R.	1-1
Norwich City v. Liverpool	1-0
Nottingham Forest v. Sheffield United	0-2
Sheffield Wed. v. Middlesbrough	2-3
Southampton v. Manchester City	0-1
Tottenham Hotspur v. Wimbledon	1-1

Sunday 2 May

Aston Villa v. Oldham Athletic	0-1

Monday 3 May

Manchester United v. Blackburn Rovers	3-1

Tuesday 4 May

Arsenal v. Queen's Park R.	0-0
Everton v. Sheffield United	0-2
Sheffield Wed. v. Leeds United	1-1

Wednesday 5 May

Manchester City v. Crystal Palace	0-0
Oldham Athletic v. Liverpool	3-2
Tottenham Hotspur v. Blackburn Rovers	1-2

Thursday 6 May

Sheffield Wed. v. Arsenal	1-0

Saturday 8 May

Arsenal v. Crystal Palace	3-0
Blackburn Rovers v. Sheffield Wed.	1-0
Coventry City v. Leeds United	3-3
Ipswich Town v. Nottingham Forest	2-1
Liverpool v. Tottenham Hotspur	6-2
Manchester City v. Everton	2-5
Middlesbrough v. Norwich City	3-3
Oldham Athletic v. Southampton	4-3
Sheffield United v. Chelsea	4-2

Sunday 9 May

Queen's Park R. v. Aston Villa	2-1
Wimbledon v. Manchester United	1-2

Tuesday 11 May

Arsenal v. Tottenham Hotspur	1-3
Queen's Park R. v. Sheffield Wed.	3-1

		P	W	D	L	F	A	Pts
1	Manchester United	42	24	12	6	67	31	84
2	Aston Villa	42	21	11	10	57	40	74
3	Norwich City	42	21	9	12	61	65	72
4	Blackburn Rovers	42	20	11	11	68	46	71
5	Queen's Park R.	42	17	12	13	63	55	63
6	Liverpool	42	16	11	15	62	55	59
7	Sheffield Wed.	42	15	14	13	55	51	59
8	Tottenham Hotspur	42	16	11	15	60	66	59
9	Manchester City	42	15	12	15	56	51	57
10	Arsenal	42	15	11	16	40	38	56
11	Chelsea	42	14	14	14	51	54	56
12	Wimbledon	42	14	12	16	56	55	54
13	Everton	42	15	8	19	53	55	53
14	Sheffield United	42	14	10	18	54	53	52
15	Coventry City	42	13	13	16	52	57	52
16	Ipswich Town	42	12	16	14	50	55	52
17	Leeds United	42	12	15	15	57	62	51
18	Southampton	42	13	11	18	54	61	50
19	Oldham Athletic	42	13	10	19	63	74	49
20	Crystal Palace	42	11	16	15	48	61	49
21	Middlesbrough	42	11	11	20	54	75	44
22	Nottingham Forest	42	10	10	22	41	62	40

Promoted from Barclays League Division One

Newcastle

West Ham United

Swindon Town (via play-offs)

SHEFFIELD UNITED begin their Houdini-like escape from relegation when they open the final month of the season with a win at Nottingham Forest that confirms relegation for the home side, who bid a tearful farewell to Brian Clough. Middlesbrough join Forest for the drop, despite a gallant victory at Sheffield Wednesday.

Manchester United celebrate their first league title since 1967 due to Oldham's win at Aston Villa, Villa's second successive reverse. Alex Ferguson makes history as the first manager to win the title both sides of the border. The next day United mark their triumph as first-ever Premiership champions by beating Blackburn. Sheffield United win at Everton to retain their top-flight status and 24 hours later Oldham win at Liverpool and remain on course to stay up, since Crystal Palace are held by Manchester City.

Most issues are settled on the final Saturday with the outstanding performance being Oldham's win over Southampton, despite a Matt Le Tissier hat-trick, their third successive league victory. It means that Crystal Palace are down, on goal difference, because of a defeat at Highbury that was set up by a goal from their former striker Ian Wright, taking his final tally for the season to 20, 15 in the league. Sheffield United complete their escape from the drop by registering their third consecutive league victory against Chelsea.

Norwich claim third place in the Premiership table, and a place in the UEFA Cup if Arsenal take the FA Cup, by drawing with Middlesbrough, and Aston Villa, despite ending the campaign with a hat-trick of defeats, the last one by QPR, are runners-up, 10 points behind Manchester United, following the champions' win at Wimbledon. Villa's last seven games yielded just three victories; United reeled off seven in a row.

It's a poignant day at Anfield where Ian Rush marks the final game before the world-famous Kop is demolished by scoring his 300th goal for Liverpool as they hammer Spurs. Graeme Souness isn't there but the club call a press conference the next day to confirm that the Scot is staying on as manager for another three years.

Terry Venables is sacked by Tottenham then reinstated pending further High Court hearings. Two weeks later an uneasy peace prevails between Venables, who remains as manager at White Hart Lane, and his chairman Alan Sugar.

Andy Ritchie's goal helps Oldham to safety in a seven-goal thriller against Saints.

Manchester United, FA Premier League Champions.

End of season round-up

Top Premiership Goalscorers 1992–93

Teddy Sheringham	Tottenham Hotspur	22
(1 for Nottingham Forest)		
Les Ferdinand	QPR	20
Mick Quinn	Coventry	19
(2 for Newcastle)		
Dean Holdsworth	Wimbledon	19
Alan Shearer	Blackburn Rovers	16
David White	Manchester City	16
Ian Wright	Arsenal	15
Brian Deane	Sheffield United	15
Mark Hughes	Manchester United	15
Eric Cantona	Mancherster United	15
(6 for Leeds)		

Coca-Cola League Cup Final

Arsenal 2   Sheffield Wednesday 1

Steve Morrow's Wembley dream turned into a nightmare when his arm was broken by Tony Adams as Arsenal celebrated Morrow's winner. John Harkes put Wednesday ahead after nine minutes but Merson's powerful volley ensured parity by half-time. Morrow, only playing because of injuries to senior players, latched on to a poor clearance to fire home the winner but after the final whistle Tony Adams lifted the youngster on to his shoulders only to drop him with a sickening crack that broke the full-back's arm and robbed him of a possible second Wembley appearance in May.

FA Cup Final

Arsenal 1   Sheffield Wednesday 1
Arsenal 2   Sheffield Wedneday 1
                        (aet) – replay

The draw in the first FA Cup Final was a dour affair. Arsenal took the lead midway through the first half when Andy Linighan's headed pass set up Ian Wright for a powerful scoring header, by which the Gunners led at the interval. Wednesday improved in the second half and they equalised through David Hirst, but neither side could break the ensuing deadlock and a replay five days later was ensured.

The replay was no better as a spectacle, but again Ian Wright put Arsenal ahead. It was his fourth goal in four FA Cup Final appearances, but he never completed a full 90 minutes. As in the first game Wednesday improved after the interval and the ball cannoned off Linighan's shoulder, then off Dixon's knee, to Chris Waddle, who fired home the equaliser via Dixon's leg. Andy Linighan headed Arsenal's winner in the last minute of extra-time.

Football Writers' Footballer of the Year

Chris Waddle   Sheffield Wednesday

PFA Player of the Year

Paul McGrath   Aston Villa

PFA Young Player of the Year

Ryan Giggs   Manchester United

Manager of the Year

Alex Ferguson   Manchester United

> **FACT FILE**
>
> Arsenal boss George Graham becomes the first person to win the League Championship and both cups, as both player and manager.

Close season 1993

Peter Beardsley rejoins Newcastle when he signs from Everton for £1.4 million and Carlton Palmer agrees a new five-year deal at Sheffield Wednesday.

West Bromwich Albion threaten legal action as Ossie Ardiles walks out on them to become Spurs' manager. Almost his first action at his new club is to sack Ray Clemence and appoint Steve Perryman as his assistant.

Leeds pay a club record £2.9 million for Brian Deane and Sheffield United directors Derek Dooley and Bernard Proctor resign in protest.

The Premiership will be known as the FA Carling Premiership for the coming season and Des Walker leaves Sampdoria for Sheffield Wednesday in a deal worth £2.7 million.

Manchester United pay Nottingham Forest £3.75 million for Roy Keane while Neil Ruddock's move to Liverpool is held up by Spurs' refusal to pay a £100,000 loyalty bonus to the player for his one year spent at White Hart Lane.

A compromise is finally reached and Ruddock moves to Anfield for £2.5 million, but there's further controversy as Ruddock's previous club, Southampton, protest that their £1.5 million valuation of the player was halved by a tribunal when they sold him to Tottenham a year earlier.

Manchester United win the Charity Shield when they beat Arsenal 5–4 on penalties after a 1–1 draw, and Alan Shearer takes a big step towards recovery from injury when he nets twice in a pre-season friendly.

Chris Waddle, double cup loser but player of the year.

August

Saturday 14 August	
Arsenal v. Coventry City	0-3
Aston Villa v. Queen's Park R.	4-1
Chelsea v. Blackburn Rovers	1-2
Liverpool v. Sheffield Wed.	2-0
Manchester City v. Leeds United	1-1
Newcastle United v. Tottenham Hotspur	0-1
Oldham Athletic v. Ipswich Town	0-3
Sheffield United v. Swindon Town	3-1
Southampton v. Everton	0-2
West Ham United v. Wimbledon	0-2
Sunday 15 August	
Norwich City v. Manchester United	0-2
Monday 16 August	
Tottenham Hotspur v. Arsenal	0-1
Tuesday 17 August	
Everton v. Manchester City	1-0
Ipswich Town v. Southampton	1-0
Leeds United v. West Ham United	1-0
Wimbledon v. Chelsea	1-1
Wednesday 18 August	
Blackburn Rovers v. Norwich City	2-3
Coventry City v. Newcastle United	2-1
Manchester United v. Sheffield United	3-0
Queen's Park R. v. Liverpool	1-3
Sheffield Wed. v. Aston Villa	0-0
Swindon Town v. Oldham Athletic	0-1
Saturday 21 August	
Blackburn Rovers v. Oldham Athletic	1-0
Coventry City v. West Ham United	1-1
Everton v. Sheffield United	4-2
Ipswich Town v. Chelsea	1-0
Leeds United v. Norwich City	0-4
Manchester United v. Newcastle United	1-1
Queen's Park R. v. Southampton	2-1
Sheffield Wed. v. Arsenal	0-1
Tottenham Hotspur v. Manchester City	1-0
Wimbledon v. Aston Villa	2-2
Sunday 22 August	
Swindon Town v. Liverpool	0-5
Monday 23 August	
Aston Villa v. Manchester United	1-2
Tuesday 24 August	
Arsenal v. Leeds United	2-1
Manchester City v. Blackburn Rovers	0-2
Oldham Athletic v. Coventry City	3-3
Sheffield United v. Wimbledon	2-1
Wednesday 25 August	
Chelsea v. Queen's Park R.	2-0
Liverpool v. Tottenham Hotspur	1-2
Newcastle United v. Everton	1-0
Norwich City v. Ipswich Town	1-0
Southampton v. Swindon Town	5-1
West Ham United v. Sheffield Wed.	2-0
Friday 27 August	
Manchester City v. Coventry City	1-1
Saturday 28 August	
Arsenal v. Everton	2-0
Aston Villa v. Tottenham Hotspur	1-0
Chelsea v. Sheffield Wed.	1-1
Liverpool v. Leeds United	2-0
Norwich City v. Swindon Town	0-0
Oldham Athletic v. Wimbledon	1-1
Sheffield United v. Ipswich Town	1-1
Southampton v. Manchester United	1-3
West Ham United v. Queen's Park R.	0-4
Sunday 29 August	
Newcastle United v. Blackburn Rovers	1-1
Monday 30 August	
Leeds United v. Oldham Athletic	1-0
Tuesday 31 August	
Everton v. Aston Villa	0-1
Ipswich Town v. Newcastle United	1-1
Wimbledon v. Southampton	1-0

		P	W	D	L	F	A	Pts
1	Manchester United	5	4	1	0	11	3	13
2	Liverpool	5	4	0	1	13	3	12
3	Arsenal	5	4	0	1	6	4	12
4	Aston Villa	6	3	2	1	9	5	11
5	Ipswich Town	6	3	2	1	7	3	11
6	Norwich City	5	3	1	1	8	4	10
7	Blackburn Rovers	5	3	1	1	8	5	10
8	Coventry City	5	2	3	0	10	6	9
9	Wimbledon	6	2	3	1	8	6	9
10	Everton	6	3	0	3	7	6	9
11	Tottenham Hotspur	5	3	0	2	4	3	9
12	Sheffield United	5	2	1	2	8	10	7
13	Leeds United	6	2	1	3	4	9	7
14	Newcastle United	6	1	3	2	5	6	6
15	Queen's Park R.	5	2	0	3	8	10	6
16	Chelsea	5	1	2	2	5	5	5
17	Oldham Athletic	6	1	2	3	5	9	5
18	West Ham United	5	1	1	3	3	8	4
19	Southampton	6	1	0	5	7	10	3
20	Manchester City	5	0	2	3	2	6	2
21	Sheffield Wed.	5	0	2	3	1	6	2
22	Swindon Town	5	0	1	4	2	14	1

THE SEASON opens with a remarkable sequence of six away wins from the 10-game programme with the biggest shock coming at Highbury where Micky Quinn's hat-trick shocks Arsenal. New boy Nigel Clough gets both goals as Liverpool beat Sheffield Wednesday. Manchester United commence the defence of their Premiership crown by beating Norwich but City's East Anglian rivals Ipswich go top with their second consecutive victory, while Everton match Town's start and go second with another victory.

With Manchester United's second win in four days taking them top, on goal difference, Roy Keane hits two goals on his home debut. Coventry and Liverpool also make it two wins in two games with victories over Newcastle and QPR respectively, but a Tony Cottee hat-trick takes Everton top of the table, on goal difference from Ipswich.

Of the new boys it's the stormiest welcome for Swindon, who open with defeat at Bramall Lane and then lose their first home game to Oldham. Liverpool then complete an unhappy baptism for the Robins with a thrashing that sees Liverpool displace their Mersey neighbours at the top of the Premiership. The other new clubs, Newcastle and West Ham, fare little better when they both lose their first two Premiership fixtures.

The leadership changes again as Manchester United go back to the top with their win at Villa Park and it's a position that is strengthened when all three teams previously with 100 percent records: Liverpool, Everton and Ipswich, lose to leave the champions a point clear.

Manchester City's poor start to the campaign continues with their third consecutive defeat, which leads to manager Peter Reid becoming the first Premiership managerial casualty. The sacking is on the recommendation of the new general manager at Maine Road, John Maddock. Police then have to quell riots at the ground, protesting against chairman Peter Swales. Brian Horton is the surprise choice to replace Reid, although City stalwart Tony Book leads the team for the game against Coventry that yields only the team's second point from five games.

Manchester United retain the lead in the Premiership by beating Southampton and stay ahead of Liverpool and Arsenal, who both win. Ian Rush scores his 200th league goal for Liverpool in the victory over Leeds. Norwich's winning sequence is surprisingly ended by Swindon, who register their first Premiership point with a goalless draw at Carrow Road.

Newcastle finally gain their first win of the campaign, over Everton, who slump to eighth when they are beaten again in the next game, by Arsenal. West Ham also manage a first win when they beat Sheffield Wednesday, but they end the month in 18th after a hammering at home to QPR.

Brian Horton, Manchester City's new boss.

September

Wednesday 1 September

Blackburn Rovers v. Arsenal	1-1
Coventry City v. Liverpool	1-0
Manchester United v. West Ham United	3-0
Queen's Park R. v. Sheffield United	2-1
Sheffield Wed. v. Norwich City	3-3
Swindon Town v. Manchester City	1-3
Tottenham Hotspur v. Chelsea	1-1

Saturday 11 September

Arsenal v. Ipswich Town	4-0
Aston Villa v. Coventry City	0-0
Chelsea v. Manchester United	1-0
Manchester City v. Queen's Park R.	3-0
Norwich City v. Wimbledon	0-1
Oldham Athletic v. Everton	0-1
Sheffield United v. Tottenham Hotspur	2-2
Southampton v. Leeds United	0-2
West Ham United v. Swindon Town	0-0

Sunday 12 September

Liverpool v. Blackburn Rovers	0-1

Monday 13 September

Newcastle United v. Sheffield Wed.	4-2

Saturday 18 September

Blackburn Rovers v. West Ham United	0-2
Coventry City v. Chelsea	1-1
Everton v. Liverpool	2-0
Ipswich Town v. Aston Villa	1-2
Leeds United v. Sheffield United	2-1
Queen's Park R. v. Norwich City	2-2
Sheffield Wed. v. Southampton	2-0
Swindon Town v. Newcastle United	2-2
Tottenham Hotspur v. Oldham Athletic	5-0

Sunday 19 September

Manchester United v. Arsenal	1-0

Monday 20 September

Wimbledon v. Manchester City	1-0

Saturday 25 September

Arsenal v. Southampton	1-0
Blackburn Rovers v. Sheffield Wed.	1-1
Chelsea v. Liverpool	1-0
Coventry City v. Leeds United	0-2
Everton v. Norwich City	1-5
Manchester United v. Swindon Town	4-2
Newcastle United v. West Ham United	2-0
Oldham Athletic v. Aston Villa	1-1
Sheffield United v. Manchester City	0-1

Sunday 26 September

Ipswich Town v. Tottenham Hotspur	2-2

Monday 27 September

Wimbledon v. Queen's Park R.	1-1

		P	W	D	L	F	A	Pts
1	Manchester United	9	7	1	1	19	6	22
2	Arsenal	9	6	1	2	12	6	19
3	Aston Villa	9	4	4	1	12	7	16
4	Wimbledon	9	4	4	1	11	7	16
5	Leeds United	9	5	1	3	10	10	16
6	Norwich City	9	4	3	2	18	11	15
7	Tottenham Hotspur	9	4	3	2	14	8	15
8	Blackburn Rovers	9	4	3	2	11	9	15
9	Everton	9	5	0	4	11	11	15
10	Coventry City	9	3	5	1	12	9	14
11	Newcastle United	9	3	4	2	13	10	13
12	Chelsea	9	3	4	2	9	7	13
13	Liverpool	9	4	0	5	13	8	12
14	Ipswich Town	9	3	3	3	10	11	12
15	Manchester City	9	3	2	4	9	8	11
16	Queen's Park R.	9	3	2	4	13	17	11
17	Sheffield United	9	2	5	2	12	17	8
18	West Ham United	9	2	2	5	5	13	8
19	Sheffield Wed.	9	1	4	4	9	14	7
20	Oldham Athletic	9	1	3	5	6	16	6
21	Southampton	9	1	0	8	7	15	3
22	Swindon Town	9	0	3	6	7	23	3

Chris Sutton of Norwich City celebrates scoring the equaliser against Sheffield Wednesday.

MANCHESTER UNITED extend their lead at the top to three points by beating West Ham; Lee Sharpe and Eric Cantona are the scorers for the second successive match. Sheffield Wednesday are denied their first victory of the season when they let slip a 3–0 lead to allow Norwich to draw, with three goals in 13 minutes. Shortly afterwards Wednesday sell Paul Warhurst to Blackburn Rovers for £2.7 million, three weeks after the player signed a new four-year contract with the Yorkshire club.

Chelsea inflict a first defeat, in 17 games, on Manchester United, which ends the champions' unbeaten record. Arsenal move level with United with a Kevin Campbell hat-trick helping them to victory over Ipswich and Leeds end a miserable run of 24 games without an away win by winning at Southampton.

Blackburn's home defeat by West Ham prevents them from joining Arsenal and Manchester United at the top of the table and Liverpool lose to Everton, but the headlines at Goodison are made by a bout of 'near-fisticuffs' between Liverpool's Steve McManaman and Bruce Grobbelaar, who dispute where the blame lies for Everton's opening goal.

First beats second as an Eric Cantona goal gives Manchester United victory over Arsenal and sends United three points clear again. Efan Ekoku produces the best scoring feat of the season thus far with four goals as Norwich slam fourth-placed Everton at Goodison, and the Canaries had to come from a goal down.

Andrei Kanchelskis is among the goals, with his first strike of the season, as Manchester United crush Swindon to stay three points ahead of Arsenal, a result that keeps Swindon bottom. Southampton are just one place better off after a run of three defeats, and no goals scored, while Oldham complete the basement trio although they manage a draw at the end of the month after losing to Everton and shipping five goals to Spurs.

Saturday 2 October	
Aston Villa v. Newcastle United	0-2
Leeds United v. Wimbledon	4-0
Liverpool v. Arsenal	0-0
Norwich City v. Coventry City	1-0
Queen's Park R. v. Ipswich Town	3-0
Sheffield Wed. v. Manchester United	2-3
Southampton v. Sheffield United	3-3
Swindon Town v. Blackburn Rovers	1-3
West Ham United v. Chelsea	1-0
Sunday 3 October	
Tottenham Hotspur v. Everton	3-2
Monday 4 October	
Manchester City v. Oldham Athletic	1-1
Saturday 16 October	
Arsenal v. Manchester City	0-0
Chelsea v. Norwich City	1-2
Coventry City v. Southampton	1-1
Liverpool v. Oldham Athletic	2-1
Manchester United v. Tottenham Hotspur	2-1
Newcastle United v. Queen's Park R.	1-2
Sheffield Wed. v. Wimbledon	2-2
Swindon Town v. Everton	1-1
West Ham United v. Aston Villa	0-0
Sunday 17 October	
Ipswich Town v. Leeds United	0-0
Monday 18 October	
Blackburn Rovers v. Sheffield United	0-0
Saturday 23 October	
Aston Villa v. Chelsea	1-0
Everton v. Manchester United	0-1
Leeds United v. Blackburn Rovers	3-3
Manchester City v. Liverpool	1-1
Norwich City v. West Ham United	0-0
Oldham Athletic v. Arsenal	0-0
Queen's Park R. v. Coventry City	5-1
Sheffield United v. Sheffield Wed.	1-1
Tottenham Hotspur v. Swindon Town	1-1
Sunday 24 October	
Southampton v. Newcastle United	2-1
Monday 25 October	
Wimbledon v. Ipswich Town	0-2
Saturday 30 October	
Arsenal v. Norwich City	0-0
Blackburn Rovers v. Tottenham Hotspur	1-0
Chelsea v. Oldham Athletic	0-1
Ipswich Town v. Everton	0-2
Liverpool v. Southampton	4-2
Manchester United v. Queen's Park R.	2-1
Newcastle United v. Wimbledon	4-0
Sheffield Wed. v. Leeds United	3-3
Swindon Town v. Aston Villa	1-2
Sunday 31 October	
Coventry City v. Sheffield United	0-0

		P	W	D	L	F	A	Pts
1	Manchester United	13	11	1	1	27	10	34
2	Norwich City	13	6	5	2	21	12	23
3	Arsenal	13	6	5	2	12	6	23
4	Blackburn Rovers	13	6	5	2	18	13	23
5	Aston Villa	13	6	5	2	15	10	23
6	Leeds United	13	6	4	3	20	16	22
7	Liverpool	13	6	2	5	20	12	20
8	Queen's Park R.	13	6	2	5	24	21	20
9	Newcastle United	13	5	4	4	21	14	19
10	Tottenham Hotspur	13	5	4	4	19	14	19
11	Everton	13	6	1	6	16	16	19
12	Wimbledon	13	4	5	4	13	19	17
13	Coventry City	13	3	7	3	14	16	16
14	Ipswich Town	13	4	4	5	12	16	16
15	Manchester City	12	3	5	4	11	10	14
16	Chelsea	13	3	4	6	10	12	13
17	West Ham United	12	3	4	5	6	13	13
18	Sheffield United	13	2	6	5	16	21	12
19	Oldham Athletic	13	2	5	6	9	19	11
20	Sheffield Wed.	13	1	7	5	17	23	10
21	Southampton	13	2	2	9	15	24	8
22	Swindon Town	13	0	5	8	11	30	5

Bobby Gould and 'friend' as he quits the Sky Blues.

MANCHESTER UNITED increase their lead over Arsenal at the top of the table to five points by beating Sheffield Wednesday, while Liverpool end their run of four consecutive defeats with an Anfield draw against Arsenal. But, significantly, it is now five games without a goal for Liverpool, who drop to 13th as a consequence.

Paul Warhurst's season seems over when he breaks a leg in Blackburn's victory at Swindon.

Spurs trail Everton 2–1 with only two minutes left but recover to win and move into fifth place in the table. Next game they come up against Manchester United, who win their fourth game in a row to consolidate top spot and open up a seven-point lead at the top. Arsenal drop to third after being held by Manchester City and Norwich go second on goal difference after winning at Stamford Bridge.

Jim Holton, former United centre-half, dies of a heart attack, aged 42. In his Old Trafford heyday the defender was a cult hero of the Stretford End, who cheered him with the song, 'six foot two, eyes of blue, Big Jim Holton's after you'.

After European action for Premiership clubs it's back to league action and United's Lee Sharpe scores his fifth goal of the campaign to beat Everton and send United a massive nine points clear of nearest challengers Arsenal and Norwich, who can only manage goalless draws. Alan Shearer nets his first hat-trick of the season, against Leeds, but United twice overturn a two-goal deficit to earn a draw. QPR move fifth with their third win in a row and their highest score of the season thus far, over Coventry, a result that prompts the immediate resignation of Sky Blues' manager Bobby Gould.

Sheffield United slip towards the relegation zone with four consecutive draws and Swindon are still seeking their first Premiership victory and remain bottom. Southampton are one place above after just one win, over Newcastle, with a brace of Matt Le Tissier goals. The Channel Islander nets two in the following game but Saints crash at Liverpool. Le Tissier is now Southampton's leading scorer with all six goals coming in twos. Oldham also manage just one win in October, against Chelsea, so they stay in trouble, although the win at Stamford Bridge lifts the Latics to 19th.

Manchester United end the month an incredible 11 points clear, after coming from a goal down to beat QPR, thanks to nearest challengers Arsenal and Norwich drawing at Highbury. Robbie Fowler's first hat-trick of the campaign inspires Liverpool to victory over Southampton and moves them up to a respectable 7th place.

FACT FILE

When Jim Holton was recovering from a broken leg he was trying to park his car in the garage when that leg, encased in plaster, slipped off the footbrake and onto the accelerator. The result was his car slamming through the wall of his garage.

Monday 1 November		
West Ham United v. Manchester City	3-1	
Saturday 6 November		
Arsenal v. Aston Villa	1-2	
Coventry City v. Everton	2-1	
Ipswich Town v. Sheffield Wed.	1-4	
Leeds United v. Chelsea	4-1	
Liverpool v. West Ham United	2-0	
Queen's Park R. v. Blackburn Rovers	1-0	
Sheffield United v. Norwich City	1-2	
Southampton v. Tottenham Hotspur	1-0	
Wimbledon v. Swindon Town	3-0	
Sunday 7 November		
Manchester City v. Manchester United	2-3	
Monday 8 November		
Oldham Athletic v. Newcastle United	1-3	
Saturday 20 November		
Aston Villa v. Sheffield United	1-0	
Blackburn Rovers v. Southampton	2-0	
Chelsea v. Arsenal	0-2	
Everton v. Queen's Park R.	0-3	
Manchester United v. Wimbledon	3-1	
Norwich City v. Manchester City	1-1	
Sheffield Wed. v. Coventry City	0-0	
Swindon Town v. Ipswich Town	2-2	
Tottenham Hotspur v. Leeds United	1-1	
West Ham United v. Oldham Athletic	2-0	
Sunday 21 November		
Newcastle United v. Liverpool	3-0	
Monday 22 November		
Chelsea v. Manchester City	0-0	
Tuesday 23 November		
Blackburn Rovers v. Coventry City	2-1	
Everton v. Leeds United	1-1	
Wednesday 24 November		
Aston Villa v. Southampton	0-2	
Manchester United v. Ipswich Town	0-0	
Newcastle United v. Sheffield United	4-0	
Sheffield Wed. v. Oldham Athletic	3-0	
Swindon Town v. Queen's Park R.	1-0	
Tottenham Hotspur v. Wimbledon	1-1	
West Ham United v. Arsenal	0-0	
Saturday 27 November		
Arsenal v. Newcastle United	2-1	
Coventry City v. Manchester United	0-1	
Ipswich Town v. Blackburn Rovers	1-0	
Leeds United v. Swindon Town	3-0	
Manchester City v. Sheffield Wed.	1-3	
Oldham Athletic v. Norwich City	2-1	
Queen's Park R. v. Tottenham Hotspur	1-1	
Sheffield United v. Chelsea	1-0	
Wimbledon v. Everton	1-1	
Sunday 28 November		
Liverpool v. Aston Villa	2-1	
Monday 29 November		
Southampton v. West Ham United	0-2	

		P	W	D	L	F	A	Pts
1	Manchester United	17	14	2	1	34	13	44
2	Leeds United	17	8	6	3	29	19	30
3	Arsenal	17	8	6	3	17	9	30
4	Blackburn Rovers	17	8	5	4	22	16	29
5	Aston Villa	17	8	5	4	19	15	29
6	Newcastle United	17	8	4	5	32	17	28
7	Norwich City	16	7	6	3	25	16	27
8	Queen's Park R.	17	8	3	6	29	23	27
9	Liverpool	16	8	2	6	24	16	26
10	West Ham United	17	6	5	6	13	16	23
11	Tottenham Hotspur	17	5	7	5	22	18	22
12	Wimbledon	17	5	7	5	19	24	22
13	Everton	17	6	3	8	19	23	21
14	Ipswich Town	17	5	6	6	16	22	21
15	Sheffield Wed.	17	4	8	5	27	25	20
16	Coventry City	17	4	8	5	17	20	20
17	Manchester City	17	3	7	7	16	20	16
18	Sheffield United	17	3	6	8	18	28	15
19	Chelsea	17	3	5	9	11	19	14
20	Southampton	17	4	2	11	18	28	14
21	Oldham Athletic	17	3	5	9	12	28	14
22	Swindon Town	17	1	6	10	14	38	9

Andy Cole, Newcastle United, scores past Bruce Grobbelaar, of Liverpool.

TOTTENHAM are found guilty of misconduct for approaching Ossie Ardiles without the permission of his then club, West Bromwich Albion. They are fined £25,000 and warned about their future conduct.

Tim Flowers leaves Southampton in a new British record fee for a goalkeeper of £2 million. Dave Beasant moves to the Dell from Chelsea.

Aston Villa cut the gap on Manchester United to eight points by beating another of the chasing pack, Arsenal. But consolation for the Gunners comes from the Ian Wright goal that is the team's first in five league games. A fifth scoreless match would have given Arsenal an unwanted record. Norwich stay second after beating Sheffield United; Villa then leapfrog the Canaries, also by beating the Blades.

An exciting Manchester derby sees United come back from 2–0 down to beat City and restore their 11 point advantage at the summit. A brace of Niall Quinn goals is matched by Eric Cantona and Roy Keane gets a late winner.

The Football Managers' Association submits a plan to the FA Premier League that includes recommendations for a reduction in teams to 18, a midwinter break and transfer windows twice a year.

When the Premiership resumes after the international break Manchester United retain their 11 point lead at the top by beating Wimbledon and Newcastle beat Liverpool, with Andy Cole netting his first hat-trick of the season to take his tally to 15 in 15 games since the campaign kicked off.

Former Liverpool star Phil Neal is confirmed as the new Coventry manager and then sees his team lose to a couple of Alan Shearer goals that take Blackburn up to second in the table.

After eight successive Premiership victories Manchester United are held by Ipswich but it doesn't dent their lead at the top as Villa lose to Southampton, a result which increases United's advantage to 12 points. For the fourth time in the season Matt Le Tissier bags a brace of goals but this time the result takes the Saints out of the relegation zone.

At the 16th attempt Swindon finally register their first Premiership victory when a Keith Scott goal, his first for Swindon, nets a win over visitors QPR, and the Robins do it with 10 men after Luke Nijholt is sent off after 15 minutes.

Arsenal 'keeper David Seaman is sent off for a professional foul in the draw with West Ham and Gary Mabbutt badly fractures a cheekbone in a clash with Wimbledon's John Fashanu. Spurs then get news that Teddy Sheringham will need a cartilage operation.

Manchester United get back to winning ways with a victory at Coventry that extends their lead at the top to a massive 14 points because of Blackburn's defeat at Ipswich. But it's sad news in the Blue half of Manchester as Peter Swales, citing death threats against him and his family, severs his 20-year link with Manchester City by resigning.

Oldham finish the month by beating Norwich but they stay 21st.

Saturday 4 December	
Coventry City v. Arsenal	1-0
Everton v. Southampton	1-0
Ipswich Town v. Oldham Athletic	0-0
Leeds United v. Manchester City	3-2
Manchester United v. Norwich City	2-2
Queen's Park R. v. Aston Villa	2-2
Sheffield Wed. v. Liverpool	3-1
Swindon Town v. Sheffield United	0-0
Tottenham Hotspur v. Newcastle United	1-2
Wimbledon v. West Ham United	1-2

Sunday 5 December	
Blackburn Rovers v. Chelsea	2-0

Monday 6 December	
Arsenal v. Tottenham Hotspur	1-1

Tuesday 7 December	
Oldham Athletic v. Swindon Town	2-1
Sheffield United v. Manchester United	0-3

Wednesday 8 December	
Aston Villa v. Sheffield Wed.	2-2
Liverpool v. Queen's Park R.	3-2
Manchester City v. Everton	1-0
Southampton v. Ipswich Town	0-1
West Ham United v. Leeds United	0-1

Saturday 11 December	
Aston Villa v. Wimbledon	0-1
Chelsea v. Ipswich Town	1-1
Liverpool v. Swindon Town	2-2
Manchester City v. Tottenham Hotspur	0-2
Newcastle United v. Manchester United	1-1
Oldham Athletic v. Blackburn Rovers	1-2
Sheffield United v. Everton	0-0
Southampton v. Queen's Park R.	0-1
West Ham United v. Coventry City	3-2

Sunday 12 December	
Arsenal v. Sheffield Wed.	1-0

Monday 13 December	
Norwich City v. Leeds United	2-1

Saturday 18 December	
Blackburn Rovers v. Manchester City	2-0
Coventry City v. Oldham Athletic	1-1
Everton v. Newcastle United	0-2
Ipswich Town v. Norwich City	2-1
Leeds United v. Arsenal	2-1
Sheffield Wed. v. West Ham United	5-0
Swindon Town v. Southampton	2-1
Tottenham Hotspur v. Liverpool	3-3
Wimbledon v. Sheffield United	2-0

Sunday 19 December	
Manchester United v. Aston Villa	3-1

Wednesday 22 December	
Newcastle United v. Leeds United	1-1

Sunday 26 December	
Manchester United v. Blackburn Rovers	1-1
Sheffield United v. Liverpool	0-0
Wimbledon v. Coventry City	1-2

Monday 27 December	
Everton v. Sheffield Wed.	0-2
Ipswich Town v. West Ham United	1-1
Queen's Park R. v. Oldham Athletic	2-0
Southampton v. Chelsea	3-1
Swindon Town v. Arsenal	0-4
Tottenham Hotspur v. Norwich City	1-3

Tuesday 28 December	
Chelsea v. Newcastle United	1-0
Liverpool v. Wimbledon	1-1
Manchester City v. Southampton	1-1
West Ham United v. Tottenham Hotspur	1-3

Wednesday 29 December	
Arsenal v. Sheffield United	3-0
Blackburn Rovers v. Everton	2-0
Leeds United v. Queen's Park R.	1-1
Norwich City v. Aston Villa	1-2
Oldham Athletic v. Manchester United	2-5
Sheffield Wed. v. Swindon Town	3-3

		P	W	D	L	F	A	Pts
1	Manchester United	23	17	5	1	49	20	56
2	Blackburn Rovers	22	12	6	4	31	18	42
3	Leeds United	23	11	8	4	38	26	41
4	Arsenal	23	11	7	5	27	13	40
5	Newcastle United	22	10	6	6	38	21	36
6	Queen's Park R.	22	10	5	7	37	29	35
7	Norwich City	21	9	7	5	34	24	34
8	Aston Villa	22	9	7	6	26	24	34
9	Liverpool	22	9	6	7	34	27	33
10	Sheffield Wed.	23	7	10	6	42	32	31
11	Tottenham Hotspur	23	7	9	7	33	28	30
12	Ipswich Town	22	7	9	6	21	25	30
13	West Ham United	23	8	6	9	20	29	30
14	Wimbledon	22	7	8	7	25	29	29
15	Coventry City	21	6	9	6	23	25	27
16	Everton	23	7	4	12	20	30	25
17	Manchester City	22	4	8	10	20	28	20
18	Oldham Athletic	23	4	7	12	18	39	19
19	Chelsea	21	4	6	11	14	25	18
20	Southampton	23	5	3	15	23	35	18
21	Sheffield United	23	3	9	11	18	36	18
22	Swindon Town	23	2	9	12	22	50	15

THE CHAIRMEN of Premiership clubs vote against reducing the Premiership's numbers to 18, by a majority of 20–2. And, for the first time, video evidence sees a player's booking removed when referee Joe Worrall reviews video footage of Leeds United's John Pemberton's challenge on Nicky Barmby in November.

Everton manager Howard Kendall resigns after his side claim their first Goodison victory since beating Liverpool 10 weeks earlier, against Southampton, with a Tony Cottee goal. Manchester United stay top despite being held by Norwich. Brian McClair marks only his second start of the campaign with one of United's goals, his first of the season.

The following game, a win at Bramall Lane, takes United a colossal 15 points clear and puts Sheffield United just outside the relegation zone. But Blackburn cut back United's lead when a brace of Alan Shearer goals, taking his total to 14 in the league, beat Oldham. Manchester United are then held by Newcastle but they still have a 13-point lead over second-placed Leeds United, who are beaten by Norwich the day after.

At the foot of the table Swindon are just four minutes from beating Liverpool at Anfield when Mark Wright pops up with a late header to register his first goal of the season and earn his side a point.

Manchester United have their advantage at the top cut by victories for Leeds and Blackburn but, inside 24 hours, Alex Ferguson's team justify their domination of the Premiership by turning a 1–0 deficit against Aston Villa into a 3–1 win by scoring three times in the last few minutes to restore the 13-point lead over the chasing pack. Eric Cantona scores twice and Paul Ince nets for the second game running. Ince then makes it three goals in three games when he gets a late Boxing Day equaliser against Blackburn, to earn a point and rescue United's unbeaten home record.

Chelsea, who dropped into the bottom three when they drew with Ipswich, fall another place when they are beaten by Southampton, who leap over the Londoners into 19th.

Swindon end the year bottom, where they have been since August, and seeing out the old year one place ahead of the Robins are Sheffield United, who haven't scored a Premiership goal for more than 540 minutes.

After a run of 11 matches without a win, Chelsea finally register three points when Mark Stein scores the only goal of the game against Newcastle to take his side out of the relegation zone. At the top Manchester United continue their title cruise and end 1993 14 points clear, with a hammering of Oldham Athletic.

Strugglers Southampton 'call in the troops' in the person of former manager Lawrie McMenemy. The ex-guardsman joins his former club as a director but his input is expected to take the heat out of manager Ian Branfoot's precarious position.

Manchester United's Eric Cantona scores against Aston Villa.

Saturday 1 January	
Aston Villa v. Blackburn Rovers	0-1
Everton v. West Ham United	0-1
Ipswich Town v. Liverpool	1-2
Manchester United v. Leeds United	0-0
Newcastle United v. Manchester City	2-0
Queen's Park R. v. Sheffield Wed.	1-2
Sheffield United v. Oldham Athletic	2-1
Southampton v. Norwich City	0-1
Swindon Town v. Chelsea	1-3
Tottenham Hotspur v. Coventry City	1-2
Wimbledon v. Arsenal	0-3

Monday 3 January	
Arsenal v. Queen's Park R.	0-0
Chelsea v. Everton	4-2
Coventry City v. Swindon Town	1-1
Sheffield Wed. v. Tottenham Hotspur	1-0
West Ham United v. Sheffield United	0-0

Tuesday 4 January	
Liverpool v. Manchester United	3-3
Norwich City v. Newcastle United	1-2

Saturday 15 January	
Aston Villa v. West Ham United	3-1
Everton v. Swindon Town	6-2
Leeds United v. Ipswich Town	0-0
Manchester City v. Arsenal	0-0
Norwich City v. Chelsea	1-1
Oldham Athletic v. Liverpool	0-3
Sheffield United v. Blackburn Rovers	1-2
Southampton v. Coventry City	1-0
Tottenham Hotspur v. Manchester United	0-1
Wimbledon v. Sheffield Wed.	2-1

Sunday 16 January	
Queen's Park R. v. Newcastle United	1-2

Saturday 22 January	
Arsenal v. Oldham Athletic	1-1
Chelsea v. Aston Villa	1-1
Coventry City v. Queen's Park R.	0-1
Ipswich Town v. Wimbledon	0-0
Liverpool v. Manchester City	2-1
Manchester United v. Everton	1-0
Newcastle United v. Southampton	1-2
Sheffield Wed. v. Sheffield United	3-1
Swindon Town v. Tottenham Hotspur	2-1

Sunday 23 January	
Blackburn Rovers v. Leeds United	2-1

Monday 24 January	
West Ham United v. Norwich City	3-3

		P	W	D	L	F	A	Pts
1	Manchester United	27	19	7	1	54	23	64
2	Blackburn Rovers	25	15	6	4	36	20	51
3	Arsenal	27	12	10	5	31	14	46
4	Newcastle United	26	13	6	7	45	25	45
5	Liverpool	26	12	7	7	44	32	43
6	Leeds United	26	11	10	5	39	28	43
7	Sheffield Wed.	27	10	10	7	49	36	40
8	Norwich City	25	10	9	6	40	30	39
9	Queen's Park R.	26	11	6	9	40	33	39
10	Aston Villa	25	10	8	7	30	27	38
11	West Ham United	27	9	8	10	25	35	35
12	Wimbledon	25	8	9	8	27	33	33
13	Ipswich Town	25	7	11	7	22	27	32
14	Coventry City	25	7	10	8	26	29	31
15	Tottenham Hotspur	27	7	9	11	35	34	30
16	Everton	27	8	4	15	28	38	28
17	Chelsea	25	6	8	11	23	30	26
18	Southampton	26	7	3	16	26	37	24
19	Sheffield United	27	4	10	13	22	42	22
20	Manchester City	25	4	9	12	21	32	21
21	Oldham Athletic	26	4	8	14	20	45	20
22	Swindon Town	27	3	10	14	28	61	19

Manchester United and Everton players stand in front of a silent Old Trafford crowd during the minute's silence in honour of former Manchester United manager Matt Busby.

THE YEAR starts with Manchester United being held to two draws, first by Leeds, and then at Anfield, where they throw away a 3–0 advantage and Liverpool hit back to earn a point. In between Blackburn close the points gap at the top to 12 when they beat Aston Villa. But the point at Liverpool does at least restore United's lead to 13 points.

Norwich accuse Everton of poaching their manager, Mike Walker, as he resigns and signs a new three-and-a-half year contract to take over at Goodison Park. Another manager leaves his job as Ian Branfoot resigns at struggling Southampton to become the first managerial casualty in the Premiership in 1994.

After cup action Manchester United hold on to their 13-point lead at the top by winning at Spurs, while Blackburn go second with a brace of Alan Shearer goals, not to mention a brace of Sheffield United dismissals, that gain Rovers a win at Bramall Lane.

At the foot of the table it just gets worse for Swindon as they remain rooted to the bottom after a thrashing by Everton, helped by a Tony Cottee hat-trick. After starting the year in 20th place Southampton improve their lot with consecutive victories over Coventry and Newcastle, and move up to 18th. Manchester City are on the slide after two defeats in three games send them down to 20th and there are worries at Boundary Park after Oldham take just one point from three games this month to occupy 21st place.

With Manchester United romping away with the championship the club is saddened by the death of Sir Matt Busby, aged 84. United beat Everton two days later in a display of football that is a tribute to the man who made Manchester United. The win takes United 16 points clear of Blackburn, their biggest lead of the campaign, but Rovers peg it back to 13 the very next day when they beat Leeds, with another brace from Alan Shearer that takes his running total to 23. Shearer's last-minute winner is his seventh goal in four games.

Graeme Souness resigns after less than three years as Liverpool manager and the club delve, once more, into the famed 'boot room' for a successor and appoint Roy Evans.

February

Wednesday 2 February		
Coventry City v. Ipswich Town		1-0
Saturday 5 February		
Blackburn Rovers v. Wimbledon		3-0
Everton v. Chelsea		4-2
Manchester City v. Ipswich Town		2-1
Norwich City v. Liverpool		2-2
Oldham Athletic v. Southampton		2-1
Queen's Park R. v. Manchester United		2-3
Swindon Town v. Coventry City		3-1
Tottenham Hotspur v. Sheffield Wed.		1-3
Sunday 6 February		
Aston Villa v. Leeds United		1-0
Saturday 12 February		
Aston Villa v. Swindon Town		5-0
Everton v. Ipswich Town		0-0
Manchester City v. West Ham United		0-0
Oldham Athletic v. Chelsea		2-1
Sheffield United v. Coventry City		0-0
Tottenham Hotspur v. Blackburn Rovers		0-2
Wimbledon v. Newcastle United		4-2
Sunday 13 February		
Norwich City v. Arsenal		1-1
Monday 14 February		
Southampton v. Liverpool		4-2
Saturday 19 February		
Blackburn Rovers v. Newcastle United		1-0
Coventry City v. Manchester City		4-0
Everton v. Arsenal		1-1
Leeds United v. Liverpool		2-0
Swindon Town v. Norwich City		3-3
Tuesday 22 February		
Aston Villa v. Manchester City		0-0
Ipswich Town v. Sheffield United		3-2
Norwich City v. Blackburn Rovers		2-2
Wednesday 23 February		
Newcastle United v. Coventry City		4-0
Saturday 26 February		
Arsenal v. Blackburn Rovers		1-0
Liverpool v. Coventry City		1-0
Manchester City v. Swindon Town		2-1
Norwich City v. Sheffield Wed.		1-1
Southampton v. Wimbledon		1-0
West Ham United v. Manchester United		2-2
Sunday 27 February		
Chelsea v. Tottenham Hotspur		4-3
Monday 28 February		
Oldham Athletic v. Leeds United		1-1

		P	W	D	L	F	A	Pts
1	Manchester United	29	20	8	1	59	27	68
2	Blackburn Rovers	30	18	7	5	44	23	61
3	Arsenal	30	13	12	5	34	16	51
4	Newcastle United	29	14	6	9	51	30	48
5	Leeds United	29	12	11	6	42	30	47
6	Liverpool	30	13	8	9	49	40	47
7	Aston Villa	28	12	9	7	36	27	45
8	Sheffield Wed.	29	11	11	7	53	38	44
9	Norwich City	30	10	14	6	49	39	44
10	Queen's Park R.	27	11	6	10	42	36	39
11	Coventry City	31	9	11	11	32	37	38
12	West Ham United	29	9	10	10	27	37	37
13	Ipswich Town	29	8	12	9	26	32	36
14	Wimbledon	28	9	9	10	31	39	36
15	Everton	30	9	6	15	33	41	33
16	Tottenham Hotspur	30	7	9	14	39	43	30
17	Southampton	29	9	3	17	32	41	30
18	Chelsea	28	7	8	13	30	39	29
19	Manchester City	30	6	11	13	25	38	29
20	Oldham Athletic	29	6	9	14	25	48	27
21	Sheffield United	29	4	11	14	24	45	23
22	Swindon Town	31	4	11	16	35	72	23

MANCHESTER UNITED extend their unbeaten run to 21 matches with a win over QPR that also maintains their 13-point lead at the top of the table. Blackburn stay second with a victory over Wimbledon. At the bottom five clubs are covered by just two points and there is some joy for Swindon, who register their fourth win of the campaign when a Jan Aage Fjortoft hat-trick sinks Coventry. A week later, however, the Sky Blues draw with Sheffield United and that point takes the Blades above Swindon into 21st place. Oldham open the month with a couple of wins that improve their position to 18th.

Blackburn cut the deficit on United to 10 points by beating Spurs, and Rovers have a game in hand. At the other end of the Premiership Southampton celebrate their first game under new manager Alan Ball with a Matt Le Tissier hat-trick, including two penalties, inspiring the Saints to a victory over Liverpool that takes them out of the bottom three.

Blackburn beat Newcastle to close the gap on Manchester United to seven points but it's the first time in seven games that Alan Shearer hasn't been on the scoresheet. Rovers are then held by 10-man Norwich and although the gap on United is now just six points, Kenny Dalglish's side have played one game more. Andy Cole nets his second hat-trick of the campaign to take his tally to 26 and Newcastle move into third place, above Arsenal and Leeds, by beating Coventry.

FIFA's Sepp Blatter declares that tackles from behind are to be punished with a straight red card, providing such challenges are deemed to have no chance of getting the ball.

The last Saturday of the month proves a significant one in the title race. Although Manchester United are held at West Ham, where a late goal from former Hammer Paul Ince earns the draw, they stretch their lead to seven points because Blackburn crash at Arsenal.

Southampton move even further away from relegation with a Matt Le Tissier goal that beats Wimbledon. It's the fifth game in a row that Le Tissier has scored and his tally in that run is seven. Swindon stay bottom, with Sheffield United one place better off, but Manchester City are in danger of being pulled into the relegation struggle after poor results against Coventry and Aston Villa, although City finish the month with a morale-boosting win over rock-bottom Swindon.

Norwich City's Brian Gunn gets a red card in the game against Liverpool.

Wednesday 2 March		
Tottenham Hotspur v. Aston Villa		1-1
Saturday 5 March		
Blackburn Rovers v. Liverpool		2-0
Everton v. Oldham Athletic		2-1
Ipswich Town v. Arsenal		1-5
Leeds United v. Southampton		0-0
Manchester United v. Chelsea		0-1
Queen's Park R. v. Manchester City		1-1
Sheffield Wed. v. Newcastle United		0-1
Swindon Town v. West Ham United		1-1
Tottenham Hotspur v. Sheffield United		2-2
Wimbledon v. Norwich City		3-1
Sunday 6 March		
Coventry City v. Aston Villa		0-1
Saturday 12 March		
Aston Villa v. Ipswich Town		0-1
Manchester City v. Wimbledon		0-1
Newcastle United v. Swindon Town		7-1
Norwich City v. Queen's Park R.		3-4
Southampton v. Sheffield Wed.		1-1
Sunday 13 March		
Liverpool v. Everton		2-1
Sheffield United v. Leeds United		2-2
Wednesday 16 March		
Chelsea v. Wimbledon		2-0
Leeds United v. Aston Villa		2-0
Manchester United v. Sheffield Wed.		5-0
Sheffield United v. Queen's Park R.		1-1
Saturday 19 March		
Aston Villa v. Oldham Athletic		1-2
Leeds United v. Coventry City		1-0
Liverpool v. Chelsea		2-1
Manchester City v. Sheffield United		0-0
Queen's Park R. v. Wimbledon		1-0
Southampton v. Arsenal		0-4
Swindon Town v. Manchester United		2-2
Tottenham Hotspur v. Ipswich Town		1-1
West Ham United v. Newcastle United		2-4
Sunday 20 March		
Sheffield Wed. v. Blackburn Rovers		1-2
Monday 21 March		
Norwich City v. Everton		3-0
Tuesday 22 March		
Arsenal v. Manchester United		2-2
Wednesday 23 March		
Newcastle United v. Ipswich Town		2-0
Saturday 26 March		
Arsenal v. Liverpool		1-0
Blackburn Rovers v. Swindon Town		3-1
Chelsea v. West Ham United		2-0
Coventry City v. Norwich City		2-1
Everton v. Tottenham Hotspur		0-1
Ipswich Town v. Queen's Park R.		1-3
Oldham Athletic v. Manchester City		0-0
Sheffield United v. Southampton		0-0
Wimbledon v. Leeds United		1-0
Monday 28 March		
Sheffield United v. West Ham United		3-2
Tuesday 29 March		
Ipswich Town v. Manchester City		2-2
Newcastle United v. Norwich City		3-0
Wimbledon v. Blackburn Rovers		4-1
Wednesday 30 March		
Aston Villa v. Everton		0-0
Manchester United v. Liverpool		1-0
Sheffield Wed. v. Chelsea		3-1
Southampton v. Oldham Athletic		1-3

		P	W	D	L	F	A	Pts
1	Manchester United	34	22	10	2	69	32	76
2	Blackburn Rovers	34	21	7	6	52	29	70
3	Newcastle United	34	19	6	9	68	33	63
4	Arsenal	34	16	13	5	46	19	61
5	Leeds United	34	14	13	7	47	33	55
6	Liverpool	35	15	8	12	53	46	53
7	Queen's Park R.	32	14	8	10	52	42	50
8	Aston Villa	34	13	11	10	39	33	50
9	Sheffield Wed.	34	12	12	10	58	48	48
10	Wimbledon	34	13	9	12	40	44	48
11	Norwich City	35	11	14	10	57	51	47
12	Coventry City	34	10	11	13	34	40	41
13	Ipswich Town	35	9	14	12	32	45	41
14	Chelsea	33	10	8	15	37	44	38
15	West Ham United	33	9	11	13	32	47	38
16	Everton	35	10	7	18	36	48	37
17	Tottenham Hotspur	34	8	12	14	47	47	36
18	Oldham Athletic	33	8	10	15	31	52	34
19	Manchester City	35	6	15	14	28	42	33
20	Southampton	34	9	6	19	34	49	33
21	Sheffield United	35	5	16	14	32	52	31
22	Swindon Town	35	4	13	18	40	85	25

AFTER a run of 22 matches without defeat Manchester United are finally beaten, and lose their home record too, when Chelsea complete the league double over them. Gavin Peacock, who scored the only goal in September's victory at Stamford Bridge, is also the match-winner at Old Trafford. Blackburn move to within four points of United as a consequence, by beating Liverpool, and Arsenal move third by thrashing Ipswich, assisted by an Ian Wright hat-trick, including a penalty. Wright then repeats the feat, exactly, when the Gunners beat Southampton, but it's Blackburn who remain in second place with successive victories over Sheffield Wednesday and Swindon, the latter remaining bottom.

Sheffield United stay 21st despite remaining unbeaten throughout the month, but their only win comes in their sixth and final game of the six they play, against West Ham. Oldham complete the bottom three despite picking up four points from six against Aston Villa and Manchester City.

Manchester United have to wait 11 days to resume Premiership action but when they do it's poor old Sheffield Wednesday who suffer, with a thrashing at Old Trafford that takes United seven points clear of Blackburn. The fact that Eric Cantona is in sparkling form, with two goals, of course has nothing to do with the time he was wanted by Wednesday but didn't take kindly to being asked by the Hillsborough club to subject himself to a trial period. Three days later it's 'Eric the Red' as the volatile Frenchman is sent off for stamping on an opponent when bottom club Swindon hold the league leaders to a draw.

Sheffield Wednesday are again on the receiving end when they fall to Blackburn in their next game, allowing Rovers to close the gap on the leaders once more, to only five points.

United have Eric Cantona sent off for the second time in four days when he is dismissed for a second bookable offence as Arsenal claim a Highbury draw.

Transfer deadline day sees a flurry of activity, with Darren Peacock's departure from QPR for Newcastle United, in a club record £2.7 million deal, topping the record sales total of £7 million.

Blackburn take advantage of their game in hand over Coca-Cola Cup finalists Manchester United by reducing the gap on top spot, with a victory over Swindon Town, to a mere three points.

Spurs, who have forgotten what it's like to win, register their first victory for 11 games when Steve Sedgley nets the only goal of the game at Goodison.

Blackburn's title hopes are set back by a Wimbledon walloping, after the Dons overturn a 1–0 deficit, and to rub that in Manchester United win at Liverpool, the very next day, with a Paul Ince goal, to go six points clear.

Manchester United's Eric Cantona tangles with Swindon's John Moncur in the incident which led to Cantona's sending off.

Friday 1 April
Leeds United v. Newcastle United	1-1

Saturday 2 April
Arsenal v. Swindon Town	1-1
Blackburn Rovers v. Manchester United	2-0
Chelsea v. Southampton	2-0
Coventry City v. Wimbledon	1-2
Liverpool v. Sheffield United	1-2
Manchester City v. Aston Villa	3-0
Norwich City v. Tottenham Hotspur	1-2
Oldham Athletic v. Queen's Park R.	4-1
Sheffield Wed. v. Everton	5-1
West Ham United v. Ipswich Town	2-1

Monday 4 April
Aston Villa v. Norwich City	0-0
Everton v. Blackburn Rovers	0-3
Ipswich Town v. Coventry City	0-2
Manchester United v. Oldham Athletic	3-2
Newcastle United v. Chelsea	0-0
Queen's Park R. v. Leeds United	0-4
Sheffield United v. Arsenal	1-1
Southampton v. Manchester City	0-1
Swindon Town v. Sheffield Wed.	0-1
Tottenham Hotspur v. West Ham United	1-4
Wimbledon v. Liverpool	1-1

Saturday 9 April
Coventry City v. Tottenham Hotspur	1-0
Liverpool v. Ipswich Town	1-0
Manchester City v. Newcastle United	2-1
Norwich City v. Southampton	4-5
Sheffield Wed. v. Queen's Park R.	3-1
West Ham United v. Everton	0-1

Monday 11 April
Blackburn Rovers v. Aston Villa	1-0

Wednesday 13 April
Queen's Park R. v. Chelsea	1-1

Saturday 16 April
Arsenal v. Chelsea	1-0
Coventry City v. Sheffield Wed.	1-1
Ipswich Town v. Swindon Town	1-1
Liverpool v. Newcastle United	0-2
Manchester City v. Norwich City	1-1
Oldham Athletic v. West Ham United	1-2
Queen's Park R. v. Everton	2-1
Sheffield United v. Aston Villa	1-2
Southampton v. Blackburn Rovers	3-1
Wimbledon v. Manchester United	1-0

Sunday 17 April
Leeds United v. Tottenham Hotspur	2-0

Tuesday 19 April
Arsenal v. Wimbledon	1-1

Saturday 23 April
Aston Villa v. Arsenal	1-2
Chelsea v. Leeds United	1-1
Everton v. Coventry City	0-0
Manchester United v. Manchester City	2-0
Newcastle United v. Oldham Athletic	3-2
Norwich City v. Sheffield United	0-1
Sheffield Wed. v. Ipswich Town	5-0
Swindon Town v. Wimbledon	2-4
Tottenham Hotspur v. Southampton	3-0
West Ham United v. Liverpool	1-2

Sunday 24 April
Blackburn Rovers v. Queen's Park R.	1-1

Tuesday 26 April
Wimbledon v. Oldham Athletic	3-0

Wednesday 27 April
Chelsea v. Swindon Town	2-0
Leeds United v. Manchester United	0-2
Newcastle United v. Aston Villa	5-1
Queen's Park R. v. Arsenal	1-1
West Ham United v. Blackburn Rovers	1-2

Saturday 30 April
Arsenal v. West Ham United	0-2
Leeds United v. Everton	3-0
Liverpool v. Norwich City	0-1
Manchester City v. Chelsea	2-2
Oldham Athletic v. Sheffield Wed.	0-0
Queen's Park R. v. Swindon Town	1-3
Sheffield United v. Newcastle United	2-0
Southampton v. Aston Villa	4-1
Wimbledon v. Tottenham Hotspur	2-1

		P	W	D	L	F	A	Pts
1	Manchester United	39	25	10	4	76	37	85
2	Blackburn Rovers	40	25	8	7	62	34	83
3	Newcastle United	41	22	8	11	80	41	74
4	Arsenal	41	18	17	6	53	26	71
5	Leeds United	40	17	15	8	58	37	66
6	Wimbledon	41	18	11	12	54	50	65
7	Sheffield Wed.	40	16	14	10	73	51	62
8	Liverpool	41	17	9	15	58	53	60
9	Queen's Park R.	40	15	11	14	60	60	56
10	Aston Villa	41	14	12	15	44	49	54
11	Norwich City	41	12	16	13	64	60	52
12	West Ham United	40	13	11	16	44	55	50
13	Coventry City	39	12	13	14	39	43	49
14	Chelsea	40	12	12	16	45	49	48
15	Manchester City	41	9	17	15	37	48	44
16	Tottenham Hotspur	40	10	12	18	51	57	42
17	Southampton	40	12	6	22	46	61	42
18	Ipswich Town	40	9	15	16	34	56	42
19	Sheffield United	40	8	17	15	39	56	41
20	Everton	41	11	8	22	39	61	41
21	Oldham Athletic	39	9	11	19	40	64	38
22	Swindon Town	41	5	15	21	47	95	30

Alan Shearer of Blackburn Rovers scores the first goal against Manchester United.

BLACKBURN are right back in the title race with a sensational victory over Manchester United. A brace of Alan Shearer goals takes Rovers to within three points of the leaders, with seven games left. At the foot of the table only Southampton, of the relegation-threatened clubs, lose, while Sheffield United celebrate their first win at Anfield for more than two decades as a couple of Tore Andre Flo goals move the Blades up to 20th.

Teddy Sheringham celebrates his return to action, after a five month absence, by scoring shortly after coming on as a substitute at Norwich to help Spurs to their second successive victory. But things are looking dicey for Everton, who slip towards the drop zone after a drubbing at Sheffield Wednesday. Swindon hold Arsenal but still look doomed. Oldham give themselves hope with their best win of the season, over QPR, but follow up by starting the Bank Holiday programme with a defeat by Manchester United that starts a downward spiral.

Blackburn keep up the pressure on United when a brace of Mike Newell goals at Goodison helps send his former club into deeper trouble, just above the relegation zone.

It's very tight at the foot of the Premiership and Southampton come back from 3–1 down to edge Norwich in a nine-goal thriller at Carrow Road, which finishes 4–5, to move up to 20th. Matt Le Tissier takes his season's goal tally to 20 with a hat-trick, then creates a last-minute winner for Ken Monkou. Sheffield United drop to one place above Swindon after losing to Aston Villa.

FACT FILE

Andy Cole's goal in Newcastle's 5–0 win over Aston Villa is his 40th of the season and overtakes the club record, set by Hughie Gallacher in 1927 and equalled by George Robledo in 1952.

Back at the top it couldn't be any closer. At one time Manchester United's lead over Blackburn was 16 points, but Rovers draw level on 79 points when a late Alan Shearer goal defeats Villa. It is Shearer's 30th goal of the campaign but Rovers still trail on goal difference and have played one game more than United.

Five days later Shearer's former club, Southampton, throw the title race wide open by beating Rovers at the Dell to move out of the relegation zone. But United fail to take advantage when, later the same day, John Fashanu scores the only goal as Wimbledon beat the leaders.

Spurs are dropping like a stone and defeat at Leeds means they are fifth from bottom and fast running out of games. Fixtures against two of the clubs below them, Oldham and Southampton, follow and could decide Tottenham's fate. But Spurs beat Southampton to climb to 16th and keep the Saints 19th, and in trouble.

At the top Cantona marks his return from suspension with a St George's Day brace that beats Manchester City and takes United three points clear of Blackburn, who then fail to beat QPR and the title race is all but over. With three matches left they trail United, who have a game in hand, by two points. Shearer scores for the last time in this campaign to finish on 31 goals.

Swindon are relegated in a defeat by Wimbledon and then Oldham are crushed by Dean Holdsworth's first Premiership hat-trick for the Dons, to keep the Latics 21st.

Everton are in serious trouble after losing to Leeds. Southampton and Sheffield United then both win, to leave the Toffees third from bottom with one match left.

Oldham are three points adrift of Everton, after drawing with Sheffield Wednesday, but have two games in hand.

Relegated Swindon register their first, and last, away win in the Premiership, completing their only league double of the season over QPR, and there is a certain symmetry to the end of Arsenal's long unbeaten run. Their 2–0 reverse to West Ham is a first defeat in 20 games.

Sunday 1 May

Ipswich Town v. Manchester United	1-2

Monday 2 May

Coventry City v. Blackburn Rovers	2-1

Tuesday 3 May

Leeds United v. Sheffield Wed.	2-2
Oldham Athletic v. Sheffield United	1-1
Queen's Park R. v. West Ham United	0-0

Wednesday 4 May

Chelsea v. Coventry City	1-2
Manchester United v. Southampton	2-0

Thursday 5 May

Oldham Athletic v. Tottenham Hotspur	0-2

Saturday 7 May

Aston Villa v. Liverpool	2-1
Blackburn Rovers v. Ipswich Town	0-0
Chelsea v. Sheffield United	3-2
Everton v. Wimbledon	3-2
Newcastle United v. Arsenal	2-0
Norwich City v. Oldham Athletic	1-1
Sheffield Wed. v. Manchester City	1-1
Swindon Town v. Leeds United	0-5
Tottenham Hotspur v. Queen's Park R.	1-2
West Ham United v. Southampton	3-3

Sunday 8 May

Manchester United v. Coventry City	0-0

		P	W	D	L	F	A	Pts
1	Manchester United	42	27	11	4	80	38	92
2	Blackburn Rovers	42	25	9	8	63	36	84
3	Newcastle United	42	23	8	11	82	41	77
4	Arsenal	42	18	17	7	53	28	71
5	Leeds United	42	18	16	8	65	39	70
6	Wimbledon	42	18	11	13	56	53	65
7	Sheffield Wed.	42	16	16	10	76	54	64
8	Liverpool	42	17	9	16	59	55	60
9	Queen's Park R.	42	16	12	14	62	61	60
10	Aston Villa	42	15	12	15	46	50	57
11	Coventry City	42	14	14	14	43	45	56
12	Norwich City	42	12	17	13	65	61	53
13	West Ham United	42	13	13	16	47	58	52
14	Chelsea	42	13	12	17	49	53	51
15	Tottenham Hotspur	42	11	12	19	54	59	45
16	Manchester City	42	9	18	15	38	49	45
17	Everton	42	12	8	22	42	63	44
18	Southampton	42	12	7	23	49	66	43
19	Ipswich Town	42	9	16	17	35	58	43
20	Sheffield United	42	8	18	16	42	60	42
21	Oldham Athletic	42	9	13	20	42	68	40
22	Swindon Town	42	5	15	22	47	100	30

Promoted from Endsleigh Insurance League Division One

Crystal Palace

Nottingham Forest

Leicester City (via play-offs)

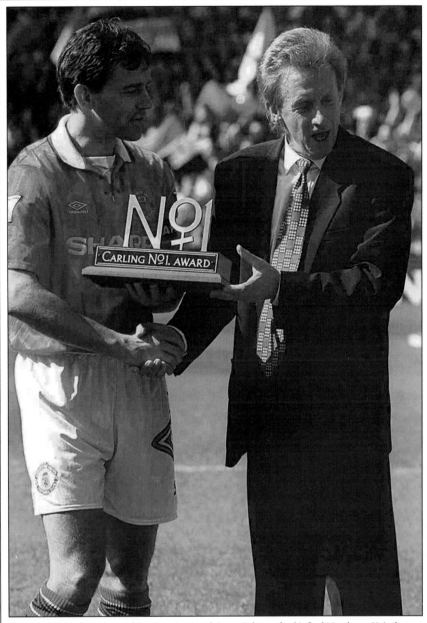

'The King', Denis Law, congratulates Captain Marvel, Bryan Robson, after his final Manchester United game.

MANCHESTER UNITED move a step closer to retaining their title with a win at Ipswich but an injury to Peter Schmeichel puts a question mark over his fitness for the FA Cup Final. With just two games left Blackburn trail the leaders by five points. Rovers finally concede the title to United after losing to a brace of Julian Darby goals at Coventry. It's a ninth championship for Old Trafford.

Newcastle clinch third place with a final game win against Arsenal in which Andy Cole takes his season's goal tally to 41 at his former club. Top Premiership scorer Cole earns a new four-year deal and Newcastle also sign up manager Kevin Keegan, on a remarkable 10-year contract.

At Boundary Park Spurs win to stave off relegation but virtually condemn Oldham to the First Division. But the escape of the season is carried out by Everton on the final Saturday of the campaign. Wimbledon lead 2–0 at Goodison, but Everton fight back, with Graham Stuart netting the crucial winner just nine minutes from time. That win, plus Ipswich's draw at Blackburn and Southampton's draw with West Ham, relegates Sheffield United, who are 2–1 ahead against Chelsea until the last 15 minutes when Mark Stein's brace wins the game for Chelsea. Oldham draw at Norwich but a point isn't enough and the Latics complete the relegated trio.

Champions Manchester United bring an end to the Premiership season at Old Trafford with a draw which marks Bryan Robson's 340th and last appearance for the club.

End of season round-up

Top Premiership Goalscorers 1993–94

Andy Cole	Newcastle United	34
Alan Shearer	Blackburn Rovers	31
Chris Sutton	Norwich City	25
Matt Le Tissier	Southampton	25
Ian Wright	Arsenal	23
Peter Beardsley	Newcastle United	21
Mark Bright	Sheffield Wednesday	19
Eric Cantona	Manchester United	18
Dean Holdsworth	Wimbledon	17
Rod Wallace	Leeds	17

Coca-Cola League Cup Final

Aston Villa 3   Manchester United 1

Aston Villa equalled the League Cup record of four wins, held jointly by Liverpool and Nottingham Forest, with a comprehensive victory over Manchester United. One goal from Dalian Atkinson plus two from Dean Saunders, one a penalty, against a consolation by Mark Hughes, stopped United's pursuit of the 'Treble' in its tracks. Andrei Kanchelskis was sent off for handling on the line in the last minute, becoming the fourth United player to be dismissed in five games.

FA Cup Final

Manchester United 4   Chelsea 0

After completing the league double over United, without conceding a goal, no one was expecting Chelsea to suffer a defeat that equalled the post-war record, also held by United. Eric Cantona scored two penalties but it was the second, and most contentious, that turned the game, as it gave United a 2–0 lead. Andrei Kanchelskis was tripped by Frank Sinclair and although it appeared outside the area the spot-kick was awarded and converted by Cantona. It got worse for Sinclair when he slipped, allowing Mark Hughes to make it 3–0, and substitute Brian McClair completed the rout with a tap-in.

FWA Footballer of the Year

Alan Shearer   Blackburn Rovers

PFA Player of the Year

Eric Cantona   Manchester United

PFA Young Player of the Year

Andy Cole   Manchester United

Manager of the Year

Alex Ferguson   Manchester United

Close Season 1994

After being found guilty of financial irregularities Spurs are banned from next season's FA Cup, have 12 points deducted at the start of the Premiership season and are fined £600,000. The FA Appeals Board reduces the points deduction to six but increases the fine to £1.5 million and confirms the FA Cup ban.

Manchester City sign Nicky Summerbee from Swindon for £1.5 million and Leeds sign Sheffield Wednesday's Carlton Palmer for £2.6 million.

Norwich place a record fee of £5 million on Chris Sutton and Manchester United withdraw from the race for his signature, leaving Blackburn and Arsenal as favourites to capture the player. The Gunners pull out leaving the field clear for Rovers.

After 27 years, man and boy, at Upton Park, West Ham sack Billy Bonds and replace him with his assistant Harry Redknapp. John Fashanu, for so long an integral part of the 'Crazy Gang', leaves Wimbledon and signs for Aston Villa, and Bruce Grobbelaar leaves Liverpool after 13 trophy-packed seasons and signs for Southampton, while Newcastle fail to get a work permit for US goalkeeper Brad Friedel. In a portent of things to come, Manchester United's Eric Cantona is sent off in a pre-season tournament in Scotland.

The fraud inquiry investigating bribery allegations at Tottenham Hotspur is dropped and Spurs will not lose six points at the start of the campaign. Instead those points will be deducted at the end of the season. The curtain-raiser for the Premiership season, the Charity Shield, is a stormy affair as referee Philip Don brandishes seven yellow cards. Eric Cantona scores his third penalty in consecutive Wembley matches to help defeat Blackburn Rovers.

Paul Ince finally signs his new contract at Old Trafford, two weeks after United's 'take it or leave' edict. Ince is then warned about his conduct during the Charity Shield when he went over the top in his celebrations after scoring.

Aston Villa manager Ron Atkinson celebrates with his player, Dean Saunders, after winning the League cup.

Saturday 20 August	
Arsenal v. Manchester City	3-0
Chelsea v. Norwich City	2-0
Coventry City v. Wimbledon	1-1
Crystal Palace v. Liverpool	1-6
Everton v. Aston Villa	2-2
Ipswich Town v. Nottingham Forest	0-1
Manchester United v. Queen's Park R.	2-0
Sheffield Wed. v. Tottenham Hotspur	3-4
Southampton v. Blackburn Rovers	1-1
West Ham United v. Leeds United	0-0
Sunday 21 August	
Leicester City v. Newcastle United	1-3
Monday 22 August	
Nottingham Forest v. Manchester United	1-1
Tuesday 23 August	
Blackburn Rovers v. Leicester City	3-0
Leeds United v. Arsenal	1-0
Wimbledon v. Ipswich Town	1-1
Wednesday 24 August	
Aston Villa v. Southampton	1-1
Manchester City v. West Ham United	3-0
Newcastle United v. Coventry City	4-0
Norwich City v. Crystal Palace	0-0
Queen's Park R. v. Sheffield Wed.	3-2
Tottenham Hotspur v. Everton	2-1
Saturday 27 August	
Aston Villa v. Crystal Palace	1-1
Blackburn Rovers v. Coventry City	4-0
Leeds United v. Chelsea	2-3
Manchester City v. Everton	4-0
Newcastle United v. Southampton	5-1
Norwich City v. West Ham United	1-0
Nottingham Forest v. Leicester City	1-0
Queen's Park R. v. Ipswich Town	1-2
Tottenham Hotspur v. Manchester United	0-1
Wimbledon v. Sheffield Wed.	0-1
Sunday 28 August	
Liverpool v. Arsenal	3-0
Monday 29 August	
Coventry City v. Aston Villa	0-1
Tuesday 30 August	
Crystal Palace v. Leeds United	1-2
Everton v. Nottingham Forest	1-2
Ipswich Town v. Tottenham Hotspur	1-3
Wednesday 31 August	
Arsenal v. Blackburn Rovers	0-0
Chelsea v. Manchester City	3-0
Leicester City v. Queen's Park R.	1-1
Manchester United v. Wimbledon	3-0
Sheffield Wed. v. Norwich City	0-0
Southampton v. Liverpool	0-2
West Ham United v. Newcastle United	1-3

		P	W	D	L	F	A	Pts
1	Newcastle United	4	4	0	0	15	3	12
2	Manchester United	4	3	1	0	7	1	10
3	Nottingham Forest	4	3	1	0	5	2	10
4	Liverpool	3	3	0	0	11	1	9
5	Chelsea	3	3	0	0	8	2	9
6	Tottenham Hotspur	4	3	0	1	9	6	9
7	Blackburn Rovers	4	2	2	0	8	1	8
8	Leeds United	4	2	1	1	5	4	7
9	Manchester City	4	2	0	2	7	6	6
10	Aston Villa	4	1	3	0	5	4	6
11	Norwich City	4	1	2	1	1	2	5
12	Sheffield Wed.	4	1	1	2	6	7	4
13	Arsenal	4	1	1	2	3	4	4
14	Queen's Park R.	4	1	1	2	5	7	4
15	Ipswich Town	4	1	1	2	4	6	4
16	Wimbledon	4	0	2	2	2	6	2
17	Crystal Palace	4	0	2	2	3	9	2
18	Southampton	4	0	2	2	3	9	2
19	Everton	4	0	1	3	4	10	1
20	Leicester City	4	0	1	3	2	8	1
21	West Ham United	4	0	1	3	1	7	1
22	Coventry City	4	0	1	3	1	10	1

Jürgen Klinsmann celebrates scoring his first goal for Tottenham Hotspur at Sheffield Wednesday.

LIVERPOOL kick off with an impressive win at Crystal Palace with 'Sorcerer' Ian Rush netting two and apprentice Robbie Fowler getting half the goals. 1990 World Cup winner Jürgen Klinsmann marks his Spurs debut with a goal in the win at Hillsborough.

New £5 million signing Chris Sutton opens his account by scoring in Blackburn's victory over Leicester. Alan Shearer also gets a goal and the 'SAS' duo is born. Newcastle top the table after two games, on goal difference from Spurs, for whom Jürgen Klinsmann nets twice in the win over Everton.

Chris Sutton continues his goal-laden start to life at Ewood Park with a hat-trick that helps defeat Coventry. Newcastle storm ahead after thumping Southampton in a game where Andy Cole scores twice, but Liverpool join the Magpies at the summit after a Robbie Fowler hat-trick against his favourite Premiership opposition downs Arsenal. Nottingham Forest, who win at Everton, draw level with the top two.

Jürgen Klinsmann excedes Chris Sutton's four-goal start to the campaign with another brace as Spurs beat Ipswich. Newcastle's victory at West Ham sees them end the month as league leaders but Chelsea and Liverpool, with Robbie Fowler netting his fifth goal in three games, continue their 100 percent starts.

FACT FILE

Robbie Fowler's hat-trick against Arsenal, taking him just four minutes, against the 'meanest' Premiership defence, is the fastest hat-trick in the league's history. Two of the 19-year-old's goals come inside two minutes.

Saturday 10 September	
Aston Villa v. Ipswich Town	2-0
Blackburn Rovers v. Everton	3-0
Liverpool v. West Ham United	0-0
Manchester City v. Crystal Palace	1-1
Newcastle United v. Chelsea	4-2
Norwich City v. Arsenal	0-0
Nottingham Forest v. Sheffield Wed.	4-1
Queen's Park R. v. Coventry City	2-2
Wimbledon v. Leicester City	2-1

Sunday 11 September	
Leeds United v. Manchester United	2-1

Monday 12 September	
Tottenham Hotspur v. Southampton	1-2

Saturday 17 September	
Coventry City v. Leeds United	2-1
Crystal Palace v. Wimbledon	0-0
Everton v. Queen's Park R.	2-2
Leicester City v. Tottenham Hotspur	3-1
Manchester United v. Liverpool	2-0
Sheffield Wed. v. Manchester City	1-1
Southampton v. Nottingham Forest	1-1
West Ham United v. Aston Villa	1-0

Sunday 18 September	
Arsenal v. Newcastle United	2-3
Chelsea v. Blackburn Rovers	1-2

Monday 19 September	
Ipswich Town v. Norwich City	1-2

Saturday 24 September	
Blackburn Rovers v. Aston Villa	3-1
Coventry City v. Southampton	1-3
Crystal Palace v. Chelsea	0-1
Everton v. Leicester City	1-1
Ipswich Town v. Manchester United	3-2
Manchester City v. Norwich City	2-0
Newcastle United v. Liverpool	1-1
Queen's Park R. v. Wimbledon	0-1
Tottenham Hotspur v. Nottingham Forest	1-4

Sunday 25 September	
West Ham United v. Arsenal	0-2

Monday 26 September	
Sheffield Wed. v. Leeds United	1-1

		P	W	D	L	F	A	Pts
1	Newcastle United	7	6	1	0	23	8	19
2	Blackburn Rovers	7	5	2	0	16	3	17
3	Nottingham Forest	7	5	2	0	14	5	17
4	Manchester United	7	4	1	2	12	6	13
5	Chelsea	6	4	0	2	12	8	12
6	Liverpool	6	3	2	1	12	4	11
7	Manchester City	7	3	2	2	11	8	11
8	Leeds United	7	3	2	2	9	8	11
9	Aston Villa	7	2	3	2	8	8	9
10	Wimbledon	7	2	3	2	5	7	9
11	Norwich City	7	2	3	2	3	5	9
12	Tottenham Hotspur	7	3	0	4	12	15	9
13	Southampton	7	2	3	2	9	12	9
14	Arsenal	7	2	2	3	7	7	8
15	Ipswich Town	7	2	1	4	8	12	7
16	Queen's Park R.	7	1	3	3	9	12	6
17	Sheffield Wed.	7	1	3	3	9	13	6
18	Leicester City	7	1	2	4	7	12	5
19	West Ham United	7	1	2	4	2	9	5
20	Coventry City	7	1	2	4	6	16	5
21	Crystal Palace	7	0	4	3	4	11	4
22	Everton	7	0	3	4	7	16	3

PHIL BABB becomes the most expensive defender in British football when he joins Liverpool in a £3.75 million transfer from Coventry. Twenty-four hours later John Scales arrives from Wimbledon, taking Liverpool's outlay on central defenders to £7 million in two days. Travelling in the opposite direction Tony Cottee rejoins West Ham in an exchange deal that takes David Burrows to Goodison, allowing him to join a select band of players who have appeared for both Merseyside clubs.

On the field Newcastle take their perfect record to five wins out of five with a home win that shatters Chelsea's 100 percent start. Liverpool fail to win for the first time when they are held at home by West Ham, who have Tony Cottee sent off on his second debut for the Hammers. Leeds United secure their first win over Manchester United for 13 matches, but United recover to beat Liverpool at Old Trafford and move into fourth place. Then Newcastle make it six out of six as their victory away to Arsenal takes them four points clear of second-placed Blackburn, who win at Chelsea.

Blackburn end the month in second place thanks to the 'SAS' taking their combined goals total to 11 with a win over Aston Villa. Newcastle's winning streak is ended by Liverpool, who take a point at St James' Park, but Blackburn are joined just two points adrift of the Magpies by Nottingham Forest, who thump Spurs at White Hart Lane. Manchester United fail to improve on fourth place when they suffer a shock reverse at Ipswich.

At the other end of the table a win over Spurs and a draw with Everton take Leicester up to 18th and dump the Goodison outfit bottom. Coventry lose at home to Southampton and are 20th, with West Ham one place above after losing to Arsenal, and Crystal Palace, still without a win, sink to 21st after losing to Chelsea.

Bryan Roy, Nottingham Forest, scores his second goal against Spurs. Dutchman Roy was signed from Italian club Foggia and scored 13 League goals in his first season.

October

Saturday 1 October
Arsenal v. Crystal Palace	1-2
Aston Villa v. Newcastle United	0-2
Leeds United v. Manchester City	2-0
Liverpool v. Sheffield Wed.	4-1
Manchester United v. Everton	2-0
Norwich City v. Blackburn Rovers	2-1
Southampton v. Ipswich Town	3-1
Wimbledon v. Tottenham Hotspur	1-2

Sunday 2 October
Chelsea v. West Ham United	1-2
Nottingham Forest v. Queen's Park R.	3-2

Monday 3 October
Leicester City v. Coventry City	2-2

Saturday 8 October
Chelsea v. Leicester City	4-0
Liverpool v. Aston Villa	3-2
Manchester City v. Nottingham Forest	3-3
Norwich City v. Leeds United	2-1
Sheffield Wed. v. Manchester United	1-0
Southampton v. Everton	2-0
Tottenham Hotspur v. Queen's Park R.	1-1
West Ham United v. Crystal Palace	1-0
Wimbledon v. Arsenal	1-3

Sunday 9 October
Newcastle United v. Blackburn Rovers	1-1

Monday 10 October
Coventry City v. Ipswich Town	2-0

Saturday 15 October
Arsenal v. Chelsea	3-1
Aston Villa v. Norwich City	1-1
Blackburn Rovers v. Liverpool	3-2
Crystal Palace v. Newcastle United	0-1
Everton v. Coventry City	0-2
Leeds United v. Tottenham Hotspur	1-1
Leicester City v. Southampton	4-3
Manchester United v. West Ham United	1-0
Queen's Park R. v. Manchester City	1-2

Sunday 16 October
Ipswich Town v. Sheffield Wed.	1-2

Monday 17 October
Nottingham Forest v. Wimbledon	3-1

Saturday 22 October
Aston Villa v. Nottingham Forest	0-2
Crystal Palace v. Everton	1-0
Liverpool v. Wimbledon	3-0
Manchester City v. Tottenham Hotspur	5-2
Newcastle United v. Sheffield Wed.	2-1
Norwich City v. Queen's Park R.	4-2
West Ham United v. Southampton	2-0

Sunday 23 October
Arsenal v. Coventry City	2-1
Blackburn Rovers v. Manchester United	2-4
Chelsea v. Ipswich Town	2-0

Monday 24 October
Leeds United v. Leicester City	2-1

Saturday 29 October
Coventry City v. Manchester City	1-0
Everton v. Arsenal	1-1
Ipswich Town v. Liverpool	1-3
Leicester City v. Crystal Palace	0-1
Manchester United v. Newcastle United	2-0
Nottingham Forest v. Blackburn Rovers	0-2
Queen's Park R. v. Aston Villa	2-0
Sheffield Wed. v. Chelsea	1-1
Southampton v. Leeds United	1-3
Tottenham Hotspur v. West Ham United	3-1

Sunday 30 October
Wimbledon v. Norwich City	1-0

Monday 31 October
Queen's Park R. v. Liverpool	2-1

		P	W	D	L	F	A	Pts
1	Newcastle United	12	9	2	1	29	12	29
2	Nottingham Forest	12	8	3	1	25	13	27
3	Manchester United	12	8	1	3	21	9	25
4	Blackburn Rovers	12	7	3	2	25	12	24
5	Liverpool	12	7	2	3	28	13	23
6	Leeds United	12	6	3	3	18	13	21
7	Chelsea	11	6	1	4	21	14	19
8	Norwich City	12	5	4	3	12	11	19
9	Manchester City	12	5	3	4	21	17	18
10	Arsenal	12	5	3	4	17	13	18
11	Tottenham Hotspur	12	5	2	5	21	24	17
12	Southampton	12	4	3	5	18	22	15
13	Coventry City	12	4	3	5	14	20	15
14	West Ham United	12	4	2	6	8	14	14
15	Queen's Park R.	13	3	4	6	19	23	13
16	Sheffield Wed.	12	3	4	5	15	21	13
17	Crystal Palace	12	3	4	5	8	14	13
18	Wimbledon	12	3	3	6	9	18	12
19	Aston Villa	12	2	4	6	11	18	10
20	Leicester City	12	2	3	7	14	24	9
21	Ipswich Town	12	2	1	9	11	24	7
22	Everton	12	0	4	8	8	24	4

Newcastle's Peter Beardsley celebrates his goal against Crystal Palace.

AFTER midweek European victories it's back down to earth for both Arsenal and Aston Villa as both lose. Newcastle win at Villa Park and extend their lead at the top to five points and Crystal Palace enjoy a shock first win of the season, at Highbury. It's a milestone for Ian Wright, who nets his 100th Arsenal goal against his first club. Nottingham Forest move to second by beating QPR.

A second-half hat-trick from Steve McManaman beats Sheffield Wednesday and takes Liverpool fifth. Blackburn slip to third after losing to Norwich and Manchester United are fourth after beating Everton.

Leicester's PRO Alan Birchenall uses the Filbert Street PA system to criticise the referee after the first-half dismissal of two players in the game against Coventry. Forest climb to within a point of Newcastle after drawing with Manchester City but Newcastle have to rely on a late Steve Howey goal to preserve their unbeaten record.

An 89th-minute Peter Beardsley goal extends Newcastle's lead at the top to five points as they win at Crystal Palace, their fifth away game in a row, leaving the Eagles 20th. Blackburn's win over Liverpool takes them second. Everton go four points adrift at the bottom after they lose to Coventry and Stan Collymore nets for the third consecutive game as Forest beat Wimbledon to cut Newcastle's lead at the top to three points.

Bottom club Everton, still seeking their first win of the campaign, reveal they are paying Glasgow Rangers £35,000 a week for the loan of Duncan Ferguson, *plus* the player's wages.

It's still neck and neck at the top as both Newcastle and Forest win, but Everton's fourth successive defeat, their 11th game without a win, at Selhurst Park, keeps Mike Walker's team rooted to the foot of the table while the Eagles soar out of the drop zone.

Manchester United ruin Blackburn's perfect home record and jump into third place. Eric Cantona scores an equaliser from the spot after Henning Berg is red-carded by Gerald Ashby and Blackburn drop to fourth. Ian Wright scores for the 10th game in a row as Arsenal beat Coventry and in so doing Wright draws level with Highbury legend David Jack, whose record was set in 1931.

The last Saturday of the month sees the four leading teams playing in the day's top two games and the season's last two unbeaten records fall. Newcastle lose at Old Trafford as Manchester United retain third place and Forest lose to Blackburn, who stay fourth. Although the top four positions stay the same there are only six points between first and fifth as Liverpool close the gap by beating Ipswich, who remain 21st. But the Anfield club can't improve on that position as they follow up by losing at QPR.

On the other side of Stanley Park the pressure mounts on Mike Walker despite grabbing a point from visitors Arsenal and Everton stay bottom. Leicester end the month 20th after losing to Palace.

November

Tuesday 1 November		
Everton v. West Ham United		1-0
Ipswich Town v. Leeds United		2-0
Wednesday 2 November		
Coventry City v. Crystal Palace		1-4
Sheffield Wed. v. Blackburn Rovers		0-1
Southampton v. Norwich City		1-1
Saturday 5 November		
Blackburn Rovers v. Tottenham Hotspur		2-0
Crystal Palace v. Ipswich Town		3-0
Leeds United v. Wimbledon		3-1
Liverpool v. Nottingham Forest		1-0
Manchester City v. Southampton		3-3
Newcastle United v. Queen's Park R.		2-1
Norwich City v. Everton		0-0
West Ham United v. Leicester City		1-0
Sunday 6 November		
Arsenal v. Sheffield Wed.		0-0
Aston Villa v. Manchester United		1-2
Chelsea v. Coventry City		2-2
Monday 7 November		
Nottingham Forest v. Newcastle United		0-0
Wednesday 9 November		
Liverpool v. Chelsea		3-1
Wimbledon v. Aston Villa		4-3
Thursday 10 November		
Manchester United v. Manchester City		5-0
Saturday 19 November		
Coventry City v. Norwich City		1-0
Ipswich Town v. Blackburn Rovers		1-3
Manchester United v. Crystal Palace		3-0
Nottingham Forest v. Chelsea		0-1
Queen's Park R. v. Leeds United		3-2
Sheffield Wed. v. West Ham United		1-0
Southampton v. Arsenal		1-0
Tottenham Hotspur v. Aston Villa		3-4
Wimbledon v. Newcastle United		3-2
Sunday 20 November		
Leicester City v. Manchester City		0-1
Monday 21 November		
Everton v. Liverpool		2-0
Wednesday 23 November		
Leicester City v. Arsenal		2-1
Tottenham Hotspur v. Chelsea		0-0
Saturday 26 November		
Arsenal v. Manchester United		0-0
Blackburn Rovers v. Queen's Park R.		4-0
Chelsea v. Everton		0-1
Crystal Palace v. Southampton		0-0
Leeds United v. Nottingham Forest		1-0
Liverpool v. Tottenham Hotspur		1-1
Manchester City v. Wimbledon		2-0
Newcastle United v. Ipswich Town		1-1
Norwich City v. Leicester City		2-1
West Ham United v. Coventry City		0-1
Sunday 27 November		
Aston Villa v. Sheffield Wed.		1-1

		P	W	D	L	F	A	Pts
1	Blackburn Rovers	16	11	3	2	35	13	36
2	Manchester United	16	11	2	3	31	10	35
3	Newcastle United	16	10	4	2	34	17	34
4	Liverpool	16	9	3	4	33	17	30
5	Nottingham Forest	16	8	4	4	25	16	28
6	Leeds United	16	8	3	5	24	19	27
7	Manchester City	16	7	4	5	27	25	25
8	Chelsea	16	7	3	6	25	20	24
9	Norwich City	16	6	6	4	15	14	24
10	Coventry City	16	6	4	6	19	26	22
11	Southampton	16	5	6	5	23	26	21
12	Arsenal	16	5	5	6	18	16	20
13	Crystal Palace	16	5	5	6	15	18	20
14	Tottenham Hotspur	16	5	4	7	25	31	19
15	Sheffield Wed.	16	4	6	6	17	23	18
16	Wimbledon	16	5	3	8	17	28	18
17	West Ham United	16	5	2	9	9	17	17
18	Queen's Park R.	16	4	4	8	23	31	16
19	Aston Villa	16	3	5	8	20	28	14
20	Everton	16	3	5	8	12	24	14
21	Leicester City	16	3	3	10	17	29	12
22	Ipswich Town	16	3	2	11	15	31	11

SPURS sack Ossie Ardiles and Steve Perryman takes over as caretaker manager of the club that drops to 13th in the table after losing their 13th league game of the season, to Blackburn, who go second, but Newcastle also win to stay top. Manchester United beat Aston Villa and go third. Meanwhile, despite Everton claiming their first victory of the season, at the 13th attempt, by beating West Ham, Mike Walker is also sacked, but that news is dwarfed by newspaper allegations accusing Bruce Grobbelaar of taking bribes to fix matches while he was at Liverpool.

At the other end of the table Leicester's defeat by West Ham drops them to 21st; Ipswich are one place above them and, although they pick up a point against Norwich, Everton remain bottom.

The FA promise an investigation into the bribery accusations against Bruce Grobbelaar as his old club Liverpool win their game in hand, over Chelsea, to move into third place in the table, just four points adrift of Newcastle.

The 'sacking season' moves on apace and former stars step into the breach at Aston Villa and Everton. Brian Little eventually replaces Ron Atkinson at Villa Park, after protracted animosity between Villa and his current club, Leicester City. Joe Royle, who made his Everton debut at 16, returns to Goodison Park to replace Mike Walker. But the big news is made on the park, where Manchester United rattle up their best-ever derby win over City, with an Andrei Kanchelskis hat-trick, to move second to Newcastle by just two points.

After David Pleat declines the role of general manager Spurs move for Gerry Francis once he is released by QPR, but Francis only gets a one-year rolling contract and he promptly sacks Steve Perryman, who had 16 years as a player at the club.

Newcastle are knocked off the top of the Premiership for the first time as they crash to Wimbledon, so Manchester United's win over Crystal Palace takes them to the summit and Blackburn slip into second with their victory at Ipswich. Bruce Grobbelaar puts his troubles behind him and gives a flawless performance to keep a clean sheet as Southampton beat Arsenal.

Leicester lose to Manchester City and remain 21st but Everton's momentum gathers with a dream start for Joe Royle, who masterminds the derby victory over Liverpool. Goalkeeper Neville Southall celebrates his record 35th derby appearance with a clean sheet and on-loan Duncan Ferguson nets his first goal for the club. But things are looking bad for Ipswich, who sink to the bottom despite holding Newcastle. After losing Brian Little, who has resigned for 'personal' reasons, managerless Leicester beat Arsenal to move off the foot of the table.

Alan Shearer hits his first hat-trick of the season to down QPR and Blackburn move to the top thanks to United's draw at Arsenal. The Gunners are then rocked by news that a book in Denmark alleges that a top official received a payment as part of the transfer of John Jensen to Highbury.

Southampton's Bruce Grobbelaar comes out onto the pitch in the game against Arsenal. He kept a clean sheet.

Saturday 3 December	
Coventry City v. Liverpool	1-1
Ipswich Town v. Manchester City	1-2
Leicester City v. Aston Villa	1-1
Manchester United v. Norwich City	1-0
Nottingham Forest v. Arsenal	2-2
Sheffield Wed. v. Crystal Palace	1-0
Southampton v. Chelsea	0-1
Tottenham Hotspur v. Newcastle United	4-2
Wimbledon v. Blackburn Rovers	0-3
Sunday 4 December	
Queen's Park R. v. West Ham United	2-1
Monday 5 December	
Everton v. Leeds United	3-0
Saturday 10 December	
Aston Villa v. Everton	0-0
Blackburn Rovers v. Southampton	3-2
Leeds United v. West Ham United	2-2
Newcastle United v. Leicester City	3-1
Norwich City v. Chelsea	3-0
Nottingham Forest v. Ipswich Town	4-1
Queen's Park R. v. Manchester United	2-3
Tottenham Hotspur v. Sheffield Wed.	3-1
Wimbledon v. Coventry City	2-0
Sunday 11 December	
Liverpool v. Crystal Palace	0-0
Monday 12 December	
Manchester City v. Arsenal	1-2
Friday 16 December	
Ipswich Town v. Wimbledon	2-2
Saturday 17 December	
Arsenal v. Leeds United	1-3
Coventry City v. Newcastle United	0-0
Crystal Palace v. Norwich City	0-1
Everton v. Tottenham Hotspur	0-0
Leicester City v. Blackburn Rovers	0-0
Manchester United v. Nottingham Forest	1-2
Sheffield Wed. v. Queen's Park R.	0-2
West Ham United v. Manchester City	3-0
Sunday 18 December	
Chelsea v. Liverpool	0-0
Monday 19 December	
Southampton v. Aston Villa	2-1
Monday 26 December	
Arsenal v. Aston Villa	0-0
Chelsea v. Manchester United	2-3
Coventry City v. Nottingham Forest	0-0
Crystal Palace v. Queen's Park R.	0-0
Everton v. Sheffield Wed.	1-4
Leeds United v. Newcastle United	0-0
Leicester City v. Liverpool	1-2
Manchester City v. Blackburn Rovers	1-3
Norwich City v. Tottenham Hotspur	0-2
Southampton v. Wimbledon	2-3
West Ham United v. Ipswich Town	1-1
Tuesday 27 December	
Nottingham Forest v. Norwich City	1-0
Tottenham Hotspur v. Crystal Palace	0-0
Wednesday 28 December	
Aston Villa v. Chelsea	3-0
Ipswich Town v. Arsenal	0-2
Liverpool v. Manchester City	2-0
Manchester United v. Leicester City	1-1
Queen's Park R. v. Southampton	2-2
Sheffield Wed. v. Coventry City	5-1
Wimbledon v. West Ham United	1-0
Saturday 31 December	
Arsenal v. Queen's Park R.	1-3
Chelsea v. Wimbledon	1-1
Coventry City v. Tottenham Hotspur	0-4
Crystal Palace v. Blackburn Rovers	0-1
Everton v. Ipswich Town	4-1
Leeds United v. Liverpool	0-2
Leicester City v. Sheffield Wed.	0-1
Manchester City v. Aston Villa	2-2
Norwich City v. Newcastle United	2-1
Southampton v. Manchester United	2-2
West Ham United v. Nottingham Forest	3-1

		P	W	D	L	F	A	Pts
1	Blackburn Rovers	21	15	4	2	45	16	49
2	Manchester United	22	14	4	4	42	19	46
3	Liverpool	22	12	6	4	40	19	42
4	Newcastle United	21	11	6	4	40	24	39
5	Nottingham Forest	22	11	6	5	35	23	39
6	Tottenham Hotspur	22	9	6	7	38	34	33
7	Norwich City	22	9	6	7	21	19	33
8	Leeds United	21	9	5	7	29	27	32
9	Sheffield Wed.	22	8	6	8	29	30	30
10	Chelsea	22	8	5	9	29	30	29
11	Manchester City	22	8	5	9	33	38	29
12	Wimbledon	22	8	5	9	26	36	29
13	Arsenal	22	7	7	8	26	25	28
14	Queen's Park R.	22	7	6	9	34	38	27
15	Southampton	22	6	8	8	33	38	26
16	West Ham United	22	7	4	11	19	24	25
17	Coventry City	22	6	7	9	21	38	25
18	Crystal Palace	22	5	8	9	15	21	23
19	Everton	21	5	7	9	20	29	22
20	Aston Villa	22	4	9	9	27	33	21
21	Leicester City	22	3	6	13	21	37	15
22	Ipswich Town	22	3	4	15	21	46	13

V INNIE JONES, courtesy of his long-departed grandfather, is selected for the Welsh squad, while Ulster-born Martin O'Neill declines to leave Wycombe for Leicester City. The FA Premier League decides, after three months, that Ian Wright's goal against Newcastle does in fact belong to the Arsenal striker and he can now claim a club record of scoring in 12 consecutive league and cup games.

There is excitement at the top of the table, where Blackburn's win at Wimbledon keeps them a point in front of Manchester United and Alan Shearer takes his goal tally to 14, but Newcastle slip to third after losing to Spurs, and Teddy Sheringham hits Tottenham's first hat-trick of the campaign.

Everton's winning run, under new manager Joe Royle, stumbles with successive draws, but they move up to 18th. Ipswich stay bottom, with Leicester just above them, as both teams seek a pre-Christmas win in vain. Town manager John Lyall bows to fan pressure and resigns, and Paul Goddard takes over as caretaker manager. The warning bells ring at Villa Park where Brian Little's new side go into the festive programme in 20th place.

The top two both win and Alan Shearer takes his tally to 16 with a brace against his old club, Southampton, to keep Rovers ahead of Manchester United, for whom Roy Keane nets his first goal of the campaign.

Corruption rears its head once again as George Graham denies he received a secret payment during the transfer of John Jensen to Highbury. Reports say the Arsenal manager has been under investigation by the Inland Revenue.

It must be the date, again, as Everton sign on-loan Duncan Ferguson for £4 million on 13 December, despite the fact he has a 12-match suspension hanging over him as an investigation continues into an alleged criminal assault.

Leaders Blackburn have their seven-game winning streak ended as they are held by 21st-placed Leicester but Rovers move two points clear of Manchester United, who not only lose their 100 percent home record but also concede their first league goals at Old Trafford since the first week of April. Stan Collymore and Stuart Pearce are Forest's scorers, for the second successive match.

Everton set a new club record of seven games without conceding a goal when they hold Spurs, but the team is still

Tim Sherwood, Blackburn Rovers.

19th. Aston Villa take seven points from nine over the holiday programme but still end the year in 20th place. Leicester's winless sequence extends to six and they enter 1995 in 21st place.

Liverpool end the year with a flourish and three successive wins sees them tuck nicely into third place behind Blackburn, who stay top for the second consecutive month, and Manchester United, who miss their chance to go top when Leicester hold them at Old Trafford.

Arsenal's John Jensen, becoming notorious at Highbury for his inability to score, finally breaks his duck after 97 games, but this is scant consolation as Arsenal crash to QPR.

Monday 2 January

Aston Villa v. Leeds United	0-0
Blackburn Rovers v. West Ham United	4-2
Ipswich Town v. Leicester City	4-1
Liverpool v. Norwich City	4-0
Newcastle United v. Manchester City	0-0
Nottingham Forest v. Crystal Palace	1-0
Sheffield Wed. v. Southampton	1-1
Tottenham Hotspur v. Arsenal	1-0
Wimbledon v. Everton	2-1

Tuesday 3 January

Manchester United v. Coventry City	2-0

Saturday 14 January

Arsenal v. Everton	1-1
Aston Villa v. Queen's Park R.	2-1
Blackburn Rovers v. Nottingham Forest	3-0
Chelsea v. Sheffield Wed.	1-1
Crystal Palace v. Leicester City	2-0
Leeds United v. Southampton	0-0
Liverpool v. Ipswich Town	0-1
Manchester City v. Coventry City	0-0
Norwich City v. Wimbledon	1-2
West Ham United v. Tottenham Hotspur	1-2

Sunday 15 January

Newcastle United v. Manchester United	1-1

Saturday 21 January

Coventry City v. Arsenal	0-1
Everton v. Crystal Palace	3-1
Ipswich Town v. Chelsea	2-2
Nottingham Forest v. Aston Villa	1-2
Sheffield Wed. v. Newcastle United	0-0

Sunday 22 January

Manchester United v. Blackburn Rovers	1-0

Monday 23 January

West Ham United v. Sheffield Wed.	0-2

Tuesday 24 January

Arsenal v. Southampton	1-1
Leeds United v. Queen's Park R.	4-0
Liverpool v. Everton	0-0

Wednesday 25 January

Aston Villa v. Tottenham Hotspur	1-0
Chelsea v. Nottingham Forest	0-2
Crystal Palace v. Manchester United	1-1
Manchester City v. Leicester City	0-1
Newcastle United v. Wimbledon	2-1
Norwich City v. Coventry City	2-2

Saturday 28 January

Blackburn Rovers v. Ipswich Town	4-1

		P	W	D	L	F	A	Pts
1	Blackburn Rovers	25	18	4	3	56	20	58
2	Manchester United	26	16	6	4	47	21	54
3	Liverpool	25	13	7	5	44	20	46
4	Newcastle United	25	12	9	4	43	26	45
5	Nottingham Forest	26	13	6	7	39	28	45
6	Tottenham Hotspur	25	11	6	8	41	36	39
7	Leeds United	24	10	7	7	33	27	37
8	Sheffield Wed.	26	9	9	8	33	32	36
9	Wimbledon	25	10	5	10	31	40	35
10	Norwich City	25	9	7	9	24	27	34
11	Arsenal	26	8	9	9	29	28	33
12	Aston Villa	26	7	10	9	32	35	31
13	Chelsea	25	8	7	10	32	35	31
14	Manchester City	25	8	7	10	33	39	31
15	Southampton	25	6	11	8	35	40	29
16	Crystal Palace	26	6	9	11	19	26	27
17	Everton	25	6	9	10	25	32	27
18	Queen's Park R.	24	7	6	11	35	44	27
19	Coventry City	26	6	9	11	23	43	27
20	West Ham United	25	7	4	14	22	32	25
21	Ipswich Town	26	5	5	16	29	53	20
22	Leicester City	25	4	6	15	23	43	18

Eric Cantona jumps back onto the pitch after attacking a fan after being sent off against Crystal Palace.

ALAN SHEARER'S second hat-trick of the season defeats West Ham and sends Blackburn six points clear but Manchester United reduce the deficit the next day by beating Coventry. Southampton pay a club record £1.2 million to sign Neil Shipperley from Chelsea and struggling Aston Villa bring in Derby pair Tommy Johnson and Gary Charles, for a combined fee of £2.9 million. Leeds set a new club record in signing Tony Yeboah for £3.4 million, but the story of the year so far is news from Malaysia that a 50-year-old blind man is the mastermind behind the recent match-fixing scandal that saw several Premiership games interrupted by power failure.

More transfer records fall as Manchester United sign Andy Cole from title rivals Newcastle for a new British high of £7 million, though £1 million of the fee is accounted for by Keith Gillespie, who moves to St James' Park.

The Premier League investigating team spend several hours talking to Norwegian agent Rune Hauge as part of their inquiry into the George Graham 'bung allegations'.

Blackburn restore their lead to six points with victory over Forest, and neither of the 'SAS' partnership is on the scoresheet, while Liverpool are jolted by Ipswich's first-ever win at Anfield, although Town remain 21st. Andy Cole has to sit out the clash between his new club and his former employers, by agreement, as they draw at St James' Park.

The top two clash and Manchester United's victory over Blackburn sees them close to within two points of Rovers at the summit, though United have played one game more. At the other end of the Premiership West Ham's relegation plight isn't helped by the dismissals of Tim Breaker and Alvin Martin as the Hammers lose to Sheffield Wednesday.

Eric Cantona blows his stack 'big time' when he launches a 'kung fu' attack on a fan at Selhurst Park and follows up with flailing fists before he is dragged away. The draw with Palace damages United's pursuit of Blackburn, who are still one point ahead of Fergie's side, but with two games in hand.

Cantona is given two weeks to answer FA charges over his attack on the Palace fan. United keep quiet until the next day, when they announce they are suspending the Frenchman from all first-team games for the rest of the season and fining him the maximum amount: two weeks' wages. Eric is also relieved of the captaincy of the French national side. The fan involved at Selhurst Park doesn't get away scot free and after it's discovered he has a criminal record for assault he is banned by Crystal Palace for the rest of the season. Things are not looking good for Leicester and Ipswich, who occupy the two bottom places, while West Ham aren't much better off above them.

Wednesday 1 February		
Blackburn Rovers v. Leeds United		1-1
Newcastle United v. Everton		2-0
Saturday 4 February		
Coventry City v. Chelsea		2-2
Everton v. Norwich City		2-1
Ipswich Town v. Crystal Palace		0-2
Leicester City v. West Ham United		1-2
Manchester United v. Aston Villa		1-0
Nottingham Forest v. Liverpool		1-1
Queen's Park R. v. Newcastle United		3-0
Sheffield Wed. v. Arsenal		3-1
Southampton v. Manchester City		2-2
Wimbledon v. Leeds United		0-0
Sunday 5 February		
Tottenham Hotspur v. Blackburn Rovers		3-1
Saturday 11 February		
Arsenal v. Leicester City		1-1
Aston Villa v. Wimbledon		7-1
Chelsea v. Tottenham Hotspur		1-1
Crystal Palace v. Coventry City		0-2
Liverpool v. Queen's Park R.		1-1
Manchester City v. Manchester United		0-3
Newcastle United v. Nottingham Forest		2-1
Norwich City v. Southampton		2-2
Sunday 12 February		
Blackburn Rovers v. Sheffield Wed.		3-1
Monday 13 February		
West Ham United v. Everton		2-2
Saturday 18 February		
Coventry City v. West Ham United		2-0
Sheffield Wed. v. Aston Villa		1-2
Tuesday 21 February		
Arsenal v. Nottingham Forest		1-0
Wednesday 22 February		
Aston Villa v. Leicester City		4-4
Blackburn Rovers v. Wimbledon		2-1
Leeds United v. Everton		1-0
Manchester City v. Ipswich Town		2-0
Norwich City v. Manchester United		0-2
Saturday 25 February		
Blackburn Rovers v. Norwich City		0-0
Coventry City v. Leicester City		4-2
Crystal Palace v. Arsenal		0-3
Everton v. Manchester United		1-0
Ipswich Town v. Southampton		2-1
Manchester City v. Leeds United		0-0
Newcastle United v. Aston Villa		3-1
Sheffield Wed. v. Liverpool		1-2
Tottenham Hotspur v. Wimbledon		1-2
West Ham United v. Chelsea		1-2
Sunday 26 February		
Queen's Park R. v. Nottingham Forest		1-1
Tuesday 28 February		
Ipswich Town v. Newcastle United		0-2

		P	W	D	L	F	A	Pts
1	Blackburn Rovers	30	20	6	4	63	26	66
2	Manchester United	30	19	6	5	53	22	63
3	Newcastle United	30	16	9	5	52	31	57
4	Liverpool	28	14	9	5	48	23	51
5	Nottingham Forest	30	13	8	9	42	33	47
6	Leeds United	28	11	10	7	35	28	43
7	Tottenham Hotspur	28	12	7	9	46	40	43
8	Arsenal	30	10	10	10	35	32	40
9	Sheffield Wed.	30	10	9	11	39	40	39
10	Wimbledon	29	11	6	12	35	50	39
11	Aston Villa	31	9	11	11	46	45	38
12	Coventry City	30	9	10	11	33	47	37
13	Chelsea	28	9	9	10	37	39	36
14	Norwich City	29	9	9	11	27	33	36
15	Manchester City	29	9	9	11	37	44	36
16	Everton	30	8	10	12	30	39	34
17	Queen's Park R.	27	8	8	11	40	46	32
18	Southampton	28	6	13	9	40	46	31
19	Crystal Palace	29	7	9	13	21	31	30
20	West Ham United	29	8	5	16	27	39	29
21	Ipswich Town	30	6	5	19	31	60	23
22	Leicester City	29	4	8	17	31	54	20

Arsenal manager George Graham, whose Highbury tenure is almost over.

ONLY TWO Premiership games survive the weather but tempers flare as 14 players are booked and Tim Flowers is red-carded after just two minutes of the draw with Leeds that sees Blackburn go five points clear of second-placed Manchester United. In the other fixture Earl Barrett and Barry Horne see red as Everton lose at Newcastle but it's referee David Elleray who makes the headlines: giving 12 yellow cards to 10 different players.

Andy Cole's first goal for Manchester United beats Aston Villa and closes the gap on Blackburn to two points. Rovers then lose, for only the fourth time in the league, at Spurs, to keep the pressure on Fergie's side, who are unbeaten in eight games. Meanwhile, despite his suspension Eric Cantona keeps 'hitting' the headlines. This time he takes a family holiday to the Caribbean instead of attending a police interview. It gets worse for the errant Frenchman when he is alleged to have reprised his now infamous kung fu kick on a reporter trying to film him.

Bad weather again affects the fixture list but it doesn't stop Manchester United, who leapfrog Blackburn into pole position with their win over City. Tommy Johnson nets his first Villa hat-trick as they crush Wimbledon. Leicester claim a point at Highbury but stay bottom. Blackburn retain top spot by beating Sheffield Wednesday and restore their two-point advantage. Coventry's precarious position – they are 17th despite beating Crystal Palace – is enough for the board, who end Phil Neal's tenure after 15 months.

Reports leak out that the Premier League Commission has found George Graham guilty of taking a bung and has reported its findings to the Highbury board. Arsenal sack their most successful manager the very next day but Graham vows to clear his name and in a twist the Gunners win their first home Premiership game for four months after Arsenal promote Graham's assistant, Stewart Houston, to caretaker manager.

Eric Cantona is charged with assault after his attack on a Crystal Palace fan in January. Meanwhile United are getting into their stride, easily beating Norwich while Blackburn stay level with them by beating Wimbledon.

In the relegation zone Leicester move off the bottom as they claim a point in an incredible eight-goal draw at Villa Park, by scoring three times in the last 13 minutes. Ipswich fall to 22nd after they lose to Manchester City.

The Premier League confirm the findings of the George Graham investigation but say that the former Arsenal boss isn't the only one guilty of taking bungs.

The race for the championship continues to be a two-horse affair, but United's defeat against Everton isn't too damaging as Blackburn are held by Norwich while neighbours Ipswich begin their descent into Division One by losing to Newcastle. West Ham lose their last two games of the month to complete the bottom three.

March

Saturday 4 March		
Aston Villa v. Blackburn Rovers		0-1
Leeds United v. Sheffield Wed.		0-1
Leicester City v. Everton		2-2
Liverpool v. Newcastle United		2-0
Manchester United v. Ipswich Town		9-0
Norwich City v. Manchester City		1-1
Nottingham Forest v. Tottenham Hotspur		2-2
Southampton v. Coventry City		0-0
Wimbledon v. Queen's Park R.		1-3
Sunday 5 March		
Arsenal v. West Ham United		0-1
Chelsea v. Crystal Palace		0-0
Monday 6 March		
Aston Villa v. Coventry City		0-0
Tuesday 7 March		
Wimbledon v. Manchester United		0-1
Wednesday 8 March		
Blackburn Rovers v. Arsenal		3-1
Manchester City v. Chelsea		1-2
Newcastle United v. West Ham United		2-0
Norwich City v. Sheffield Wed.		0-0
Nottingham Forest v. Everton		2-1
Queen's Park R. v. Leicester City		2-0
Tottenham Hotspur v. Ipswich Town		3-0
Saturday 11 March		
Chelsea v. Leeds United		0-3
Coventry City v. Blackburn Rovers		1-1
Leicester City v. Nottingham Forest		2-4
Sheffield Wed. v. Wimbledon		0-1
West Ham United v. Norwich City		2-2
Tuesday 14 March		
Crystal Palace v. Sheffield Wed.		2-1
Liverpool v. Coventry City		2-3
Wednesday 15 March		
Everton v. Manchester City		1-1
Leicester City v. Leeds United		1-3
Manchester United v. Tottenham Hotspur		0-0
Queen's Park R. v. Norwich City		2-0
Southampton v. West Ham United		1-1
Saturday 18 March		
Aston Villa v. West Ham United		0-2
Blackburn Rovers v. Chelsea		2-1
Leeds United v. Coventry City		3-0
Manchester City v. Sheffield Wed.		3-2
Nottingham Forest v. Southampton		3-0
Queen's Park R. v. Everton		2-3
Tottenham Hotspur v. Leicester City		1-0
Wimbledon v. Crystal Palace		2-0
Sunday 19 March		
Liverpool v. Manchester United		2-0
Newcastle United v. Arsenal		1-0
Monday 20 March		
Norwich City v. Ipswich Town		3-0
Tuesday 21 March		
Wimbledon v. Manchester City		2-0
Wednesday 22 March		
Manchester United v. Arsenal		3-0
Nottingham Forest v. Leeds United		3-0
Queen's Park R. v. Chelsea		1-0
Southampton v. Newcastle United		3-1
Tottenham Hotspur v. Liverpool		0-0

		P	W	D	L	F	A	Pts
1	Blackburn Rovers	34	23	7	4	70	29	76
2	Manchester United	35	22	7	6	66	24	73
3	Newcastle United	34	18	9	7	56	36	63
4	Nottingham Forest	35	17	9	9	56	38	60
5	Liverpool	32	16	10	6	54	26	58
6	Leeds United	33	14	10	9	44	33	52
7	Tottenham Hotspur	33	14	10	9	52	42	52
8	Wimbledon	34	14	6	14	41	54	48
9	Queen's Park R.	32	12	8	12	50	50	44
10	Sheffield Wed.	35	11	10	14	43	46	43
11	Coventry City	35	10	13	12	37	53	43
12	Norwich City	34	10	12	12	33	38	42
13	Manchester City	34	10	11	13	43	52	41
14	Arsenal	34	10	10	14	36	40	40
15	Chelsea	33	10	10	13	40	46	40
16	Aston Villa	34	9	12	13	46	48	39
17	Everton	34	9	12	13	37	46	39
18	West Ham United	34	10	7	17	33	44	37
19	Southampton	32	7	15	10	44	51	36
20	Crystal Palace	32	8	10	14	23	34	34
21	Ipswich Town	33	6	5	22	31	75	23
22	Leicester City	34	4	9	21	36	66	21

MIKE WALKER wins his case for breach of contract against Everton after he takes legal action against the club that sacked him with nearly three years left on his contract. The FA warns players not to celebrate scoring goals by taking their shirts off.

Manchester United and Andy Cole establish Premiership records in the 9–0 hammering of Ipswich. Cole's contribution is a new individual record haul of five goals, but Blackburn retain their three-point lead at the top with a more modest victory at Villa Park. The relegation dogfight at Filbert Street sees Leicester fight back from a 2–0 deficit but only after Duncan Ferguson and Vinny Samways are red-carded. Everton move to 17th while City stay bottom.

Manchester United go top, on goal difference, after a late winner at Wimbledon, but Blackburn resume pole position 24 hours later with a win over Arsenal in which a brace takes Alan Shearer to 28 goals so far. Liverpool lose ground as Peter Ndlovu nets what proves to be Coventry's only hat-trick of the season in City's shock win at Anfield.

Alan Shearer nets his 100th league goal as Blackburn beat Chelsea to move six points clear of second place Manchester United and the most significant result of the campaign occurs the next day when United lose to Liverpool. Three days later United bounce back to within three points of Blackburn by beating Arsenal, and although Southampton hit three goals in the last five minutes against Newcastle, to overturn a 1–0 deficit, they remain in the bottom four.

Eric Cantona gets bail pending an appeal against his two-week jail sentence for the kung fu attack at Selhurst Park. The appeal proves successful and Eric receives 120 hours community service instead. At a subsequent press conference Eric makes his famous pronouncement: 'When the seagulls follow a trawler it is because they think sardines will be thrown into the sea.' Few people had the slightest idea what he meant!

It's all the fours as Nottingham Forest consolidate fourth place and Stan Collymore makes it four goals in four games, all won, as Liverpool slip up, drawing goalless at Spurs. Leicester's losing streak extends to four and they stay bottom, just behind Ipswich who crash in the East Anglian derby. Southampton look capable of escaping the drop as they impress by beating third-placed Newcastle.

Manchester United's Andy Cole scores his hat-trick goal in the 9–0 defeat of Ipswich Town.

Saturday 1 April	
Arsenal v. Norwich City	5-1
Chelsea v. Newcastle United	1-1
Coventry City v. Queen's Park R.	0-1
Crystal Palace v. Manchester City	2-1
Everton v. Blackburn Rovers	1-2
Ipswich Town v. Aston Villa	0-1
Leicester City v. Wimbledon	3-4
Sheffield Wed. v. Nottingham Forest	1-7
Sunday 2 April	
Manchester United v. Leeds United	0-0
Southampton v. Tottenham Hotspur	4-3
Tuesday 4 April	
Crystal Palace v. Aston Villa	0-0
Queen's Park R. v. Blackburn Rovers	0-1
Wednesday 5 April	
Leeds United v. Ipswich Town	4-0
Leicester City v. Norwich City	1-0
Liverpool v. Southampton	3-1
Saturday 8 April	
Newcastle United v. Norwich City	3-0
Nottingham Forest v. West Ham United	1-1
Queen's Park R. v. Arsenal	3-1
Sheffield Wed. v. Leicester City	1-0
Sunday 9 April	
Liverpool v. Leeds United	0-1
Monday 10 April	
Wimbledon v. Chelsea	1-1
Tuesday 11 April	
Ipswich Town v. Queen's Park R.	0-1
Tottenham Hotspur v. Manchester City	2-1
Wednesday 12 April	
Arsenal v. Liverpool	0-1
Chelsea v. Southampton	0-2
Norwich City v. Nottingham Forest	0-1
Thursday 13 April	
West Ham United v. Wimbledon	3-0
Friday 14 April	
Crystal Palace v. Tottenham Hotspur	1-1
Everton v. Newcastle United	2-0
Manchester United v. Liverpool	2-1
Saturday 15 April	
Arsenal v. Ipswich Town	4-1
Chelsea v. Aston Villa	1-0
Coventry City v. Sheffield Wed.	2-0
Leeds United v. Blackburn Rovers	1-1
Leicester City v. Manchester United	0-4
Southampton v. Queen's Park R.	2-1
Monday 17 April	
Aston Villa v. Arsenal	0-4
Blackburn Rovers v. Manchester City	2-3
Ipswich Town v. West Ham United	1-1
Liverpool v. Leicester City	2-0
Manchester United v. Chelsea	0-0
Newcastle United v. Leeds United	1-2
Nottingham Forest v. Coventry City	2-0
Queen's Park R. v. Crystal Palace	0-1
Sheffield Wed. v. Everton	0-0
Tottenham Hotspur v. Norwich City	1-0
Wimbledon v. Southampton	0-2
Thursday 20 April	
Blackburn Rovers v. Crystal Palace	2-1
Saturday 29 April	
Arsenal v. Tottenham Hotspur	1-1
Chelsea v. Queen's Park R.	1-0
Crystal Palace v. Nottingham Forest	1-2
Everton v. Wimbledon	0-0
Leeds United v. Aston Villa	1-0
Leicester City v. Ipswich Town	2-0
Manchester City v. Newcastle United	0-0
Norwich City v. Liverpool	1-2
Southampton v. Sheffield Wed.	0-0
Sunday 30 April	
West Ham United v. Blackburn Rovers	2-0

		P	W	D	L	F	A	Pts
1	Blackburn Rovers	40	26	8	6	78	37	86
2	Manchester United	38	23	9	6	70	24	78
3	Nottingham Forest	40	21	10	9	69	41	73
4	Liverpool	38	20	10	8	63	31	70
5	Newcastle United	39	19	11	9	61	41	68
6	Leeds United	39	18	12	9	53	35	66
7	Tottenham Hotspur	38	16	12	10	60	49	60
8	Queen's Park R.	39	15	8	16	56	56	53
9	Wimbledon	39	15	8	16	46	63	53
10	Arsenal	40	13	11	16	51	47	50
11	Southampton	38	11	16	11	55	58	49
12	Chelsea	39	12	13	14	44	50	49
13	Manchester City	39	12	12	15	50	59	48
14	Sheffield Wed.	40	12	12	16	45	55	48
15	Coventry City	38	11	13	14	39	56	46
16	West Ham United	38	12	9	17	40	46	45
17	Everton	38	10	14	14	40	48	44
18	Aston Villa	39	10	13	16	47	54	43
19	Crystal Palace	38	10	12	16	29	40	42
20	Norwich City	40	10	12	18	35	51	42
21	Leicester City	40	6	9	25	42	77	27
22	Ipswich Town	39	6	6	27	33	88	24

BLACKBURN open up a six-point lead at the top while Nottingham Forest move up to fourth after inflicting a worst-ever home defeat on Sheffield Wednesday. Stan Collymore scores for the fifth consecutive game and takes his tally in that run to six. Manchester United fall further back in the title race when they are held by Leeds and are five points behind Rovers having played one game more. The next day Blackburn have one hand on the trophy after they open up an eight-point lead by beating QPR with only six games to go.

Southampton's Bruce Grobbelaar makes an emotional return to Anfield but there is no sentiment as Liverpool win and things gets worse for Ipswich, who crash to bottom after being crushed by Leeds and a Tony Yeboah hat-trick. Leicester look odds-on to join them in Division One after defeat by Sheffield Wednesday.

Spurs rob Crystal Palace of two extra points after a late equaliser from Jürgen Klinsmann. It is the German's third consecutive scoring game and his 18th goal of the season, which pushes Palace down to 19th. Leicester look doomed as Manchester United rekindle their title pursuit with a crushing win as Blackburn's lead is reduced to six points by Brian Deane's late equaliser for Leeds.

An eventful Easter Monday programme adds another twist to the title race as Manchester United are held at Old Trafford by Chelsea, but Alex Ferguson is delighted when an evening fixture sees Blackburn fall to Manchester City, meaning the gap between the two is down to five points. Newcastle drop to fifth after they suffer their first Premiership home defeat for a year, by Leeds. Aston Villa are in trouble as their defeat by Arsenal sends them to within one point of the drop zone, but they have two games in hand. Norwich look surprise candidates for the drop after they lose to Spurs and plunge to 20th while Palace gain renewed hope by winning at QPR to go 19th.

Palace then lose to Blackburn, leaving Rovers eight points clear needing just five points from their remaining three games to claim the title. Kevin Gallacher scores the winner and breaks his leg – the same leg (left) and in the same place as 15 months earlier. In the drop zone Norwich are virtually down after successive defeats by Nottingham Forest and Liverpool, who move third and fourth respectively. Aston Villa are in real trouble after their defeat at Leeds leaves them 18th.

Blackburn Rovers' nerves are getting frayed as they lose at West Ham, giving Manchester United, who have two games in hand, hopes of catching Kenny Dalglish's team. But West Ham are to figure in the nail-biting climax to the Premiership title race in the weeks ahead.

Stan Collymore performs an aerial ballet as he scores the second goal for Nottingham Forest against Coventry.

May

Monday 1 May	
Coventry City v. Manchester United	2-3
Tuesday 2 May	
Wimbledon v. Liverpool	0-0
Wednesday 3 May	
Aston Villa v. Manchester City	1-1
Everton v. Chelsea	3-3
Newcastle United v. Tottenham Hotspur	3-3
Southampton v. Crystal Palace	3-1
West Ham United v. Queen's Park R.	0-0
Thursday 4 May	
Arsenal v. Wimbledon	0-0
Saturday 6 May	
Aston Villa v. Liverpool	2-0
Crystal Palace v. West Ham United	1-0
Everton v. Southampton	0-0
Ipswich Town v. Coventry City	2-0
Leeds United v. Norwich City	2-1
Leicester City v. Chelsea	1-1
Nottingham Forest v. Manchester City	1-0
Queen's Park R. v. Tottenham Hotspur	2-1
Sunday 7 May	
Manchester United v. Sheffield Wed.	1-0
Monday 8 May	
Blackburn Rovers v. Newcastle United	1-0
Tuesday 9 May	
Ipswich Town v. Everton	0-1
Leeds United v. Crystal Palace	3-1
Tottenham Hotspur v. Coventry City	1-3
Wednesday 10 May	
Manchester United v. Southampton	2-1
West Ham United v. Liverpool	3-0
Saturday 13 May	
Wimbledon v. Nottingham Forest	2-2
Sunday 14 May	
Chelsea v. Arsenal	2-1
Coventry City v. Everton	0-0
Liverpool v. Blackburn Rovers	2-1
Manchester City v. Queen's Park R.	2-3
Newcastle United v. Crystal Palace	3-2
Norwich City v. Aston Villa	1-1
Sheffield Wed. v. Ipswich Town	4-1
Southampton v. Leicester City	2-2
Tottenham Hotspur v. Leeds United	1-1
West Ham United v. Manchester United	1-1

		P	W	D	L	F	A	Pts
1	Blackburn Rovers	42	27	8	7	80	39	89
2	Manchester United	42	26	10	6	77	28	88
3	Nottingham Forest	42	22	11	9	72	43	77
4	Liverpool	42	21	11	10	65	37	74
5	Leeds United	42	20	13	9	59	38	73
6	Newcastle United	42	20	12	10	67	47	72
7	Tottenham Hotspur	42	16	14	12	66	58	62
8	Queen's Park R.	42	17	9	16	61	59	60
9	Wimbledon	42	15	11	16	48	65	56
10	Southampton	42	12	18	12	61	63	54
11	Chelsea	42	13	15	14	50	55	54
12	Arsenal	42	13	12	17	52	49	51
13	Sheffield Wed.	42	13	12	17	49	57	51
14	West Ham United	42	13	11	18	44	48	50
15	Everton	42	11	17	14	44	51	50
16	Coventry City	42	12	14	16	44	62	50
17	Manchester City	42	12	13	17	53	64	49
18	Aston Villa	42	11	15	16	51	56	48
19	Crystal Palace	42	11	12	19	34	49	45
20	Norwich City	42	10	13	19	37	54	43
21	Leicester City	42	6	11	25	45	80	29
22	Ipswich Town	42	7	6	29	36	93	27

Promoted from Endsleigh Insurance League Division One

Middlesbrough

Bolton Wanderers (via play-offs)

MANCHESTER UNITED convert their first game in hand into maximum points by winning at Coventry, despite half a dozen first-choice players being out through injury and suspension.

The relegation fight hots up as Crystal Palace are defeated by Southampton and draws for Villa, Everton and West Ham boost those clubs' survival chances. Norwich become the second relegated club when they fall to a seventh successive defeat, at Leeds, but Palace are boosted by a win over West Ham and Villa have a chance of staying up when they beat Liverpool. Liverpool are so disgusted with their performance at Villa Park that they refuse a copy of the match video.

Blackburn win their last home game, with Alan Shearer's 36th goal of the season beating Newcastle, but they may need a final-day victory at Anfield to become champions. In the relegation zone Palace are virtually down after losing to Leeds while West Ham ensure safety by beating Liverpool.

John Burridge, Manchester City's goalkeeper, becomes the oldest Premiership player to take to the field in the match against QPR. He is 43 years and 5 months old.

West Ham have the final say on the title when they hold Manchester United at Upton Park – the Premier League send a replica trophy to Upton Park just in case, but it isn't needed and Blackburn are crowned top-flight champions for the first time since 1914, despite losing at Liverpool. Alan Shearer, who scored Rovers' first goal of the season, completes the campaign with his 37th goal and Blackburn become the first club, other than Manchester United, to win the Premiership. Palace finally lose their relegation fight after losing to Newcastle, but results elsewhere would have sent them down even if they had won at St James' Park.

John Burridge, Manchester City.

Blackburn Rovers' Alan Shearer and Chris Sutton celebrate with the FA Carling Premiership trophy. Between them they scored 49 goals in the league that year.

End of season round-up

Top Premiership Goalscorers 1994–95

Alan Shearer	Blackburn Rovers	34
Robbie Fowler	Liverpool	25
Les Ferdinand	QPR	24
Stan Collymore	Nottingham Forest	22
Andy Cole	Newcastle United	21
Jürgen Klinsmann	Tottenham	20
Matt Le Tissier	Southampton	19
Ian Wright	Arsenal	18
Teddy Sheringham	Tottenham Hotspur	18
Ashley Ward	Norwich City	16
(8 for Crewe)		

Coca-Cola League Cup Final

Liverpool 2   Bolton Wanderers 1

A brace of superb individual goals from Steve McManaman saw Liverpool create a new League Cup record of five wins with a comfortable victory over First Division Bolton Wanderers. Alan Thompson hit the consolation goal for Bolton.

FA Cup Final

Everton 1   Manchester United 0

Defeat at Wembley ensured a trophy-less season for United, just days after they lost their other piece of silverware, the Premiership trophy. Everton had flirted with relegation right up to May but keenly contested the final, thwarting repeated United attacks before taking the winning lead after half an hour.

Graham Stuart's shot beat Schmeichel but hit the bar. Everton's Paul Rideout reacted quicker than United defenders and nodded home the rebound. Without the suspended Eric Cantona United relied on second-half substitute Ryan Giggs for inspiration but with Neville Southall outstanding Everton held on to end their run of five successive Wembley final defeats and record the club's first FA Cup Final success since 1984, leaving United without a trophy for the first time in six years.

FWA Footballer of the Year

Jürgen Klinsmann   Tottenham Hotspur

PFA Player of the Year

Alan Shearer   Blackburn Rovers

PFA Young Player of the Year

Robbie Fowler   Liverpool

Manager of the Year

Kenny Dalglish   Blackburn Rovers

Close Season 1995

Liverpool set a new British transfer record in paying £8.5 million to Nottingham Forest for Stan Collymore, staving off interest from Everton, although the deal is jeopardised by Forest's refusal to pay Collymore five percent of the fee.

Arsenal pay £7.5 million for Inter Milan's Dennis Bergkamp. Paul Ince leaves Old Trafford for Milan for £7 million.

Bolton Wanderers appoint Roy McFarland as manager and Chelsea pay Manchester United £1.5 million for Mark Hughes in the same week they introduce Ruud Gullit as their new manager.

Kenny Dalglish's role at Premiership champions Blackburn Rovers is 'redefined' as Director of Football, with his assistant Ray Harford becoming team manager.

Aston Villa pay a new club record, £3.5 million, to Partizan Belgrade for Savo Milosevic and Newcastle pay Paris St Germain £2.5 million for David Ginola. Arsenal buy David Platt from Sampdoria for £4.75 million, making him the world's most expensive player. His aggregate transfers now total a staggering £22.15 million.

George Graham is banned for a year for 'misconduct' after being found guilty of taking illegal payments while Arsenal manager, though the FA do accept he did not do so for personal gain.

John Fashanu, Bruce Grobbelaar and Hans Segers are charged with match-fixing and bailed to appear in court in October. Villa striker Fashanu is then forced to retire due to a knee injury.

Manchester United turn down Eric Cantona's transfer request and, after the FA decide not to take action over the Frenchman's appearance in a behind-closed-doors match against Rochdale, they give permission for Eric to play in… behind-closed-doors friendlies.

Jürgen Klinsmann, Tottenham Hotspur and Colin Cooper, Nottingham Forest.

August

Saturday 19 August	
Aston Villa v. Manchester United	3-1
Blackburn Rovers v. Queen's Park R.	1-0
Chelsea v. Everton	0-0
Liverpool v. Sheffield Wed.	1-0
Manchester City v. Tottenham Hotspur	1-1
Newcastle United v. Coventry City	3-0
Southampton v. Nottingham Forest	3-4
West Ham United v. Leeds United	1-2
Wimbledon v. Bolton Wanderers	3-2
Sunday 20 August	
Arsenal v. Middlesbrough	1-1
Monday 21 August	
Leeds United v. Liverpool	1-0
Tuesday 22 August	
Bolton Wanderers v. Newcastle United	1-3
Wednesday 23 August	
Coventry City v. Manchester City	2-1
Everton v. Arsenal	0-2
Manchester United v. West Ham United	2-1
Nottingham Forest v. Chelsea	0-0
Queen's Park R. v. Wimbledon	0-3
Sheffield Wed. v. Blackburn Rovers	2-1
Tottenham Hotspur v. Aston Villa	0-1
Saturday 26 August	
Bolton Wanderers v. Blackburn Rovers	2-1
Coventry City v. Arsenal	0-0
Everton v. Southampton	2-0
Leeds United v. Aston Villa	2-0
Manchester United v. Wimbledon	3-1
Middlesbrough v. Chelsea	2-0
Nottingham Forest v. West Ham United	1-1
Queen's Park R. v. Manchester City	1-0
Tottenham Hotspur v. Liverpool	1-3
Sunday 27 August	
Sheffield Wed. v. Newcastle United	0-2
Monday 28 August	
Blackburn Rovers v. Manchester United	1-2
Tuesday 29 August	
Arsenal v. Nottingham Forest	1-1
Wednesday 30 August	
Aston Villa v. Bolton Wanderers	1-0
Chelsea v. Coventry City	2-2
Liverpool v. Queen's Park R.	1-0
Manchester City v. Everton	0-2
Newcastle United v. Middlesbrough	1-0
Southampton v. Leeds United	1-1
West Ham United v. Tottenham Hotspur	1-1
Wimbledon v. Sheffield Wed.	2-2

		P	W	D	L	F	A	Pts
1	Newcastle United	4	4	0	0	9	1	12
2	Leeds United	4	3	1	0	6	2	10
3	Liverpool	4	3	0	1	5	2	9
4	Manchester United	4	3	0	1	8	6	9
5	Aston Villa	4	3	0	1	5	3	9
6	Wimbledon	4	2	1	1	9	7	7
7	Everton	4	2	1	1	4	2	7
8	Arsenal	4	1	3	0	4	2	6
9	Nottingham Forest	4	1	3	0	6	5	6
10	Coventry City	4	1	2	1	4	6	5
11	Middlesbrough	3	1	1	1	3	2	4
12	Sheffield Wed.	4	1	1	2	4	6	4
13	Blackburn Rovers	4	1	0	3	4	6	3
14	Chelsea	4	0	3	1	2	4	3
15	Bolton Wanderers	4	1	0	3	5	8	3
16	Queen's Park R.	4	1	0	3	1	5	3
17	West Ham United	4	0	2	2	4	6	2
18	Tottenham Hotspur	4	0	2	2	3	6	2
19	Southampton	3	0	1	2	4	7	1
20	Manchester City	4	0	1	3	2	6	1

THE OPENING day of the season sees champions Blackburn lose their 'keeper Tim Flowers but an Alan Shearer penalty ensures victory over QPR. Leeds United open with a win and a brace from Tony Yeboah while Manchester United crash at Aston Villa. New British transfer record holder, £8.5 million Stan Collymore, nets his first Premiership goal for Liverpool as they beat Sheffield Wednesday. Without Stan Nottingham Forest earn the points from a seven-goal thriller at Southampton where Matt Le Tissier nets the first hat-trick of the new campaign, including two penalties, for the home side. Those goals represent nearly half of Le Tissier's final total for the campaign come May.

Fast-food chain McDonalds agree a two-year £1.75 million sponsorship deal with the Premier League, which represents approximately 900,000 Big Macs.

Manchester United recover to record back-to-back victories over London sides to go fifth after three games. Newcastle are top of the table with a 100 percent record from their first three games while Liverpool are boosted by a John Barnes brace that gets the Anfield outfit back on the winning trail after their defeat at Leeds.

Middlesbrough mark the opening of their new Cellnet Riverside Stadium with victory over Chelsea. The new sponsorship became a necessity when British Steel withdrew after discovering only 2,000 tons of British steel was being used in construction of the stadium, with the other 18,000 tons coming from Germany! Craig Hignett is the scorer of the historic first goal.

Ten-man Manchester United beat Blackburn despite Roy Keane being sent off for 'diving'. Referee David Elleray books seven players in the game and across Manchester the warning signs begin to flash at Maine Road as City end the month with three consecutive defeats to drop into the bottom three. Southampton, with just one point from three games, are similarly concerned.

Spurs chairman Alan Sugar declares he will sell the club if he and his family continue to be abused by the fans.

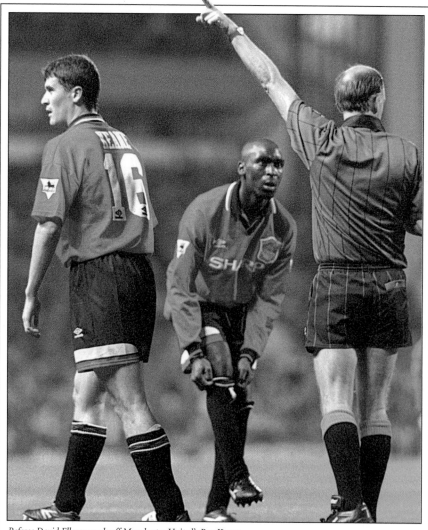

Referee David Elleray sends off Manchester United's Roy Keane.

Saturday 9 September	
Blackburn Rovers v. Aston Villa	1-1
Bolton Wanderers v. Middlesbrough	1-1
Coventry City v. Nottingham Forest	1-1
Everton v. Manchester United	2-3
Queen's Park R. v. Sheffield Wed.	0-3
Southampton v. Newcastle United	1-0
Tottenham Hotspur v. Leeds United	2-1
Wimbledon v. Liverpool	1-0

Sunday 10 September	
Manchester City v. Arsenal	0-1

Monday 11 September	
West Ham United v. Chelsea	1-3

Tuesday 12 September	
Middlesbrough v. Southampton	0-0

Saturday 16 September	
Arsenal v. West Ham United	1-0
Aston Villa v. Wimbledon	2-0
Chelsea v. Southampton	3-0
Leeds United v. Queen's Park R.	1-3
Liverpool v. Blackburn Rovers	3-0
Manchester United v. Bolton Wanderers	3-0
Middlesbrough v. Coventry City	2-1
Newcastle United v. Manchester City	3-1
Sheffield Wed. v. Tottenham Hotspur	1-3

Sunday 17 September	
Nottingham Forest v. Everton	3-2

Saturday 23 September	
Arsenal v. Southampton	4-2
Aston Villa v. Nottingham Forest	1-1
Blackburn Rovers v. Coventry City	5-1
Liverpool v. Bolton Wanderers	5-2
Manchester City v. Middlesbrough	0-1
Sheffield Wed. v. Manchester United	0-0
West Ham United v. Everton	2-1
Wimbledon v. Leeds United	2-4

Sunday 24 September	
Newcastle United v. Chelsea	2-0

Monday 25 September	
Queen's Park R. v. Tottenham Hotspur	2-3

Saturday 30 September	
Bolton Wanderers v. Queen's Park R.	0-1
Chelsea v. Arsenal	1-0
Coventry City v. Aston Villa	0-3
Leeds United v. Sheffield Wed.	2-0
Middlesbrough v. Blackburn Rovers	2-0
Nottingham Forest v. Manchester City	3-0
Tottenham Hotspur v. Wimbledon	3-1

		P	W	D	L	F	A	Pts
1	Newcastle United	7	6	0	1	14	3	18
2	Aston Villa	8	5	2	1	12	5	17
3	Manchester United	7	5	1	1	14	8	16
4	Leeds United	8	5	1	2	14	9	16
5	Liverpool	7	5	0	2	13	5	15
6	Arsenal	8	4	3	1	10	5	15
7	Middlesbrough	8	4	3	1	9	4	15
8	Nottingham Forest	8	3	5	0	14	9	14
9	Tottenham Hotspur	8	4	2	2	14	11	14
10	Chelsea	8	3	3	2	9	7	12
11	Wimbledon	8	3	1	4	13	16	10
12	Queen's Park R.	8	3	0	5	7	12	9
13	Sheffield Wed.	8	2	2	4	8	11	8
14	Everton	7	2	1	4	9	10	7
15	Blackburn Rovers	8	2	1	5	10	13	7
16	Coventry City	8	1	3	4	7	17	6
17	West Ham United	7	1	2	4	7	11	5
18	Southampton	7	1	2	4	7	14	5
19	Bolton Wanderers	8	1	1	6	8	18	4
20	Manchester City	8	0	1	7	3	14	1

Jean-Marc Bosman after the ruling that blows the transfer market apart.

NEWCASTLE lose the last 100 percent record in the league, but stay top, when they are beaten at Southampton by Jim Magilton's first goal of the season, but it's fun and games at Selhurst Park. The serious part is Vinnie Jones being sent off for the 10th time in his career, in Wimbledon's win over Liverpool, but the comedy comes when Andy Thorn is also red-carded, mistakenly, and then has to be recalled from the dressing room when the error is realised. Jones eventually has the red card overturned and replaced with a booking after the linesman views video evidence and decides that there had been no head contact and he, Ray Gould, had advised the referee incorrectly.

Manchester United keep up their winning sequence and stay second with victory at Everton, while Aston Villa go third by beating Wimbledon.

Manchester City continue to struggle and lose to Arsenal to remain rock bottom while QPR are just one place better off following their defeat at Sheffield Wednesday. West Ham complete the bottom three after consecutive London defeats.

It seems to be the month for Wimbledon making the news. After the team are crushed at 'home' (Selhurst Park) by Leeds United, one fan turns on owner Sam Hammam and demands his money back. Sam promptly puts his hand in his pocket and hands over the cash before tearing the ticket up on the spot.

It's goals all the way as the Premiership goes crazy. There are 31 goals in total, with three hat-tricks; Robbie Fowler hits four as Liverpool beat Bolton, Alan Shearer nets three to lift Blackburn to their first victory since the opening day, and Tony Yeboah hits a cracker in his second treble in two weeks in the win that left Wimbledon pointless and Sam Hammam a

few quid light. At the other end of the Premiership Manchester City lose their sixth consecutive game, but West Ham record their first win of the season, thanks to a couple of Julian Dicks penalties, and move out of the bottom three to be replaced by Southampton, who are on the receiving end as Dennis Bergkamp breaks his scoring duck with a brace at Highbury.

But the major news is made in the European Court of Justice when their verdict is given in favour of Jean-Marc Bosman's restraint of trade claim against his Belgian club FC Liège, which promises to have wide-ranging repercussions in the transfer market. The court said that existing transfer regulations were in breach of European Union law governing the free movement of workers between member states and it means that players will be free to sell themselves once they reach the end of a contract.

October

Sunday 1 October	
Everton v. Newcastle United	1-3
Manchester United v. Liverpool	2-2
Monday 2 October	
Southampton v. West Ham United	0-0
Saturday 14 October	
Aston Villa v. Chelsea	0-1
Blackburn Rovers v. Southampton	2-1
Bolton Wanderers v. Everton	1-1
Leeds United v. Arsenal	0-3
Liverpool v. Coventry City	0-0
Manchester United v. Manchester City	1-0
Queen's Park R. v. Newcastle United	2-3
Tottenham Hotspur v. Nottingham Forest	0-1
Sunday 15 October	
Sheffield Wed. v. Middlesbrough	0-1
Monday 16 October	
Wimbledon v. West Ham United	0-1
Saturday 21 October	
Arsenal v. Aston Villa	2-0
Chelsea v. Manchester United	1-4
Coventry City v. Sheffield Wed.	0-1
Manchester City v. Leeds United	0-0
Middlesbrough v. Queen's Park R.	1-0
Newcastle United v. Wimbledon	6-1
Nottingham Forest v. Bolton Wanderers	3-2
West Ham United v. Blackburn Rovers	1-1
Sunday 22 October	
Everton v. Tottenham Hotspur	1-1
Southampton v. Liverpool	1-3
Saturday 28 October	
Aston Villa v. Everton	1-0
Blackburn Rovers v. Chelsea	3-0
Leeds United v. Coventry City	3-1
Liverpool v. Manchester City	6-0
Manchester United v. Middlesbrough	2-0
Queen's Park R. v. Nottingham Forest	1-1
Sheffield Wed. v. West Ham United	0-1
Wimbledon v. Southampton	1-2
Sunday 29 October	
Tottenham Hotspur v. Newcastle United	1-1
Monday 30 October	
Bolton Wanderers v. Arsenal	1-0

		P	W	D	L	F	A	Pts
1	Newcastle United	11	9	1	1	27	8	28
2	Manchester United	11	8	2	1	23	11	26
3	Liverpool	11	7	2	2	24	8	23
4	Arsenal	11	6	3	2	15	6	21
5	Nottingham Forest	11	5	6	0	19	12	21
6	Middlesbrough	11	6	3	2	11	6	21
7	Aston Villa	11	6	2	3	13	8	20
8	Leeds United	11	6	2	3	17	13	20
9	Tottenham Hotspur	11	4	4	3	16	14	16
10	Chelsea	11	4	3	4	11	14	15
11	Blackburn Rovers	11	4	2	5	16	15	14
12	West Ham United	11	3	4	4	10	12	13
13	Sheffield Wed.	11	3	2	6	9	13	11
14	Queen's Park R.	11	3	1	7	10	17	10
15	Wimbledon	11	3	1	7	15	25	10
16	Everton	11	2	3	6	12	16	9
17	Southampton	11	2	3	6	11	20	9
18	Bolton Wanderers	11	2	2	7	12	22	8
19	Coventry City	11	1	4	6	8	21	7
20	Manchester City	11	0	2	9	3	21	2

ERIC CANTONA is back. After his eight-month suspension the *Enfant Terrible* returns in triumph and scores from a penalty to equalise against Liverpool, helping Manchester United to a draw at a packed Old Trafford. But it costs, as United lose top spot to Newcastle United, who impress as Les Ferdinand scores his 100th goal for them in the victory at Everton.

Middlesbrough player-manager Bryan Robson pulls off the transfer coup of the season when he signs Brazilian Player of the Year, Juninho, for £4.75 million.

Manchester United stay second despite beating City, an eighth consecutive defeat for the Blues that keeps them rock bottom of the Premiership. Southampton's defeat at Blackburn, in which former Saint Alan Shearer nets his eighth goal in nine starts, keeps them in the bottom three just ahead of Bolton, who draw with Everton.

The Premier League announces that, from next season, teams will be able to name five substitutes.

Bolton Wanderers' John McGinlay. His winning goal inflicts a first home defeat on Arsenal.

Les Ferdinand just can't stop scoring and leaders Newcastle can't stop winning. The hammering of Wimbledon is the Magpies' ninth win in 10 since the start of the campaign and Ferdinand, with his first hat-trick of the season, equals the post-war Newcastle record of scoring in seven consecutive games, an honour he now shares with Len White and Paul Goddard. Newcastle's cause is helped by Vinnie Jones having to take over between the sticks after Paul Heald is sent off.

Manchester United keep up the chase, in second place, by thumping Chelsea at Stamford Bridge and Arsenal hang on to third spot by beating Aston Villa.

At the foot of the table Manchester City still hold up the rest when held by Leeds, Bolton are one place higher after losing to Nottingham Forest, who move sixth, and Southampton complete the basement three after they are beaten by Liverpool. The Anfield outfit then crush Manchester City, who finish bottom for the third month in a row.

But Southampton end the month out of the drop zone thanks to their win at Wimbledon with a Neil Shipperley brace, his first goals of the campaign, in his 10th game. Bolton are still in trouble but a John McGinlay goal gives them a shock win against the Gunners, keeping Arsenal third.

Newcastle finish top of the table for the third month running after drawing at Spurs the day after Manchester United beat Middlesbrough with the help of a goal from former 'Boro defender Gary Pallister, who nets what proves to be his only entry on the scoresheet all season. But 'Boro can at least celebrate the news that Juninho is granted a work permit and is cleared to play in the next game.

November

Saturday 4 November	
Arsenal v. Manchester United	1-0
Chelsea v. Sheffield Wed.	0-0
Coventry City v. Tottenham Hotspur	2-3
Manchester City v. Bolton Wanderers	1-0
Middlesbrough v. Leeds United	1-1
Newcastle United v. Liverpool	2-1
Southampton v. Queen's Park R.	2-0
West Ham United v. Aston Villa	1-4
Sunday 5 November	
Everton v. Blackburn Rovers	1-0
Monday 6 November	
Nottingham Forest v. Wimbledon	4-1
Wednesday 8 November	
Newcastle United v. Blackburn Rovers	1-0
Saturday 18 November	
Aston Villa v. Newcastle United	1-1
Blackburn Rovers v. Nottingham Forest	7-0
Bolton Wanderers v. West Ham United	0-3
Leeds United v. Chelsea	1-0
Liverpool v. Everton	1-2
Manchester United v. Southampton	4-1
Sheffield Wed. v. Manchester City	1-1
Tottenham Hotspur v. Arsenal	2-1
Wimbledon v. Middlesbrough	0-0
Sunday 19 November	
Queen's Park R. v. Coventry City	1-1
Monday 20 November	
Southampton v. Aston Villa	0-1
Tuesday 21 November	
Arsenal v. Sheffield Wed.	4-2
Middlesbrough v. Tottenham Hotspur	0-1
Wednesday 22 November	
Chelsea v. Bolton Wanderers	3-2
Coventry City v. Manchester United	0-4
Everton v. Queen's Park R.	2-0
Manchester City v. Wimbledon	1-0
West Ham United v. Liverpool	0-0
Saturday 25 November	
Chelsea v. Tottenham Hotspur	0-0
Coventry City v. Wimbledon	3-3
Everton v. Sheffield Wed.	2-2
Manchester City v. Aston Villa	1-0
Middlesbrough v. Liverpool	2-1
Newcastle United v. Leeds United	2-1
Southampton v. Bolton Wanderers	1-0
West Ham United v. Queen's Park R.	1-0
Sunday 26 November	
Arsenal v. Blackburn Rovers	0-0
Monday 27 November	
Nottingham Forest v. Manchester United	1-1

		P	W	D	L	F	A	Pts
1	Newcastle United	15	12	2	1	33	11	38
2	Manchester United	15	10	3	2	32	14	33
3	Arsenal	15	8	4	3	21	10	28
4	Aston Villa	15	8	3	4	19	11	27
5	Tottenham Hotspur	15	7	5	3	22	17	26
6	Middlesbrough	15	7	5	3	14	9	26
7	Nottingham Forest	14	6	7	1	24	21	25
8	Liverpool	15	7	3	5	27	14	24
9	Leeds United	14	7	3	4	20	16	24
10	West Ham United	15	5	5	5	15	16	20
11	Chelsea	15	5	5	5	14	17	20
12	Everton	15	5	4	6	19	19	19
13	Blackburn Rovers	15	5	3	7	23	17	18
14	Southampton	15	4	3	8	15	25	15
15	Sheffield Wed.	15	3	5	7	14	20	14
16	Wimbledon	15	3	3	9	19	33	12
17	Manchester City	15	3	3	9	7	22	12
18	Queen's Park R.	15	3	2	10	11	23	11
19	Coventry City	15	1	6	8	14	32	9
20	Bolton Wanderers	15	2	2	11	14	30	8

JUNINHO makes an impressive debut but Middlesbrough are held by Leeds. Newcastle stay top with victory over Liverpool, who remain fourth, and Manchester United are still second, after losing for only the second time this season to a Dennis Bergkamp goal that keeps Arsenal third.

At the other end of the Premiership Manchester City celebrate victory for the first time when a Nicky Summerbee goal, his first and only the team's fourth of the season, beats Bolton, who are 18th. But City remain 20th, below Coventry, who lose against Spurs.

Two days later Vinnie Jones is sent off for the 10th time in his career (after his red card against Liverpool in September was revoked) as Wimbledon crash to a club record seventh consecutive defeat at Forest, who are now the only unbeaten side in the country.

Everton's Duncan Ferguson fails in his appeal against the Scottish FA's 12-match ban for his assault on Raith's John McStay, for which he is currently serving a jail term. Leeds complete the signing of Swedish international Tomas Brolin from Parma.

Nottingham Forest's impressive 25-match unbeaten run, including 12 games this season, is ended unceremoniously when they are hammered at Ewood Park. Alan Shearer, with his second hat-trick of the campaign, takes his tally to 13 goals in 16 matches, a fact that is certainly unlucky for Forest. On the scoresheet for Manchester United, in their drubbing of Southampton, is Ryan Giggs, who takes just 16 seconds to score the first of his brace to help keep United second. Arsenal lose the North London derby, but stay third.

Manchester City extend their unbeaten sequence to two games when Steve Lomas earns a point at Sheffield Wednesday with his first goal of the season. Coventry's draw at QPR keeps them 19th and Bolton's defeat by West Ham, in which Hammers' Ian Bishop moves onto the scoresheet for the first time, keeps them 18th.

Arsenal bounce back to beat Sheffield Wednesday, with the help of Dennis Bergkamp, who scores for the third game running to keep up the pressure on the top two. Manchester United stay one place higher when they score four goals against Southampton, but Newcastle still top the table, for the fourth month in a row, when they beat Leeds.

Manchester City move out of the drop zone when they beat Aston Villa to record consecutive wins for the first time in the campaign. Bolton drop to bottom after losing to Southampton and Coventry stage a remarkable comeback against Wimbledon when they overturn a 3–1 deficit, scoring their last goal just seven minutes from time to earn a point, but the Sky Blues stay 19th. QPR complete the bottom three when they lose to West Ham.

Newcastle maintain their place at the summit with a draw at Aston Villa; Les Ferdinand scores his 15th goal of the campaign. Manchester United score four goals, again, in crushing Coventry, but remain second.

Arsenal's Dennis Bergkamp scores despite a late lunge by Denis Irwin of Manchester United and ends United's unbeaten run.

45

December

Saturday 2 December		
Aston Villa v. Arsenal	1-1	
Blackburn Rovers v. West Ham United	4-2	
Bolton Wanderers v. Nottingham Forest	1-1	
Leeds United v. Manchester City	0-1	
Liverpool v. Southampton	1-1	
Manchester United v. Chelsea	1-1	
Queen's Park R. v. Middlesbrough	1-1	
Tottenham Hotspur v. Everton	0-0	
Sunday 3 December		
Wimbledon v. Newcastle United	3-3	
Monday 4 December		
Sheffield Wed. v. Coventry City	4-3	
Saturday 9 December		
Bolton Wanderers v. Liverpool	0-1	
Chelsea v. Newcastle United	1-0	
Coventry City v. Blackburn Rovers	5-0	
Leeds United v. Wimbledon	1-1	
Manchester United v. Sheffield Wed.	2-2	
Middlesbrough v. Manchester City	4-1	
Southampton v. Arsenal	0-0	
Tottenham Hotspur v. Queen's Park R.	1-0	
Sunday 10 December		
Nottingham Forest v. Aston Villa	1-1	
Monday 11 December		
Everton v. West Ham United	3-0	
Saturday 16 December		
Arsenal v. Chelsea	1-1	
Aston Villa v. Coventry City	4-1	
Blackburn Rovers v. Middlesbrough	1-0	
Newcastle United v. Everton	1-0	
Queen's Park R. v. Bolton Wanderers	2-1	
Sheffield Wed. v. Leeds United	6-2	
West Ham United v. Southampton	2-1	
Wimbledon v. Tottenham Hotspur	0-1	
Sunday 17 December		
Liverpool v. Manchester United	2-0	
Monday 18 December		
Manchester City v. Nottingham Forest	1-1	
Saturday 23 December		
Coventry City v. Everton	2-1	
Liverpool v. Arsenal	3-1	
Manchester City v. Chelsea	0-1	
Middlesbrough v. West Ham United	4-2	
Newcastle United v. Nottingham Forest	3-1	
Queen's Park R. v. Aston Villa	1-0	
Sheffield Wed. v. Southampton	2-2	
Tottenham Hotspur v. Bolton Wanderers	2-2	
Wimbledon v. Blackburn Rovers	1-1	
Sunday 24 December		
Leeds United v. Manchester United	3-1	
Tuesday 26 December		
Arsenal v. Queen's Park R.	3-0	
Blackburn Rovers v. Manchester City	2-0	
Chelsea v. Wimbledon	1-2	
Everton v. Middlesbrough	4-0	
Nottingham Forest v. Sheffield Wed.	1-0	
Southampton v. Tottenham Hotspur	0-0	
Wednesday 27 December		
Bolton Wanderers v. Leeds United	0-2	
Manchester United v. Newcastle United	2-0	
Saturday 30 December		
Arsenal v. Wimbledon	1-3	
Blackburn Rovers v. Tottenham Hotspur	2-1	
Bolton Wanderers v. Coventry City	1-2	
Chelsea v. Liverpool	2-2	
Everton v. Leeds United	2-0	
Manchester United v. Queen's Park R.	2-1	
Nottingham Forest v. Middlesbrough	1-0	

		P	W	D	L	F	A	Pts
1	Newcastle United	20	14	3	3	40	18	45
2	Manchester United	21	12	5	4	40	23	41
3	Liverpool	20	10	5	5	36	18	35
4	Tottenham Hotspur	21	9	8	4	27	21	35
5	Arsenal	21	9	7	5	28	18	34
6	Nottingham Forest	20	8	10	2	30	27	34
7	Middlesbrough	21	9	6	6	23	19	33
8	Aston Villa	19	9	5	5	25	15	32
9	Blackburn Rovers	21	9	4	8	33	26	31
10	Leeds United	20	9	4	7	28	27	31
11	Everton	21	8	5	8	29	22	29
12	Chelsea	21	7	8	6	21	23	29
13	West Ham United	19	6	5	8	21	28	23
14	Sheffield Wed.	20	5	7	8	28	30	22
15	Wimbledon	21	5	6	10	29	41	21
16	Southampton	20	4	7	9	19	30	19
17	Coventry City	20	4	6	10	27	42	18
18	Queen's Park R.	21	5	3	13	16	31	18
19	Manchester City	20	4	4	12	10	30	16
20	Bolton Wanderers	21	2	4	15	19	40	10

LEADERS Newcastle are held at Wimbledon the day after second-placed Manchester United draw with Chelsea and Arsenal complete a hat-trick of draws for the top three when they are held at Villa, who stay fourth. At the other end of the Premiership Bolton move above Coventry, following their draw at home to Nottingham Forest, but are replaced by Coventry two days later when the Sky Blues lose 4–3 at Sheffield Wednesday, despite a Dion Dublin hat-trick. QPR complete the basement trio after they draw with Middlesbrough. Alan Shearer's second hat-trick, in successive home games, takes his tally to 16 and moves Blackburn up to 10th.

Blackburn suffer their worst defeat of the season when they crash at Coventry, a result which avenges the 5–1 defeat at Ewood Park back in September. The Sky Blues remain 19th, but are still ahead of Bolton, who lose at home to Stan Collymore's second goal in successive games, which takes Liverpool to seventh. QPR's defeat at Tottenham keeps them top of the bottom three.

Newcastle lose for only the second time this campaign when Dan Petrescu gets his first goal of the season for Chelsea, but the Magpies retain top spot as Manchester United fail to capitalise and are held by Sheffield Wednesday, while Arsenal grind out a draw at Southampton to maintain the status quo at the top of the table.

Duncan Ferguson finally makes it back into an Everton shirt when he comes on as a substitute against West Ham. Despite Julian Dicks having to go in goal for the Hammers after Ludek Miklosko is sent off, Ferguson fails to make the scoresheet.

Despite scoring 11 goals in their last three games Coventry break their club record when they pay Leeds United £2 million for striker Noel Whelan and Crystal Palace sell centre-half Chris Coleman to Blackburn for a shade under £3 million.

In the aftermath of the Bosman ruling the European Court of Justice rules that clubs don't have the right to buy and sell players as commodities once their contracts expire. Although the ruling is relevant to moves between players of clubs in different EU countries, it won't be long before there is a knock-on effect domestically.

Coventry games are the ones to watch for goals at present. Their thrashing by Aston Villa takes the aggregate total, in the last five games in which the Sky Blues have played, to a staggering 27. But the dismissal of former Villa man Kevin Richardson doesn't help Coventry's cause at all. Leeds United suffer their worst defeat under Howard Wilkinson when they are at the wrong end of Sheffield Wednesday's best result of the campaign.

Newcastle win their 10th consecutive home game, against Nottingham Forest, to go 10 points clear at the top and player-manager Bryan Robson makes an impressive full debut, partnering Juninho, in Middlesbrough's win over West Ham, which takes 'Boro fifth. Arsenal lose at Liverpool and drop to seventh, with the Anfield outfit going third thanks to a Robbie Fowler hat-trick.

Wimbledon players celebrate their first win bonus for 15 matches but their victory, at Stamford Bridge, is marred by Vinnie Jones being sent off for a tackle from behind on Ruud Gullit. Jones is then charged by the FA for bringing the game into disrepute when he makes comments about Gullit, and other foreign players, in a newspaper article.

Manchester United reduce the gap on Newcastle to seven points with a win over the Magpies at Old Trafford and the last unbeaten away record in the Premiership falls when Alan Shearer becomes the first player to score 100 goals in the Premier League, by netting during Blackburn's defeat of Tottenham Hotspur.

Bolton lose their last two games of 1995 to end the year bottom of the table. Their last defeat, at Coventry, lifts the Sky Blues out of the bottom three for the first time since October.

Manchester City's defeat at Blackburn means they see in the New Year in the bottom three with QPR, who end the year in the relegation zone after losing to Manchester United at Old Trafford.

Savo Milosevic chips the Coventry keeper to score his hat-trick and Villa's fourth goal.

January

Monday 1 January

Coventry City v. Southampton	1-1
Leeds United v. Blackburn Rovers	0-0
Liverpool v. Nottingham Forest	4-2
Manchester City v. West Ham United	2-1
Middlesbrough v. Aston Villa	0-2
Sheffield Wed. v. Bolton Wanderers	4-2
Tottenham Hotspur v. Manchester United	4-1
Wimbledon v. Everton	2-3

Tuesday 2 January

Newcastle United v. Arsenal	2-0
Queen's Park R. v. Chelsea	1-2

Saturday 13 January

Bolton Wanderers v. Wimbledon	1-0
Everton v. Chelsea	1-1
Leeds United v. West Ham United	2-0
Manchester United v. Aston Villa	0-0
Middlesbrough v. Arsenal	2-3
Nottingham Forest v. Southampton	1-0
Queen's Park R. v. Blackburn Rovers	0-1
Sheffield Wed. v. Liverpool	1-1
Tottenham Hotspur v. Manchester City	1-0

Sunday 14 January

Coventry City v. Newcastle United	0-1

Saturday 20 January

Arsenal v. Everton	1-2
Blackburn Rovers v. Sheffield Wed.	3-0
Chelsea v. Nottingham Forest	1-0
Liverpool v. Leeds United	5-0
Manchester City v. Coventry City	1-1
Newcastle United v. Bolton Wanderers	2-1
Southampton v. Middlesbrough	2-1
Wimbledon v. Queen's Park R.	2-1

Sunday 21 January

Aston Villa v. Tottenham Hotspur	2-1

Monday 22 January

West Ham United v. Manchester United	0-1

Wednesday 31 January

Aston Villa v. Liverpool	0-2
Nottingham Forest v. Leeds United	2-1
Southampton v. Manchester City	1-1
West Ham United v. Coventry City	3-2

		P	W	D	L	F	A	Pts
1	Newcastle United	23	17	3	3	45	19	54
2	Liverpool	24	13	6	5	48	21	45
3	Manchester United	24	13	6	5	42	27	45
4	Tottenham Hotspur	24	11	8	5	33	24	41
5	Nottingham Forest	24	10	10	4	35	33	40
6	Aston Villa	23	11	6	6	29	18	39
7	Blackburn Rovers	24	11	5	8	37	26	38
8	Arsenal	24	10	7	7	32	24	37
9	Everton	24	10	6	8	35	26	36
10	Chelsea	24	9	9	6	25	25	36
11	Leeds United	24	10	5	9	31	34	35
12	Middlesbrough	24	9	6	9	26	26	33
13	Sheffield Wed.	23	6	8	9	33	36	26
14	West Ham United	23	7	5	11	25	35	26
15	Southampton	24	5	9	10	23	34	24
16	Wimbledon	24	6	6	12	33	46	24
17	Manchester City	24	5	6	13	14	34	21
18	Coventry City	24	4	8	12	31	48	20
19	Queen's Park R.	24	5	3	16	18	36	18
20	Bolton Wanderers	24	3	4	17	23	46	13

Leeds United v Blackburn Rovers: Leeds's Tomas Brolin beats Blackburn's Stuart Ripley.

MANCHESTER UNITED suffer their biggest league defeat for four years when they are beaten at White Hart Lane and lose ground, four points adrift of Newcastle, as the Magpies now have two games in hand. Liverpool go third when Stan Collymore, taunted by visiting fans, scores and inspires his side to victory over his former club, Nottingham Forest. Liverpool are now just three points short of United, with a game in hand.

Newcastle go four points clear of Manchester United when they convert one of their games in hand into victory over Arsenal and at the other end of the Premiership Bolton, who are eight points adrift in last place, sack manager Roy McFarland. QPR are just above Wanderers after they start the New Year with a third consecutive defeat and Manchester City complete the basement trio after they start 1996 with defeat by West Ham.

Villa hold United at Old Trafford and Spurs make it a Manchester 'double' when they follow up their victory over United with a win against City and move into third place.

Bolton claim their first win since 30 October but remain last. QPR lose again to stay 19th and Manchester City complete the relegation trio with a draw against Coventry.

Newcastle increase their advantage over Manchester United to nine points when a Steve Watson goal earns victory at Coventry and they still have a game in hand.

Nigel Clough joins Manchester City from Liverpool for £1.5 million.

Newcastle extend their astonishing winning sequence at St James' Park to a 100 percent record from 12 games and extend their lead over Manchester United to 12 points. Liverpool go second with a thrashing of Leeds United in which Robbie Fowler, with two goals, takes his tally to 20. Two days later United reduce the deficit on the top to single figures, but they have Nicky Butt sent off in the process of winning at West Ham.

For many Newcastle fans, with the benefit of end-of-season hindsight, the seminal moment in Newcastle's title chase occurs when the club signs Faustino Asprilla from Parma for £7.5 million.

Manchester United drop down to third, on goal difference, after Liverpool win at Aston Villa to go second, nine points behind Newcastle.

Bolton occupy last place at the end of the second month running. QPR are one place above and Coventry City are also in the relegation zone.

February

Saturday 3 February	
Arsenal v. Coventry City	1-1
Aston Villa v. Leeds United	3-0
Blackburn Rovers v. Bolton Wanderers	3-1
Liverpool v. Tottenham Hotspur	0-0
Manchester City v. Queen's Park R.	2-0
Newcastle United v. Sheffield Wed.	2-0
Southampton v. Everton	2-2
West Ham United v. Nottingham Forest	1-0
Wimbledon v. Manchester United	2-4

Sunday 4 February	
Chelsea v. Middlesbrough	5-0

Saturday 10 February	
Bolton Wanderers v. Aston Villa	0-2
Coventry City v. Chelsea	1-0
Everton v. Manchester City	2-0
Manchester United v. Blackburn Rovers	1-0
Middlesbrough v. Newcastle United	1-2
Nottingham Forest v. Arsenal	0-1
Sheffield Wed. v. Wimbledon	2-1

Sunday 11 February	
Queen's Park R. v. Liverpool	1-2

Monday 12 February	
Tottenham Hotspur v. West Ham United	0-1

Saturday 17 February	
Chelsea v. West Ham United	1-2
Middlesbrough v. Bolton Wanderers	1-4
Sheffield Wed. v. Queen's Park R.	1-3

Wednesday 21 February	
Manchester United v. Everton	2-0
West Ham United v. Newcastle United	2-0

Saturday 24 February	
Blackburn Rovers v. Liverpool	2-3
Coventry City v. Middlesbrough	0-0
Everton v. Nottingham Forest	3-0
Manchester City v. Newcastle United	3-3
Southampton v. Chelsea	2-3
Tottenham Hotspur v. Sheffield Wed.	1-0
West Ham United v. Arsenal	0-1
Wimbledon v. Aston Villa	3-3

Sunday 25 February	
Bolton Wanderers v. Manchester United	0-6

Wednesday 28 February	
Aston Villa v. Blackburn Rovers	2-0

		P	W	D	L	F	A	Pts
1	Newcastle United	27	19	4	4	52	25	61
2	Manchester United	28	17	6	5	55	29	57
3	Liverpool	27	15	7	5	53	24	52
4	Aston Villa	27	14	7	6	39	21	49
5	Tottenham Hotspur	27	12	9	6	34	25	45
6	Arsenal	27	12	8	7	35	25	44
7	Everton	28	12	7	9	42	30	43
8	Chelsea	28	11	9	8	34	30	42
9	Blackburn Rovers	28	12	5	11	42	33	41
10	Nottingham Forest	27	10	10	7	35	38	40
11	West Ham United	28	11	5	12	31	37	38
12	Leeds United	25	10	5	10	31	37	35
13	Middlesbrough	28	9	7	12	28	37	34
14	Sheffield Wed.	27	7	8	12	36	43	29
15	Southampton	26	5	10	11	27	39	25
16	Wimbledon	27	6	7	14	39	55	25
17	Coventry City	27	5	10	12	33	49	25
18	Manchester City	27	6	7	14	19	39	25
19	Queen's Park R.	27	6	3	18	22	41	21
20	Bolton Wanderers	28	4	4	20	28	58	16

THE DUNCAN FERGUSON saga is finally over, for now. The Everton striker has the remaining seven matches of his suspension quashed after a Scottish judge ruled that the Scottish FA acted beyond their powers.

Leaders Newcastle maintain their nine-point advantage over Manchester United, who beat Wimbledon, with victory over Sheffield Wednesday, but Liverpool fall behind the top two when they are held by Spurs. Aston Villa, who have had an erratic patch in the last couple of months, start the month well and with Dwight Yorke in form – a brace of goals in consecutive victories over Leeds and Bolton – Villa move up to fourth.

Alan Shearer's fourth hat-trick of the season wins the Lancashire derby against Bolton to move Blackburn up to sixth and keep Wanderers rock bottom. QPR lose for the sixth successive game, at Manchester City, and remain 19th, but, helped by Nigel Clough's first goal for his new club, City move out of the bottom three for the first time since before Christmas. Chelsea's Gavin Peacock's hat-trick, as they crush Middlesbrough, is not only the club's first of the season, but also Chelsea's first-ever Premiership triple.

Manchester United's long-term plans receive a financial boost when the club announces a 10-year kit deal with Umbro, said to be worth £60 million. On the field United beat Blackburn but make no impact on the leaders who, inspired by a debut appearance from the bench of Faustino Asprilla, sink 'Boro with a couple of late goals. Things are looking bleak for the Riverside outfit, who have now lost seven Premiership games in a row.

Arsenal end Nottingham Forest's unbeaten 26-match sequence at home when Dennis Bergkamp nets the only goal at the City Ground.

Bolton lose for the third game running and stay bottom. QPR stay one place higher when they lose to Liverpool; Robbie Fowler hits his 22nd goal of the campaign and Mark Wright nets his first. Manchester City drop back into the bottom three when they lose at Everton.

Liverpool, and arguably English football's, most successful manager Bob Paisley dies aged 77, fittingly reflecting the first time Liverpool won the European Cup under him in 1977.

Manchester United close the gap on the leaders to six points, with victory over Everton, because Newcastle lose for only the fourth time at West Ham, although the Magpies still have a game in hand. Two days later Kevin Keegan takes his spending to £44 million in four years when he pays Blackburn nearly £4 million for David Batty. Aston Villa are fourth after two own-goals and a Dwight Yorke penalty earn a draw at Wimbledon.

Newcastle stay top but they have to come back three times at Maine Road to earn a draw. Faustino Asprilla scores his first goal for the club, but there is a late clash between the Colombian and City skipper Keith Curle, prompting the FA to ask for video footage of the incident, which results in a misconduct charge for both players.

Liverpool win at Blackburn to close the gap on second-placed Manchester United, themselves seven points behind Newcastle, to just two points. Then Fergie's men throw out a 'don't write us off yet' warning to Newcastle when they reduce the deficit on the leaders to just four points with a best away win since 1960, at rock-bottom Bolton.

Faustino Asprilla (Newcastle United) head butts Keith Curle (Manchester City).

Saturday 2 March

Coventry City v. West Ham United	2-2
Leeds United v. Bolton Wanderers	0-1
Manchester City v. Blackburn Rovers	1-1
Middlesbrough v. Everton	0-2
Queen's Park R. v. Arsenal	1-1
Sheffield Wed. v. Nottingham Forest	1-3
Tottenham Hotspur v. Southampton	1-0
Wimbledon v. Chelsea	1-1

Sunday 3 March

Liverpool v. Aston Villa	3-0

Monday 4 March

Newcastle United v. Manchester United	0-1

Tuesday 5 March

Arsenal v. Manchester City	3-1

Wednesday 6 March

Aston Villa v. Sheffield Wed.	3-2
Queen's Park R. v. Leeds United	1-2

Saturday 9 March

Aston Villa v. Queen's Park R.	4-2
Everton v. Coventry City	2-2
West Ham United v. Middlesbrough	2-0

Tuesday 12 March

Chelsea v. Manchester City	1-1

Wednesday 13 March

Blackburn Rovers v. Leeds United	1-0
Liverpool v. Wimbledon	2-2

Saturday 16 March

Coventry City v. Bolton Wanderers	0-2
Liverpool v. Chelsea	2-0
Manchester City v. Southampton	2-1
Middlesbrough v. Nottingham Forest	1-1
Queen's Park R. v. Manchester United	1-1
Sheffield Wed. v. Aston Villa	2-0
Tottenham Hotspur v. Blackburn Rovers	2-3
Wimbledon v. Arsenal	0-3

Sunday 17 March

Leeds United v. Everton	2-2

Monday 18 March

Newcastle United v. West Ham United	3-0

Tuesday 19 March

Aston Villa v. Middlesbrough	0-0

Wednesday 20 March

Bolton Wanderers v. Tottenham Hotspur	2-3
Manchester United v. Arsenal	1-0
Southampton v. Sheffield Wed.	0-1

Saturday 23 March

Arsenal v. Newcastle United	2-0
Bolton Wanderers v. Sheffield Wed.	2-1
Chelsea v. Queen's Park R.	1-1
Everton v. Wimbledon	2-4
Nottingham Forest v. Liverpool	1-0
West Ham United v. Manchester City	4-2

Sunday 24 March

Manchester United v. Tottenham Hotspur	1-0

Monday 25 March

Southampton v. Coventry City	1-0

Saturday 30 March

Blackburn Rovers v. Everton	0-3
Bolton Wanderers v. Manchester City	1-1
Leeds United v. Middlesbrough	0-1
Queen's Park R. v. Southampton	3-0
Tottenham Hotspur v. Coventry City	3-1
Wimbledon v. Nottingham Forest	1-0

		P	W	D	L	F	A	Pts
1	Manchester United	32	20	7	5	59	30	67
2	Newcastle United	30	20	4	6	55	28	64
3	Liverpool	31	17	8	6	60	27	59
4	Aston Villa	32	16	8	8	46	30	56
5	Arsenal	32	15	9	8	44	28	54
6	Tottenham Hotspur	32	15	9	8	43	32	54
7	Everton	33	14	9	10	53	38	51
8	Blackburn Rovers	32	14	6	12	47	39	48
9	Nottingham Forest	31	12	11	8	40	41	47
10	Chelsea	32	11	12	9	37	35	45
11	West Ham United	32	13	6	13	39	44	45
12	Leeds United	30	11	6	13	35	43	39
13	Middlesbrough	33	10	9	14	30	42	39
14	Sheffield Wed.	32	9	8	15	43	51	35
15	Wimbledon	32	8	9	15	47	63	33
16	Manchester City	33	7	10	16	27	50	31
17	Southampton	31	6	10	15	29	46	28
18	Queen's Park R.	33	7	6	20	31	50	27
19	Coventry City	32	5	12	15	38	59	27
20	Bolton Wanderers	33	7	5	21	36	63	26

NEWCASTLE'S unbeaten home record – all 13 games this campaign have been victories – ends when an Eric Cantona goal wins the clash between the top two teams, leaving Manchester United just one point adrift of the leaders. Liverpool, with a burst of three goals in the opening 10 minutes, beat Villa to move above the Midlands side, who are fourth. Bolton remain bottom, despite winning at Leeds. QPR are one place higher despite holding Arsenal and Southampton complete the basement trio with defeat at Tottenham.

Manchester United go top of the Premiership, on goal difference from Newcastle, for the first time in six months, when a Cantona equaliser earns a point at struggling QPR, who remain 19th. Bolton stay bottom despite recording a third successive away win, at Coventry, and a fourth consecutive defeat for Southampton leaves them still in the bottom three. Alan Shearer scores in stoppage time, in Blackburn's win at Spurs, to complete his fifth hat-trick of the campaign.

Newcastle reclaim top spot, by three points, with a comfortable win at home to West Ham, but the cracks are showing in the Magpies' title pursuit. Manchester United keep up the pressure with a narrow win over Arsenal; Eric Cantona is again their talisman, but victory isn't enough to go top and the Reds stay second, on goal difference.

Blackburn sign Garry Flitcroft from Manchester City for £3 million and there is a certain symmetry when, on his debut, the midfielder is sent off after three minutes, as Rovers lose 3–0 to Everton. Flitcroft is subsequently suspended for… three matches.

There's movement at both ends of the Premiership as Manchester United go top, without kicking a ball, following Newcastle's shock defeat at Highbury and on the scoresheet is Ian Wright, 10 days after having his transfer request turned down by Arsenal. Bolton move off the bottom for the first time in four months when they climb above QPR by beating Sheffield Wednesday.

Manchester United turn up the heat on Newcastle with victory over Spurs, thanks to Eric Cantona's fourth goal in four games, and go three points clear of Kevin Keegan's side.

Bolton drop back to bottom after being held by Manchester City but QPR move up two places when they follow up their draw at Chelsea by beating Southampton, who are 17th as a consequence. Manchester City's draw with Bolton is a result that does neither side any favours, with just one complete month to go.

Tottenham Hotspur defenders can't catch Manchester United's Eric Cantona as he breaks through to score.

April

Wednesday 3 April	
Leeds United v. Southampton	1-0
Liverpool v. Newcastle United	4-3
Friday 5 April	
Middlesbrough v. Sheffield Wed.	3-1
Saturday 6 April	
Arsenal v. Leeds United	2-1
Chelsea v. Aston Villa	1-2
Coventry City v. Liverpool	1-0
Everton v. Bolton Wanderers	3-0
Manchester City v. Manchester United	2-3
Newcastle United v. Queen's Park R.	2-1
Nottingham Forest v. Tottenham Hotspur	2-1
Southampton v. Blackburn Rovers	1-0
West Ham United v. Wimbledon	1-1
Monday 8 April	
Aston Villa v. Southampton	3-0
Blackburn Rovers v. Newcastle United	2-1
Bolton Wanderers v. Chelsea	2-1
Leeds United v. Nottingham Forest	1-3
Liverpool v. West Ham United	2-0
Manchester United v. Coventry City	1-0
Queen's Park R. v. Everton	3-1
Sheffield Wed. v. Arsenal	1-0
Tottenham Hotspur v. Middlesbrough	1-1
Wimbledon v. Manchester City	3-0
Saturday 13 April	
Chelsea v. Leeds United	4-1
Coventry City v. Queen's Park R.	1-0
Manchester City v. Sheffield Wed.	1-0
Middlesbrough v. Wimbledon	1-2
Nottingham Forest v. Blackburn Rovers	1-5
Southampton v. Manchester United	3-1
West Ham United v. Bolton Wanderers	1-0
Sunday 14 April	
Newcastle United v. Aston Villa	1-0
Monday 15 April	
Arsenal v. Tottenham Hotspur	0-0
Tuesday 16 April	
Everton v. Liverpool	1-1
Wednesday 17 April	
Aston Villa v. West Ham United	1-1
Blackburn Rovers v. Wimbledon	3-2
Manchester United v. Leeds United	1-0
Newcastle United v. Southampton	1-0
Nottingham Forest v. Coventry City	0-0
Sheffield Wed. v. Chelsea	0-0
Saturday 27 April	
Aston Villa v. Manchester City	0-1
Blackburn Rovers v. Arsenal	1-1
Bolton Wanderers v. Southampton	0-1
Liverpool v. Middlesbrough	1-0
Queen's Park R. v. West Ham United	3-0
Sheffield Wed. v. Everton	2-5
Tottenham Hotspur v. Chelsea	1-1
Wimbledon v. Coventry City	0-2
Sunday 28 April	
Manchester United v. Nottingham Forest	5-0
Monday 29 April	
Leeds United v. Newcastle United	0-1

		P	W	D	L	F	A	Pts
1	Manchester United	37	24	7	6	70	35	79
2	Newcastle United	36	24	4	8	64	35	76
3	Liverpool	36	20	9	7	68	32	69
4	Aston Villa	37	18	9	10	52	34	63
5	Arsenal	36	16	11	9	47	31	59
6	Everton	37	16	10	11	63	44	58
7	Blackburn Rovers	37	17	7	13	58	45	58
8	Tottenham Hotspur	36	15	12	9	46	36	57
9	Nottingham Forest	36	14	12	10	46	53	54
10	Chelsea	37	12	14	11	44	41	50
11	West Ham United	37	14	8	15	42	51	50
12	Middlesbrough	37	11	10	16	35	47	43
13	Leeds United	36	12	6	18	39	54	42
14	Wimbledon	37	10	10	17	55	70	40
15	Sheffield Wed.	37	10	9	18	47	60	39
16	Coventry City	37	8	13	16	42	60	37
17	Southampton	37	9	10	18	34	52	37
18	Manchester City	37	9	10	18	31	56	37
19	Queen's Park R.	37	9	6	22	38	54	33
20	Bolton Wanderers	37	8	5	24	38	69	29

THE CRACKS are appearing in Newcastle's title dream as they crash at Anfield, despite leading 2–1 at half-time, where Stan Collymore's last minute goal wins a seven-goal thriller. It is the Magpies' fourth defeat in six matches and they are now three points behind Manchester United with an inferior goal difference, although they do still have a game in hand. Liverpool's position improves as they are now just five points behind top spot. Aston Villa win at Chelsea to stay fourth.

Bolton lose at Everton to stay bottom of the table while QPR push Newcastle all the way and are leading until a late brace from Peter Beardsley clinches victory and keeps Rangers 19th and the Magpies second, but Manchester United scent victory as they win the Manchester derby to retain pole position and keep City perilously close to the drop.

Manchester United open the Bank Holiday programme with a win over Coventry that increases their lead over second-placed Newcastle to six points and the match winner is Eric Cantona, who scores for the sixth consecutive match, to keep the Sky Blues 19th. Newcastle, despite leading 1–0 until five minutes from time, are caught cold by a couple of Graham Fenton goals that give Blackburn victory at Ewood Park. Liverpool, with John Barnes scoring his first goal for eight months, retain third place by beating West Ham.

Despite beating Chelsea Bolton stay 20th and QPR give themselves a little hope with victory over Everton that lifts them to 18th.

The date could be nothing other than the 13th when Manchester United change their despised grey strip at half-time during the match at the Dell because, according to manager Alex Ferguson, his players couldn't see each other.

Robbie Fowler's 26th goal of the campaign opens the scoring against Newcastle.

The Saints, 3–0 ahead at the time, still ran out winners, although the new strip inspired United to a consolation goal from Ryan Giggs. The win keeps Southampton out of the drop zone but Coventry's victory over QPR virtually assures relegation for Rangers although Manchester City's victory over Sheffield Wednesday keeps the Sky Blues in the relegation zone. Bolton look doomed after defeat at West Ham keeps them 20th.

Newcastle profit from Manchester United's reverse at Southampton with a Les Ferdinand goal that beats Aston Villa and moves the Magpies to within three points of the leaders, and they have a game in hand.

Both leading Uniteds win to maintain the status quo at the top, but the news is made by another scoring milestone for Alan Shearer. The first of his two goals, against Wimbledon, makes him the first player to score 30 goals in the Premiership in three consecutive seasons.

Ian Rush bids farewell to Anfield when he comes on as a substitute against Middlesbrough, but fails to finish with a goal. It's left to Stan Collymore to earn the points, with his 14th and final goal of the campaign, keeping Liverpool third. But it's the opposite end of the table that takes centre stage and Bolton's home defeat by Southampton confirms relegation for Wanderers and they are joined by QPR, despite their victory over West Ham.

With Manchester City, Coventry and Southampton winning there is a surprise new candidate for the final relegation berth in Sheffield Wednesday, who are just two points above the drop line, following their thrashing at home to Everton, for whom Andrei Kanchelskis scores the only hat-trick of the campaign.

Manchester United thrash Nottingham Forest to stand on the title threshold. They are six points clear and have a superior goal difference of seven.

United have just one game to play; Newcastle have three. The Magpies then win at Leeds to stay in contention and afterwards Kevin Keegan's passionate 'I would love it if we beat them to the title' speech is TV manna for Sky Sports.

Wednesday 1 May

Arsenal v. Liverpool	0-0

Thursday 2 May

Leeds United v. Tottenham Hotspur	1-3
Nottingham Forest v. Newcastle United	1-1

Sunday 5 May

Arsenal v. Bolton Wanderers	2-1
Chelsea v. Blackburn Rovers	2-3
Coventry City v. Leeds United	0-0
Everton v. Aston Villa	1-0
Manchester City v. Liverpool	2-2
Middlesbrough v. Manchester United	0-3
Newcastle United v. Tottenham Hotspur	1-1
Nottingham Forest v. Queen's Park R.	3-0
Southampton v. Wimbledon	0-0
West Ham United v. Sheffield Wed.	1-1

		P	W	D	L	F	A	Pts
1	Manchester United	38	25	7	6	73	35	82
2	Newcastle United	38	24	6	8	66	37	78
3	Liverpool	38	20	11	7	70	34	71
4	Aston Villa	38	18	9	11	52	35	63
5	Arsenal	38	17	12	9	49	32	63
6	Everton	38	17	10	11	64	44	61
7	Blackburn Rovers	38	18	7	13	61	47	61
8	Tottenham Hotspur	38	16	13	9	50	38	61
9	Nottingham Forest	38	15	13	10	50	54	58
10	West Ham United	38	14	9	15	43	52	51
11	Chelsea	38	12	14	12	46	44	50
12	Middlesbrough	38	11	10	17	35	50	43
13	Leeds United	38	12	7	19	40	57	43
14	Wimbledon	38	10	11	17	55	70	41
15	Sheffield Wed.	38	10	10	18	48	61	40
16	Coventry City	38	8	14	16	42	60	38
17	Southampton	38	9	11	18	34	52	38
18	Manchester City	38	9	11	18	33	58	38
19	Queen's Park R.	38	9	6	23	38	57	33
20	Bolton Wanderers	38	8	5	25	39	71	29

Promoted from Endsleigh Insurance League Division One

Sunderland
Derby County
Leicester City (via play-offs)

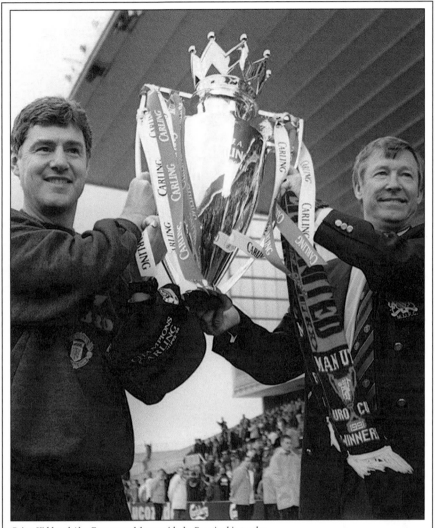

Brian Kidd and Alex Ferguson celebrate with the Premiership trophy.

NEWCASTLE'S draw at Nottingham Forest means that Manchester United need just a point from their final game to clinch the championship, even if Keegan's side win their last fixture. Leeds lose to Spurs and the sixth consecutive defeat is the worst run for the club since 1947.

There are contrasting emotions in Manchester on the final day of the Premiership. United make no mistake and secure the title with their 10th away win of the season, at Middlesbrough, while Newcastle fail to win at St James' Park for only the second time in the campaign, against Tottenham. Significantly, the other occasion was when they lost to Manchester United in March, which proved the ultimate difference between the teams and ensured the final gap of four points. Arsenal get the win over relegated Bolton that they need to clinch the final UEFA Cup place, but they leave it very late to turn a 1–0 deficit into victory with David Platt and Dennis Bergkamp scoring in the final eight minutes. Liverpool clinch third place with a draw that sees gloom descend on the blue half of Manchester.

Three days after former chairman Peter Swales dies of a heart attack, aged 62, Manchester City are relegated with Alan Ball's instructions to his team making the headlines alongside the club's descent into Division One. The City manager tells his players, late in the match, having come back from 2–0 down at the break to level the game against Liverpool, to keep the ball because he had 'heard a rumour' that one of the other sides in trouble was losing! The fact that Coventry and Southampton were both drawing 0–0 proves that you should not always believe what you hear. At least it was a scoring 'leaving of Liverpool' for Ian Rush, who marks his final game for the club with one of their goals at Maine Road.

Aston Villa, despite losing their final game, finish fourth ahead of Arsenal, who have the same number of points and the same goal difference. Villa finish one place higher because they have scored more goals, 52 against 49 for the Gunners.

End of season round-up

Top Premiership Goalscorers 1995–96

Alan Shearer	Blackburn Rovers	31
Robbie Fowler	Liverpool	28
Les Ferdinand	Newcastle United	25
Dwight Yorke	Aston Villa	17
Teddy Sheringham	Tottenham Hotspur	16
Andrei Kanchelskis	Everton	16
Ian Wright	Arsenal	15
Chris Armstrong	Tottenham Hotspur	15
Eric Cantona	Manchester United	14
Stan Collymore	Liverpool	14
Dion Dublin	Coventry City	14

Coca-Cola League Cup Final

Aston Villa 3   Leeds United 0

Although they only led 1–0 at half-time, Aston Villa went on to record an easy victory over Leeds to equal Liverpool's record of five wins in the competition, in a very one-sided game. Savo Milosevic at last seemed to justify his record £3.5 million transfer fee with a stunning goal. Ian Taylor and Dwight Yorke were Villa's other scorers against a disappointing Leeds side.

FA Cup Final

Manchester United 1 Liverpool 0

The final between two of the top three sides in the Premiership produced a poor game that was scoreless until five minutes from time, when Eric Cantona scored the only goal. David Beckham's corner was punched out by David James but only as far as the enigmatic Frenchman, via Rush's shoulder. Eric, reading the situation perfectly, took one step backwards to create time and space. He used both to fire home through a crowded area and the first Frenchman to become Footballer of the Year lifted the FA Cup to secure United's second 'double' in five years.

FWA Footballer of the Year

Eric Cantona   Manchester United

PFA Player of the Year

Les Ferdinand   Newcastle United

PFA Young Player of the Year

Robbie Fowler   Liverpool

Manager of the Year

Alex Ferguson   Manchester United

Mark Bosnich and Mark Draper of Aston Villa celebrate with the Coca-Cola Cup.

Close Season 1996

Alex Ferguson signs a new four-year deal to manage Manchester United.

Graeme Souness signs a three-year contract to manage Southampton and Leeds United make Lee Bowyer the most expensive teenage player when they pay Charlton £2.5 million for the midfielder.

Bryan Robson pays £7 million, to Juventus, for Fabrizio Ravanelli, and the flood of foreign imports accelerates when Chelsea buy Roberto di Matteo, for £4.9 million, from Lazio, Manchester United sign Ole Gunnar Solskjaer, from Molde, for a give-away £1.5 million and Ronnie Johnsen moves to Old Trafford from Besiktas.

After nearly two years of working without a formal contract Gerry Francis signs a two-year deal with Spurs.

Football headlines are made when the name Alan Shearer appears on a passenger list for Manchester United's pre-season trip to Milan, but the truth finally emerges that it was a prank, or wishful thinking, by someone at United's travel company.

United's final bid of £12 million for the England striker is rejected and Blackburn counter with a £4 million offer for Eric Cantona.

Coventry agree a fee of £3 million for Leeds' skipper Gary McAllister and Manchester United sign Jordi 'son of Johan' Cruyff for £800,000 after the player forces Barcelona to drop their asking price.

Kevin Keegan stuns football, and Alex Ferguson, when he pays a world record £15 million to take Alan Shearer to Newcastle.

Saturday 17 August	
Arsenal v. West Ham United	2-0
Blackburn Rovers v. Tottenham Hotspur	0-2
Coventry City v. Nottingham Forest	0-3
Derby County v. Leeds United	3-3
Everton v. Newcastle United	2-0
Middlesbrough v. Liverpool	3-3
Sheffield Wed. v. Aston Villa	2-1
Sunderland v. Leicester City	0-0
Wimbledon v. Manchester United	0-3
Sunday 18 August	
Southampton v. Chelsea	0-0
Monday 19 August	
Liverpool v. Arsenal	2-0
Tuesday 20 August	
Leeds United v. Sheffield Wed.	0-2
Wednesday 21 August	
Aston Villa v. Blackburn Rovers	1-0
Chelsea v. Middlesbrough	1-0
Leicester City v. Southampton	2-1
Manchester United v. Everton	2-2
Newcastle United v. Wimbledon	2-0
Nottingham Forest v. Sunderland	1-4
Tottenham Hotspur v. Derby County	1-1
West Ham United v. Coventry City	1-1
Saturday 24 August	
Aston Villa v. Derby County	2-0
Chelsea v. Coventry City	2-0
Leicester City v. Arsenal	0-2
Liverpool v. Sunderland	0-0
Newcastle United v. Sheffield Wed.	1-2
Nottingham Forest v. Middlesbrough	1-1
Tottenham Hotspur v. Everton	0-0
West Ham United v. Southampton	2-1
Sunday 25 August	
Manchester United v. Blackburn Rovers	2-2
Monday 26 August	
Leeds United v. Wimbledon	1-0

		P	W	D	L	F	A	Pts
1	Sheffield Wed.	3	3	0	0	6	2	9
2	Chelsea	3	2	1	0	3	0	7
3	Aston Villa	3	2	0	1	4	2	6
4	Arsenal	3	2	0	1	4	2	6
5	Manchester United	3	1	2	0	7	4	5
6	Sunderland	3	1	2	0	4	1	5
7	Liverpool	3	1	2	0	5	3	5
8	Everton	3	1	2	0	4	2	5
9	Tottenham Hotspur	3	1	2	0	3	1	5
10	Nottingham Forest	3	1	1	1	5	5	4
11	Leeds United	3	1	1	1	4	5	4
12	West Ham United	3	1	1	1	3	4	4
13	Leicester City	3	1	1	1	2	3	4
14	Newcastle United	3	1	0	2	3	4	3
15	Middlesbrough	3	0	2	1	4	5	2
16	Derby County	3	0	2	1	4	6	2
17	Southampton	3	0	1	2	2	4	1
18	Blackburn Rovers	3	0	1	2	2	5	1
19	Coventry City	3	0	1	2	1	6	1
20	Wimbledon	3	0	0	3	0	6	0

THERE are two hat-tricks on the opening day of the Premiership: from Fabrizio Ravanelli, on his Middlesbrough debut, against Liverpool, and Kevin Campbell for Forest as they beat Coventry, but the day's headline is created by David Beckham scoring at Wimbledon from the halfway line. Don's 'keeper Neil Sullivan will never live it down as the champions open the defence of their title with a win. The nine fixtures yield a total of 27 goals with five of the six, in Derby's home draw with Leeds, coming in the last 20 minutes. Two days later a Steve McManaman brace sees Liverpool beat Arsenal.

Sheffield Wednesday follow up their opening win over Aston Villa with a derby victory at Leeds to top the table and after five successive days of Premiership action they are the only side with a 100 percent record after two games. The world's most expensive player, £15 million Alan Shearer, has to wait until his second game to score his first goal for his new club, Newcastle United. There are just two minutes left when he nets the Magpies' second against Wimbledon. Manchester United's 30-match unbeaten record at Old Trafford is under threat as they trail at half-time to a couple of Duncan Ferguson goals, but Jordi Cruyff, and a David Unsworth own-goal, eight minutes from time, rescue United.

Kenny Dalglish and Blackburn Rovers part company by mutual consent. The next day Arsenal reveal that their new manager is Arsene Wenger and the Gunners admit they approached the Frenchman before sacking Bruce Rioch.

Sheffield Wednesday make it a hat-trick of victories as they hold on to top spot with a win at St James' Park and Chelsea are tucked into second after seven points from their three opening fixtures. At the foot of the table Blackburn are 18th after three games and only pick up a first point in game number three when they hold Manchester United. One place below them are Coventry.

Wimbledon are the only team with no points after three matches.

FACT FILE

Kevin Campbell's hat-trick is officially the first of the Premiership season as he completes his treble two minutes into the second half, while Ravanelli's third goal comes in the 81st minute. Stig Inge Bjornebye is the Premiership's first goalscorer of the season with his fourth minute strike at the Riverside.

An 'Ab Fab' 'Boro debut. Ravanelli scores against Liverpool from the penalty spot.

September

Monday 2 September		
Sheffield Wed. v. Leicester City		2-1
Wednesday 4 September		
Arsenal v. Chelsea		3-3
Blackburn Rovers v. Leeds United		0-1
Coventry City v. Liverpool		0-1
Derby County v. Manchester United		1-1
Everton v. Aston Villa		0-1
Middlesbrough v. West Ham United		4-1
Southampton v. Nottingham Forest		2-2
Sunderland v. Newcastle United		1-2
Wimbledon v. Tottenham Hotspur		1-0
Saturday 7 September		
Aston Villa v. Arsenal		2-2
Leeds United v. Manchester United		0-4
Liverpool v. Southampton		2-1
Middlesbrough v. Coventry City		4-0
Nottingham Forest v. Leicester City		0-0
Sheffield Wed. v. Chelsea		0-2
Tottenham Hotspur v. Newcastle United		1-2
Wimbledon v. Everton		4-0
Sunday 8 September		
Sunderland v. West Ham United		0-0
Monday 9 September		
Blackburn Rovers v. Derby County		1-2
Saturday 14 September		
Coventry City v. Leeds United		2-1
Derby County v. Sunderland		1-0
Everton v. Middlesbrough		1-2
Manchester United v. Nottingham Forest		4-1
Newcastle United v. Blackburn Rovers		2-1
Southampton v. Tottenham Hotspur		0-1
West Ham United v. Wimbledon		0-2
Sunday 15 September		
Chelsea v. Aston Villa		1-1
Leicester City v. Liverpool		0-3
Monday 16 September		
Arsenal v. Sheffield Wed.		4-1
Saturday 21 September		
Aston Villa v. Manchester United		0-0
Blackburn Rovers v. Everton		1-1
Leeds United v. Newcastle United		0-1
Liverpool v. Chelsea		5-1
Middlesbrough v. Arsenal		0-2
Nottingham Forest v. West Ham United		0-2
Sheffield Wed. v. Derby County		0-0
Sunderland v. Coventry City		1-0
Sunday 22 September		
Tottenham Hotspur v. Leicester City		1-2
Monday 23 September		
Wimbledon v. Southampton		3-1
Saturday 28 September		
Arsenal v. Sunderland		2-0
Chelsea v. Nottingham Forest		1-1
Coventry City v. Blackburn Rovers		0-0
Derby County v. Wimbledon		0-2
Everton v. Sheffield Wed.		2-0
Leicester City v. Leeds United		1-0
Southampton v. Middlesbrough		4-0
Sunday 29 September		
Manchester United v. Tottenham Hotspur		2-0
West Ham United v. Liverpool		1-2
Monday 30 September		
Newcastle United v. Aston Villa		4-3

		P	W	D	L	F	A	Pts
1	Liverpool	8	6	2	0	18	6	20
2	Newcastle United	8	6	0	2	14	10	18
3	Arsenal	8	5	2	1	17	8	17
4	Manchester United	8	4	4	0	18	6	16
5	Wimbledon	8	5	0	3	12	7	15
6	Chelsea	8	3	4	1	11	10	13
7	Sheffield Wed.	8	4	1	3	9	11	13
8	Aston Villa	8	3	3	2	11	9	12
9	Middlesbrough	8	3	2	3	14	13	11
10	Leicester City	8	3	2	3	6	9	11
11	Derby County	8	2	4	2	8	10	10
12	Sunderland	8	2	3	3	6	6	9
13	Everton	8	2	3	3	8	10	9
14	Tottenham Hotspur	8	2	2	4	6	8	8
15	West Ham United	8	2	2	4	7	12	8
16	Nottingham Forest	8	1	4	3	9	14	7
17	Leeds United	8	2	1	5	6	13	7
18	Southampton	8	1	2	5	10	12	5
19	Coventry City	8	1	2	5	3	13	5
20	Blackburn Rovers	8	0	3	5	5	11	3

SHEFFIELD WEDNES-DAY continue their 100 percent start to the season with a win over Leicester that extends the Owls' lead at the top to five points. Wimbledon register their first win of the campaign but lose Vinnie Jones to the 12th red card of his career as the Dons beat Spurs.

Chelsea end Sheffield Wednesday's perfect record with a victory that puts them second, just a point behind the leaders, and Liverpool go third on goal difference from Chelsea after beating Southampton. After three consecutive draws Manchester United finally click with a hammering of Leeds that takes the reigning champions fifth; two days later Leeds sack manager Howard Wilkinson after eight years in charge. Inside 24 hours George Graham is installed as the new manager at Elland Road, after 19 months out of the game.

Manchester United go top after crushing Nottingham Forest, but only on goal difference from Sheffield Wednesday and Newcastle, who send Blackburn to the bottom with Alan Shearer on the scoresheet against his old club. Leeds lose their first game under new manager George Graham despite scoring in the first minute against Coventry.

Liverpool take over at the top – Chelsea are held by Villa – and go two points clear, as Patrik Berger scores twice in less than 20 minutes, after coming on as substitute at Leicester. Berger then has only an hour to get from Filbert Street to Birmingham airport in time to catch a plane so that he can play for the Czech Republic in a World Cup qualifier.

Arsenal's victory over Sheffield Wednesday, after going 1–0 down, represents a milestone in the career of Ian Wright. His hat-trick includes his 100th league goal for the Gunners and his 150th for the club in just 226 matches.

Patrik Berger hits his second brace in two matches as Liverpool crush Chelsea to maintain their two-point lead over Newcastle. Arsenal go third by winning at Middlesbrough as Manchester United are held at Villa.

Team of the month are Wimbledon, who go sixth after a fourth consecutive Premiership victory. It's a remarkable turn around for the 'Crazy Gang', who were bottom at the start of September after losing their first three matches.

Arsenal close the gap on leaders Liverpool to goal difference after they beat nine-man Sunderland. Wimbledon's fifth win in a row takes them third and at long last Southampton win a Premiership game, after seven unsuccessful attempts. 'Boro are the vanquished side and, naturally, Matt Le Tissier is on the scoresheet, with a brace that takes his tally to four. Saints move up to 18th above Coventry, who only have one win to their name in eight matches. That's still one more victory than bottom club Blackburn: no surprise then that the two sides end the month sharing a goalless draw.

At the other end of the Premiership Liverpool go three points clear of Arsenal after they beat West Ham and Manchester United go third after a Solskjaer double sinks Tottenham. Newcastle slip into second place when they win for the fifth game in a row, despite a Dwight Yorke hat-trick for Aston Villa.

Liverpool's Patrik Berger scores his second goal, which beats Leicester to keep Liverpool top.

October

Saturday 12 October	
Blackburn Rovers v. Arsenal	0-2
Derby County v. Newcastle United	0-1
Everton v. West Ham United	2-1
Leeds United v. Nottingham Forest	2-0
Leicester City v. Chelsea	1-3
Manchester United v. Liverpool	1-0
Tottenham Hotspur v. Aston Villa	1-0
Wimbledon v. Sheffield Wed.	4-2

Sunday 13 October	
Coventry City v. Southampton	1-1

Monday 14 October	
Sunderland v. Middlesbrough	2-2

Saturday 19 October	
Arsenal v. Coventry City	0-0
Aston Villa v. Leeds United	2-0
Chelsea v. Wimbledon	2-4
Middlesbrough v. Tottenham Hotspur	0-3
Nottingham Forest v. Derby County	1-1
Sheffield Wed. v. Blackburn Rovers	1-1
Southampton v. Sunderland	3-0
West Ham United v. Leicester City	1-0

Sunday 20 October	
Newcastle United v. Manchester United	5-0

Saturday 26 October	
Arsenal v. Leeds United	3-0
Chelsea v. Tottenham Hotspur	3-1
Coventry City v. Sheffield Wed.	0-0
Leicester City v. Newcastle United	2-0
Middlesbrough v. Wimbledon	0-0
Southampton v. Manchester United	6-3
Sunderland v. Aston Villa	1-0
West Ham United v. Blackburn Rovers	2-1

Sunday 27 October	
Liverpool v. Derby County	2-1

Monday 28 October	
Nottingham Forest v. Everton	0-1

		P	W	D	L	F	A	Pts
1	Arsenal	11	7	3	1	22	8	24
2	Newcastle United	11	8	0	3	20	12	24
3	Liverpool	10	7	2	1	20	8	23
4	Wimbledon	11	7	1	3	20	11	22
5	Manchester United	11	5	4	2	22	17	19
6	Chelsea	11	5	4	2	19	16	19
7	Aston Villa	11	4	3	4	13	11	15
8	Everton	10	4	3	3	11	11	15
9	Sheffield Wed.	11	4	3	4	12	16	15
10	Tottenham Hotspur	11	4	2	5	11	11	14
11	West Ham United	11	4	2	5	11	15	14
12	Leicester City	11	4	2	5	9	13	14
13	Middlesbrough	11	3	4	4	16	18	13
14	Sunderland	11	3	4	4	9	11	13
15	Southampton	11	3	3	5	20	16	12
16	Derby County	11	2	5	4	10	14	11
17	Leeds United	11	3	1	7	8	18	10
18	Nottingham Forest	11	1	5	5	10	18	8
19	Coventry City	11	1	5	5	4	14	8
20	Blackburn Rovers	11	0	4	7	7	16	4

Egil Ostenstad beats Schmeichel to score Southampton's fifth goal.

A David Beckham goal beats leaders Liverpool, who are the only top-six side not to win. United are tucked in third, behind Arsenal, on goal difference, but Newcastle take over at the top for the first time in the campaign, as an Alan Shearer goal beats Derby. Wimbledon keep up their winning run with a sixth consecutive victory and move up to fifth.

At the foot of the table Blackburn are 20th following defeat by Arsenal, Rovers' ninth game without a win. Coventry rescue a point with a last-minute Dion Dublin goal against Southampton and stay 19th, while Saints are just one place above.

Mark Bosnich gets himself into trouble with a Nazi salute at White Hart Lane during Spurs' 1–0 win and, despite a later apology, the Villa 'keeper is later charged with misconduct by the FA.

Having dropped as far as seventh, Sheffield Wednesday break their transfer record by signing Benito Carbone from Inter Milan for £3 million. Two days later Southampton break their record when they pay £1.3 million to sign Ulrich van Gobbel from Galatasaray.

Arsenal go top despite being held by second from bottom Coventry, and are only ahead of Wimbledon on goal difference. The victory at Chelsea is the Dons' seventh consecutive league win and Robbie Earle scores for a third successive game. The following day Manchester United suffer defeat for the first time this campaign when they suffer their worst defeat in 12 matches at St James' Park, a win that takes Newcastle three points clear of Arsenal and Wimbledon. Alan Shearer nets his seventh goal of the season but suffers a groin injury that requires surgery and means up to eight weeks out. At the other end of the pitch Newcastle appoint Mark Lawrenson as a full-time defensive coach. Manchester United suffer their second heavy defeat inside a week when they crash at the Dell. Egil Ostenstad hits a hat-trick but United are handicapped by the dismissal of Roy Keane, which means the visitors having to play for most of the game with 10 men.

A 'Shearer-less' Newcastle go down to Leicester allowing Arsenal, who beat Leeds, to go top on goal difference. Wimbledon stay third but their winning sequence ends with a draw at Middlesbrough.

Liverpool convert one of their games in hand to three points, against Derby, and go third behind Arsenal and Newcastle, although they still have another game in hand.

Blackburn end the month bottom, still without a league win. A run of draws keeps Coventry 19th and Nottingham Forest, without a win since the opening day, complete the relegation zone.

November

Saturday 2 November

Aston Villa v. Nottingham Forest	2-0
Derby County v. Leicester City	2-0
Leeds United v. Sunderland	3-0
Manchester United v. Chelsea	1-2
Sheffield Wed. v. Southampton	1-1
Tottenham Hotspur v. West Ham United	1-0
Wimbledon v. Arsenal	2-2

Sunday 3 November

Blackburn Rovers v. Liverpool	3-0
Newcastle United v. Middlesbrough	3-1

Monday 4 November

Everton v. Coventry City	1-1

Saturday 16 November

Aston Villa v. Leicester City	1-3
Blackburn Rovers v. Chelsea	1-1
Everton v. Southampton	7-1
Leeds United v. Liverpool	0-2
Manchester United v. Arsenal	1-0
Newcastle United v. West Ham United	1-1
Tottenham Hotspur v. Sunderland	2-0
Wimbledon v. Coventry City	2-2

Sunday 17 November

Derby County v. Middlesbrough	2-1

Monday 18 November

Sheffield Wed. v. Nottingham Forest	2-0

Wednesday 20 November

Liverpool v. Everton	1-1

Saturday 23 November

Chelsea v. Newcastle United	1-1
Coventry City v. Aston Villa	1-2
Leicester City v. Everton	1-2
Liverpool v. Wimbledon	1-1
Middlesbrough v. Manchester United	2-2
Southampton v. Leeds United	0-2
Sunderland v. Sheffield Wed.	1-1
West Ham United v. Derby County	1-1

Sunday 24 November

Arsenal v. Tottenham Hotspur	3-1

Monday 25 November

Nottingham Forest v. Blackburn Rovers	2-2

Saturday 30 November

Aston Villa v. Middlesbrough	1-0
Blackburn Rovers v. Southampton	2-1
Derby County v. Coventry City	2-1
Everton v. Sunderland	1-3
Manchester United v. Leicester City	3-1
Newcastle United v. Arsenal	1-2
Sheffield Wed. v. West Ham United	0-0
Wimbledon v. Nottingham Forest	1-0

		P	W	D	L	F	A	Pts
1	Arsenal	15	9	4	2	29	13	31
2	Newcastle United	15	9	2	4	26	17	29
3	Liverpool	14	8	4	2	24	13	28
4	Wimbledon	15	8	4	3	26	16	28
5	Manchester United	15	7	5	3	29	22	26
6	Chelsea	14	6	6	2	23	19	24
7	Aston Villa	15	7	3	5	19	15	24
8	Everton	15	6	5	4	23	18	23
9	Derby County	15	5	6	4	17	17	21
10	Sheffield Wed.	15	5	6	4	16	18	21
11	Tottenham Hotspur	14	6	2	6	15	14	20
12	West Ham United	15	4	5	6	13	18	17
13	Sunderland	15	4	5	6	13	18	17
14	Leicester City	15	5	2	8	14	21	17
15	Leeds United	14	5	1	8	13	20	16
16	Middlesbrough	15	3	5	7	20	26	14
17	Southampton	15	3	4	8	23	28	13
18	Blackburn Rovers	15	2	6	7	15	20	12
19	Coventry City	15	1	7	7	9	21	10
20	Nottingham Forest	15	1	6	8	12	25	9

ARSENAL stay top of table after drawing with Wimbledon, who go third while Chelsea are winning at Old Trafford, a third successive Premiership defeat for Manchester United and their first at Old Trafford since December 1994. It is also the first time United have lost three Premiership games in a row and the team drop to sixth as a consequence. Chelsea move up into fifth place.

Liverpool drop to fourth after they are the victims of Blackburn's first win of the campaign, but Rovers stay bottom. Newcastle go top after a Peter Beardsley brace helps them to victory over Middlesbrough and they replace Arsenal as leaders and have a two-point advantage over the Gunners.

Former Arsenal and Everton centre-forward Tommy Lawton, often referred to as the most complete English centre-forward, dies aged 77.

Newcastle, with a late Beardsley equaliser the saviour, are held by West Ham, but stay top. Liverpool go second when Neil Ruddock gets on the scoresheet, for the first time this season, as they beat Leeds. Arsenal drop to third after a Nigel Winterburn own-goal gifts Manchester United victory at Old Trafford. Wimbledon also drop a place, to fourth, when they allow Coventry to fight back from 2–0 down and climb to 18th, where they replace Nottingham Forest, who suffer a second successive 2–0 defeat. Blackburn move off the bottom by drawing with Chelsea, who stay fifth. Gary Speed hits a hat-trick as Everton thrash Southampton in the biggest win of Joe Royle's reign.

Chelsea strengthen their squad, and brighten up the Premiership to boot, with the £4.5 million acquisition of Gianfranco Zola from Parma.

Aston Villa goalkeeper Mark Bosnich gets off lightly, with a £1,000 fine and a warning, after the FA accept his explanation of 'a joke that went wrong' for his Nazi salute at Spurs.

Liverpool are just eight minutes from going top of the Premiership when Everton's Gary Speed cancels out Robbie Fowler's fifth goal of the campaign.

Newcastle then go top, despite the first red card of David Batty's career, as they are held at Chelsea, because Liverpool are also held, by bogey side Wimbledon, and are third. Arsenal take advantage and move second, above the Anfield outfit, on goal difference, with two goals in the last three minutes that give them victory in the North London derby. They are just a point adrift of top spot.

The bottom two, Nottingham Forest and Blackburn, draw at the City Ground and fail to gain any advantage on each other, while Coventry continue their membership of the bottom three when they lose to Aston Villa.

Arsenal lead the table by two points when they win the clash between the top two at St James' Park, despite the controversial dismissal of Tony Adams following a clash with Alan Shearer. Wimbledon beat Nottingham Forest and keep them bottom, thanks to a Robbie Earle goal that takes the Dons third. Meanwhile Coventry lose the East Midlands derby to Derby County and remain 19th, despite Dion Dublin's third goal in successive games, and Blackburn move up to 18th when the new 'SAS', Sherwood and Sutton, score to beat Southampton. Sutton's winner comes just three minutes from time.

Stan Collymore receives the heaviest financial punishment in Liverpool's history when he is fined £30,000 for refusing to play in a reserve game.

Liverpool defender Neil Ruddock's first goal of the campaign opens the scoring against Leeds United.

December

Sunday 1 December		
Leeds United v. Chelsea		2-0
Monday 2 December		
Tottenham Hotspur v. Liverpool		0-2
Tuesday 3 December		
Middlesbrough v. Leicester City		0-2
Wednesday 4 December		
Arsenal v. Southampton		3-1
West Ham United v. Aston Villa		0-2
Saturday 7 December		
Arsenal v. Derby County		2-2
Chelsea v. Everton		2-2
Coventry City v. Tottenham Hotspur		1-2
Leicester City v. Blackburn Rovers		1-1
Liverpool v. Sheffield Wed.		0-1
Middlesbrough v. Leeds United		0-0
Southampton v. Aston Villa		0-1
Sunderland v. Wimbledon		1-3
Sunday 8 December		
West Ham United v. Manchester United		2-2
Monday 9 December		
Nottingham Forest v. Newcastle United		0-0
Saturday 14 December		
Leeds United v. Tottenham Hotspur		0-0
Liverpool v. Middlesbrough		5-1
Wimbledon v. Blackburn Rovers		1-0
Sunday 15 December		
Sunderland v. Chelsea		3-0
Monday 16 December		
Derby County v. Everton		0-1
Tuesday 17 December		
Coventry City v. Newcastle United		2-1
Liverpool v. Nottingham Forest		4-2
Wednesday 18 December		
Sheffield Wed. v. Manchester United		1-1
Saturday 21 December		
Chelsea v. West Ham United		3-1
Everton v. Leeds United		0-0
Leicester City v. Coventry City		0-2
Manchester United v. Sunderland		5-0
Nottingham Forest v. Arsenal		2-1
Southampton v. Derby County		3-1
Tottenham Hotspur v. Sheffield Wed.		1-1
Sunday 22 December		
Aston Villa v. Wimbledon		5-0
Monday 23 December		
Newcastle United v. Liverpool		1-1
Thursday 26 December		
Aston Villa v. Chelsea		0-2
Blackburn Rovers v. Newcastle United		1-0
Leeds United v. Coventry City		1-3
Liverpool v. Leicester City		1-1
Middlesbrough v. Everton		4-2
Nottingham Forest v. Manchester United		0-4
Sheffield Wed. v. Arsenal		0-0
Sunderland v. Derby County		2-0
Tottenham Hotspur v. Southampton		3-1
Saturday 28 December		
Arsenal v. Aston Villa		2-2
Chelsea v. Sheffield Wed.		2-2
Coventry City v. Middlesbrough		3-0
Derby County v. Blackburn Rovers		0-0
Everton v. Wimbledon		1-3
Leicester City v. Nottingham Forest		2-2
Manchester United v. Leeds United		1-0
Newcastle United v. Tottenham Hotspur		7-1
West Ham United v. Sunderland		2-0
Sunday 29 December		
Southampton v. Liverpool		0-1

		P	W	D	L	F	A	Pts
1	Liverpool	21	12	6	3	38	19	42
2	Manchester United	20	10	7	3	42	25	37
3	Arsenal	20	10	7	3	37	20	37
4	Wimbledon	19	11	4	4	33	23	37
5	Newcastle United	20	10	4	6	35	22	34
6	Aston Villa	20	10	4	6	29	19	34
7	Chelsea	20	8	8	4	32	29	32
8	Everton	20	7	7	6	29	27	28
9	Sheffield Wed.	20	6	10	4	21	22	28
10	Tottenham Hotspur	20	8	4	8	22	26	28
11	Derby County	20	5	8	7	20	25	23
12	Leicester City	20	6	5	9	20	27	23
13	Sunderland	20	6	5	9	19	28	23
14	Coventry City	20	5	7	8	20	25	22
15	Leeds United	20	6	4	10	16	24	22
16	West Ham United	19	5	6	8	18	25	21
17	Middlesbrough	20	4	6	10	25	38	18
18	Blackburn Rovers	19	3	8	8	17	22	17
19	Southampton	20	4	4	12	28	37	16
20	Nottingham Forest	20	2	8	10	18	36	14

IAN RUSH opens his account for his new club, Leeds, after a run of 15 scoreless games, as they beat Chelsea. The following day Rush's former club, Liverpool, win at Tottenham to go second on goal difference behind Arsenal. Middlesbrough's winless run extends to 10 as they lose to Leicester and the side that was sixth, back in mid-September, is perilously close to the drop zone.

Arsenal restore their three-point lead at the top by beating Southampton.

Liverpool are shock losers to Sheffield Wednesday, but Arsenal, despite being held by Derby, who are only denied a shock win at Highbury by Patrick Vieira's last-minute equaliser, extend their lead at the top to four points. Wimbledon move above Liverpool on goal difference with their win at Sunderland, and both clubs have a game in hand on the Gunners.

Blackburn climb out of the bottom three for the first time this season with a draw at Leicester, but Coventry suffer their third defeat in a row and stay 19th.

Newcastle are held at Forest and in doing so experience their first goalless draw in 73 matches, but climb to fourth on goal difference. Forest escape the bottom, moving above Coventry on goals scored.

Postponements, due to World Cup qualifying action, give Liverpool and Wimbledon the chance to improve their position near the top and both move to within a point of Arsenal. Robbie Fowler hits four in the win over Middlesbrough, with his second strike being his 100th for the club in 165 matches, thus achieving the milestone in one less game than it took Ian Rush. Wimbledon's win over Blackburn is more mundane and it takes an 85th-minute Dean Holds-worth goal to maintain parity on points with the Anfield outfit.

Liverpool take over at the top, following their win over Nottingham Forest, to lead Arsenal, who have a game in hand, by two points. Forest, who stay bottom, have now gone a Premiership record of 16 games without a win. Newcastle lose at Coventry after a first goal for the Sky Blues from Darren Huckerby, sold to Coventry by Kevin Keegan.

Former Newcastle defender Frank Clarke resigns as manager of Nottingham Forest and Stuart Pearce steps into the breach at the City Ground.

Middlesbrough manager Bryan Robson cancels their forthcoming game against Blackburn, claiming that 23 players are injured or ill.

Stuart Pearce inspires Forest to their first victory in 17 games when they come from a goal down to beat Arsenal with a brace from Alf-Inge Haaland, the winner coming in the 89th minute. Forest's cause is helped by Ian Wright's dismissal after he scores and the defeat prevents Arsenal from going top. Forest are still bottom.

Southampton beat Derby to move out of the bottom three and Coventry win a second successive game for the first time this season, with a Dion Dublin brace at Leicester.

The following day Aston Villa end the 19-match unbeaten run of third-placed Wimbledon and move fourth as a consequence. Manchester United, ominously, are on the move and their thrashing of Sunderland takes them fourth. Liverpool draw at Newcastle to move three points clear of Arsenal.

Manchester United maintain their new-found momentum with a thrashing of Nottingham Forest that takes them third, five points behind Liverpool, who are held by Leicester. Second-placed Arsenal also draw, at Sheffield Wednesday, and are three points behind Liverpool with a game in hand. Newcastle drop to sixth, their lowest position of the season, when they lose to Blackburn, who are 18th. Middlesbrough win for the first time in 13 games and Juninho scores twice but other results see 'Boro drop a place to 17th, while Southampton's defeat by Spurs sends them down to 19th.

Eric Cantona gets the only goal against his old club Leeds, from the spot, and Manchester United go second, two points behind Liverpool and above Arsenal on goals scored.

Liverpool restore their five-point lead with an extraordinary winner at Southampton. Saints' 'keeper Dave Beasant hits a poor clearance from the right-hand side of his penalty area straight to John Barnes, and the Liverpool skipper steers the ball into the empty goal from 40 yards.

Dean Sturridge, Derby County.

January

Wednesday 1 January	
Arsenal v. Middlesbrough	2-0
Chelsea v. Liverpool	1-0
Coventry City v. Sunderland	2-2
Everton v. Blackburn Rovers	0-2
Manchester United v. Aston Villa	0-0
Newcastle United v. Leeds United	3-0
West Ham United v. Nottingham Forest	0-1
Saturday 11 January	
Aston Villa v. Newcastle United	2-2
Blackburn Rovers v. Coventry City	4-0
Leeds United v. Leicester City	3-0
Liverpool v. West Ham United	0-0
Middlesbrough v. Southampton	0-1
Nottingham Forest v. Chelsea	2-0
Sheffield Wed. v. Everton	2-1
Sunderland v. Arsenal	1-0
Wimbledon v. Derby County	1-1
Sunday 12 January	
Tottenham Hotspur v. Manchester United	1-2
Saturday 18 January	
Chelsea v. Derby County	3-1
Coventry City v. Manchester United	0-2
Leicester City v. Wimbledon	1-0
Liverpool v. Aston Villa	3-0
Middlesbrough v. Sheffield Wed.	4-2
Southampton v. Newcastle United	2-2
Sunderland v. Blackburn Rovers	0-0
Sunday 19 January	
Arsenal v. Everton	3-1
Nottingham Forest v. Tottenham Hotspur	2-1
Monday 20 January	
West Ham United v. Leeds United	0-2
Wednesday 29 January	
Aston Villa v. Sheffield Wed.	0-1
Leeds United v. Derby County	0-0
Leicester City v. Sunderland	1-1
Manchester United v. Wimbledon	2-1
Newcastle United v. Everton	4-1
Nottingham Forest v. Coventry City	0-1
Tottenham Hotspur v. Blackburn Rovers	2-1
West Ham United v. Arsenal	1-2

		P	W	D	L	F	A	Pts
1	Manchester United	24	13	8	3	48	27	47
2	Arsenal	24	13	7	4	44	23	46
3	Liverpool	24	13	7	4	41	20	46
4	Newcastle United	24	12	6	6	46	27	42
5	Wimbledon	22	11	5	6	35	27	38
6	Chelsea	23	10	8	5	36	32	38
7	Aston Villa	24	10	6	8	31	25	36
8	Sheffield Wed.	23	8	10	5	26	27	34
9	Tottenham Hotspur	23	9	4	10	26	31	31
10	Leeds United	24	8	5	11	21	27	29
11	Sunderland	24	7	8	9	23	31	29
12	Everton	24	7	7	10	32	38	28
13	Leicester City	23	7	6	10	22	31	27
14	Coventry City	24	6	8	10	23	33	26
15	Derby County	23	5	10	8	22	29	25
16	Blackburn Rovers	23	5	9	9	24	24	24
17	Nottingham Forest	24	5	8	11	23	38	23
18	West Ham United	23	5	7	11	19	30	22
19	Middlesbrough	23	5	6	12	29	43	21
20	Southampton	22	5	5	12	31	39	20

ARSENAL take advantage of slip-ups by Liverpool, who lose at Chelsea, and Manchester United, held at home by Aston Villa, to go second, two points behind the Merseysiders, with a game in hand. It's a 'good day, bad day' for Arsenal strikers as Ian Wright nets his 200th league goal in the win over Middlesbrough, but John Hartson becomes the fourth Gunner to be sent off in the last eight matches. Alan Shearer takes his goal tally to 15, with his second brace in consecutive games, to take Newcastle up to fourth.

Nottingham Forest start the year by moving off the bottom, with victory over West Ham, and Blackburn move out of the drop zone with their first away win of the campaign, at Everton.

Kevin Keegan stuns the football world by suddenly resigning as Newcastle manager, after five years in the job. Terry McDermott becomes joint caretaker manager with Arthur Cox. Another Geordie, Barcelona manager Bobby Robson, turns down the job at St James' Park and, completing a unique quartet of Geordie headline makers, 'Boro's Bryan Robson announces his retirement from playing on his 40th birthday.

West Ham, 17th in the table, claim a draw at Anfield but Liverpool stay top, by three points, as Arsenal lose to Sunderland and have Dennis Bergkamp sent off in the process. Newcastle throw away a 2–0 lead and draw at Villa Park but it could have been worse had Shaka Hislop not saved a spot-kick from his London-born adopted countryman, Dwight Yorke.

Away from the top of the Premiership table Blackburn improve to their highest placing of the campaign, 14th, when they crush Coventry City, who have Dion Dublin red carded for the second successive match.

Nottingham Forest win consecutive matches for the first time this campaign when they beat Chelsea, with Stuart Pearce netting his first goal as player-manager, and move up to 18th. Middlesbrough go bottom with their third defeat in a row, at Southampton.

Manchester United move second, with a game in hand over leaders Liverpool, above Arsenal, by beating Spurs.

The north-east is once again making the headlines as Kenny Dalglish becomes manager of Newcastle United and follows Kevin Keegan, as he did as a player 20 years earlier at Liverpool. But there

is consternation down the road at Middlesbrough when the club is docked three points and fined £50,000 for failing to fulfil their fixture at Blackburn. The penalty, which will have dire consequences, leaves 'Boro four points adrift at the foot of the table.

Liverpool beat Aston Villa to maintain their two-point lead over Manchester United, who win at Coventry, but Newcastle fail to give new manager Kenny Dalglish a winning start as they throw away a 2–0 lead, for the second match running, when they concede twice in the last two minutes to draw with Southampton.

Nottingham Forest put some daylight between themselves and the relegation zone with a third consecutive win, over Spurs, that takes the team up to 17th.

Dennis Bergkamp signs off in style as he scores in the win over Everton, in his last game before a three-match ban, to keep Arsenal third.

Manchester United take over as Premiership leaders but they have to come from a goal down to do it. With a quarter of an hour left United trail Wimbledon but goals from Andy Cole and Ryan Giggs claim victory and a point lead over Arsenal, who win at Upton Park.

Kenny Dalglish succeeds Kevin Keegan again. Newcastle United's new manager is mobbed by fans at St James' Park.

Saturday 1 February	
Aston Villa v. Sunderland	1-0
Blackburn Rovers v. West Ham United	2-1
Derby County v. Liverpool	0-1
Everton v. Nottingham Forest	2-0
Leeds United v. Arsenal	0-0
Manchester United v. Southampton	2-1
Sheffield Wed. v. Coventry City	0-0
Tottenham Hotspur v. Chelsea	1-2
Wimbledon v. Middlesbrough	1-1
Sunday 2 February	
Newcastle United v. Leicester City	4-3
Saturday 15 February	
Derby County v. West Ham United	1-0
Tottenham Hotspur v. Arsenal	0-0
Wednesday 19 February	
Arsenal v. Manchester United	1-2
Aston Villa v. Coventry City	2-1
Derby County v. Sheffield Wed.	2-2
Liverpool v. Leeds United	4-0
Saturday 22 February	
Chelsea v. Manchester United	1-1
Coventry City v. Everton	0-0
Leicester City v. Derby County	4-2
Liverpool v. Blackburn Rovers	0-0
Middlesbrough v. Newcastle United	0-1
Nottingham Forest v. Aston Villa	0-0
Southampton v. Sheffield Wed.	2-3
Sunderland v. Leeds United	0-1
Sunday 23 February	
Arsenal v. Wimbledon	0-1
Monday 24 February	
West Ham United v. Tottenham Hotspur	4-3
Wednesday 26 February	
Southampton v. Wimbledon	0-0

		P	W	D	L	F	A	Pts
1	Manchester United	27	15	9	3	53	30	54
2	Liverpool	27	15	8	4	46	20	53
3	Newcastle United	26	14	6	6	51	30	48
4	Arsenal	28	13	9	6	45	26	48
5	Wimbledon	25	12	7	6	37	28	43
6	Aston Villa	27	12	7	8	34	26	43
7	Chelsea	25	11	9	5	39	34	42
8	Sheffield Wed.	26	9	12	5	31	31	39
9	Leeds United	27	9	6	12	22	31	33
10	Everton	26	8	8	10	34	38	32
11	Tottenham Hotspur	26	9	5	12	30	37	32
12	Leicester City	25	8	6	11	29	37	30
13	Derby County	27	6	11	10	27	36	29
14	Sunderland	26	7	8	11	23	33	29
15	Blackburn Rovers	25	6	10	9	26	25	28
16	Coventry City	27	6	10	11	24	35	28
17	West Ham United	26	6	7	13	24	36	25
18	Nottingham Forest	26	5	9	12	23	40	24
19	Middlesbrough	25	5	7	13	30	45	22
20	Southampton	25	5	6	14	34	44	21

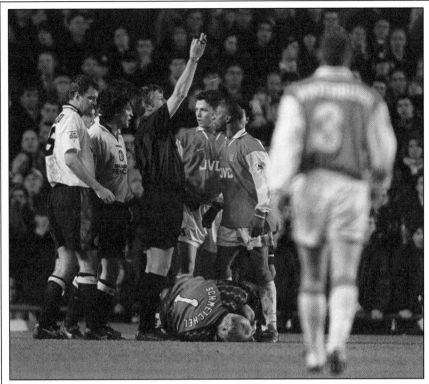

Referee Martin Bodenham waves away Ian Wright of Arsenal after his clash with Peter Schmeichel of Manchester United.

ERIC CANTONA keeps Manchester United top when they come from a goal down to beat Southampton, who remain 19th, with the Frenchman getting the decisive strike 10 minutes from time. Liverpool are one point behind after Stan Collymore nets the only goal at Derby. Arsenal are third after drawing at Leeds.

Nottingham Forest stay out of the relegation zone despite losing at Everton, West Ham's defeat at Blackburn keeps them 18th, and Middlesbrough grab a late equaliser that earns a point at Wimbledon, but stay bottom.

Newcastle move up to fourth place after a sensational seven-goal thriller at St James' Park. After taking a 1–0 lead the Magpies ship three goals in 13 second-half minutes to trail Leicester by a two-goal margin, with 22 minutes left. Alan Shearer then takes over and a 14-minute hat-trick sends the bulk of the 36,000 crowd into transports of delight.

West Ham pay Arsenal £3.2 million for John Hartson but he draws a blank on his debut as defeat at Derby County keeps the Hammers in the bottom three. Arsenal, held by Spurs, miss the chance of going top.

It then gets worse for Arsenal as they lose their unbeaten home record when Manchester United triumph at Highbury, and the game is marred by a continuation of the long-standing feud between Peter Schmeichel and Ian Wright. After a two-footed challenge by the Arsenal striker goes unpunished, the two players continue their disagreement as the teams leave the field. The result means that the Gunners are now five points adrift of the leaders having played one game more. Liverpool stay in touch with United, just one point behind, with a thrashing of Leeds.

The newspaper headlines after the Arsenal-United game are full of accusations and counter-accusations of racism and violence regarding the spat between Peter Schmeichel and Ian Wright.

Southampton lose at home to Sheffield Wednesday and Middlesbrough lose at home to Newcastle to an early Les Ferdinand goal.

Manchester United stay one point ahead at the top despite being held at Chelsea because Liverpool also draw, at home to Blackburn, to remain second.

Arsenal's second home defeat in a week, to Wimbledon, seriously damages their title aspirations and they drop to fourth. Vinnie Jones, with his third and final goal of the season, is the goalscorer.

West Ham move out of the relegation zone when goals for Paul Kitson and John Hartson, on their home debuts, allied to a brace from the inspirational Julian Dicks, sink Spurs and Southampton draw at Wimbledon to stay 20th.

Blackburn announce that Roy Hodgson, currently coach at Inter Milan, will be their new manager.

Saturday 1 March	
Blackburn Rovers v. Sunderland	1-0
Derby County v. Chelsea	3-2
Everton v. Arsenal	0-2
Leeds United v. West Ham United	1-0
Manchester United v. Coventry City	3-1
Newcastle United v. Southampton	0-1
Sheffield Wed. v. Middlesbrough	3-1
Tottenham Hotspur v. Nottingham Forest	0-1
Wimbledon v. Leicester City	1-3
Sunday 2 March	
Aston Villa v. Liverpool	1-0
Monday 3 March	
Coventry City v. Wimbledon	1-1
Tuesday 4 March	
Sunderland v. Tottenham Hotspur	0-4
Wednesday 5 March	
Chelsea v. Blackburn Rovers	1-1
Leicester City v. Aston Villa	1-0
Middlesbrough v. Derby County	6-1
Nottingham Forest v. Sheffield Wed.	0-3
Southampton v. Everton	2-2
Saturday 8 March	
Arsenal v. Nottingham Forest	2-0
Coventry City v. Leicester City	0-0
Leeds United v. Everton	1-0
Sunderland v. Manchester United	2-1
Monday 10 March	
Liverpool v. Newcastle United	4-3
Tuesday 11 March	
Blackburn Rovers v. Nottingham Forest	1-1
Wednesday 12 March	
Leeds United v. Southampton	0-0
Sheffield Wed. v. Sunderland	2-1
West Ham United v. Chelsea	3-2
Saturday 15 March	
Aston Villa v. West Ham United	0-0
Blackburn Rovers v. Wimbledon	3-1
Everton v. Derby County	1-0
Leicester City v. Middlesbrough	1-3
Manchester United v. Sheffield Wed.	2-0
Newcastle United v. Coventry City	4-0
Nottingham Forest v. Liverpool	1-1
Southampton v. Arsenal	0-2
Tottenham Hotspur v. Leeds United	1-0
Sunday 16 March	
Chelsea v. Sunderland	6-2
Tuesday 18 March	
Wimbledon v. West Ham United	1-1
Wednesday 19 March	
Chelsea v. Southampton	1-0
Leicester City v. Tottenham Hotspur	1-1
Middlesbrough v. Blackburn Rovers	2-1
Saturday 22 March	
Blackburn Rovers v. Aston Villa	0-2
Coventry City v. West Ham United	1-3
Derby County v. Tottenham Hotspur	4-2
Everton v. Manchester United	0-2
Middlesbrough v. Chelsea	1-0
Sheffield Wed. v. Leeds United	2-2
Southampton v. Leicester City	2-2
Sunderland v. Nottingham Forest	1-1
Sunday 23 March	
Wimbledon v. Newcastle United	1-1
Monday 24 March	
Arsenal v. Liverpool	1-2
Middlesbrough v. Nottingham Forest	1-1

		P	W	D	L	F	A	Pts
1	Manchester United	31	18	9	4	61	33	63
2	Liverpool	31	17	9	5	53	26	60
3	Arsenal	32	16	9	7	52	28	57
4	Newcastle United	30	15	7	8	59	36	52
5	Aston Villa	31	14	8	9	37	27	50
6	Chelsea	31	13	10	8	51	44	49
7	Sheffield Wed.	31	12	13	6	41	37	49
8	Wimbledon	30	12	10	8	42	37	46
9	Leeds United	32	11	8	13	26	34	41
10	Tottenham Hotspur	31	11	6	14	38	43	39
11	Leicester City	31	10	9	12	37	44	39
12	Blackburn Rovers	31	8	12	11	33	32	36
13	Everton	31	9	9	13	37	45	36
14	Middlesbrough	31	9	8	14	44	52	35
15	Derby County	31	8	11	12	35	47	35
16	West Ham United	31	8	9	14	31	41	33
17	Sunderland	32	8	9	15	29	48	33
18	Nottingham Forest	33	6	13	14	28	49	31
19	Coventry City	32	6	12	14	27	46	30
20	Southampton	31	6	9	16	39	51	27

Ian Taylor (right) hits Aston Villa's winner against Liverpool.

WITH LIVERPOOL not playing Manchester United extend their lead at the top by four points by beating Coventry and Karol Poborsky scores his first goal of the season.

At the other end of the table Nottingham Forest hand Dave Bassett a debut win at Spurs that lifts them out of the relegation zone. Dean Saunders is the match-winner with his first goal for five months.

At the Baseball Ground Derby twice come back from a goal down to beat Chelsea; Scott Minto scores for both sides, Ashley Ward hits a last-minute winner and Frank Leboeuf is sent off. Middlesbrough stay bottom when they lose at Sheffield Wednesday and Matt Le Tissier shocks St James' Park with the goal that beats Newcastle, a result which is only the third home reverse for the Magpies this season. Newcastle drop to fourth as a result. West Ham are also in the basement trio after defeat at Leeds.

Ian Taylor's goal at Villa Park is the first that Liverpool concede in the Premiership since 1 January, and it condemns the Anfield outfit to a defeat that means they are now four points behind leaders Manchester United.

The corruption trial involving Bruce Grobbelaar, John Fashanu and Hans Segers fails to reach a verdict, leaving the footballers facing a retrial.

Steffen Iverson hits his side's first hat-trick of the season as Spurs thrash Sunderland and the following day Fabrizio Ravanelli hits his second hat-trick of the campaign as Middlesbrough thrash Derby and record their best win of the season, but 'Boro stay bottom, three points adrift.

There are significant results at the other end of the Premiership where Arsenal's win over Forest cuts Manchester United's lead – they lose at Sunderland – to just three points.

It's déjà vu for Newcastle as they lose a seven-goal thriller at Anfield for the second year running. After going 3–0 down the Magpies draw level but are shattered by a Robbie Fowler winner, in the last minute, that takes Liverpool to within a point of Manchester United.

Nottingham Forest stay 18th despite holding Liverpool at the City Ground while the other top three sides, Manchester United, Arsenal and Newcastle, all win.

Chelsea hit six goals for the first time in more than six years when they crush Sunderland. Middlesbrough win a second successive game, at Leicester, but remain 20th.

Manchester United exploit the fact that the other leading clubs are not in action by winning at Everton to increase their advantage to six points, but the next day, in controversial circumstances, Liverpool win at Arsenal to go three points clear of the Gunners and to within the same margin of the leaders. David Seaman fells Robbie Fowler and, despite protests by the striker that the 'keeper never touched him, referee Gerald Ashby awards a penalty and when Fowler's kick is saved by Seaman Jason McAteer nets from the rebound for the decisive goal.

'Boro claim a fourth consecutive victory, over Chelsea, to move out of the drop zone for the first time since the end of December. Nottingham Forest's third draw in a row drops them to 19th while successive defeats, by London clubs, keep Southampton in the bottom three. They drop to the very bottom when held at home by Leicester.

Coventry drop into the bottom three when they are held at home by West Ham and a fourth consecutive draw sees Forest in 18th.

A new transfer deadline-day record of £8 million is set with the top moves being Steve Lomas joining West Ham from Manchester City for £1.6 million, and Des Hamilton leaving Bradford City for Newcastle for £1.5 million.

Saturday 5 April	
Aston Villa v. Everton	3-1
Chelsea v. Arsenal	0-3
Manchester United v. Derby County	2-3
Newcastle United v. Sunderland	1-1
Nottingham Forest v. Southampton	1-3
Tottenham Hotspur v. Wimbledon	1-0
Sunday 6 April	
Liverpool v. Coventry City	1-2
Monday 7 April	
Leeds United v. Blackburn Rovers	0-0
Wednesday 9 April	
Coventry City v. Chelsea	3-1
Derby County v. Southampton	1-1
Everton v. Leicester City	1-1
Sheffield Wed. v. Tottenham Hotspur	2-1
West Ham United v. Middlesbrough	0-0
Wimbledon v. Aston Villa	0-2
Saturday 12 April	
Arsenal v. Leicester City	2-0
Blackburn Rovers v. Manchester United	2-3
Derby County v. Aston Villa	2-1
Everton v. Tottenham Hotspur	1-0
Southampton v. West Ham United	2-0
Sunday 13 April	
Sheffield Wed. v. Newcastle United	1-1
Sunderland v. Liverpool	1-2
Wednesday 16 April	
Everton v. Liverpool	1-1
Newcastle United v. Chelsea	3-1
Wimbledon v. Leeds United	2-0
Saturday 19 April	
Arsenal v. Blackburn Rovers	1-1
Aston Villa v. Tottenham Hotspur	1-1
Chelsea v. Leicester City	2-1
Liverpool v. Manchester United	1-3
Middlesbrough v. Sunderland	0-1
Newcastle United v. Derby County	3-1
Nottingham Forest v. Leeds United	1-1
Sheffield Wed. v. Wimbledon	3-1
Southampton v. Coventry City	2-2
West Ham United v. Everton	2-2
Monday 21 April	
Coventry City v. Arsenal	1-1
Tuesday 22 April	
Blackburn Rovers v. Sheffield Wed.	4-1
Leeds United v. Aston Villa	0-0
Sunderland v. Southampton	0-1
Wimbledon v. Chelsea	0-1
Wednesday 23 April	
Derby County v. Nottingham Forest	0-0
Leicester City v. West Ham United	0-1
Thursday 24 April	
Tottenham Hotspur v. Middlesbrough	1-0

		P	W	D	L	F	A	Pts
1	Manchester United	34	20	9	5	69	39	69
2	Arsenal	36	18	11	7	59	30	65
3	Liverpool	35	18	10	7	58	33	64
4	Newcastle United	34	17	9	8	67	40	60
5	Aston Villa	36	16	10	10	44	31	58
6	Sheffield Wed.	35	14	14	7	48	44	56
7	Chelsea	36	15	10	11	56	54	55
8	Wimbledon	35	13	10	12	45	44	49
9	Tottenham Hotspur	36	13	7	16	42	47	46
10	Leeds United	36	11	11	14	27	37	44
11	Derby County	36	10	13	13	42	54	43
12	Everton	36	10	12	14	43	52	42
13	Blackburn Rovers	35	9	14	12	40	37	41
14	Leicester City	35	10	10	15	39	50	40
15	Southampton	36	9	11	16	48	55	38
16	West Ham United	35	9	11	15	34	45	38
17	Coventry City	36	8	14	14	35	51	38
18	Sunderland	36	9	10	17	32	52	37
19	Middlesbrough	34	9	9	16	44	54	36
20	Nottingham Forest	36	6	15	15	30	53	33

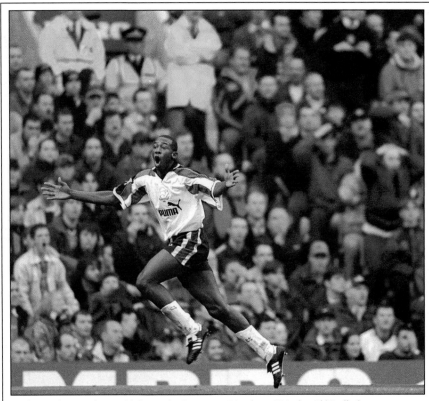

Paulo Wanchope is a 'Ram raider' as Derby County stun Manchester United at Old Trafford.

MANCHESTER UNITED'S title hopes are jolted, although they retain top spot, when they lose at home to Derby County, with Dean Sturridge hitting the decisive goal that takes the Rams up to 12th. Earlier Costa Rican debutant Paulo Wanchope had run half the length of Old Trafford to score. Arsenal close the gap on United with a victory at Chelsea in which Ian Wright's strike takes his tally to 20. Nottingham Forest lose to Southampton and are 19th while the Saints are still bottom.

Liverpool miss the chance of leapfrogging Arsenal and United to the top when they lose to Coventry, only the second defeat at Anfield all season. Dion Dublin nets the winning goal in the 90th minute that takes City off the bottom and up to 17th.

Coventry then follow up with a win over Chelsea to keep some breathing space between themselves and the bottom three.

The FA decides against punishing Peter Schmeichel and Ian Wright for their feuding but warns the pair about their future conduct. The FA also turns down Manchester United's request to extend the season beyond May but, undaunted, United face up to fixture congestion by beating Blackburn to maintain a three-point advantage over Arsenal, who beat Leicester to stay in touch with the leaders. At the other end of the table Southampton beat West Ham and shoot up to 16th, exiting the bottom three for the first time since the end of November.

Liverpool show they are not to be written off with a win at Sunderland that keeps them in contention in third place. But three days later a draw with Everton, in which Robbie Fowler is sent off with David Unsworth for fighting, robs Liverpool of their top scorer for the last three games of the campaign.

Liverpool's title hopes finally disappear with a comprehensive Manchester United victory at Anfield that, due to Arsenal's draw with Blackburn, leaves them five points clear and almost home and dry. Newcastle beat Derby to go fourth. In the relegation battle Nottingham Forest draw with Leeds and stay bottom, 'Boro are 19th after losing to Sunderland and Southampton's draw with Coventry drops them back to 17th.

Coventry then hold Arsenal, to stay safe in 15th place, and all of a sudden second place isn't a certainty for the Gunners.

In significant games involving the bottom three the relegation places are becoming more defined. Southampton win at Sunderland, with an Egil Ostenstad goal, to stay out of the drop zone; Nottingham Forest draw at Derby and remain bottom, and 'Boro's defeat at Spurs leaves them 19th with just four games to play. West Ham's win at Leicester, with John Moncur netting the only goal, puts them level on points with Coventry, just one point away from the drop zone.

May

Saturday 3 May

Arsenal v. Newcastle United	0-1
Chelsea v. Leeds United	0-0
Coventry City v. Derby County	1-2
Leicester City v. Manchester United	2-2
Liverpool v. Tottenham Hotspur	2-1
Middlesbrough v. Aston Villa	3-2
Nottingham Forest v. Wimbledon	1-1
Southampton v. Blackburn Rovers	2-0
Sunderland v. Everton	3-0
West Ham United v. Sheffield Wed.	5-1

Monday 5 May

Manchester United v. Middlesbrough	3-3

Tuesday 6 May

West Ham United v. Newcastle United	0-0
Wimbledon v. Liverpool	2-1

Wednesday 7 May

Leicester City v. Sheffield Wed.	1-0

Thursday 8 May

Blackburn Rovers v. Middlesbrough	0-0
Manchester United v. Newcastle United	0-0

Sunday 11 May

Aston Villa v. Southampton	1-0
Blackburn Rovers v. Leicester City	2-4
Derby County v. Arsenal	1-3
Everton v. Chelsea	1-2
Leeds United v. Middlesbrough	1-1
Manchester United v. West Ham United	2-0
Newcastle United v. Nottingham Forest	5-0
Sheffield Wed. v. Liverpool	1-1
Tottenham Hotspur v. Coventry City	1-2
Wimbledon v. Sunderland	1-0

		P	W	D	L	F	A	Pts
1	Manchester United	38	21	12	5	76	44	75
2	Newcastle United	38	19	11	8	73	40	68
3	Arsenal	38	19	11	8	62	32	68
4	Liverpool	38	19	11	8	62	37	68
5	Aston Villa	38	17	10	11	47	34	61
6	Chelsea	38	16	11	11	58	55	59
7	Sheffield Wed.	38	14	15	9	50	51	57
8	Wimbledon	38	15	11	12	49	46	56
9	Leicester City	38	12	11	15	46	54	47
10	Tottenham Hotspur	38	13	7	18	44	51	46
11	Leeds United	38	11	13	14	28	38	46
12	Derby County	38	11	13	14	45	58	46
13	Blackburn Rovers	38	9	15	14	42	43	42
14	West Ham United	38	10	12	16	39	48	42
15	Everton	38	10	12	16	44	57	42
16	Southampton	38	10	11	17	50	56	41
17	Coventry City	38	9	14	15	38	54	41
18	Sunderland	38	10	10	18	35	53	40
19	Middlesbrough	38	10	12	16	51	60	39
20	Nottingham Forest	38	6	16	16	31	59	34

Promoted from Nationwide Football League Division One

Bolton Wanderers
Barnsley
Crystal Palace (via play-offs)

Liverpool's Michael Owen scores his first ever league goal past Wimbledon's Neil Sullivan.

MANCHESTER UNITED pull back a 2–0 deficit to draw at Leicester. Ole Gunnar Solskjaer is the two-goal hero, and the club go three points clear of Liverpool, who beat Spurs. Newcastle are hotly pursuing the runners-up spot after winning their third game on the trot and Robbie Elliott, with the only goal at Highbury, is on the scoresheet for the second consecutive game.

In the drop zone Forest draw with Wimbledon and are relegated. Ravanelli hits two goals, including a last-minute penalty, as 'Boro beat Aston Villa to keep their hopes alive, but they remain 19th and Coventry suffer a massive blow to their survival hopes when they lose at home to Derby County, with the help of an own-goal from David Burrows, and drop into the bottom three. Performance of the day is West Ham's thrashing of Sheffield Wednesday, in which Paul Kitson hits the Hammers' only hat-trick of the season,

rocketing them up to the safety of 15th place.

Sunderland, who have been dropping steadily towards the relegation zone since March, bid farewell to Roker Park after 99 years with a victory over Everton in which Allan Johnstone hits the historic last goal at the stadium before the club moves to the Stadium of Light. The three points take Sunderland out of the bottom three.

Incredibly, Middlesbrough lead Manchester United 3–1 at Old Trafford until just before half-time, but Gary Neville's only goal of the campaign, three minutes before the break, puts 'Boro on the back foot and Solskjaer's second-half goal forces a draw.

The next day United are crowned champions because Liverpool are beaten at Wimbledon and Newcastle are held at West Ham. Liverpool's chase for the runner-up place may have suffered but a star is born as 17-year-old Michael Owen nets a debut goal after coming on as a substitute at

Selhurst Park. Middlesbrough draw with Blackburn and the result, from the fixture that had already cost them a deduction of three points, leaves 'Boro two points adrift in 18th place.

On the final day of the league programme there are contrasting fortunes for the north-east's three Premiership clubs. After the joy of Newcastle pinching the runners-up spot, due to Liverpool's failure to win at Hillsborough, and a thrashing of relegated Nottingham Forest, in which Alan Shearer's strike takes his tally to 25, there's despair for Sunderland and Middlesbrough. Sunderland lose at Wimbledon and are relegated and they are joined by 'Boro, who draw with Leeds. Coventry City escape the drop with a crucial win at Spurs.

Manchester United's joy at winning the Premiership for the fourth time is tempered by the shock retirement of Eric Cantona, still only 30, to pursue a career as an actor.

End of season round-up

Top Premiership Goalscorers 1996–97

Alan Shearer	Newcastle United	25
Ian Wright	Arsenal	23
Robbie Fowler	Liverpool	18
Ole Gunnar Solskjaer	Manchester United	18
Dwight Yorke	Aston Villa	17
Fabrizio Ravanelli	Middlesbrough	16
Les Ferdinand	Newcastle United	16
Matt Le Tissier	Southampton	13
Dion Dublin	Coventry City	13
Stan Collymore	Liverpool	12
Juninho	Middlesbrough	12
Dennis Bergkamp	Arsenal	12

Coca-Cola League Cup

Leicester City 1	Middlesbrough 1
Leicester City 1	Middlesbrough 0

(aet) – replay

The first final, at Wembley, finished 1–1 after extra-time when Fabrizio Ravanelli's 95th minute goal was cancelled out by Emile Heskey, two minutes from the end of extra-time. 'Boro had never before reached a domestic cup final and in the replay at Hillsborough a Steve Claridge winner, 10 minutes into extra-time, ensured they would have to wait a little longer for the club's first trophy. The goal was only the second in that season's competition and it gave Leicester their first major trophy for 33 years and put them into Europe for the first time since 1962.

FA Cup Final

Chelsea 2	Middlesbrough 0

Chelsea took the lead with the quickest-ever goal in an FA Cup Final. Roberto di Matteo fired home a dipping shot, via the bar, with just 42 seconds on the clock. Although 'Boro lost two players injured, Chelsea never got their second goal until eight minutes from time when Eddie Newton fired home after Zola's cheeky flick set up the chance.

FWA Footballer of the Year

Gianfranco Zola   Chelsea

PFA Player of the Year

Alan Shearer   Newcastle United

PFA Young Player of the Year

David Beckham   Manchester United

Manager of the Year

Alex Ferguson   Manchester United

Close Season 1997

At 30 years and 220 days Les Ferdinand is the 13th most expensive '30-something' to sign for over a million pounds when he becomes Tottenham's record £6 million man in a move from Newcastle United. The fee is not quite double what Manchester United pay Spurs for Teddy Sheringham, later in the close season.

Graeme Souness resigns as Southampton manager and Lawrie McMenemy steps down as director of football.

Harrods owner Mohamed Al Fayed buys a controlling interest in Fulham for an initial £30 million.

Arsenal take their French complement to five when they buy Emmanuel Petit for £3 million and Gilles Grimandi for £2 million from Monaco.

Leeds sign Jimmy Floyd Hasselbaink, from Boavista, for £2 million.

Marc Overmars moves from Ajax to Arsenal for £7 million, taking the Gunners' investment in foreign players, inside a fortnight, to more than £14 million.

Andy Gray rejects Everton advances to make the former Goodison favourite their new manager and stays a football pundit with Sky TV. The club instead turns to Howard Kendall, who starts his third stint as manager.

David Ginola joins Spurs from Newcastle for £ 2.5 million. Liverpool pay Crewe an initial fee of £1.5 million, rising to £3 million, for midfielder Danny Murphy.

Alex Ferguson makes Roy Keane captain of Manchester United.

Fabrizio Ravanelli's proposed £7.5 million move to Everton collapses when the club refuses to meet his wage demands. The 'White Feather' then decides to stay at Middlesbrough.

Liverpool sign Paul Ince from Inter Milan for £4.2 million and Stuart Pearce signs a two-year deal with Newcastle after being given a free transfer by Nottingham Forest.

Manchester United beat Chelsea 4–2 on penalties to win the Charity Shield but United spell David's name Beckam on his number 7 shirt, clearly visible after he spends 77 minutes on the bench.

Leicester City's Steve Claridge volleys past Middlesbrough's goalkeeper Ben Roberts to score the winning goal in the Coca-Cola Cup final.

August

Saturday 9 August

Barnsley v. West Ham United	1-2
Blackburn Rovers v. Derby County	1-0
Coventry City v. Chelsea	3-2
Everton v. Crystal Palace	1-2
Leeds United v. Arsenal	1-1
Leicester City v. Aston Villa	1-0
Newcastle United v. Sheffield Wed.	2-1
Southampton v. Bolton Wanderers	0-1
Wimbledon v. Liverpool	1-1

Sunday 10 August

Tottenham Hotspur v. Manchester United	0-2

Monday 11 August

Arsenal v. Coventry City	2-0

Tuesday 12 August

Crystal Palace v. Barnsley	0-1

Wednesday 13 August

Aston Villa v. Blackburn Rovers	0-4
Liverpool v. Leicester City	1-2
Manchester United v. Southampton	1-0
Sheffield Wed. v. Leeds United	1-3
West Ham United v. Tottenham Hotspur	2-1

Saturday 23 August

Blackburn Rovers v. Liverpool	1-1
Coventry City v. Bolton Wanderers	2-2
Everton v. West Ham United	2-1
Leeds United v. Crystal Palace	0-2
Leicester City v. Manchester United	0-0
Newcastle United v. Aston Villa	1-0
Southampton v. Arsenal	1-3
Tottenham Hotspur v. Derby County	1-0
Wimbledon v. Sheffield Wed.	1-1

Sunday 24 August

Barnsley v. Chelsea	0-6

Monday 25 August

Blackburn Rovers v. Sheffield Wed.	7-2

Tuesday 26 August

Leeds United v. Liverpool	0-2

Wednesday 27 August

Barnsley v. Bolton Wanderers	2-1
Coventry City v. West Ham United	1-1
Everton v. Manchester United	0-2
Leicester City v. Arsenal	3-3
Southampton v. Crystal Palace	1-0
Tottenham Hotspur v. Aston Villa	3-2
Wimbledon v. Chelsea	0-2

Saturday 30 August

Arsenal v. Tottenham Hotspur	0-0
Aston Villa v. Leeds United	1-0
Chelsea v. Southampton	4-2
Crystal Palace v. Blackburn Rovers	1-2
Derby County v. Barnsley	1-0
Manchester United v. Coventry City	3-0
Sheffield Wed. v. Leicester City	1-0
West Ham United v. Wimbledon	3-1

		P	W	D	L	F	A	Pts
1	Blackburn Rovers	5	4	1	0	15	4	13
2	Manchester United	5	4	1	0	8	0	13
3	West Ham United	5	3	1	1	9	6	10
4	Chelsea	4	3	0	1	14	5	9
5	Arsenal	5	2	3	0	9	5	9
6	Leicester City	5	2	2	1	6	5	8
7	Tottenham Hotspur	5	2	1	2	5	6	7
8	Newcastle United	2	2	0	0	3	1	6
9	Crystal Palace	5	2	0	3	5	5	6
10	Barnsley	5	2	0	3	4	10	6
11	Liverpool	4	1	2	1	5	4	5
12	Coventry City	5	1	2	2	6	10	5
13	Leeds United	5	1	1	3	4	7	4
14	Sheffield Wed.	5	1	1	3	6	13	4
15	Derby County	3	1	0	2	1	2	3
16	Everton	3	1	0	2	3	5	3
17	Southampton	5	1	0	4	4	9	3
18	Aston Villa	5	1	0	4	3	9	3
19	Wimbledon	4	0	2	2	3	7	2
20	Bolton Wanderers	3	1	1	1	4	4	4

DION DUBLIN secures the opening day headlines with a hat-trick in Coventry's victory over Chelsea in which the Sky Blues twice come back from a goal down before Dublin hits the clincher, two minutes from time.

Teddy Sheringham gets a frosty reception on his return to White Hart Lane, but despite missing a penalty helps Manchester United to victory over Spurs. The next day Ian Wright scores in Arsenal's win over Coventry, taking him to within one goal of Cliff Bastin's Gunners record.

Henning Berg moves from Blackburn to Manchester United for £5 million, just four days after Rovers drop their asking price to allow Graham Le Saux to return to Chelsea for the same price. Barnsley get their first win in the top flight with a Neil Redfearn goal that beats Crystal Palace.

Blackburn Rovers go top of the table after Chris Sutton hits a hat-trick in their win at Villa Park. On the same night Leicester make it six points out of six with a shock win at Anfield and share leadership of the Premiership with Rovers, and Manchester United, who need a goal from substitute David Beckham to beat Southampton.

Derby County's opening game at their new Pride Park Stadium is abandoned due to floodlight failure after less than an hour, with the Rams leading Wimbledon 2–1.

At the age of 33 John Barnes leaves Liverpool, on a free transfer, to sign for Newcastle United, where he teams up with Anfield old boys Kenny Dalglish, manager at St James' Park, and his assistant Terry McDermott. Five days later Peter Beardsley moves from Newcastle to join Bolton Wanderers.

Blackburn are held at home by Liverpool but stay top and Newcastle beat Aston Villa, who drop to bottom of the table after their third successive defeat, with a John Beresford goal, to retain their 100 percent record. Arsenal's victory at Southampton takes them second and dumps the Saints to 19th. Gianluca Vialli hits four as Chelsea crush top-flight new boys Barnsley.

Blackburn swamp Sheffield Wednesday to confirm their place at the top of the table. Wednesday's Benito Carbone is sent off and Rovers 'keeper John Filan breaks his arm.

Barnsley win at home to Bolton, for whom Peter Beardsley scores on his debut, and remain mid-table.

Liverpool finally get their first win, at Leeds, with first goals of the campaign for Steve McManaman and Karl Heinz Riedle.

Manchester United win at Everton to go second while Arsenal squander a 2–0 lead against Leicester, who don't get their first goal until the 84th minute. Despite a Dennis Bergkamp hat-trick, the Gunners concede a goal in the sixth minute of stoppage time to miss out on the chance of going top.

Blackburn and Manchester United both win to go three points clear at the top, while Aston Villa claim a first win of the season, at the fifth attempt, over Leeds United. Dwight Yorke scores Villa's first goal of the campaign after nearly 300 minutes of trying.

Chelsea end the month in fourth place after clocking up their third successive victory, and take their goal tally to 14 from four matches, at home to Southampton. Derby get their first victory of the campaign when Stefan Eranio's penalty, their first Premiership goal, beats newcomers Barnsley, and Leicester drop out of the top four by losing at Sheffield Wednesday, who climb up to 14th as a consequence. Southampton's woeful start continues and defeat at Chelsea, their fourth reverse in five games, leaves the Saints 17th. Wimbledon and Bolton prop up the rest.

Gianlucca Vialli's header loops over Dave Watson in the Barnsley goal to score Chelsea's third and his second goal.

September

Monday 1 September	
Bolton Wanderers v. Everton	0-0
Saturday 13 September	
Arsenal v. Bolton Wanderers	4-1
Barnsley v. Aston Villa	0-3
Coventry City v. Southampton	1-0
Crystal Palace v. Chelsea	0-3
Derby County v. Everton	3-1
Leicester City v. Tottenham Hotspur	3-0
Liverpool v. Sheffield Wed.	2-1
Manchester United v. West Ham United	2-1
Newcastle United v. Wimbledon	1-3
Sunday 14 September	
Blackburn Rovers v. Leeds United	3-4
Saturday 20 September	
Aston Villa v. Derby County	2-1
Bolton Wanderers v. Manchester United	0-0
Everton v. Barnsley	4-2
Leeds United v. Leicester City	0-1
Sheffield Wed. v. Coventry City	0-0
Southampton v. Liverpool	1-1
Tottenham Hotspur v. Blackburn Rovers	0-0
West Ham United v. Newcastle United	0-1
Wimbledon v. Crystal Palace	0-1
Sunday 21 September	
Chelsea v. Arsenal	2-3
Monday 22 September	
Liverpool v. Aston Villa	3-0
Tuesday 23 September	
Bolton Wanderers v. Tottenham Hotspur	1-1
Wimbledon v. Barnsley	4-1
Wednesday 24 September	
Arsenal v. West Ham United	4-0
Coventry City v. Crystal Palace	1-1
Leicester City v. Blackburn Rovers	1-1
Manchester United v. Chelsea	2-2
Newcastle United v. Everton	1-0
Sheffield Wed. v. Derby County	2-5
Southampton v. Leeds United	0-2
Saturday 27 September	
Aston Villa v. Sheffield Wed.	2-2
Barnsley v. Leicester City	0-2
Chelsea v. Newcastle United	1-0
Crystal Palace v. Bolton Wanderers	2-2
Derby County v. Southampton	4-0
Everton v. Arsenal	2-2
Leeds United v. Manchester United	1-0
Tottenham Hotspur v. Wimbledon	0-0
West Ham United v. Liverpool	2-1
Sunday 28 September	
Blackburn Rovers v. Coventry City	0-0

		P	W	D	L	F	A	Pts
1	Arsenal	9	5	4	0	22	10	19
2	Manchester United	9	5	3	1	12	4	18
3	Leicester City	9	5	3	1	13	6	18
4	Chelsea	8	5	1	2	22	10	16
5	Blackburn Rovers	9	4	4	1	19	9	16
6	Leeds United	9	4	1	4	11	11	13
7	West Ham United	9	4	1	4	12	14	13
8	Derby County	7	4	0	3	14	7	12
9	Liverpool	8	3	3	2	12	8	12
10	Newcastle United	6	4	0	2	6	5	12
11	Crystal Palace	9	3	2	4	9	11	11
12	Coventry City	9	2	5	2	8	11	11
13	Tottenham Hotspur	9	2	4	3	6	10	10
14	Aston Villa	9	3	1	5	10	15	10
15	Wimbledon	8	2	3	3	10	10	9
16	Everton	8	2	2	4	10	13	8
17	Bolton Wanderers	8	1	5	2	8	11	8
18	Sheffield Wed.	9	1	3	5	11	22	6
19	Barnsley	9	2	0	7	7	23	6
20	Southampton	9	1	1	7	5	17	4

Leeds United's Nigel Martyn (left) holds back teammate Alf-Inge Haaland (centre) as Haaland shouts at Manchester United's Roy Keane (on floor).

BOLTON open their new 'space age' Reebok Stadium with a 0–0 draw against Everton. A goal from Nathan Blake, 'confirmed' by television replay, is not given. Liverpool's teenage striking sensation, Michael Owen, is sent off in an England Under-18 international against Yugoslavia.

13 September is a lucky date for Ian Wright as he finally beats Cliff Bastin's Arsenal record of 178 goals. Wright's hat-trick, against Bolton, takes his tally to 180, but it's Manchester United who top the table after they beat West Ham. John Hartson's goal for the Hammers is the first conceded by United, and the first past Peter Schmeichel, in more than 11 and a half hours, since April. Derby win at home to Everton to go 11th and dump the Goodison outfit down to 18th.

Aston Villa jump six places, and out of the relegation zone, by winning at Barnsley, and Wimbledon also exit the basement group with a shock victory at Newcastle. But Southampton are bottom after losing at Coventry.

A fourth successive victory, over Crystal Palace, sees Chelsea go second, where Blackburn replace them the very next day, despite losing their first game of the season, a seven-goal thriller at home to Leeds. All the goals come in a breathtaking 34 first-half minutes and Rovers are three points behind the leaders.

Barnsley lose to Everton, a result that plummets the Tykes down to 17th but rockets the Goodison outfit up to 13th. Wimbledon slip into the relegation zone when Attilio Lombardo nets the only goal for the 'landlords' against the 'lodgers', the Italian's third goal in his seventh game. Southampton are still bottom despite holding Liverpool. Manchester United are held by Bolton and Gary Pallister and Nathan Blake are sent off. Blackburn are three points behind leaders Manchester United after drawing with Spurs and Leicester achieve parity with Rovers after beating Leeds with a Steve Walsh goal, his second in successive matches, which takes him ahead of fellow defender Matt Elliott as the Foxes' leading scorer.

Arsenal go second, two points behind Manchester United, when a rare Nigel Winterburn goal in the last minute earns victory over Chelsea. The Gunners top the table, for the first time this campaign, on goal difference, with a crushing victory over West Ham, because Manchester United are held by Chelsea. Newcastle are creeping up as their victory over Everton takes them up to seventh and although the Magpies are six points adrift they do have three games in hand.

Derby achieve their best top-flight result with a comprehensive victory over Sheffield Wednesday.

Wimbledon improve their position in the basement group with a crushing defeat of fellow strugglers Barnsley, but Southampton remain bottom after losing to Leeds.

Leeds win for the second time in four days when David Wetherall's first goal of the season inflicts a first defeat on Manchester United, who are overtaken by Arsenal, who move a point clear after drawing at Everton, despite the Gunners squandering a 2–0 lead. United's defeat at Elland Road is even more costly as Roy Keane leaves the ground on crutches following a rash challenge. Leicester win at Barnsley and move third, just behind Manchester United, on goal difference.

Wednesday 'top' the bottom three by drawing at Aston Villa. Southampton are still bottom after they are thrashed by Derby County, who take their goal tally, inside four days, to nine. Barnsley are one place higher than the Saints after they suffer a fifth consecutive league defeat to Leicester.

Blackburn miss the chance of going second when they fail to score for only the second time this campaign, and drop to fifth as a consequence of drawing with Coventry.

Roy Keane's injury turns out to be a ruptured cruciate ligament, which means he is out for the rest of the season.

Saturday 4 October	
Arsenal v. Barnsley	5-0
Bolton Wanderers v. Aston Villa	0-1
Coventry City v. Leeds United	0-0
Manchester United v. Crystal Palace	2-0
Newcastle United v. Tottenham Hotspur	1-0
Sheffield Wed. v. Everton	3-1
Southampton v. West Ham United	3-0
Wimbledon v. Blackburn Rovers	0-1

Sunday 5 October	
Liverpool v. Chelsea	4-2

Monday 6 October	
Leicester City v. Derby County	1-2

Saturday 18 October	
Aston Villa v. Wimbledon	1-2
Blackburn Rovers v. Southampton	1-0
Chelsea v. Leicester City	1-0
Crystal Palace v. Arsenal	0-0
Derby County v. Manchester United	2-2
Everton v. Liverpool	2-0
Leeds United v. Newcastle United	4-1
West Ham United v. Bolton Wanderers	3-0

Sunday 19 October	
Tottenham Hotspur v. Sheffield Wed.	3-2

Monday 20 October	
Barnsley v. Coventry City	2-0

Wednesday 22 October	
Derby County v. Wimbledon	1-1

Saturday 25 October	
Coventry City v. Everton	0-0
Liverpool v. Derby County	4-0
Manchester United v. Barnsley	7-0
Newcastle United v. Blackburn Rovers	1-1
Sheffield Wed. v. Crystal Palace	1-3
Southampton v. Tottenham Hotspur	3-2
Wimbledon v. Leeds United	1-0

Sunday 26 October	
Arsenal v. Aston Villa	0-0
Bolton Wanderers v. Chelsea	1-0

Monday 27 October	
Leicester City v. West Ham United	2-1

		P	W	D	L	F	A	Pts
1	Manchester United	12	7	4	1	23	6	25
2	Arsenal	12	6	6	0	27	10	24
3	Blackburn Rovers	12	6	5	1	22	10	23
4	Leicester City	12	6	3	3	16	10	21
5	Chelsea	11	6	1	4	25	15	19
6	Liverpool	11	5	3	3	20	12	18
7	Derby County	11	5	2	4	19	15	17
8	Leeds United	12	5	2	5	15	13	17
9	Wimbledon	12	4	4	4	14	13	16
10	Newcastle United	9	5	1	3	9	10	16
11	West Ham United	12	5	1	6	16	19	16
12	Crystal Palace	12	4	3	5	12	14	15
13	Aston Villa	12	4	2	6	12	17	14
14	Tottenham Hotspur	12	3	4	5	11	16	13
15	Coventry City	12	2	7	3	8	13	13
16	Everton	11	3	3	5	13	16	12
17	Bolton Wanderers	11	2	5	4	9	15	11
18	Southampton	12	3	1	8	11	20	10
19	Sheffield Wed.	12	2	3	7	17	29	9
20	Barnsley	12	3	0	9	9	35	9

TABLE-TOPPERS Arsenal crush Barnsley and send the Yorkshire side to the bottom but Manchester United keep up the pressure with victory over Crystal Palace that keeps them in second place. Spurs suffer inconvenience when Ruel Fox and Les Ferdinand are locked in the toilets at St James' Park at half-time, and the visitors start the second period with nine men. Restored to full complement Tottenham are beaten by a late Warren Barton goal, his second of the campaign, which puts him level with Tino Asprilla as leading scorer. Chris Sutton's strike beats Wimbledon and Blackburn leap from fifth to third.

Steve Ogrizovic marks his record 488th league appearance for Coventry with a clean sheet against Leeds. It's the 40-year-old 'keeper's fourth clean sheet in five games.

Bolton, still without a win since the opening day, lose to Villa and hover just above the bottom trio, which is topped by Everton after they lose to Sheffield Wednesday. South-ampton beat West Ham but move just one place off the bottom.

Leicester fail to improve on third place when they lose to Derby, who secure a fifth win in six games that moves them up to sixth and just seven points adrift of Arsenal. The Rams have two games in hand.

Arsenal are held at Crystal Palace and a fifth booking for Dennis Bergkamp means a three-match suspension looms. Manchester United come back from 2–0 down to take a point at Derby County, for whom Francesco Baiano scores for the fifth consecutive game, and lose second place to Blackburn, who win at Southampton, keeping the Saints 19th. Bolton lose at West Ham to stay 18th. Barnsley then beat Coventry and move off the bottom of the Premiership, to be replaced by Southampton.

Barnsley are brought back to earth with a thumping at Old Trafford in which Andy Cole hits a hat-trick that helps Manchester United go top and sends the Tykes back to the foot of the table. Blackburn move third after drawing with Newcastle and Liverpool swamp Derby to move fifth, their highest position of the campaign. Derby retain seventh place.

Southampton improve by one place to 18th with victory over Spurs, in which £2 million record signing David Hirst nets two second-half goals on his home debut. Sheffield Wednesday, the club that sold Hirst, drop to 19th after losing at home to Crystal Palace.

Bolton beat Chelsea, with Dean Holdsworth scoring his first goal of the campaign, to move out of the bottom three; Chelsea stay fourth. Arsenal are held by Aston Villa and fail to recapture top spot. Emmanuel Petit is red-carded for putting hands on referee Paul Durkin.

The Tomas Brolin on-off love affair with English football finally ends when Leeds cut their losses and off-load the Swedish World Cup star, bought from Parma for £4.5 million, on a free transfer, after just four goals in 27 appearances.

Steve Ogrizovic of Coventry City saves from Leeds United's Rodney Wallace to earn Coventry a draw.

November

Saturday 1 November	
Aston Villa v. Chelsea	0-2
Barnsley v. Blackburn Rovers	1-1
Bolton Wanderers v. Liverpool	1-1
Derby County v. Arsenal	3-0
Manchester United v. Sheffield Wed.	6-1
Newcastle United v. Leicester City	3-3
Tottenham Hotspur v. Leeds United	0-1
Wimbledon v. Coventry City	1-2
Sunday 2 November	
Everton v. Southampton	0-2
Saturday 8 November	
Blackburn Rovers v. Everton	3-2
Coventry City v. Newcastle United	2-2
Crystal Palace v. Aston Villa	1-1
Leeds United v. Derby County	4-3
Liverpool v. Tottenham Hotspur	4-0
Sheffield Wed. v. Bolton Wanderers	5-0
Southampton v. Barnsley	4-1
Sunday 9 November	
Arsenal v. Manchester United	3-2
Chelsea v. West Ham United	2-1
Monday 10 November	
Leicester City v. Wimbledon	0-1
Saturday 22 November	
Aston Villa v. Everton	2-1
Blackburn Rovers v. Chelsea	1-0
Derby County v. Coventry City	3-1
Leicester City v. Bolton Wanderers	0-0
Liverpool v. Barnsley	0-1
Newcastle United v. Southampton	2-1
Sheffield Wed. v. Arsenal	2-0
Wimbledon v. Manchester United	2-5
Sunday 23 November	
Leeds United v. West Ham United	3-1
Monday 24 November	
Tottenham Hotspur v. Crystal Palace	0-1
Wednesday 26 November	
Chelsea v. Everton	2-0
Saturday 29 November	
Barnsley v. Leeds United	2-3
Bolton Wanderers v. Wimbledon	1-0
Chelsea v. Derby County	4-0
Coventry City v. Leicester City	0-2
Crystal Palace v. Newcastle United	1-2
Everton v. Tottenham Hotspur	0-2
Southampton v. Sheffield Wed.	2-3
West Ham United v. Aston Villa	2-1
Sunday 30 November	
Arsenal v. Liverpool	0-1
Manchester United v. Blackburn Rovers	4-0

		P	W	D	L	F	A	Pts
1	Manchester United	16	10	4	2	40	12	34
2	Chelsea	16	10	1	5	35	17	31
3	Blackburn Rovers	16	8	6	2	27	17	30
4	Leeds United	16	9	2	5	26	19	29
5	Arsenal	16	7	6	3	30	18	27
6	Leicester City	16	7	5	4	21	14	26
7	Liverpool	15	7	4	4	26	14	25
8	Newcastle United	13	7	3	3	18	17	24
9	Derby County	15	7	2	6	28	24	23
10	Crystal Palace	15	5	4	6	15	17	19
11	Wimbledon	16	5	4	7	18	21	19
12	West Ham United	15	6	1	8	20	25	19
13	Aston Villa	16	5	3	8	16	23	18
14	Sheffield Wed.	16	5	3	8	28	37	18
15	Coventry City	16	3	8	5	13	21	17
16	Southampton	16	5	1	10	20	26	16
17	Tottenham Hotspur	16	4	4	8	13	22	16
18	Bolton Wanderers	15	3	7	5	11	21	16
19	Barnsley	16	4	1	11	14	43	13
20	Everton	16	3	3	10	16	27	12

DERBY COUNTY climb to sixth when they end the last unbeaten record in the league with a comprehensive victory over Arsenal. Arsenal's defence: Dixon, Bould, Adams and Winterburn, with more than 2,200 games between them, can't cope with Paulo Wanchope, who scores twice. Manchester United profit with a blitzing of Sheffield Wednesday that takes the Reds four points clear at the top. Blackburn are held by Barnsley, who move off the foot of the table as a consequence; Rovers stay third.

Bolton are held by Liverpool and drop to 18th while Southampton move up to the lofty height of 16th after their first away win of the campaign at Everton.

Rock-bottom Sheffield Wednesday surprise no one when they sack David Pleat. Floodlight failure causes the abandonment of the West Ham-Crystal Palace game, with the scores level at 2–2, after just over an hour.

Blackburn Rovers ease into second place, splitting Manchester United and Arsenal, with victory over Everton. Derby, 3–0 up inside 34 minutes, squander that lead and lose at Leeds, for whom Lee Bowyer hits a 90th-minute winner. Sheffield Wednesday climb off the bottom in style with a thrashing of fellow-strugglers Bolton, in which Andy Booth hits a hat-trick and all the goals come in the first half. Spurs suffer a third consecutive defeat, at Anfield, and drop towards the relegation zone. Barnsley are crushed at Southampton and remain 20th.

Arsenal are twice pegged back by Manchester United but a late David Platt winner, against his first club, takes the Gunners to within a point of the leaders. Chelsea beat West Ham to close to within three points of United, with a game

Barnsley's Martin Bullock (second left), Ashley Ward (third left) and Eric Tinkler (centre) celebrate Barnsley's winning goal at Anfield.

in hand, but the action isn't confined to football and Hammers' teammates Eyal Berkovic and Nigel Winterburn have to be separated following a frank and physical exchange of views.

Ron Atkinson succeeds David Pleat as manager of Sheffield Wednesday but he rejects a three-year contract in favour of a deal until the end of the season with speculation surrounding a massive bonus if he keeps the club in the Premiership.

John Burridge, the oldest goalkeeper to play in the Premiership, for Manchester City, announces his retirement at the age of 46. Gerry Francis is replaced as Tottenham manager by Christian Gross.

Manchester United confirm their place at the top with victory over Wimbledon, with all the goals coming in the second half, but Blackburn stay within a point and move second after beating Chelsea, who drop to fifth. Arsenal are shocked by a rejuvenated Sheffield Wednesday, who present new boss Ron Atkinson with a first victory, in the first game of his second spell at Hillsborough, a result that drops the Gunners to third.

Bolton win for the first time in four games when an 89th-minute Nathan Blake goal beats Wimbledon, but Wanderers don't, and stay 18th. The biggest shock of the day is a debut goal for Ashley Ward that gives Barnsley victory at Anfield, but they remain 19th just above Everton, who are bottom after a third consecutive defeat, at Aston Villa, who climb to 11th.

Chelsea ascend to third after a couple of late penalties clinch victory over struggling Everton, who stay bottom. Three days later Chelsea improve to second, on goal difference behind United, with a hammering of Derby County in which the Italian wizard Gianfranco Zola hits his first hat-trick of the season. Leeds are fourth when they stage another comeback and turn over a 2–0 deficit to Barnsley with Derek Lilley hitting the winner, eight minutes from time, his only goal of the season. Christan Gross celebrates his first victory as Spurs' manager, at bottom club Everton, but Tottenham are just outside the relegation zone. Another first for new Sheffield Wednesday boss Ron Atkinson comes as his team chalk up a first away win, at Southampton.

Manchester United maintain pole position by crushing Blackburn, with half the goals contributed by Rovers' defenders Stephane Henchoz and Jeff Kenna. United go three points clear of second-placed Arsenal, who lose at home to Liverpool.

Monday 1 December	
Bolton Wanderers v. Newcastle United	1-0
Wednesday 3 December	
West Ham United v. Crystal Palace	4-1
Saturday 6 December	
Aston Villa v. Coventry City	3-0
Blackburn Rovers v. Bolton Wanderers	3-1
Derby County v. West Ham United	2-0
Leeds United v. Everton	0-0
Leicester City v. Crystal Palace	1-1
Liverpool v. Manchester United	1-3
Newcastle United v. Arsenal	0-1
Tottenham Hotspur v. Chelsea	1-6
Sunday 7 December	
Wimbledon v. Southampton	1-0
Monday 8 December	
Sheffield Wed. v. Barnsley	2-1
Saturday 13 December	
Arsenal v. Blackburn Rovers	1-3
Barnsley v. Newcastle United	2-2
Chelsea v. Leeds United	0-0
Coventry City v. Tottenham Hotspur	4-0
Crystal Palace v. Liverpool	0-3
Everton v. Wimbledon	0-0
Southampton v. Leicester City	2-1
West Ham United v. Sheffield Wed.	1-0
Sunday 14 December	
Bolton Wanderers v. Derby County	3-3
Monday 15 December	
Manchester United v. Aston Villa	1-0
Wednesday 17 December	
Newcastle United v. Derby County	0-0
Saturday 20 December	
Aston Villa v. Southampton	1-1
Blackburn Rovers v. West Ham United	3-0
Derby County v. Crystal Palace	0-0
Leeds United v. Bolton Wanderers	2-0
Leicester City v. Everton	0-1
Liverpool v. Coventry City	1-0
Sheffield Wed. v. Chelsea	1-4
Tottenham Hotspur v. Barnsley	3-0
Sunday 21 December	
Newcastle United v. Manchester United	0-1
Friday 26 December	
Arsenal v. Leicester City	2-1
Aston Villa v. Tottenham Hotspur	4-1
Bolton Wanderers v. Barnsley	1-1
Chelsea v. Wimbledon	1-1
Crystal Palace v. Southampton	1-1
Derby County v. Newcastle United	1-0
Liverpool v. Leeds United	3-1
Manchester United v. Everton	2-0
Sheffield Wed. v. Blackburn Rovers	0-0
West Ham United v. Coventry City	1-0
Sunday 28 December	
Barnsley v. Derby County	1-0
Blackburn Rovers v. Crystal Palace	2-2
Coventry City v. Manchester United	3-2
Everton v. Bolton Wanderers	3-2
Leeds United v. Aston Villa	1-1
Leicester City v. Sheffield Wed.	1-1
Newcastle United v. Liverpool	1-2
Tottenham Hotspur v. Arsenal	1-1
Wimbledon v. West Ham United	1-2
Monday 29 December	
Southampton v. Chelsea	1-0

		P	W	D	L	F	A	Pts
1	Manchester United	21	14	4	3	49	16	46
2	Blackburn Rovers	21	11	8	2	38	21	41
3	Chelsea	21	12	3	6	46	21	39
4	Liverpool	20	11	4	5	36	19	37
5	Leeds United	21	10	5	6	30	23	35
6	Arsenal	20	9	7	4	35	23	34
7	Derby County	21	9	5	7	34	28	32
8	West Ham United	21	10	1	10	28	32	31
9	Leicester City	21	7	7	7	25	21	28
10	Aston Villa	21	7	5	9	25	27	26
11	Newcastle United	20	7	5	8	21	25	26
12	Wimbledon	20	6	6	8	21	24	24
13	Southampton	21	7	3	11	25	30	24
14	Coventry City	21	5	8	8	20	28	23
15	Crystal Palace	21	5	8	8	20	28	23
16	Sheffield Wed.	21	6	5	10	32	44	23
17	Bolton Wanderers	21	4	9	8	19	33	21
18	Everton	21	5	5	11	20	31	20
19	Tottenham Hotspur	21	5	5	11	19	37	20
20	Barnsley	21	5	3	13	19	51	18

BOLTON win successive matches for the first time this season, Nathan Blake is again the match-winner.

Manchester United maintain their three-point lead at the top, with a comprehensive victory over Liverpool, while second-placed Chelsea impress with a thrashing of London rivals Tottenham in which a Tore Andre Flo hat-trick ruins Christian Gross's first home game and keeps Spurs in the bottom three. Third-placed Blackburn keep up the chase with victory over Bolton, while Everton's point at Leeds moves them one place off the bottom and Southampton lose to Wimbledon and drop a place to 17th.

Blackburn go second, one point behind United, after beating Arsenal. Chelsea drop down to third after being held by Leeds, who play with nine men for the entire second half after referee Graham Poll sends off Gary Kelly and Alf-Inge Haaland. Leeds move fourth while Liverpool's victory over Crystal Palace takes them up to sixth.

Barnsley are held by Newcastle and remain bottom and Everton stay 19th after drawing with Wimbledon while things just go from bad to worse for Tottenham under new manager Christian Gross; they stay in the bottom three, three points from the safety line, after being crushed by Coventry, who score twice in the last six minutes.

Manchester United move further away and can even afford a Teddy Sheringham penalty miss as they beat Aston Villa with a Ryan Giggs goal that secures a fourth successive victory.

Blackburn and Chelsea close the gap on United with victories over West Ham and Sheffield Wednesday respectively. Rovers are now just a point behind the leaders, while Chelsea are one point further behind. In a basement battle Spurs beat bottom-placed Barnsley but stay 18th. One place better off are Everton who celebrate a bunch of firsts. The victory, at Leicester, with an 89th-minute Gary Speed penalty, is the side's first away win in a year, their first goal in a month (the last was also a Speed penalty) and their first victory in nine games.

It's a case of Cole to Newcastle as Andy returns to St James' Park and nets the winner to restore Manchester United's four-point lead at the top of the table.

Spurs, with just 17 goals in 19 Premiership matches, pluck Jürgen Klinsmann from the doldrums of the Sampdoria bench on a six-month contract in a move that means no small measure of humble pie for chairman Alan Sugar, who bade farewell to the German striker by saying he wouldn't wash his car with Klinsmann's jersey!

For the third time this season a Premiership game is abandoned because of floodlight failure, this time the Wimbledon v Arsenal game at Selhurst Park.

Coventry pay a club record £3.25 million to Grasshoppers, Zurich, for Romanian striker Viorel Moldovan. Boxing Day victory for Manchester United over Everton, who stay 19th, increases their lead to six points because the two chasing sides, Blackburn and Chelsea, are held by Sheffield Wednesday and Wimbledon respectively. Georgi Hristov scores his first goal for 12 games and it earns rock-bottom Barnsley a point at Bolton.

Manchester United concede two goals in the last five minutes to lose at Coventry – Darren Huckerby nets the 88th-minute winner – but second-placed Blackburn fail to profit as they are held by Crystal Palace. Everton increase the pressure on Christian Gross by beating Bolton, with a Duncan Ferguson 'headed' hat-trick, which sees them swap places with Tottenham, now 19th. Spurs are looking nervously over their shoulders as even bottom club Barnsley win, against Derby.

Chelsea lose at Southampton and fall to third, seven points behind table-toppers Manchester United, and the year ends with speculation that beleaguered Tottenham manager Christian Gross is wanted by the Swiss national team.

FACT FILE

Tottenham's 6–1 drubbing by Chelsea is the club's worst home defeat since 6 May 1935 when they lost 6–0 to Arsenal.

Darren Huckerby of Coventry City celebrates scoring the winning goal in the last minute.

Saturday 10 January

Arsenal v. Leeds United	2-1
Aston Villa v. Leicester City	1-1
Bolton Wanderers v. Southampton	0-0
Chelsea v. Coventry City	3-1
Crystal Palace v. Everton	1-3
Liverpool v. Wimbledon	2-0
Manchester United v. Tottenham Hotspur	2-0
Sheffield Wed. v. Newcastle United	2-1
West Ham United v. Barnsley	6-0

Sunday 11 January

Derby County v. Blackburn Rovers	3-1

Saturday 17 January

Barnsley v. Crystal Palace	1-0
Blackburn Rovers v. Aston Villa	5-0
Coventry City v. Arsenal	2-2
Leeds United v. Sheffield Wed.	1-2
Leicester City v. Liverpool	0-0
Newcastle United v. Bolton Wanderers	2-1
Tottenham Hotspur v. West Ham United	1-0
Wimbledon v. Derby County	0-0

Sunday 18 January

Everton v. Chelsea	3-1

Monday 19 January

Southampton v. Manchester United	1-0

Tuesday 20 January

Liverpool v. Newcastle United	1-0

Saturday 31 January

Arsenal v. Southampton	3-0
Bolton Wanderers v. Coventry City	1-5
Chelsea v. Barnsley	2-0
Crystal Palace v. Leeds United	0-2
Derby County v. Tottenham Hotspur	2-1
Liverpool v. Blackburn Rovers	0-0
Manchester United v. Leicester City	0-1
Sheffield Wed. v. Wimbledon	1-1
West Ham United v. Everton	2-2

		P	W	D	L	F	A	Pts
1	Manchester United	24	15	4	5	51	18	49
2	Chelsea	24	14	3	7	52	25	45
3	Blackburn Rovers	24	12	9	3	44	24	45
4	Liverpool	24	13	6	5	39	19	45
5	Arsenal	23	11	8	4	42	26	41
6	Derby County	24	11	6	7	39	30	39
7	Leeds United	24	11	5	8	34	27	38
8	West Ham United	24	11	2	11	36	35	35
9	Leicester City	24	8	9	7	27	22	33
10	Sheffield Wed.	24	8	6	10	37	47	30
11	Newcastle United	23	8	5	10	24	29	29
12	Southampton	24	8	4	12	26	33	28
13	Coventry City	24	6	9	9	28	34	27
14	Everton	24	7	6	11	28	35	27
15	Aston Villa	23	7	6	10	26	33	27
16	Wimbledon	23	6	8	9	22	27	26
17	Crystal Palace	24	5	8	11	21	34	23
18	Tottenham Hotspur	24	6	5	13	21	41	23
19	Bolton Wanderers	24	4	10	10	21	40	22
20	Barnsley	24	6	3	15	20	59	21

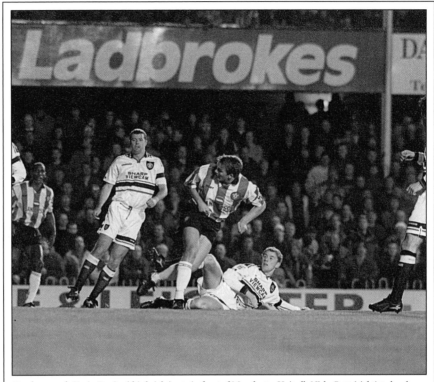

Southampton's Kevin Davies (third right) gets in front of Manchester United's Nicky Butt (right) to head home the winner.

MANCHESTER United increase their lead at the top to seven points with an easy victory over Tottenham that leaves Spurs 19th. Chelsea beat Coventry to go second and Blackburn fail to keep pace and fall to third when they lose at Derby, who move up to sixth.

Barnsley suffer their second heaviest defeat of the campaign at West Ham. Everton's second successive win, against Crystal Palace, with Nicky Barmby scoring his first goal of the season after 18 games, sends the Merseysiders soaring out of the bottom three to 15th and Bolton drop to 18th after drawing with Southampton.

Faustino Asprilla ends his unhappy stay at St James' Park and returns to Parma for £6 million.

Blackburn make the most of being the only top three side in action with a thumping victory over Aston Villa in which Kevin Gallagher nets a hat-trick. It's the worst defeat of the campaign for Villa since a Rovers win at Villa Park in August, in which Gallagher also scored. Blackburn's aggregate increases to nine goals, without reply, and they go second, five points adrift of the leaders.

Alan Shearer returns after six months out when he comes on as substitute in Newcastle's win over Bolton that drops Wanderers a place to 19th. Barnsley record only their third win in nine games, against Crystal Palace, and as in the previous two, the only goal of the match comes from Ashley Ward. The Tykes are still marooned in 20th place.

Everton's climb to safety continues with a third consecutive win over Chelsea, which takes them to 13th. Jürgen Klinsmann finally gets his first goal in three games since his return to White Hart Lane and it's enough to take Spurs up to 18th. Liverpool maintain fourth place by drawing at Leicester and Southampton give the chasing pack hope when Kevin Davies scores a third-minute goal which proves enough to beat Manchester United. But Chelsea's defeat by Everton limits the damage to the leaders' advantage at the top.

It's a tale of two strikers as Alan Shearer makes another substitute appearance, at Anfield, but cannot prevent a Michael Owen goal consigning Newcastle to defeat.

Manchester United suffer a second successive defeat, for the first time in 15 months, when Leicester's Tony Cottee's first goal of the season inflicts a first home reverse of the season on the leaders to give hope to the chasing pack. But only Chelsea, who beat Barnsley and move up a place to second, four points behind United, profit as Blackburn and Liverpool cancel each other out with an Anfield draw and remain third and fourth respectively.

Bolton are thrashed at home by Coventry and stay 19th and Spurs complete the basement trio after defeat at Derby, which keeps the Rams sixth.

February

Sunday 1 February		
Aston Villa v. Newcastle United		0-1
Saturday 7 February		
Barnsley v. Everton		2-2
Blackburn Rovers v. Tottenham Hotspur		0-3
Coventry City v. Sheffield Wed.		1-0
Derby County v. Aston Villa		0-1
Leicester City v. Leeds United		1-0
Liverpool v. Southampton		2-3
Manchester United v. Bolton Wanderers		1-1
Newcastle United v. West Ham United		0-1
Sunday 8 February		
Arsenal v. Chelsea		2-0
Monday 9 February		
Crystal Palace v. Wimbledon		0-3
Saturday 14 February		
Everton v. Derby County		1-2
Sheffield Wed. v. Liverpool		3-3
Tottenham Hotspur v. Leicester City		1-1
Wednesday 18 February		
Aston Villa v. Manchester United		0-2
Southampton v. Coventry City		1-2
Saturday 21 February		
Arsenal v. Crystal Palace		1-0
Bolton Wanderers v. West Ham United		1-1
Coventry City v. Barnsley		1-0
Leicester City v. Chelsea		2-0
Manchester United v. Derby County		2-0
Sheffield Wed. v. Tottenham Hotspur		1-0
Southampton v. Blackburn Rovers		3-0
Wimbledon v. Aston Villa		2-1
Sunday 22 February		
Newcastle United v. Leeds United		1-1
Monday 23 February		
Liverpool v. Everton		1-1
Saturday 28 February		
Aston Villa v. Liverpool		2-1
Barnsley v. Wimbledon		2-1
Blackburn Rovers v. Leicester City		5-3
Chelsea v. Manchester United		0-1
Crystal Palace v. Coventry City		0-3
Derby County v. Sheffield Wed.		3-0
Everton v. Newcastle United		0-0
Leeds United v. Southampton		0-1

		P	W	D	L	F	A	Pts
1	Manchester United	28	18	5	5	57	19	59
2	Blackburn Rovers	27	13	9	5	49	33	48
3	Arsenal	25	13	8	4	45	26	47
4	Liverpool	28	13	8	7	46	28	47
5	Chelsea	27	14	3	10	52	30	45
6	Derby County	28	13	6	9	44	34	45
7	Leicester City	28	10	10	8	34	28	40
8	Leeds United	27	11	6	10	35	30	39
9	West Ham United	26	12	3	11	38	36	39
10	Coventry City	28	10	9	9	35	35	39
11	Southampton	28	11	4	13	34	37	37
12	Newcastle United	27	9	7	11	26	31	34
13	Sheffield Wed.	28	9	7	12	41	54	34
14	Aston Villa	28	9	6	13	30	39	33
15	Wimbledon	26	8	8	10	28	30	32
16	Everton	28	7	9	12	32	40	30
17	Tottenham Hotspur	27	7	6	14	25	43	27
18	Barnsley	27	7	4	16	24	63	25
19	Bolton Wanderers	26	4	12	10	23	42	24
20	Crystal Palace	27	5	8	14	21	41	23

BLACKBURN player Chris Sutton's reaction to being omitted from the senior England squad is to withdraw from the 'B' team despite attempts to dissuade him by his managers at club and country.

Newcastle sign Gary Speed, from Everton, for £5.5 million.

Manchester United are held by 19th-placed Bolton but their lead at the head of the table actually increases, due to shock home defeats for Blackburn and Liverpool. Rovers crash to struggling Spurs, who move up a place to 17th, with two of the visitors' goals coming in the last two minutes of the game. Liverpool, despite two Michael Owen goals, are beaten by the Saints, who also net twice in the final minutes.

Chelsea lose to Arsenal but stay second and Arsenal close to within six points of United, with a game in hand. In another all-London clash Crystal Palace lose to Wimbledon and drop into the bottom three.

Michael Owen becomes the youngest international of the 20th century when he makes his debut against Chile but England lose 2–0. Gianluca Vialli is the shock replacement as Chelsea remove Ruud Gullit.

Michael Owen returns from England duty to continue his purple patch of scoring with a hat-trick that allows Liverpool to come back from 3–1 down at Sheffield Wednesday to take a point and move second, four points adrift of Manchester United. Spurs are held by Leicester and stay 17th.

Manchester United increase their advantage when they win at Villa, with David Beckham and Ryan Giggs netting in the last eight minutes.

Arsenal, with more than a dozen first-teamers missing, are still too strong for Crystal Palace and a win takes the Gunners second and leaves Palace, after a fifth consecutive defeat, 19th. Barnsley lose to Coventry and prop up the table while Bolton manage a draw with West Ham that keeps Wanderers 18th. Spurs don't move either, as they lose to Sheffield Wednesday to remain 17th. Chelsea lose for the second game running, to Leicester, for the first time this campaign, and drop to fourth. But there's no stopping Manchester United who beat Derby County to take a massive nine-point lead at the top.

Liverpool join Arsenal in second place with a draw against Everton that leaves them still without a 'derby'

win since 1994. Phil Neville's first senior goal for Manchester United, which will prove to be his only goal of the season, is enough to beat Chelsea and not only increase the leaders' advantage at the top to 11 points but effectively remove the Stamford Bridge club from the title race. Blackburn go second when Chris Sutton's second hat-trick of the campaign helps Rovers beat Leicester. Liverpool drop to fourth when they are beaten by a brace from former striker Stan Collymore at Villa Park.

Barnsley climb to their highest position since September, 18th, by beating Wimbledon, and striker Jan-Aage Fjortoft makes history by becoming the first Barnsley player to hit two goals in one Premiership game. Crystal Palace are dumped to the foot of the Premiership after losing their sixth consecutive game, against Coventry. Dion Dublin's goal is his 63rd for the club and makes him the Sky Blues' most prolific top-flight scorer in their 31 years in the top tier of English football.

Bryan Robson's Middlesbrough upstage his former club by launching the first dedicated club football channel, six months ahead of Manchester United's MUTV.

Aston Villa's two-goal Stan Collymore and Liverpool's Paul Ince battle for the ball.

Sunday 1 March	
Tottenham Hotspur v. Bolton Wanderers	1-0
Monday 2 March	
West Ham United v. Arsenal	0-0
Wednesday 4 March	
Leeds United v. Tottenham Hotspur	1-0
Saturday 7 March	
Liverpool v. Bolton Wanderers	2-1
Sheffield Wed. v. Manchester United	2-0
Southampton v. Everton	2-1
Sunday 8 March	
Chelsea v. Aston Villa	0-1
Wednesday 11 March	
Aston Villa v. Barnsley	0-1
Chelsea v. Crystal Palace	6-2
Leeds United v. Blackburn Rovers	4-0
West Ham United v. Manchester United	1-1
Wimbledon v. Arsenal	0-1
Saturday 14 March	
Aston Villa v. Crystal Palace	3-1
Barnsley v. Southampton	4-3
Bolton Wanderers v. Sheffield Wed.	3-2
Everton v. Blackburn Rovers	1-0
Manchester United v. Arsenal	0-1
Newcastle United v. Coventry City	0-0
Tottenham Hotspur v. Liverpool	3-3
West Ham United v. Chelsea	2-1
Wimbledon v. Leicester City	2-1
Sunday 15 March	
Derby County v. Leeds United	0-5
Wednesday 18 March	
Newcastle United v. Crystal Palace	1-2
Saturday 28 March	
Arsenal v. Sheffield Wed.	1-0
Barnsley v. Liverpool	2-3
Bolton Wanderers v. Leicester City	2-0
Coventry City v. Derby County	1-0
Crystal Palace v. Tottenham Hotspur	1-3
Everton v. Aston Villa	1-4
Manchester United v. Wimbledon	2-0
Southampton v. Newcastle United	2-1
Monday 30 March	
West Ham United v. Leeds United	3-0
Tuesday 31 March	
Blackburn Rovers v. Barnsley	2-1
Bolton Wanderers v. Arsenal	0-1
Wimbledon v. Newcastle United	0-0

		P	W	D	L	F	A	Pts
1	Manchester United	32	19	6	7	60	23	63
2	Arsenal	30	17	9	4	49	26	60
3	Liverpool	31	15	9	7	54	34	54
4	Blackburn Rovers	30	14	9	7	51	39	51
5	Chelsea	30	15	3	12	59	35	48
6	Leeds United	31	14	6	11	45	33	48
7	West Ham United	30	14	5	11	44	38	47
8	Derby County	30	13	6	11	44	40	45
9	Coventry City	30	11	10	9	36	35	43
10	Southampton	31	13	4	14	41	43	43
11	Aston Villa	32	12	6	14	38	42	42
12	Leicester City	30	10	10	10	35	32	40
13	Sheffield Wed.	31	10	7	14	45	58	37
14	Wimbledon	30	9	9	12	30	34	36
15	Newcastle United	31	9	9	13	28	35	36
16	Tottenham Hotspur	31	9	7	15	32	48	34
17	Everton	31	8	9	14	35	46	33
18	Barnsley	31	9	4	18	32	71	31
19	Bolton Wanderers	31	6	12	13	29	48	30
20	Crystal Palace	31	6	8	17	27	54	26

ALAN NIELSEN'S third and final goal of the season is enough for Spurs to win the crucial relegation battle with Bolton, although the clubs stay 17th and 19th respectively.

Arsenal draw with West Ham and go above Blackburn, on goal difference, into second place, but are still 11 points adrift of the leaders. Manchester United's advantage at the top is big enough to persuade one Manchester bookmaker to pay up on all bets laid on the team for the Premiership title.

Aston Villa's Stan Collymore confirms that there was an altercation between himself and Steve Harkness after the recent game at Villa Park, and accuses his former Liverpool teammate of racial prejudice.

Relegation worries intensify for Tottenham with defeat at Leeds. Manchester United have their lead over Liverpool, who beat Bolton, cut to nine points when they lose to Sheffield Wednesday. Wanderers remain 19th.

Arsenal recover to within nine points of Manchester United by winning at Wimbledon because the leaders are held by West Ham, who continue to affect the title race.

The biggest result of the season occurs at Old Trafford where a Marc Overmars goal beats Manchester United and cuts their lead on Arsenal to six points, and the Gunners have three games in hand. Liverpool lose ground when they can only salvage a draw at White Hart Lane with an 89th-minute goal from Steve McManaman, but Spurs are still just outside the relegation zone. Barnsley top the basement trio with victory over Southampton, Bolton beat Sheffield Wednesday but stay 19th, and bottom club Crystal Palace lose for the eighth consecutive game at Aston Villa.

Crystal Palace finally win a Premiership game, for the first time since 24 November, when they beat Newcastle at St James' Park. Twenty-year-old Carlisle-born Matt Jansen nets for the second consecutive game and his goal proves the winner.

Barnsley lose at home to Liverpool and have three players sent off in the process: Darren Barnard, Darren Sheridan and Chris Morgan. Steve McManaman is again the Reds' saviour with a last-minute winner. Match referee Gary Willard has to suspend play for a while after angry home fans invade the pitch. Old Trafford's biggest gate of the season, 55,306, sees United maintain their six-point lead at the top but they leave it late against serial 'party poopers' Wimbledon, with Ronnie Johnsen and Paul Scholes goals in the last eight minutes. Bolton beat Leicester but stay 19th. Tottenham win another crucial relegation game when they beat fellow strugglers Crystal Palace, a 10th home defeat that virtually condemns the Eagles to the drop.

Arsenal keep up the pressure on United and move to within three points of the leaders, with two games still in hand, with a fourth successive 1–0 win over Bolton that keeps Wanderers 19th, one place behind Barnsley, who stay 18th despite losing at Blackburn. The Gunners also establish a new Premiership record, with an eighth consecutive clean sheet that also equals the club record, set in 1902–03.

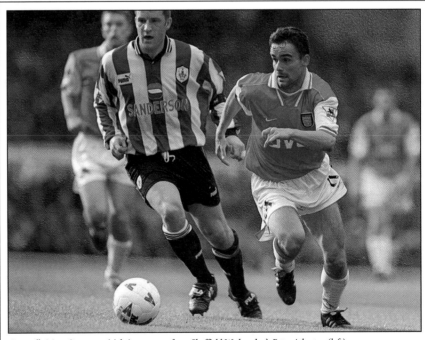

Arsenal's Marc Overmars (right) gets away from Sheffield Wednesday's Peter Atherton (left).

April

Saturday 4 April	
Aston Villa v. West Ham United	2-0
Leeds United v. Barnsley	2-1
Leicester City v. Coventry City	1-1
Sheffield Wed. v. Southampton	1-0
Tottenham Hotspur v. Everton	1-1
Wimbledon v. Bolton Wanderers	0-0
Sunday 5 April	
Derby County v. Chelsea	0-1
Monday 6 April	
Blackburn Rovers v. Manchester United	1-3
Wednesday 8 April	
Leeds United v. Chelsea	3-1
Friday 10 April	
Manchester United v. Liverpool	1-1
Saturday 11 April	
Arsenal v. Newcastle United	3-1
Barnsley v. Sheffield Wed.	2-1
Bolton Wanderers v. Blackburn Rovers	2-1
Chelsea v. Tottenham Hotspur	2-0
Coventry City v. Aston Villa	1-2
Crystal Palace v. Leicester City	0-3
Everton v. Leeds United	2-0
Southampton v. Wimbledon	0-1
West Ham United v. Derby County	0-0
Monday 13 April	
Blackburn Rovers v. Arsenal	1-4
Derby County v. Bolton Wanderers	4-0
Liverpool v. Crystal Palace	2-1
Newcastle United v. Barnsley	2-1
Sheffield Wed. v. West Ham United	1-1
Tottenham Hotspur v. Coventry City	1-1
Wimbledon v. Everton	0-0
Tuesday 14 April	
Leicester City v. Southampton	3-3
Saturday 18 April	
Arsenal v. Wimbledon	5-0
Barnsley v. Tottenham Hotspur	1-1
Bolton Wanderers v. Leeds United	2-3
Crystal Palace v. Derby County	3-1
Everton v. Leicester City	1-1
Manchester United v. Newcastle United	1-1
Southampton v. Aston Villa	1-2
West Ham United v. Blackburn Rovers	2-1
Sunday 19 April	
Chelsea v. Sheffield Wed.	1-0
Coventry City v. Liverpool	1-1
Saturday 25 April	
Aston Villa v. Bolton Wanderers	1-3
Barnsley v. Arsenal	0-2
Blackburn Rovers v. Wimbledon	0-0
Chelsea v. Liverpool	4-1
Everton v. Sheffield Wed.	1-3
Leeds United v. Coventry City	3-3
Tottenham Hotspur v. Newcastle United	2-0
West Ham United v. Southampton	2-4
Sunday 26 April	
Derby County v. Leicester City	0-4
Monday 27 April	
Crystal Palace v. Manchester United	0-3
Wednesday 29 April	
Arsenal v. Derby County	1-0
Chelsea v. Blackburn Rovers	0-1
Coventry City v. Wimbledon	0-0
Leicester City v. Newcastle United	0-0

		P	W	D	L	F	A	Pts
1	Arsenal	35	22	9	4	64	28	75
2	Manchester United	36	21	8	7	68	26	71
3	Chelsea	36	19	3	14	68	40	60
4	Liverpool	35	16	11	8	59	41	59
5	Leeds United	36	17	7	12	56	42	58
6	Blackburn Rovers	36	15	10	11	56	50	55
7	West Ham United	35	15	7	13	49	46	52
8	Aston Villa	36	15	6	15	45	47	51
9	Leicester City	36	12	14	10	47	37	50
10	Derby County	36	14	7	15	49	49	49
11	Coventry City	36	11	15	10	43	43	48
12	Southampton	36	14	5	17	49	52	47
13	Sheffield Wed.	36	12	8	16	51	63	44
14	Wimbledon	36	10	13	13	33	43	43
15	Newcastle United	36	10	11	15	32	42	41
16	Tottenham Hotspur	36	10	10	16	37	53	40
17	Everton	36	9	12	15	40	51	39
18	Bolton Wanderers	36	8	13	15	36	57	37
19	Barnsley	36	10	5	21	37	79	35
20	Crystal Palace	35	7	8	20	31	63	29

THERE is still no clarity at the foot of the table as Spurs draw with Everton to remain 16th, while Bolton draw at Wimbledon to stay 18th and Barnsley, 19th, suffer a third consecutive defeat, to Leeds.

Manchester United come back from a goal down to win at Blackburn and restore their six-point lead over Arsenal.

United then miss out on extending their lead over Arsenal to nine points when they are held at home by Liverpool, despite goalscorer Michael Owen being sent off, leaving the visitors to play the second half with 10 men.

Arsenal press on relentlessly and record their fifth consecutive victory, with Nicolas Anelka netting twice against Newcastle, who drop to 16th, their lowest position of the campaign. There is consolation for the Magpies, however, as Warren Barton's goal is the first conceded by the Gunners in nine matches. Arsene Wenger's side are now just four points behind leaders Manchester United, with three games in hand, and have their championship odds cut to 1–2 on, as they replace United as title favourites.

Spurs' defeat by Chelsea cuts their advantage over Bolton and Barnsley to just a point. The Tykes and Bolton, despite rare wins over Sheffield Wednesday and Blackburn respectively, don't move in the table and poor old Palace crash to their 11th home defeat and are eight points adrift at the bottom.

Blackburn run into Arsenal in rampant mood and are unable to stem the Gunners' relentless march to the championship. Four-nil up by half-time, the first from the returning Dennis Bergkamp in the second minute, the title aspirants, hampered by a snowstorm, take their collective foot off the pedal and allow Rovers a second-half

Colin Calderwood's fourth goal of the season earns 10-man Spurs a vital point at Barnsley.

consolation goal by Kevin Gallagher. United's lead is down to a single point and Arsenal have two games in hand.

Arsenal keep up their momentum and, in sweeping aside Wimbledon, helped by Nigel Winterburn playing his 500th game, they go top of the table. It is the first time in six months that Manchester United, who slip up to draw against Newcastle, have not led the Premiership. The Gunners are a point clear. Ten-man Spurs – Ramon Vega is sent off – claim a crucial point in the relegation battle at Oakwell thanks to Colin Calderwood's equaliser cancelling out a Neil Redfearn goal that turns out to be the Tykes' final Premiership goal. It was a fitting strike, as Redfearn also netted the club's first-ever Premiership goal. Barnsley move up a place, to 18th, while Tottenham stay just outside the relegation zone. Bolton crash to Leeds and remain 19th and doomed Crystal Palace beat Derby to record their first home win of the campaign, and all the goals come in the last 17 minutes.

Liverpool consolidate third place with a draw at Coventry, where Michael Owen's 16th goal of the season is cancelled out by Dion Dublin's second-half penalty.

Bolton give themselves hope with a win at Aston Villa that moves them up a place to 18th, replacing Barnsley, who lose to Arsenal, who take another giant step towards the title. The win at Oakwell puts the Gunners four points ahead of Manchester United, with a home game in hand. Liverpool suffer their worst defeat of the campaign, to Chelsea, with three goals in 11 minutes doing the damage. Chelsea go third and Liverpool drop to fourth.

Away from home United show no mercy as their win condemns Crystal Palace to Division One and closes the gap on Arsenal to a point.

Arsene Wenger's side take a four-point lead over chasing United with a narrow win over Derby County, despite Dennis Bergkamp missing his first penalty for the club. One more victory will take the title to Highbury. At the other end of the table Attilio Lombardo relinquishes his post at Crystal Palace leaving chairman Ron Noades and coach Ray Lewington in charge of team affairs at the relegated club.

May

Saturday 2 May

Bolton Wanderers v. Crystal Palace	5-2
Coventry City v. Blackburn Rovers	2-0
Leicester City v. Barnsley	1-0
Liverpool v. West Ham United	5-0
Newcastle United v. Chelsea	3-1
Sheffield Wed. v. Aston Villa	1-3
Southampton v. Derby County	0-2
Wimbledon v. Tottenham Hotspur	2-6

Sunday 3 May

Arsenal v. Everton	4-0

Monday 4 May

Manchester United v. Leeds United	3-0

Tuesday 5 May

Crystal Palace v. West Ham United	3-3

Wednesday 6 May

Liverpool v. Arsenal	4-0

Sunday 10 May

Aston Villa v. Arsenal	1-0
Barnsley v. Manchester United	0-2
Blackburn Rovers v. Newcastle United	1-0
Chelsea v. Bolton Wanderers	2-0
Crystal Palace v. Sheffield Wed.	1-0
Derby County v. Liverpool	1-0
Everton v. Coventry City	1-1
Leeds United v. Wimbledon	1-1
Tottenham Hotspur v. Southampton	1-1
West Ham United v. Leicester City	4-3

		P	W	D	L	F	A	Pts
1	Arsenal	38	23	9	6	68	33	78
2	Manchester United	38	23	8	7	73	26	77
3	Liverpool	38	18	11	9	68	42	65
4	Chelsea	38	20	3	15	71	43	63
5	Leeds United	38	17	8	13	57	46	59
6	Blackburn Rovers	38	16	10	12	57	52	58
7	Aston Villa	38	17	6	15	49	48	57
8	West Ham United	38	16	8	14	56	57	56
9	Derby County	38	16	7	15	52	49	55
10	Leicester City	38	13	14	11	51	41	53
11	Coventry City	38	12	16	10	46	44	52
12	Southampton	38	14	6	18	50	55	48
13	Newcastle United	38	11	11	16	35	44	44
14	Tottenham Hotspur	38	11	11	16	44	56	44
15	Wimbledon	38	10	14	14	34	46	44
16	Sheffield Wed.	38	12	8	18	52	67	44
17	Everton	38	9	13	16	41	56	40
18	Bolton Wanderers	38	9	13	16	41	61	40
19	Barnsley	38	10	5	23	37	82	35
20	Crystal Palace	38	8	9	21	37	71	33

Promoted from Nationwide Football League Division One

Nottingham Forest
Middlesbrough
Charlton Athletic (via play-offs)

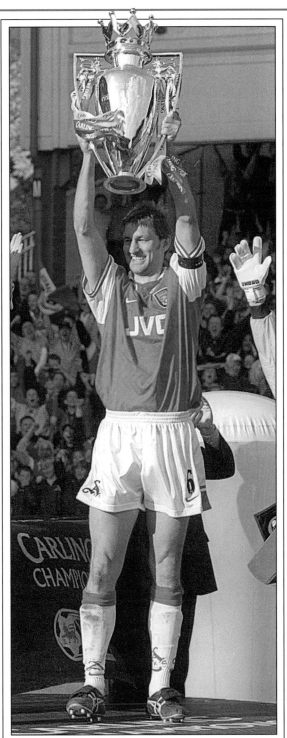

Tony Adams of Arsenal holds the Premiership trophy aloft.

THE SECOND relegation place is filled by Barnsley after they lose at Leicester and the prodigal German Jürgen Klinsmann rescues Tottenham's season with a four-goal blast, his second, third and fourth goals coming inside six second-half minutes, which helps beat Wimbledon and virtually assures Spurs of Premiership survival, moving them up to 15th. Bolton give themselves late hope and move out of the relegation zone with their best result in the top flight, and a season's best, as they thrash Crystal Palace. It is also the first time Bolton have scored five goals in a Premiership match.

Arsenal clinch their 11th league championship in style with a crushing victory over Everton that is a 10th consecutive win, equals a club record and is a new Premiership record. Fittingly the Highbury result is completed by a sensational 89th-minute goal from skipper Tony Adams, who bursts forward to volley past a statue-like Thomas Myhre. Arsene Wenger becomes the first foreign manager to win the English league title. The defeat plunges Everton into relegation trouble as it puts them a point behind Bolton, in 18th place. But the result ensures Premiership safety for Tottenham and Wimbledon, although Wimbledon's tally of just 34 Premiership goals in the season is fewer than any of the relegated teams.

FACT FILE

Arsenal's defeat at Liverpool is the first time they have conceded four goals since the very first day of the Premiership, in 1992, when they lost 4–2 at home to Norwich City. It is also the Gunners' worst-ever defeat in six seasons of the Premiership.

Manchester United get on with the job of securing second place with a professional victory over Leeds and the next day they shatter the club record by signing Jaap Stam for £10.75 million, which is also a world record for a defender.

Arsenal's 18-match unbeaten run finally comes to an end when they rest a number of players and suffer their worst defeat of the season to Liverpool.

The final relegation issue is decided when Bolton are relegated after they lose at Chelsea and Everton survive, on goal difference, with a home draw against Coventry City.

End of season round-up

Top Premiership Goalscorers 1997–98

Dion Dublin	Coventry City	18
Michael Owen	Liverpool	18
Chris Sutton	Blackburn Rovers	18
Dennis Bergkamp	Arsenal	16
Jimmy Floyd Hasselbaink		
	Leeds United	16
Andy Cole	Manchester United	16
Kevin Gallacher	Blackburn Rovers	16
John Hartson	West Ham United	15
Darren Huckerby	Coventry City	14
Paulo Wanchope	Derby County	13

Coca-Cola League Cup

Chelsea 2   Middlesbrough 0

Chelsea won the last Coca-Cola League Cup with a repeat of the previous season's FA Cup Final against 'Boro. Paul Gascoigne made his debut for 'Boro as a second-half substitute but his main contribution to the game was a booking. Gazza gave his losers' medal to Craig Hignett, who had played all the games up to the final. The game was scoreless at the interval and at 90 minutes, but five minutes into extra-time Frank Sinclair put Chelsea ahead. Twelve minutes later Roberto Di Matteo made it 2–0.

FA Cup Final

Arsenal 2   Newcastle United 0

Arsenal clinched the 'Double' with victory over a disappointing Newcastle United. The Gunners took the lead through a Marc Overmars goal, midway through the first half, and sealed the game halfway through the second period when Nicolas Anelka scored number two. The closest Newcastle came to scoring was when Alan Shearer hit the post but Chelsea were never really troubled and made Ruud Gullit the first foreign manager to win the FA Cup.

FWA Footballer of the Year

Dennis Bergkamp   Arsenal

PFA Player of the Year

Dennis Bergkamp   Arsenal

PFA Young Player of the Year

Michael Owen   Liverpool

Manager of the Year

Arsene Wenger   Arsenal

Arsenal's Dennis Bergkamp with the PFA Player of the year award.

Close Season 1998

Chelsea sign Pierluigi Casiraghi from Lazio for £5.4 million while Blackburn pay a club record £7.5 million for Southampton's Kevin Davies.

Newcastle lose their second chairman in less than a week as Sir John Hall steps down from the board six days after Sir Terence Harrison resigned.

Aston Villa sign Alan Thompson, from Bolton Wanderers, for £4.5 million.

Walter Smith becomes Everton's fourth manager in four years when he agrees a three-year contract.

David Platt, despite having a year left on his Arsenal contract, retires at the age of 32. And Ian Wright, the Gunners' record goalscorer, moves to West Ham.

Ronnie Moran, 50 years at Anfield and one of the famous 'Boot room' boys, retires and Liverpool announce that Gerard Houllier is on his way to share managerial duties with another long-serving member of the 'Boot room' club, Roy Evans.

Arsenal bring the curtain down on the close season with a comprehensive 3–0 victory over Manchester United to win the Charity Shield.

August

Saturday 15 August	
Blackburn Rovers v. Derby County	0-0
Coventry City v. Chelsea	2-1
Everton v. Aston Villa	0-0
Manchester United v. Leicester City	2-2
Middlesbrough v. Leeds United	0-0
Newcastle United v. Charlton Athletic	0-0
Sheffield Wed. v. West Ham United	0-1
Wimbledon v. Tottenham Hotspur	3-1

Sunday 16 August	
Southampton v. Liverpool	1-2

Monday 17 August	
Arsenal v. Nottingham Forest	2-1

Saturday 22 August	
Charlton Athletic v. Southampton	5-0
Chelsea v. Newcastle United	1-1
Derby County v. Wimbledon	0-0
Leicester City v. Everton	2-0
Liverpool v. Arsenal	0-0
Nottingham Forest v. Coventry City	1-0
Tottenham Hotspur v. Sheffield Wed.	0-3
West Ham United v. Manchester United	0-0

Sunday 23 August	
Aston Villa v. Middlesbrough	3-1

Monday 24 August	
Leeds United v. Blackburn Rovers	1-0

Saturday 29 August	
Arsenal v. Charlton Athletic	0-0
Blackburn Rovers v. Leicester City	1-0
Coventry City v. West Ham United	0-0
Everton v. Tottenham Hotspur	0-1
Middlesbrough v. Derby County	1-1
Sheffield Wed. v. Aston Villa	0-1
Southampton v. Nottingham Forest	1-2
Wimbledon v. Leeds United	1-1

Sunday 30 August	
Newcastle United v. Liverpool	1-4

		P	W	D	L	F	A	Pts
1	Liverpool	3	2	1	0	6	2	7
2	Aston Villa	3	2	1	0	4	1	7
3	Nottingham Forest	3	2	0	1	4	3	6
4	Charlton Athletic	3	1	2	0	5	0	5
5	Wimbledon	3	1	2	0	4	2	5
6	Arsenal	3	1	2	0	2	1	5
7	Leeds United	3	1	2	0	2	1	5
8	West Ham United	3	1	2	0	1	0	5
9	Leicester City	3	1	1	1	4	3	4
10	Coventry City	3	1	1	1	2	2	4
11	Blackburn Rovers	3	1	1	1	1	1	4
12	Sheffield Wed.	3	1	0	2	3	2	3
13	Derby County	3	0	3	0	1	1	3
14	Tottenham Hotspur	3	1	0	2	2	6	3
15	Manchester United	2	0	2	0	2	2	2
16	Middlesbrough	3	0	2	1	2	4	2
17	Newcastle United	3	0	2	1	2	5	2
18	Chelsea	2	0	1	1	2	3	1
19	Everton	3	0	1	2	0	3	1
20	Southampton	3	0	0	3	2	9	0

Julian Joachim's two goals in three games helped Aston Villa to an unbeaten start.

RUMOURS of a planned breakaway European League, involving Manchester United, Liverpool, and Arsenal, plus more than a dozen top European clubs, see UEFA issue an ultimatum threatening expulsion of those clubs from Euro competition. The Premiership kicks off regardless and reigning champions Arsenal make a start that gets worse before it gets better. Despite opening with a home win over the previous season's First Division champions Nottingham Forest, the next two fixtures in August are draws, at Liverpool and at home to promoted Charlton Athletic. Manchester United fare little better, drawing both of their opening fixtures at home to Leicester City and at West Ham. Of the three Premiership 'new boys' Charlton make the most promising start.

Charlton, who came up behind Nottingham Forest and Middlesbrough via the play-offs, open with a goalless draw at Newcastle before celebrating the return of top-flight football to the Valley, for the first time since 1947, with a thumping of Southampton that takes the Addicks to the top of the Premiership. Clive Mendonca is the hero of the day with the season's first hat-trick, inside 25 second-half minutes. It is a second consecutive August defeat for the Saints, who slump to the bottom of the table as a consequence.

Other notable scores of the opening month include Sheffield Wednesday's 3–0 win at Tottenham, with goals from Peter Atherton, Paolo Di Canio and Andy Hinchcliffe. Aston Villa take seven points from a possible nine with a 0–0 draw at Everton followed by a 3–1 home win over 'Boro, then a 1–0 win at Sheffield Wednesday, thanks to Joachim's second goal in consecutive matches, a run which takes them into second place.

August sees the first managerial casualty when Kenny Dalglish is sacked by Newcastle United, just two games into the season, after 19 months in charge. It then gets worse for the Magpies when they slump to 17th in the table, their lowest position in the campaign, following a 4–1 home drubbing by Liverpool, Dalglish's old club, in front of new manager Ruud Gullit. Michael Owen nets the Premiership's second hat-trick of the season, 10 minutes faster than Clive Mendonca, completing his first-half triple in just a quarter of an hour.

September

Tuesday 8 September	
Leeds United v. Southampton	3-0
Nottingham Forest v. Everton	0-2
Wednesday 9 September	
Aston Villa v. Newcastle United	1-0
Chelsea v. Arsenal	0-0
Derby County v. Sheffield Wed.	1-0
Leicester City v. Middlesbrough	0-1
Liverpool v. Coventry City	2-0
Manchester United v. Charlton Athletic	4-1
Tottenham Hotspur v. Blackburn Rovers	2-1
West Ham United v. Wimbledon	3-4
Saturday 12 September	
Aston Villa v. Wimbledon	2-0
Charlton Athletic v. Derby County	1-2
Chelsea v. Nottingham Forest	2-1
Everton v. Leeds United	0-0
Leicester City v. Arsenal	1-1
Manchester United v. Coventry City	2-0
Newcastle United v. Southampton	4-0
Sheffield Wed. v. Blackburn Rovers	3-0
West Ham United v. Liverpool	2-1
Sunday 13 September	
Tottenham Hotspur v. Middlesbrough	0-3
Saturday 19 September	
Coventry City v. Newcastle United	1-5
Derby County v. Leicester City	2-0
Leeds United v. Aston Villa	0-0
Liverpool v. Charlton Athletic	3-3
Middlesbrough v. Everton	2-2
Nottingham Forest v. West Ham United	0-0
Southampton v. Tottenham Hotspur	1-1
Wimbledon v. Sheffield Wed.	2-1
Sunday 20 September	
Arsenal v. Manchester United	3-0
Monday 21 September	
Blackburn Rovers v. Chelsea	3-4
Thursday 24 September	
Manchester United v. Liverpool	2-0
Saturday 26 September	
Aston Villa v. Derby County	1-0
Charlton Athletic v. Coventry City	1-1
Chelsea v. Middlesbrough	2-0
Everton v. Blackburn Rovers	0-0
Newcastle United v. Nottingham Forest	2-0
Sheffield Wed. v. Arsenal	1-0
Tottenham Hotspur v. Leeds United	3-3
Sunday 27 September	
Leicester City v. Wimbledon	1-1
Monday 28 September	
West Ham United v. Southampton	1-0

		P	W	D	L	F	A	Pts
1	Aston Villa	7	5	2	0	8	1	17
2	Derby County	7	3	3	1	6	3	12
3	Wimbledon	7	3	3	1	11	9	12
4	West Ham United	7	3	3	1	7	5	12
5	Newcastle United	7	3	2	2	13	7	11
6	Manchester United	6	3	2	1	10	6	11
7	Leeds United	7	2	5	0	8	4	11
8	Liverpool	7	3	2	2	12	9	11
9	Chelsea	6	3	2	1	10	7	11
10	Arsenal	7	2	4	1	6	3	10
11	Sheffield Wed.	7	3	0	4	8	5	9
12	Middlesbrough	7	2	3	2	8	8	9
13	Tottenham Hotspur	7	2	2	3	8	14	8
14	Charlton Athletic	7	1	4	2	11	10	7
15	Everton	7	1	4	2	4	5	7
16	Nottingham Forest	7	2	1	4	5	9	7
17	Leicester City	7	1	3	3	6	8	6
18	Blackburn Rovers	7	1	2	4	5	10	5
19	Coventry City	7	1	2	4	4	12	5
20	Southampton	7	0	1	6	3	18	1

EARLY leaders Charlton take a reality check when they open September with a 4–1 thrashing at Manchester United, while Aston Villa continue their good start with a win at home to Newcastle. Liverpool are not left behind either as their home victory over Coventry keeps them in touch with the pace-setters. Arsenal fall down to ninth, with a goalless draw at Chelsea. The Premier League announce that referees are to undergo fitness and diet tests and Steven Lodge certainly needs stamina and appetite as he shows six yellow cards and dismisses Lee Dixon in a stormy Stamford Bridge encounter.

Aston Villa go top of the table when they win their fourth consecutive game, at home to Wimbledon, with new £6.75 million signing Paul Merson scoring on his debut. Villa's great start to the campaign earns manager John Gregory a new four-year deal worth a reported £2 million.

Liverpool miss the chance to go joint top when they are beaten at West Ham while Derby County go second when they win their third game in a row, at home to Leicester, extending their unbeaten start to the season to six games.

At the opposite end of the table Southampton's losing streak, from the start of the campaign, goes to five with a 4–0 mauling at Newcastle that leaves them rooted to the foot of the Premiership. Coventry are just one place above after Newcastle make it nine goals and six points inside eight days with a 5–1 win at Highfield Road. Alan Shearer helps himself to four of those goals and finishes the month with a brace in three consecutive games with the goals that register a home win over Nottingham Forest. Meanwhile, Shearer's former club Blackburn complete the bottom three when they can only draw at Everton.

Arsenal are involved in some stormy games this month and there are two high-profile red cards. When the Gunners beat Manchester United in the 'big game', Nicky Butt is sent off for the second time in five days. And when Paul Alcock sends off Paolo Di Canio, in Sheffield Wednesday's win at Hillsborough, the Italian responds by pushing the official to the ground.

Sheffield Wednesday's Paolo Di Canio (left) leaves referee Paul Alcock on the floor after pushing him over, after being sent off.

Saturday 3 October	
Blackburn Rovers v. West Ham United	3-0
Coventry City v. Aston Villa	1-2
Derby County v. Tottenham Hotspur	0-1
Leeds United v. Leicester City	0-1
Middlesbrough v. Sheffield Wed.	4-0
Nottingham Forest v. Charlton Athletic	0-1
Southampton v. Manchester United	0-3
Wimbledon v. Everton	1-2
Sunday 4 October	
Arsenal v. Newcastle United	3-0
Liverpool v. Chelsea	1-1
Saturday 17 October	
Arsenal v. Southampton	1-1
Chelsea v. Charlton Athletic	2-1
Everton v. Liverpool	0-0
Manchester United v. Wimbledon	5-1
Middlesbrough v. Blackburn Rovers	2-1
Newcastle United v. Derby County	2-1
Nottingham Forest v. Leeds United	1-1
West Ham United v. Aston Villa	0-0
Sunday 18 October	
Coventry City v. Sheffield Wed.	1-0
Monday 19 October	
Leicester City v. Tottenham Hotspur	2-1
Saturday 24 October	
Aston Villa v. Leicester City	1-1
Charlton Athletic v. West Ham United	4-2
Derby County v. Manchester United	1-1
Liverpool v. Nottingham Forest	5-1
Sheffield Wed. v. Everton	0-0
Southampton v. Coventry City	2-1
Tottenham Hotspur v. Newcastle United	2-0
Wimbledon v. Middlesbrough	2-2
Sunday 25 October	
Blackburn Rovers v. Arsenal	1-2
Leeds United v. Chelsea	0-0
Saturday 31 October	
Coventry City v. Arsenal	0-1
Derby County v. Leeds United	2-2
Everton v. Manchester United	1-4
Leicester City v. Liverpool	1-0
Newcastle United v. West Ham United	0-3
Sheffield Wed. v. Southampton	0-0
Wimbledon v. Blackburn Rovers	1-1

		P	W	D	L	F	A	Pts
1	Aston Villa	10	6	4	0	11	3	22
2	Manchester United	10	6	3	1	23	9	21
3	Arsenal	11	5	5	1	13	5	20
4	Liverpool	11	4	4	3	18	12	16
5	Middlesbrough	10	4	4	2	16	11	16
6	Chelsea	9	4	4	1	13	9	16
7	Leicester City	11	4	4	3	11	10	16
8	West Ham United	11	4	4	3	12	12	16
9	Leeds United	11	2	8	1	11	8	14
10	Derby County	11	3	5	3	10	9	14
11	Newcastle United	11	4	2	5	15	16	14
12	Wimbledon	11	3	5	3	16	19	14
13	Tottenham Hotspur	10	4	2	4	12	16	14
14	Charlton Athletic	10	3	4	3	17	14	13
15	Everton	11	2	6	3	7	10	12
16	Sheffield Wed.	11	3	2	6	8	10	11
17	Blackburn Rovers	11	2	3	6	11	15	9
18	Nottingham Forest	10	2	2	6	7	16	8
19	Coventry City	11	2	2	7	7	17	8
20	Southampton	11	1	3	7	6	23	6

ON 1 October George Graham is installed as manager of Spurs on a four-year deal said to be worth £6 million and Tottenham respond by winning at Derby.

Although Aston Villa maintain top spot throughout the month they win just one of their three fixtures, but that success at Coventry, with a brace of Ian Taylor goals, makes it six wins in a row. Subsequent draws, at West Ham and at home to Leicester, do little to affect Villa's status, although the gap is being closed. Derby lost their unbeaten sequence when they lost at Villa at the end of September and October is even worse for the Rams. After losing at home to Spurs and at Newcastle United, County slump to 10th by the end of the month after consecutive home draws with Manchester United and Leeds United. Dave Watson had become only the third player to reach 500 appearances for Everton when he helped them to a draw at 'Boro.

Arsenal begin October in third place with an emphatic Highbury win over Newcastle and amass 10 points from 12 in the month with a draw at Southampton and victories at Blackburn and Coventry. Nicholas Anelka scores in all four Premiership games. But the Gunners have to be content with third as Manchester United, ominously, mirror their points total with three wins and a draw during the month.

United open with a win at Southampton and follow up with a thrashing of Wimbledon at Old Trafford. Only a late equaliser by Jordi Cruyff prevent a Deon Burton goal from proving the winner at Pride Park before United get back to winning ways with a success at Everton that sees them end the month in second place.

Southampton remain rooted to the foot of the table despite picking up five points from nine with a home win over Coventry sandwiched between draws at Arsenal and Sheffield Wednesday. Coventry maintain their penultimate position though they do well to lose just 1–0 at Highbury. Nottingham Forest have the misfortune to run into Liverpool's Michael Owen in full flight and the teenage strike sensation takes his tally to eight with four of the goals in a 5–1 victory at Anfield.

As the month draws to a close Chelsea incur seven bookings when they draw at Leeds, traditionally a volatile fixture. Leeds, on their way to a season's total of 47 bookings and two dismissals, fare marginally better with just five yellow cards. Referee Mike Reed certainly proves his fitness in this one.

Disciplinary matters hit the headlines as the month closes with an 11-match ban and a £5,000 fine on Paolo Di Canio for his push on referee Paul Alcock.

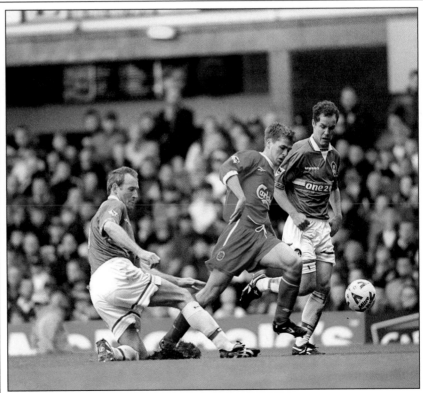

Liverpool's Michael Owen threads his way past Everton's Dave Watson, who a month earlier had passed 500 appearances for the Goodison club.

November

Sunday 1 November	
Middlesbrough v. Nottingham Forest	1-1
Monday 2 November	
Tottenham Hotspur v. Charlton Athletic	2-2
Saturday 7 November	
Aston Villa v. Tottenham Hotspur	3-2
Blackburn Rovers v. Coventry City	1-2
Charlton Athletic v. Leicester City	0-0
Liverpool v. Derby County	1-2
Nottingham Forest v. Wimbledon	0-1
Southampton v. Middlesbrough	3-3
Sunday 8 November	
Arsenal v. Everton	1-0
Leeds United v. Sheffield Wed.	2-1
Manchester United v. Newcastle United	0-0
West Ham United v. Chelsea	1-1
Saturday 14 November	
Arsenal v. Tottenham Hotspur	0-0
Charlton Athletic v. Middlesbrough	1-1
Chelsea v. Wimbledon	3-0
Liverpool v. Leeds United	1-3
Manchester United v. Blackburn Rovers	3-2
Newcastle United v. Sheffield Wed.	1-1
Southampton v. Aston Villa	1-4
West Ham United v. Leicester City	3-2
Sunday 15 November	
Coventry City v. Everton	3-0
Monday 16 November	
Nottingham Forest v. Derby County	2-2
Saturday 21 November	
Aston Villa v. Liverpool	2-4
Blackburn Rovers v. Southampton	0-2
Leeds United v. Charlton Athletic	4-1
Leicester City v. Chelsea	2-4
Middlesbrough v. Coventry City	2-0
Sheffield Wed. v. Manchester United	3-1
Tottenham Hotspur v. Nottingham Forest	2-0
Wimbledon v. Arsenal	1-0
Sunday 22 November	
Derby County v. West Ham United	0-2
Monday 23 November	
Everton v. Newcastle United	1-0
Saturday 28 November	
Charlton Athletic v. Everton	1-2
Chelsea v. Sheffield Wed.	1-1
Coventry City v. Leicester City	1-1
Newcastle United v. Wimbledon	3-1
Nottingham Forest v. Aston Villa	2-2
Southampton v. Derby County	0-1
West Ham United v. Tottenham Hotspur	2-1
Sunday 29 November	
Arsenal v. Middlesbrough	1-1
Liverpool v. Blackburn Rovers	2-0
Manchester United v. Leeds United	3-2

		P	W	D	L	F	A	Pts
1	Aston Villa	14	8	5	1	22	12	29
2	Manchester United	14	8	4	2	30	16	28
3	West Ham United	15	7	5	3	20	16	26
4	Arsenal	15	6	7	2	15	7	25
5	Chelsea	13	6	6	1	22	13	24
6	Leeds United	15	5	8	2	22	14	23
7	Middlesbrough	15	5	8	2	24	17	23
8	Liverpool	15	6	4	5	26	19	22
9	Derby County	15	6	4	5	14	14	21
10	Wimbledon	15	5	5	5	19	25	20
11	Newcastle United	15	5	4	6	19	19	19
12	Tottenham Hotspur	15	5	4	6	19	23	19
13	Leicester City	15	4	6	5	16	18	18
14	Everton	15	4	6	5	10	15	18
15	Charlton Athletic	15	3	7	5	22	23	16
16	Sheffield Wed.	15	4	4	7	14	15	16
17	Coventry City	15	4	3	8	13	21	15
18	Nottingham Forest	15	2	5	8	12	24	11
19	Southampton	15	2	4	9	12	31	10
20	Blackburn Rovers	15	2	3	10	14	24	9

MUCH-WANTED Coventry striker Dion Dublin turns down Blackburn and Leeds to sign for Aston Villa in a £5.75 million, five and a half year deal, then celebrates his debut with two goals as Villa beat Spurs 3–2 to remain top. Kop fans jeer Liverpool as they crash at home to Derby. Arsenal move to within two points of Villa with a Nicolas Anelka goal, his fifth in consecutive games, which earns a home win over Everton.

Peter Schmeichel announces his retirement at the end of the season and the managerial duo that no one in football thought would work finally fails. 'Joint manager' Roy Evans leaves Anfield after 34 years, and Gerard Houllier is in sole charge at the Merseyside club.

Dion Dublin continues his scoring spree with a hat-trick that helps beat struggling Southampton, and Villa stay top despite following up with a home defeat to Liverpool, in which Robbie Fowler hits a hat-trick and former teammates Stan Collymore and Liverpool's Steve Harkness are sent off for a physically frank exchange of views. Chelsea extend their unbeaten run to 17 with a win at Leicester while Blackburn, who sink to the bottom after losing at home to fellow strugglers Southampton, in 19th place, sack Roy Hodgson after just 16 months at the helm. The former manager of the Swiss national side says he 'never saw the axe coming'. Two days later Blackburn announce perennial caretaker Tony Parkes as temporary manager, for the fourth time in 12 years. Forest's draw with Derby sees them top the bottom three and although Forest then lose to Spurs, to remain 18th, they end the month by drawing at home to Villa, although John Gregory's team still finish November top of the table. But Manchester United close the gap as they go second with a home win over Leeds. Blackburn stay bottom with a defeat at Liverpool but then announce they are to make an official bid for Alex Ferguson's assistant, Brian Kidd.

Arsenal's Nicolas Anelka and Tottenham Hotspur's Sol Campbell hold hands during North London derby.

December

Saturday 5 December

Aston Villa v. Manchester United	1-1
Blackburn Rovers v. Charlton Athletic	1-0
Derby County v. Arsenal	0-0
Everton v. Chelsea	0-0
Leeds United v. West Ham United	4-0
Leicester City v. Southampton	2-0
Tottenham Hotspur v. Liverpool	2-1
Wimbledon v. Coventry City	2-1

Sunday 6 December

Middlesbrough v. Newcastle United	2-2

Monday 7 December

Sheffield Wed. v. Nottingham Forest	3-2

Wednesday 9 December

Chelsea v. Aston Villa	2-1

Saturday 12 December

Blackburn Rovers v. Newcastle United	0-0
Derby County v. Chelsea	2-2
Everton v. Southampton	1-0
Leicester City v. Nottingham Forest	3-1
Middlesbrough v. West Ham United	1-0
Sheffield Wed. v. Charlton Athletic	3-0
Tottenham Hotspur v. Manchester United	2-2

Sunday 13 December

Aston Villa v. Arsenal	3-2
Wimbledon v. Liverpool	1-0

Monday 14 December

Leeds United v. Coventry City	2-0

Wednesday 16 December

Manchester United v. Chelsea	1-1

Saturday 19 December

Chelsea v. Tottenham Hotspur	2-0
Coventry City v. Derby County	1-1
Liverpool v. Sheffield Wed.	2-0
Manchester United v. Middlesbrough	2-3
Newcastle United v. Leicester City	1-0
Nottingham Forest v. Blackburn Rovers	2-2
Southampton v. Wimbledon	3-1
West Ham United v. Everton	2-1

Sunday 20 December

Arsenal v. Leeds United	3-1

Monday 21 December

Charlton Athletic v. Aston Villa	0-1

Saturday 26 December

Arsenal v. West Ham United	1-0
Blackburn Rovers v. Aston Villa	2-1
Coventry City v. Tottenham Hotspur	1-1
Everton v. Derby County	0-0
Manchester United v. Nottingham Forest	3-0
Middlesbrough v. Liverpool	1-3
Newcastle United v. Leeds United	0-3
Sheffield Wed. v. Leicester City	0-1
Southampton v. Chelsea	0-2
Wimbledon v. Charlton Athletic	2-1

Monday 28 December

Aston Villa v. Sheffield Wed.	2-1
Charlton Athletic v. Arsenal	0-1
Derby County v. Middlesbrough	2-1
Leicester City v. Blackburn Rovers	1-1
Liverpool v. Newcastle United	4-2
Nottingham Forest v. Southampton	1-1
Tottenham Hotspur v. Everton	4-1
West Ham United v. Coventry City	2-0

Tuesday 29 December

Chelsea v. Manchester United	0-0
Leeds United v. Wimbledon	2-2

		P	W	D	L	F	A	Pts
1	Aston Villa	20	11	6	3	31	20	39
2	Chelsea	20	9	10	1	31	17	37
3	Manchester United	20	9	8	3	39	23	35
4	Arsenal	20	9	8	3	22	11	35
5	Leeds United	20	8	9	3	34	19	33
6	West Ham United	20	9	5	6	24	23	32
7	Liverpool	20	9	4	7	36	25	31
8	Middlesbrough	20	7	9	4	32	26	30
9	Wimbledon	20	8	6	6	27	32	30
10	Leicester City	20	7	7	6	23	21	28
11	Derby County	20	6	10	4	20	18	28
12	Tottenham Hotspur	20	7	6	7	28	30	27
13	Newcastle United	20	6	6	8	24	28	24
14	Everton	20	5	8	7	13	21	23
15	Sheffield Wed.	20	6	4	10	21	22	22
16	Blackburn Rovers	20	4	6	10	20	28	18
17	Coventry City	20	4	5	11	16	29	17
18	Charlton Athletic	20	3	7	10	23	31	16
19	Southampton	20	3	5	12	16	38	14
20	Nottingham Forest	20	2	7	11	18	36	13

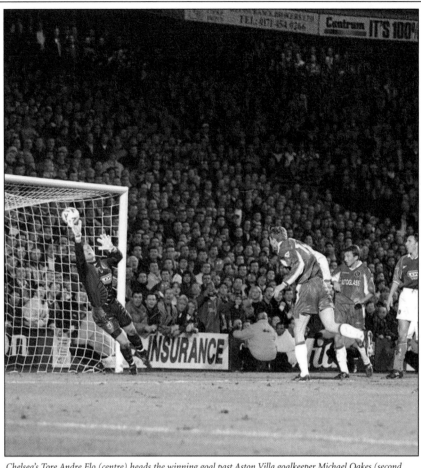

Chelsea's Tore Andre Flo (centre) heads the winning goal past Aston Villa goalkeeper Michael Oakes (second left) in the last minute.

JUST FOUR days into the month, Brian Kidd severs his 33-year association with Manchester United to become manager at Ewood Park. Dion Dublin's seven goals in his first four Aston Villa games earn him the Player of the Month award for November.

Leeds United's young guns – six of the team are under 21 – move into third place with a win over West Ham, while Blackburn give their new manager a welcoming present, a home victory over Charlton, their first win in eight games. Chelsea drop to sixth after a dull goalless draw at Everton is headlined by Dennis Wise's third red card of the season. Four days later Chelsea beat Aston Villa with Tore Andre Flo netting the winner in the fourth minute of added time. It's his 35th appearance as substitute.

At the other end of the table Everton's victory at the Dell keeps Southampton rock bottom and while Blackburn manage a couple of draws they stay 18th. Nottingham Forest don't manage a single win in the five games they play in December and by the turn of the year they have replaced Southampton at the foot of the table.

It's a momentous month for Chelsea as the home win over Spurs takes them top for the first time in a decade, although the dismissal of Tottenham striker Chris Armstrong is a contributory factor. But Aston Villa regain top spot and go three points clear of Chelsea with a win at Charlton, courtesy of a Richard Rufus own-goal. Five days later Chelsea return to the summit with a Boxing Day win at Southampton, while Villa lose at Blackburn, due, in

the main, to the sending-off of goalkeeper Michael Oakes. Nottingham Forest lose at Old Trafford as United move third. It is this defeat that sends Forest bottom, where they are to remain for the duration of the season.

As the year draws to an end Villa, Chelsea and Manchester United occupy the leading positions that, historically, indicate from where the eventual champions emerge, while the bottom three, Charlton Athletic, Southampton and Nottingham Forest, nervously reflect that a place in the bottom three, prior to the ringing in of the New Year, usually means getting out route-maps to First Division grounds come August.

Didier Doni becomes the 23rd French Premiership player when he completes his £3.25 million move from Paris St Germain to Newcastle United.

Saturday 9 January	
Arsenal v. Liverpool	0-0
Blackburn Rovers v. Leeds United	1-0
Coventry City v. Nottingham Forest	4-0
Everton v. Leicester City	0-0
Middlesbrough v. Aston Villa	0-0
Newcastle United v. Chelsea	0-1
Sheffield Wed. v. Tottenham Hotspur	0-0
Southampton v. Charlton Athletic	3-1
Wimbledon v. Derby County	2-1
Sunday 10 January	
Manchester United v. West Ham United	4-1
Saturday 16 January	
Chelsea v. Coventry City	2-1
Derby County v. Blackburn Rovers	1-0
Leeds United v. Middlesbrough	2-0
Leicester City v. Manchester United	2-6
Liverpool v. Southampton	7-1
Nottingham Forest v. Arsenal	0-1
Tottenham Hotspur v. Wimbledon	0-0
West Ham United v. Sheffield Wed.	0-4
Sunday 17 January	
Charlton Athletic v. Newcastle United	2-2
Monday 18 January	
Aston Villa v. Everton	3-0
Saturday 30 January	
Blackburn Rovers v. Tottenham Hotspur	1-1
Coventry City v. Liverpool	2-1
Everton v. Nottingham Forest	0-1
Middlesbrough v. Leicester City	0-0
Newcastle United v. Aston Villa	2-1
Sheffield Wed. v. Derby County	0-1
Southampton v. Leeds United	3-0
Wimbledon v. West Ham United	0-0
Sunday 31 January	
Arsenal v. Chelsea	1-0
Charlton Athletic v. Manchester United	0-1

		P	W	D	L	F	A	Pts
1	Manchester United	23	12	8	3	50	26	44
2	Chelsea	23	11	10	2	34	19	43
3	Aston Villa	23	12	7	4	35	22	43
4	Arsenal	23	11	9	3	24	11	42
5	Leeds United	23	9	9	5	36	23	36
6	Liverpool	23	10	5	8	44	28	35
7	Wimbledon	23	9	8	6	29	33	35
8	Derby County	23	8	10	5	23	20	34
9	West Ham United	23	9	6	8	25	31	33
10	Middlesbrough	23	7	11	5	32	28	32
11	Tottenham Hotspur	23	7	9	7	29	31	30
12	Leicester City	23	7	9	7	25	27	30
13	Newcastle United	23	7	7	9	28	32	28
14	Sheffield Wed.	23	7	5	11	25	23	26
15	Everton	23	5	9	9	13	25	24
16	Coventry City	23	6	5	12	23	32	23
17	Blackburn Rovers	23	5	7	11	22	30	22
18	Southampton	23	5	5	13	23	46	20
19	Charlton Athletic	23	3	8	12	26	37	17
20	Nottingham Forest	23	3	7	13	19	41	16

BOTTOM club Nottingham Forest and Dave Bassett part company and he becomes the seventh Premiership manager to lose his job since the end of last season.

The Premier League announce that next season referees and assistants will wear radio-mike links to improve communication.

Blackburn Rovers' resurgence earns Brian Kidd the Manager of the Month award for December.

Nottingham Forest make it 18 games without a win when they are hammered at Coventry with Darren Huckerby scoring a hat-trick. Chelsea take their unbeaten run to 20 by beating Newcastle and join Aston Villa, separated only by goal difference, at the top.

Although 17-year-old Joe Cole makes his much anticipated Premiership debut for West Ham, in the 4–1 hammering by Manchester United, the headlines are made by the power cut at Old Trafford that delays the start by 45 minutes.

Nottingham Forest appoint Ron Atkinson and the new manager flies in from his Barbados hotel to meet his new team. In the same week the Football Association confirm they have secured the purchase of Wembley and its site for £320 million. For a little less, by some £313 million, Wimbledon break their transfer record in signing John Hartson from West Ham on a six-year deal.

Without Hartson the Hammers crash to Sheffield Wednesday and a Dwight Yorke triple helps Manchester United swamp Leicester, while Robbie Fowler completes his second hat-trick of the season to devastate Southampton, who slump to 19th. Fellow strugglers Charlton are just seconds away from a new Premiership record of nine successive defeats when they stage a comeback to draw with Newcastle, Martin Pringle getting the point-saver in the 90th minute. Meanwhile Julian Joachim nets a brace as Villa beat Everton to join Chelsea at the top.

A sign of the times, perhaps, as Aston Villa's record signing Stan Collymore reveals he is to seek stress counselling. Presumably the Premier League sanctioning an extension of the domestic season for 1999–2000 will only add to the pressures on top-flight footballers. But Steve McManaman won't suffer such problems, domestically, as he announces his signing of a transfer agreement with Real Madrid and looks set to be the first high-profile British beneficiary of the Bosman ruling.

Back on the field Alan Shearer ends a near three-month goal drought when he scores after just four minutes to help Newcastle to victory over Aston Villa, who drop to third. At the other end of the table Nottingham Forest end their 19-game run without a victory by beating Everton at Goodison: Pierre Van Hooijdonk is the match-winner. Fellow strugglers Blackburn Rovers climb out of the drop zone with a draw at Spurs but have a player sent off for the third successive game, Jason Wilcox.

Chelsea hand a boost to the other title-chasers by losing for the first time since the opening day of the campaign. Dennis Bergkamp nets the Highbury winner as Arsenal stretch their record for not conceding a league goal to nearly eight hours.

Coventry City's manager Gordon Strachan argues with officials.

February

Wednesday 3 February		
Manchester United v. Derby County		1-0
Saturday 6 February		
Aston Villa v. Blackburn Rovers		1-3
Chelsea v. Southampton		1-0
Leeds United v. Newcastle United		0-1
Leicester City v. Sheffield Wed.		0-2
Liverpool v. Middlesbrough		3-1
Nottingham Forest v. Manchester United		1-8
Tottenham Hotspur v. Coventry City		0-0
West Ham United v. Arsenal		0-4
Sunday 7 February		
Derby County v. Everton		2-1
Monday 8 February		
Charlton Athletic v. Wimbledon		2-0
Saturday 13 February		
Charlton Athletic v. Liverpool		1-0
West Ham United v. Nottingham Forest		2-1
Wednesday 17 February		
Aston Villa v. Leeds United		1-2
Chelsea v. Blackburn Rovers		1-1
Everton v. Middlesbrough		5-0
Manchester United v. Arsenal		1-1
Newcastle United v. Coventry City		4-1
Saturday 20 February		
Arsenal v. Leicester City		5-0
Blackburn Rovers v. Sheffield Wed.		1-4
Coventry City v. Manchester United		0-1
Derby County v. Charlton Athletic		0-2
Leeds United v. Everton		1-0
Liverpool v. West Ham United		2-2
Middlesbrough v. Tottenham Hotspur		0-0
Nottingham Forest v. Chelsea		1-3
Southampton v. Newcastle United		2-1
Sunday 21 February		
Wimbledon v. Aston Villa		0-0
Saturday 27 February		
Aston Villa v. Coventry City		1-4
Charlton Athletic v. Nottingham Forest		0-0
Chelsea v. Liverpool		2-1
Everton v. Wimbledon		1-1
Manchester United v. Southampton		2-1
Sheffield Wed. v. Middlesbrough		3-1
Tottenham Hotspur v. Derby County		1-1
West Ham United v. Blackburn Rovers		2-0
Sunday 28 February		
Newcastle United v. Arsenal		1-1

		P	W	D	L	F	A	Pts
1	Manchester United	28	16	9	3	63	29	57
2	Chelsea	27	14	11	2	41	22	53
3	Arsenal	27	13	11	3	35	13	50
4	Aston Villa	27	12	8	7	38	31	44
5	Leeds United	26	11	9	6	39	25	42
6	West Ham United	27	11	7	9	31	38	40
7	Liverpool	27	11	6	10	50	34	39
8	Derby County	27	9	11	7	26	25	38
9	Wimbledon	26	9	10	7	30	36	37
10	Sheffield Wed.	26	10	5	11	34	25	35
11	Newcastle United	27	9	8	10	35	36	35
12	Tottenham Hotspur	26	7	12	7	30	32	33
13	Middlesbrough	27	7	12	8	34	39	33
14	Leicester City	25	7	9	9	25	34	30
15	Everton	27	6	10	11	20	29	28
16	Charlton Athletic	27	6	9	12	31	37	27
17	Coventry City	27	7	6	14	28	38	27
18	Blackburn Rovers	27	6	8	13	27	38	26
19	Southampton	26	6	5	15	26	50	23
20	Nottingham Forest	27	3	8	16	22	54	17

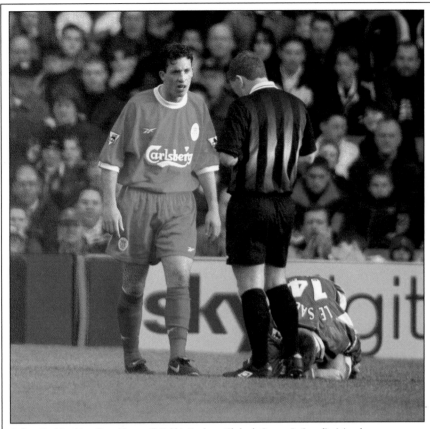

Referee Paul Durkin talks to Liverpool's Robbie Fowler as Chelsea's Graeme Le Saux lies injured.

JOHN HARTSON has to fork out £20,000 as the FA equal their highest-ever fine in punishing the new Wimbledon striker for his training-ground kick in the head on Eyal Berkovic, while he was at West Ham. Hartson is also hit with a three-match ban. At the other end of the financial scale Manchester United are acclaimed as the world's richest club with a turnover of £90 million. Alex Ferguson and Dwight Yorke are respectively named as Manager and Player of the month for January. And the month just gets better for United as substitute Ole Gunnar Solskjaer nets four quick goals to sink Nottingham Forest. Southampton lose to Chelsea and Arsenal move into third with victory over West Ham.

Mark Hughes, who has the worst disciplinary record in the Premiership, is hit with a £2,000 fine, a two-match ban and a warning as to future conduct, for amassing 14 yellow cards. Added winter gloom is prevented at the Valley, where three Malaysians and a member of staff are arrested after a break-in at the club's power room is linked to a Far Eastern syndicate betting on Premiership games. Flood-light 'failures' at previous fixtures caused delays at Old Trafford last month, and, in 1997, at Pride Park, Upton Park and Selhurst Park.

A bad-tempered 'top v bottom' clash sees Blackburn draw at Chelsea. There are seven yellow cards and Gianluca Vialli sees red, along with Marlon Broome. Nicolas Anelka hits his first Prem-iership hat-trick as Arsenal sweep aside Leicester City and Coventry sink into the bottom three with defeat to Manchester United. South-ampton net a precious win after beating Newcastle and Charlton gain hope with a victory at Derby.

Chelsea christen their newly laid pitch with a win over Liverpool but the game is marred by a Graham Le Saux elbow on Robbie Fowler that is missed by referee Paul Durkin but not by millions of tele-vision viewers. Manchester United rest a number of players but still beat Sout-hampton. Former pacesetters Aston Villa continue their fall from grace with a derby ham-mering at home to Coventry, the first Sky Blues win at Villa Park after 25 matches trying.

A first goal for new signing Tim Sherwood earns Spurs a home draw with Derby and extends their unbeaten run to eight, although the last six have all been draws. There is a phoenix-like return to action for Mark Crossley as he gets his first outing for 22 months and the top flight's best penalty stopper promptly saves a spot-kick to earn Forest a draw at Charlton. Only Southampton's Matt Le Tissier has scored a penalty against Crossley.

March

	Monday 1 March	
	Leicester City v. Leeds United	1-2
	Tuesday 2 March	
	Tottenham Hotspur v. Southampton	3-0
	Wednesday 3 March	
	Sheffield Wed. v. Wimbledon	1-2
	Saturday 6 March	
	Coventry City v. Charlton Athletic	2-1
	Southampton v. West Ham United	1-0
	Wimbledon v. Leicester City	0-1
	Tuesday 9 March	
	Arsenal v. Sheffield Wed.	3-0
	Wednesday 10 March	
	Blackburn Rovers v. Everton	1-2
	Derby County v. Aston Villa	2-1
	Leeds United v. Tottenham Hotspur	2-0
	Nottingham Forest v. Newcastle United	1-2
	Saturday 13 March	
	Chelsea v. West Ham United	0-1
	Coventry City v. Blackburn Rovers	1-1
	Derby County v. Liverpool	3-2
	Everton v. Arsenal	0-2
	Leicester City v. Charlton Athletic	1-1
	Newcastle United v. Manchester United	1-2
	Sheffield Wed. v. Leeds United	0-2
	Tottenham Hotspur v. Aston Villa	1-0
	Wimbledon v. Nottingham Forest	1-3
	Sunday 14 March	
	Middlesbrough v. Southampton	3-0
	Saturday 20 March	
	Arsenal v. Coventry City	2-0
	Blackburn Rovers v. Wimbledon	3-1
	Leeds United v. Derby County	4-1
	Nottingham Forest v. Middlesbrough	1-2
	Southampton v. Sheffield Wed.	1-0
	West Ham United v. Newcastle United	2-0
	Sunday 21 March	
	Aston Villa v. Chelsea	0-3
	Manchester United v. Everton	3-1

		P	W	D	L	F	A	Pts
1	Manchester United	30	18	9	3	68	31	63
2	Arsenal	30	16	11	3	42	13	59
3	Chelsea	29	15	11	3	44	23	56
4	Leeds United	30	15	9	6	49	27	54
5	West Ham United	30	13	7	10	34	39	46
6	Aston Villa	30	12	8	10	39	37	44
7	Derby County	30	11	11	8	32	32	44
8	Wimbledon	30	10	10	10	34	44	40
9	Liverpool	28	11	6	11	52	37	39
10	Tottenham Hotspur	29	9	12	8	34	34	39
11	Middlesbrough	29	9	12	8	39	40	39
12	Newcastle United	30	10	8	12	38	41	38
13	Sheffield Wed.	30	10	5	15	35	33	35
14	Leicester City	28	8	10	10	28	37	34
15	Coventry City	30	8	7	15	31	42	31
16	Everton	30	7	10	13	23	35	31
17	Blackburn Rovers	30	7	9	14	32	42	30
18	Southampton	30	8	5	17	28	56	29
19	Charlton Athletic	29	6	10	13	33	40	28
20	Nottingham Forest	30	4	8	18	27	59	20

TONY COTTEE nets his 199th league goal but Leicester still fall to fast-improving Leeds United, who are destined to win all their games this month. The FA announce misconduct charges for Graham Le Saux and Robbie Fowler.

Wimbledon's win at Sheffield Wednesday is too much for manager Joe Kinnear, who is rushed to hospital after complaining of severe chest pains. At the foot of the table Coventry and Southampton both claim vital wins while Arsenal extend their unbeaten run to 24 by beating Sheffield Wednesday to move second, ahead of Chelsea.

Derby inflict a second successive defeat on Aston Villa to severely damage their title hopes. Further defeats, before the month is out, drop Villa to sixth.

The total Premier League wage bill, for 1996–97, is revealed at £361 million, a rise of 25 percent on the previous season. The warning signs are posted when it's revealed that 70 Premiership players earned £1 million when just two earned that sum the year before, but many top-flight clubs ignore forecasts of problems ahead.

Manchester United keep up their momentum at the top of the table when an Andy Cole brace extends their unbeaten run to 17 at Newcastle. Arsenal net a comfortable win over Everton, despite Emmanuel Petit's red card, to remain second, but Chelsea's defeat by West Ham drops them to third. It's Petit's fourth red card in his 17 months at Highbury.

At the foot of the table Blackburn climb out of the drop zone with a win over Wimbledon. Two wins out of three see Southampton top the bottom three, while Nottingham Forest, despite winning at eighth-placed Wimbledon, remain rock bottom.

Arsenal reduce the deficit on United to a point when Lee Dixon, on his 500th club appearance, helps them to a win over Coventry, and Chelsea effectively remove Villa from the championship race with a couple of Tore Andre Flo goals in their win at Villa Park.

Derby County's Jacob Laursen tackles Leeds United's Harry Kewell.

82

April

Friday 2 April	
Aston Villa v. West Ham United	0-0
Saturday 3 April	
Blackburn Rovers v. Middlesbrough	0-0
Charlton Athletic v. Chelsea	0-1
Derby County v. Newcastle United	3-4
Leeds United v. Nottingham Forest	3-1
Liverpool v. Everton	3-2
Sheffield Wed. v. Coventry City	1-2
Southampton v. Arsenal	0-0
Tottenham Hotspur v. Leicester City	0-2
Wimbledon v. Manchester United	1-1
Monday 5 April	
Coventry City v. Southampton	1-0
Everton v. Sheffield Wed.	1-2
Middlesbrough v. Wimbledon	3-1
Newcastle United v. Tottenham Hotspur	1-1
Nottingham Forest v. Liverpool	2-2
West Ham United v. Charlton Athletic	0-1
Tuesday 6 April	
Arsenal v. Blackburn Rovers	1-0
Leicester City v. Aston Villa	2-2
Saturday 10 April	
Aston Villa v. Southampton	3-0
Derby County v. Nottingham Forest	1-0
Leicester City v. West Ham United	0-0
Middlesbrough v. Charlton Athletic	2-0
Sunday 11 April	
Everton v. Coventry City	2-0
Wimbledon v. Chelsea	1-2
Monday 12 April	
Leeds United v. Liverpool	0-0
Wednesday 14 April	
Middlesbrough v. Chelsea	0-0
Saturday 17 April	
Charlton Athletic v. Leeds United	1-1
Coventry City v. Middlesbrough	1-2
Liverpool v. Aston Villa	0-1
Manchester United v. Sheffield Wed.	3-0
Newcastle United v. Everton	1-3
Nottingham Forest v. Tottenham Hotspur	0-1
Southampton v. Blackburn Rovers	3-3
West Ham United v. Derby County	5-1
Sunday 18 April	
Chelsea v. Leicester City	2-2
Monday 19 April	
Arsenal v. Wimbledon	5-1
Tuesday 20 April	
Charlton Athletic v. Tottenham Hotspur	1-4
Wednesday 21 April	
Liverpool v. Leicester City	0-1
Sheffield Wed. v. Newcastle United	1-1
Saturday 24 April	
Aston Villa v. Nottingham Forest	2-0
Blackburn Rovers v. Liverpool	1-3
Derby County v. Southampton	0-0
Everton v. Charlton Athletic	4-1
Leicester City v. Coventry City	1-0
Middlesbrough v. Arsenal	1-6
Tottenham Hotspur v. West Ham United	1-2
Wimbledon v. Newcastle United	1-1
Sunday 25 April	
Leeds United v. Manchester United	1-1
Sheffield Wed. v. Chelsea	0-0

		P	W	D	L	F	A	Pts
1	Arsenal	34	19	12	3	54	15	69
2	Manchester United	33	19	11	3	73	33	68
3	Chelsea	34	17	14	3	49	26	65
4	Leeds United	34	16	12	6	54	30	60
5	Aston Villa	35	15	10	10	47	39	55
6	West Ham United	35	15	9	11	41	42	54
7	Middlesbrough	35	12	14	9	47	48	50
8	Derby County	34	12	12	10	37	41	48
9	Liverpool	34	13	8	13	60	44	47
10	Tottenham Hotspur	34	11	13	10	41	40	46
11	Leicester City	34	11	13	10	36	41	46
12	Newcastle United	35	11	11	13	46	50	44
13	Wimbledon	35	10	12	13	39	56	42
14	Sheffield Wed.	35	11	7	17	39	40	40
15	Everton	35	10	10	15	35	42	40
16	Coventry City	35	10	7	18	35	48	37
17	Blackburn Rovers	34	7	11	16	36	49	32
18	Charlton Athletic	35	7	11	17	37	52	32
19	Southampton	35	8	8	19	31	63	32
20	Nottingham Forest	35	4	9	22	30	68	21

LEEDS secure their seventh consecutive Premiership victory to keep Nottingham Forest bottom and David O'Leary earns his first Manager of the Month award, for March, and his team's run equals Don Revie's record, set 26 years ago. Tony Cottee scores his 200th career league goal as Leicester win at Spurs. His first goal was against Tottenham in 1983, and his 100th was for Everton against Tottenham. With this latest strike he completes a unique trio against the north London club. Derby County lose a seven-goal thriller at Pride Park, in which Gary Speed nets a hat-trick.

Robbie Fowler invites more misery as he mimics 'coke-snorting' along the byline and nets two goals in the Merseyside derby win over Everton. He apologises the next day but trouble looms and he is fined a record £32,000 by the FA and given a four-match ban. It gets worse as the Liverpool striker receives a further two-match suspension for 'distasteful gestures' towards Graham Le Saux in February. Liverpool fine Fowler heavily and give him a formal warning. Le Saux gets a one-match ban and a £5,000 fine for his elbow on Fowler in that same match.

Arsenal beat Blackburn and Martin Keown and Keith Gillespie are sent off. Chelsea beat Wimbledon to keep up the pressure on the top two, while Aston Villa end their miserable 11-match run without a win by beating Southampton, a reverse that keeps the Saints 19th and praying for a miracle. Nottingham Forest lose to an 85th-minute Derby goal, stay bottom and have Pierre Van Hooijdonk sent off. There is no joy for Charlton either, as they drop closer to the relegation zone with a defeat at 'Boro.

Another sign of changing times comes when the list of six nominees for the PFA Player of the Year Award contains just one Englishman, David Beckham. Dennis Bergkamp, Dwight Yorke, Roy Keane, Emmanuel Petit and David Ginola complete the list.

Manchester United retain pole position with a win over Sheffield Wednesday while Arsenal savage Wimbledon with four goals in a 10-minute burst that closes the gap to a point. Meanwhile the cracks begin to show in Chelsea's title challenge as they squander a 2–0 lead, conceding twice in last eight minutes, to Leicester. Coach Vialli admits tactical errors he feels have cost them the title.

Meanwhile, Arsenal steam on and register their best away win since 1954 when they demolish Middlesbrough to go top. United can only muster a draw at Leeds the day after, and remain second.

At the other end of the table Charlton crash to Everton and stay 18th. Southampton take a point at Derby but remain 19th and Forest's third consecutive reverse leaves them holding up the rest, as they have since before Christmas. But, despite gifting goals to Liverpool, Blackburn stay outside the drop zone.

There is another portent of money worries to come when figures show that 75 percent of Premiership clubs paid out in excess of half of their income on wages, with Chelsea's wage bill topping the chart at nearly £30 million. On 1 April Leeds chairman Peter Ridsdale had warned that spiralling players' wages could price fans out of football.

Alex Ferguson ends the month with his second Manager of the Month Award for the season, a record eighth such award for the Scot.

Leicester City's Tony Cottee celebrates career goal 201, the equaliser against Aston Villa.

Saturday 1 May

Charlton Athletic v. Blackburn Rovers	0-0
Chelsea v. Everton	3-1
Coventry City v. Wimbledon	2-1
Liverpool v. Tottenham Hotspur	3-2
Manchester United v. Aston Villa	2-1
Newcastle United v. Middlesbrough	1-1
Nottingham Forest v. Sheffield Wed.	2-0
Southampton v. Leicester City	2-1
West Ham United v. Leeds United	1-5

Sunday 2 May

Arsenal v. Derby County	1-0

Wednesday 5 May

Chelsea v. Leeds United	1-0
Leicester City v. Derby County	1-2
Liverpool v. Manchester United	2-2
Tottenham Hotspur v. Arsenal	1-3

Saturday 8 May

Aston Villa v. Charlton Athletic	3-4
Blackburn Rovers v. Nottingham Forest	1-2
Derby County v. Coventry City	0-0
Everton v. West Ham United	6-0
Leicester City v. Newcastle United	2-0
Sheffield Wed. v. Liverpool	1-0
Wimbledon v. Southampton	0-2

Sunday 9 May

Middlesbrough v. Manchester United	0-1

Monday 10 May

Tottenham Hotspur v. Chelsea	2-2

Tuesday 11 May

Leeds United v. Arsenal	1-0

Wednesday 12 May

Blackburn Rovers v. Manchester United	0-0

Sunday 16 May

Arsenal v. Aston Villa	1-0
Charlton Athletic v. Sheffield Wed.	0-1
Chelsea v. Derby County	2-1
Coventry City v. Leeds United	2-2
Liverpool v. Wimbledon	3-0
Manchester United v. Tottenham Hotspur	2-1
Newcastle United v. Blackburn Rovers	1-1
Nottingham Forest v. Leicester City	1-0
Southampton v. Everton	2-0
West Ham United v. Middlesbrough	4-0

		P	W	D	L	F	A	Pts
1	Manchester United	38	22	13	3	80	37	79
2	Arsenal	38	22	12	4	59	17	78
3	Chelsea	38	20	15	3	57	30	75
4	Leeds United	38	18	13	7	62	34	67
5	West Ham United	38	16	9	13	46	53	57
6	Aston Villa	38	15	10	13	51	46	55
7	Liverpool	38	15	9	14	68	49	54
8	Derby County	38	13	13	12	40	45	52
9	Middlesbrough	38	12	15	11	48	54	51
10	Leicester City	38	12	13	13	40	46	49
11	Tottenham Hotspur	38	11	14	13	47	50	47
12	Sheffield Wed.	38	13	7	18	41	42	46
13	Newcastle United	38	11	13	14	48	54	46
14	Everton	38	11	10	17	42	47	43
15	Coventry City	38	11	9	18	39	51	42
16	Wimbledon	38	10	12	16	40	63	42
17	Southampton	38	11	8	19	37	64	41
18	Charlton Athletic	38	8	12	18	41	56	36
19	Blackburn Rovers	38	7	14	17	38	52	35
20	Nottingham Forest	38	7	9	22	35	69	30

Promoted from Nationwide Football League Division One

Sunderland

Bradford City

Watford (via play-offs)

Manchester United's Dwight Yorke (left) tries the crown from the Premiership trophy on for size, much to the amusement of goalkeeper Peter Schmeichel (right).

DAVID BECKHAM nets a free-kick winner to beat Aston Villa but United remain second as Arsenal defeat Derby with Nicolas Anelka's 16th goal of the season. But Fergie is still smiling as he signs a new four-year £5 million deal, and reputedly becomes Britain's highest-paid manager.

An explosive Anfield encounter sees ex-United player Paul Ince net a very late equaliser, in the 89th minute, after Denis Irwin is sent off, a quarter of an hour after his penalty puts United 2–0 up. Alex Ferguson blames referee David Elleray: nothing new there, then. Arsenal benefit and close in on the championship by beating Spurs.

Shortly after Fergie's attack on David Elleray comes the news that there is a proposal for Premier League referees to be driven to and from games in 'safe' cars.

Southampton win their second game in succession, against Wimbledon, to move out of the relegation zone. Already relegated, Nottingham Forest stun Blackburn to pull Rovers one place closer to the drop and Charlton give themselves hope as they top the bottom three thanks to a Danny Mills free-kick winner in a seven-goal extravaganza at Villa Park.

Manchester United regain top spot with a victory over Middlesbrough while the most significant result of the season occurs at Leeds, where Jimmy Floyd Hasselbaink ends Arsenal's 19-match unbeaten run and virtually sends the Premiership trophy back to Old Trafford.

Blackburn hold United at Ewood Park but a point is not enough and the Premiership winners of 1995 are relegated. They are the first team to achieve the dubious distinction of having both won the Premiership title and been relegated from the league. There is a tense end to the title race as United then beat Spurs to claim the championship by a single point: had Tottenham managed to equalise they would have enabled Arsenal to retain their title thanks to the win over Aston Villa.

It is Alex Ferguson's fifth Premiership title and Chelsea claim third place, their highest finish in 29 years, with a home win over Derby. At the other end of the table Charlton go into the final day needing a home win over Sheffield Wednesday and hoping that Southampton will slip up at the Dell, against Everton. Neither happens so it is a swift return to Division One for the Addicks. Southampton's win over Everton completes the club's fourth final-day escape from relegation in the last six years.

FACT FILE

Kevin Campbell hits a hat-trick in Everton's win over West Ham and becomes the first player to score a Premiership hat-trick for three different clubs. Arsenal and Nottingham Forest are the others.

End of season round-up

Top Premiership Goalscorers 1998–99

Dwight Yorke	Manchester United	18
Michael Owen	Liverpool	18
Jimmy Floyd Hasselbaink	Leeds United	18
Andy Cole	Manchester United	17
Nicolas Anelka	Arsenal	17
Hamilton Ricard	Middlesbrough	15
Alan Shearer	Newcastle United	14
Robbie Fowler	Liverpool	14
Julian Joachim	Aston Villa	14
Dion Dublin	Aston Villa	14
(3 for Coventry)		

Worthington League Cup

Tottenham Hotspur 1   Leicester City 0
Wembley served up another disappointing League Cup Final, the first under new sponsorship, and Spurs' victory was the first trophy won under new manager George Graham. Justin Edinburgh was sent off just past the hour mark but Leicester failed to make their numerical advantage pay and the game looked to be heading for extra-time for the second successive year when Allan Nielsen threw himself full-length to head home the winner in stoppage time.

FA Cup Final

Manchester United 2   Newcastle United 0
Manchester United skipper Roy Keane limped out of the final after just nine minutes, but his replacement Teddy Sheringham turned the game when he scored two minutes after coming on, after being set up by Paul Scholes, to become only the sixth scoring substitute in an FA Cup Final. Newcastle tried hard to get back into the game with a second-half revival but it was Fergie's team that clinched the game. The same two players who were involved in the opening goal swapped roles and Sheringham set up Scholes for the winning strike. United achieved their second double and stage two of their historic treble – they added the European Cup four days later.

FWA Footballer of the Year

David Ginola   Tottenham Hotspur

PFA Player of the Year

David Ginola   Tottenham Hotspur

PFA Young Player of the Year

Nicolas Anelka   Arsenal

Manager of the Year

Sir Alex Ferguson   Manchester United

Close Season 1999

Liverpool sign Finnish international Sammy Hyypia, for £3.25 million, from Dutch club Willem II. Derby pay a club-record £3 million for Crewe's Seth Johnson, a deal delayed by the midfielder wanting to remain with the Cheshire club to help them avoid relegation from Division One, which they achieve.

Joe Kinnear, the game's fourth longest-serving manager, leaves Wimbledon after seven years.

Manchester United complete the free transfer signing of Mark Bosnich from Aston Villa, who then sign David James as the Australian's replacement.

Alex Ferguson receives his knighthood in the Queens' Birthday Honours list.

Chelsea's Gianluca Vialli retires from the 'player' part of his player-manager role. 'Luca' then signs Marion Melchiot from Ajax on a Bosman free.

Premiership referees are to get a pay-rise, of £200 to £600 per match.

Liverpool break the British transfer record for a goalkeeper when they pay £4 million to Vitesse Arnhem for Sander Westerveldt. Chelsea pay £3 million for France's World Cup-winning captain Didier Deschamps, who signs a three-year deal. Chelsea pay the third-largest fee, among British clubs, of £10 million when they sign Chris Sutton from Blackburn Rovers. Manager Vialli's spending, on nine players, is now more than £22 million.

Steve Bould, part of the legendary Arsenal 'back five', leaves Highbury after 11 years to sign for Sunderland.

Gerard Houllier tells Paul Ince he has no future at Anfield.

Newcastle sign Kieron Dyer, from Ipswich, for £6 million and then sell Dietmar Hamann to Liverpool for £7.5 million.

The Charity Shield is won by Arsenal after they come back from a goal down to beat Manchester United. Manchester United players had held a sweepstake for the team that would end their 33-game unbeaten run – it isn't known who drew Arsenal.

Arsenal pay £10 million to Juventus for 21-year-old French World Cup-winner Thierry Henry, on a five-year deal.

Manchester United manager Alex Ferguson gives a thumbs-up to the crowd.

Saturday 7 August	
Arsenal v. Leicester City	2-1
Chelsea v. Sunderland	4-0
Coventry City v. Southampton	0-1
Leeds United v. Derby County	0-0
Middlesbrough v. Bradford City	0-1
Newcastle United v. Aston Villa	0-1
Sheffield Wed. v. Liverpool	1-2
Watford v. Wimbledon	2-3
West Ham United v. Tottenham Hotspur	1-0

Sunday 8 August	
Everton v. Manchester United	1-1

Monday 9 August	
Tottenham Hotspur v. Newcastle United	3-1

Tuesday 10 August	
Derby County v. Arsenal	1-2
Sunderland v. Watford	2-0
Wimbledon v. Middlesbrough	2-3

Wednesday 11 August	
Aston Villa v. Everton	3-0
Leicester City v. Coventry City	1-0
Manchester United v. Sheffield Wed.	4-0
Southampton v. Leeds United	0-3

Saturday 14 August	
Bradford City v. Sheffield Wed.	1-1
Derby County v. Middlesbrough	1-3
Leicester City v. Chelsea	2-2
Liverpool v. Watford	0-1
Manchester United v. Leeds United	2-0
Sunderland v. Arsenal	0-0
Tottenham Hotspur v. Everton	3-2
Wimbledon v. Coventry City	1-1

Sunday 15 August	
Southampton v. Newcastle United	4-2

Monday 16 August	
Aston Villa v. West Ham United	2-2

Saturday 21 August	
Chelsea v. Aston Villa	1-0
Coventry City v. Derby County	2-0
Everton v. Southampton	4-1
Leeds United v. Sunderland	2-1
Middlesbrough v. Liverpool	1-0
Newcastle United v. Wimbledon	3-3
Sheffield Wed. v. Tottenham Hotspur	1-2
Watford v. Bradford City	1-0
West Ham United v. Leicester City	2-1

Sunday 22 August	
Arsenal v. Manchester United	1-2

Monday 23 August	
Leeds United v. Liverpool	1-2

Tuesday 24 August	
Middlesbrough v. Leicester City	0-3
Watford v. Aston Villa	0-1

Wednesday 25 August	
Arsenal v. Bradford City	2-0
Coventry City v. Manchester United	1-2
Everton v. Wimbledon	4-0
Newcastle United v. Sunderland	1-2
Sheffield Wed. v. Derby County	0-2

Saturday 28 August	
Aston Villa v. Middlesbrough	1-0
Bradford City v. West Ham United	0-3
Derby County v. Everton	1-0
Liverpool v. Arsenal	2-0
Southampton v. Sheffield Wed.	2-0
Tottenham Hotspur v. Leeds United	1-2
Wimbledon v. Chelsea	0-1

Sunday 29 August	
Sunderland v. Coventry City	1-1

Monday 30 August	
Leicester City v. Watford	1-0
Manchester United v. Newcastle United	5-1

		P	W	D	L	F	A	Pts
1	Manchester United	6	5	1	0	16	4	16
2	Aston Villa	6	4	1	1	8	3	13
3	Chelsea	4	3	1	0	8	2	10
4	West Ham United	4	3	1	0	8	3	10
5	Leicester City	6	3	1	2	9	6	10
6	Leeds United	6	3	1	2	8	6	10
7	Arsenal	6	3	1	2	7	6	10
8	Tottenham Hotspur	5	3	0	2	9	7	9
9	Liverpool	5	3	0	2	6	4	9
10	Southampton	5	3	0	2	8	9	9
11	Middlesbrough	6	3	0	3	7	8	9
12	Sunderland	6	2	2	2	6	8	8
13	Everton	6	2	1	3	11	9	7
14	Derby County	6	2	1	3	5	7	7
15	Watford	6	2	0	4	4	7	6
16	Coventry City	6	1	2	3	5	6	5
17	Wimbledon	6	1	2	3	9	14	5
18	Bradford City	5	1	1	3	2	7	4
19	Newcastle United	6	0	1	5	8	18	1
20	Sheffield Wed.	6	0	1	5	3	13	1

THE NEW season begins with a staggering statistic. The number of foreign players has risen from nine on the opening day of the first Premiership season, to 65 just seven years later.

Chelsea stun new boys Sunderland, with all the goals coming from overseas players. In fact, of the 21 goals on the first day of this campaign, 12 are scored by foreign players.

Champions Manchester United are held at Everton while Arsenal beat Leicester thanks to the only own-goal of the opening day, from Frank Sinclair, in the 90th minute.

Bradford open their Premiership account with a Dean Saunders winner at Middlesbrough in the Bantams' first top-flight fixture for 77 years. The third promoted club, Watford, lose to Wimbledon. There's a first career red card for Alan Shearer – not the best way to mark his 100th start for Newcastle – as Villa win at St James' Park.

Manchester United are held at Goodison, where a Jaap Stam own-goal, four minutes from time, robs the champions of victory.

A Dennis Bergkamp winner at Derby makes it two wins out of two for the Gunners.

Manchester United win their first game and Dwight Yorke scores for the second game running as Sheffield Wednesday are trounced. United join Arsenal, who can only draw at Sunderland, as leaders when Dwight Yorke's brace beats Leeds.

Only days after receiving a 'vote of confidence', Ruud Gullit's tenure looks increasingly fragile as Newcastle are ripped apart by Southampton and drop to the bottom of the table while the Saints go sixth.

Derby fall to 17th after losing to Middlesbrough and Everton are one place below when they lose at Spurs, despite being 2–1 ahead until the 82nd minute.

Aston Villa are just seconds away from going top of the table but Trevor Sinclair thwarts them with a 90th-minute equaliser for West Ham.

19-year-old Robbie Keane leaves Wolves for Coventry and becomes the most expensive teenager at £6 million. He makes a two-goal debut as the Sky Blues beat Derby County.

Chelsea benefit from an own-goal for the second match running as a Ugo Ehiogu own-goal takes them fourth. Everton leap from 18th to 14th after thrashing Southampton for a first win of the campaign. Only one place better off are Merseyside neighbours Liverpool, who are 17th after defeat by Middlesbrough, a result that takes 'Boro third. Newcastle replace Everton in the bottom three when they surrender a 3–1 lead and concede a 90th-minute goal to draw with Wimbledon. Sheffield Wednesday prop up the table after losing to Spurs.

Arsenal plummet to eighth after losing to Manchester United, who reinforce top spot with a rare brace from Roy Keane, which means a first Highbury defeat for the Gunners since December 1997.

The Alan Shearer–Ruud Gullit power struggle comes to a head as the Newcastle striker is benched for the Tyne-Tees derby, which Sunderland win. Three days later the Dutchman quits as manager at St James' Park after losing more games than he won: 21 against 18. Steve Clarke takes temporary control and in his first game Newcastle are thrashed by Manchester United and ex-Magpie Andy Cole nets four, the last three coming after Nicos Dabizas is sent off. Even the Magpies' consolation goal comes from United's Henning Berg.

Derby record a first win when they take the points at Sheffield Wednesday, and the Owls stay 20th, behind Bradford and Newcastle in 18th and 19th respectively.

FACT FILE

Bradford's 'Dad's Army' side contains a host of players in their thirties. Goalscorer Dean Saunders (35) is three months older than his manager Paul Jewell, 34. The others making Bradford the oldest team in the Premiership are: Neil Redfern, 34; John Dreyer, 36; Gunnar Halle, 33; Peter Beagrie, 33; Gary Walsh, 31; Wayne Jacobs, 30; Dean Windass, 30. Stuart McCall, 35, is kept out by injury until the fourth game, when he replaces Redfern.

Unhappy Alan Shearer, benched by Ruud Gullit as Newcastle crash to Sunderland.

September

Saturday 11 September	
Arsenal v. Aston Villa	3-1
Chelsea v. Newcastle United	1-0
Coventry City v. Leeds United	3-4
Liverpool v. Manchester United	2-3
Middlesbrough v. Southampton	3-2
Sheffield Wed. v. Everton	0-2
Sunderland v. Leicester City	2-0
West Ham United v. Watford	1-0
Wimbledon v. Derby County	2-2

Sunday 12 September	
Bradford City v. Tottenham Hotspur	1-1

Saturday 18 September	
Aston Villa v. Bradford City	1-0
Derby County v. Sunderland	0-5
Leicester City v. Liverpool	2-2
Manchester United v. Wimbledon	1-1
Southampton v. Arsenal	0-1
Watford v. Chelsea	1-0

Sunday 19 September	
Everton v. West Ham United	1-0
Leeds United v. Middlesbrough	2-0
Newcastle United v. Sheffield Wed.	8-0
Tottenham Hotspur v. Coventry City	3-2

Saturday 25 September	
Arsenal v. Watford	1-0
Coventry City v. West Ham United	1-0
Derby County v. Bradford City	0-1
Leeds United v. Newcastle United	3-2
Leicester City v. Aston Villa	3-1
Manchester United v. Southampton	3-3
Middlesbrough v. Chelsea	0-1
Sunderland v. Sheffield Wed.	1-0

Sunday 26 September	
Wimbledon v. Tottenham Hotspur	1-1

Monday 27 September	
Liverpool v. Everton	0-1

		P	W	D	L	F	A	Pts
1	Manchester United	9	6	3	0	23	10	21
2	Leeds United	9	6	1	2	17	11	19
3	Arsenal	9	6	1	2	12	7	19
4	Sunderland	9	5	2	2	14	8	17
5	Chelsea	7	5	1	1	10	3	16
6	Everton	9	5	1	3	15	9	16
7	Aston Villa	9	5	1	3	11	9	16
8	Tottenham Hotspur	8	4	2	2	14	11	14
9	Leicester City	9	4	2	3	14	11	14
10	West Ham United	7	4	1	2	9	5	13
11	Middlesbrough	9	4	0	5	10	13	12
12	Liverpool	8	3	1	4	10	10	10
13	Southampton	8	3	1	4	13	16	10
14	Watford	9	3	0	6	5	9	9
15	Coventry City	9	2	2	5	11	13	8
16	Wimbledon	9	1	5	3	13	18	8
17	Bradford City	8	2	2	4	4	9	8
18	Derby County	9	2	2	5	7	15	8
19	Newcastle United	9	1	1	7	18	22	4
20	Sheffield Wed.	9	0	1	8	3	24	1

BOTTOM-of-the-table Newcastle unveil 66-year-old Bobby Robson as their new manager, but the contract is only until the end of the season.

Mikael Silvestre snubs Liverpool in preference to Manchester United and signs for £3.2 million from Inter Milan. His arrival softens, somewhat, the blow of the administrative error that means the other new arrival at Old Trafford, £4.5 million Italian goalkeeper Massimo Taibi, wasn't signed in time for the opening games in the Champions League.

The electronic age arrives in the Premiership as match officials are wired up with two-way communications.

West Ham's win over Watford, which takes them third, is marred by Stuart Pearce breaking that famous left leg. Manchester United win the battle of the reds when a couple of Jamie Carragher own-goals, at either end of the first half, put the leaders in the driving seat at Anfield. Liverpool slump to 12th. Arsenal move up a place, to fifth, after beating Aston Villa.

Sheffield Wednesday lose, for the seventh time in eight outings, to Everton, and still prop up the Premiership. Newcastle's sixth reverse, in seven games, leaves them just one place higher, and Bradford draw with Spurs but stay 18th.

Former Liverpool and England full-back Rob Jones is forced into retirement, at 27, after four knee operations.

After the intervention of Prime Minister Tony Blair Juninho finally gets his work permit.

Manchester United are just 17 minutes away from defeat by Wimbledon until substitute Jordi Cruyff rescues a point and keeps United top. Chelsea slump to sixth after a shock Watford win due to Alan Smart's first goal of the season, but Thierry Henry's first goal for Arsenal beats Southampton and takes the Gunners third.

Bottom club Sheffield Wednesday are on the receiving end of Newcastle's pent-up frustrations and are hammered at St James' Park, where Alan Shearer nets five goals, including two penalties. But the Magpies stay 19th, despite the club's biggest win since 1946. Bradford lose to Villa and remain 18th.

Manchester United are lucky to escape with a home draw against Southampton, after an error-prone performance from goalkeeper Massimo Taibi. It's the first time the Saints have emerged from Old Trafford without defeat in 11 visits. United stay top but second-placed Arsenal reduce the gap with victory over Watford.

Derby slump into the bottom three when they lose to Bradford, who move up to 17th, due to a Horatio Carbonari own-goal. Newcastle, despite a brace from Alan Shearer, making it seven goals in two games for him, lose to Leeds and remain 19th while Sheffield Wednesday's sixth consecutive reverse keeps them bottom.

A stormy affair at Anfield sees Everton triumph in the Merseyside derby, thanks to an early Kevin Campbell goal. Liverpool have Steven Gerrard and Sandor Westerveld sent off. Steve Staunton dons the 'keeper's gloves and Everton striker Francis Jeffers is also red-carded.

> **FACT FILE**
>
> Len Shackleton scored six goals on his Newcastle debut, in the 13–0 win over Newport County, on Saturday 5 October 1946.

Sunderland's Kevin Phillips clips the ball past Derby County goalkeeper Russell Hoult to net the first goal of his hat-trick.

October

Saturday 2 October		
Aston Villa v. Liverpool		0-0
Bradford City v. Sunderland		0-4
Everton v. Coventry City		1-1
Sheffield Wed. v. Wimbledon		5-1
Sunday 3 October		
Chelsea v. Manchester United		5-0
Newcastle United v. Middlesbrough		2-1
Tottenham Hotspur v. Leicester City		2-3
Watford v. Leeds United		1-2
West Ham United v. Arsenal		2-1
Monday 4 October		
Southampton v. Derby County		3-3
Saturday 16 October		
Arsenal v. Everton		4-1
Coventry City v. Newcastle United		4-1
Derby County v. Tottenham Hotspur		0-1
Leeds United v. Sheffield Wed.		2-0
Leicester City v. Southampton		2-1
Liverpool v. Chelsea		1-0
Manchester United v. Watford		4-1
Wimbledon v. Bradford City		3-2
Sunday 17 October		
Middlesbrough v. West Ham United		2-0
Monday 18 October		
Sunderland v. Aston Villa		2-1
Saturday 23 October		
Aston Villa v. Wimbledon		1-1
Bradford City v. Leicester City		3-1
Chelsea v. Arsenal		2-3
Sheffield Wed. v. Coventry City		0-0
Southampton v. Liverpool		1-1
Tottenham Hotspur v. Manchester United		3-1
Sunday 24 October		
Everton v. Leeds United		4-4
Watford v. Middlesbrough		1-3
West Ham United v. Sunderland		1-1
Monday 25 October		
Newcastle United v. Derby County		2-0
Wednesday 27 October		
Liverpool v. West Ham United		1-0
Saturday 30 October		
Arsenal v. Newcastle United		0-0
Derby County v. Chelsea		3-1
Leeds United v. West Ham United		1-0
Leicester City v. Sheffield Wed.		3-0
Manchester United v. Aston Villa		3-0
Middlesbrough v. Everton		2-1
Wimbledon v. Southampton		1-1
Sunday 31 October		
Coventry City v. Watford		4-0
Sunderland v. Tottenham Hotspur		2-1

		P	W	D	L	F	A	Pts
1	Leeds United	13	9	2	2	26	16	29
2	Manchester United	13	8	3	2	31	19	27
3	Sunderland	13	8	3	2	23	11	27
4	Arsenal	13	8	2	3	20	12	26
5	Leicester City	13	7	2	4	23	17	23
6	Middlesbrough	13	7	0	6	18	17	21
7	Tottenham Hotspur	12	6	2	4	21	17	20
8	Chelsea	11	6	1	4	18	10	19
9	Everton	13	5	3	5	22	20	18
10	Liverpool	12	5	3	4	13	11	18
11	Aston Villa	13	5	3	5	13	15	18
12	West Ham United	12	5	2	5	12	11	17
13	Coventry City	13	4	4	5	20	15	16
14	Southampton	12	3	4	5	19	23	13
15	Wimbledon	13	2	7	4	19	27	13
16	Derby County	13	3	3	7	13	22	12
17	Newcastle United	13	3	2	8	23	27	11
18	Bradford City	11	3	2	6	9	17	11
19	Watford	13	3	0	10	8	22	9
20	Sheffield Wed.	13	1	2	10	8	30	5

Leeds United's Alan Smith rounds the Sheffield Wednesday goalkeeper Pavel Srnicek to score their opening goal.

SUNDERLAND move up to third as in-form striker Kevin Phillips takes his goal tally to 10, to lead the Premiership scoring chart, with a brace that helps sink struggling Bradford and drop the Bantams to 18th. Sheffield Wednesday finally secure a first victory of the campaign, and end their run of six consecutive defeats, with a shock win over Wimbledon, although they stay bottom. A pair of Alan Shearer goals, taking his total to nine in just three games, is enough to beat Middlesbrough but Newcastle stay 19th.

Chelsea crush Manchester United, who have Nicky Butt sent off midway through the first half. Gus Poyet hits the first of his two goals with just 27 seconds on the clock. Chelsea go fourth and pull United down a peg to second as Leeds United take over at the top with a win at Watford in which Harry Kewell scores for the third game in a row.

Chelsea have Marcel Desailly and Dennis Wise, for the ninth time in his Stamford Bridge career, sent off as they drop to sixth after losing at Liverpool. Dwight Yorke nets his 10th goal of the season as Manchester United beat Watford to stay second but Leeds United retain top spot with a sixth consecutive win, with two Alan Smith goals,

FACT FILE

Wendy Toms, the only female assistant referee in the Premiership, became violently sick and had to be replaced at the Aston Villa–Liverpool game. The reason was an adverse reaction to her ear-piece, for communication between the match officials, which had caused inner-ear damage.

that keeps Sheffield Wednesday bottom. Arsenal move up to third when they thump Everton with Lee Dixon netting his first goal since 1996.

Newcastle are crushed at Coventry to remain 19th and Bradford are one place higher after losing to Wimbledon, a first win since the opening day of the campaign for the Dons.

London's top two teams meet at Stamford Bridge where a Kanu hat-trick, in the last 15 minutes, overturns a Chelsea lead to take the Gunners third and push the home side down to seventh. At White Hart Lane Spurs dent Manchester United's title aspirations with a win that pushes them up to fifth and pulls the champions down to fourth.

Leeds are just seconds away from extending their club

record winning sequence to 11 games, six in the league, but are denied by David Weir's 90th-minute equaliser at Goodison Park, although David O'Leary's team stay top. Sunderland miss out on the chance of heading the table when a Trevor Sinclair equaliser, in the 89th minute, prevents Kevin Phillips's 13th goal of the season beating West Ham. Having Steve Bould sent off, after 19 minutes, doesn't help the Black Cats' cause.

Newcastle move out of the relegation zone, for the first time, by beating Derby County. Titi Camara scores the winner for Liverpool against West Ham, just a few hours after learning of the death of his father and declining the club's offer of compassionate leave.

Leeds maintain leadership of the Premiership with victory over West Ham. Arsenal slump to fourth after they are held by Newcastle, who claim their first away point of the season and move up to 17th. Manchester United beat Aston Villa to go second.

Sunderland confirm third place with a Niall Quinn brace beating Tottenham, while struggling Sheffield Wednesday lose their fifth away game in a row, at Leicester, who move up to fifth, to stay rooted to the bottom.

November

Monday 1 November	
Liverpool v. Bradford City	3-1

Saturday 6 November	
Aston Villa v. Southampton	0-1
Bradford City v. Coventry City	1-1
Liverpool v. Derby County	2-0
Manchester United v. Leicester City	2-0
Middlesbrough v. Sunderland	1-1
Sheffield Wed. v. Watford	2-2

Sunday 7 November	
Chelsea v. West Ham United	0-0
Newcastle United v. Everton	1-1
Tottenham Hotspur v. Arsenal	2-1
Wimbledon v. Leeds United	2-0

Saturday 20 November	
Arsenal v. Middlesbrough	5-1
Derby County v. Manchester United	1-2
Everton v. Chelsea	1-1
Leeds United v. Bradford City	2-1
Leicester City v. Wimbledon	2-1
Southampton v. Tottenham Hotspur	0-1
Sunderland v. Liverpool	0-2
Watford v. Newcastle United	1-1

Sunday 21 November	
West Ham United v. Sheffield Wed.	4-3

Monday 22 November	
Coventry City v. Aston Villa	2-1

Saturday 27 November	
Coventry City v. Leicester City	0-1
Everton v. Aston Villa	0-0
Middlesbrough v. Wimbledon	0-0
Watford v. Sunderland	2-3
West Ham United v. Liverpool	1-0

Sunday 28 November	
Arsenal v. Derby County	2-1
Chelsea v. Bradford City	1-0
Leeds United v. Southampton	1-0
Newcastle United v. Tottenham Hotspur	2-1

		P	W	D	L	F	A	Pts
1	Leeds United	16	11	2	3	29	19	35
2	Manchester United	15	10	3	2	35	20	33
3	Arsenal	16	10	2	4	28	16	32
4	Sunderland	16	9	4	3	27	16	31
5	Leicester City	16	9	2	5	26	20	29
6	Liverpool	16	8	3	5	20	13	27
7	Tottenham Hotspur	15	8	2	5	25	20	26
8	Chelsea	14	7	3	4	20	11	24
9	West Ham United	15	7	3	5	17	14	24
10	Middlesbrough	16	7	2	7	20	23	23
11	Everton	16	5	6	5	24	22	21
12	Coventry City	16	5	5	6	23	18	20
13	Aston Villa	16	5	4	7	14	18	19
14	Wimbledon	16	3	8	5	22	29	17
15	Newcastle United	16	4	4	8	27	30	16
16	Southampton	15	4	4	7	20	25	16
17	Bradford City	15	3	3	9	12	24	12
18	Derby County	16	3	3	10	15	28	12
19	Watford	16	3	2	11	13	28	11
20	Sheffield Wed.	15	1	3	11	13	36	6

Leeds United's Michael Bridges' 90th-minute winner beats Southampton for Leeds to resume pole position.

GARY WILLARD becomes the first referee to be dropped by the Premier League for failing a fitness test.

Manchester United go top of the table with an Andy Cole brace that beats Leicester. A record Riverside crowd of 34,793 sees a bad-tempered Middlesbrough-Sunderland derby in which there are 11 bookings and the Black Cats' Chris Makin is dismissed, but the visitors stay third.

Sheffield Wednesday start a third consecutive month on the bottom as they draw with Watford, who stay 19th. Derby slump into the bottom three, 18th, with defeat at Anfield, where they haven't kept a clean sheet for 29 years. Liverpool move up to fifth.

Leeds are knocked off the top when they lose for the first time since the end of August, at Wimbledon, who keep a clean sheet for the first time in 29 matches. Arsenal miss the chance of gaining ground when they lose a bad-tempered North London derby to Spurs. The Gunners have six booked and Martin Keown and Freddie Ljungberg are sent off.

Newcastle continue their climb up the table when Alan Shearer's 13th goal in 11 matches, a penalty, earns a draw with Everton that takes the Magpies up to 16th, their highest placing of the campaign.

Manchester United receive a cash boost from Highbury when Croatian striker Davor Suker, a player on the stock market, reveals he has made a £20,000 investment in the Old Trafford club. Arsenal could perhaps have done with the money, as they announce plans to move to a new purpose-built stadium at Ashburton Grove.

Leeds get back to winning ways with victory over Bradford that keeps them second, behind Manchester United, who beat Derby to keep the Rams 18th and hold on to top place. Bradford stay just outside the drop zone. Arsenal hit their highest score of the season to crush Middlesbrough and move up to third, helped by a Marc Overmars hat-trick. Dennis

Bergkamp's brace puts him on the scoresheet for the first time since the second game of the campaign.

Sheffield Wednesday twice lead against West Ham but lose to remain bottom of the Premiership and have Danny Sonner red-carded.

The day after Roma coach Fabio Capello brands Alan Shearer a 'diver', Michael Owen is cautioned for diving in Liverpool's defeat at West Ham, which lifts the Hammers into ninth place and drops Liverpool one place to sixth. Sunderland move up to third as a couple of goals from ex-Hornets striker Kevin Phillips earn Sunderland victory at Watford and keep the home side 19th.

Michael Bridges nets his 10th goal of the season to beat Southampton and take Leeds back to the top of the table and a Thierry Henry brace that beats Derby County keeps the Gunners third and the Rams 18th. Bradford's defeat at Stamford Bridge, which keeps them 17th, is a first win in seven for Chelsea, who move up a place to eighth.

December

Saturday 4 December

Aston Villa v. Newcastle United	0-1
Bradford City v. Middlesbrough	1-1
Leicester City v. Arsenal	0-3
Manchester United v. Everton	5-1
Southampton v. Coventry City	0-0
Sunderland v. Chelsea	4-1
Wimbledon v. Watford	5-0

Sunday 5 December

Derby County v. Leeds United	0-1
Liverpool v. Sheffield Wed.	4-1

Monday 6 December

Tottenham Hotspur v. West Ham United	0-0

Saturday 18 December

Arsenal v. Wimbledon	1-1
Aston Villa v. Sheffield Wed.	2-1
Bradford City v. Newcastle United	2-0
Leicester City v. Derby County	0-1
Liverpool v. Coventry City	2-0
Middlesbrough v. Tottenham Hotspur	2-1
Sunderland v. Southampton	2-0
Watford v. Everton	1-3
West Ham United v. Manchester United	2-4

Sunday 19 December

Chelsea v. Leeds United	0-2

Sunday 26 December

Coventry City v. Arsenal	3-2
Derby County v. Aston Villa	0-2
Everton v. Sunderland	5-0
Leeds United v. Leicester City	2-1
Manchester United v. Bradford City	4-0
Newcastle United v. Liverpool	2-2
Sheffield Wed. v. Middlesbrough	1-0
Southampton v. Chelsea	1-2
Tottenham Hotspur v. Watford	4-0
Wimbledon v. West Ham United	2-2

Tuesday 28 December

Arsenal v. Leeds United	2-0
Bradford City v. Everton	0-0
Leicester City v. Newcastle United	1-2
Liverpool v. Wimbledon	3-1
Sunderland v. Manchester United	2-2
Watford v. Southampton	3-2
West Ham United v. Derby County	1-1

Wednesday 29 December

Aston Villa v. Tottenham Hotspur	1-1
Chelsea v. Sheffield Wed.	3-0

		P	W	D	L	F	A	Pts
1	Leeds United	20	14	2	4	34	22	44
2	Manchester United	19	13	4	2	50	25	43
3	Arsenal	20	12	3	5	36	20	39
4	Sunderland	20	11	5	4	35	24	38
5	Liverpool	20	11	4	5	31	17	37
6	Tottenham Hotspur	19	9	4	6	31	23	31
7	Chelsea	18	9	3	6	26	18	30
8	Leicester City	20	9	2	9	28	28	29
9	Everton	20	7	7	6	33	28	28
10	West Ham United	19	7	6	6	22	21	27
11	Middlesbrough	19	8	3	8	23	26	27
12	Aston Villa	20	7	5	8	19	21	26
13	Coventry City	19	6	6	7	26	22	24
14	Newcastle United	20	6	5	9	32	35	23
15	Wimbledon	20	4	10	6	31	35	22
16	Southampton	19	4	5	10	23	32	17
17	Bradford City	19	4	5	10	15	29	17
18	Derby County	20	4	4	12	17	32	16
19	Watford	20	4	2	14	17	42	14
20	Sheffield Wed.	19	2	3	14	16	45	9

MANCHESTER UNITED crush Everton and are second, with Ole Gunnar Solskjaer becoming the second United player, this campaign, to hit four goals in a game. Sunderland hit their highest score of the season in avenging their opening day defeat at Chelsea with a pair of goals each for Niall Quinn and Kevin Phillips, who takes his tally to 17, but the Black Cats are static in fourth place. Arsenal are one place higher after beating Leicester, who drop to sixth. Watford suffer their worst defeat of the season, at Wimbledon, and remain 19th.

Leeds retain top spot but it takes a stoppage-time Ian Harte penalty to win at Derby, who stay 18th as a consequence. Sheffield Wednesday concede four goals for the second match running as they are crushed at Liverpool, after taking a 1–0 lead in just 17 minutes. Midfielders Danny Murphy and Steven Gerrard net their first goals of the campaign as Liverpool climb a place to fifth leaving Wednesday rock-bottom.

Roy Keane breaks the £50,000 per week barrier when he signs a new four-year contract at Manchester United.

After the recent accusations about high-profile players Alan Shearer and Michael Owen diving, the players' union, the PFA, urges managers to stop their players from indulging in the practice.

Sunderland pay £2.5 million for West Brom winger Kevin Kilbane and another wingman, Jason Wilcox, leaves Blackburn for Leeds United in a £3 million transfer. Struggling Derby County pay Genk £3 million for striker Branko Strupar.

Off the field, Manchester United chairman Martin Edwards is quoted as saying that Alex Ferguson is a troublemaker and is useless with money!

Derby County win for the first time in five outings as Darryl Powell's first goal for three years earns a win over Leicester, but the Rams stay 18th. Sheffield Wednesday lose again, to Aston Villa, and continue to prop up the Premiership. The two strugglers still have Watford separating them after the Hornets lose to Everton. Villa then reveal that Dion Dublin broke his neck in the game at Villa Park.

At the other end of the table Arsenal lose ground and drop to fourth following the draw with Wimbledon while Manchester United go to town at West Ham with a brace each for Dwight Yorke and Ryan Giggs that keeps United second. Kevin Phillips scores two for the third game in a row as Sunderland beat Southampton and move back up to third. Liverpool's sixth consecutive Anfield victory, over Coventry, moves them up to fifth.

Leeds continue to head the Premiership when a pair of Stephen McPhail goals is too much for Chelsea, who have Frank Leboeuf sent off.

There's a Christmas Eve thespian takeover at Everton where former Coronation Street actor turned theatre impresario, Bill Kenwright, announces a £20 million deal to buy his beloved club from Peter Johnson.

Another takeover, of sorts, occurs at the Dell, where history is made when Chelsea face Southampton without a single British player in their starting line-up. Norwegian Tore Andre Flo scores twice to move Chelsea up a place to ninth. Above them Leeds maintain top spot with victory over Leicester and Manchester United crush Bradford with a four-goal blast in the last quarter of an hour to stay second. Sunderland remain third despite their shock hammering at Everton.

There's Boxing Day cheer for Sheffield Wednesday, who record their first win in eight games when a Peter Atherton goal beats Middlesbrough, but the Owls are still bottom. Watford's goals-against record rises to 12 in just three games when they are swamped at White Hart Lane. David Ginola is on the scoresheet for the first time in the campaign but he then sees the board showing number 11 and the Frenchman is substituted, for the 11th time, by manager George Graham.

Watford stay 19th and there's no Christmas joy for Derby, who are still 18th, for the second complete month, following defeat by Aston Villa.

A Stadium of Light record crowd of 42,026 sees Sunderland go 2–0 up against Manchester United inside 13 minutes. Roy Keane reduces the arrears but it takes an 86th-minute Nicky Butt goal to earn United a draw, which keeps them second and pushes Sunderland down a place to fourth.

Goals from Henry and Ljungberg end a winning run by Leeds, who field nine players under the age of 22 at Highbury. But David O'Leary's side stay top while the Gunners move up a slot to third.

Robbie Fowler nets his 150th goal for Liverpool as they beat Wimbledon but heir-apparent to Fowler's crown, Michael Owen, also nets for the third game running and Liverpool remain fifth.

Chelsea once again start a Premiership game with a 'foreign XI' but it takes Anglo-Saxon Dennis Wise, who replaces French World Cup-winning captain Didier Deschamps, to inspire the team to the victory over Sheffield Wednesday that means the Owls end the year bottom of the table.

January

Monday 3 January	
Derby County v. Watford	2-0
Everton v. Leicester City	2-2
Leeds United v. Aston Villa	1-2
Newcastle United v. West Ham United	2-2
Sheffield Wed. v. Arsenal	1-1
Southampton v. Bradford City	1-0
Tottenham Hotspur v. Liverpool	1-0
Wimbledon v. Sunderland	1-0
Tuesday 4 January	
Coventry City v. Chelsea	2-2
Saturday 8 January	
Bradford City v. Chelsea	1-1
Wednesday 12 January	
Chelsea v. Tottenham Hotspur	1-0
Saturday 15 January	
Arsenal v. Sunderland	4-1
Chelsea v. Leicester City	1-1
Coventry City v. Wimbledon	2-0
Everton v. Tottenham Hotspur	2-2
Middlesbrough v. Derby County	1-4
Sheffield Wed. v. Bradford City	2-0
Watford v. Liverpool	2-3
West Ham United v. Aston Villa	1-1
Sunday 16 January	
Newcastle United v. Southampton	5-0
Saturday 22 January	
Aston Villa v. Chelsea	0-0
Bradford City v. Watford	3-2
Derby County v. Coventry City	0-0
Leicester City v. West Ham United	1-3
Liverpool v. Middlesbrough	0-0
Southampton v. Everton	2-0
Tottenham Hotspur v. Sheffield Wed.	0-1
Wimbledon v. Newcastle United	2-0
Sunday 23 January	
Sunderland v. Leeds United	1-2
Monday 24 January	
Manchester United v. Arsenal	1-1
Saturday 29 January	
Manchester United v. Middlesbrough	1-0

		P	W	D	L	F	A	Pts
1	Manchester United	21	14	5	2	52	26	47
2	Leeds United	22	15	2	5	37	25	47
3	Arsenal	23	13	5	5	42	23	44
4	Liverpool	23	12	5	6	34	20	41
5	Sunderland	23	11	5	7	37	31	38
6	Chelsea	23	10	7	6	31	22	37
7	Tottenham Hotspur	23	10	5	8	34	27	35
8	West Ham United	22	8	8	6	28	25	32
9	Aston Villa	23	8	7	8	22	23	31
10	Leicester City	23	9	4	10	32	34	31
11	Everton	23	7	9	7	37	34	30
12	Coventry City	22	7	8	7	30	24	29
13	Wimbledon	23	6	10	7	34	37	28
14	Middlesbrough	22	8	4	10	24	31	28
15	Newcastle United	23	7	6	10	39	39	27
16	Derby County	23	6	5	12	23	33	23
17	Southampton	22	6	5	11	26	37	23
18	Bradford City	23	5	6	12	19	35	21
19	Sheffield Wed.	22	4	4	14	20	46	16
20	Watford	23	4	2	17	21	50	14

Manchester United's Jaap Stam (partially hidden), Nicky Butt, David Beckham and Roy Keane suround referee Andy D'Urso (l) after he had awarded a penalty against them.

THERE IS an interesting postscript to Dennis Wise's replacement of Didier Deschamps in the win over Sheffield Wednesday, as the Frenchman declares that Serie 'A' football is superior to the Premiership.

Leeds lose a second consecutive game, for the first time in the campaign, but stay top despite defeat at home to Aston Villa, for whom Gareth Southgate is a rare scorer, netting twice.

Branko Strupar scores twice for Derby County as they beat Watford to move out of the bottom three and keep the Hornets 19th. Bottom club Sheffield Wednesday claim a point against Arsenal and the clubs stay 20th and third respectively.

Chelsea are held at Bradford City, where a Lee Mills goal in the first minute looks like giving the Bantams a fifth home win of the season, but Dan Petrescu spoils that with a second-half equaliser that keeps City 18th.

George Weah joins Chelsea on a six-month loan, from AC Milan, and makes a dream start. He scores the winner against Spurs, three minutes from time, after his registration comes through only a few hours before kick-off.

As if Danny Wilson doesn't

have enough problems with his Sheffield Wednesday team propping up the Premiership, four Sheffield MPs call for him to be sacked!

Arsenal move second, level on points with Manchester United, when they thrash Sunderland with two goals apiece for Thierry Henry and Davor Suker. The Black Cats drop a place to fifth. Liverpool move up to fourth as Vladimir Smicer nets his first goal for the club in the victory at Watford that keeps the Hornets 19th.

Sheffield Wednesday win the basement battle against Bradford City but the Owls stay bottom, while the Bantams are two places higher. Watford are still sandwiched between the two Yorkshire clubs.

The League Managers' Association calls on the government to censure the four Sheffield MPs, David Blunkett, Joe Ashton, Clive Betts and Bill Michie, who are campaigning for the removal of Wednesday manager Danny Wilson.

There's controversy among Manchester United fans after the club's website announces Eric Cantona has pipped George Best as United's player of the 20th century.

Sheffield Wednesday climb off the bottom of the Premiership, for the first time

this campaign, by winning their first away game of the season at Spurs. Niklas Alexandersson is the goalscorer, for the second game running, as the Owls secure successive victories for the first time in the current season. Bradford win for the first time in six games against fellow-strugglers Watford and although the Bantams stay 18th defeat plunges the Hornets to the bottom of the Premiership, with 50 goals conceded.

Leeds stay top by beating Sunderland, who remain fifth. Liverpool only manage a draw with Middlesbrough but stay fourth.

The much-awaited clash between Arsenal and Manchester United ends all square at Old Trafford. The Gunners lead until the 73rd minute, through Freddie Ljungberg, but substitute Teddy Sheringham earns a point.

A record Premiership attendance of 61,267, at Old Trafford, sees Manchester United beat Middlesbrough with David Beckham's first goal of the season to go top, but the home side disgrace themselves by hounding referee Andy D'Urso for awarding 'Boro a penalty. It's the first time in six years a visiting side has been awarded a spot-kick at Old Trafford.

Wednesday 2 February

Sheffield Wed. v. Manchester United	0-1

Saturday 5 February

Aston Villa v. Watford	4-0
Bradford City v. Arsenal	2-1
Derby County v. Sheffield Wed.	3-3
Leicester City v. Middlesbrough	2-1
Liverpool v. Leeds United	3-1
Manchester United v. Coventry City	3-2
Southampton v. West Ham United	2-1
Sunderland v. Newcastle United	2-2
Tottenham Hotspur v. Chelsea	0-1

Sunday 6 February

Wimbledon v. Everton	0-3

Saturday 12 February

Chelsea v. Wimbledon	3-1
Coventry City v. Sunderland	3-2
Everton v. Derby County	2-1
Leeds United v. Tottenham Hotspur	1-0
Newcastle United v. Manchester United	3-0
Sheffield Wed. v. Southampton	0-1
Watford v. Leicester City	1-1
West Ham United v. Bradford City	5-4

Sunday 13 February

Arsenal v. Liverpool	0-1

Monday 14 February

Middlesbrough v. Aston Villa	0-4

Saturday 19 February

Middlesbrough v. Coventry City	2-0

Sunday 20 February

Leeds United v. Manchester United	0-1

Saturday 26 February

Arsenal v. Southampton	3-1
Bradford City v. Aston Villa	1-1
Chelsea v. Watford	2-1
Coventry City v. Tottenham Hotspur	0-1
Middlesbrough v. Leeds United	0-0
Sheffield Wed. v. Newcastle United	0-2
Sunderland v. Derby County	1-1
West Ham United v. Everton	0-4
Wimbledon v. Manchester United	2-2

		P	W	D	L	F	A	Pts
1	Manchester United	26	17	6	3	59	33	57
2	Leeds United	26	16	3	7	39	29	51
3	Arsenal	26	14	5	7	46	27	47
4	Liverpool	25	14	5	6	38	21	47
5	Chelsea	26	13	7	6	37	24	46
6	Sunderland	26	11	7	8	42	37	40
7	Everton	26	10	9	7	46	35	39
8	Aston Villa	26	10	8	8	31	24	38
9	Tottenham Hotspur	26	11	5	10	35	29	38
10	Leicester City	25	10	5	10	35	36	35
11	West Ham United	25	9	8	8	34	35	35
12	Newcastle United	26	9	7	10	46	41	34
13	Coventry City	26	8	8	10	35	32	32
14	Middlesbrough	26	9	5	12	27	37	32
15	Wimbledon	26	6	11	9	37	45	29
16	Southampton	25	8	5	12	30	41	29
17	Derby County	26	6	7	13	28	39	25
18	Bradford City	26	6	7	13	26	42	25
19	Sheffield Wed.	26	4	5	17	23	53	17
20	Watford	26	4	3	19	23	57	15

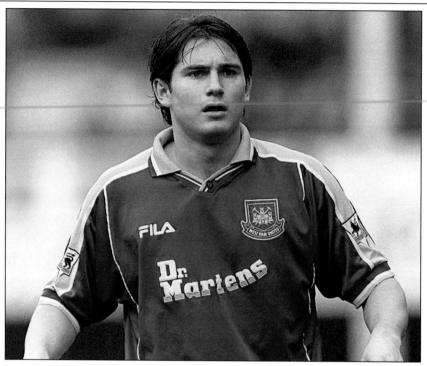

Frank Lampard, West Ham United.

SEVEN points from January's unbeaten run earns Sheffield Wednesday boss Danny Wilson Manager of the Month, while another manager, Chelsea's Gianluca Vialli, announces he is coming out of retirement and registers himself for European and domestic football.

The Manager of the Month 'curse' strikes again as Sheffield Wednesday are beaten by the leaders, Manchester United, who move three points clear of Leeds United with their first league victory at Hillsborough for seven years.

Arsenal lose ground in third place when they are beaten at struggling Bradford. It is the Gunners' first visit there since 1922, and Dean Saunders scores the winner with only his third goal of the campaign, but the Bantams stay in the bottom three. To make matters worse for Arsenal, Manchester United extend their lead at the top to six points with victory over Coventry and Liverpool's win over Leeds drops David O'Leary's side down to second

and consolidates fourth place for the Anfield outfit.

Manchester United lose at Newcastle and have Roy Keane sent off but they retain top place, ahead of Leeds, who beat Spurs.

Arsenal are beaten for a second successive game, for the first time this season, when Titi Camara's goal is enough to give Liverpool victory and the two clubs swap positions: Arsenal are now fourth, behind the Anfield club.

Upton Park goes goal crazy as the Hammers share nine goals with Bradford City. They come back from 4–2 down and Frank Lampard's 83rd-minute winner takes West Ham ninth and leaves City in 18th place. One place lower are Sheffield Wednesday, losers at Southampton. Watford, still seeking their first victory of the year, draw with Leicester and stay bottom.

Aston Villa extend their unbeaten run to eight games but a second successive 4–0 victory, over 'Boro, is marred by yet another self-inflicted Paul Gascoigne injury, as the former England star breaks his

left arm by elbowing George Boateng.

A number of Leicester City players are sent home from the La Manga complex after misbehaviour in which Stan Collymore lets off a fire extinguisher.

Following a training ground fall-out Alex Ferguson drops David Beckham from the top-of-the-table clash with Leeds United. Becks has to watch from the stands as an Andy Cole strike, his 100th for the club, proves the winner and extends the gap between the two Uniteds.

Manchester United retain top place despite being held by Wimbledon and Leeds stay second with a draw at the Riverside Stadium. Arsenal's victory over Southampton, the Gunners' first win in four games, takes them up a place to third.

Watford continue to prop up the table after losing at Chelsea, a 13th unbeaten game for Vialli's side. Sheffield Wednesday are a place higher when they lose to Newcastle and Bradford City complete the bottom trio despite drawing with Aston Villa.

Saturday 4 March

Derby County v. Wimbledon	4-0
Everton v. Sheffield Wed.	1-1
Manchester United v. Liverpool	1-1
Newcastle United v. Chelsea	0-1
Southampton v. Middlesbrough	1-1
Tottenham Hotspur v. Bradford City	1-1
Watford v. West Ham United	1-2

Sunday 5 March

Aston Villa v. Arsenal	1-1
Leeds United v. Coventry City	3-0
Leicester City v. Sunderland	5-2

Wednesday 8 March

West Ham United v. Southampton	2-0

Saturday 11 March

Aston Villa v. Coventry City	1-0
Chelsea v. Everton	1-1
Liverpool v. Sunderland	1-1
Manchester United v. Derby County	3-1
Newcastle United v. Watford	1-0
Sheffield Wed. v. West Ham United	3-1
Tottenham Hotspur v. Southampton	7-2
Wimbledon v. Leicester City	2-1

Sunday 12 March

Bradford City v. Leeds United	1-2
Middlesbrough v. Arsenal	2-1

Wednesday 15 March

Coventry City v. Everton	1-0
Liverpool v. Aston Villa	0-0

Saturday 18 March

Coventry City v. Bradford City	4-0
Derby County v. Liverpool	0-2
Leicester City v. Manchester United	0-2
Southampton v. Aston Villa	2-0
Sunderland v. Middlesbrough	1-1
Watford v. Sheffield Wed.	1-0
West Ham United v. Chelsea	0-0

Sunday 19 March

Arsenal v. Tottenham Hotspur	2-1
Everton v. Newcastle United	0-2
Leeds United v. Wimbledon	4-1

Saturday 25 March

Aston Villa v. Derby County	2-0
Bradford City v. Manchester United	0-4
Chelsea v. Southampton	1-1
Liverpool v. Newcastle United	2-1
Middlesbrough v. Sheffield Wed.	1-0
Sunderland v. Everton	2-1
Watford v. Tottenham Hotspur	1-1

Sunday 26 March

Arsenal v. Coventry City	3-0
Leicester City v. Leeds United	2-1
West Ham United v. Wimbledon	2-1

		P	W	D	L	F	A	Pts
1	Manchester United	30	20	7	3	69	35	67
2	Leeds United	30	19	3	8	49	33	60
3	Liverpool	30	16	8	6	44	24	56
4	Arsenal	30	16	6	8	53	31	54
5	Chelsea	30	14	10	6	40	26	52
6	Aston Villa	31	12	10	9	35	27	46
7	Sunderland	30	12	9	9	48	45	45
8	West Ham United	30	12	9	9	41	40	45
9	Tottenham Hotspur	30	12	7	11	45	35	43
10	Everton	31	10	11	10	49	42	41
11	Leicester City	29	12	5	12	43	43	41
12	Newcastle United	30	11	7	12	50	44	40
13	Middlesbrough	30	11	7	12	32	40	40
14	Coventry City	31	10	8	13	40	39	38
15	Southampton	30	9	7	14	36	52	34
16	Wimbledon	30	7	11	12	41	56	32
17	Derby County	30	7	7	16	33	46	28
18	Bradford City	30	6	8	16	28	53	26
19	Sheffield Wed.	30	5	6	19	27	57	21
20	Watford	30	5	4	21	26	61	19

Ed De Goey, Chelsea goalkeeper.

E D DE GOEY sets a new record of 22 when he keeps another clean sheet as Chelsea win at Newcastle and move up to third. Leeds brush aside Coventry and remain second while Manchester United are held by Liverpool but stay top and set another Premiership best attendance of 61,592.

Bradford stay top of the bottom three by drawing at Spurs and Derby improve their survival chances with a season's best score against Wimbledon that keeps them above the drop zone and pulls the Dons down to 16th, one place above the Rams. Sheffield Wednesday are still 19th after drawing with Everton and Watford remain rock bottom after losing to West Ham.

Sunderland's descent con-

tinues as they are rocked by a Stan Collymore hat-trick, a season's first for the Foxes, and fall to seventh.

Leeds close the gap on Manchester United to four points by beating Coventry, while Arsenal drop to fourth after a late Lee Dixon goal rescues a point against Aston Villa.

John Hartson's £6 million move from Wimbledon to Tottenham collapses when a medical reveals doubts over an old knee injury.

Stuart Pearce breaks his left leg for the second time in six months as West Ham beat Southampton.

Manchester United's value breaks the £1 billion barrier.

Emile Heskey becomes the third most expensive player to move between Premiership clubs when he leaves Leicester to join Liverpool for £11 million.

Dwight Yorke's first hat-trick of the campaign helps Manchester United beat Derby to retain top spot. Chelsea are held by Everton but remain third, while Liverpool draw at home to Sunderland, for whom Kevin Phillips nets his 25th goal of the season, a penalty, but the Black Cats' fall down the table continues and they are now ninth. Watford lose, for the 21st time in 28 league outings, to Newcastle and stay bottom. Sheffield Wednesday, despite winning for the first time in six games against West Ham, don't improve from 19th.

Leeds retain second place with victory over Bradford City, thanks to a brace of goals from Michael Bridges that takes his tally to 15, leaving the Bantams 18th. Goalkeeping coach Neville Southall, 41, is pressed into action for Bradford after their usual 'keeper Matt Clarke is injured, falling down the stairs at home.

Arsenal drop to fifth after they are beaten by Middles-

brough. Liverpool are unable to break down Aston Villa and a third consecutive draw dents Anfield aspirations of achieving a Champions League place and Michael Owen is substituted after missing a penalty. Everton lose to a late Gary McAllister goal, which is Coventry's first for more than 500 minutes.

It's business as usual for both Liverpool and Michael Owen as the Reds beat Derby County and disappoint the 350 die-hard members of the Branko Strupar fan club, who trek over to Anfield from Belgium. Goals from Owen – his first in nine games – and Titi Camara move the team up to third and keep the Rams just above the drop zone.

Things are looking bleaker for Bradford after they crash to Coventry, especially as Watford close the gap with an 89th-minute Alan Smart winner that wins the battle of the bottom two and keeps Sheffield Wednesday 19th.

Leeds crush Wimbledon and stay second and Arsenal move up to third by beating Spurs.

Wednesday boss Danny Wilson, the club's fourth manager in five years, pays the price for just five Premiership wins and is sacked.

Manchester United increase their lead at the top with a comprehensive win at Bradford that keeps the Bantams in the bottom three, 18th. Liverpool confirm third place with victory over Newcastle, thanks to an 88th-minute winner from substitute Jamie Redknapp.

Leeds' defeat at Leicester prompts David O'Leary to concede that Manchester United will win the championship.

Steve Ogrizovic, aged 42, deputies for Magnus Hedman in Coventry's defeat at Highbury that confirms the Gunners' fourth place.

April

Saturday 1 April	
Coventry City v. Liverpool	0-3
Everton v. Watford	4-2
Leeds United v. Chelsea	0-1
Manchester United v. West Ham United	7-1
Newcastle United v. Bradford City	2-0
Southampton v. Sunderland	1-2
Wimbledon v. Arsenal	1-3
Sunday 2 April	
Derby County v. Leicester City	3-0
Monday 3 April	
Tottenham Hotspur v. Middlesbrough	2-3
Wednesday 5 April	
Sheffield Wed. v. Aston Villa	0-1
Saturday 8 April	
Bradford City v. Southampton	1-2
Leicester City v. Everton	1-1
Sunderland v. Wimbledon	2-1
Watford v. Derby County	0-0
Sunday 9 April	
Aston Villa v. Leeds United	1-0
Liverpool v. Tottenham Hotspur	2-0
Monday 10 April	
Middlesbrough v. Manchester United	3-4
Wednesday 12 April	
Chelsea v. Coventry City	2-1
West Ham United v. Newcastle United	2-1
Wimbledon v. Sheffield Wed.	0-2
Saturday 15 April	
Coventry City v. Middlesbrough	2-1
Derby County v. West Ham United	1-2
Everton v. Bradford City	4-0
Manchester United v. Sunderland	4-0
Newcastle United v. Leicester City	0-2
Sheffield Wed. v. Chelsea	1-0
Southampton v. Watford	2-0
Tottenham Hotspur v. Aston Villa	2-4
Sunday 16 April	
Leeds United v. Arsenal	0-4
Wimbledon v. Liverpool	1-2
Wednesday 19 April	
Leicester City v. Tottenham Hotspur	0-1
Friday 21 April	
Bradford City v. Derby County	4-4
Everton v. Liverpool	0-0
Saturday 22 April	
Aston Villa v. Leicester City	2-2
Chelsea v. Middlesbrough	1-1
Sheffield Wed. v. Sunderland	0-2
Southampton v. Manchester United	1-3
Tottenham Hotspur v. Wimbledon	2-0
West Ham United v. Coventry City	5-0
Sunday 23 April	
Newcastle United v. Leeds United	2-2
Watford v. Arsenal	2-3
Monday 24 April	
Derby County v. Southampton	2-0
Manchester United v. Chelsea	3-2
Sunderland v. Bradford City	0-1
Saturday 29 April	
Aston Villa v. Sunderland	1-1
Chelsea v. Liverpool	2-0
Everton v. Arsenal	0-1
Newcastle United v. Coventry City	2-0
Southampton v. Leicester City	1-2
Tottenham Hotspur v. Derby County	1-1
Watford v. Manchester United	2-3
West Ham United v. Middlesbrough	0-1
Sunday 30 April	
Bradford City v. Wimbledon	3-0
Sheffield Wed. v. Leeds United	0-3

		P	W	D	L	F	A	Pts
1	Manchester United	36	26	7	3	93	44	85
2	Arsenal	34	20	6	8	64	34	66
3	Liverpool	35	19	9	7	51	27	66
4	Leeds United	35	20	4	11	54	41	64
5	Chelsea	36	17	11	8	48	32	62
6	Aston Villa	36	15	12	9	44	32	57
7	Sunderland	36	15	10	11	55	53	55
8	West Ham United	35	15	9	11	51	50	54
9	Tottenham Hotspur	36	14	8	14	53	45	50
10	Everton	36	12	13	11	58	46	49
11	Leicester City	35	14	7	14	50	51	49
12	Newcastle United	35	13	8	14	57	50	47
13	Middlesbrough	35	13	8	14	41	49	47
14	Coventry City	36	11	8	17	43	52	41
15	Southampton	36	11	7	18	43	62	40
16	Derby County	36	9	10	17	44	53	37
17	Bradford City	36	8	9	19	37	65	33
18	Wimbledon	36	7	11	18	44	70	32
19	Sheffield Wed.	35	7	6	22	30	63	27
20	Watford	35	5	5	25	32	73	20

WEST HAM have the effrontery to score first at Old Trafford but the leaders make them pay with a haul of goals that is the biggest of the Premiership season. Paul Scholes becomes the fourth different United player to score a hat-trick this campaign and his team extends its advantage over second-placed Leeds, who lose at home to Chelsea. Emile Heskey nets his first goal as Liverpool extend their unbeaten run to 10 with victory over Coventry.

Bradford lose for the fifth game in a row, to Newcastle, and top the basement trio. Watford remain 19th after they lose their 14th away game, to Everton, despite scoring twice. Alan Smart nets for the third consecutive game.

Derby stay just above the drop zone with victory over Leicester, who lose Stan Collymore with a broken leg.

Sheffield Wednesday are rooted between Bradford and Watford after they lose to Aston Villa. But things get worse for the Bantams as they go down to Southampton, for whom Matt Le Tissier scores a penalty, his 48th for the club from 49 attempts, and his 100th Premiership goal.

Manchester United increase their lead at the top to 11 points with victory at Middlesbrough.

The Premier League announces that the Premiership is to introduce rugby's 10-yard advancement rule for dissent next season.

The lowest Premiership attendance, 8,248, is recorded at Selhurst Park, where Wimbledon lose to Sheffield Wednesday. The Owls are still deep in relegation trouble.

Spurs crash to a fifth defeat in six games, to Aston Villa, prompting their fans to protest after the game. Manchester United rest a number of players but are still too strong for Sunderland and victory means a 14-point lead and at least one hand on the championship trophy.

Things are looking bleak for Bradford as a sixth defeat in a row drops them a place to 19th. Sheffield Wednesday move up to 18th after a shock win over Chelsea and Watford remain bottom after losing at Southampton.

Leeds are crushed at Arsenal, a fourth straight defeat, and the teams swap places with the Gunners moving up a place to third. Liverpool rack up their fifth consecutive victory, at Wimbledon, and go third with a brace from Emile Heskey.

Derby complete the signing of Georgi Kinkladze from Ajax for £3 million but Manchester United shatter the British transfer record in agreeing to pay PSV Eindhoven £18.5 million for striker Ruud Van Nistelrooy.

The Merseyside derby ends scoreless but there is no such drought at Valley Parade, where Derby draw with struggling Bradford, for whom Dean Windass scores the club's first Premiership hat-trick, in

a result that helps neither team. The Rams are still perilously close to the drop zone. Manchester United celebrate a sixth Premiership title in eight seasons by winning at Southampton to present Sir Alex Ferguson with his 15th trophy in 10 years at Old Trafford.

Arsenal's fifth consecutive win keeps them third and Watford bottom, while Leeds stay fourth with a draw at Newcastle, who fight back from 2–0 down with an Alan Shearer brace that takes his tally to 21. Bradford move up a place to 18th following John Dreyer's winning goal at Sunderland and Derby improve with a win over Southampton.

A blow for the new Premiership champions comes as Ruud Van Nistelrooy fails a medical on a knee injury he suffered in February and puts a huge question mark over his record move to Manchester United. The club call off the deal, saying they want to see the striker in action before the move goes ahead. The situation then gets worse for Van Nistelrooy, who collapses in agony during a PSV training session. He is rushed to hospital, where he undergoes an operation to repair a ruptured anterior ligament, which will not only put him out for a year but also jeopardise his career.

A Marc Overmars goal beats Everton, extending the Gunners' winning sequence to six and taking the team second, while Liverpool drop to third after losing at Chelsea, who stay fifth.

Leeds, with a first win in five games, stay fourth but virtually condemn Sheffield Wednesday to relegation. Bradford revive survival hopes with a convincing victory over Wimbledon that takes the Bantams out of the relegation zone for the first time since the end of December.

Bradford City's John Dreyer leaps high at the back post to head the winning goal.

May

	P	W	D	L	F	A	Pts

Tuesday 2 May

Arsenal v. West Ham United	2-1
Middlesbrough v. Newcastle United	2-2

Wednesday 3 May

Leeds United v. Watford	3-1
Liverpool v. Leicester City	0-2

Saturday 6 May

Arsenal v. Chelsea	2-1
Coventry City v. Sheffield Wed.	4-1
Derby County v. Newcastle United	0-0
Leicester City v. Bradford City	3-0
Manchester United v. Tottenham Hotspur	3-1
Middlesbrough v. Watford	1-1
Sunderland v. West Ham United	1-0
Wimbledon v. Aston Villa	2-2

Sunday 7 May

Liverpool v. Southampton	0-0

Monday 8 May

Leeds United v. Everton	1-1

Tuesday 9 May

Arsenal v. Sheffield Wed.	3-3

Sunday 14 May

Aston Villa v. Manchester United	0-1
Bradford City v. Liverpool	1-0
Chelsea v. Derby County	4-0
Everton v. Middlesbrough	0-2
Newcastle United v. Arsenal	4-2
Sheffield Wed. v. Leicester City	4-0
Southampton v. Wimbledon	2-0
Tottenham Hotspur v. Sunderland	3-1
Watford v. Coventry City	1-0
West Ham United v. Leeds United	0-0

		P	W	D	L	F	A	Pts
1	Manchester United	38	28	7	3	97	45	91
2	Arsenal	38	22	7	9	73	43	73
3	Leeds United	38	21	6	11	58	43	69
4	Liverpool	38	19	10	9	51	30	67
5	Chelsea	38	18	11	9	53	34	65
6	Aston Villa	38	15	13	10	46	35	58
7	Sunderland	38	16	10	12	57	56	58
8	Leicester City	38	16	7	15	55	55	55
9	West Ham United	38	15	10	13	52	53	55
10	Tottenham Hotspur	38	15	8	15	57	49	53
11	Newcastle United	38	14	10	14	63	54	52
12	Middlesbrough	38	14	10	14	46	52	52
13	Everton	38	12	14	12	59	49	50
14	Coventry City	38	12	8	18	47	54	44
15	Southampton	38	12	8	18	45	62	44
16	Derby County	38	9	11	18	44	57	38
17	Bradford City	38	9	9	20	38	68	36
18	Wimbledon	38	7	12	19	46	74	33
19	Sheffield Wed.	38	8	7	23	38	70	31
20	Watford	38	6	6	26	35	77	24

Promoted from Nationwide Football League Division One

Charlton Athletic
Manchester City
Ipswich Town (via play-offs)

Wimbledon's Ben Thatcher leaves the pitch with his head down after the Dons 2-0 defeat consigns them to the First Division next season.

WIMBLEDON manager Egil Olsen is sacked by the club's Norwegian owners after an eight-game losing streak, ending an 11-month tenure.

Arsenal move three points closer to runners-up place with a stoppage time winner from 'Manu' Petit against West Ham.

Leeds look favourites for third place after they beat doomed Watford while Liverpool's European ambitions are hit by defeat at Leicester.

Bradford are dumped back into the bottom three after losing to Leicester and look set to join Sheffield Wednesday and Watford in the drop.

Manchester United receive the Premiership trophy after easing to a 10th successive league victory, over Spurs. Wimbledon gain a priceless point at Villa, with a stoppage-time equaliser from substitute John Hartson, and move out of the bottom three. Derby ensure safety with a draw against Newcastle and an eighth successive Arsenal win, with another Thierry Henry brace, means second place for the Gunners and keeps Chelsea fifth.

Liverpool, even with Robbie Fowler starting for the first time since September, are held by Southampton and can't budge from third. Leeds can't improve either, and despite Michael Bridges scoring for the fourth consecutive game to take his final tally to 19, they remain fourth after drawing with Everton.

Sheffield Wednesday are relegated at Highbury, but at one stage they lead Arsenal 3–1, only to be pegged back by two goals in the last 12 minutes.

It's an emotional day in the Premiership as the final issues are settled. Wimbledon are relegated from the top flight with defeat at Southampton. Ironically it's 23 years since the Dons joined the Football League and 12 years since the club enjoyed it's finest moment, FA Cup success against Liverpool. And it's Liverpool who are on the receiving end as Bradford confound all expectations. They have only been out of the bottom three once since the turn of the year, but victory from a David Wetherall header preserves the Bantams' Premiership status.

Despite suffering their worst defeat of the season, at Newcastle, Arsenal earn second place ahead of Leeds, who gain entry into the Champions League by finishing third. Newcastle's win over the Gunners is special for Alan Shearer, who nets his 30th goal of the season, his 23rd in the Premiership, with his 22nd-minute strike.

Sheffield Wednesday bid farewell to the Premiership with a 'pressure off' thrashing of Leicester.

Team of the season, Manchester United, sign off in style. Their victory at Aston Villa, who finish sixth, gives them the title by 18 points, equals the club record of only three defeats, and surpasses the Busby Babes' mark of 27 league wins in one campaign.

End of season round-up

Top Premiership Goalscorers 1999–2000

Kevin Phillips	Sunderland	30
Alan Shearer	Newcastle United	23
Dwight Yorke	Manchester United	20
Andy Cole	Manchester United	19
Michael Bridges	Leeds United	19
Thierry Henry	Arsenal	17
Paolo Di Canio	West Ham	16
Steffan Iversen	Tottenham Hotspur	14
Chris Armstrong	Tottenham Hotspur	14
Niall Quinn	Sunderland	14

Worthington League Cup

Leicester City 2   Tranmere Rovers 1

Both Leicester goals came from set pieces which Matt Elliott headed home, but the game turned on the second-half dismissal of Tranmere's Clint Hill. Elliott scored his first goal just short of the half hour but the First Division side hit back with just 13 minutes left, when David 'Ned' Kelly equalised. But with the game just nine minutes from extra-time the one-man advantage paid off for the Premiership side and Elliott scored to put City into a winning lead, which they maintained. Hill wasn't the only one to leave the field as Alan Wilkie pulled a calf muscle and became the first referee to be stretchered off at Wembley.

FA Cup Final

Chelsea 1   Aston Villa 0

The last cup final at Wembley proved to be one of the worst football matches staged there, perhaps spoiled by the playing of both semi-finals at the same venue for the first time. The first half was poor but after the interval Chelsea increased the pressure on Villa and it paid off with just 17 minutes remaining. Zola's free-kick was poorly punched by David James and bounced off Gareth Southgate for Di Matteo to crash the ball into the roof of the net. It was a sad occasion for football, reflected in the lowest FA Cup Final attendance since the last pre-Wembley final at Stamford Bridge in 1922.

FWA Footballer of the Year

Roy Keane   Manchester United

PFA Player of the Year

Roy Keane   Manchester United

PFA Young Player of the Year

Harry Kewell   Leeds United

Manager of the Year

Alan Curbishley   Charlton Athletic

Close Season 2000

Steve McManaman becomes the first Englishman to score for a foreign club in a European final when he nets Real Madrid's second goal as they beat Valencia in the All-Spanish Champions' League Final in Paris.

Fabian Barthez joins Manchester United in a new British record fee for a goalkeeper, £7.8 million.

Chelsea pay £15 million to Atletico Madrid for Jimmy Floyd Hasselbaink.

Next season Premiership referees will have their match-fee doubled to £1,200, more than six times that of Nationwide referees, who pick up £195.

Sunderland's 30-goal striker Kevin Phillips is named Carling Player of the Year.

It's the end of an era as the BBC is outbid by ITV for Premier League highlights. *Match of the Day*, a football fixture on Saturday nights for 35 years, is no more.

Chelsea buy Bolton's Icelandic striker, Eidur Gudjohnsen, for £4 million.

Nigel Winterburn leaves Arsenal after 13 years, on a free transfer to West Ham.

Mario Stanic moves from Parma to Chelsea for £5.6 million and Alessandro Pistone signs for Everton from Newcastle for £3 million.

Robert Pires snubs Real Madrid in favour of Arsenal and moves from Marseilles to Highbury for £6 million. Newcastle pay £1 million more to sign Wimbledon's Carl Cort. The Dons also bank £5 million when Ben Thatcher joins Tottenham.

Chris Sutton completes a Scottish record transfer when he leaves Chelsea for Celtic in a £6 million deal. The same amount is paid by Arsenal for Edu but the player is deported to Brazil on arrival at Heathrow, when he is found to have a forged passport.

Paul Gascoigne completes a shock move from Middlesbrough to Everton, where he teams up with Walter Smith, who was his manager at Rangers. Nicky Barmby becomes the first Everton player to sign for Liverpool for 40 years when he completes a £6 million move.

Inter Milan pay £13 million for Coventry's Robbie Keane, less than a year after Sir Alex Ferguson said the player was only worth £500,000.

Arsenal pair 'Manu' Petit and Marc Overmars join Barcelona for £30 million. Three million pounds is what Aston Villa pay Spurs for David Ginola.

Chelsea win the Charity Shield against Manchester United, who have Roy Keane sent off for a seventh time.

'I thought you were marking him?' – Villa defenders are in confusion as Di Matteo scores the goal that wins the FA Cup.

August

Saturday 19 August	
Charlton Athletic v. Manchester City	4-0
Chelsea v. West Ham United	4-2
Coventry City v. Middlesbrough	1-3
Derby County v. Southampton	2-2
Leeds United v. Everton	2-0
Leicester City v. Aston Villa	0-0
Liverpool v. Bradford City	1-0
Sunderland v. Arsenal	1-0
Tottenham Hotspur v. Ipswich Town	3-1

Sunday 20 August	
Manchester United v. Newcastle United	2-0

Monday 21 August	
Arsenal v. Liverpool	2-0

Tuesday 22 August	
Bradford City v. Chelsea	2-0
Ipswich Town v. Manchester United	1-1
Middlesbrough v. Tottenham Hotspur	1-1

Wednesday 23 August	
Everton v. Charlton Athletic	3-0
Manchester City v. Sunderland	4-2
Newcastle United v. Derby County	3-2
Southampton v. Coventry City	1-2
West Ham United v. Leicester City	0-1

Saturday 26 August	
Arsenal v. Charlton Athletic	5-3
Bradford City v. Leicester City	0-0
Everton v. Derby County	2-2
Ipswich Town v. Sunderland	1-0
Manchester City v. Coventry City	1-2
Middlesbrough v. Leeds United	1-2
Newcastle United v. Tottenham Hotspur	2-0
Southampton v. Liverpool	3-3
West Ham United v. Manchester United	2-2

Sunday 27 August	
Aston Villa v. Chelsea	1-1

		P	W	D	L	F	A	Pts
1	Arsenal	3	2	0	1	7	4	6
2	Leeds United	2	2	0	0	4	1	6
3	Newcastle United	3	2	0	1	5	4	6
4	Coventry City	3	2	0	1	5	5	6
5	Manchester United	3	1	2	0	5	3	5
6	Leicester City	3	1	2	0	1	0	5
7	Everton	3	1	1	1	5	4	4
8	Middlesbrough	3	1	1	1	5	4	4
9	Bradford City	3	1	1	1	2	1	4
10	Chelsea	3	1	1	1	5	5	4
11	Tottenham Hotspur	3	1	1	1	4	4	4
12	Liverpool	3	1	1	1	4	5	4
13	Ipswich Town	3	1	1	1	3	4	4
14	Charlton Athletic	3	1	0	2	7	8	3
15	Sunderland	3	1	0	2	3	5	3
16	Manchester City	3	1	0	2	5	8	3
17	Aston Villa	2	0	2	0	1	1	2
18	Southampton	3	0	2	1	6	7	2
19	Derby County	3	0	2	1	6	7	2
20	West Ham United	3	0	1	2	4	7	1

PATRICK Vieira gets a fifth red card of his Arsenal career in the last minute as the Gunners open the season with defeat by a goal from Highbury old boy Niall Quinn. Mario Stanic makes a scoring debut for Chelsea with two goals in the win over West Ham. Charlton Athletic enjoy the day's biggest win when they thrash Manchester City and Everton, who haven't won at Elland Road since 1951, are beaten by Leeds. Les Ferdinand makes a scoring debut as Spurs beat Ipswich.

Manchester United enjoy a comfortable win over Newcastle with former Magpie Andy Cole on the mark against his old club.

Liverpool lose a bad-tempered game at Arsenal in which Patrick Vieira is red carded for the second time in four days. Gary McAllister and Dietmar Hamann also get their marching orders. But the German is later reprieved as referee Graham Poll rescinds Hamann's second yellow card.

Sir Alex Ferguson lambasts Premiership referees as 'prima donnas' after the champions are held by Ipswich. Coventry register their first away win in 22 attempts with victory at Southampton. Duncan Ferguson comes off the bench to mark his Everton return with a brace that helps beat Charlton and Warren Barton is sent off on his 350th league appearance as Newcastle defeat Derby in front of St James' Park's biggest attendance for 24 years, 51,327. £7 million striker Carl Cort nets on his Magpies' debut.

Patrick Vieira makes the right kind of headlines with two goals as Arsenal beat Charlton to go top. Leeds win again, at Middlesbrough, and go second, while Liverpool squander a 3–0 lead and concede three goals in the last 17 minutes in being held by Southampton, who are just one place off the bottom. Manchester United are fifth after drawing with West Ham, who are bottom of the table, and Newcastle beat Spurs to go third while Coventry reach the heady heights of fourth place by beating Manchester City.

Another John Hartson transfer falls through as the Wimbledon striker fails a medical and his dream £7 million move to Glasgow Rangers is called off.

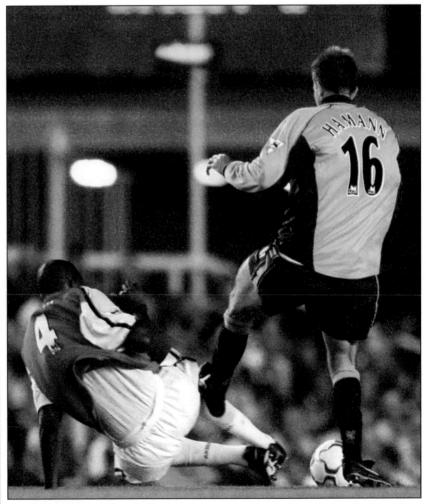

Arsenal's Patrick Vieira clashes with Liverpool's Dietmar Hamann in an incident which led to Vieira receiving his second yellow card in as many minutes.

September

Tuesday 5 September	
Leeds United v. Manchester City	1-2
Manchester United v. Bradford City	6-0
Sunderland v. West Ham United	1-1
Tottenham Hotspur v. Everton	3-2
Wednesday 6 September	
Charlton Athletic v. Southampton	1-1
Chelsea v. Arsenal	2-2
Coventry City v. Newcastle United	0-2
Derby County v. Middlesbrough	3-3
Leicester City v. Ipswich Town	2-1
Liverpool v. Aston Villa	3-1
Saturday 9 September	
Bradford City v. Arsenal	1-1
Coventry City v. Leeds United	0-0
Ipswich Town v. Aston Villa	1-2
Leicester City v. Southampton	1-0
Liverpool v. Manchester City	3-2
Manchester United v. Sunderland	3-0
Middlesbrough v. Everton	1-2
Newcastle United v. Chelsea	0-0
Sunday 10 September	
Derby County v. Charlton Athletic	2-2
Monday 11 September	
Tottenham Hotspur v. West Ham United	1-0
Saturday 16 September	
Arsenal v. Coventry City	2-1
Aston Villa v. Bradford City	2-0
Charlton Athletic v. Tottenham Hotspur	1-0
Everton v. Manchester United	1-3
Leeds United v. Ipswich Town	1-2
Southampton v. Newcastle United	2-0
Sunderland v. Derby County	2-1
Sunday 17 September	
Chelsea v. Leicester City	0-2
Manchester City v. Middlesbrough	1-1
West Ham United v. Liverpool	1-1
Saturday 23 September	
Bradford City v. Southampton	0-1
Coventry City v. West Ham United	0-3
Derby County v. Leeds United	1-1
Ipswich Town v. Arsenal	1-1
Liverpool v. Sunderland	1-1
Manchester United v. Chelsea	3-3
Middlesbrough v. Aston Villa	1-1
Newcastle United v. Charlton Athletic	0-1
Tottenham Hotspur v. Manchester City	0-0
Sunday 24 September	
Leicester City v. Everton	1-1
Saturday 30 September	
Aston Villa v. Derby County	4-1
Charlton Athletic v. Coventry City	2-2
Everton v. Ipswich Town	0-3
Leeds United v. Tottenham Hotspur	4-3
Manchester City v. Newcastle United	0-1
Southampton v. Middlesbrough	1-3
West Ham United v. Bradford City	1-1

		P	W	D	L	F	A	Pts
1	Manchester United	7	4	3	0	20	7	15
2	Leicester City	7	4	3	0	7	2	15
3	Newcastle United	8	4	1	3	8	7	13
4	Arsenal	7	3	3	1	13	9	12
5	Aston Villa	7	3	3	1	11	7	12
6	Liverpool	7	3	3	1	12	10	12
7	Charlton Athletic	8	3	3	2	14	13	12
8	Leeds United	7	3	2	2	11	9	11
9	Ipswich Town	8	3	2	3	11	10	11
10	Tottenham Hotspur	8	3	2	3	11	11	11
11	Middlesbrough	8	2	4	2	14	12	10
12	Southampton	8	2	3	3	11	12	9
13	Everton	8	2	2	4	11	15	8
14	Manchester City	8	2	2	4	10	14	8
15	Sunderland	7	2	2	3	7	11	8
16	Coventry City	8	2	2	4	8	14	8
17	West Ham United	8	1	4	3	10	11	7
18	Chelsea	7	1	4	2	10	12	7
19	Bradford City	8	1	3	4	4	12	6
20	Derby County	8	0	5	3	14	19	5

MANCHESTER United hammer Bradford and Arsenal rescue a point at Chelsea with a Silvinho equaliser four minutes from time. Leeds lose ground after losing to Manchester City and a Michael Owen hat-trick for Liverpool, taking his tally to five in two games, means Aston Villa are still without a win. Newcastle go top, for the first time since November 1996, with Alan Shearer netting his 200th league goal, in 275 games, in the win at Coventry.

West Ham claim a point at Sunderland but fail to move off the bottom while Southampton draw at Charlton and stay 19th. Derby, still awaiting a first win, overcome a 3–0 deficit at home to 'Boro to force a draw, with the Rams netting twice in the final seven minutes.

Arsenal, with £13 million Sylvain Wiltord making his bow, are held at Bradford and fall to fifth as a consequence. Unbeaten Leicester go second with Gerry Taggart's first goal of the campaign earning the points against Southampton, who are 18th and without a win. Liverpool are fourth after beating Manchester City, helped by Michael Owen's sixth goal in three games and a brace from Dietmar Hamann. Manchester United go top with victory over Sunderland, who drop into the bottom three to join West Ham and Southampton. Aston Villa get their first win at Ipswich.

Derby, still without a win, draw for the fourth time in five games against Charlton, to move out of the relegation zone.

Chelsea, without a win since the opening day, sack Gianluca Vialli amid speculation about rifts in the Stamford Bridge dressing room. Within days Chelsea install little-known Claudio Ranieri, whose initial problems centre around his lack of English rather than his managerial acumen.

Manchester United stay top with a comfortable win at Everton and already this season nine different United players have scored.

Premiership newcomers Ipswich get a first away win when they take the points in a shock win at Leeds, who drop three places to ninth. Southampton finally win against Newcastle, with a brace from Marian Pahars taking his tally in four games to five goals.

Ken Bates, using the platform of his national newspaper column, aims a parting shot at Vialli, stating that he could not, as chairman, allow the Chelsea club to disintegrate, so the manager had to go.

Paolo Di Canio's penalty earns West Ham a point against Liverpool, after they lead through Steven Gerrard's first goal of the season, but the Hammers remain 20th.

West Ham finally end their winless streak with a victory at Coventry that lifts them two places, but they are still in the bottom three.

Manchester United recover from 3–1 down to Chelsea to claim a point and stay top of the table, but unbeaten Leicester keep up the pressure in second place with a draw against Everton. The Foxes' 15 points, thus far, have been earned by seven different scorers, with no one player registering more than a single goal.

Manchester United announce an awesome £300 million shirt deal with Nike.

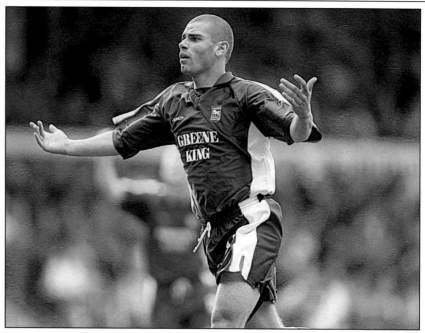

Ipswich Town's Jermaine Wright celebrates his winner at Leeds.

October

Sunday 1 October	
Arsenal v. Manchester United	1-0
Chelsea v. Liverpool	3-0
Sunderland v. Leicester City	0-0
Saturday 14 October	
Arsenal v. Aston Villa	1-0
Coventry City v. Tottenham Hotspur	2-1
Everton v. Southampton	1-1
Ipswich Town v. West Ham United	1-1
Leeds United v. Charlton Athletic	3-1
Leicester City v. Manchester United	0-3
Manchester City v. Bradford City	2-0
Sunderland v. Chelsea	1-0
Sunday 15 October	
Derby County v. Liverpool	0-4
Monday 16 October	
Middlesbrough v. Newcastle United	1-3
Saturday 21 October	
Bradford City v. Ipswich Town	0-2
Charlton Athletic v. Middlesbrough	1-0
Chelsea v. Coventry City	6-1
Liverpool v. Leicester City	1-0
Manchester United v. Leeds United	3-0
Newcastle United v. Everton	0-1
Tottenham Hotspur v. Derby County	3-1
West Ham United v. Arsenal	1-2
Sunday 22 October	
Aston Villa v. Sunderland	0-0
Monday 23 October	
Southampton v. Manchester City	0-2
Saturday 28 October	
Arsenal v. Manchester City	5-0
Aston Villa v. Charlton Athletic	2-1
Chelsea v. Tottenham Hotspur	3-0
Ipswich Town v. Middlesbrough	2-1
Leicester City v. Derby County	2-1
Manchester United v. Southampton	5-0
Sunderland v. Coventry City	1-0
West Ham United v. Newcastle United	1-0
Sunday 29 October	
Bradford City v. Leeds United	1-1
Liverpool v. Everton	3-1

		P	W	D	L	F	A	Pts
1	Manchester United	11	7	3	1	31	8	24
2	Arsenal	11	7	3	1	22	10	24
3	Liverpool	11	6	3	2	20	14	21
4	Leicester City	11	5	4	2	9	7	19
5	Ipswich Town	11	5	3	3	16	12	18
6	Chelsea	11	4	4	3	22	14	16
7	Aston Villa	10	4	4	2	13	9	16
8	Newcastle United	11	5	1	5	11	10	16
9	Sunderland	11	4	4	3	9	11	16
10	Leeds United	10	4	3	3	15	14	15
11	Charlton Athletic	11	4	3	4	17	18	15
12	Tottenham Hotspur	11	4	2	5	15	17	14
13	Manchester City	11	4	2	5	14	19	14
14	Everton	11	3	3	5	14	19	12
15	West Ham United	11	2	5	4	13	14	11
16	Coventry City	11	3	2	6	11	22	11
17	Middlesbrough	11	2	4	5	16	18	10
18	Southampton	11	2	4	5	12	20	10
19	Bradford City	11	1	4	6	5	17	7
20	Derby County	11	0	5	6	16	28	5

MANCHESTER UNITED are beaten for the first time since February when a Thierry Henry goal helps Arsenal close the gap on second place, but unbeaten Leicester are the surprise new table-toppers thanks to a draw with Sunderland. Chelsea earn new manager Claudio Ranieri an impressive first win over Liverpool, who are rocked by an early Sandor Westerveld own-goal and Jimmy Floyd Hasselbaink's fourth goal of the season inside two minutes.

Leicester City's tenure at the top ends when they are replaced by Manchester United, who win comfortably at Filbert Street. The Foxes drop below Arsenal, for whom Henry is again the match-winner, against Aston Villa. Graham Le Saux and Kevin Kilbane are sent off as Sunderland beat Chelsea and Spurs fans rage at George Graham after their team lose to Coventry.

West Ham draw with Ipswich but stay 18th. Everton fall to just above the drop zone after drawing with Southampton.

Liverpool go fourth with the help of an Emile Heskey hat-trick that sinks bottom of the table Derby.

Manchester United and Arsenal are level on points at the top of the table, but United are ahead on goal difference after the sides beat Leeds and West Ham respectively. Leicester drop further down the table when they lose to a goal from old boy Emile Heskey, which takes Liverpool third. Newcastle lose to Everton but stay fourth. Jimmy Floyd Hasselbaink hits four, and doubles his tally, as Chelsea thrash Coventry.

Manchester United and Arsenal go goal crazy as they confirm their respective first and second placings. United entertain a Premiership record attendance of 67,581 when they crush Southampton, who drop into the bottom three, helped by a Teddy Sheringham hat-trick, United's first treble of the campaign. Arsenal match United's score against their City rivals. Newcastle slump four places, to eighth, when they lose to a Freddie Kanoute goal, only his second of the season, at West Ham. The Hammers leap out of the relegation zone to 15th.

Derby suffer a fourth consecutive defeat, to Leicester, who move up a place to fourth, and the Rams stay bottom.

Muzzy Izzit hits the Foxes' opener and becomes the first player to score more than one goal. His second of the season makes him the club's top scorer! Ipswich take their unbeaten run to six with a win over Middlesbrough that takes them up a place to fifth.

Liverpool consolidate third place with victory in the Merseyside derby, helped by a Nick Barmby goal against his former club.

Bradford pick up their only point of the month with a spectacular Stan Collymore goal earning a draw with Leeds, but the Bantams remain 19th.

Thierry Henry's fifth goal of the season beats Manchester United.

November

Saturday 4 November	
Charlton Athletic v. Bradford City	2-0
Coventry City v. Manchester United	1-2
Leeds United v. Liverpool	4-3
Manchester City v. Leicester City	0-1
Middlesbrough v. Arsenal	0-1
Newcastle United v. Ipswich Town	2-1
Southampton v. Chelsea	3-2
Tottenham Hotspur v. Sunderland	2-1

Sunday 5 November	
Everton v. Aston Villa	0-1

Monday 6 November	
Derby County v. West Ham United	0-0

Saturday 11 November	
Arsenal v. Derby County	0-0
Aston Villa v. Tottenham Hotspur	2-0
Bradford City v. Everton	0-1
Ipswich Town v. Charlton Athletic	2-0
Leicester City v. Newcastle United	1-1
Manchester United v. Middlesbrough	2-1
Sunderland v. Southampton	2-2
West Ham United v. Manchester City	4-1

Sunday 12 November	
Chelsea v. Leeds United	1-1
Liverpool v. Coventry City	4-1

Saturday 18 November	
Charlton Athletic v. Chelsea	2-0
Derby County v. Bradford City	2-0
Everton v. Arsenal	2-0
Leeds United v. West Ham United	0-1
Manchester City v. Manchester United	0-1
Middlesbrough v. Leicester City	0-3
Newcastle United v. Sunderland	1-2
Southampton v. Aston Villa	2-0

Sunday 19 November	
Tottenham Hotspur v. Liverpool	2-1

Monday 20 November	
Coventry City v. Ipswich Town	0-1

Saturday 25 November	
Charlton Athletic v. Sunderland	0-1
Coventry City v. Aston Villa	1-1
Derby County v. Manchester United	0-3
Everton v. Chelsea	2-1
Manchester City v. Ipswich Town	2-3
Middlesbrough v. Bradford City	2-2
Southampton v. West Ham United	2-3
Tottenham Hotspur v. Leicester City	3-0

Sunday 26 November	
Leeds United v. Arsenal	1-0
Newcastle United v. Liverpool	2-1

		P	W	D	L	F	A	Pts
1	Manchester United	15	11	3	1	39	10	36
2	Arsenal	15	8	4	3	23	13	28
3	Ipswich Town	15	8	3	4	23	16	27
4	Leicester City	15	7	5	3	14	11	26
5	Liverpool	15	7	3	5	29	23	24
6	Aston Villa	14	6	5	3	17	12	23
7	Newcastle United	15	7	2	6	17	15	23
8	Tottenham Hotspur	15	7	2	6	22	21	23
9	Sunderland	15	6	5	4	15	16	23
10	Leeds United	14	6	4	4	21	19	22
11	West Ham United	15	5	6	4	21	17	21
12	Charlton Athletic	15	6	3	6	21	21	21
13	Everton	15	6	3	6	19	21	21
14	Chelsea	15	4	5	6	26	22	17
15	Southampton	15	4	5	6	21	27	17
16	Manchester City	15	4	2	9	17	28	14
17	Coventry City	15	3	3	9	14	30	12
18	Middlesbrough	15	2	5	8	19	26	11
19	Derby County	15	1	7	7	18	31	10
20	Bradford City	15	1	5	9	7	24	8

Leeds United's Mark Viduka (centre) heads his second goal past Liverpool goalkeeper Sander Westerveld as Liverpool's Markus Babbel (second right) looks on.

MANCHESTER UNITED beat Coventry to stay top. Arsenal remain second with a Thierry Henry winner at Middlesbrough. Leicester move up to third after Robbie Savage's first goal of the season beats Manchester City, and Liverpool fall to fourth after being blitzed by a four-goal blast from Mark Viduka for Leeds.

Roy Keane bemoans the lack of vocal support at Old Trafford, labelling corporate supporters the 'prawn sandwich brigade'.

A 90th-minute rocket from Paul Merson earns Aston Villa victory over Everton and fifth place.

A fifth successive victory, over Middlesbrough, confirms Manchester United in top spot but Arsenal lose ground when they are held by battling Derby County, who are now 19th. Leicester drop a place, to fourth, after they draw with Newcastle.

Liverpool climb to third with a comprehensive victory over Coventry, for whom David Thompson scores a sentimental consolation goal on his return to his former club.

Sir Alex Ferguson misses a David Beckham free-kick winner in the Manchester derby to attend his son's wedding in South Africa. United stay top. Everton, with former Gunner Kevin Campbell on the scoresheet, inflict only the second defeat of the season on Arsenal, who stay second. Leicester climb a place to third by beating Middlesbrough, a sixth consecutive defeat for Bryan Robson's team that keeps them 18th.

Derby, with goals from Malcolm Christie and Rory Delap, beat Bradford in the basement battle but the clubs remain 19th and 20th respectively.

Ipswich climb to fifth with victory at Coventry, with a Fabian Wilnis 90th-minute winner.

Chelsea's out-of-favour Tore Andre Flo, two days after submitting a transfer request, completes a record £12 million switch to Glasgow Rangers.

Ipswich continue their impressive climb up the Premiership table with a Marcus Stewart brace. His second goal proves the winner at Manchester City and helps take the club third, Town's highest top-flight position for nearly 20 years.

In a throw back to the 1960s and 70s Arsenal lose a pulsating match with Leeds, in which seven are booked, and fail to score for a third consecutive game but stay second. Liverpool drop a place to fifth, when they lose to Newcastle, who move up a slot to seventh. Leicester also slip a place, to fourth, when they lose at Spurs. But Manchester United's seventh consecutive victory, at Derby, keeps them in pole position and the Rams 19th.

Bradford claim their first point in four games but they squander a 2–0 lead, gained in the first 10 minutes, against Middlesbrough. For 'Boro their first point in two months comes courtesy of an 89th-minute Paul Ince goal. City and 'Boro remain 20th and 18th respectively.

December

Saturday 2 December

Arsenal v. Southampton	1-0
Aston Villa v. Newcastle United	1-1
Bradford City v. Coventry City	2-1
Ipswich Town v. Derby County	0-1
Leicester City v. Leeds United	3-1
Liverpool v. Charlton Athletic	3-0
Manchester United v. Tottenham Hotspur	2-0
West Ham United v. Middlesbrough	1-0

Sunday 3 December

Chelsea v. Manchester City	2-1

Monday 4 December

Sunderland v. Everton	2-0

Saturday 9 December

Arsenal v. Newcastle United	5-0
Bradford City v. Tottenham Hotspur	3-3
Charlton Athletic v. Manchester United	3-3
Chelsea v. Derby County	4-1
Manchester United v. Everton	5-0
Southampton v. Leeds United	1-0
Sunderland v. Middlesbrough	1-0
West Ham United v. Aston Villa	1-1

Sunday 10 December

Coventry City v. Leicester City	1-0
Liverpool v. Ipswich Town	0-1

Saturday 16 December

Aston Villa v. Manchester City	2-2
Derby County v. Coventry City	1-0
Everton v. West Ham United	1-1
Ipswich Town v. Southampton	3-1
Leeds United v. Sunderland	2-0
Leicester City v. Charlton Athletic	3-1
Middlesbrough v. Chelsea	1-0
Newcastle United v. Bradford City	2-1

Sunday 17 December

Manchester United v. Liverpool	0-1

Monday 18 December

Tottenham Hotspur v. Arsenal	1-1

Friday 22 December

Coventry City v. Southampton	1-1

Saturday 23 December

Charlton Athletic v. Everton	1-0
Chelsea v. Bradford City	3-0
Derby County v. Newcastle United	2-0
Leeds United v. Aston Villa	1-2
Leicester City v. West Ham United	2-1
Liverpool v. Arsenal	4-0
Manchester United v. Ipswich Town	2-0
Sunderland v. Manchester City	1-0
Tottenham Hotspur v. Middlesbrough	0-0

Tuesday 26 December

Arsenal v. Leicester City	6-1
Aston Villa v. Manchester United	0-1
Bradford City v. Sunderland	1-4
Everton v. Coventry City	1-2
Ipswich Town v. Chelsea	2-2
Manchester City v. Derby County	0-0
Middlesbrough v. Liverpool	1-0
Newcastle United v. Leeds United	2-1
West Ham United v. Charlton Athletic	5-0

Wednesday 27 December

Southampton v. Tottenham Hotspur	2-0

Saturday 30 December

Arsenal v. Sunderland	2-2
Ipswich Town v. Tottenham Hotspur	3-0
Manchester City v. Charlton Athletic	1-4
Middlesbrough v. Coventry City	1-1
Newcastle United v. Manchester United	1-1
Southampton v. Derby County	1-0

		P	W	D	L	F	A	Pts
1	Manchester United	21	14	5	2	48	15	47
2	Arsenal	21	11	6	4	38	21	39
3	Ipswich Town	21	11	4	6	32	22	37
4	Sunderland	21	10	6	5	25	21	36
5	Leicester City	20	10	5	5	23	21	35
6	Liverpool	20	10	3	7	37	25	33
7	Newcastle United	21	9	4	8	23	26	31
8	West Ham United	20	7	8	5	30	21	29
9	Aston Villa	19	7	8	4	23	18	29
10	Charlton Athletic	21	8	4	9	30	36	28
11	Chelsea	20	7	6	7	37	27	27
12	Southampton	21	7	6	8	27	32	27
13	Tottenham Hotspur	21	7	5	9	26	32	26
14	Leeds United	19	7	4	8	26	27	25
15	Everton	20	6	4	10	21	32	22
16	Derby County	21	4	8	9	23	36	20
17	Coventry City	21	5	5	11	20	36	20
18	Middlesbrough	21	4	7	10	22	29	19
19	Manchester City	21	5	4	12	26	37	19
20	Bradford City	20	2	6	12	14	37	12

MIDDLESBROUGH chairman Steve Gibson abandons plans to bring in Terry Venables and retains Bryan Robson as manager.

Derby County shock high-flying Ipswich and Rory Delap enters the record books in notching up the Rams' 200th Premiership goal, which takes them out of the relegation zone. Bradford City defeat Coventry and pull the Sky Blues into the bottom three although the win doesn't alter the Bantams' 20th position. 'Boro lose to West Ham and stay 19th.

Leicester spoil £18 million Rio Ferdinand's debut with victory over Leeds that lifts them into third place but Manchester United confirm top spot with an eighth consecutive win over Tottenham. Arsenal win for the first time in four games to stay second, but it takes a Kachloul own-goal to beat Southampton.

There is a U-turn at the Riverside as Terry Venables is brought in to work alongside Bryan Robson while Robbo's former club, Manchester United, are declared the world's richest club for the third year running.

The new 'Boro managerial pair doesn't seem to work as the team crashes to the foot of the table following defeat by Sunderland.

Manchester United are pegged back when they squander a 2–0 advantage over Charlton and concede twice in the last 11 minutes. Arsenal take advantage by thrashing Newcastle with the help of Ray Parlour's first Premiership hat-trick. Ipswich retain third place with victory over Southampton, their 10th league win.

Bradford rise one place, to 19th, after a six-goal thriller with Spurs. Benito Carbone is the Bantams' hero with an 89th-minute equaliser. Derby drop back into the relegation zone after a Chelsea thrashing. Manchester City end their six-game losing streak with a shock hammering of Everton that results in Walter Smith cancelling the Merseysiders' Christmas party and forcing his players to watch the match video.

Everton are on the receiving end of one of the most sporting incidents in Premiership history. West Ham's Paolo Di Canio, instead of capitalising on prostrate 'keeper Paul Gerrard and converting a cross, catches the ball to allow treatment to the Everton 'keeper, a gesture which earns the Italian universal acclaim.

Middlesbrough's Dean Gordon scores the only goal against Chelsea.

Middlesbrough finally win, after 10 games, when Dean Gordon's first goal of the season beats Chelsea to lift 'Boro one place off the bottom. Bradford slump back to 20th after defeat at Newcastle and Derby escape the drop zone, again, with victory over Coventry, thanks to a Malcolm Christie goal, which sends the Sky Blues into the bottom three.

Liverpool mark Houllier's 100th match, and throw the title-race wide open, by inflicting a first home defeat on Manchester United in two days short of two years, with a stunning Danny Murphy free-kick.

Arsenal rescue a point against Spurs with an 89th-minute Patrick Vieira equaliser that sends the Gunners into the Christmas programme in second place.

Liverpool stun second-placed Arsenal with a season's-best Anfield win that lifts Houllier's side to fourth and boosts Manchester United, who stretch their lead to eight points with victory over Ipswich, who drop to fifth. Fergie declares his team the best United have ever had.

Bradford are still bottom after losing to Chelsea, 'Boro earn a point at Spurs and remain 19th, and alarm bells sound at Maine Road as Manchester City are pulled down to 17th by defeat at Sunderland.

Solskjaer's late goal beats Aston Villa and prompts John Gregory to declare that the title race is over. Second-placed Arsenal bounce back to record a season's best score against Leicester, who drop to fourth, with Thierry Henry netting his first hat-trick of the campaign. Sunderland leap three places to third when a Kevin Phillips hat-trick beats Bradford and keeps the Bantams bottom. Liverpool slump to sixth after losing at 'Boro.

United end the year still top after drawing at Newcastle. Arsenal stay second after drawing with Sunderland and Ipswich are third after beating Spurs.

Middlesbrough climb to 18th after drawing with Coventry, who exit the relegation zone. Manchester City drop to 19th after crashing to Charlton, conceding four goals to the Addicks for the second time this season. City's only goal is a stoppage-time penalty from debutant Darren Huckerby.

Monday 1 January	
Charlton Athletic v. Arsenal	1-0
Chelsea v. Aston Villa	1-0
Coventry City v. Manchester City	1-1
Derby County v. Everton	1-0
Leeds United v. Middlesbrough	1-1
Leicester City v. Bradford City	1-2
Liverpool v. Southampton	2-1
Manchester United v. West Ham United	3-1
Sunderland v. Ipswich Town	4-1
Tuesday 2 January	
Tottenham Hotspur v. Newcastle United	4-2
Saturday 13 January	
Arsenal v. Chelsea	1-1
Aston Villa v. Liverpool	0-3
Bradford City v. Manchester United	0-3
Everton v. Tottenham Hotspur	0-0
Manchester City v. Leeds United	0-4
Middlesbrough v. Derby County	4-0
Newcastle United v. Coventry City	3-1
Southampton v. Charlton Athletic	0-0
West Ham United v. Sunderland	0-2
Sunday 14 January	
Ipswich Town v. Leicester City	2-0
Saturday 20 January	
Chelsea v. Ipswich Town	4-1
Coventry City v. Everton	1-3
Derby County v. Manchester City	1-1
Leeds United v. Newcastle United	1-3
Leicester City v. Arsenal	0-0
Liverpool v. Middlesbrough	0-0
Manchester United v. Aston Villa	2-0
Tottenham Hotspur v. Southampton	0-0
Sunday 21 January	
Sunderland v. Bradford City	0-0
Monday 22 January	
Charlton Athletic v. West Ham United	1-1
Wednesday 24 January	
Aston Villa v. Leeds United	1-2
Tuesday 30 January	
Arsenal v. Bradford City	2-0
Charlton Athletic v. Derby County	2-1
Wednesday 31 January	
Chelsea v. Newcastle United	3-1
Everton v. Middlesbrough	2-2
Leeds United v. Coventry City	1-0
Manchester City v. Liverpool	1-1
Southampton v. Leicester City	1-0
Sunderland v. Manchester United	0-1
West Ham United v. Tottenham Hotspur	0-0

		P	W	D	L	F	A	Pts
1	Manchester United	25	18	5	2	57	16	59
2	Arsenal	25	12	8	5	41	23	44
3	Sunderland	25	12	7	6	31	23	43
4	Liverpool	24	12	5	7	43	27	41
5	Ipswich Town	24	12	4	8	36	30	40
6	Chelsea	24	10	7	7	46	30	37
7	Newcastle United	25	11	4	10	32	35	37
8	Leicester City	24	10	6	8	24	26	36
9	Charlton Athletic	25	10	6	9	34	38	36
10	Leeds United	24	10	5	9	35	32	35
11	Tottenham Hotspur	25	8	8	9	30	34	32
12	Southampton	25	8	8	9	29	34	32
13	West Ham United	24	7	10	7	32	27	31
14	Aston Villa	23	7	8	8	24	26	29
15	Everton	24	7	6	11	26	36	27
16	Middlesbrough	25	5	10	10	29	32	25
17	Derby County	25	5	9	11	26	43	24
18	Manchester City	25	5	7	13	29	44	22
19	Coventry City	25	5	6	14	23	44	21
20	Bradford City	24	3	7	14	16	43	16

Sunderland's Don Hutchison celebrates scoring the second goal against West Ham.

FACT FILE

After Villa pay £9.5 million for Juan Pablo Angel chairman Doug Ellis institutes cost-cutting measures. Scouts are requested to take sandwiches on long journeys and trips abroad are to be on Easy-jet flights from Luton.

MANCHESTER UNITED extend their lead to 11 points, with victory over West Ham, after Arsenal lose to Charlton. Robbie Keane makes a scoring debut for Leeds, with a penalty in the draw with Middlesbrough, who remain 18th. Sunderland move up to third, swapping places with vanquished Ipswich, with a season's best home win.

Bradford claim a first away win by shocking Leicester, who drop two places to sixth as a consequence, but the Bantams remain bottom. Manchester City stay 19th after a draw with Coventry.

Liverpool pull off the free transfer of the season with the signing of Jari Litmanen, from Barcelona.

New England coach Sven-Goran Eriksson makes West Ham versus Sunderland his first game and sees Scottish international Don Hutchison hit the winner that takes the Black Cats into second place. Luke Chadwick scores his first goal for Manchester United but the leaders have to wait until the last 18 minutes for their goals against bottom club Bradford City. Arsenal drop a place to third when they are held by Chelsea.

Middlesbrough leap out of the relegation zone, to 15th, with their best win of the season against Derby, who drop to one place above the basement trio. Manchester City are 19th after being crushed by Leeds, and the goals-against column now shows 42 conceded in 23 games by Joe Royle's team. Coventry complete the relegation zone after losing to Newcastle.

Marcus Stewart hits his 14th Premiership goal, in his fourth successive scoring game, to impress the watching Sven-Goran Eriksson, and go top of the scoring chart as Ipswich beat Leicester to stay fourth.

Sir Alex Ferguson announces his intention to retire next summer, prompting widespread speculation about who will succeed him at Old Trafford.

Arsenal's poor run continues as they are held at Leicester, who give Roberto Mancini his debut, and remain third. Manchester United are top for the third month running when they win again, and Gary Neville is a rare name on the scoresheet against Villa. Sunderland stay second despite being held by Bradford, who are still bottom.

Everton arrive at Highfield Road with just 11 fit first-teamers. Coventry drop to 19th after they lose to Everton and Manchester City climb a place after drawing with Derby, but they are still in the drop zone just behind the Rams.

A stormy game at the Stadium of Light between first and second place sees goalscorer Andy Cole and Sunderland pair Alex Rae and Michael Gray red-carded as Manchester United win to extend their lead at the top. Arsenal stay in contention with victory over Bradford, who remain 20th. Manchester City and Coventry are still in trouble after a draw with Liverpool and defeat by Leeds respectively.

February

Saturday 3 February

Bradford City v. Aston Villa	0-3
Coventry City v. Arsenal	0-1
Derby County v. Sunderland	1-0
Ipswich Town v. Leeds United	1-2
Leicester City v. Chelsea	2-1
Liverpool v. West Ham United	3-0
Manchester United v. Everton	1-0
Middlesbrough v. Manchester City	1-1
Tottenham Hotspur v. Charlton Athletic	0-0

Wednesday 7 February

Everton v. Leeds United	2-2

Saturday 10 February

Arsenal v. Ipswich Town	1-0
Aston Villa v. Middlesbrough	1-1
Chelsea v. Manchester United	1-1
Everton v. Leicester City	2-1
Leeds United v. Derby County	0-0
Manchester City v. Tottenham Hotspur	0-1
Southampton v. Bradford City	2-0
Sunderland v. Liverpool	1-1

Sunday 11 February

Charlton Athletic v. Newcastle United	2-0

Monday 12 February

West Ham United v. Coventry City	1-1

Saturday 24 February

Bradford City v. West Ham United	1-2
Coventry City v. Charlton Athletic	2-2
Derby County v. Aston Villa	1-0
Ipswich Town v. Everton	2-0
Leicester City v. Sunderland	2-0
Middlesbrough v. Southampton	0-1
Newcastle United v. Manchester City	0-1
Tottenham Hotspur v. Leeds United	1-2

Sunday 25 February

Manchester United v. Arsenal	6-1

		P	W	D	L	F	A	Pts
1	Manchester United	28	20	6	2	65	18	66
2	Arsenal	28	14	8	6	44	29	50
3	Liverpool	26	13	6	7	47	28	45
4	Sunderland	28	12	8	8	32	27	44
5	Ipswich Town	27	13	4	10	39	33	43
6	Leeds United	28	12	7	9	41	36	43
7	Leicester City	27	12	6	9	29	29	42
8	Charlton Athletic	28	11	8	9	38	40	41
9	Chelsea	26	10	8	8	48	33	38
10	Southampton	27	10	8	9	32	34	38
11	Newcastle United	27	11	4	12	32	38	37
12	Tottenham Hotspur	28	9	9	10	32	36	36
13	West Ham United	27	8	11	8	35	32	35
14	Aston Villa	26	8	9	9	28	28	33
15	Everton	28	8	7	13	30	42	31
16	Derby County	28	7	10	11	28	43	31
17	Middlesbrough	28	5	12	11	31	35	27
18	Manchester City	28	6	8	14	31	46	26
19	Coventry City	28	5	8	15	26	48	23
20	Bradford City	27	3	7	17	17	50	16

MANCHESTER UNITED maintain their 15-point lead at the top when a Dave Watson own-goal secures victory at Everton. Fergie blames the pitch at Old Trafford, which has been staging rugby league matches, for his team's poorest display of the season. Arsenal are second after Dennis Bergkamp hits the winner against Coventry, who remain 19th. Liverpool go third with a Robbie Fowler brace helping defeat West Ham.

Manchester City draw at 'Boro but stay 18th and Bradford, after a fourth consecutive scoreless outing, remain rock-bottom after losing to Aston Villa, for whom Darius Vassell scores his first Premiership brace.

'Boro coach Terry Venables becomes the first 'non manager' to win the Carling Manager of the Month award.

Andy Cole rescues a point, and United stay top, with his ninth goal of the season at Chelsea. Thierry Henry keeps Arsenal second with a goal that beats Ipswich, who drop a place to sixth. Jari Litmanen scores his first goal for Liverpool, from the spot, to earn a point against Sunderland that keeps Houllier's side third and the Black Cats, for whom former Red Don Hutchison scores, fourth. Sergei Rebrov's 89th-minute winner against Manchester City gives Spurs their first win on the road for 10 months. It's also the team's first league goal in nearly eight hours of football and keeps City in the bottom three. Bradford stay bottom after losing to Southampton.

Middlesbrough extend their unbeaten run, under Terry Venables, to a dozen games, cup and league, with a point at Villa Park, due to a goal from former Villain Ugo Ehiogu. 'Boro stay clear of the drop zone.

Coventry claim a point against West Ham courtesy of a last-minute Christian Dailly own-goal, but stay 19th.

The top two meet and Arsenal are kept in their place, second, by a Manchester United thrashing in which Dwight Yorke scores his first hat-trick of the season, to extend the leaders' advantage to 16 points. This equals Arsenal's worst-ever defeat – 6–1 against United in 1952 – since the 19th century.

Bradford lose their 17th game of the campaign, against West Ham, and stay rooted in 20th place. Manchester City gain a shock win at Newcastle with Shaun Goater's first goal of the year but stay 18th and Coventry are held by Charlton and remain 19th.

Sergei Rebrov gets between Manchester City's Danny Granville and goalkeeper Nicky Weaver to score Spurs' winner and seal a first away victory of the season.

Saturday 3 March	
Arsenal v. West Ham United	3-0
Coventry City v. Chelsea	0-0
Derby County v. Tottenham Hotspur	2-1
Everton v. Newcastle United	1-1
Leeds United v. Manchester United	1-1
Leicester City v. Liverpool	2-0
Manchester City v. Southampton	0-1
Middlesbrough v. Charlton Athletic	0-0
Sunday 4 March	
Ipswich Town v. Bradford City	3-1
Monday 5 March	
Sunderland v. Aston Villa	1-1
Wednesday 7 March	
West Ham United v. Chelsea	0-2
Saturday 10 March	
Aston Villa v. Ipswich Town	2-1
Saturday 17 March	
Bradford City v. Manchester City	2-2
Charlton Athletic v. Leeds United	1-2
Chelsea v. Sunderland	2-4
Manchester United v. Leicester City	2-0
Newcastle United v. Middlesbrough	1-2
Southampton v. Everton	1-0
Tottenham Hotspur v. Coventry City	3-0
West Ham United v. Ipswich Town	0-1
Sunday 18 March	
Aston Villa v. Arsenal	0-0
Liverpool v. Derby County	1-1
Saturday 31 March	
Arsenal v. Tottenham Hotspur	2-0
Bradford City v. Newcastle United	2-2
Chelsea v. Middlesbrough	2-1
Coventry City v. Derby County	2-0
Liverpool v. Manchester United	2-0
Manchester City v. Aston Villa	1-3
Sunderland v. Leeds United	0-2
West Ham United v. Everton	0-2

		P	W	D	L	F	A	Pts
1	Manchester United	31	21	7	3	68	21	70
2	Arsenal	31	16	9	6	49	29	57
3	Leeds United	31	14	8	9	46	38	50
4	Liverpool	29	14	7	8	50	31	49
5	Ipswich Town	30	15	4	11	44	36	49
6	Sunderland	31	13	9	9	37	32	48
7	Chelsea	30	12	9	9	54	38	45
8	Leicester City	29	13	6	10	31	31	45
9	Southampton	29	12	8	9	34	34	44
10	Charlton Athletic	30	11	9	10	39	42	42
11	Aston Villa	30	10	11	9	34	31	41
12	Tottenham Hotspur	31	10	9	12	36	40	39
13	Newcastle United	30	11	6	13	36	43	39
14	West Ham United	31	8	11	12	35	40	35
15	Everton	31	9	8	14	33	44	35
16	Derby County	31	8	11	12	31	47	35
17	Middlesbrough	31	6	13	12	34	38	31
18	Manchester City	31	6	9	16	34	52	27
19	Coventry City	31	6	9	16	28	51	27
20	Bradford City	30	3	9	18	22	57	18

John Hartson, Coventry City.

MANCHESTER UNITED are held at Leeds, due to a late Mark Viduka equaliser, after Luke Chadwick's second goal of the campaign, but the leaders are grateful for a Barthez penalty save to remain unbeaten this year. Arsenal beat West Ham with a Wiltord hat-trick to close the gap. Liverpool lose third place to Ipswich after going down to Leicester, and drop a place after Town beat bottom club Bradford.

Dan Petrescu's goal takes Southampton into the top 10 and keeps Manchester City in the relegation zone. Coventry claim a third successive draw, against Chelsea, but are still 19th. Pride Park's 100th game sees Derby claim victory over Spurs to move eight points clear of the drop zone.

Stan Collymore, at 30, retires from football. Also leaving his job, but not voluntarily, is George Graham, who is sacked after a brief and stormy meeting with Tottenham's new executive vice-chairman David Buchler.

Under caretaker manager David Pleat Spurs beat Coventry and keep the Sky Blues 19th, just ahead of rock-bottom Bradford, who draw with Manchester City, also still in the drop zone.

Things stay the same at the top of the table after Manchester United beat Leicester with goals in the last two minutes. But Arsenal lose ground in second place when they draw at Villa. Ipswich retain third place with victory over West Ham and Liverpool slump two places to sixth when they are held by Derby, who extend their unbeaten run to five.

Tottenham confirm Glenn Hoddle as their new manager and the former White Hart Lane hero has to endure Arsenal marking Wenger's 250th game in charge with victory in the North London derby. There's more joy for the Gunners' boss as Liverpool complete their first league double over Manchester United for 22 years to climb back up to fourth. Leeds move up to third after beating Sunderland, who drop to sixth.

At the bottom Bradford remain 20th after drawing with Newcastle. Coventry claim a first win in 11 games, and first of the year, over Derby, with £15,000 a game John Hartson netting his first goal for the club, but the Sky Blues stay 19th. Manchester City remain 18th after losing to Aston Villa.

David Rocastle, who won two championships with Arsenal, and 14 England caps, loses his fight against cancer.

Sunday 1 April	
Charlton Athletic v. Leicester City	2-0
Monday 2 April	
Southampton v. Ipswich Town	0-3
Wednesday 4 April	
Aston Villa v. Leicester City	2-1
Saturday 7 April	
Aston Villa v. West Ham United	2-2
Derby County v. Chelsea	0-4
Leeds United v. Southampton	2-0
Leicester City v. Coventry City	1-3
Sunday 8 April	
Everton v. Manchester City	3-1
Monday 9 April	
Middlesbrough v. Sunderland	0-0
Tuesday 10 April	
Ipswich Town v. Liverpool	1-1
Manchester United v. Charlton Athletic	2-1
Tottenham Hotspur v. Bradford City	2-1
Wednesday 11 April	
Manchester City v. Arsenal	0-4
Friday 13 April	
Bradford City v. Charlton Athletic	2-0
Liverpool v. Leeds United	1-2
Saturday 14 April	
Arsenal v. Middlesbrough	0-3
Aston Villa v. Everton	2-1
Chelsea v. Southampton	1-0
Ipswich Town v. Newcastle United	1-0
Leicester City v. Manchester City	1-2
Manchester United v. Coventry City	4-2
Sunderland v. Tottenham Hotspur	2-3
West Ham United v. Derby County	3-1
Monday 16 April	
Coventry City v. Sunderland	1-0
Derby County v. Leicester City	2-0
Everton v. Liverpool	2-3
Middlesbrough v. Ipswich Town	1-2
Newcastle United v. West Ham United	2-1
Tuesday 17 April	
Charlton Athletic v. Aston Villa	3-3
Tottenham Hotspur v. Chelsea	0-3
Saturday 21 April	
Arsenal v. Everton	4-1
Aston Villa v. Southampton	0-0
Bradford City v. Derby County	2-0
Chelsea v. Charlton Athletic	0-1
Ipswich Town v. Coventry City	2-0
Leicester City v. Middlesbrough	0-3
Manchester United v. Manchester City	1-1
Sunderland v. Newcastle United	1-1
West Ham United v. Leeds United	0-2
Sunday 22 April	
Liverpool v. Tottenham Hotspur	3-1
Saturday 28 April	
Coventry City v. Liverpool	0-2
Derby County v. Arsenal	1-2
Everton v. Bradford City	2-1
Leeds United v. Chelsea	2-0
Manchester City v. West Ham United	1-0
Middlesbrough v. Manchester United	0-2
Newcastle United v. Leicester City	1-0
Southampton v. Sunderland	0-1
Tottenham Hotspur v. Aston Villa	0-0
Monday 30 April	
Charlton Athletic v. Ipswich Town	2-1

		P	W	D	L	F	A	Pts
1	Manchester United	35	24	8	3	77	25	80
2	Arsenal	35	19	9	7	59	34	66
3	Leeds United	35	18	8	9	54	39	62
4	Ipswich Town	36	19	5	12	54	40	62
5	Liverpool	34	17	8	9	60	37	59
6	Chelsea	35	15	9	11	62	41	54
7	Sunderland	36	14	11	11	41	37	53
8	Charlton Athletic	36	14	10	12	48	50	52
9	Aston Villa	36	12	15	9	43	38	51
10	Newcastle United	34	13	7	14	40	46	46
11	Tottenham Hotspur	36	12	10	14	42	49	46
12	Southampton	34	12	9	13	34	41	45
13	Leicester City	36	13	6	17	34	46	45
14	Everton	36	11	8	17	42	55	41
15	West Ham United	36	9	12	15	41	48	39
16	Middlesbrough	36	8	14	14	41	42	38
17	Derby County	36	9	11	16	35	58	38
18	Manchester City	36	8	10	18	39	61	34
19	Coventry City	36	8	9	19	34	60	33
20	Bradford City	34	5	9	20	28	61	24

IPSWICH canter to victory at Southampton on the back of the club's first hat-trick of the season, from Marcus Stewart, to confirm third place.

John Hartson scores his fifth goal, in four matches, as Coventry beat Leicester to move up one place to 18th.

Manchester City crash to 19th after losing to Everton.

Manchester United stay top but need an 82nd-minute Solskjaer winner to beat Charlton. Ipswich stay third after drawing with Liverpool, who are one place behind.

Arsenal crush Manchester City, who remain 19th with relegation looming. Leeds complete their first double over Liverpool since 1971 with a victory at Anfield, in which Steven Gerrard is sent off.

Bradford get their first victory since New Year's Day when they beat Charlton but stay bottom. The next day Manchester City win at Leicester and are 18th.

Manchester United clinch the championship for a record third successive season, in front of the highest-ever Premiership attendance of 67,637, with a thrashing of Coventry that leaves the Sky Blues one place off the bottom. John Hartson scores another two goals. United also equal Liverpool's record of seven titles in nine years.

The Mersey derby is marred by disrespect in the minute's silence to mark the anniversary of Hillsborough. A stormy game, won by Liverpool, sees 12 yellow cards and the dismissal of Igor Biscan, in contentious added time.

John Hartson scores for the fourth consecutive game, taking his tally to six in seven matches, to beat Sunderland, but Coventry stay 18th.

The Manchester derby is overshadowed by Roy Keane's 'over-the-top' challenge, which leaves Alf-Inge Haaland badly injured, earning the United skipper his eighth red card in United colours and keeping City in 19th place.

Arsenal close in on the runners-up spot with victory over Everton, while third-placed Ipswich push Coventry closer to relegation with a win that leaves the Sky Blues 18th. Bradford win consecutive games for the first time in the campaign, against Derby, with former Ram Ashley Ward netting twice, but the Bantams look doomed in 20th place.

Champions Manchester United complete a British transfer record deal, of £19 million, for PSV Eindhoven's 24-year-old striker Ruud Van Nistelrooy, on a five-year contract. The deal comes one year after a cruciate ligament injury threatened the Dutch player's career.

Leeds finalise the £12 million signing of Robbie Keane from Inter Milan, who agree to staged payments over a three-year period.

Bradford City bid farewell to the Premiership, after two years, following defeat by Everton. The Bantams, bottom since before Christmas, have been in the relegation zone since mid-September. Coventry drop to 19th after losing to Liverpool, who stay fifth. Gary McAllister is a scorer for the third game running to drop his former club to one place off the bottom. Arsenal stay second after beating Derby, who are just one place above the relegation zone. A Stuart Pearce own-goal gives Manchester City victory, and hope, against West Ham, and moves Joe Royle's team up to 18th. Leeds' sixth successive victory, over Chelsea, with goals from Robbie Keane and Mark Viduka in the last four minutes, takes them third.

Leicester's losing sequence continues with a worst-ever ninth successive defeat, to Newcastle.

Manchester United's Ole Gunnar Solskjaer tries to bring the ball down.

Tuesday 1 May	
Bradford City v. Liverpool	0-2
Newcastle United v. Southampton	1-1
Saturday 5 May	
Arsenal v. Leeds United	2-1
Aston Villa v. Coventry City	3-2
Bradford City v. Middlesbrough	1-1
Chelsea v. Everton	2-1
Leicester City v. Tottenham Hotspur	4-2
Liverpool v. Newcastle United	3-0
Manchester United v. Derby County	0-1
Sunderland v. Charlton Athletic	3-2
West Ham United v. Southampton	3-0
Monday 7 May	
Ipswich Town v. Manchester City	2-1
Tuesday 8 May	
Liverpool v. Chelsea	2-2
Sunday 13 May	
Leeds United v. Bradford City	6-1
Southampton v. Manchester United	2-1
Tuesday 15 May	
Newcastle United v. Arsenal	0-0
Saturday 19 May	
Charlton Athletic v. Liverpool	0-4
Coventry City v. Bradford City	0-0
Derby County v. Ipswich Town	1-1
Everton v. Sunderland	2-2
Leeds United v. Leicester City	3-1
Manchester City v. Chelsea	1-2
Middlesbrough v. West Ham United	2-1
Newcastle United v. Aston Villa	3-0
Southampton v. Arsenal	3-2
Tottenham Hotspur v. Manchester United	3-1

		P	W	D	L	F	A	Pts
1	Manchester United	38	24	8	6	79	31	80
2	Arsenal	38	20	10	8	63	38	70
3	Liverpool	38	20	9	9	71	39	69
4	Leeds United	38	20	8	10	64	43	68
5	Ipswich Town	38	20	6	12	57	42	66
6	Chelsea	38	17	10	11	68	45	61
7	Sunderland	38	15	12	11	46	41	57
8	Aston Villa	38	13	15	10	46	43	54
9	Charlton Athletic	38	14	10	14	50	57	52
10	Southampton	38	14	10	14	40	48	52
11	Newcastle United	38	14	9	15	44	50	51
12	Tottenham Hotspur	38	13	10	15	47	54	49
13	Leicester City	38	14	6	18	39	51	48
14	Middlesbrough	38	9	15	14	44	44	42
15	West Ham United	38	10	12	16	45	50	42
16	Everton	38	11	9	18	45	59	42
17	Derby County	38	10	12	16	37	59	42
18	Manchester City	38	8	10	20	41	65	34
19	Coventry City	38	8	10	20	36	63	34
20	Bradford City	38	5	11	22	30	70	26

Promoted from Nationwide Football League Division One

Fulham

Blackburn Rovers

Bolton Wanderers (via play-offs)

DERBY COUNTY end lingering relegation worries with a shock victory over champions Manchester United. Malcolm Christie nets the only goal at Old Trafford, and seals only the second home defeat of the season for Fergie's team.

Coventry City's 34-year stay in the top flight ends after they let slip a 2–0 lead, by the 26th minute, with Aston Villa's decisive last two goals coming in the final nine minutes.

Arsenal stay second after ending Leeds' winning sequence of seven games, and United drop a place to fourth. Michael Owen hits his second hat-trick of the season to sink Newcastle.

Exactly one year since they clinched promotion to the Premiership Manchester City are relegated after they lose to Ipswich.

Leeds hammer Bradford with a season's best scoreline that keeps United fourth.

Despite being held to a draw, by Newcastle, Arsenal are runners-up in the Premiership and secure a place in the Champions League for the third year running.

Southampton bring the curtain down on 103 years of football at the Dell with a victory over Arsenal that is marked, fittingly, by Matt Le Tissier scoring the last goal on the ground, in the last minute of the last game. Liverpool clinch a Champions League place when a Robbie Fowler brace helps brush aside Charlton.

Southampton's Matt Le Tissier controls the ball in the penalty box before his historic goal sinks Arsenal. It is his 209th in 534 appearances.

End of season round-up

Top Premiership Goalscorers 2000–2001

Jimmy Floyd Hasselbaink

	Chelsea	23
Marcus Stewart	Ipswich Town	19
Thierry Henry	Arsenal	17
Mark Viduka	Leeds United	17
Michael Owen	Liverpool	16
Teddy Sheringham	Manchester United	15
Emile Heskey	Liverpool	14
Kevin Phillips	Sunderland	14
Alen Boksic	Middlesbrough	12
Alan Smith	Leeds United	11
Jonatan Johansson	Charlton Athletic	11
Frederic Kanoute	West Ham	11
James Beattie	Southampton	11
Gustavo Poyet	Chelsea	11

Worthington League Cup

Liverpool 1   Birmingham City 1
(Liverpool won 5–4 on penalties)

This was the first League Cup Final to be played outside England, in Cardiff, and also the first domestic final to be settled by a penalty shoot-out. Robbie Fowler put Liverpool ahead after half an hour with stunning long-range volley and Liverpool were just seconds from victory when Birmingham's Darren Purse kept his nerve to score from a 90th-minute penalty to send the game into extra-time.

Neither side could score in the extra half-hour so it went to penalties and it was all-square with McAllister, Barmby, Ziege and Fowler netting for Liverpool, with only Hamman missing his kick. The German international revealed later that he has 'never scored a penalty' in senior football. Grainger missed Birmingham's first spot-kick but after Purse, Marcelo, Lazaridis and Hughes scored it came down to the last two penalties. Jamie Carragher scored for Liverpool but Andrew Johnson's kick was saved by Westerveld to create a new record with a sixth League Cup win for the Anfield club.

FA Cup Final

Liverpool 2   Arsenal 1

Freddie Ljungberg put Arsenal ahead with the game's first goal, with 18 minutes remaining, after his side squandered numerous chances to clinch the trophy. The Gunners were just seven minutes away from winning the first FA Cup Final to be staged outside England when Michael Owen's quicksilver pace turned the game. Owen equalised with just seven minutes remaining and with the game heading for extra-time Owen struck again when he turned the Arsenal defence, in the 88th minute, to score the winner.

FWA Footballer of the Year

Teddy Sheringham   Manchester United

PFA Player of the Year

Teddy Sheringham   Manchester United

PFA Young Player of the Year

Steven Gerrard   Liverpool

Manager of the Year

George Burley   Ipswich Town

Close Season 2001

Manchester City sack Joe Royle after three years in the job. A row then ensues as to whether he is entitled to compensation as a Premier League manager or as the departing manager of a Nationwide League Division One side. Three days later Kevin Keegan takes over at Maine Road. Royle then considers legal action against Manchester City over claims he ran the side like a pub team.

After four years Teddy Sheringham rejoins Tottenham on a free transfer from Manchester United.

Bryan Robson resigns after seven years as Middlesbrough manager.

Sir Alex Ferguson's assistant, Steve McClaren, leaves to become Middlesbrough manager on a five-year, £8 million deal.

An elite group of 24 Premiership referees is formed and their full-time earnings, from 2001–02, will be up to £70,000 per annum. Salaries will be based on a match-fee of £900 plus bonuses based on good performances.

Chelsea pay £11 million for West Ham's Frank Lampard. Everton's Francis Jeffers joins Arsenal for £10 million. The Gunners then spend £8.5 million on Rangers' Giovanni Van Bronckhorst.

Coventry's Craig Bellamy joins Newcastle for £6.5 million and Emmanuel Petit leaves Barcelona for Chelsea, for £7.5 million.

Sol Campbell joins Arsenal on a Bosman free transfer and walks into Highbury commanding a huge salary, thought to be in excess of £100,000 a week.

Paul Scholes and Nicky Butt commit their futures to Old Trafford by signing six and five-year contracts respectively. Wes Brown follows suit by agreeing a four-year deal.

Southampton break their club record in signing Derby's Rory Delap for £4 million.

Juan Sebastian Veron's £28.5 million move from Lazio takes Sir Alex Ferguson's summer spending to £42 million while former United 'keeper Peter Schmeichel is Aston Villa's new signing.

Junichi Inamoto joins Arsenal for £3.5 million, from Gamba Osaka, and becomes the first Japanese Premiership player.

Fabrizio Ravanelli joins Derby County from Lazio.

Fulham sign goalkeeper Edwin van der Sar from Juventus for £7 million.

Laurent Robert joins Newcastle, from PSG, for £10 million.

New manager of Manchester City, Kevin Keegan, with a Man City flag .

		P	W	D	L	F	A	Pts

Saturday 18 August

Charlton Athletic v. Everton	1-2
Derby County v. Blackburn Rovers	2-1
Leeds United v. Southampton	2-0
Leicester City v. Bolton Wanderers	0-5
Liverpool v. West Ham United	2-1
Middlesbrough v. Arsenal	0-4
Sunderland v. Ipswich Town	1-0
Tottenham Hotspur v. Aston Villa	0-0

Sunday 19 August

Chelsea v. Newcastle United	1-1
Manchester United v. Fulham	3-2

Monday 20 August

Everton v. Tottenham Hotspur	1-1

Tuesday 21 August

Arsenal v. Leeds United	1-2
Bolton Wanderers v. Middlesbrough	1-0
Ipswich Town v. Derby County	3-1

Wednesday 22 August

Blackburn Rovers v. Manchester United	2-2
Fulham v. Sunderland	2-0

Saturday 25 August

Arsenal v. Leicester City	4-0
Blackburn Rovers v. Tottenham Hotspur	2-1
Everton v. Middlesbrough	2-0
Fulham v. Derby County	0-0
Ipswich Town v. Charlton Athletic	0-1
Southampton v. Chelsea	0-2
West Ham United v. Leeds United	0-0

Sunday 26 August

Aston Villa v. Manchester United	1-1
Newcastle United v. Sunderland	1-1

Monday 27 August

Bolton Wanderers v. Liverpool	2-1

		P	W	D	L	F	A	Pts
1	Bolton Wanderers	3	3	0	0	8	1	9
2	Everton	3	2	1	0	5	2	7
3	Leeds United	3	2	1	0	4	1	7
4	Arsenal	3	2	0	1	9	2	6
5	Manchester United	3	1	2	0	6	5	5
6	Chelsea	2	1	1	0	3	1	4
7	Fulham	3	1	1	1	4	3	4
8	Blackburn Rovers	3	1	1	1	5	5	4
9	Derby County	3	1	1	1	3	4	4
10	Sunderland	3	1	1	1	2	3	4
11	Ipswich Town	3	1	0	2	3	3	3
12	Liverpool	2	1	0	1	3	3	3
13	Charlton Athletic	2	1	0	1	2	2	3
14	Newcastle United	2	0	2	0	2	2	2
15	Aston Villa	2	0	2	0	1	1	2
16	Tottenham Hotspur	3	0	2	1	2	3	2
17	West Ham United	2	0	1	1	1	2	1
18	Southampton	2	0	0	2	0	4	0
19	Middlesbrough	3	0	0	3	0	7	0
20	Leicester City	2	0	0	2	0	9	0

ARSENAL open with a crushing victory at Middlesbrough in which the Gunners score three times in the final three minutes, including two from Dennis Bergkamp. Bolton go one better with their victory over Leicester in which Kevin Nolan nets the first Premiership goal of the season, after 15 minutes, and Sunderland draw the day's best attendance, 47,370, for their victory over Ipswich. Michael Owen's brace gives Liverpool a winning start against West Ham.

Fulham nearly pull off a shock at Old Trafford, twice taking the lead through Louis Saha, but champions Manchester United, with their own two-goal hero, Ruud Van Nistelrooy, hit back to win.

ITV's replacement for BBC's *Match of the Day*, *The Premiership*, is slaughtered for broadcasting just 28 minutes of football action, only 60 seconds less than the time spent talking about the games shown, with the rest of the 68-minute programme being adverts.

Nine-man Spurs grind out a draw with Everton, after Gary Doherty and Gus Poyet are sent off within three minutes of each other, just past the hour.

More disciplinary problems come as Leeds beat Arsenal. Referee Jeff Winter brandishes 11 yellow cards and dismisses United pair Danny Mills and Lee Bowyer.

Following a mass of complaints ITV increases the football action in *The Premiership* programme to 38 minutes!

Sir Alex Ferguson drops Jaap Stam for the Blackburn game and says it has nothing to do with the Dutch defender's revelations, in his recent autobiography, that he met secretly with the United manager before his move to Old Trafford. The champions then struggle, with David Beckham scoring for both sides, to a draw. Fulham beat Sunderland and Saha scores again.

The opening week of Premiership football sees a total of 63 yellow cards and nine red.

Arsenal swamp Leicester to go third but Everton are the early leaders after beating Middlesbrough, who slump to 19th, still scoreless.

Alan Shearer returns, after a five-month injury absence, when he comes on as a substitute in the Tyne-Tees derby. Manchester United, again minus Jaap Stam, only avoid defeat at Villa thanks to a 90th-minute Alpay own-goal. Stam then admits shock at the speed of his hastily conducted transfer to Lazio, for £16.5 million, just six months after signing a new five-year deal at Old Trafford.

Bolton, with Michael Ricketts scoring for the third successive game, beat Liverpool, with Dean Holdsworth's last-minute winner taking Wanderers top.

Gary Doherty's red card against Everton is wiped out after referee David Elleray admits making a mistake in sending the Irishman off.

The month ends with a flurry of transfer activity. Fulham top the lot by paying Olympique Lyon £11.5 million for striker Steve Marlet. Laurent Blanc, 35, joins Manchester United for £2 million and Gerard Houllier starts his goalkeeper 'collection' when he spends nearly £10 million on Jerzey Dudek, from Feyenoord, and Coventry City's Chris Kirkland. The Englishman's fee is set to rise to £8 million, depending on appearances. Anfield incumbent Sander Westerveld naturally expresses concern about his position.

Fulham's Louis Saha chips Fabien Barthez in the Manchester United goal to score the opening goal of the game.

September

Saturday 8 September

Chelsea v. Arsenal	1-1
Derby County v. West Ham United	0-0
Leeds United v. Bolton Wanderers	0-0
Leicester City v. Ipswich Town	1-1
Liverpool v. Aston Villa	1-3
Manchester United v. Everton	4-1
Middlesbrough v. Newcastle United	1-4
Sunderland v. Blackburn Rovers	1-0

Sunday 9 September

Charlton Athletic v. Fulham	1-1
Tottenham Hotspur v. Southampton	2-0

Saturday 15 September

Bolton Wanderers v. Southampton	0-1
Derby County v. Leicester City	2-3
Everton v. Liverpool	1-3
Fulham v. Arsenal	1-3
Middlesbrough v. West Ham United	2-0
Newcastle United v. Manchester United	4-3

Sunday 16 September

Aston Villa v. Sunderland	0-0
Charlton Athletic v. Leeds United	0-2
Ipswich Town v. Blackburn Rovers	1-1
Tottenham Hotspur v. Chelsea	2-3

Monday 17 September

Leicester City v. Middlesbrough	1-2

Wednesday 19 September

Blackburn Rovers v. Bolton Wanderers	1-1
Sunderland v. Tottenham Hotspur	1-2

Saturday 22 September

Arsenal v. Bolton Wanderers	1-1
Blackburn Rovers v. Everton	1-0
Leicester City v. Fulham	0-0
Liverpool v. Tottenham Hotspur	1-0
Manchester United v. Ipswich Town	4-0
Sunderland v. Charlton Athletic	2-2

Sunday 23 September

Chelsea v. Middlesbrough	2-2
Leeds United v. Derby County	3-0
West Ham United v. Newcastle United	3-0

Monday 24 September

Southampton v. Aston Villa	1-3

Wednesday 26 September

Newcastle United v. Leicester City	1-0

Saturday 29 September

Bolton Wanderers v. Sunderland	0-2
Charlton Athletic v. Leicester City	2-0
Derby County v. Arsenal	0-2
Everton v. West Ham United	5-0
Middlesbrough v. Southampton	1-3
Tottenham Hotspur v. Manchester United	3-5

Sunday 30 September

Aston Villa v. Blackburn Rovers	2-0
Fulham v. Chelsea	1-1
Ipswich Town v. Leeds United	1-2
Newcastle United v. Liverpool	0-2

		P	W	D	L	F	A	Pts
1	Leeds United	7	5	2	0	11	2	17
2	Arsenal	7	4	2	1	16	5	14
3	Manchester United	7	4	2	1	22	13	14
4	Aston Villa	6	3	3	0	9	3	12
5	Bolton Wanderers	8	3	3	2	10	6	12
6	Liverpool	6	4	0	2	10	7	12
7	Sunderland	8	3	3	2	8	7	12
8	Newcastle United	7	3	2	2	11	11	11
9	Chelsea	6	2	4	0	10	7	10
10	Everton	7	3	1	3	12	10	10
11	Blackburn Rovers	8	2	3	3	8	10	9
12	Charlton Athletic	6	2	2	2	7	7	8
13	Tottenham Hotspur	8	2	2	4	11	13	8
14	Fulham	7	1	4	2	7	8	7
15	Middlesbrough	8	2	1	5	8	17	7
16	Southampton	6	2	0	4	5	10	6
17	Ipswich Town	7	1	2	4	6	11	5
18	West Ham United	6	1	2	3	4	9	5
19	Derby County	7	1	2	4	5	12	5
20	Leicester City	8	1	2	5	5	17	5

Sunderland's Kevin Phillips celebrates scoring their opening goal against Bolton in front of the Sunderland fans.

GERARD HOULLIER confirms Jerzey Dudek as his number-one goalkeeper. Former Liverpool player Don Hutchison becomes West Ham's record signing when he moves from Sunderland for £5 million.

Bolton manager Sam Allardyce and Fulham striker Louis Saha take the first monthly awards of the season. Wanderers retain top spot by drawing with Leeds, who drop a place to third. Liverpool crash to Aston Villa, and have Steven Gerrard sent off for a lunge at George Boateng. Veron, Cole and Fortune all net their first goals of the season, and David Beckham's strike makes him Manchester United's top scorer as they beat Everton to move up three places to second, sending the Goodison outfit four places down to fifth.

West Ham drop to 17th after drawing with Derby County. Colin Cooper nets Middlesbrough's first goal of the season but Newcastle hit back to crush the home side, who plunge to the foot of the table, without a point to their name. Leicester claim a first point of the campaign, against Ipswich, and climb to 18th.

Southampton, still goalless, drop to 19th after their third consecutive 2–0 defeat, at Tottenham.

Roy Keane is sent off for the ninth time as Manchester United lose to Newcastle. Shearer doesn't score but Wes Brown's own-goal is the decisive one. United drop three places, to fifth, one place below the Magpies, who climb above the champions. Bolton lose for the first time, to Southampton, and drop to third, while Saints move up a place to 18th. Leeds go top by beating Charlton Athletic, with former Addick Danny Mills a scorer.

Middlesbrough win for the first time, against West Ham, and move one place off the bottom to be replaced by the Hammers. Leicester beat Derby to climb out of the relegation zone but Robbie Savage winds up the Rams fans and is involved in a tunnel fracas.

'Boro, with goals in the last five minutes from Paul Ince and Jonathan Greening, come back to beat Leicester and move out of the drop zone, leaving City in the bottom three.

Jari Litmanen hits the winner against Spurs but the headlines are made by Michael Owen's departure from Anfield on crutches. Francis Jeffers scores his first Arsenal goal, against Bolton, but the Gunners drop a place, to third, and are leapfrogged by Wanderers.

Leeds stay top after beating Derby, who drop three places, into the relegation zone. Southampton join them in the bottom three after losing to Villa.

Manchester United stage one of the greatest comebacks in Premiership history when they overturn Spurs' 3–0 interval lead, with a second-half blitz that has Fergie declaring it his best away result as United's manager. United move up to third. Thierry Henry takes his goal tally to six with a brace that beats Derby, to send the Rams down a place to 19th and move the Gunners up to second, but Martin Keown is sent off with the 36th Arsenal red card of Arsene Wenger's tenure. Bolton slump to fifth after losing to Sunderland, for whom Kevin Phillips scores his 100th Sunderland goal, in 147 games. Southampton, with Marian Pahars scoring for the third game in a row, beat Middlesbrough to move out of the bottom three. West Ham slip into the drop zone after being thrashed by Everton. Leeds stay top after beating Ipswich.

October

Season 2001-02

Saturday 13 October	
Bolton Wanderers v. Newcastle United	0-4
Charlton Athletic v. Middlesbrough	0-0
Chelsea v. Leicester City	2-0
Ipswich Town v. Everton	0-0
Liverpool v. Leeds United	1-1
Southampton v. Arsenal	0-2
Sunderland v. Manchester United	1-3
Sunday 14 October	
Aston Villa v. Fulham	2-0
Blackburn Rovers v. West Ham United	7-1
Monday 15 October	
Tottenham Hotspur v. Derby County	3-1
Saturday 20 October	
Arsenal v. Blackburn Rovers	3-3
Derby County v. Charlton Athletic	1-1
Everton v. Aston Villa	3-2
Leicester City v. Liverpool	1-4
Manchester United v. Bolton Wanderers	1-2
West Ham United v. Southampton	2-0
Sunday 21 October	
Fulham v. Ipswich Town	1-1
Leeds United v. Chelsea	0-0
Newcastle United v. Tottenham Hotspur	0-2
Monday 22 October	
Middlesbrough v. Sunderland	2-0
Wednesday 24 October	
Aston Villa v. Charlton Athletic	1-0
Southampton v. Ipswich Town	3-3
West Ham United v. Chelsea	2-1
Saturday 27 October	
Aston Villa v. Bolton Wanderers	3-2
Charlton Athletic v. Liverpool	0-2
Everton v. Newcastle United	1-3
Fulham v. Southampton	2-1
Manchester United v. Leeds United	1-1
Sunderland v. Arsenal	1-1
Tottenham Hotspur v. Middlesbrough	2-1
Sunday 28 October	
Derby County v. Chelsea	1-1
Ipswich Town v. West Ham United	2-3
Monday 29 October	
Blackburn Rovers v. Leicester City	0-0

		P	W	D	L	F	A	Pts
1	Aston Villa	10	6	3	1	17	8	21
2	Leeds United	10	5	5	0	13	4	20
3	Arsenal	10	5	4	1	22	9	19
4	Liverpool	9	6	1	2	17	9	19
5	Manchester United	10	5	3	2	27	17	18
6	Newcastle United	10	5	2	3	18	14	17
7	Tottenham Hotspur	11	5	2	4	18	15	17
8	Chelsea	10	3	6	1	14	10	15
9	Bolton Wanderers	11	4	3	4	14	14	15
10	Blackburn Rovers	11	3	5	3	18	14	14
11	Everton	10	4	2	4	16	15	14
12	West Ham United	10	4	2	4	12	19	14
13	Sunderland	11	3	4	4	10	13	13
14	Fulham	10	2	5	3	10	12	11
15	Middlesbrough	11	3	2	6	11	19	11
16	Charlton Athletic	10	2	4	4	8	11	10
17	Ipswich Town	11	1	5	5	12	18	8
18	Derby County	10	1	4	5	8	17	7
19	Southampton	10	2	1	7	9	19	7
20	Leicester City	11	1	3	7	6	23	6

Fabien Barthez can't stop Michael Ricketts as Bolton stun Old Trafford.

DION DUBLIN becomes the sixth Premiership player to have a red card rescinded this season.

The row between the Premier League and the PFA gathers momentum as the governing body claim their £10 million per annum offer is reasonable.

Liverpool's draw with Leeds is overshadowed by news that Gerard Houllier has been rushed to hospital, after his half-time team talk, for heart surgery. Leeds stay top, Liverpool are seventh. Manchester United remain third after beating Sunderland. Thierry Henry scores his seventh goal of the season as Arsenal beat Southampton to stay second, while the Saints drop to 17th.

Leicester remain bottom after they fail to score a goal for the fourth successive game. They are defeated by Chelsea, who go sixth. Blackburn post the biggest win of the campaign, with seven different scorers, as they swamp West Ham. Hammers' Michael Carrick contributes with an own-goal that helps dump them to 19th.

Bolton add another surprise to their best-ever start to a Premiership season when they beat Manchester United, with Michael Ricketts hitting the 84th-minute winner, to move up to sixth, but United stay third. Arsenal, with Henry scoring again, are held by Blackburn but remain second. Liverpool move up to fourth on the back of a stunning Robbie Fowler hat-trick that helps sink Leicester, who stay bottom. There is some consolation for the Foxes as Dennis Wise nets the side's first goal in five games.

Southampton drop to one place off the bottom after losing to West Ham, who leap out of the bottom three to 16th. Fabrizio Ravanelli's fifth goal of the season earns a point against Charlton but the Rams stay 18th. Aston Villa drop to fifth after losing to Everton and Peter Schmeichel makes the headlines with yet another career goal, a 90th-minute volley following a corner.

Leeds march on in pole position despite being held by Chelsea. Southampton sack Stuart Gray. Aston Villa beat Bolton to top the Premiership for the first time in three years. Leeds are held by Manchester United and drop to second, while Fergie's side fall to fifth. Arsenal drop a place to third after drawing with Sunderland.

Southampton stay 19th after losing to Fulham and Leicester end the month by finally getting a point, against Blackburn, although they remain bottom.

November

Saturday 3 November

Bolton Wanderers v. Everton	2-2
Leicester City v. Sunderland	1-0
Middlesbrough v. Derby County	5-1
Newcastle United v. Aston Villa	3-0
Southampton v. Blackburn Rovers	1-2
West Ham United v. Fulham	0-2

Sunday 4 November

Arsenal v. Charlton Athletic	2-4
Chelsea v. Ipswich Town	2-1
Leeds United v. Tottenham Hotspur	2-1
Liverpool v. Manchester United	3-1

Saturday 17 November

Aston Villa v. Middlesbrough	0-0
Blackburn Rovers v. Liverpool	1-1
Derby County v. Southampton	1-0
Fulham v. Newcastle United	3-1
Manchester United v. Leicester City	2-0
Tottenham Hotspur v. Arsenal	1-1

Sunday 18 November

Everton v. Chelsea	0-0
Ipswich Town v. Bolton Wanderers	1-2
Sunderland v. Leeds United	2-0

Monday 19 November

Charlton Athletic v. West Ham United	4-4

Saturday 24 November

Bolton Wanderers v. Fulham	0-0
Chelsea v. Blackburn Rovers	0-0
Leicester City v. Everton	0-0
Newcastle United v. Derby County	1-0
Southampton v. Charlton Athletic	1-0
West Ham United v. Tottenham Hotspur	0-1

Sunday 25 November

Arsenal v. Manchester United	3-1
Leeds United v. Aston Villa	1-1
Liverpool v. Sunderland	1-0
Middlesbrough v. Ipswich Town	0-0

		P	W	D	L	F	A	Pts
1	Liverpool	12	8	2	2	22	11	26
2	Leeds United	13	6	6	1	16	8	24
3	Arsenal	13	6	5	2	28	15	23
4	Newcastle United	13	7	2	4	23	17	23
5	Aston Villa	13	6	5	2	18	12	23
6	Manchester United	13	6	3	4	31	23	21
7	Tottenham Hotspur	14	6	3	5	21	18	21
8	Chelsea	13	4	8	1	16	11	20
9	Bolton Wanderers	14	5	5	4	18	17	20
10	Blackburn Rovers	14	4	7	3	21	16	19
11	Fulham	13	4	6	3	15	13	18
12	Everton	13	4	5	4	18	17	17
13	Sunderland	14	4	4	6	12	15	16
14	Middlesbrough	14	4	4	6	16	20	16
15	West Ham United	13	4	3	6	16	26	15
16	Charlton Athletic	13	3	5	5	16	18	14
17	Southampton	13	3	1	9	11	22	10
18	Derby County	13	2	4	7	10	23	10
19	Leicester City	14	2	4	8	7	25	10
20	Ipswich Town	14	1	6	7	14	22	9

Liverpool's Emile Heskey gets between Sunderland's Emerson Thome and Michael Gray to head home the winning goal past Thomas Sorensen.

LEICESTER win, for the first time in nine games, against Sunderland, and Ade Akinbiyi scores his first league goal for 203 days as the Foxes move out of the bottom three. Ravanelli nets on his return to the Riverside, his fourth consecutive scoring game, in the 89th minute, but it's small consolation for Derby County, who slump to the bottom of the table as a result of their heaviest defeat of the season. Southampton stay 19th after losing to Blackburn.

An awesome display by Liverpool, with two goals from Michael Owen, beats Manchester United, who drop to sixth, and puts the Anfield outfit top, for a few hours at least. Leeds go back to the summit after beating Spurs. Aston Villa fall two places to third after they lose to Newcastle, who go fourth. Arsenal slump to fifth after they suffer a shock defeat by Charlton, who hit four goals in 18 minutes.

Ipswich lose at Chelsea and drop into the bottom three. Samuele Dalla Bona hits the last-minute winner, his first goal for the club.

The impending storm over television rights money is worsened by the PFA's announcement that 99 percent of their members would vote in favour of strike action. Liverpool go top of the Premiership after a Michael Owen goal, his seventh of the season, earns a point at Blackburn. Manchester United climb two places to fourth after victory over Leicester, who drop a place, into the bottom three, as a consequence. Arsenal, after a fourth game without a win, stay fifth after a drawn North London derby. Newcastle's defeat by Fulham is United's 27th visit to the capital without a victory.

Leeds drop a place to second after losing, for the first time this campaign, at Sunderland. Ipswich sink to their lowest position of the season so far, 19th, when their defeat by Bolton extends their winless league run to 11 games.

Paul Kitson marks his first game for 21 months by scoring only the second Premiership hat-trick of the season as West Ham draw with Charlton. Only a 90th-minute Jonatan Johansson leveller prevents the Hammers' second away win.

The PFA announce strike action for the first weekend of December. But this is called off after the Premier League promises £52.5 million over three years. The players' union then reveal the deal is for 10 years, not three as first announced. Southampton win for the first time at their new St Mary's Stadium before a club record crowd of 31,198. Marian Pahars gets the only goal that beats Charlton and takes the Saints out of the bottom three, pulling the Addicks to 16th.

Leicester drop a place to 19th after drawing with Everton.

Liverpool remain top with an Emile Heskey goal that beats Sunderland and Leeds stay second with a draw against Aston Villa, but goalscorer Alan Smith is red-carded for the fifth time in his career. Fabien Barthez has a nightmare game at Highbury as two late Henry goals help Arsenal to a victory over Manchester United that takes the Gunners third and drops United two places to sixth.

Newcastle go fourth with a victory over Derby that plunges the Rams into the bottom three.

Ipswich drop to bottom of the table after drawing with Middlesbrough.

Table-topping Liverpool sell 'God', Robbie Fowler, to championship rivals Leeds United in an £11 million transfer that shocks Anfield fans. Fowler then reveals, after 171 goals for the club, that there was no contract on the table from Liverpool.

December

Saturday 1 December
Aston Villa v. Leicester City	0-2
Blackburn Rovers v. Middlesbrough	0-1
Charlton Athletic v. Newcastle United	1-1
Derby County v. Liverpool	0-1
Ipswich Town v. Arsenal	0-2
Manchester United v. Chelsea	0-3
Sunderland v. West Ham United	1-0

Sunday 2 December
Everton v. Southampton	2-0
Fulham v. Leeds United	0-0

Monday 3 December
Tottenham Hotspur v. Bolton Wanderers	3-2

Wednesday 5 December
Chelsea v. Charlton Athletic	0-1
West Ham United v. Aston Villa	1-1

Saturday 8 December
Charlton Athletic v. Tottenham Hotspur	3-1
Derby County v. Bolton Wanderers	1-0
Fulham v. Everton	2-0
Leicester City v. Southampton	0-4
Liverpool v. Middlesbrough	2-0
Manchester United v. West Ham United	0-1

Sunday 9 December
Arsenal v. Aston Villa	3-2
Blackburn Rovers v. Leeds United	1-2
Ipswich Town v. Newcastle United	0-1
Sunderland v. Chelsea	0-0

Wednesday 12 December
Liverpool v. Fulham	0-0
Manchester United v. Derby County	5-0

Saturday 15 December
Bolton Wanderers v. Charlton Athletic	0-0
Everton v. Derby County	1-0
Middlesbrough v. Manchester United	0-1
Newcastle United v. Blackburn Rovers	2-1
Southampton v. Sunderland	2-0
Tottenham Hotspur v. Fulham	4-0
West Ham United v. Arsenal	1-1

Sunday 16 December
Chelsea v. Liverpool	4-0
Leeds United v. Leicester City	2-2

Monday 17 December
Aston Villa v. Ipswich Town	2-1

Tuesday 18 December
Arsenal v. Newcastle United	1-3

Wednesday 19 December
Leeds United v. Everton	3-2

Saturday 22 December
Charlton Athletic v. Blackburn Rovers	0-2
Derby County v. Aston Villa	3-1
Leeds United v. Newcastle United	3-4
Leicester City v. West Ham United	1-1
Manchester United v. Southampton	6-1
Sunderland v. Everton	1-0
Tottenham Hotspur v. Ipswich Town	1-2

Sunday 23 December
Chelsea v. Bolton Wanderers	5-1
Liverpool v. Arsenal	1-2

Wednesday 26 December
Arsenal v. Chelsea	2-1
Aston Villa v. Liverpool	1-2
Blackburn Rovers v. Sunderland	0-3
Bolton Wanderers v. Leeds United	0-3
Everton v. Manchester United	0-2
Fulham v. Charlton Athletic	0-0
Ipswich Town v. Leicester City	2-0
Newcastle United v. Middlesbrough	3-0
Southampton v. Tottenham Hotspur	1-0
West Ham United v. Derby County	4-0

Saturday 29 December
Arsenal v. Middlesbrough	2-1
Aston Villa v. Tottenham Hotspur	1-1
Blackburn Rovers v. Derby County	0-1
Bolton Wanderers v. Leicester City	2-2
Everton v. Charlton Athletic	0-3
Ipswich Town v. Sunderland	5-0
Newcastle United v. Chelsea	1-2
Southampton v. Leeds United	0-1
West Ham United v. Liverpool	1-1

Sunday 30 December
Fulham v. Manchester United	2-3

		P	W	D	L	F	A	Pts
1	Arsenal	20	11	6	3	41	24	39
2	Newcastle United	20	12	3	5	38	25	39
3	Leeds United	20	10	8	2	30	17	38
4	Liverpool	19	11	4	4	29	19	37
5	Manchester United	20	11	3	6	48	30	36
6	Chelsea	20	8	9	3	31	16	33
7	Tottenham Hotspur	20	8	4	8	31	27	28
8	Aston Villa	20	7	7	6	26	25	28
9	Charlton Athletic	20	6	8	6	24	22	26
10	Sunderland	20	7	5	8	17	22	26
11	West Ham United	20	6	7	7	25	31	25
12	Fulham	19	5	9	5	19	20	24
13	Everton	20	6	5	9	23	28	23
14	Blackburn Rovers	20	5	7	8	25	25	22
15	Bolton Wanderers	20	5	7	8	23	31	22
16	Middlesbrough	19	5	4	10	18	28	19
17	Southampton	19	6	1	12	19	31	19
18	Derby County	20	5	4	11	15	35	19
19	Ipswich Town	20	4	6	10	24	28	18
20	Leicester City	20	3	7	10	14	36	16

MICHAEL OWEN'S fifth goal in five games beats Derby County to keep Liverpool top and Derby 19th. Arsenal move up to second after victory over Ipswich, who stay bottom. Chelsea shock Manchester United with a comprehensive victory that takes them up three places to fifth, two places above United, beaten in successive games for the first time this season.

Leeds drop another place, to third, after drawing with Fulham. Alan Shearer's dismissal, in the draw with Charlton, is wiped out after referee Andy D'Urso views video footage. Southampton lose to Everton and drop back into the bottom three.

Liverpool maintain pole position with a win over Middlesbrough, in which Michael Owen scores again.

Manchester United lose to London opposition for the third game in a row against West Ham and plunge to ninth, their lowest position of the season.

Leicester are crushed by Southampton, the fourth time already this season that they have conceded four or more goals, and drop to bottom of the table.

Thierry Henry is on the scoresheet for the third game running as Arsenal beat Aston Villa and stay second. A Harry Kewell brace beats Blackburn and keeps Leeds third.

Liverpool stay top after a draw with Fulham. Derby County have the misfortune to be on the receiving end of a wounded Manchester United, who record their best win of the campaign. Even Roy Keane scores, with his first goal of the season.

Arsenal remain second after drawing with West Ham, with Ashley Cole getting his first Gunners' goal of the season. Newcastle move up to third after beating Blackburn and there is a milestone for former Magpie Les Ferdinand. His opener, in Spurs' defeat of Fulham, is the 10,000th goal in the nine-year history of the Premiership and earns a £10,000 cheque for charity from sponsors Barclaycard.

Liverpool suffer their worst defeat of the season, to Chelsea, but stay top of the table, while Chelsea remain fifth. Leeds drop again, to fourth, after drawing with Leicester, who improve a place to 18th.

Ipswich's third consecutive defeat, to Villa, keeps them bottom.

Newcastle win again and their victory over Arsenal is a record-breaking win in London, at the 30th attempt, which puts the Geordies top of the table, but they have to come back from a goal down, scoring three times in the last half hour.

Newcastle again come back from a deficit, 3–1, to beat Leeds and retain top spot, and, again, they hit three goals in the final 30 minutes, 'Nobby' Solano nets the 90th-minute winner. Ruud Van Nistelrooy nets the fastest Premiership goal of the season, after 30 seconds, to put Manchester United on the road to a comprehensive win over Southampton. The Dutchman goes on to complete his hat-trick in what is now United's biggest victory of the campaign that moves them up a place to fifth.

Derby beat Aston Villa and improve one place to 18th. Leicester drop a place to 19th after drawing with West Ham. Poor old Ipswich get their first win in 16 games, against Spurs, but stay bottom for Christmas.

Liverpool's second consecutive defeat, to Arsenal, knocks them down to third and keeps the Gunners second. But Giovanni Van Bronckhorst is sent off for diving, the 40th red card during Arsene Wenger's Highbury reign.

Leaders Newcastle beat Middlesbrough and Arsenal beat Chelsea to stay second. Liverpool get their first win in four games by beating Aston Villa to go third. Leeds beat Bolton, with a Robbie Fowler hat-trick, and go fourth.

Derby stay 18th when they lose to West Ham. Leicester drop to bottom when they lose to Ipswich, who move above them.

Michael Owen comes on as substitute, against West Ham, to deny the Hammers victory with his 100th goal for Liverpool in the 88th minute, but the draw drops Liverpool to fourth.

Arsenal beat Middlesbrough to end the year on top of the Premiership with the decisive goal, his second in a fortnight, coming from Ashley Cole.

Manchester United secure their fifth successive victory, over Fulham, and are just three points adrift of leaders Arsenal. Ipswich win their last two games of the year, against Leicester and Sunderland, to climb off the bottom.

FACT FILE

The last time United lost three Premiership games in a row was in the last three fixtures of 2000–01, after they had already clinched the title. The last time the team were as low as ninth in the table was the opening day of 1999–2000. In the season proper, United had not been this low since 20 September 1998, when they were actually 10th.

January

Tuesday 1 January

Charlton Athletic v. Ipswich Town	3-2
Chelsea v. Southampton	2-4
Leeds United v. West Ham United	3-0
Liverpool v. Bolton Wanderers	1-1
Middlesbrough v. Everton	1-0
Sunderland v. Aston Villa	1-1
Tottenham Hotspur v. Blackburn Rovers	1-0

Wednesday 2 January

Derby County v. Fulham	0-1
Manchester United v. Newcastle United	3-1

Wednesday 9 January

Southampton v. Liverpool	2-0

Saturday 12 January

Aston Villa v. Derby County	2-1
Blackburn Rovers v. Charlton Athletic	4-1
Bolton Wanderers v. Chelsea	2-2
Everton v. Sunderland	1-0
Fulham v. Middlesbrough	2-1
Ipswich Town v. Tottenham Hotspur	2-1
Newcastle United v. Leeds United	3-1
West Ham United v. Leicester City	1-0

Sunday 13 January

Arsenal v. Liverpool	1-1
Southampton v. Manchester United	1-3

Saturday 19 January

Derby County v. Ipswich Town	1-3
Leicester City v. Newcastle United	0-0
Liverpool v. Southampton	1-1
Manchester United v. Blackburn Rovers	2-1
Middlesbrough v. Bolton Wanderers	1-1
Sunderland v. Fulham	1-1
Tottenham Hotspur v. Everton	1-1

Sunday 20 January

Chelsea v. West Ham United	5-1
Leeds United v. Arsenal	1-1

Monday 21 January

Charlton Athletic v. Aston Villa	1-2

Tuesday 22 January

Manchester United v. Liverpool	0-1

Wednesday 23 January

Leicester City v. Arsenal	1-3

Tuesday 29 January

Bolton Wanderers v. Manchester United	0-4
Charlton Athletic v. Derby County	1-0
Sunderland v. Middlesbrough	0-1

Wednesday 30 January

Aston Villa v. Everton	0-0
Blackburn Rovers v. Arsenal	2-3
Chelsea v. Leeds United	2-0
Ipswich Town v. Fulham	1-0
Liverpool v. Leicester City	1-0
Southampton v. West Ham United	2-0
Tottenham Hotspur v. Newcastle United	1-3

		P	W	D	L	F	A	Pts
1	Manchester United	25	15	3	7	60	34	48
2	Arsenal	24	13	8	3	49	29	47
3	Newcastle United	24	14	4	6	45	30	46
4	Liverpool	25	13	7	5	34	24	46
5	Leeds United	24	11	9	4	35	23	42
6	Chelsea	24	10	10	4	42	23	40
7	Aston Villa	24	9	9	6	31	28	36
8	Tottenham Hotspur	24	9	5	10	35	33	32
9	Charlton Athletic	24	8	8	8	30	30	32
10	Fulham	23	7	10	6	23	23	31
11	Southampton	24	9	2	13	29	37	29
12	Everton	24	7	7	10	25	30	28
13	Sunderland	24	7	7	10	19	26	28
14	West Ham United	24	7	7	10	27	41	28
15	Ipswich Town	24	7	6	11	32	33	27
16	Middlesbrough	23	7	5	11	22	31	26
17	Blackburn Rovers	24	6	7	11	32	32	25
18	Bolton Wanderers	24	5	10	9	27	39	25
19	Derby County	24	5	4	15	17	42	19
20	Leicester City	24	3	8	13	15	41	17

SUNDERLAND'S Niall Quinn decides his £1 million testimonial will be donated to children's charities.

Leeds take over at the top by beating West Ham. Liverpool are held by Bolton and stay fourth.

Ruud Van Nistelrooy scores for the sixth league game running as United close in on leaders Arsenal with victory over Newcastle. Alan Shearer's goal gives him a fifth consecutive scoring game.

Derby lose to Fulham and stay in the bottom three.

Alan Smith's goal for Leeds, after 24 seconds, is the fastest of the Premiership, but 'comeback kings' Newcastle secure a victory that takes them second and drops Leeds to fourth.

Ipswich beat Spurs to stay just above Leicester, on goal difference, after the Foxes lose to West Ham and stay bottom.

Derby, after losing for the 11th time in 17 matches, to Aston Villa, end Colin Todd's reign after 98 days.

Manchester United top the table, for the first time this season, and Ruud Van Nistelrooy scores for the seventh consecutive game as Southampton are beaten. Arsenal drop to fourth when they are held by Liverpool, who are one place behind.

Ruud Van Nistelrooy nets for a record eighth consecutive Premiership game in the win over Blackburn that keeps Manchester United top. Newcastle remain second despite being held by Leicester, who stay bottom. Middlesbrough drop into the bottom three when they are held by Bolton.

Derby lose to Ipswich and remain 19th but Town climb out of the bottom three as a consequence. Marcus Bent scores for the victors for the third game running.

Leeds are held by Arsenal and the clubs stay third and fourth respectively, but the Gunners become the first Premiership club to reach 50 yellow cards this campaign.

Liverpool's defeat of Manchester United, with Danny Murphy hitting an 85th-minute winner, throws the title race wide open.

Arsenal beat Leicester and stay fourth. The Foxes remain bottom. John Gregory resigns at Villa, just short of his fourth anniversary as manager, citing a lack of transfer funds as the reason.

Solskjaer hits his first hat-trick of the season as Manchester United beat Bolton and maintain pole position.

Derby lose their fourth game of the month to stay in trouble, in 19th place.

Marcus Bent scores again as Ipswich beat Fulham, but skipper Matt Holland makes history by playing his 200th consecutive game for the club since he arrived at Portman Road from Bournemouth in July 1997. Emile Heskey is the match-winner for Liverpool and keeps his former club, Leicester, bottom of the table.

Six days after leaving Villa, the club that beat Derby to end the tenure of Colin Todd, John Gregory takes over as Derby manager.

Manchester United's Ruud Van Nistelrooy sees his header go past Blackburn Rovers' goalkeeper Brad Friedel but wide of the goal.

February

Saturday 2 February	
Arsenal v. Southampton	1-1
Derby County v. Tottenham Hotspur	1-0
Everton v. Ipswich Town	1-2
Fulham v. Aston Villa	0-0
Leicester City v. Chelsea	2-3
Manchester United v. Sunderland	4-1
Newcastle United v. Bolton Wanderers	3-2
West Ham United v. Blackburn Rovers	2-0

Sunday 3 February	
Leeds United v. Liverpool	0-4
Middlesbrough v. Charlton Athletic	0-0

Saturday 9 February	
Aston Villa v. Chelsea	1-1
Bolton Wanderers v. West Ham United	1-0
Derby County v. Sunderland	0-1
Fulham v. Blackburn Rovers	2-0
Ipswich Town v. Liverpool	0-6
Middlesbrough v. Leeds United	2-2
Newcastle United v. Southampton	3-1
Tottenham Hotspur v. Leicester City	2-1

Sunday 10 February	
Charlton Athletic v. Manchester United	0-2
Everton v. Arsenal	0-1

Tuesday 19 February	
Middlesbrough v. Fulham	2-1

Saturday 23 February	
Arsenal v. Fulham	4-1
Leicester City v. Derby County	0-3
Liverpool v. Everton	1-1
Manchester United v. Aston Villa	1-0
Southampton v. Bolton Wanderers	0-0
West Ham United v. Middlesbrough	1-0

Sunday 24 February	
Leeds United v. Charlton Athletic	0-0
Sunderland v. Newcastle United	0-1

		P	W	D	L	F	A	Pts
1	Manchester United	28	18	3	7	67	35	57
2	Newcastle United	27	17	4	6	52	33	55
3	Arsenal	27	15	9	3	55	31	54
4	Liverpool	28	15	8	5	45	25	53
5	Chelsea	26	11	11	4	46	26	44
6	Leeds United	27	11	11	5	37	29	44
7	Aston Villa	27	9	11	7	32	30	38
8	Tottenham Hotspur	26	10	5	11	37	35	35
9	Fulham	27	8	11	8	27	29	35
10	Charlton Athletic	27	8	10	9	30	32	34
11	West Ham United	27	9	7	11	30	42	34
12	Middlesbrough	27	8	7	12	26	35	31
13	Southampton	27	9	4	14	31	41	31
14	Sunderland	27	8	7	12	21	31	31
15	Ipswich Town	26	8	6	12	34	40	30
16	Everton	27	7	8	12	27	34	29
17	Bolton Wanderers	27	6	11	10	30	42	29
18	Blackburn Rovers	26	6	7	13	32	36	25
19	Derby County	27	7	4	16	21	43	25
20	Leicester City	27	3	8	16	18	49	17

MANCHESTER UNITED cruise to victory over Sunderland and confirm leadership of the Premiership. Although Ruud Van Nistelrooy hits two to take his tally to 18 it's David Beckham, who abandons his trademark white boots, who makes the headlines with a free-kick scored wearing all-black footwear. Alan Shearer also hits two as Newcastle beat Bolton to stay second, sending Wanderers into the bottom three. Arsenal are held by Southampton and remain fourth.

Leicester give Chelsea a run for their money before going down to a Jimmy Floyd Hasselbaink 90th-minute winner. Chelsea go fifth while Leicester stay bottom. Derby end their losing run with a Lee Morris goal, beating Spurs to climb up to 19th.

Liverpool keep a third consecutive clean sheet as they inflict Leeds' worst home defeat for nearly two years and take third place.

Newcastle make 18-year-old Jermaine Jenas English football's most expensive teenager when they pay Nottingham Forest £5 million for him.

Graham Taylor signs a two and a half year contract to take over as Aston Villa manager. Sir Alex Ferguson does a U-turn and reveals that his 'wife and family' persuaded him to postpone his planned retirement.

After becoming only the third player in 67 years to move from Everton to Liverpool Abel Xavier marks his debut with the opening goal in the thrashing of Ipswich which Town manager George Burley sums up by saying: 'we were lucky to get away with 6–0'. Liverpool move up to second while Ipswich drop to 13th. Newcastle drop to third despite a victory over Southampton in which Alan Shearer nets twice against his first club.

Leicester lose again, to Spurs, and stay bottom. Derby are one place better off after

losing to Sunderland and Ricardo Gardner gets the goal that beats West Ham and takes Bolton out of the bottom three. Blackburn replace Wanderers after their fourth successive defeat, against Fulham, plunges them into trouble.

Solskjaer's brace beats Charlton and provides a change of Premiership leader for the 25th time this campaign as Manchester United take pole position.

Nicolas Anelka scores his first goal for Liverpool in the drawn Mersey derby that drops Liverpool down to fourth. Arsenal climb above Liverpool by beating Fulham and Thierry Henry's brace takes his tally to 20. But Manchester United are still leaders after Ruud Van Nistelrooy nets the winner against Villa.

Newcastle beat Sunderland and climb to second.

Sir Alex Ferguson signs a three-year deal to remain as Manchester United's manager.

Newcastle United's Jermaine Jenas at the press conference to announce his arrival from Nottingham Forest, with Newcastle manager Bobby Robson.

March

Saturday 2 March

Aston Villa v. West Ham United	2-1
Bolton Wanderers v. Blackburn Rovers	1-1
Charlton Athletic v. Chelsea	2-1
Fulham v. Liverpool	0-2
Ipswich Town v. Southampton	1-3
Middlesbrough v. Leicester City	1-0
Newcastle United v. Arsenal	0-2
Tottenham Hotspur v. Sunderland	2-1

Sunday 3 March

Derby County v. Manchester United	2-2
Everton v. Leeds United	0-0

Tuesday 5 March

Arsenal v. Derby County	1-0
Blackburn Rovers v. Aston Villa	3-0
Sunderland v. Bolton Wanderers	1-0

Wednesday 6 March

Chelsea v. Fulham	3-2
Leeds United v. Ipswich Town	2-0
Liverpool v. Newcastle United	3-0
Manchester United v. Tottenham Hotspur	4-0
Southampton v. Middlesbrough	1-1
West Ham United v. Everton	1-0

Saturday 9 March

Leicester City v. Charlton Athletic	1-1

Wednesday 13 March

Blackburn Rovers v. Ipswich Town	2-1
Chelsea v. Tottenham Hotspur	4-0

Saturday 16 March

Bolton Wanderers v. Derby County	1-3
Chelsea v. Sunderland	4-0
Everton v. Fulham	2-1
Middlesbrough v. Liverpool	1-2
Newcastle United v. Ipswich Town	2-2
Southampton v. Leicester City	2-2
West Ham United v. Manchester United	3-5

Sunday 17 March

Aston Villa v. Arsenal	1-2
Leeds United v. Blackburn Rovers	3-1

Monday 18 March

Tottenham Hotspur v. Charlton Athletic	0-1

Saturday 23 March

Charlton Athletic v. Bolton Wanderers	1-2
Derby County v. Everton	3-4
Ipswich Town v. Aston Villa	0-0
Leicester City v. Leeds United	0-2
Manchester United v. Middlesbrough	0-1
Sunderland v. Southampton	1-1

Sunday 24 March

Fulham v. Tottenham Hotspur	0-2
Liverpool v. Chelsea	1-0

Friday 29 March

Newcastle United v. Everton	6-2

Saturday 30 March

Arsenal v. Sunderland	3-0
Bolton Wanderers v. Aston Villa	3-2
Chelsea v. Derby County	2-1
Leeds United v. Manchester United	3-4
Leicester City v. Blackburn Rovers	2-1
Liverpool v. Charlton Athletic	2-0
Middlesbrough v. Tottenham Hotspur	1-1
Southampton v. Fulham	1-1
West Ham United v. Ipswich Town	3-1

		P	W	D	L	F	A	Pts
1	Liverpool	33	20	8	5	55	26	68
2	Manchester United	33	21	4	8	82	44	67
3	Arsenal	31	19	9	3	63	32	66
4	Newcastle United	31	18	5	8	60	42	59
5	Chelsea	32	15	11	6	60	32	56
6	Leeds United	32	14	12	6	47	34	54
7	Aston Villa	32	10	12	10	37	39	42
8	Tottenham Hotspur	32	12	6	14	42	46	42
9	Charlton Athletic	32	10	11	11	35	38	41
10	West Ham United	31	11	7	13	38	50	40
11	Middlesbrough	32	10	9	13	31	39	39
12	Southampton	32	10	8	14	39	47	38
13	Fulham	32	8	12	12	31	39	36
14	Everton	32	9	9	14	35	45	36
15	Bolton Wanderers	32	8	12	12	37	50	36
16	Sunderland	32	9	8	15	24	41	35
17	Blackburn Rovers	31	8	8	15	40	43	32
18	Ipswich Town	32	8	8	16	39	52	32
19	Derby County	32	8	5	19	30	53	29
20	Leicester City	32	4	10	18	23	56	22

ROY KEANE follows his manager's example and signs a new contract, the most expensive in Manchester United's history, reputedly worth £90,000 per week, to stay at Old Trafford for another four years.

Arsenal improve a place to second after winning at Newcastle, who drop to fourth. Liverpool, with Anelka scoring again, beat Fulham and improve to third.

Manchester United are fortunate not to lose at Derby, where the home side have a dramatic last-minute goal ruled out, but the draw keeps United top and the Rams stay one place off the bottom. Blackburn draw with Bolton but stay 18th; Wanderers are 17th. A sixth consecutive Leicester defeat, to Middlesbrough, keeps the Foxes rooted to the bottom.

David Beckham and Ruud Van Nistelrooy share the goals as Manchester United retain pole position with victory over Spurs.

Leeds announce a loss of nearly £14 million, which prompts fears of player sales.

Walter Smith and Everton part company, after three and a half years. Two days later David Moyes, Preston's highly rated 39-year-old manager, is installed as manager at Goodison Park, but only after a compensation settlement said to be in the order of £1 million. Paul Gascoigne leaves Everton for Burnley for the remainder of the season.

Another eight-goal capital thriller sees Manchester United claim the points against West Ham and David Beckham nets a brace for the second game running to keep United top. Liverpool win at 'Boro and are third.

An 87th-minute Marian Pahars penalty, his second goal of the game, robs Leicester of a crucial away win and keeps them 20th. Derby are winners at Bolton but stay 19th, one place behind Wanderers.

Arsenal suffer a hammer-blow to their title chances when Robert Pires is stretchered off with damaged knee ligaments, ending his season. But the Gunners beat Villa in a fifth consecutive victory and climb to second, with, paradoxically, Pires's goal proving the winner. Manchester United suffer a crucial defeat when they lose at home to Middlesbrough, who take the points with an Alan Boksic winner.

Leicester are still bottom after losing to Leeds, who climb a place to fifth. Ipswich draw with Aston Villa and drop into the relegation zone but Derby are in real trouble after they crash at home to Everton, and remain 19th.

Liverpool go top of the table after a last-minute Vladimir Smicer winner beats Chelsea. The club then stay top after their next game, with goals from Smicer and Owen ensuring a fifth win in a row. Manchester United win a real 'ding-dong' game at Elland Road, and remain second. Despite another victory, over Sunderland, in which Tony Adams plays his 500th Gunners' game, Arsenal drop to third.

Leicester win for the first time in 18 games, with a Paul Dickov brace beating Blackburn, but the Foxes look doomed in 20th place.

Derby lose at Chelsea and look odds-on to join their East Midlands neighbours in the drop. Ipswich lose at West Ham and complete the bottom three.

Liverpool's Vladimir Smicer is mobbed by teammates after scoring the winning goal in the last minute of play against Chelsea.

April

Monday 1 April

Blackburn Rovers v. Southampton	2-0
Charlton Athletic v. Arsenal	0-3
Derby County v. Middlesbrough	0-1
Everton v. Bolton Wanderers	3-1
Fulham v. West Ham United	0-1
Ipswich Town v. Chelsea	0-0
Sunderland v. Leicester City	2-1
Tottenham Hotspur v. Leeds United	2-1

Tuesday 2 April

Aston Villa v. Newcastle United	1-1

Saturday 6 April

Arsenal v. Tottenham Hotspur	2-1
Bolton Wanderers v. Ipswich Town	4-1
Chelsea v. Everton	3-0
Leicester City v. Manchester United	0-1
Middlesbrough v. Aston Villa	2-1
Southampton v. Derby County	2-0
West Ham United v. Charlton Athletic	2-0

Sunday 7 April

Leeds United v. Sunderland	2-0

Monday 8 April

Newcastle United v. Fulham	1-1

Wednesday 10 April

Blackburn Rovers v. Chelsea	0-0

Saturday 13 April

Aston Villa v. Leeds United	0-1
Charlton Athletic v. Southampton	1-1
Derby County v. Newcastle United	2-3
Everton v. Leicester City	2-2
Sunderland v. Liverpool	0-1
Tottenham Hotspur v. West Ham United	1-1

Saturday 20 April

Bolton Wanderers v. Tottenham Hotspur	1-1
Chelsea v. Manchester United	0-3
Leeds United v. Fulham	0-1
Leicester City v. Aston Villa	2-2
Liverpool v. Derby County	2-0
Middlesbrough v. Blackburn Rovers	1-3
Newcastle United v. Charlton Athletic	3-0
Southampton v. Everton	0-1
West Ham United v. Sunderland	3-0

Sunday 21 April

Arsenal v. Ipswich Town	2-0

Tuesday 23 April

Blackburn Rovers v. Newcastle United	2-2
Fulham v. Bolton Wanderers	3-0

Wednesday 24 April

Arsenal v. West Ham United	2-0
Ipswich Town v. Middlesbrough	1-0

Saturday 27 April

Aston Villa v. Southampton	2-1
Charlton Athletic v. Sunderland	2-2
Derby County v. Leeds United	0-1
Fulham v. Leicester City	0-0
Ipswich Town v. Manchester United	0-1
Middlesbrough v. Chelsea	0-2
Newcastle United v. West Ham United	3-1
Tottenham Hotspur v. Liverpool	1-0

Sunday 28 April

Everton v. Blackburn Rovers	1-2

Monday 29 April

Bolton Wanderers v. Arsenal	0-2

		P	W	D	L	F	A	Pts
1	Arsenal	36	24	9	3	74	33	81
2	Manchester United	36	24	4	8	87	44	76
3	Liverpool	36	22	8	6	58	27	74
4	Newcastle United	37	21	8	8	73	49	71
5	Chelsea	37	17	13	7	65	35	64
6	Leeds United	37	17	12	8	52	37	63
7	Tottenham Hotspur	37	14	8	15	48	51	50
8	West Ham United	37	14	8	15	46	56	50
9	Aston Villa	37	11	14	12	43	46	47
10	Middlesbrough	37	12	9	16	35	46	45
11	Fulham	37	10	14	13	36	41	44
12	Blackburn Rovers	36	11	10	15	49	47	43
13	Everton	37	11	10	16	42	53	43
14	Charlton Athletic	37	10	13	14	38	49	43
15	Southampton	37	11	9	17	43	53	42
16	Bolton Wanderers	37	9	13	15	43	60	40
17	Sunderland	37	10	9	18	28	50	39
18	Ipswich Town	37	9	9	19	41	59	36
19	Derby County	37	8	5	24	32	62	29
20	Leicester City	37	4	13	20	28	63	25

Arsenal's Freddie Ljungberg is chased down by Bolton's Kevin Nolan.

ARSENAL go top, for the first time in the year, by winning their sixth consecutive away game against Charlton. Thierry Henry scores twice, for the sixth time in the campaign, taking his tally to 22.

Derby's home defeat, by Middlesbrough, seems to have settled their fate as the Rams stay 19th, just above Leicester, who lose to Sunderland. Ipswich get a draw with Chelsea but are still 18th.

An 86th-minute Lauren penalty gives Arsenal victory over Spurs and keeps them top. Manchester United maintain the pressure on the leaders with a Solskjaer winner that keeps them in second place and Leicester are rooted to the foot of the table. Ipswich stay 18th after being hammered by Bolton.

Liverpool drop to second despite a sixth consecutive win, over Sunderland, with Michael Owen getting the only goal of the game.

Jamie Redknapp pulls the curtain down on his 11-year career at Liverpool and moves to Spurs on a free transfer.

Liverpool's seventh win on the bounce, with Michael Owen's brace too much for Derby, keeps the Anfield side second and condemns the Rams to Division One. Manchester United win at Chelsea but drop a place to third.

Freddie Ljungberg scores twice to beat Ipswich to keep the Gunners in pole position and Town 18th.

Alan Shearer scores two goals against Blackburn, his former club, to earn Newcastle a place in the Champions League.

Arsenal steamroller on with their 10th win in succession, against West Ham, with Freddie Ljungberg

FACT FILE

Alan Shearer's 89th-minute goal, in Newcastle's win over Charlton on 20 April, is his 200th in the Premier League, 61 ahead of nearest rival Andy Cole.

scoring for the fourth consecutive game.

Manchester United need a Van Nistelrooy penalty to sink doomed Ipswich and remain second. Liverpool's title hopes end, and they drop to third, after a shock defeat at Spurs. Gus Poyet's 10th goal of the season proves the match-winner.

Ljungberg scores again as Arsenal win at Bolton leaving the Gunners requiring just one point, at Manchester United, to clinch the title.

Wednesday 8 May

Liverpool v. Blackburn Rovers		4-3
Manchester United v. Arsenal		0-1

Saturday 11 May

Arsenal v. Everton		4-3
Blackburn Rovers v. Fulham		3-0
Chelsea v. Aston Villa		1-3
Leeds United v. Middlesbrough		1-0
Leicester City v. Tottenham Hotspur		2-1
Liverpool v. Ipswich Town		5-0
Manchester United v. Charlton Athletic		0-0
Southampton v. Newcastle United		3-1
Sunderland v. Derby County		1-1
West Ham United v. Bolton Wanderers		2-1

		P	W	D	L	F	A	Pts
1	Arsenal	38	26	9	3	79	36	87
2	Liverpool	38	24	8	6	67	30	80
3	Manchester United	38	24	5	9	87	45	77
4	Newcastle United	38	21	8	9	74	52	71
5	Leeds United	38	18	12	8	53	37	66
6	Chelsea	38	17	13	8	66	38	64
7	West Ham United	38	15	8	15	48	57	53
8	Aston Villa	38	12	14	12	46	47	50
9	Tottenham Hotspur	38	14	8	16	49	53	50
10	Blackburn Rovers	38	12	10	16	55	51	46
11	Southampton	38	12	9	17	46	54	45
12	Middlesbrough	38	12	9	17	35	47	45
13	Fulham	38	10	14	14	36	44	44
14	Charlton Athletic	38	10	14	14	38	49	44
15	Everton	38	11	10	17	45	57	43
16	Bolton Wanderers	38	9	13	16	44	62	40
17	Sunderland	38	10	10	18	29	51	40
18	Ipswich Town	38	9	9	20	41	64	36
19	Derby County	38	8	6	24	33	63	30
20	Leicester City	38	5	13	20	30	64	28

Promoted from Nationwide Football League Division One

Manchester City
West Bromwich Albion
Birmingham City (via play-offs)

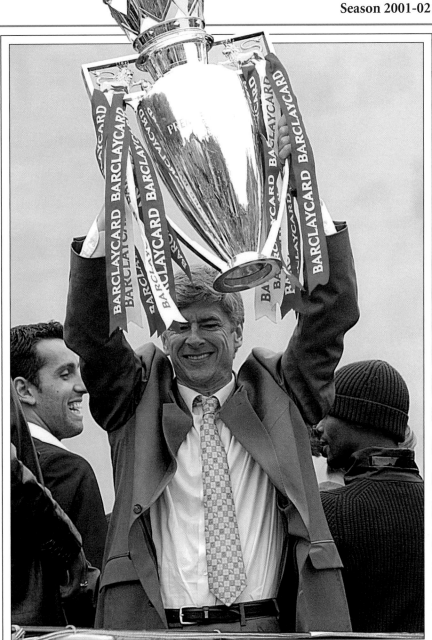

Arsenal manager Arsene Wenger lifts the Premiership trophy for the second time.

SIR ALEX FERGUSON loses his temper at a press conference when media critics question his £28 million purchase of Juan Sebastian Veron. Roy Keane follows up with an attack on certain Old Trafford teammates who he claims have not been pulling their weight.

With deep irony Arsenal clinch the Premiership title, and the 'Double', on Manchester United's patch with a Sylvain Wiltord goal that earns a 12th consecutive victory. The Gunners are eight points clear of United who finish without a trophy for only the third time in 13 years. Arsenal finish with an unbeaten away record, something not achieved in the top flight since Preston did it in 1889.

After 12 years Denis Irwin plays his 527th, and last, game for Manchester United in the draw at Charlton that gives United a third-place finish.

It's party time at Highbury, where Arsenal receive the Premiership trophy and then celebrate with their 13th consecutive victory. Ironically their winner, in a seven-goal thriller with Everton, comes from former Goodison player Francis Jeffers.

Two issues are settled at Anfield, where Liverpool's crushing victory over Ipswich earns them a Champions League place as runners-up and relegates Town. Michael Owen scores and takes his tally to 19, 10 more than the nearest challenger, Emile Heskey.

Heskey's former club, Leicester, say goodbye to the Premiership with their first win in six games, against Spurs, but they finish bottom.

Derby's six-year run in the top flight finishes with a draw against Sunderland, who finish four points above the drop line.

End of season round-up

Top Premiership Goalscorers 2001–02

Thiery Henry	Arsenal	24
Ruud Van Nisterooy	Manchester United	23
Jimmy Floyd Hasselbaink		
	Chelsea	23
Alan Shearer	Newcastle United	23
Michael Owen	Liverpool	19
Ole Gunnar Solskjaer	Manchester United	17
Robbie Fowler	Leeds United	15
(3 for Liverpool)		
Eidur Gudjohnsen	Chelsea	14
Marian Pahars	Southampton	14
Frederik Ljungberg	Arsenal	12
Michael Ricketts	Bolton Wanderers	12
Juan Pablo Angel	Aston Villa	12
James Beattie	Southampton	12
Darius Vassell	Aston Villa	12

Worthington League Cup

Blackburn Rovers 2   Tottenham Hotspur 1

Blackburn emerged victorious from the first domestic cup final to be played under cover as the retractable roof of the Millennium Stadium was closed. Matt Jensen put Rovers ahead just past the halfway point of the first half, only for Christian Ziege to equalise just five minutes later. The decisive goal came from Andy Cole, who scored with just over 20 minutes remaining to secure Blackburn's first ever League Cup.

FA Cup Final

Arsenal 2   Chelsea 0

Arsenal were given a massive advantage when Chelsea fielded a palpably unfit Jimmy Floyd Hasselbaink from the start, although the Gunners took until 20 minutes from time to open the scoring. The Premiership winners were always comfortable in the first all-London final for 21 years. The first goal came with a stunning long-range curling shot from Ray Parlour, after runs by Thierry Henry and Sylvain Wiltord created the space for the midfielder. Ten minutes later Arsenal clinched the FA Cup when Ljungberg had the strength to hold off a defender before curling his shot inside the far post. Skipper Tony Adams, 35, lifted the FA Cup on his 669th appearance for Arsenal.

FWA Footballer of the Year

Robert Pires   Arsenal

PFA Player of the Year

Ruud Van Nistelrooy

PFA Young Player of the Year

Craig Bellamy   Newcastle United

Manager of the Year

Arsene Wenger   Arsenal

Close Season 2002

Gerard Houllier decides against making Nicolas Anelka a permanent signing from PSG after his loan spell at Anfield. Manchester City line up Anelka but first sign Sylvain Distin, for £3.8 million.

Blackburn's Matt Jansen is in a coma for two days after being knocked off a motorbike in Italy.

Leeds United, £77 million in the red, sack David O'Leary.

Newcastle pay Ipswich £5 million for defender Titus Bramble.

Manchester City pay £10 million for Anelka, while United name Portuguese Carlos Queiroz as Sir Alex's assistant.

Middlesbrough re-sign Juninho, as well as Massimo Maccarone, for £13 million. Former 'Boro coach Terry Venables becomes manager at Leeds United.

Bolton's Gudni Bergsson postpones his planned retirement, to become a lawyer back home in Iceland, for a fourth year running and signs another one-year deal to stay at the Reebok Stadium.

Manchester United smash the British record and pay £30 million to Leeds for Rio Ferdinand. Arsene Wenger then claims that United paid £10 million over the odds for the England defender. Liverpool call off the proposed £8 million signing of Lee Bowyer after Gerard Houllier questions the player's commitment.

Four years after joining Manchester United for £12.6 million, from Villa, Dwight Yorke leaves Old Trafford for Blackburn in a £2 million deal. Arsenal buy Brazilian World Cup-winner Gilberto Silva for £4.5 million and the midfielder celebrates by scoring the only goal as Arsenal win the Community Shield against Liverpool.

Manchester United's new signing Rio Ferdinand, at the press conference announcing his move to Old Trafford.

Saturday 17 August	
Blackburn Rovers v. Sunderland	0-0
Charlton Athletic v. Chelsea	2-3
Everton v. Tottenham Hotspur	2-2
Fulham v. Bolton Wanderers	4-1
Leeds United v. Manchester City	3-0
Manchester United v. West Bromwich Alb.	1-0
Southampton v. Middlesbrough	0-0
Sunday 18 August	
Arsenal v. Birmingham City	2-0
Aston Villa v. Liverpool	0-1
Monday 19 August	
Newcastle United v. West Ham United	4-0
Friday 23 August	
Chelsea v. Manchester United	2-2
Saturday 24 August	
Birmingham City v. Blackburn Rovers	0-1
Bolton Wanderers v. Charlton Athletic	1-2
Liverpool v. Southampton	3-0
Manchester City v. Newcastle United	1-0
Middlesbrough v. Fulham	2-2
Sunderland v. Everton	0-1
Tottenham Hotspur v. Aston Villa	1-0
West Bromwich Alb. v. Leeds United	1-3
West Ham United v. Arsenal	2-2
Tuesday 27 August	
Arsenal v. West Bromwich Alb.	5-2
Charlton Athletic v. Tottenham Hotspur	0-1
Wednesday 28 August	
Aston Villa v. Manchester City	1-0
Blackburn Rovers v. Liverpool	2-2
Everton v. Birmingham City	1-1
Leeds United v. Sunderland	0-1
Southampton v. Chelsea	1-1
Saturday 31 August	
Birmingham City v. Leeds United	2-1
Manchester City v. Everton	3-1
Middlesbrough v. Blackburn Rovers	1-0
Sunderland v. Manchester United	1-1
Tottenham Hotspur v. Southampton	2-1
West Bromwich Alb. v. Fulham	1-0
West Ham United v. Charlton Athletic	0-2

		P	W	D	L	F	A	Pts
1	Tottenham Hotspur	4	3	1	0	6	3	10
2	Arsenal	3	2	1	0	9	4	7
3	Liverpool	3	2	1	0	6	2	7
4	Leeds United	4	2	0	2	7	4	6
5	Charlton Athletic	4	2	0	2	6	5	6
6	Manchester City	4	2	0	2	4	5	6
7	Chelsea	3	1	2	0	6	5	5
8	Manchester United	3	1	2	0	4	3	5
9	Middlesbrough	3	1	2	0	3	2	5
10	Blackburn Rovers	4	1	2	1	3	3	5
11	Sunderland	4	1	2	1	2	2	5
12	Everton	4	1	2	1	5	6	5
13	Fulham	3	1	1	1	6	4	4
14	Birmingham City	4	1	1	2	3	5	4
15	Newcastle United	2	1	0	1	4	1	3
16	Aston Villa	3	1	0	2	1	2	3
17	West Bromwich Alb.	4	1	0	3	4	9	3
18	Southampton	4	0	2	2	2	6	2
19	West Ham United	3	0	1	2	2	8	1
20	Bolton Wanderers	2	0	0	2	2	6	0

West Bromwich Albion's Darren Moore goal against Fulham takes Albion off the foot of the table.

OLE GUNNAR SOLS-KJAER nets his 100th goal as Manchester United open with a win over Premiership new boys West Bromwich Albion. Liverpool beat Aston Villa while Manchester City crash to Leeds.

Arsenal set a new Premiership best with their 14th consecutive top-flight victory, 2–0 over promoted Birmingham. Thierry Henry is on the scoresheet.

Newcastle get off to a flier with a hammering of West Ham in which Lomano Lua Lua scores twice.

Ryan Giggs nets his 100th goal for the club as Manchester United draw with Chelsea.

Leeds go top of the table and Mark Viduka scores again as West Brom are beaten and drop into the bottom three. Liverpool beat Southampton and go second. Arsenal draw with West Ham and extend their unbeaten run to 23 games, with Henry and Wiltord scorers for the second match running. Fulham go third after drawing with Middlesbrough. Newcastle are shocked as a goal from former Magpie Darren Huckerby earns Manchester City a first win of the season.

Birmingham lose to a Dwight Yorke goal for Blackburn, and are 19th. Bolton are beaten again by London opposition, at Charlton, and are bottom.

Arsenal romp to victory over West Brom. Henry doesn't score but Wiltord does, twice, taking his three-game tally to four.

Jason McAteer scores Sunderland's first goal of the campaign and it's enough for a shock victory over leaders Leeds United.

Villa get their first goal, and victory, when Darius Vassell's strike is enough to beat Manchester City.

Tottenham go top of the table when a 90th-minute Teddy Sheringham penalty beats Southampton and sends the Saints down to 19th place. Birmingham earn their first win of the season and a second successive defeat for Leeds drops them down to fourth. Nicolas Anelka scores a hat-trick as Manchester City beat Everton, though some sources give the Frenchman's third goal to Tomas Radzinski.

A Darren Moore goal earns West Brom their first-ever Premiership victory, over Fulham, to take the Baggies up to 18th. West Ham lose to Charlton and go bottom.

Spurs pay Leeds £7 million for Robbie Keane while Sunderland pay £8 million for Rangers' Tore Andre Flo. The Norwegian then scores on his debut in the draw with Manchester United but it's Roy Keane who makes the headlines, with the 11th red card of his career, for elbowing Jason McAteer, allegedly for comments the Sunderland player made about parts of Keane's book.

September

Sunday 1 September		
Bolton Wanderers v. Aston Villa		1-0
Chelsea v. Arsenal		1-1
Monday 2 September		
Liverpool v. Newcastle United		2-2
Tuesday 3 September		
Manchester United v. Middlesbrough		1-0
Tuesday 10 September		
Arsenal v. Manchester City		2-1
Middlesbrough v. Sunderland		3-0
Wednesday 11 September		
Aston Villa v. Charlton Athletic		2-0
Blackburn Rovers v. Chelsea		2-3
Fulham v. Tottenham Hotspur		3-2
Liverpool v. Birmingham City		2-2
Manchester United v. Bolton Wanderers		0-1
Newcastle United v. Leeds United		0-2
Southampton v. Everton		1-0
West Ham United v. West Bromwich Alb.		0-1
Saturday 14 September		
Bolton Wanderers v. Liverpool		2-3
Charlton Athletic v. Arsenal		0-3
Chelsea v. Newcastle United		3-0
Everton v. Middlesbrough		2-1
Leeds United v. Manchester United		1-0
Sunderland v. Fulham		0-3
West Bromwich Alb. v. Southampton		1-0
Sunday 15 September		
Manchester City v. Blackburn Rovers		2-2
Tottenham Hotspur v. West Ham United		3-2
Monday 16 September		
Birmingham City v. Aston Villa		3-0
Saturday 21 September		
Arsenal v. Bolton Wanderers		2-1
Liverpool v. West Bromwich Alb.		2-0
Manchester United v. Tottenham Hotspur		1-0
Middlesbrough v. Birmingham City		1-0
Newcastle United v. Sunderland		2-0
Southampton v. Charlton Athletic		0-0
West Ham United v. Manchester City		0-0
Sunday 22 September		
Aston Villa v. Everton		3-2
Blackburn Rovers v. Leeds United		1-0
Monday 23 September		
Fulham v. Chelsea		0-0
Saturday 28 September		
Birmingham City v. Newcastle United		0-2
Bolton Wanderers v. Southampton		1-1
Charlton Athletic v. Manchester United		1-3
Chelsea v. West Ham United		2-3
Everton v. Fulham		2-0
Leeds United v. Arsenal		1-4
Manchester City v. Liverpool		0-3
Sunderland v. Aston Villa		1-0
Tottenham Hotspur v. Middlesbrough		0-3
Monday 30 September		
West Bromwich Alb. v. Blackburn Rovers		0-2

		P	W	D	L	F	A	Pts
1	Arsenal	8	6	2	0	21	8	20
2	Liverpool	8	5	3	0	18	8	18
3	Middlesbrough	8	4	2	2	11	5	14
4	Manchester United	8	4	2	2	9	6	14
5	Chelsea	8	3	4	1	15	11	13
6	Tottenham Hotspur	8	4	1	3	11	12	13
7	Leeds United	8	4	0	4	11	9	12
8	Blackburn Rovers	8	3	3	2	10	8	12
9	Fulham	7	3	2	2	12	8	11
10	Everton	8	3	2	3	11	11	11
11	Newcastle United	7	3	1	3	10	8	10
12	Aston Villa	8	3	0	5	6	9	9
13	West Bromwich Alb.	8	3	0	5	6	13	9
14	Birmingham City	8	2	2	4	8	10	8
15	Manchester City	8	2	2	4	7	12	8
16	Sunderland	8	2	2	4	3	10	8
17	Bolton Wanderers	7	2	1	4	8	12	7
18	Southampton	8	1	4	3	4	8	7
19	Charlton Athletic	8	2	1	5	7	13	7
20	West Ham United	7	1	2	4	7	14	5

ARSENAL move into second place after drawing with Chelsea but Patrick Vieira is sent off.

Liverpool are held by Newcastle but only after they concede twice in the last 10 minutes, to Gary Speed and Alan Shearer.

A Van Nistelrooy penalty, for struggling Manchester United, beats Middlesbrough.

Another record comes for Arsenal as they equal Manchester City's 1937 record of scoring in 44 consecutive matches, against, ironically, Manchester City. Former Gunner Anelka gets City's only goal.

Kevin Nolan is the match-winner as Bolton pull off a shock victory over Manchester United and move out of the bottom three. West Brom win again, against West Ham, but the Baggies remain in the drop zone and the Hammers are 20th.

Arsenal, who have dropped only four points, confirm top spot with victory over Charlton. Harry Kewell's goal beats Manchester United and takes Leeds up to third. With just eight points from six games it's the worst-ever start to a Premiership season for Fergie's side. Zola scores his fifth goal of the season, which helps Chelsea to victory over Newcastle and boosts them up to fourth. Amazingly the Magpies plummet to 19th in the table. Liverpool extend their unbeaten run to six with a victory over Bolton that lifts them up to fifth.

West Ham stay bottom after losing to Spurs, for whom Teddy Sheringham is a scorer, for the third game running.

There is joy for Birmingham and despair for Villa's Peter Enckelman as Blues win the first second city top-flight derby for 16 years. The Villa goalkeeper concedes a bizarre own-goal, as, despite inconclusive video footage, he is deemed to have made contact as he attempted to kick a throw-in clear.

Arsenal equal Chesterfield's 1931 record of scoring in 46 consecutive league games with victory over Bolton. Henry scores for as third game in a row, keeping the Gunners top, but the Frenchman fails with a spot-kick. Liverpool end West Brom's three-game winning sequence with victory that takes them second; Michael Owen misses a penalty. Spurs drop to third after defeat by Manchester United, who climb to seventh.

West Ham stay bottom after a draw with Manchester City. Sunderland are just one place higher after losing to Newcastle. Southampton complete the basement trio after their draw with Charlton pulls them into the drop zone.

The all-time record is exclusively Arsenal's after their win over Leeds is the Gunners' 47th consecutive scoring game, and they retain pole position. Michael Owen's first hat-trick of the campaign beats Manchester City and takes Liverpool second. Middlesbrough leap three places, to third, after they beat Spurs. Manchester United are closing on the top three after victory over Charlton takes them fourth and plunges the Addicks to 19th.

West Ham continue to prop up the table despite a shock victory over Chelsea with Paolo Di Canio becoming the club's top scorer, with two goals, his first of the season. Southampton stay 18th after a draw with Bolton.

FACT FILE

Nothing to do with the Premier League, unless it is a look into the future, but Scottish Premier League referees sign a £1 million sponsorship deal with Specsavers!

A dejected Peter Enckelman, Villa's goalkeeper, watches the ball into the net for the second goal.

Saturday 5 October	
Middlesbrough v. Bolton Wanderers	2-0
Newcastle United v. West Bromwich Alb.	2-1
Southampton v. Manchester City	2-0
West Ham United v. Birmingham City	1-2
Sunday 6 October	
Arsenal v. Sunderland	3-1
Aston Villa v. Leeds United	0-0
Blackburn Rovers v. Tottenham Hotspur	1-2
Fulham v. Charlton Athletic	1-0
Liverpool v. Chelsea	1-0
Monday 7 October	
Manchester United v. Everton	3-0
Saturday 19 October	
Blackburn Rovers v. Newcastle United	5-2
Everton v. Arsenal	2-1
Fulham v. Manchester United	1-1
Leeds United v. Liverpool	0-1
Manchester City v. Chelsea	0-3
Sunderland v. West Ham United	0-1
West Bromwich Alb. v. Birmingham City	1-1
Sunday 20 October	
Charlton Athletic v. Middlesbrough	1-0
Tottenham Hotspur v. Bolton Wanderers	3-1
Monday 21 October	
Aston Villa v. Southampton	0-1
Wednesday 23 October	
Fulham v. West Ham United	0-1
Saturday 26 October	
Arsenal v. Blackburn Rovers	1-2
Birmingham City v. Manchester City	0-2
Chelsea v. West Bromwich Alb.	2-0
Liverpool v. Tottenham Hotspur	2-1
Manchester United v. Aston Villa	1-1
Middlesbrough v. Leeds United	2-2
Newcastle United v. Charlton Athletic	2-1
Sunday 27 October	
Southampton v. Fulham	4-2
West Ham United v. Everton	0-1
Monday 28 October	
Bolton Wanderers v. Sunderland	1-1

		P	W	D	L	F	A	Pts
1	Liverpool	11	8	3	0	22	9	27
2	Arsenal	11	7	2	2	26	13	23
3	Chelsea	11	5	4	2	20	12	19
4	Manchester United	11	5	4	2	14	8	19
5	Tottenham Hotspur	11	6	1	4	17	16	19
6	Middlesbrough	11	5	3	3	15	8	18
7	Blackburn Rovers	11	5	3	3	18	13	18
8	Everton	11	5	2	4	14	15	17
9	Newcastle United	10	5	1	4	16	15	16
10	Southampton	11	4	4	3	11	10	16
11	Fulham	11	4	3	4	16	14	15
12	Leeds United	11	4	2	5	13	12	14
13	Birmingham City	11	3	3	5	11	14	12
14	Aston Villa	11	3	2	6	7	11	11
15	West Ham United	11	3	2	6	10	17	11
16	Manchester City	11	3	2	6	9	17	11
17	Charlton Athletic	11	3	1	7	9	16	10
18	West Bromwich Alb.	11	3	1	7	8	18	10
19	Sunderland	11	2	3	6	5	15	9
20	Bolton Wanderers	10	2	2	6	10	18	8

WEST HAM lose to Birmingham and stay bottom. Brett Ormerod hits his first two goals for Southampton, in the win over Manchester City that catapults Saints out of the relegation zone up to 13th.

Kanu hits a brace, for the second successive match, as Arsenal beat Sunderland to stay top. The Black Cats, one place above the drop zone having spent more than £20 million in less than a year, then sack Peter Reid after a seven and a half year tenure. Zola makes his 200th league appearance for Chelsea but Michael Owen is the match-winner with a 90th-minute goal for Liverpool that keeps them second. Charlton are beaten by Fulham and stay 19th.

Manchester United score three in the last four minutes to beat Everton; Ruud Van Nistelrooy scores in the last minute for the second game running, and the Reds go fourth.

Howard Wilkinson leaves his post as FA Technical Director to be the surprise successor to Peter Reid at Sunderland.

Roy Keane receives a record £150,000 fine and a five-match ban from the Football Association.

Liverpool's fifth consecutive victory, with a Salif Diao goal that beats Leeds, takes them top for the first time this season. Ryan Giggs makes his 500th appearance for Manchester United as they draw with Fulham and stay fourth. Wayne Rooney, at 16 years and 360 days, makes history as the youngest-ever Premiership scorer with a screamer that beats Arsenal in the dying seconds. The Gunners drop down to second. Alan Shearer picks on his former club, again, as he scores his 300th club goal, at Blackburn, but Rovers win.

New signing Robbie Keane scores again, twice, to help Spurs beat Bolton, and Tottenham move up a place to third.

Sunderland crash to West Ham and drop to one place off the bottom. The Hammers move out of the bottom three for the first time since August. Manchester City drop into the relegation zone, for the first time this campaign, after losing to Chelsea.

Liverpool retain pole position by beating Tottenham. Danny Murphy and Michael Owen, with his second penalty of the season, are the scorers. Arsenal lose again, to Blackburn: Edu scores for both sides and the Gunners stay second. Chelsea move up to third with victory over West Brom that plunges the Baggies down to 18th. Manchester United cannot improve from fourth but their draw with Villa does have the consolation of a first Premiership goal from Diego Forlan after nine months and 23 games of trying by the £7.5 million striker.

Manchester City climb two places out of the drop zone with victory over Birmingham City. Southampton's first hat-trick of the season, from James Beattie, helps beat Fulham.

Sunderland, with only their fifth goal of the season, from Michael Gray, draw with Bolton but stay 19th.

Everton's Wayne Rooney celebrates scoring the winning goal against Arsenal in front of the Everton fans.

November

Saturday 2 November	
Birmingham City v. Bolton Wanderers	3-1
Liverpool v. West Ham United	2-0
Manchester United v. Southampton	2-1
West Bromwich Alb. v. Manchester City	1-2
Sunday 3 November	
Blackburn Rovers v. Aston Villa	0-0
Charlton Athletic v. Sunderland	1-1
Fulham v. Arsenal	0-1
Leeds United v. Everton	0-1
Tottenham Hotspur v. Chelsea	0-0
Monday 4 November	
Newcastle United v. Middlesbrough	2-0
Saturday 9 November	
Arsenal v. Newcastle United	1-0
Aston Villa v. Fulham	3-1
Bolton Wanderers v. West Bromwich Alb.	1-1
Chelsea v. Birmingham City	3-0
Everton v. Charlton Athletic	1-0
Manchester City v. Manchester United	3-1
Middlesbrough v. Liverpool	1-0
Southampton v. Blackburn Rovers	1-1
Sunday 10 November	
Sunderland v. Tottenham Hotspur	2-0
West Ham United v. Leeds United	3-4
Saturday 16 November	
Arsenal v. Tottenham Hotspur	3-0
Chelsea v. Middlesbrough	1-0
Manchester City v. Charlton Athletic	0-1
Newcastle United v. Southampton	2-1
West Bromwich Alb. v. Aston Villa	0-0
Sunday 17 November	
Birmingham City v. Fulham	0-0
Blackburn Rovers v. Everton	0-1
Leeds United v. Bolton Wanderers	2-4
Liverpool v. Sunderland	0-0
West Ham United v. Manchester United	1-1
Saturday 23 November	
Aston Villa v. West Ham United	4-1
Bolton Wanderers v. Chelsea	1-1
Everton v. West Bromwich Alb.	1-0
Fulham v. Liverpool	3-2
Manchester United v. Newcastle United	5-3
Middlesbrough v. Manchester City	3-1
Southampton v. Arsenal	3-2
Sunderland v. Birmingham City	0-1
Sunday 24 November	
Charlton Athletic v. Blackburn Rovers	3-1
Tottenham Hotspur v. Leeds United	2-0
Saturday 30 November	
Arsenal v. Aston Villa	3-1
Birmingham City v. Tottenham Hotspur	1-1
Blackburn Rovers v. Fulham	2-1
Chelsea v. Sunderland	3-0
Manchester City v. Bolton Wanderers	2-0
West Bromwich Alb. v. Middlesbrough	1-0

		P	W	D	L	F	A	Pts
1	Arsenal	16	11	2	3	36	17	35
2	Liverpool	15	9	4	2	26	13	31
3	Chelsea	16	8	6	2	28	13	30
4	Everton	15	9	2	4	18	15	29
5	Manchester United	15	7	5	3	23	16	26
6	Middlesbrough	16	7	3	6	19	13	24
7	Tottenham Hotspur	16	7	3	6	20	22	24
8	Blackburn Rovers	16	6	5	5	22	19	23
9	Newcastle United	14	7	1	6	23	22	22
10	Southampton	15	5	5	5	17	17	20
11	Birmingham City	16	5	5	6	16	19	20
12	Manchester City	16	6	2	8	17	23	20
13	Fulham	16	5	4	7	21	22	19
14	Aston Villa	16	5	4	7	15	16	19
15	Leeds United	15	5	2	8	19	22	17
16	Charlton Athletic	15	5	2	8	14	19	17
17	West Bromwich Alb.	16	4	3	9	11	22	15
18	Sunderland	16	3	5	8	8	20	14
19	Bolton Wanderers	15	3	4	8	17	27	13
20	West Ham United	15	3	3	9	15	28	12

TWO Michael Owen goals earn victory over West Ham and keep Liverpool top.

Manchester City beat West Bromwich Albion to drop the Baggies a place to 19th. Sunderland draw with Charlton and stay 18th. Bolton are bottom after they are beaten by Birmingham.

Second-placed Arsenal win for the first time in three games but it takes a Steve Marlet own-goal to give them victory over Fulham. Manchester United's victory over Southampton moves them up to third. Wayne Rooney makes the headlines again as his goal nets Everton their first win at Leeds in 51 years and moves Everton up to sixth.

Liverpool stay top despite their unbeaten run ending at Middlesbrough, with Gareth Southgate scoring his second goal in three games. Arsenal remain second by beating Newcastle. Manchester City win the Manchester derby for the first time in 13 years and United drop to fifth.

Bolton snatch a point from fellow strugglers West Brom with Per Frandsen's 89th-minute equaliser denying the Baggies a second away win of the season. Wanderers stay bottom; West Brom are one place higher.

West Ham drop into the bottom three, after losing a seven-goal thriller with Leeds, who score all their goals in the first half leaving the Hammers the only side, from the Premier League to the Conference, without a home win.

Arsenal win a stormy derby with Spurs to stay top. West Brom draw with Villa and are bottom of the table.

Manchester United are held by West Ham and stay fifth. Jermaine Defoe rescues a point with an 86th-minute equaliser but the Hammers drop a place to 19th. Liverpool are held by Sunderland, who don't win a single corner during the game,

West Ham United's Jermain Defoe hits his second goal of the season to rescue a point against Manchester United.

or muster a single effort on goal, while Liverpool rack up 24 attempts on target, and drop to second. Shock of the day is Bolton's crushing win against Leeds in which Wanderers score three times in the last 10 minutes to move off the bottom. Dennis Bergkamp nets his first goal of the season, in his 10th game, but Arsenal lose to Southampton and remain top. Liverpool lose ground, in second place, by losing to Fulham, while Everton move up to third with their sixth straight victory, over West Brom, who nevertheless move off the bottom to 19th. Newcastle score three at Old Trafford but a Ruud Van Nistelrooy treble, inside 15

minutes, helps Manchester United to victory and up to fifth.

West Ham drop to rock-bottom after being hammered by Aston Villa and Dion Dublin nets his 100th Premiership goal. Bolton are 18th after earning a point against Chelsea.

Arsenal recover top spot with Thierry Henry scoring twice and Robert Pires once, to beat Villa.

Sunderland drop into the bottom three after losing to Chelsea, who move up to third. But Danny Dichio's first goal of the season beats Middlesbrough to take West Brom out of the bottom three, to 17th.

December

Sunday 1 December	
Leeds United v. Charlton Athletic	1-2
Liverpool v. Manchester United	1-2
Newcastle United v. Everton	2-1
Monday 2 December	
West Ham United v. Southampton	0-1
Saturday 7 December	
Aston Villa v. Newcastle United	0-1
Bolton Wanderers v. Blackburn Rovers	1-1
Charlton Athletic v. Liverpool	2-0
Everton v. Chelsea	1-3
Fulham v. Leeds United	1-0
Manchester United v. Arsenal	2-0
Middlesbrough v. West Ham United	2-2
Southampton v. Birmingham City	2-0
Sunday 8 December	
Tottenham Hotspur v. West Bromwich Alb.	3-1
Monday 9 December	
Sunderland v. Manchester City	0-3
Saturday 14 December	
Aston Villa v. West Bromwich Alb.	2-1
Charlton Athletic v. Manchester City	2-2
Everton v. Blackburn Rovers	2-1
Manchester United v. West Ham United	3-0
Middlesbrough v. Chelsea	1-1
Southampton v. Newcastle United	1-1
Sunday 15 December	
Fulham v. Birmingham City	0-1
Sunderland v. Liverpool	2-1
Tottenham Hotspur v. Arsenal	1-1
Monday 16 December	
Bolton Wanderers v. Leeds United	0-3
Saturday 21 December	
Arsenal v. Middlesbrough	2-0
Birmingham City v. Charlton Athletic	1-1
Chelsea v. Aston Villa	2-0
Leeds United v. Southampton	1-1
Newcastle United v. Fulham	2-0
West Bromwich Alb. v. Sunderland	2-2
West Ham United v. Bolton Wanderers	1-1
Sunday 22 December	
Blackburn Rovers v. Manchester United	1-0
Liverpool v. Everton	0-0
Monday 23 December	
Manchester City v. Tottenham Hotspur	2-3
Thursday 26 December	
Birmingham City v. Everton	1-1
Bolton Wanderers v. Newcastle United	4-3
Chelsea v. Southampton	0-0
Liverpool v. Blackburn Rovers	1-1
Manchester City v. Aston Villa	3-1
Middlesbrough v. Manchester United	3-1
Sunderland v. Leeds United	1-2
Tottenham Hotspur v. Charlton Athletic	2-2
West Bromwich Alb. v. Arsenal	1-2
West Ham United v. Fulham	1-1
Saturday 28 December	
Aston Villa v. Middlesbrough	1-0
Blackburn Rovers v. West Ham United	2-2
Charlton Athletic v. West Bromwich Alb.	1-0
Everton v. Bolton Wanderers	0-0
Fulham v. Manchester City	0-1
Leeds United v. Chelsea	2-0
Manchester United v. Birmingham City	2-0
Southampton v. Sunderland	2-1
Sunday 29 December	
Arsenal v. Liverpool	1-1
Newcastle United v. Tottenham Hotspur	2-1

		P	W	D	L	F	A	Pts
1	Arsenal	21	13	4	4	42	22	43
2	Chelsea	21	10	8	3	34	17	38
3	Manchester United	21	11	5	5	33	21	38
4	Newcastle United	20	11	2	7	34	29	35
5	Everton	21	10	5	6	23	22	35
6	Liverpool	21	9	7	5	30	21	34
7	Southampton	21	8	8	5	24	20	32
8	Tottenham Hotspur	21	9	5	7	30	30	32
9	Manchester City	21	9	3	9	28	29	30
10	Middlesbrough	21	8	5	8	25	20	29
11	Blackburn Rovers	21	7	8	6	28	25	29
12	Charlton Athletic	21	8	5	8	24	25	29
13	Leeds United	21	8	3	10	28	27	27
14	Aston Villa	21	7	4	10	19	23	25
15	Birmingham City	21	6	7	8	19	25	25
16	Fulham	21	6	5	10	23	27	23
17	Bolton Wanderers	20	4	7	9	23	35	19
18	Sunderland	21	4	6	11	14	30	18
19	West Bromwich Alb.	21	4	4	13	16	32	16
20	West Ham United	21	3	7	11	21	38	16

A HOWLER by Jerzey Dudek gifts Manchester United victory over Liverpool, with Diegor Forlan netting both goals inside three minutes in the win that takes United fourth and keeps Liverpool second.

West Ham draw with Southampton and stay bottom of the table.

FACT FILE

Liverpool's defeat at the Stadium of Light is the first time a Liverpool side has lost on Wearside since 30 August 1958, when Sunderland won the Second Division fixture 2–1.

Arsenal retain pole position despite a crucial defeat by Manchester United in which Veron scores his first goal of the season, in his 14th game, to help United climb a place to third. It's the first time Arsenal have failed to score in 56 matches. Chelsea beat Everton and reach their highest placing of the campaign, second, and Hasselbaink scores for a third consecutive game. Charlton mark the 10th anniversary of their return to the Valley with their fourth consecutive victory, over Liverpool, who drop to fourth. Storm clouds gather over Leeds, who suffer their 10th Premiership defeat in 17 outings, to Fulham, and drop to just two places above the relegation zone.

Bolton climb to 18th, after drawing with Blackburn, but West Ham stay bottom, despite drawing with 'Boro.

West Brom stay out of the drop zone despite losing to Spurs.

Manchester United continue their climb towards the top with a win over West Ham that takes them second and keeps the Hammers bottom. Chelsea draw with 'Boro and drop to third.

Aston Villa's victory over West Brom pushes the Baggies back into the bottom three.

Arsenal draw with Tottenham but stay top. Liverpool lose for a fourth consecutive game and drop to fifth as a result of the club's first defeat in Sunderland for more than 40 years.

Bolton crash to Leeds and stay in the bottom three.

Arsenal retain top spot by beating Middlesbrough with a goal at the end of each half from Sol Campbell, his first of the season, and Robert Pires, his fourth. Chelsea beat Villa to go second.

West Brom's draw with Sunderland keeps them 18th but they squander a 2–0 lead with just over half an hour remaining.

Roy Keane returns for his first game in more than three months but Manchester United suffer their first defeat in a dozen games, with Garry Flitcroft scoring the only goal for Blackburn, and drop a place, to third. A draw in the Mersey derby drops Liverpool down a place to fifth and allows Everton to leapfrog their neighbours into fourth.

Arsenal stay top and Francis Jeffers gets his first goal of the season as the Gunners beat West Brom and the Baggies drop to 19th. Chelsea's draw with Southampton keeps them second. Manchester United lose again, to Middlesbrough, but stay third.

Bolton's cracking victory over Newcastle takes them out of the bottom three for the first time in three months. West Ham draw with Fulham and stay 20th. Sunderland drop into the relegation zone after losing to Leeds, for whom James Milner becomes the youngest-ever Premiership scorer, aged 16 years and 357 days. The previous youngest, Wayne Rooney, is sent off as Everton draw with Birmingham.

Dion Dublin's 200th career goal beats Middlesbrough. West Ham end the year bottom after a draw with Blackburn. West Brom see out 2002 in 19th place after losing to Charlton and Sunderland will see in the New Year 18th after defeat by Southampton.

Chelsea lose to Leeds but retain second place. Manchester United beat Birmingham to enter 2003 in third place.

Arsenal stay top after drawing with Liverpool. It's the ninth game without a win for the Anfield outfit, their worst sequence for half a century. Alan Shearer marks his 250th Newcastle game with a headed winner against Spurs that takes the Magpies fourth.

Charlton Athletic's Jason Euell celebrates scoring the opening goal against Liverpool.

Wednesday 1 January	
Arsenal v. Chelsea	3-2
Aston Villa v. Bolton Wanderers	2-0
Blackburn Rovers v. Middlesbrough	1-0
Everton v. Manchester City	2-2
Leeds United v. Birmingham City	2-0
Manchester United v. Sunderland	2-1
Newcastle United v. Liverpool	1-0
Southampton v. Tottenham Hotspur	1-0
Saturday 11 January	
Bolton Wanderers v. Fulham	0-0
Chelsea v. Charlton Athletic	4-1
Liverpool v. Aston Villa	1-1
Manchester City v. Leeds United	2-1
Middlesbrough v. Southampton	2-2
Sunderland v. Blackburn Rovers	0-0
West Bromwich Alb. v. Manchester United	1-3
West Ham United v. Newcastle United	2-2
Sunday 12 January	
Birmingham City v. Arsenal	0-4
Tottenham Hotspur v. Everton	4-3
Saturday 18 January	
Aston Villa v. Tottenham Hotspur	0-1
Blackburn Rovers v. Birmingham City	1-1
Charlton Athletic v. Bolton Wanderers	1-1
Everton v. Sunderland	2-1
Leeds United v. West Bromwich Alb.	0-0
Manchester United v. Chelsea	2-1
Newcastle United v. Manchester City	2-0
Southampton v. Liverpool	0-1
Sunday 19 January	
Arsenal v. West Ham United	3-1
Fulham v. Middlesbrough	1-0
Wednesday 22 January	
Charlton Athletic v. West Ham United	4-2
Newcastle United v. Bolton Wanderers	1-0
Tuesday 28 January	
Bolton Wanderers v. Everton	1-2
Chelsea v. Leeds United	3-2
Middlesbrough v. Aston Villa	2-5
Sunderland v. Southampton	0-1
Wednesday 29 January	
Liverpool v. Arsenal	2-2
Manchester City v. Fulham	4-1
Tottenham Hotspur v. Newcastle United	0-1
West Bromwich Alb. v. Charlton Athletic	0-1
West Ham United v. Blackburn Rovers	2-1

		P	W	D	L	F	A	Pts
1	Arsenal	25	16	5	4	54	27	53
2	Newcastle United	25	15	3	7	41	31	48
3	Manchester United	24	14	5	5	40	24	47
4	Chelsea	25	12	8	5	44	25	44
5	Everton	25	12	6	7	32	30	42
6	Liverpool	25	10	9	6	34	25	39
7	Southampton	25	10	9	6	28	23	39
8	Tottenham Hotspur	25	11	5	9	35	35	38
9	Manchester City	25	11	4	10	36	35	37
10	Charlton Athletic	25	10	6	9	31	32	36
11	Blackburn Rovers	25	8	10	7	31	28	34
12	Aston Villa	25	9	5	11	27	27	32
13	Leeds United	25	9	4	12	33	32	31
14	Middlesbrough	25	8	6	11	29	29	30
15	Fulham	24	7	6	11	25	31	27
16	Birmingham City	24	6	8	10	20	32	26
17	Bolton Wanderers	25	4	9	12	25	41	21
18	West Ham United	25	4	8	13	28	48	20
19	Sunderland	25	4	7	14	16	35	19
20	West Bromwich Alb.	24	4	5	15	17	36	17

ARSENAL beat Chelsea to stay top but the visitors drop a place to third. Despite waterlogged pitches causing postponements all over the country, the Old Trafford grass has to be watered before United beat Sunderland, with goals in the last 10 minutes, to go second. The Black Cats remain 18th.

Chelsea are still third after beating Charlton on a Stamford Bridge pitch that has more sand than grass.

Liverpool's dreadful winless run extends to 11 games with the draw against Villa that means Houllier's side has picked up just five points from a possible 33.

Sunderland draw with Blackburn and stay 18th. West Ham draw with Newcastle and are one place lower while West Brom's defeat at Old Trafford keeps them bottom and United second.

Thierry Henry scores his 100th goal, in just 180 Arsenal appearances, as the Gunners beat Birmingham City to stay top. Robbie Keane hits Tottenham's first hat-trick of the campaign as they beat Everton.

Another scoring record comes for Alan Shearer as he hits the second-fastest Premiership goal, against Manchester City, after just 10.4 seconds. Victory takes Newcastle up to third. Manchester United beat Chelsea to stay second, while Chelsea drop a place to fourth. Paul Scholes scores for the third game running. Liverpool end the club's worst run of league results since 1955 with an Emile Heskey goal beating Southampton. Sunderland stay 18th after losing to Everton.

Thierry Henry takes West Ham apart with a hat-trick taking his tally to five in two games as the Gunners stay top. The striker's treble includes his first headed goal in the Premiership after a staggering 9,639 minutes of trying. The Hammers stay rooted in 20th place. West Brom, without a win in seven games, are 19th after drawing with Leeds.

Newcastle go top of the table – they were 19th back in September – for the first time in the campaign when Jermaine Jenas scores the only goal against Bolton.

Chelsea stay fourth courtesy of an own-goal from Leeds' Dominic Matteo. Veteran Dave Watson scores a brace as Everton are fifth following victory over Bolton.

Sunderland stay in the bottom three after defeat by Southampton. West Brom are bottom after losing to Charlton and in trouble West Ham are still in 18th, despite beating Blackburn.

The transfer window closes with completion of Jonathan Woodgate's £9 million transfer from Leeds to Newcastle.

Arsenal are pegged back by a 90th-minute Emile Heskey equaliser but the Gunners still have a five-point lead over second-placed Newcastle.

FACT FILE

The fastest-ever Premiership goal, just 10 seconds from kick-off, was scored by Tottenham's Ledley King, at Bradford City, in December 2000.

Robbie Keane's trademark celebration is seen three times as his hat-trick seals a 4-3 Tottenham win over Everton.

Saturday 1 February

Arsenal v. Fulham	2-1
Bolton Wanderers v. Birmingham City	4-2
Chelsea v. Tottenham Hotspur	1-1
Everton v. Leeds United	2-0
Manchester City v. West Bromwich Alb.	1-2
Southampton v. Manchester United	0-2
Sunderland v. Charlton Athletic	1-3

Sunday 2 February

Aston Villa v. Blackburn Rovers	3-0
West Ham United v. Liverpool	0-3

Tuesday 4 February

Birmingham City v. Manchester United	0-1

Saturday 8 February

Birmingham City v. Chelsea	1-3
Blackburn Rovers v. Southampton	1-0
Charlton Athletic v. Everton	2-1
Fulham v. Aston Villa	2-1
Leeds United v. West Ham United	1-0
Liverpool v. Middlesbrough	1-1
Tottenham Hotspur v. Sunderland	4-1
West Bromwich Alb. v. Bolton Wanderers	1-1

Sunday 9 February

Manchester United v. Manchester City	1-1
Newcastle United v. Arsenal	1-1

Wednesday 19 February

Fulham v. West Bromwich Alb.	3-0

Saturday 22 February

Bolton Wanderers v. Manchester United	1-1
Charlton Athletic v. Aston Villa	3-0
Chelsea v. Blackburn Rovers	1-2
Everton v. Southampton	2-1
Leeds United v. Newcastle United	0-3
Manchester City v. Arsenal	1-5
Sunderland v. Middlesbrough	1-3

Sunday 23 February

Birmingham City v. Liverpool	2-1
West Bromwich Alb. v. West Ham United	1-2

Monday 24 February

Tottenham Hotspur v. Fulham	1-1

		P	W	D	L	F	A	Pts
1	Arsenal	28	18	6	4	62	30	60
2	Manchester United	28	16	7	5	45	26	55
3	Newcastle United	27	16	4	7	45	32	52
4	Chelsea	28	13	9	6	49	29	48
5	Everton	28	14	6	8	37	33	48
6	Charlton Athletic	28	13	6	9	39	34	45
7	Liverpool	28	11	10	7	39	28	43
8	Tottenham Hotspur	28	12	7	9	41	38	43
9	Blackburn Rovers	28	10	10	8	34	32	40
10	Southampton	28	10	9	9	29	28	39
11	Manchester City	28	11	5	12	39	43	38
12	Aston Villa	28	10	5	13	31	32	35
13	Middlesbrough	27	9	7	11	33	31	34
14	Leeds United	28	10	4	14	34	37	34
15	Fulham	28	9	7	12	32	35	34
16	Birmingham City	28	7	8	13	25	41	29
17	Bolton Wanderers	28	5	11	12	31	45	26
18	West Ham United	28	5	8	15	30	53	23
19	West Bromwich Albion	28	5	6	17	21	43	21
20	Sunderland	28	4	7	17	19	45	19

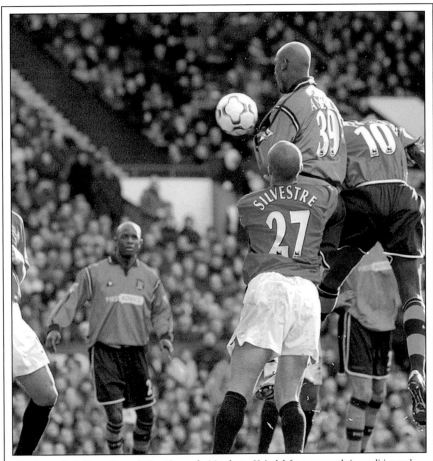

Manchester City's Shaun Goater (10) out jumps the Manchester United defence to score their equalising goal.

SOMEONE from the Stadium of Light must have run over a Black Cat because Sunderland concede three own-goals in seven minutes, two from Michael Proctor, in losing to Charlton to drop the Wearsiders to bottom of the table. West Brom rise to 18th after beating Manchester City. Bolton thrash Birmingham to stay clear of the relegation zone.

A brace from Robert Pires beats Fulham and keeps Arsenal top. Manchester United win for the fifth game running, against Southampton, and stay second.

West Ham lose to Liverpool and stay 19th.

Van Nistelrooy's goal sinks Birmingham and keeps United second.

Liverpool announce a £100 million kit deal with Reebok, the biggest in the club's history.

Teddy Sheringham scores his 300th career goal as Spurs beat Sunderland to keep the Black Cats 20th.

Arsenal are held by Newcastle but stay top. The Magpies are third but Laurent Robert is sent off after grabbing their equaliser. United are just four minutes from winning the Manchester derby but substitute Shaun Goater grabs the City equaliser and the Reds stay second.

Bolton stay clear of the bottom three with a draw that keeps West Brom 18th. West Ham lose to a Seth Johnson goal, for Leeds, and remain 19th.

Sir Alex Ferguson kicks up a storm in the press when he volleys a boot across the dressing-room into the face of David Beckham, after Arsenal beat United in the FA Cup.

Arsenal stick five past Peter Schmeichel as Manchester City fail to contain the leaders,

who record their best away win of the season, but Anelka does score against his former club. Manchester United fall two points further behind when they are held by Bolton. Newcastle stay third with victory over Leeds.

Poor old Kevin Phillips scores for the third game running but Sunderland's fifth consecutive defeat, to Middlesbrough, leaves the Black Cats rooted to the foot of the table.

West Ham improve to 18th with victory in the relegation battle over West Brom, thanks to two Trevor Sinclair goals. Paolo Di Canio 'throws his toys out of the pram' in a touchline tantrum after being substituted. Albion drop a place to 19th.

Birmingham make it four points out of six against Liverpool with a victory at St Andrews that keeps Blues well clear of the drop zone.

March

Saturday 1 March	
Blackburn Rovers v. Manchester City	1-0
Fulham v. Sunderland	1-0
Middlesbrough v. Everton	1-1
Newcastle United v. Chelsea	2-1
Southampton v. West Bromwich Alb.	1-0
West Ham United v. Tottenham Hotspur	2-0

Sunday 2 March	
Arsenal v. Charlton Athletic	2-0

Monday 3 March	
Aston Villa v. Birmingham City	0-2

Wednesday 5 March	
Manchester United v. Leeds United	2-1
Middlesbrough v. Newcastle United	1-0

Saturday 8 March	
Liverpool v. Bolton Wanderers	2-0

Saturday 15 March	
Aston Villa v. Manchester United	0-1
Blackburn Rovers v. Arsenal	2-0
Charlton Athletic v. Newcastle United	0-2
Everton v. West Ham United	0-0
Fulham v. Southampton	2-2
Leeds United v. Middlesbrough	2-3
Sunderland v. Bolton Wanderers	0-2

Sunday 16 March	
Manchester City v. Birmingham City	1-0
Tottenham Hotspur v. Liverpool	2-3
West Bromwich Alb. v. Chelsea	0-2

Saturday 22 March	
Birmingham City v. West Bromwich Alb.	1-0
Chelsea v. Manchester City	5-0
Manchester United v. Fulham	3-0
Middlesbrough v. Charlton Athletic	1-1
Newcastle United v. Blackburn Rovers	5-1
Southampton v. Aston Villa	2-2
West Ham United v. Sunderland	2-0

Sunday 23 March	
Arsenal v. Everton	2-1
Liverpool v. Leeds United	3-1

Monday 24 March	
Bolton Wanderers v. Tottenham Hotspur	1-0

		P	W	D	L	F	A	Pts
1	Arsenal	31	20	6	5	66	33	66
2	Manchester United	31	19	7	5	51	27	64
3	Newcastle United	31	19	4	8	54	35	61
4	Chelsea	31	15	9	7	57	31	54
5	Liverpool	31	14	10	7	47	31	52
6	Everton	31	14	8	9	39	36	50
7	Charlton Athletic	31	13	7	11	40	39	46
8	Blackburn Rovers	31	12	10	9	38	37	46
9	Southampton	31	11	11	9	34	32	44
10	Tottenham Hotspur	31	12	7	12	43	44	43
11	Middlesbrough	31	11	9	11	39	35	42
12	Manchester City	31	12	5	14	40	49	41
13	Fulham	31	10	8	13	35	40	38
14	Aston Villa	31	10	6	15	33	37	36
15	Birmingham City	31	9	8	14	28	42	35
16	Leeds United	31	10	4	17	38	45	34
17	Bolton Wanderers	31	7	11	13	34	47	32
18	West Ham United	31	7	9	15	34	53	30
19	West Bromwich Alb.	31	5	6	20	21	47	21
20	Sunderland	31	4	7	20	19	50	19

JUNINHO marks the start of his third 'Boro spell with a goal that earns a point against Everton. His previous game for 'Boro was on 14 May 2000, at Everton, when he also scored. Sunderland lose again, to Fulham, and stay bottom. West Brom are beaten by Southampton and are 19th. West Ham beat Spurs but stay in the bottom three.

Pires and Jeffers score as Arsenal beat Charlton to stay in pole position. Birmingham win the first second city top flight derby at Villa Park for 16 years, but Villa's Dion Dublin is sent off, for head-butting Robbie Savage, as well as Joey Gudjonsson. Manchester United defeat Leeds to stay second. Middlesbrough beat Newcastle in front of the biggest Riverside crowd in the stadium's eight-year history, a sell out 34,814, but the Magpies stay third.

Sunderland finally lose patience with Howard Wilkinson and Steve Cotterill and sack the management pair after just two wins in the 20 games they have been in charge. Two days later Mick McCarthy is installed as manager at the Stadium of Light.

Arsenal lose for the first time in 15 games, against Blackburn, but retain pole position. Manchester United beat Villa, with David Beckham's first goal in eight games, and close the gap on the Gunners. Newcastle are still third after beating Charlton.

Mick McCarthy's presence fails to ignite Sunderland, who lose to Bolton and stay bottom. West Ham draw with Everton and are one place higher.

West Brom are 19th after losing to Chelsea, who move up to fourth. A significant moment in the title race comes as Manchester United hit the top, for the first time this campaign, with a Ruud Van Nistelrooy hat-trick beating Fulham, before another Premiership record attendance of 67,706. Newcastle cruise to victory against Blackburn, with three of the Magpies' goals coming in the final five minutes. For once, Alan Shearer doesn't score against his former club.

West Brom's defeat by Birmingham keeps the Baggies 19th but West Ham move out of the relegation zone, for the first time since November, with victory over Sunderland, who stay bottom.

James Beattie becomes the first striker to reach 20 Premiership goals this season with a goal in Southampton's draw with Aston Villa.

Arsenal regain pole position with victory over Everton. Pascal Cygan scores his first goal of the season.

Struggling Bolton snatch a shock victory over Spurs with a 90th-minute penalty winner from Jay Jay Okocha.

Leeds United's under-fire chairman Peter Ridsdale, who sanctioned David O'Leary's £100 million spending spree, finally bows to fans' pressure and resigns, leaving Leeds nearly £80 million in debt.

Aston Villa's Dion Dublin head butts Birmingham City's Robbie Savage, for which he is red-carded.

April

Saturday 5 April	
Aston Villa v. Arsenal	1-1
Bolton Wanderers v. Manchester City	2-0
Charlton Athletic v. Leeds United	1-6
Manchester United v. Liverpool	4-0
Middlesbrough v. West Bromwich Alb.	3-0
Southampton v. West Ham United	1-1
Sunderland v. Chelsea	1-2
Tottenham Hotspur v. Birmingham City	2-1
Sunday 6 April	
Everton v. Newcastle United	2-1
Monday 7 April	
Fulham v. Blackburn Rovers	0-4
Saturday 12 April	
Birmingham City v. Sunderland	2-0
Blackburn Rovers v. Charlton Athletic	1-0
Chelsea v. Bolton Wanderers	1-0
Leeds United v. Tottenham Hotspur	2-2
Liverpool v. Fulham	2-0
Manchester City v. Middlesbrough	0-0
Newcastle United v. Manchester United	2-6
West Bromwich Alb. v. Everton	1-2
West Ham United v. Aston Villa	2-2
Wednesday 16 April	
Arsenal v. Manchester United	2-2
Friday 18 April	
Tottenham Hotspur v. Manchester City	0-2
Saturday 19 April	
Aston Villa v. Chelsea	2-1
Bolton Wanderers v. West Ham United	1-0
Charlton Athletic v. Birmingham City	0-2
Everton v. Liverpool	1-2
Fulham v. Newcastle United	2-1
Manchester United v. Blackburn Rovers	3-1
Middlesbrough v. Arsenal	0-2
Southampton v. Leeds United	3-2
Sunderland v. West Bromwich Alb.	1-2
Monday 21 April	
Birmingham City v. Southampton	3-2
Blackburn Rovers v. Bolton Wanderers	0-0
Chelsea v. Everton	4-1
Liverpool v. Charlton Athletic	2-1
Manchester City v. Sunderland	3-0
Newcastle United v. Aston Villa	1-1
West Bromwich Alb. v. Tottenham Hotspur	2-3
West Ham United v. Middlesbrough	1-0
Tuesday 22 April	
Leeds United v. Fulham	2-0
Saturday 26 April	
Birmingham City v. Middlesbrough	3-0
Bolton Wanderers v. Arsenal	2-2
Charlton Athletic v. Southampton	2-1
Chelsea v. Fulham	1-1
Everton v. Aston Villa	2-1
Leeds United v. Blackburn Rovers	2-3
Sunderland v. Newcastle United	0-1
West Bromwich Alb. v. Liverpool	0-6
Sunday 27 April	
Manchester City v. West Ham United	0-1
Tottenham Hotspur v. Manchester United	0-2

		P	W	D	L	F	A	Pts
1	Manchester United	36	23	8	5	68	32	77
2	Arsenal	35	21	9	5	73	38	72
3	Newcastle United	36	20	5	11	60	46	65
4	Chelsea	36	18	10	8	66	36	64
5	Liverpool	36	18	10	8	59	37	64
6	Everton	36	17	8	11	47	45	59
7	Blackburn Rovers	36	15	11	10	47	42	56
8	Tottenham Hotspur	36	14	8	14	50	53	50
9	Charlton Athletic	36	14	7	15	44	51	49
10	Southampton	35	12	12	11	41	40	48
11	Manchester City	36	14	6	16	45	52	48
12	Birmingham City	36	13	8	15	39	46	47
13	Middlesbrough	36	12	10	14	42	41	46
14	Aston Villa	36	11	9	16	40	44	42
15	Fulham	36	11	9	16	38	50	42
16	Leeds United	36	12	5	19	52	54	41
17	Bolton Wanderers	36	9	13	14	39	50	40
18	West Ham United	36	9	11	16	39	57	38
19	West Bromwich Alb.	36	6	6	24	26	62	24
20	Sunderland	36	4	7	25	21	60	19

LEEDS secure their biggest-ever Premiership away win at Charlton and Mark Viduka hits the team's first hat-trick of the campaign. Sammy Hyypia is sent off after just four minutes as Manchester United go on to record their best win over Liverpool for 50 years. Two Van Nistelrooy penalties give him five goals, including three spot-kicks, in the last two games, and United close in on leaders Arsenal, who are held by Villa.

West Ham drop back into the bottom three after drawing with Southampton. West Brom are one place lower after crashing to Middlesbrough and Sunderland lose for the ninth consecutive game, to Chelsea, who stay fourth. Shaun Thornton nets his first goal for the Black Cats, their first in four games.

Newcastle stay third, despite a shock defeat by Everton, who move up to fifth. Wayne Rooney scores for the second game running.

Manchester United post serious championship intent with a crushing victory over Newcastle, helped by a Paul Scholes hat-trick, which takes United's goal tally in three games to 13.

West Ham stay top of the relegation zone by drawing with Villa. West Brom lose to Everton and remain 19th while Sunderland's losing streak extends to double figures with defeat at Birmingham.

In the title 'decider' Manchester United move closer to leaders Arsenal with a 2–2 draw against the Gunners. Sol Cambell is red carded for an elbow on Solskjaer.

Arsenal win for the first time in three games when they beat Middlesbrough, but have to settle for second place. Manchester United take over at the top following their victory over Blackburn and Ruud Van Nistelrooy opens the scoring with his 20th league goal of the campaign. Shearer scores for the first time in four games but Newcastle stay third after losing to Fulham.

West Brom secure a first win in nine games against rock-bottom Sunderland, with skipper Derek McInnes netting his only goals of the season, but the Baggies' relegation is confirmed. West Ham are still in deep trouble after defeat by Bolton keeps them in the drop zone.

Alan Smith gets his third red card of the season as Leeds lose to Southampton.

West Ham manager Glenn Roeder is rushed to hospital, complaining of chest pains, after his side wins at 'Boro, but the Hammers remain 18th. Relegated West Brom lose to Spurs and Newcastle's victory over bottom club Sunderland takes the Magpies up to third.

Arsenal drop another two points by drawing with Bolton and the following day Manchester United extend their advantage at the top with a victory over Spurs, in which Van Nistelrooy scores for the sixth game in a row, making it nine goals in that run.

Michael Owen hits four goals, taking him to 100 goals in 185 Liverpool appearances, as Houllier's side thrash Albion, who stay 19th.

West Ham win successive games for only the third time this season, against Manchester City, but the Hammers remain 18th.

Manchester United's Paul Scholes celebrates his 23-minute hat-trick against Newcastle United with Mikael Silvestre and Nicky Butt.

Saturday 3 May

Aston Villa v. Sunderland	1-0
Blackburn Rovers v. West Bromwich Alb.	1-1
Fulham v. Everton	2-0
Liverpool v. Manchester City	1-2
Manchester United v. Charlton Athletic	4-1
Middlesbrough v. Tottenham Hotspur	5-1
Newcastle United v. Birmingham City	1-0
Southampton v. Bolton Wanderers	0-0
West Ham United v. Chelsea	1-0

Sunday 4 May

Arsenal v. Leeds United	2-3

Wednesday 7 May

Arsenal v. Southampton	6-1

Sunday 11 May

Birmingham City v. West Ham United	2-2
Bolton Wanderers v. Middlesbrough	2-1
Charlton Athletic v. Fulham	0-1
Chelsea v. Liverpool	2-1
Everton v. Manchester United	1-2
Leeds United v. Aston Villa	3-1
Manchester City v. Southampton	0-1
Sunderland v. Arsenal	0-4
Tottenham Hotspur v. Blackburn Rovers	0-4
West Bromwich Alb. v. Newcastle United	2-2

		P	W	D	L	F	A	Pts
1	Manchester United	38	25	8	5	74	34	83
2	Arsenal	38	23	9	6	85	42	78
3	Newcastle United	38	21	6	11	63	48	69
4	Chelsea	38	19	10	9	68	38	67
5	Liverpool	38	18	10	10	61	41	64
6	Blackburn Rovers	38	16	12	10	52	43	60
7	Everton	38	17	8	13	48	49	59
8	Southampton	38	13	13	12	43	46	52
9	Manchester City	38	15	6	17	47	54	51
10	Tottenham Hotspur	38	14	8	16	51	62	50
11	Middlesbrough	38	13	10	15	48	44	49
12	Charlton Athletic	38	14	7	17	45	56	49
13	Birmingham City	38	13	9	16	41	49	48
14	Fulham	38	13	9	16	41	50	48
15	Leeds United	38	14	5	19	58	57	47
16	Aston Villa	38	12	9	17	42	47	45
17	Bolton Wanderers	38	10	14	14	41	51	44
18	West Ham United	38	10	12	16	42	59	42
19	West Bromwich Alb.	38	6	8	24	29	65	26
20	Sunderland	38	4	7	27	21	65	19

Promoted from Nationwide Football League Division One:

Portsmouth

Leicester City

Wolverhampton Wanderers (via play-offs)

Manchester United's David Beckham is sprayed with champagne.

MANCHESTER UNITED are nearly there. A Van Nistelrooy hat-trick, the Dutchman's third treble of the season, helps beat Charlton and keep United ahead of Arsenal. But the news is made by what appears to be an emotional goodbye to Old Trafford fans by David Beckham, after his goal puts United on the road to victory. Newcastle again qualify for the Champions League when they clinch third place in the Premiership with victory over Birmingham City. But Sunderland's record-breaking 14th consecutive Premiership defeat, against Aston Villa, condemns them to relegation. West Ham's third consecutive victory, over Chelsea, with a Paolo Di Canio winner, keeps the Hammers' hopes of avoiding the drop alive.

Arsenal hand Manchester United their eighth Premiership title in 11 years when they crash at home to Leeds United. Mark Viduka hits the winner with two minutes left. Fergie, with 27 trophies in 29 years the most successful ever British manager, comes off the golf course to learn of his team's triumph.

In a cup final rehearsal Arsenal take out their disappointment on Southampton, crushing the Saints with hat-tricks from Jermaine Pennant and Robert Pires.

West Brom say goodbye to the Premiership with a draw against Newcastle. West Ham are down after they lose to Birmingham after leading 1–0 with 24 minutes left. And spare a thought for Sunderland, who are ruthlessly cut down by Arsenal with Thierry Henry netting his 24th goal of the campaign and Freddie Ljungberg doubling his season's tally with a hat-trick.

The Chelsea v Liverpool game, with the 'winner-takes-all' scenario of the final Champions League place, which is dubbed a £20 million game, is won by the home side, who come from 1–0 down to win.

Champions Manchester United sign off in style with their 25th victory of the campaign, at Everton. David Beckham scores again, with what proves to be his last goal for the club, and Ruud Van Nistelrooy scores for the eighth consecutive game – 13 goals in that spell – and finishes the season with 25 league goals, 40 in all competitions.

Bolton, who had been out of the bottom three since Boxing Day, finish 17th after victory over Middlesbrough.

End of season round-up

Top Premiership Goalscorers 2002–03

Ruud van Nistelrooy	Manchester United	25
Thierry Henry	Arsenal	24
James Beattie	Southampton	23
Mark Viduka	Leeds United	20
Michael Owen	Liverpool	19
Alan Shearer	Newcastle United	17
Gianfranco Zola	Chelsea	14
Paul Scholes	Manchester United	14
Robert Pires	Arsenal	14
Harry Kewell	Leeds United	14
Nicolas Anelka	Manchester City	14
Robbie Keane	Tottenham Hotspur	14
(1 for Leeds)		

Worthington Cup Final

Liverpool 2   Manchester United 0

Despite some sunshine the match was played under the closed roof at the Millennium Stadium, but it was a poor game which resulted in Liverpool's seventh League Cup success. Steven Gerrard opened the scoring with a shot that deflected off David Beckham. Jerzey Dudek then defied United's response with excellent saves to deny Giggs, Van Nistelrooy and Scholes. Liverpool made United pay for not converting their chances with a Michael Owen goal, in the 82nd minute, taking the trophy.

FA Cup Final

Arsenal 1   Southampton 0

Arsenal reached their third consecutive FA Cup Final but it turned out to be a poor game. Antti Niemi, in his first season with the club, was preferred to Paul Jones in goal but, paradoxically, the Finnish stopper had to go off injured in the second half and was replaced by the Welsh international. But Southampton were already 1–0 down having conceded a 38th-minute goal to Robert Pires. Pires scored what proved the decisive goal after Freddie Ljungberg's shot deflected into his path off Lundekvam and the Gunners went on to claim the FA Cup for the third time in six years.

FWA Footballer of the Year

Thierry Henry   Arsenal

PFA Player of the Year

Thierry Henry   Arsenal

PFA Young Player of the Year

Jermaine Jenas   Newcastle United

Manager of the Year

David Moyes   Everton

Close Season 2003

Spurs confirm the departure of Teddy Sheringham and Graham Taylor ends his second spell as Aston Villa manager, citing 'The club isn't run properly' as his reason. Fulham appoint Chris Coleman, 32, as the youngest Premiership manager.

Newcastle United sign Lee Bowyer. The media speculation surrounding a possible David Beckham move gathers momentum, with Barcelona, AC Milan and Real Madrid favourites for his signature.

Michael Owen becomes England's youngest-ever captain, at 23 years and 181 days, and he celebrates his 50th cap by scoring both goals in the 2–1 win over Slovakia.

Manchester United reveal that they offered David Beckham a new contract but Real Madrid announce that the player has already signed a pre-contract agreement. Three days later United confirm their acceptance of Madrid's £25 million offer for Beckham.

Manchester City retire their squad number 23 in tribute to their midfielder Marc-Vivien Foe, who collapsed and died while playing for Cameroon in the Confederations Cup.

Teddy Sheringham signs a one-year contract with Portsmouth and another ex-England man, 39-year-old David Seaman, signs for Manchester City.

The Russian revolution comes to London as billionaire Roman Abramovic buys Chelsea and at a stroke wipes out the club's £100 million debts. Ken Bates sells out and ends a 20-year association with Stamford Bridge, though he stays on as chairman, for now. The new regime comes days too late to prevent Gianfranco Zola leaving for Cagliari. Voted the best-ever Chelsea player, Gianfranco refuses to go back on his word to the Italian club after the new regime at the Bridge tries to lure him back.

David Beckham signs for Real Madrid for £25 million and becomes the joint 12th most expensive player in the world, with Pavel Nedved. A worldwide television audience sees the England captain undergo an intense medical.

'Chelski', the new media name for Chelsea, splash £28 million, in three days, to sign Damien Duff, Geremi and Glen Johnson. Seven million is then spent on Wayne Bridge, from Southampton. Juan Sebastian Veron then moves to Stamford Bridge for half the £28 million Manchester United paid for him, taking Chelsea's Abramovic spending spree to more than £70 million.

Arsene Wenger, financially restricted by the club's move to a new ground at Ashburton Grove, warns Premiership rivals 'not to write us off for the title'. Joe Cole moves from West Ham to Chelsea for £6.6 million and is immediately dubbed 'my natural successor' by Gianfranco Zola.

Manchester United win the Community Shield, on penalties, but the game is marred when Francis Jeffers becomes the 50th red card of Arsene Wenger's seven-year reign. Goalkeeper Jens Lehmann is the only new player in the Gunners line-up.

Manchester United sign Ronaldo but are quick to point out that it is Cristiano Ronaldo, from Sporting Lisbon. In paying their fifth highest-ever fee, £12.24 million, United make the 18-year-old the most expensive teenager in British football.

While Chelsea splash the cash Arsene Wenger secures Dennis Bergkamp, Patrick Vieira and Robert Pires on new deals

Everton's manager David Moyes, winner of the Manager of the Year award.

Saturday 16 August

Arsenal v. Everton	2-1
Birmingham City v. Tottenham Hotspur	1-0
Blackburn Rovers v. Wolverhampton W	5-1
Fulham v. Middlesbrough	3-2
Leicester City v. Southampton	2-2
Manchester United v. Bolton Wanderers	4-0
Portsmouth v. Aston Villa	2-1

Sunday 17 August

Charlton Athletic v. Manchester City	0-3
Leeds United v. Newcastle United	2-2
Liverpool v. Chelsea	1-2

Saturday 23 August

Bolton Wanderers v. Blackburn Rovers	2-2
Chelsea v. Leicester City	2-1
Everton v. Fulham	3-1
Manchester City v. Portsmouth	1-1
Newcastle United v. Manchester United	1-2
Southampton v. Birmingham City	0-0
Tottenham Hotspur v. Leeds United	2-1
Wolverhampton W v. Charlton Athletic	0-4

Sunday 24 August

Aston Villa v. Liverpool	0-0
Middlesbrough v. Arsenal	0-4

Monday 25 August

Blackburn Rovers v. Manchester City	2-3

Tuesday 26 August

Charlton Athletic v. Everton	2-2
Leeds United v. Southampton	0-0
Leicester City v. Middlesbrough	0-0
Portsmouth v. Bolton Wanderers	4-0

Wednesday 27 August

Arsenal v. Aston Villa	2-0
Liverpool v. Tottenham Hotspur	0-0
Manchester United v. Wolverhampton W	1-0

Saturday 30 August

Aston Villa v. Leicester City	3-1
Bolton Wanderers v. Charlton Athletic	0-0
Chelsea v. Blackburn Rovers	2-2
Everton v. Liverpool	0-3
Middlesbrough v. Leeds United	2-3
Newcastle United v. Birmingham City	0-1
Tottenham Hotspur v. Fulham	0-3
Wolverhampton W v. Portsmouth	0-0

Sunday 31 August

Manchester City v. Arsenal	1-2
Southampton v. Manchester United	1-0

		P	W	D	L	F	A	Pts
1	Arsenal	4	4	0	0	10	2	12
2	Manchester United	4	3	0	1	7	2	9
3	Portsmouth	4	2	2	0	7	2	8
4	Manchester City	4	2	1	1	8	5	7
5	Chelsea	3	2	1	0	6	4	7
6	Birmingham City	3	2	1	0	2	0	7
7	Fulham	3	2	0	1	7	5	6
8	Southampton	4	1	3	0	3	2	6
9	Blackburn Rovers	4	1	2	1	11	8	5
10	Liverpool	4	1	2	1	4	2	5
11	Charlton Athletic	4	1	2	1	6	5	5
12	Leeds United	4	1	2	1	6	6	5
13	Aston Villa	4	1	1	2	4	5	4
14	Everton	4	1	1	2	6	8	4
15	Tottenham Hotspur	4	1	1	2	2	5	4
16	Leicester City	4	0	2	2	4	7	2
17	Bolton Wanderers	4	0	2	2	2	10	2
18	Newcastle United	3	0	1	2	3	5	1
19	Middlesbrough	4	0	1	3	4	10	1
20	Wolverhampton W	4	0	1	3	1	10	1

Chelsea's Jimmy Floyd Hasselbaink beats Liverpool's Jamie Carragher to the ball to score their winning goal.

MANCHESTER UNITED and Arsenal open with victories, with the champions having a particularly emphatic win over Bolton. Sol Cambell's 25th-minute dismissal, in the victory over Everton, makes him the first Premiership red card of the campaign. But there are mixed fortunes for the Premiership new boys. Wolves are crushed by Blackburn and Leicester are held by Southampton, but Paul Dickov nets the first Premiership goal of the season, from the spot, after just five minutes. Portsmouth start with victory over Aston Villa, who lose Gareth Barry to an 87th-minute red card, three minutes after he scores Villa's only goal. Roman Abramovich's multi-million pound investment pays an immediate dividend as Chelsea win at Anfield, with Jimmy Floyd Hasselbaink netting an 88th-minute winner.

Wolves' introduction to top-flight football gets worse as they slump at home to Charlton and are bottom of the table. Leicester also lose, to Chelsea, who, like Manchester United and Arsenal, make it two wins out of two to top the table, with wins over Newcastle and Middlesbrough respectively. Portsmouth are third after their draw with Manchester City.

Pompey go top after they beat Bolton, with the Premiership's oldest striker, 37-year-old Teddy Sheringham, hitting the first hat-trick of the season. The next day United and Arsenal extend their 100 percent record with wins over Wolves and Villa respectively.

Successive goalless draws, against Villa and Spurs, mean just two points for winless Liverpool after three games. But United and Arsenal go clear after their third consecutive victories, over Wolves, who are bottom, and Villa.

Chelsea drop their first point in drawing with Blackburn but the first significant chapter of the season comes after United's shock defeat by Southampton coincides with Arsenal's victory at Manchester City, which moves the Gunners clear at the top. Liverpool finally get a win, over neighbours Everton.

At the foot of the table Leicester and Wolves, still without a win between them, are already looking like early strugglers after defeat by Villa and a draw with Portsmouth respectively.

September

Saturday 13 September

Arsenal v. Portsmouth	1-1
Blackburn Rovers v. Liverpool	1-3
Bolton Wanderers v. Middlesbrough	2-0
Charlton Athletic v. Manchester United	0-2
Chelsea v. Tottenham Hotspur	4-2
Everton v. Newcastle United	2-2
Southampton v. Wolverhampton W	2-0

Sunday 14 September

Birmingham City v. Fulham	2-2
Manchester City v. Aston Villa	4-1

Monday 15 September

Leicester City v. Leeds United	4-0

Saturday 20 September

Aston Villa v. Charlton Athletic	2-1
Fulham v. Manchester City	2-2
Leeds United v. Birmingham City	0-2
Liverpool v. Leicester City	2-1
Newcastle United v. Bolton Wanderers	0-0
Portsmouth v. Blackburn Rovers	1-2
Tottenham Hotspur v. Southampton	1-3
Wolverhampton W v. Chelsea	0-5

Sunday 21 September

Manchester United v. Arsenal	0-0
Middlesbrough v. Everton	1-0

Friday 26 September

Arsenal v. Newcastle United	3-2

Saturday 27 September

Birmingham City v. Portsmouth	2-0
Bolton Wanderers v. Wolverhampton W	1-1
Chelsea v. Aston Villa	1-0
Leicester City v. Manchester United	1-4
Southampton v. Middlesbrough	0-1

Sunday 28 September

Blackburn Rovers v. Fulham	0-2
Charlton Athletic v. Liverpool	3-2
Everton v. Leeds United	4-0
Manchester City v. Tottenham Hotspur	0-0

		P	W	D	L	F	A	Pts
1	Arsenal	7	5	2	0	14	5	17
2	Chelsea	6	5	1	0	16	6	16
3	Manchester United	7	5	1	1	13	3	16
4	Birmingham City	6	4	2	0	8	2	14
5	Manchester City	7	3	3	1	14	8	12
6	Southampton	7	3	3	1	8	4	12
7	Fulham	6	3	2	1	13	9	11
8	Liverpool	7	3	2	2	11	7	11
9	Portsmouth	7	2	3	2	9	7	9
10	Everton	7	2	2	3	12	11	8
11	Blackburn Rovers	7	2	2	3	14	14	8
12	Charlton Athletic	7	2	2	3	10	11	8
13	Aston Villa	7	2	1	4	7	11	7
14	Middlesbrough	7	2	1	4	6	12	7
15	Bolton Wanderers	7	1	4	2	5	11	7
16	Leicester City	7	1	2	4	10	13	5
17	Tottenham Hotspur	7	1	2	4	5	12	5
18	Leeds United	7	1	2	4	6	16	5
19	Newcastle United	6	0	3	3	7	10	3
20	Wolverhampton W	7	0	2	5	2	18	2

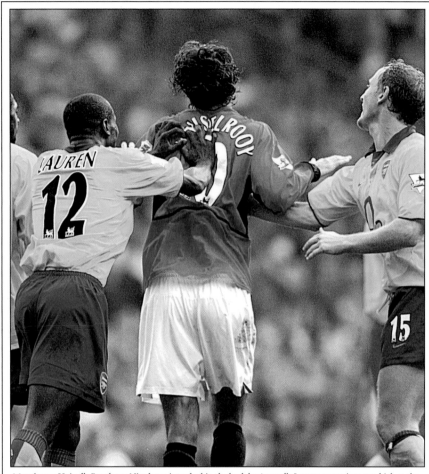

Manchester United's Ruud van Nistelrooy is pushed in the back by Arsenal's Lauren as tensions run high at the end of the match (l-r Lauren, Ruud Van Nistelrooy, Ray Parlour, Martin Keown and Ashley Cole).

ARSENAL's advantage at the top is reduced after they drop their first point of the campaign, to Portsmouth, and Manchester United's win at Charlton, in which Cristiano Ronaldo has his first 90 minutes for United, keeps them second. Chelsea's defeat of Spurs takes them above Pompey into fourth place.

Wolves stay bottom after losing to Southampton and Leicester claim a first win of the campaign, over Leeds, who are looking fragile with a points total of just five from 15. Middlesbrough stay second-bottom after they lose at Bolton.

Nicolas Anelka hits two penalties in a second-half hat-trick that sinks Aston Villa and takes City into third place. Leicester's first win of the campaign, over Leeds, moves the Foxes out of the bottom three. Newcastle stay above the bottom three by virtue of the ill-tempered draw at Everton in which there are 10 players booked and two sent off, Gary Naysmith and Laurent Robert. An Alan Shearer brace takes his tally against Everton to an astonishing 16 goals, including seven penalties. Duncan Ferguson's penalty makes him the first Everton player to reach 50 Premiership goals.

Chelsea make it nine goals in two games with a comprehensive victory over bottom club Wolves, while defeats for Leicester and Leeds, by Liverpool and Birmingham respectively, mean that this trio of clubs are the early season relegation candidates.

The top two meet in a goalless draw at Old Trafford in which Patrick Vieira is sent off and the game is marred by unsavoury scenes at the end when Ruud Van Nistelrooy is goaded by a number of Arsenal players after he misses a penalty, which they accuse him of diving to win.

Manchester United beat Leicester, who stay in the bottom three. Arsenal beat

FACT FILE

Louis Saha's goal in Fulham's 2–2 draw with Birmingham is his 50th for the Cottagers. Alan Shearer's first penalty against Everton is his 150th goal for Newcastle.

Newcastle to stay top and Chelsea keep up their momentum by beating Aston Villa to move into second place, on goal difference.

Saturday 4 October	
Fulham v. Leicester City	2-0
Leeds United v. Blackburn Rovers	2-1
Liverpool v. Arsenal	1-2
Manchester United v. Birmingham City	3-0
Newcastle United v. Southampton	1-0
Portsmouth v. Charlton Athletic	1-2
Tottenham Hotspur v. Everton	3-0
Wolverhampton W v. Manchester City	1-0

Sunday 5 October	
Aston Villa v. Bolton Wanderers	1-1
Middlesbrough v. Chelsea	1-2

Tuesday 14 October	
Birmingham City v. Chelsea	0-0

Saturday 18 October	
Arsenal v. Chelsea	2-1
Fulham v. Wolverhampton W	0-0
Leeds United v. Manchester United	0-1
Manchester City v. Bolton Wanderers	6-2
Middlesbrough v. Newcastle United	0-1
Portsmouth v. Liverpool	1-0

Sunday 19 October	
Birmingham City v. Aston Villa	0-0
Everton v. Southampton	0-0
Leicester City v. Tottenham Hotspur	1-2

Monday 20 October	
Blackburn Rovers v. Charlton Athletic	0-1

Tuesday 21 October	
Fulham v. Newcastle United	2-3

Saturday 25 October	
Aston Villa v. Everton	0-0
Bolton Wanderers v. Birmingham City	0-1
Chelsea v. Manchester City	1-0
Liverpool v. Leeds United	3-1
Manchester United v. Fulham	1-3
Newcastle United v. Portsmouth	3-0
Southampton v. Blackburn Rovers	2-0
Wolverhampton W v. Leicester City	4-3

Sunday 26 October	
Charlton Athletic v. Arsenal	1-1
Tottenham Hotspur v. Middlesbrough	0-0

		P	W	D	L	F	A	Pts
1	Arsenal	10	7	3	0	19	8	24
2	Chelsea	10	7	2	1	20	9	23
3	Manchester United	10	7	1	2	18	6	22
4	Birmingham City	10	5	4	1	9	5	19
5	Fulham	10	5	3	2	20	13	18
6	Southampton	10	4	4	2	10	5	16
7	Manchester City	10	4	3	3	20	12	15
8	Newcastle United	10	4	3	3	15	12	15
9	Charlton Athletic	10	4	3	3	14	13	15
10	Liverpool	10	4	2	4	15	11	14
11	Portsmouth	10	3	3	4	11	12	12
12	Tottenham Hotspur	10	3	3	4	10	13	12
13	Everton	10	2	4	4	12	14	10
14	Aston Villa	10	2	4	4	8	12	10
15	Wolverhampton W	10	2	3	5	7	21	9
16	Blackburn Rovers	10	2	2	6	15	19	8
17	Middlesbrough	10	2	2	6	7	15	8
18	Bolton Wanderers	10	1	5	4	8	19	8
19	Leeds United	10	2	2	6	9	21	8
20	Leicester City	10	1	2	7	14	21	5

Birmingham City's Mikael Forssell scores the opening goal past Bolton Wanderers's goalkeeper Jussi Jaaskelainen.

THERE are celebrations at the foot of the table as both Wolves and Leeds register first wins of the season, against Manchester City and Blackburn, but poor old Leicester lose again, at Fulham.

Arsenal win at Anfield: Liverpool are already nine points adrift of the top spot. Manchester United also win, against Birmingham. Chelsea make it five wins out of six, at 'Boro, to complete the leading group of three.

Claudio Ranieri, amid more speculation that he is to be replaced by Sven-Goran Eriksson, hits his first bad patch of the season as Chelsea follow up a goalless draw against Birmingham with their first defeat of the campaign, against Arsenal. Henry's 75th minute tap-in follows a Cudicini howler. The leaders stay just ahead of United, winners at Leeds, thanks to a rare headed goal by Roy Keane. Chelsea drop three points behind the Gunners into third place.

Manchester City's crushing defeat of Bolton is the team's highest Premiership win under Kevin Keegan.

Middlesbrough are 18th after losing to Newcastle. Wolves are one place lower after their draw with Fulham and Leicester are bottom after Freddie Kanoute's last-minute winner for Spurs.

Alan Shearer's brace, in the victory over Fulham which is their first Premiership defeat in two months, takes him second in Newcastle's 'all-time' list of goalscorers, with 154, behind the legendary Jackie Milburn on 200.

Manchester United suffer a shock home defeat by Fulham, and the Cottagers celebrate a first win at Old Trafford for 40 years. Arsenal fail to profit as they draw at Charlton, where Di Canio's penalty is cancelled out by Thierry Henry's sixth Premiership goal of the season. Chelsea are the only winners in the top three, beating Manchester City, and they close the gap on Arsenal to a single point. Adrian Mutu, who set up Hasselbaink's winner, cites his mother's home cooking as the reason for his resurgent form after he flew her in from Romania. Chelsea's Mikael Forssell, on loan at Birmingham, scores the goal that beats Bolton and takes Blues fourth.

Wolves' victory over Leicester plunges the Foxes to 20th and Henri Camara's 86th-minute goal, which proves the winner, is his first for the club. It caps Wolves' best winning fight-back since 1956–57, and they are 15th. Leeds are in trouble, in the bottom three, after they lose to Liverpool, for whom Sinama-Pongolle scores his first Premiership goal on his league debut. Blackburn, after a fourth successive defeat, at Southampton, only stay out of the bottom three on goal difference.

November

Saturday 1 November	
Everton v. Chelsea	0-1
Leeds United v. Arsenal	1-4
Manchester United v. Portsmouth	3-0
Middlesbrough v. Wolverhampton W	2-0
Newcastle United v. Aston Villa	1-1
Southampton v. Manchester City	0-2
Tottenham Hotspur v. Bolton Wanderers	0-1

Sunday 2 November	
Fulham v. Liverpool	1-2
Leicester City v. Blackburn Rovers	2-0

Monday 3 November	
Birmingham City v. Charlton Athletic	1-2

Saturday 8 November	
Arsenal v. Tottenham Hotspur	2-1
Aston Villa v. Middlesbrough	0-2
Bolton Wanderers v. Southampton	0-0
Charlton Athletic v. Fulham	3-1
Portsmouth v. Leeds United	6-1
Wolverhampton W v. Birmingham City	1-1

Sunday 9 November	
Chelsea v. Newcastle United	5-0
Liverpool v. Manchester United	1-2
Manchester City v. Leicester City	0-3

Monday 10 November	
Blackburn Rovers v. Everton	2-1

Saturday 22 November	
Birmingham City v. Arsenal	0-3
Everton v. Wolverhampton W	2-0
Leeds United v. Bolton Wanderers	0-2
Leicester City v. Charlton Athletic	1-1
Manchester United v. Blackburn Rovers	2-1
Middlesbrough v. Liverpool	0-0
Newcastle United v. Manchester City	3-0
Southampton v. Chelsea	0-1

Sunday 23 November	
Tottenham Hotspur v. Aston Villa	2-1

Monday 24 November	
Fulham v. Portsmouth	2-0

Saturday 29 November	
Aston Villa v. Southampton	1-0
Blackburn Rovers v. Tottenham Hotspur	1-0
Bolton Wanderers v. Everton	2-0
Charlton Athletic v. Leeds United	0-1
Portsmouth v. Leicester City	0-2
Wolverhampton W v. Newcastle United	1-1

Sunday 30 November	
Arsenal v. Fulham	0-0
Chelsea v. Manchester United	1-0
Liverpool v. Birmingham City	3-1
Manchester City v. Middlesbrough	0-1

	P	W	D	L	F	A	Pts
1 Chelsea	14	11	2	1	28	9	35
2 Arsenal	14	10	4	0	28	10	34
3 Manchester United	14	10	1	3	25	9	31
4 Fulham	14	6	4	4	24	18	22
5 Charlton Athletic	14	6	4	4	20	17	22
6 Liverpool	14	6	3	5	21	15	21
7 Newcastle United	14	5	5	4	20	19	20
8 Birmingham City	14	5	5	4	12	14	20
9 Manchester City	14	5	3	6	22	19	18
10 Middlesbrough	14	5	3	6	12	15	18
11 Bolton Wanderers	14	4	6	4	13	19	18
12 Southampton	14	4	5	5	10	9	17
13 Leicester City	14	4	3	7	22	22	15
14 Portsmouth	14	4	3	7	17	20	15
15 Tottenham Hotspur	14	4	3	7	13	18	15
16 Blackburn Rovers	14	4	2	8	19	24	14
17 Aston Villa	14	3	5	6	11	17	14
18 Everton	14	3	4	7	15	19	13
19 Wolverhampton W	14	2	5	7	9	27	11
20 Leeds United	14	3	2	9	12	33	11

Charlton Athletic's Matt Holland scores the opening goal against Birmingham City.

ARSENAL crush Leeds to top the Premiership by a point from Chelsea, who win at Everton, now goalless for six and a half hours of Premiership football. Manchester United are third after beating Portsmouth, with Cristiano Ronaldo netting his first goal for the club with a stunning free-kick.

Leicester beat Blackburn and move a place ahead of 19th-placed Rovers. Leeds are bottom of the table, on goal difference, from Graeme Souness's side, who have won just one league game in 13. Wolves are just one point above the bottom three after losing to Middlesbrough.

Birmingham City are pegged back in fourth place after losing to Charlton, the first team to win at St Andrews for nine months. Matt Holland's pair of goals are the first conceded by Blues in nearly 600 minutes.

Arsenal go four points clear at the top by winning the North London derby. Charlton are fourth after beating Fulham. Leeds are swept aside at Portsmouth and stay rock bottom. Wolves are just above the bottom three after drawing with Birmingham.

Leicester move out of the bottom three with a win at Manchester City. Manchester United have to settle for third place, after beating Liverpool, who haven't kept a clean sheet since 30 August, because of Chelsea's crushing victory over Newcastle, which closes the gap on leaders Arsenal to one point. Blackburn beat Everton to exit the relegation zone.

Peter Reid is sacked by Leeds for the second time in 12 months. Eddie Gray takes over as caretaker manager, despite not having the necessary coaching qualifications to manage in the Premiership, and promptly reinstates Mark Viduka, dropped by Reid and threatened with a £130,000 fine following a training-ground bust up. Reid's compensation package, reportedly worth £850,000, takes Leeds United's managerial bill for the last three managers to more than £7 million.

Arsenal's comprehensive victory over Birmingham, in Arsene Wenger's 400th game, with a Dennis Bergkamp goal marking his first match as skipper, keeps them a point ahead of second-placed Chelsea, who register their seventh straight league win at Southampton. Manchester United, in their best start for 10 years, are a point further behind following their win over Blackburn. Kleberson scores his first goal in English football; Van Nistelrooy's goal is his 12th of the campaign.

Leeds lose at home to Bolton and remain 20th. Wolves are 19th after losing to Everton and because Blackburn scored in their defeat at Old Trafford Aston Villa, Sunday losers at Tottenham, who hit back with two goals in the last 12 minutes, are in the bottom three.

Alan Shearer's brace against Manchester City takes his tally, under Sir Bobby Robson's four-year reign, to 100 goals.

Chelsea go top of the Premiership, with a Frank Lampard penalty beating Manchester United, one point ahead of Arsenal, who are held by Fulham, who move above Charlton to fourth. United drop to third, four points off the top.

Leeds win at Charlton but stay bottom, on goal difference, from Wolves who are held by Newcastle. Everton slump into the bottom three after losing at Bolton.

December

Saturday 6 December	
Birmingham City v. Blackburn Rovers	0-4
Fulham v. Bolton Wanderers	2-1
Leeds United v. Chelsea	1-1
Leicester City v. Arsenal	1-1
Manchester United v. Aston Villa	4-0
Middlesbrough v. Portsmouth	0-0
Newcastle United v. Liverpool	1-1
Tottenham Hotspur v. Wolverhampton W	5-2
Sunday 7 December	
Everton v. Manchester City	0-0
Southampton v. Charlton Athletic	3-2
Saturday 13 December	
Chelsea v. Bolton Wanderers	1-2
Leicester City v. Birmingham City	0-2
Liverpool v. Southampton	1-2
Manchester United v. Manchester City	3-1
Middlesbrough v. Charlton Athletic	0-0
Newcastle United v. Tottenham Hotspur	4-0
Portsmouth v. Everton	1-2
Sunday 14 December	
Arsenal v. Blackburn Rovers	1-0
Aston Villa v. Wolverhampton W	3-2
Leeds United v. Fulham	3-2
Saturday 20 December	
Blackburn Rovers v. Aston Villa	0-2
Bolton Wanderers v. Arsenal	1-1
Charlton Athletic v. Newcastle United	0-0
Everton v. Leicester City	3-2
Fulham v. Chelsea	0-1
Sunday 21 December	
Southampton v. Portsmouth	3-0
Tottenham Hotspur v. Manchester United	1-2
Monday 22 December	
Manchester City v. Leeds United	1-1
Friday 26 December	
Arsenal v. Wolverhampton W	3-0
Birmingham City v. Manchester City	2-1
Blackburn Rovers v. Middlesbrough	2-2
Charlton Athletic v. Chelsea	4-2
Fulham v. Southampton	2-0
Leeds United v. Aston Villa	0-0
Leicester City v. Newcastle United	1-1
Liverpool v. Bolton Wanderers	3-1
Manchester United v. Everton	3-2
Portsmouth v. Tottenham Hotspur	2-0
Sunday 28 December	
Aston Villa v. Fulham	3-0
Bolton Wanderers v. Leicester City	2-2
Chelsea v. Portsmouth	3-0
Everton v. Birmingham City	1-0
Manchester City v. Liverpool	2-2
Middlesbrough v. Manchester United	0-1
Newcastle United v. Blackburn Rovers	0-1
Tottenham Hotspur v. Charlton Athletic	0-1
Wolverhampton W v. Leeds United	3-1
Monday 29 December	
Southampton v. Arsenal	0-1

		P	*W*	*D*	*L*	*F*	*A*	*Pts*
1	Manchester United	19	15	1	3	38	13	46
2	Arsenal	19	13	6	0	35	12	45
3	Chelsea	19	13	3	3	36	16	42
4	Charlton Athletic	19	8	6	5	27	22	30
5	Fulham	19	8	4	7	30	26	28
6	Liverpool	18	7	5	6	28	21	26
7	Newcastle United	19	6	8	5	26	22	26
8	Southampton	19	7	5	7	18	15	26
9	Birmingham City	18	7	5	6	16	20	26
10	Aston Villa	19	6	6	7	19	23	24
11	Everton	19	6	5	8	23	25	23
12	Bolton Wanderers	19	5	8	6	20	28	23
13	Manchester City	19	5	6	8	27	27	21
14	Blackburn Rovers	19	6	3	10	26	29	21
15	Middlesbrough	18	5	6	7	14	18	21
16	Portsmouth	19	5	4	10	20	28	19
17	Leicester City	19	4	6	9	28	31	18
18	Tottenham Hotspur	19	5	3	11	19	29	18
19	Leeds United	19	4	5	10	18	40	17
20	Wolverhampton W	18	3	5	10	16	39	14

ARSENAL see Ashley Cole become the 53rd red card of Arsene Wenger's tenure as they're denied a sixth away win at Leicester. Craig Hignett equalises in the last minute to leave Chelsea as leaders, following their draw at Leeds which keeps United 19th. Manchester United cruise to victory over Aston Villa, with Forlan scoring twice in the final minute, but Fergie's men stay third, a point from the Gunners and two behind Chelsea. Wolves are crushed at Spurs with old boy Robbie Keane netting a hat-trick. The top three are now nine points ahead of fourth place and Fulham, who beat Bolton.

Everton move above Villa, who replace them in the bottom three, after a draw with Manchester City.

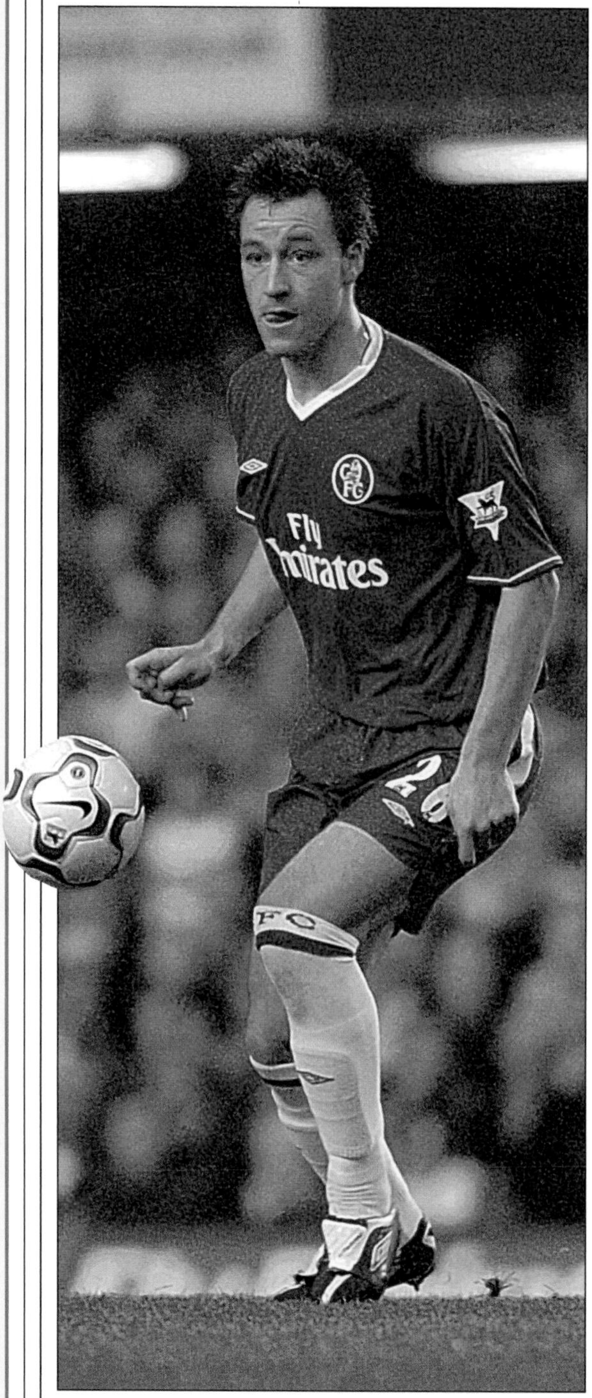

John Terry, Chelsea.

Liverpool chairman David Moores piles more pressure on Gerard Houllier by 'intimating' that Champions League qualification is the minimum acceptable target.

Fergie issues a 'hands-off' warning to Real Madrid, who are said to covet Van Nistelrooy, and United are set to offer the striker a double-your-money contract extension.

Chelsea are knocked off the top of the table when a John Terry own-goal gifts victory to Bolton Wanderers. United jump into pole position, a point ahead of Arsenal, when they win the Manchester derby against City, who haven't won at Old Trafford for 23 games. Ruud Van Nistelrooy's goal, United's third, is his 96th for the club in only 116 starts.

Southampton, without an away goal in six and a half hours, complete the league double over Liverpool with their first-ever Premiership victory at Anfield.

Alan Shearer's brace in Newcastle's thrashing of Spurs takes him to 100 league goals for the Magpies, while Everton's first away win of the season puts Portsmouth in trouble at the foot of the table. Manchester United end the year with a best first half of the season for 10 years with 46 points from 19 games, thanks to a freak Danny Mills own-goal that beats 'Boro. Arsenal move into second place, a point behind the leaders, with the Gunners' 19th consecutive league game without defeat, and Chelsea are third after beating Portsmouth.

The tradition that the bottom club in the Premiership at Christmas is marked for relegation would seem to doom Wolverhampton Wanderers, who end the year in 20th place. Things aren't much better for the other teams in the drop zone, Spurs and Leeds.

Tuesday 6 January	
Aston Villa v. Portsmouth	2-1

Wednesday 7 January	
Bolton Wanderers v. Manchester United	1-2
Chelsea v. Liverpool	0-1
Everton v. Arsenal	1-1
Manchester City v. Charlton Athletic	1-1
Middlesbrough v. Fulham	2-1
Newcastle United v. Leeds United	1-0
Southampton v. Leicester City	0-0
Tottenham Hotspur v. Birmingham City	4-1
Wolverhampton W v. Blackburn Rovers	2-2

Saturday 10 January	
Arsenal v. Middlesbrough	4-1
Birmingham City v. Southampton	2-1
Blackburn Rovers v. Bolton Wanderers	3-4
Charlton Athletic v. Wolverhampton W	2-0
Fulham v. Everton	2-1
Leeds United v. Tottenham Hotspur	0-1
Liverpool v. Aston Villa	1-0
Portsmouth v. Manchester City	4-2

Sunday 11 January	
Leicester City v. Chelsea	0-4
Manchester United v. Newcastle United	0-0

Saturday 17 January	
Bolton Wanderers v. Portsmouth	1-0
Everton v. Charlton Athletic	0-1
Manchester City v. Blackburn Rovers	1-1
Middlesbrough v. Leicester City	3-3
Southampton v. Leeds United	2-1
Tottenham Hotspur v. Liverpool	2-1
Wolverhampton W v. Manchester United	1-0

Sunday 18 January	
Aston Villa v. Arsenal	0-2
Chelsea v. Birmingham City	0-0

Monday 19 January	
Newcastle United v. Fulham	3-1

Wednesday 21 January	
Wolverhampton W v. Liverpool	1-1

Saturday 31 January	
Birmingham City v. Newcastle United	1-1
Charlton Athletic v. Bolton Wanderers	1-2
Fulham v. Tottenham Hotspur	2-1
Leeds United v. Middlesbrough	0-3
Leicester City v. Aston Villa	0-5
Liverpool v. Everton	0-0
Manchester United v. Southampton	3-2
Portsmouth v. Wolverhampton W	0-0

		P	W	D	L	F	A	Pts
1	Manchester United	23	17	2	4	43	17	53
2	Arsenal	22	15	7	0	42	14	52
3	Chelsea	22	14	4	4	40	17	46
4	Charlton Athletic	23	10	7	6	32	25	37
5	Liverpool	23	9	7	7	32	24	34
6	Newcastle United	23	8	10	5	31	24	34
7	Fulham	23	10	4	9	36	33	34
8	Bolton Wanderers	23	8	8	7	28	34	32
9	Birmingham City	22	8	7	7	20	26	31
10	Southampton	23	8	6	9	23	21	30
11	Aston Villa	23	8	6	9	26	27	30
12	Middlesbrough	22	7	7	8	23	26	28
13	Tottenham Hotspur	23	8	3	12	27	33	27
14	Everton	23	6	7	10	25	29	25
15	Manchester City	22	5	8	9	31	33	23
16	Blackburn Rovers	22	6	5	11	32	36	23
17	Portsmouth	23	6	5	12	25	33	23
18	Leicester City	23	4	8	11	31	43	20
19	Wolverhampton W	23	4	8	11	20	44	20
20	Leeds United	23	4	5	14	19	47	17

FACT FILE

It's more than a decade since the last successful penalty at Old Trafford by a visiting player. That was Ruel Fox, in his Norwich days. Since then a couple have been awarded but not converted.

YAKUBA AYEGBENI'S goal at Villa is Portsmouth's first Premiership goal in 12 hours and 24 minutes but it's a consolation as Aston Villa net a late Angel winner that plunges Pompey to within a point of the bottom three.

Manchester United win at Bolton to take over at the top from Arsenal, who are held by Everton. Tomasz Radzinski cancels out Kanu's first Premiership goal of the season and in doing so maintains his record of scoring in every game in which he has faced the Gunners. Bruno Cheyrou's first Premiership goal sinks Chelsea and revitalises Liverpool's season, taking them up to fifth.

At the other end of the Premiership, Wolves are held by Blackburn and remain bottom. Leeds crash to an Alan Shearer goal that is his 17th of the campaign, his 237th in the Premiership, and his 20th in the Premiership against Leeds, his best tally against any top-flight side. Leeds stay 19th while Portsmouth are 18th. Leicester, who fail to score for the fourth consecutive game, at Southampton, are only outside the drop zone on goal difference.

Arsenal's thrashing of Portsmouth, in which Freddie Ljungberg nets his 50th Premiership goal, keeps them ahead of United, and Fergie's side fail to convert their game in hand when they are held by Newcastle. It's the Geordies' first point at Old Trafford since 1998. Afterwards referee Paul Durkin admits he should have awarded the Magpies a penalty when Alan Shearer was felled by United 'keeper Tim Howard.

Wolves stay bottom after losing to Charlton and Leeds are only one place higher after a Robbie Keane goal gives Spurs victory. There are no celebrations from the former Elland Road striker. Leicester stay 18th after they crash to Chelsea and Adrian Mutu scores his first goal in 15 games.

It's tight at the top of the table: United and Arsenal are level on 49 points, 40 goals for, and 14 goals against.

The biggest shock of the Premiership season comes when Wolves beat Manchester United with a Kenny Miller goal, his first in the Premiership. It is Wolves' first top-flight win over United for 43 years.

Graham Stuart hits his 50th Premiership goal to give Charlton victory at Everton, his old club, 10 years after his brace on the final day of the season kept Everton in the top flight.

At the bottom of the table Leicester leapfrog Portsmouth, losers at Bolton, to 18th. Surrendering a 3–1 lead, by conceding twice in the 90th minute against Middlesbrough, stops the Foxes climbing out of the relegation zone. After losing to Southampton – Kevin Phillips's first Saints goal proves the winner – Leeds are rock bottom, five points from safety.

Arsenal extend their unbeaten run to 22 games with a controversial victory over Villa. The first of Thierry Henry's brace comes from a quickly taken free-kick while a disorganised Villa defence awaits the referee's whistle, unaware that the Frenchman had asked the official if he could take it quickly. The Gunners now lead second-placed Manchester United by two points and are six points away from third-placed Chelsea, who are held by Birmingham City.

Newcastle United's Laurent Robert scores the third goal against Fulham.

Laurent Robert scores a wonder overhead kick to clinch a Newcastle win over Fulham that takes them fifth.

Kenny Miller nets another goal as Wolves hold Liverpool to stay 19th and extend their unbeaten home record to 11 games.

Arsenal shatter their transfer record by paying Seville £20 million for Jose Antonio Reyes.

Louis Saha is credited with a debut goal in the win over Southampton that takes Manchester United top, although Kevin Phillips's head diverts the Frenchman's free-kick wickedly past Niemi. Ruud Van Nistelrooy also scores to take his United tally to 99 in 122 starts.

Leeds are now three points adrift of safety after losing their eighth 'must-win' game in a row, crashing to Middlesbrough, and United have Paul Robinson sent off. Wolves are 19th but their draw with Pompey puts them level with third-bottom Leicester, who are walloped by Aston Villa, extending their winless run at home that stretches back to 2 November.

February

Sunday 1 February		
Arsenal v. Manchester City		2-1
Blackburn Rovers v. Chelsea		2-3
Saturday 7 February		
Aston Villa v. Leeds United		2-0
Bolton Wanderers v. Liverpool		2-2
Everton v. Manchester United		3-4
Middlesbrough v. Blackburn Rovers		0-1
Newcastle United v. Leicester City		3-1
Southampton v. Fulham		0-0
Tottenham Hotspur v. Portsmouth		4-3
Wolverhampton W v. Arsenal		1-3
Sunday 8 February		
Chelsea v. Charlton Athletic		1-0
Manchester City v. Birmingham City		0-0
Tuesday 10 February		
Arsenal v. Southampton		2-0
Leeds United v. Wolverhampton W		4-1
Leicester City v. Bolton Wanderers		1-1
Wednesday 11 February		
Birmingham City v. Everton		3-0
Blackburn Rovers v. Newcastle United		1-1
Charlton Athletic v. Tottenham Hotspur		2-4
Fulham v. Aston Villa		1-2
Liverpool v. Manchester City		2-1
Manchester United v. Middlesbrough		2-3
Portsmouth v. Chelsea		0-2
Saturday 21 February		
Bolton Wanderers v. Manchester City		1-3
Charlton Athletic v. Blackburn Rovers		3-2
Chelsea v. Arsenal		1-2
Manchester United v. Leeds United		1-1
Newcastle United v. Middlesbrough		2-1
Southampton v. Everton		3-3
Wolverhampton W v. Fulham		2-1
Sunday 22 February		
Aston Villa v. Birmingham City		2-2
Tottenham Hotspur v. Leicester City		4-4
Saturday 28 February		
Arsenal v. Charlton Athletic		2-1
Blackburn Rovers v. Southampton		1-1
Everton v. Aston Villa		2-0
Fulham v. Manchester United		1-1
Leicester City v. Wolverhampton W		0-0
Manchester City v. Chelsea		0-1
Sunday 29 February		
Leeds United v. Liverpool		2-2
Portsmouth v. Newcastle United		1-1

		P	W	D	L	F	A	Pts
1	Arsenal	27	20	7	0	53	18	67
2	Chelsea	27	18	4	5	48	21	58
3	Manchester United	27	18	4	5	51	25	58
4	Newcastle United	27	10	12	5	38	28	42
5	Charlton Athletic	27	11	7	9	38	34	40
6	Liverpool	26	10	9	7	38	29	39
7	Aston Villa	27	10	7	10	32	32	37
8	Fulham	27	10	6	11	39	38	36
9	Birmingham City	25	9	9	7	25	28	36
10	Tottenham Hotspur	26	10	4	12	39	42	34
11	Bolton Wanderers	26	8	10	8	32	40	34
12	Southampton	27	8	9	10	27	27	33
13	Middlesbrough	25	8	7	10	27	31	31
14	Everton	27	7	8	12	33	39	29
15	Blackburn Rovers	27	7	7	13	39	44	28
16	Manchester City	27	6	9	12	36	39	27
17	Portsmouth	26	6	6	14	29	40	24
18	Wolverhampton W	27	5	9	13	24	52	24
19	Leicester City	27	4	11	12	37	51	23
20	Leeds United	27	5	7	15	26	53	22

ARSENAL win at Wolves and establish a new club record of 24 league games unbeaten. Thierry Henry scores his 99th Premiership goal as the Gunners move two points ahead of Manchester United, who win at Everton. Ruud Van Nistelrooy's first goal at Goodison is the 100th of his United career and, for good measure, he also nets number 101, the 89th-minute winner, to keep the Reds four points ahead of Chelsea, who beat Charlton.

At the other end of the table David O'Leary's former club, Leeds, lose their sixth game in a row, to the Irishman's present club, Aston Villa, and remain bottom. Leeds are three points adrift of Wolves. Leicester, beaten by Newcastle, are third from bottom, above Wolves on goal difference. The Magpies move into the top four for the first time this season, while the Foxes are now without a win in 12 games.

Things aren't looking too good for Portsmouth, who are now just three points above the drop zone after Gus Poyet's 89th-minute winner at White Hart Lane. Manchester City are also looking over their collective shoulder after a draw with Birmingham leaves them fifth from bottom.

Thierry Henry scores twice as Arsenal beat Southampton,

FACT FILE

Only Alan Shearer reached 100 Premiership goals quicker than Thierry Henry: 124 games as opposed to the Frenchman's 160.

extending their unbeaten run to 25, to move five points clear of Manchester United. The Frenchman's first goal is his 100th in the Premiership and his second takes him one ahead of Ruud Van Nistelrooy in the chase for the Golden Boot.

Leicester draw with Bolton to top the bottom pair by one point, but they're still two points adrift of fourth from bottom Portsmouth, who have played a game less. Les Ferdiand's goal is his 10th in 14 games for Leicester but it's cancelled out by an own-goal by Foxes 'keeper Ian Walker. Leeds crush Wolves, their first win in 10, to climb above the bottom club, but only on goal difference.

Manchester United slip up at home to Middlesbrough and are five points adrift in second place. 'Boro's first two goals, by which they lead at half-time, are headers from the smallest man on the park, Juninho. Joseph Desire Job nets the 80th-minute winner. Chelsea close the gap on second place to a point with victory over Portsmouth.

Michael Owen scores his first goal for five injury-ravaged months as Liverpool beat Manchester City. City have played 14 games without a league win, and are only three points above the drop zone.

Arsenal's win at Chelsea is a massive one, in terms of the title race, as second-placed Manchester United are held by Leeds, who stay bottom. The Gunners lead the Premiership by seven points.

At the opposite end of the table Leicester again throw away a lead. Spurs' Jermaine Defoe's 89th-minute equaliser, his second goal of the game, stops 19th-placed City from exiting the relegation zone. Wolves give themselves hope with a victory over Fulham in which Carl Cort nets his first goal for Dave Jones's side, his first for two years, and Wolves move within goal difference of fourth from bottom Pompey.

Arsenal extend their lead at the top to nine points with victory over Charlton, in which (with shades of Leeds against Southampton, under Don Revie) Arsenal string together a 40 consecutive-pass move, lasting 95 seconds, from which Pires opens the scoring. Charlton remain fifth. Manchester United are third, on goal difference from Chelsea, who win at Manchester City, after they draw with Fulham. Louis Saha nets against his old club.

Leicester draw with Wolves but Leeds also draw, with Liverpool, and the bottom two clubs are still in deep trouble.

FACT FILE

Brad Friedel scores Blackburn's 90th-minute equaliser at Charlton but seconds later the Rovers' 'keeper is beaten by Claus Jensen's stunning strike that earns the Addicks victory.

Blackburn Rovers' Brad Friedel scores the equalising goal at Charlton.

Wednesday 3 March

Birmingham City v. Middlesbrough	3-1

Saturday 6 March

Birmingham City v. Bolton Wanderers	2-0

Tuesday 9 March

Middlesbrough v. Tottenham Hotspur	1-0

Saturday 13 March

Birmingham City v. Leicester City	0-1
Blackburn Rovers v. Arsenal	0-2
Bolton Wanderers v. Chelsea	0-2
Charlton Athletic v. Middlesbrough	1-0
Everton v. Portsmouth	1-0
Fulham v. Leeds United	2-0

Sunday 14 March

Manchester City v. Manchester United	4-1
Southampton v. Liverpool	2-0
Tottenham Hotspur v. Newcastle United	1-0
Wolverhampton W v. Aston Villa	0-4

Wednesday 17 March

Liverpool v. Portsmouth	3-0

Saturday 20 March

Arsenal v. Bolton Wanderers	2-1
Aston Villa v. Blackburn Rovers	0-2
Chelsea v. Fulham	2-1
Leicester City v. Everton	1-1
Liverpool v. Wolverhampton W	1-0
Manchester United v. Tottenham Hotspur	3-0
Middlesbrough v. Birmingham City	5-3
Newcastle United v. Charlton Athletic	3-1

Sunday 21 March

Portsmouth v. Southampton	1-0

Monday 22 March

Leeds United v. Manchester City	2-1

Saturday 27 March

Birmingham City v. Leeds United	4-1
Blackburn Rovers v. Portsmouth	1-2
Charlton Athletic v. Aston Villa	1-2
Chelsea v. Wolverhampton W	5-2
Everton v. Middlesbrough	1-1
Manchester City v. Fulham	0-0
Southampton v. Tottenham Hotspur	1-0

Sunday 28 March

Arsenal v. Manchester United	1-1
Bolton Wanderers v. Newcastle United	1-0
Leicester City v. Liverpool	0-0

		P	W	D	L	F	A	Pts
1	Arsenal	30	22	8	0	58	20	74
2	Chelsea	30	21	4	5	57	24	67
3	Manchester United	30	19	5	6	56	30	62
4	Liverpool	30	12	10	8	42	31	46
5	Newcastle United	30	11	12	7	41	31	45
6	Birmingham City	30	12	9	9	37	36	45
7	Aston Villa	30	12	7	11	38	35	43
8	Charlton Athletic	30	12	7	11	41	39	43
9	Fulham	30	11	7	12	42	40	40
10	Southampton	30	10	9	11	30	28	39
11	Middlesbrough	30	10	8	12	35	39	38
12	Tottenham Hotspur	30	11	4	15	40	47	37
13	Bolton Wanderers	30	9	10	11	34	46	37
14	Everton	30	8	10	12	36	41	34
15	Manchester City	30	7	10	13	41	42	31
16	Blackburn Rovers	30	8	7	15	42	48	31
17	Portsmouth	30	8	6	16	32	45	30
18	Leicester City	30	5	13	12	39	52	28
19	Leeds United	30	6	7	17	29	60	25
20	Wolverhampton W	30	5	9	16	26	62	24

Aston Villa's Juan Pablo Angel celebrates scoring their fourth goal.

FOOTBALL is rocked by the detention of three Leicester players, on sexual assault charges, at the club's Spanish training camp in La Manga. Charges against Frank Sinclair, Keith Gillespie and Paul Dickov are subsequently dropped after Leicester are relegated.

Arsenal are nine points ahead of second-placed Chelsea after winning at Blackburn. Thierry Henry has a 'foot-up' block goal, à la George Best 1971, ruled out, but then scores from a stunning 30-yard free-kick. Chelsea stage a late 'smash and grab' to beat Bolton after Wanderers dominate. Manchester United are three points adrift

FACT FILE

Rory Delap's spectacular overhead winner, against Spurs, is his first goal in 66 games: nearly two years and very nearly 6,000 minutes without scoring.

in third after they lose the Manchester derby and their title quest is virtually over. City's win is their first at home for five months and United's defeat is their worst reverse since losing 5–0 to Chelsea in 1999. Newcastle's hopes of fourth place are damaged by an 86th-minute O'Brien own-goal that means a first away defeat in eight games at Spurs.

James Beattie's 13th goal of the campaign and a sixth in seven games for Kevin Phillips mean a first Southampton Premiership double over Liverpool, whose cause isn't helped by Michael Owen's 13th penalty miss in 22 attempts.

Leicester's win at Birmingham is their first for more than three months. Les Ferdinand's winner takes the Foxes out of the bottom three. Wolves are crushed by Aston Villa and Juan Pablo Angel's brace makes him the first Villa player since Dwight Yorke, in 1996–97, to reach 20 goals in one season. Fulham beat Leeds to keep Eddie Gray's strugglers anchored to the foot of the table, two points behind Wolves.

Liverpool move fifth, one point behind Charlton, following their win over Portsmouth, who stay in the bottom three. Michael Owen scores twice, to make only three this year.

Arsenal's victory over Bolton keeps them nine points clear and matches the 29-game unbeaten run, from the start of a season, held by Leeds and Liverpool. Chelsea are still second after beating Fulham and Manchester United are 12 points behind the Gunners but get back to winning ways with victory over Spurs in which they keep a first clean sheet for 12 games.

Portsmouth beat Southampton for the first time in 16 years to head the basement trio, three points ahead of Wolves, who are beaten by

FACT FILE

Mikael Forsell, on loan from Chelsea, scores twice in Birmingham's defeat by Middlesbrough. His tally of 12 exceeds the combined total of the £30 million Chelsea strike pair of Adrian Mutu and Hernan Crespo. Forsell is the first Birmingham player to score 15 top-flight goals since Tony Evans in 1982.

Sammy Hyypia's last-minute winner at Anfield. Leicester move out of the relegation zone, on goal difference, when they claim a point against Everton with a last-minute equaliser. But David Moyes's team have Duncan Ferguson sent off for shaking Steffen Freund 'warmly' by the throat. Leeds beat Manchester City but climb just one place off the foot of the table, splitting Wolves and Portsmouth.

Arsenal and Manchester United draw to stay top and third, respectively. The Gunners establish a new top-flight record of 30 consecutive league games unbeaten. Thierry Henry's stunning 30-yard goal, his 30th in all competitions for the season, is cancelled out by Louis Saha's 86th-minute equaliser. Jimmy Floyd Hasselbaink hits a 13-minute hat-trick, after coming off the bench, to help Chelsea to victory over Wolves, who are without an away win all season; Wanderers actually lead 2–1 by the hour. Jimmy's first goal is his 100th in the Premiership, and Frank Lampard marks his 100th consecutive Premiership start with a goal.

Fourth placed Liverpool are held by Leicester, who move to within two points of fourth from bottom Portsmouth, who move out of the drop zone with victory at Blackburn.

Saturday 3 April

Fulham v. Birmingham City	0-0
Middlesbrough v. Bolton Wanderers	2-0
Newcastle United v. Everton	4-2
Tottenham Hotspur v. Chelsea	0-1
Wolverhampton W v. Southampton	1-4

Sunday 4 April

Aston Villa v. Manchester City	1-1
Liverpool v. Blackburn Rovers	4-0

Monday 5 April

Leeds United v. Leicester City	3-2

Friday 9 April

Arsenal v. Liverpool	4-2
Everton v. Tottenham Hotspur	3-1

Saturday 10 April

Birmingham City v. Manchester United	1-2
Blackburn Rovers v. Leeds United	1-2
Bolton Wanderers v. Aston Villa	2-2
Charlton Athletic v. Portsmouth	1-1
Chelsea v. Middlesbrough	0-0
Leicester City v. Fulham	0-2
Manchester City v. Wolverhampton W	3-3

Sunday 11 April

Newcastle United v. Arsenal	0-0

Monday 12 April

Aston Villa v. Chelsea	3-2
Fulham v. Blackburn Rovers	3-4
Liverpool v. Charlton Athletic	0-1
Middlesbrough v. Southampton	3-1
Portsmouth v. Birmingham City	3-1
Tottenham Hotspur v. Manchester City	1-1
Wolverhampton W v. Bolton Wanderers	1-2

Tuesday 13 April

Leeds United v. Everton	1-1
Manchester United v. Leicester City	1-0

Friday 16 April

Arsenal v. Leeds United	5-0

Saturday 17 April

Blackburn Rovers v. Leicester City	1-0
Bolton Wanderers v. Tottenham Hotspur	2-0
Charlton Athletic v. Birmingham City	1-1
Chelsea v. Everton	0-0
Liverpool v. Fulham	0-0
Manchester City v. Southampton	1-3
Portsmouth v. Manchester United	1-0
Wolverhampton W v. Middlesbrough	2-0

Sunday 18 April

Aston Villa v. Newcastle United	0-0

Tuesday 20 April

Manchester United v. Charlton Athletic	2-0

Saturday 24 April

Everton v. Blackburn Rovers	0-1
Fulham v. Charlton Athletic	2-0
Leicester City v. Manchester City	1-1
Manchester United v. Liverpool	0-1
Middlesbrough v. Aston Villa	1-2
Southampton v. Bolton Wanderers	1-2

Sunday 25 April

Birmingham City v. Wolverhampton W	2-2
Leeds United v. Portsmouth	1-2
Newcastle United v. Chelsea	2-1
Tottenham Hotspur v. Arsenal	2-2

		P	W	D	L	F	A	Pts
1	Arsenal	34	24	10	0	69	24	82
2	Chelsea	35	22	6	7	61	29	72
3	Manchester United	35	22	5	8	61	33	71
4	Liverpool	35	14	11	10	49	36	53
5	Newcastle United	34	13	14	7	47	34	53
6	Aston Villa	35	14	10	11	46	41	52
7	Fulham	35	13	9	13	49	44	48
8	Charlton Athletic	35	13	9	13	44	45	48
9	Birmingham City	35	12	12	11	42	44	48
10	Bolton Wanderers	35	12	11	12	42	52	47
11	Southampton	34	12	9	13	39	35	45
12	Middlesbrough	35	12	9	14	41	44	45
13	Blackburn Rovers	35	11	7	17	49	57	40
14	Portsmouth	34	11	7	16	39	48	40
15	Everton	35	9	12	14	42	48	39
16	Tottenham Hotspur	35	11	6	18	44	56	39
17	Manchester City	35	7	14	14	48	51	35
18	Leeds United	35	8	8	19	36	71	32
19	Leicester City	35	5	14	16	42	60	29
20	Wolverhampton W	35	6	11	18	35	73	29

ALAN SMITH hits the 86th-minute winner as Leeds beat Leicester to climb within goal difference of the 18th-placed Foxes. But victory is tainted by two yellow cards for Mark Viduka, which put him out of Leeds' next 'six-pointer', against Portsmouth.

Arsenal twice come from behind to beat Liverpool and extend their record unbeaten run to 31. Thierry Henry's hat-trick takes his league total to 25 (33 in all competitions) and extends the Gunners' lead over Chelsea to seven points. Claudio Ranieri promptly concedes the title, an assessment that is reinforced the next day when Middlesbrough hold Chelsea to leave Roman's 'army' six points adrift in second place. Manchester United come from a goal down, at half-time, to beat Birmingham to move within six points of Chelsea.

Wolves stay bottom after drawing with Manchester City, after conceding a last-minute equaliser to Shaun Wright-Phillips that prevents a first away win for the Molineux outfit.

Leicester are second bottom after Collins John hits his first goals for Fulham. Leeds win a second game running, at Blackburn, and are only in the bottom three on goal difference from Portsmouth; Rovers are 16th. Steve Caldwell's opener for Eddie Gray's side is his first for the club.

Newcastle become the first side, for 18 games, to stop Arsenal scoring, as the teams draw. The Gunners are seven points clear of the field while Newcastle move to fifth.

Blackburn win a thrilling encounter against Fulham. For the first time in a year Rovers come from behind to win but they are still 16th, above Portsmouth on goal difference. John Stead's winner is his fourth goal in eight starts.

Gary Neville's first league

FACT FILE

Thierry Henry's goal-fest against Leeds makes him the first Arsenal player to score four goals in a Premiership game. His fifth hat-trick for the club was completed by a 'cheeky chip' penalty. His fourth was his 150th Gunners goal, in his 251st appearance, and was also his 29th Premiership goal of the campaign and his 38th in all competitions.

goal for three years, and only his fifth in 428 games, is enough for Manchester United to beat Leicester and close, with a game in hand, to within three points of Chelsea. Ranieri's side seem to have blown their championship hopes by losing to Villa, and trail Arsenal by seven points, having played one game more.

Leicester are 19th, six points adrift of 16th-placed Portsmouth and safety. Leeds draw with Everton and are top of the basement trio, two points from Pompey, but they have played one game more than Harry Redknapp's team.

Arsenal crush Leeds in a one-sided game that keeps United bottom, leaving the Gunners needing just four points to clinch the Premiership title. Pires hits his 18th goal of the season before Henry goes on a four-goal spree to send Arsenal 10 points clear of Chelsea, who then fall nine points behind by drawing with Everton. Manchester United lose to Portsmouth for the first time since 1955 at Fratton Park and stay third. Pompey move up to 16th, three points above Manchester City, who lose to Southampton.

Wolves stay 20th despite beating 'Boro but are just behind Leicester, on goal difference, who lose at Blackburn, a result that leaves Rovers 15th.

Gary Neville scores in

United's win over Charlton to give him a scoring record of two in three games, six in 430 for the club. The victory that moves Fergie's side to within a point of second place, but 10 behind the leaders.

Danny Murphy hits the penalty winner as Liverpool beat United. It's the third time Danny has hit the clincher at Old Trafford. The irony of Gary Neville, self-confessed 'scouse-hater', conceding the spot-kick isn't lost on the visitors' supporters.

John Stead hits his fifth goal in 10 games to clinch Blackburn's third consecutive victory, over Everton, to take Rovers 13th, eight points clear of the last relegation place. Leicester are held by Manchester City, who stay above them, outside the drop zone, three points clear of 18th-placed Leeds. The Foxes, for whom Paul Dickov's penalty is saved, are three points and one place further behind the Yorkshire club. The mass brawl at the Walkers Stadium, involving all 22 players, following the award of the spot-kick, is to be investigated by the FA.

Arsenal clinch their second championship title in three years, and extend their unbeaten run to 34, although they throw away a two-goal lead at White Hart Lane. Two hours earlier Newcastle beat Chelsea leaving the Gunners needing just a point against Spurs. The Magpies' winner is a Shearer stunner, from 30 yards, his 173rd Newcastle goal. Ranieri's side, five games without a win, are now just a point ahead of Manchester United.

Wolves are all but down after they stay bottom following the draw with Birmingham in which Mikael Forsell nets his 19th goal of the season. Leeds look set to join Wolves in the drop after losing to Portsmouth leaves them three points from safety.

Saturday 1 May	
Arsenal v. Birmingham City	0-0
Blackburn Rovers v. Manchester United	1-0
Charlton Athletic v. Leicester City	2-2
Chelsea v. Southampton	4-0
Manchester City v. Newcastle United	1-0
Portsmouth v. Fulham	1-1
Wolverhampton W v. Everton	2-1
Sunday 2 May	
Aston Villa v. Tottenham Hotspur	1-0
Bolton Wanderers v. Leeds United	4-1
Liverpool v. Middlesbrough	2-0
Tuesday 4 May	
Portsmouth v. Arsenal	1-1
Saturday 8 May	
Birmingham City v. Liverpool	0-3
Everton v. Bolton Wanderers	1-2
Leeds United v. Charlton Athletic	3-3
Leicester City v. Portsmouth	3-1
Manchester United v. Chelsea	1-1
Middlesbrough v. Manchester City	2-1
Southampton v. Aston Villa	1-1
Tottenham Hotspur v. Blackburn Rovers	1-0
Sunday 9 May	
Fulham v. Arsenal	0-1
Newcastle United v. Wolverhampton W	1-1
Wednesday 12 May	
Southampton v. Newcastle United	3-3
Saturday 15 May	
Arsenal v. Leicester City	2-1
Aston Villa v. Manchester United	0-2
Blackburn Rovers v. Birmingham City	1-1
Bolton Wanderers v. Fulham	0-2
Charlton Athletic v. Southampton	2-1
Chelsea v. Leeds United	1-0
Liverpool v. Newcastle United	1-1
Manchester City v. Everton	5-1
Portsmouth v. Middlesbrough	5-1
Wolverhampton W v. Tottenham Hotspur	0-2

		P	W	D	L	F	A	Pts
1	Arsenal	38	26	12	0	73	26	90
2	Chelsea	38	24	7	7	67	30	79
3	Manchester United	38	23	6	9	64	35	75
4	Liverpool	38	16	12	10	55	37	60
5	Newcastle United	38	13	17	8	52	40	56
6	Aston Villa	38	15	11	12	48	44	56
7	Charlton Athletic	38	14	11	13	51	51	53
8	Bolton Wanderers	38	14	11	13	48	56	53
9	Fulham	38	14	10	14	52	46	52
10	Birmingham City	38	12	14	12	43	48	50
11	Middlesbrough	38	13	9	16	44	52	48
12	Southampton	38	12	11	15	44	45	47
13	Portsmouth	38	12	9	17	47	54	45
14	Tottenham Hotspur	38	13	6	19	47	57	45
15	Blackburn Rovers	38	12	8	18	51	59	44
16	Manchester City	38	9	14	15	55	54	41
17	Everton	38	9	12	17	45	57	39
18	Leicester City	38	6	15	17	48	65	33
19	Leeds United	38	8	9	21	40	79	33
20	Wolverhampton W	38	7	12	19	38	77	33

Promoted from Nationwide Football League Division One:

Norwich

West Bromwich Albion

Crystal Palace (via play-offs)

WOLVES, despite beating Everton, are relegated unless they win their last two games and score 30 goals in the process. Leicester draw with Charlton and are also relegated.

Paulo Wanchope's first Sky Blue Premiership goal at home earns Manchester City the victory over Newcastle that ensures Premiership survival.

Arsenal fail to get a proper shot on target as they are held by Birmingham but still extend their record unbeaten run to 35 games. Chelsea crush Southampton to confirm second position, eight points behind the Gunners. Manchester United blow their chances of being runners-up by losing at Blackburn. Jonathan Stead's winner is his sixth goal in 11 starts.

Leeds, Champions League semi-finalists in 2000, are relegated, ending their 14-year top-flight stay, when they are thrashed by Bolton after taking a 1–0 lead. Mark Viduka is sent off again.

Danny Murphy maintains his 100 percent penalty success and Emile Heskey, scoring seven minutes after coming on as substitute, earns Liverpool victory over Middlesbrough to go fourth, four hours after Villa beat Spurs, with Angel scoring his 15th Premiership goal of the campaign, to occupy that slot.

Arsenal's draw with Portsmouth stretches their unbeaten run to 36 games. Whatever the results of their last two matches, it's another record for Highbury. Yakuba Ayegbeni's opener, his seventh goal in eight games, puts Pompey ahead, but it is cancelled out by Juan Antonio Reyes's first away goal, also his first in the Premiership. The draw means a new Premiership points record is now beyond the Gunners.

Chelsea earn the draw at Old Trafford that guarantees

Despite defeat to Fulham Bolton Wanderers' manager Sam Allardyce celebrates the Trotters' highest Premiership finish.

them the runners-up spot in the Premiership, their highest top-flight finish since 1955 when they were league Division One champions. Gronkjaer's first Premiership goal for a year is cancelled out by Van Nistelrooy, who also misses a penalty, after a mistake by Cudicini. United must settle for third place: it is only the second time in 12 years that they finish outside the top two.

Liverpool's win at Birmingham keeps them fourth while Villa's draw against Southampton leaves them three points behind in fifth.

There are emotional scenes at Elland Road, where Alan Smith nets a penalty to put relegated Leeds 3–1 up, but again the defence lets United down and folds to concede two goals in three minutes to Jason Euell. Leicester's last home game in the Premiership sees them beat Portsmouth with Nigel Quasie's goal, for Pompey, being his first in the Premiership.

Alan Shearer misses a late penalty as Newcastle are held by Wolves, whose relegation is confirmed.

Newcastle are held at Southampton, with Saints' third-choice 'keeper, Alan Blaney, marking his debut with a series of superb saves to hand Liverpool a fourth-place finish and entry into the Champions League.

Arsenal join the immortals when they come back from a

goal down, to former Gunner Paul Dickov, to beat relegated Leicester. Fittingly the champions' goals come from Thierry Henry, who equalises from the penalty-spot, with his 30th Premiership goal of the season, and the winner, meaning a complete Premiership season unbeaten, is scored by the inspirational Patrick Vieira.

Jesper Gronkjaer scores again to ensure a Chelsea victory against relegated Leeds. Third-placed Manchester United beat Villa after two early gift goals from Aston Villa, but Darren Fletcher and Ronaldo are sent off by an over-officious Rob Styles. The Premiership's most 'card-sharp' referee takes his red card count to 12 in just 20 games. Styles also books nine at Villa Park.

Liverpool's draw with Newcastle narrowly averts a worst home league record since 1954. The Magpies get the last UEFA Cup place due to Villa's defeat by Manchester United.

Manchester City finish finish two places above the relegation zone after crushing Everton, who are only one place and six points better off than third-bottom Leicester.

Wolves have Paul Ince sent off as they wave goodbye after just one Premiership season and are beaten by Spurs, who only just avoid their worst-ever points total in the Premiership. Wolves veteran Denis Irwin retires with a career total of 902 games.

End of season round-up

Top Premiership Goalscorers 2003–2004

Thierry Henry	Arsenal	30
Alan Shearer	Newcastle United	22
Ruud Van Nistelrooy	Manchester United	20
Nicolas Anelka	Manchester City	17
Mikael Forssell	Birmingham City	17
Juan Pablo Angel	Aston Villa	16
Yakuba Ayegbeni	Portsmouth	16
Michael Owen	Liverpool	16
Robert Pires	Arsenal	14
James Beattie	Southampton	14
Robbie Keane	Tottenham	14

Carling League Cup

Middlesbrough 2   Bolton Wanderers 1
Middlesbrough won the first trophy in the club's 129-year history when they beat Bolton Wanderers. A blistering start saw 'Boro 2–0 up inside seven minutes. Joseph Desire Job opened the scoring with just two minutes gone then Boudewijn Zenden, on loan from Chelsea, scored with a 'double-hit' penalty after Emerson Thome was adjudged to have fouled Job.

Kevin Davies pulled one back for Bolton midway through the first half, and Per Frandsen hit a post, but 'Boro always seemed to have the upper hand and Steve McClaren become the first English manager since Brian Little in 1996 to win a domestic trophy, also the League Cup. Gareth Southgate, who was in that Villa side under Little, lifted the trophy that took Middlesbrough into Europe in 2004–05.

FA Cup Final

Manchester United 3   Millwall 0
The final turned out to be as one-sided as neutral observers had feared. But it took until just before half-time for United to take the lead, with Cristiano Ronaldo heading home from a Gary Neville cross. Manchester United, in their 16th FA Cup Final, another record, were never troubled by Millwall, who were playing the first final in their 109-year history.

Despite their superiority United were denied by several good saves from Andy Marshall in the Millwall goal and the game wasn't secured until Ruud Van Nistelrooy made it 2–0, from the penalty spot, after 64 minutes, after Livermore felled Giggs. Van Nistelrooy then tapped home from a Giggs cross, in a suspiciously off-side position, with nine minutes left. It was the Dutchman's 30th goal of the season, making him the first player in Manchester United history to hit 30 goals in each of three successive seasons. United extended their own record of FA Cup Final triumphs to 11.

FWA Footballer of the Year

Thierry Henry	Arsenal

PFA Player of the Year

Thierry Henry	Arsenal

PFA Young Player of the Year

Scott Parker	Chelsea

Manager of the Year

Arsene Wenger	Arsenal

Close Season 2004

Gerard Houllier is sacked by Liverpool almost as soon as the season is over. Liverpool complete a Premiership 'Continental treble' when they eventually announce that Valencia's Rafael Benitez as the new manager at Anfield. At the other Merseyside club Everton boss David Moyes pays £300,000 to Ipswich for striker Marcus Bent.

Alan Smith leaves Leeds for Manchester United for a fee in the region of £7 million, with Danny Pugh heading in the opposite direction as £1 million makeweight in the deal. Auxerre striker Phillipe Mexes rejects a £15 million move to Old Trafford because Sir Alex Ferguson cannot guarantee him a first-team place.

Emile Heskey joins Birmingham from Liverpool and Blues also sign Julian Gray from Premiership new boys Crystal Palace.

Claudio Ranieri is sacked by Chelsea to be replaced by Jose Mourinho, after taking Porto to Champions League success over Monaco. Chelsea sign Porto's Portuguese international full-back Paulo Ferreira for £13.2 million in a five-year deal, and also secure Dutch winger Arjen Robben from PSV Eindhoven for £12 million.

Spurs announce that Jacques Santini, the coach of the French national team, will become the new manager at White Hart Lane after Euro 2004.

Charlton sign PSV player Dennis Rommedahl for around £5 million.

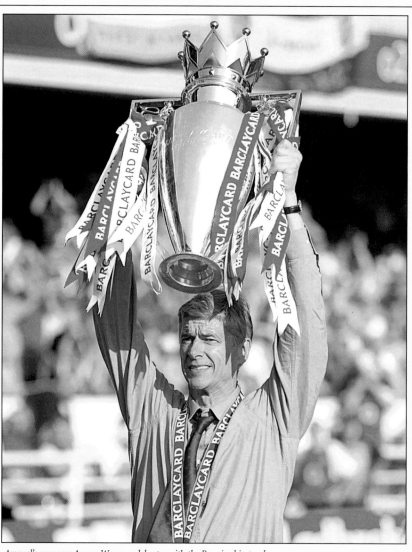

Arsenal's manager Arsene Wenger celebrates with the Premiership trophy.

Section 2
Premiership Performance Club by Club

Best Home Record:

		% Wins
1	Manchester United	71.4%
2	Arsenal	61.5%
3	Newcastle United	61.5%
4	Liverpool	59.8%
5	Chelsea	54.7%
6	Blackburn Rovers	53.6%
7	Portsmouth	52.6%
8	Leeds United	50.4%
9	Aston Villa	47.9%
10	Fulham	47.4%

Most Home Draws:

		% Draws
1	Bradford City	39.5%
2	Sheffield United	38.1%
3	Bolton Wanderers	36.8%
4	Norwich City	36.5%
5	Oldham Athletic	33.3%
6	Swindon Town	33.3%
7	Leicester City	33.1%
8	Manchester City	33.1%
9	Crystal Palace	32.8%
10	Nottingham Forest	32.3%

Best Away Record:

		% Wins
1	Manchester United	53.4%
2	Arsenal	42.7%
3	Liverpool	35.5%
4	Chelsea	32.1%
5	Leeds United	30.3%
6	Aston Villa	29.5%
7	Blackburn Rovers	29.1%
8	Norwich City	28.6%
9	Newcastle United	28.2%
10	Queen's Park R.	28.0%

Most Away Draws

		% Draws
1	Swindon Town	38.1%
2	Wolverhampton W	36.8%
3	Birmingham City	34.2%
4	Fulham	33.3%
5	Coventry City	31.6%
6	Newcastle United	31.5%
7	Arsenal	31.2%
8	Blackburn Rovers	31.1%
9	Chelsea	30.8%
10	Wimbledon	30.4%

Most Points per Game

1	Manchester United	2.10
2	Arsenal	1.84
3	Liverpool	1.69
4	Newcastle United	1.61
5	Chelsea	1.59
6	Blackburn Rovers	1.51
7	Leeds United	1.48
8	Aston Villa	1.45
9	Norwich City	1.33
10	Queen's Park R.	1.32

Best Away Record:

		% Wins
1	West Bromwich Alb.	15.8%
2	Swindon Town	19.0%
3	Crystal Palace	23.0%
4	Bradford City	26.3%
5	Watford	26.3%
6	Bolton Wanderers	31.6%
7	Manchester City	33.1%
8	Leicester City	33.1%
9	Ipswich Town	34.7%
10	Nottingham Forest	35.4%

Fewest Home Draws:

		% Draws
1	Manchester United	19.7%
2	Newcastle United	20.7%
3	Barnsley	21.1%
4	Portsmouth	21.1%
5	Watford	21.1%
6	Blackburn Rovers	21.9%
7	Liverpool	23.5%
8	Queen's Park R.	24.4%
9	Fulham	24.6%
10	Arsenal	24.8%

Worst Away Record:

		% Wins
1	Wolverhampton W	0.0%
2	Swindon Town	4.8%
3	Watford	5.3%
4	Bradford City	10.5%
5	Portsmouth	10.5%
6	Sheffield United	14.3%
7	West Bromwich Alb.	15.8%
8	Barnsley	15.8%
9	Oldham Athletic	16.7%
10	Derby County	17.5%

Fewest Away Draws

		% Draws
1	Barnsley	5.3%
2	Watford	10.5%
3	Bradford City	13.2%
4	West Bromwich Alb.	15.8%
5	Oldham Athletic	21.4%
6	Sunderland	22.1%
7	Bolton Wanderers	22.1%
8	Queen's Park R.	23.2%
9	Ipswich Town	23.8%
10	Sheffield Wed.	24.7%

Records for each club:

Team	P	W		D		L		F	Gls For/Game	A	Gls Agst/Game	W		D		L		F	Gls For/Game	A	Gls Agst/Game	Pts	Pts/Game
Arsenal	468	144	61.5%	58	24.8%	32	13.7%	436	1.86	194	0.83	100	42.7%	73	31.2%	61	26.1%	320	1.37	220	0.94	863	1.84
Aston Villa	468	112	47.9%	66	23.9%	56	28.2%	325	1.39	220	0.94	69	29.5%	69	29.5%	96	41.0%	256	1.09	305	1.30	678	1.45
Barnsley	38	7	36.8%	4	21.1%	8	42.1%	25	1.32	35	1.84	3	15.8%	1	5.3%	15	78.9%	12	0.63	47	2.47	35	0.92
Birmingham City	76	16	42.1%	10	26.3%	12	31.6%	51	1.34	47	1.24	9	23.7%	13	34.2%	16	42.1%	33	0.87	50	1.32	98	1.29
Blackburn Rovers	392	105	53.6%	43	21.9%	48	24.5%	338	1.72	208	1.06	57	29.1%	61	31.1%	78	39.8%	229	1.17	260	1.33	590	1.51
Bolton Wanderers	190	30	31.6%	35	36.8%	30	31.6%	112	1.18	129	1.36	20	21.1%	21	22.1%	54	56.8%	101	1.06	172	1.81	206	1.08
Bradford City	76	10	26.3%	15	39.5%	13	34.2%	46	1.21	58	1.53	4	10.5%	5	13.2%	29	76.3%	22	0.58	80	2.11	62	0.82
Charlton Athletic	190	35	36.8%	27	28.4%	33	34.7%	129	1.36	128	1.35	25	26.3%	27	28.4%	43	45.3%	96	1.01	141	1.48	234	1.23
Chelsea	468	128	54.7%	63	26.9%	43	18.4%	411	1.76	216	0.92	75	32.1%	72	30.8%	87	37.2%	293	1.25	303	1.29	744	1.59
Coventry City	354	65	36.7%	56	31.6%	56	31.6%	219	1.24	199	1.12	34	19.2%	56	31.6%	87	49.2%	168	0.95	291	1.64	409	1.16
Crystal Palace	122	14	23.0%	20	32.8%	27	44.3%	58	0.95	87	1.43	16	26.2%	17	27.9%	28	45.9%	61	1.00	94	1.54	127	1.04
Derby County	228	47	41.2%	30	26.3%	37	32.5%	145	1.27	134	1.18	20	17.5%	32	28.1%	62	54.4%	106	0.93	197	1.73	263	1.15
Everton	468	93	39.7%	72	30.8%	69	29.5%	335	1.43	270	1.15	52	22.2%	59	25.2%	123	52.6%	237	1.01	374	1.60	566	1.21
Fulham	114	27	47.4%	14	24.6%	16	28.1%	76	1.33	55	0.96	10	17.5%	19	33.3%	28	49.1%	53	0.93	85	1.49	144	1.26
Ipswich Town	202	35	34.7%	29	28.7%	37	36.6%	125	1.24	127	1.26	22	21.8%	24	23.8%	55	54.5%	94	0.93	185	1.83	224	1.11
Leeds United	468	118	50.4%	60	25.6%	56	23.9%	357	1.53	231	0.99	71	30.3%	65	27.8%	98	41.9%	284	1.21	342	1.46	692	1.48
Leicester City	308	51	33.1%	51	33.1%	52	33.8%	189	1.23	212	1.38	33	21.4%	39	25.3%	82	53.2%	165	1.07	244	1.58	342	1.11
Liverpool	468	140	59.8%	55	23.5%	39	16.7%	442	1.89	198	0.85	83	35.5%	67	28.6%	84	35.9%	317	1.35	288	1.23	791	1.69
Manchester City	278	46	33.1%	46	33.1%	47	33.8%	191	1.37	175	1.26	31	22.3%	38	27.3%	70	50.4%	132	0.95	220	1.58	315	1.13
Manchester United	468	167	71.4%	46	19.7%	21	9.0%	508	2.17	156	0.67	125	53.4%	61	26.1%	48	20.5%	419	1.79	273	1.17	983	2.10
Middlesbrough	346	68	39.3%	50	28.9%	55	31.8%	244	1.41	216	1.25	37	21.4%	51	29.5%	85	49.1%	161	0.93	262	1.51	413	1.19
Newcastle United	426	131	61.5%	44	20.7%	38	17.8%	414	1.94	199	0.93	60	28.2%	67	31.5%	86	40.4%	253	1.19	308	1.45	684	1.61
Norwich City	126	25	39.7%	23	36.5%	15	23.8%	84	1.33	69	1.10	18	28.6%	16	25.4%	29	46.0%	79	1.25	111	1.76	168	1.33
Nottingham Forest	198	35	35.4%	32	32.3%	32	32.3%	115	1.16	118	1.19	25	25.3%	27	27.3%	47	47.5%	114	1.15	169	1.71	239	1.21
Oldham Athletic	84	15	35.7%	14	33.3%	13	31.0%	67	1.60	63	1.50	7	16.7%	9	21.4%	26	61.9%	38	0.90	79	1.88	89	1.06
Portsmouth	38	10	52.6%	4	21.1%	5	26.3%	35	1.84	19	1.00	2	10.5%	5	26.3%	12	63.2%	12	0.63	35	1.84	45	1.18
Queen's Park R	164	36	43.9%	20	24.4%	26	31.7%	134	1.63	113	1.38	23	28.0%	19	23.2%	40	48.8%	90	1.10	119	1.45	216	1.32
Sheffield United	84	16	38.1%	16	38.1%	10	23.8%	57	1.36	42	1.00	6	14.3%	12	28.6%	24	57.1%	39	0.93	71	1.69	94	1.12
Sheffield Wed.	316	63	39.9%	50	31.6%	45	28.5%	234	1.48	187	1.18	38	24.1%	39	24.7%	81	51.3%	175	1.11	266	1.68	392	1.24
Southampton	468	102	43.6%	61	26.1%	71	30.3%	328	1.40	269	1.15	42	17.9%	62	26.5%	130	55.6%	225	0.96	403	1.72	555	1.19
Sunderland	190	36	37.9%	28	29.5%	31	32.6%	101	1.06	98	1.03	19	20.0%	21	22.1%	55	57.9%	87	0.92	168	1.77	214	1.13
Swindon Town	42	4	19.0%	7	33.3%	10	47.6%	25	1.19	45	2.14	1	4.8%	8	38.1%	12	57.1%	22	1.05	55	2.62	30	0.71
Tottenham Hotspur	468	105	44.9%	63	26.9%	66	28.2%	363	1.55	289	1.24	58	24.8%	59	25.2%	117	50.0%	253	1.08	364	1.56	611	1.31
Watford	38	5	26.3%	4	21.1%	10	52.6%	24	1.26	31	1.63	1	5.3%	2	10.5%	16	84.2%	11	0.58	46	2.42	24	0.63
West Bromwich A	38	3	15.8%	5	26.3%	11	57.9%	17	0.89	34	1.79	3	15.8%	3	15.8%	13	68.4%	12	0.63	31	1.63	26	0.68
West Ham United	388	89	45.9%	53	27.3%	52	26.8%	287	1.48	221	1.14	43	22.2%	51	26.3%	100	51.5%	175	0.90	314	1.62	500	1.29
Wimbledon	316	62	39.2%	46	29.1%	50	31.6%	218	1.38	198	1.25	37	23.4%	48	30.4%	73	46.2%	166	1.05	274	1.73	391	1.24
Wolverhampton W	38	7	36.8%	5	26.3%	7	36.8%	23	1.21	35	1.84	0	0.0%	7	36.8%	12	63.2%	15	0.79	42	2.21	33	0.87
Grand Total	9612	2202		1325		1279		7288		5325		1279		1325		2202		5325		7288		13090	1.36

Arsenal

ARSENAL'S RECORD IN THE PREMIERSHIP

Pos.	Season	P	Home: W	D	L	F	A	Away: W	D	L	F	A	Total Goals F	A	Pts
10th	1992-93	42	8	6	7	25	20	7	5	9	15	18	40	38	56
4th	1993-94	42	10	8	3	25	15	8	9	4	28	13	53	28	71
12th	1994-95	42	6	9	6	27	21	7	3	11	25	28	52	49	51
5th	1995-96	38	10	7	2	30	16	7	5	7	19	16	49	32	63
3rd	1996-97	38	10	5	4	36	18	9	6	4	26	14	62	32	68
1st	1997-98	38	15	2	2	43	10	8	7	4	25	23	68	33	78
2nd	1998-99	38	14	5	0	34	5	8	7	4	25	12	59	17	78
2nd	1999-2000	38	14	3	2	42	17	8	4	7	31	26	73	43	73
2nd	2000-01	38	15	3	1	45	13	5	7	7	18	25	63	38	70
1st	2001-02	38	12	4	3	42	25	14	5	0	37	11	79	36	87
2nd	2002-03	38	15	2	2	47	20	8	7	4	38	22	85	42	78
1st	2003-04	38	15	4	0	40	14	11	8	0	33	12	73	26	90

WHEN Arsenal clinched their third Premiership title in five years in 2003–04, the club that had set numerous records on their way to that triumph saved the most awesome achievement until the final day, when they became the first team since Preston North End, in 1889, to go through an entire top-flight season unbeaten. The Gunners joined the immortals of football history by becoming the first Premiership team to have a zero in the losses column. That they became the first side to claim the title, unbeaten, with four games to go, was yet another record. No team in the history of world football has ever remained unbeaten in a 38-match league programme.

Ironically, Premiership founder members Arsenal began that membership with one of their heaviest defeats, 4–2 at home to Norwich. But after defeat in half of their opening eight fixtures, Arsenal won six consecutive games to top the table by November. It was the only time they topped the Premiership in that inaugural season and they finished 10th.

The next campaign, thanks to Ian Wright's goals and the legendary 'back five' defence of Seaman, Dixon, Winterburn, Bould and Adams, brought Arsenal a fourth place finish.

Losing Tony Adams, to an Achilles operation, for two months, hindered the 1994–95 campaign and Arsenal finished in mid-table.

Bruce Rioch, appointed to succeed the disgraced George Graham, began his short Highbury tenure in June 1995 and while his reign isn't fondly recalled by Arsenal fans it was significant for the signing of Dennis Bergkamp, who was to prove the catalyst for future success, post-Rioch. The Dutch master's 11 goals, coupled with 15 from Ian Wright, pushed Arsenal to their second-best Premiership finish, fifth.

Following the departure of Rioch the appointment of Arsene Wenger paid immediate dividends and with Ian Wright (23) and Dennis Bergkamp (12) contributing more than half of their goals total, the Gunners posted a best-ever Premiership finish of third place, just behind runners-up Newcastle on goal difference.

Early signs in 1997–98 suggested a possible first championship, as the team went 12 games unbeaten and dropped just 12 points in that run. But three November defeats, all without scoring, dropped the team from first to fifth. Wenger stabilised the ship and after victory over Newcastle, followed by defeat by Blackburn, the Gunners went on an unbeaten run of 18 games that included a sequence of 10 consecutive victories, the last of them a title-clinching victory over Everton, capped by a Tony Adams wonder-goal.

The following season Arsenal were never out of the top three after February, and were unbeaten from 13 December, but they suffered a crucial defeat in the penultimate fixture at Leeds. That said, Manchester United lost just once in their last 24 games, the unbeaten run covering the final 20 matches, as they pipped the Gunners, in one of the tightest championship finishes, by just a single point. There was a moral victory for Arsenal, though, who took four points off Fergie's team. The significance of too many draws, half of the season's total in the opening 16 games, wasn't lost on Arsene Wenger, but neither was the legendary defensive meanness, with 23 clean sheets and a Premiership record of just

Safe hands. David Seaman made 566 Gunners appearances between 1990 and 2003.

Everton's Craig Short can only look on as Tony Adams scores the title-clinching goal in May 1998.

17 goals conceded in 38 games.

Arsenal were unable to retain their title the following season as the Gunners found Manchester United, without FA Cup action, too strong and had to settle for second place, but the big plus for Arsenal was the settling-in of Thierry Henry, who scored in seven consecutive fixtures on his way to a total of 17 Premiership goals.

Henry repeated that tally the following season and Arsenal went top in the first month, but, despite only dipping out of the top two briefly, in January, the Gunners suffered a significant 6–1 defeat at Old Trafford in February. Five games later they virtually handed United the title when own-goals by Edu and Silvinho ensured a first home defeat, to Middlesbrough.

Arsenal ensured there was no repeat in 2001–02 as they swept records aside on their way to the double. They had 13 consecutive wins, were unbeaten away from home and scored in every single Premiership fixture, suffering their final defeat of the campaign in December. The key to that season's success was balanced squad rotation by Arsene Wenger. Resting key players at the right time proved as crucial as the squad's acceptance of such necessity.

Once again Arsenal were unable to retain their crown, despite being top of the table for most of the season. A run of nine unbeaten games saw the Gunners top in mid-October but defeat by Everton and Blackburn dropped the side to second. They recovered pole position with victory in the north London derby and stayed there until the significant 2–2 draw at Old Trafford on 16 April. The Gunners only lost one of their last six games but the defeat by Leeds, due to a late Mark Viduka goal, proved decisive and Arsenal finished five points behind Manchester United.

Throughout another record-breaking season, 2003–04, Arsene Wenger declared that his players had learnt from their capitulation the season before. His players proved it on the field, where their stunning football was often from another dimension as they overwhelmed Premiership opponents with breathtaking play. Arsene Wenger, who had inherited a legendary defence when he became manager, succeeded in galvanising the work ethic and undoubted flair of his foreign imports and the cocktail was explosively potent as the title was secured with four games to go.

With all of football willing them to invincibility, the Gunners came back from a goal down to beat relegated Leicester, on the final day of the 2003–04 season. Arsenal's immortality was assured.

MANAGERS

George Graham	1986–1995
Bruce Rioch	1995–1996
Arsene Wenger	September 1996–present

Aston Villa

ASTON VILLA'S RECORD IN THE PREMIERSHIP

Pos.	Season	P	W	D	L	F	A	W	D	L	F	A	F	A	Pts
					Home:					Away:			Total Goals		
2nd	1992-93	42	13	5	3	36	16	8	6	7	21	24	57	40	74
10th	1993-94	42	8	5	8	23	18	7	7	7	23	32	46	50	57
18th	1994-95	42	6	9	6	27	24	5	6	10	24	32	51	56	48
4th	1995-96	38	11	5	3	32	15	7	4	8	20	20	52	35	63
5th	1996-97	38	11	5	3	27	13	6	5	8	20	21	47	34	61
7th	1997-98	38	9	3	7	26	24	8	3	8	23	24	49	48	57
6th	1998-99	38	10	3	6	33	28	5	7	7	18	18	51	46	55
6th	1999-2000	38	8	8	3	23	12	7	5	7	23	23	46	35	58
8th	2000-01	38	8	8	3	27	20	5	7	7	19	23	46	43	54
8th	2001-02	38	8	7	4	22	17	4	7	8	24	30	46	47	50
16th	2002-03	38	11	2	6	25	14	1	7	11	17	33	42	47	45
6th	2003-04	38	9	6	4	24	19	6	5	8	24	25	48	44	56

ASTON VILLA have, for almost the entire duration of their 12-year membership of the Premiership, been caught between a rock and a hard place. Villa have been wedged between Doug Ellis's pragmatic running of the club on a sound business footing, without expenditure exceeding income, and the desire of fans, and his managers, to build on the top-six status they enjoyed in the early Premiership years. That clash of vision has cost nine managers their job and, although it has kept Villa in the top flight, times have changed since Doug Ellis returned for his second stint at Villa Park two decades ago. Nine is also the number of times Villa have finished in the top 10 of the Premiership, although,

ironically, the club's best campaign was the first, 1992–93.

Under Ron Atkinson Villa, after waiting until the fifth game for a win, stormed through the first half of the campaign and by Christmas were second having won seven games out of 11, losing just once. Despite the hiccup of a couple of defeats the team rallied and went top in February with victory over Chelsea. Eleven points from a possible 15 confirmed the lead in the Premiership, but losing to Norwich severely damaged Villa's title hopes. They got back into the championship race with three wins and a draw before their season turned on one game.

With three games left, losing 3–0 at Blackburn effectively ended Villa's dreams of glory and the team collapsed, losing the last two games to finish 10 points behind champions Manchester United, who they had taken four points from.

Aston Villa manager Ron Atkinson and player Dalian Atkinson celebrate with the Coca-Cola League Cup.

The next campaign saw Villa second in November, but focus on the league took second place to the Coca-Cola Cup, which they won, and their season fizzled out, leaving them in 10th place in the Premiership. The following season, under Brian Little, the 'R' word first came into Villa Park's Premiership vocabulary as the team flirted with relegation. Only two games were won in the first 14 and Villa were 19th in November. The year ended with the team in the relegation zone.

Although they weren't to know it at the time, three wins and a draw in February kept Aston Villa among the elite. After that boost there were only two more victories in the last 12 games and the drop was avoided by just three points.

Then came a couple of good seasons when Villa did indeed establish themselves as a top-six club. In the first half of 1995–96 they were always in the top seven, as high as second in September, and the team was fourth by February. But the lack of a sustained winning sequence, two games at most, consigned Villa to that fourth place.

The following season Villa finished fifth, after being as high as fourth at Christmas. They then failed to improve on their previous good seasons and were 15th in February. Brian Little resigned and was succeeded by John Gregory, who engineered nine victories in the last 11 games for a respectable finish of seventh.

John Gregory proved a moderate success at Villa Park, and the team did not improve during his four-year reign. In 1998–99 Villa looked, for a long time, like genuine title contenders. They went top with three wins and a draw from the first four games and remained in pole position until Boxing Day when they were beaten by Blackburn. But a dreadful second half of the

campaign, in which there were seven defeats in one eight-game spell, meant the side were fortunate to finish sixth.

Villa then slipped a place in each of the three subsequent seasons and in 2002 John Gregory decided he had had enough and resigned, just short of his fourth anniversary in the job, citing a lack of funds for players as his main reason for going. Gregory felt a cash injection was necessary to mount a serious challenge for the title. Doug Ellis wasn't prepared to open his chequebook and so former manager Graham Taylor stepped back into the breach from his place on the board, but despite being seventh in April, the team ended the campaign eighth.

Graham Taylor did his best for the team, but the bulk of 2002–03 was spent in the lower half of the table, relying on the goals from veteran Dion Dublin because of the failure of John Gregory's record £9.5 million signing Juan Pablo Angel to

adjust to the Premiership. Even new international star Darius Vassell struggled to replicate his England form in his day job. Just two wins in the last 12 games ensured a disappointing 16th place finish. And finish was what Graham Taylor did when he resigned after 15 months as manager, saying that Villa, as a club, 'was not run properly'. Six days later David O'Leary ended his 11-month exile by becoming the new manager.

There were many who criticised O'Leary for being a chequebook manager when he spent nearly £100 million at Leeds. But he grabbed the chance at Villa Park to prove his coaching and managerial

acumen on a relative shoestring, because Doug still kept a tight hold on the purse-strings, and took Villa to within one game of qualifying for the UEFA Cup. However, the team lost to Manchester United on the last day of the season and missed out on a place in Europe on goal difference from Newcastle.

Doug Ellis may be regarded as a dinosaur in some quarters, but he is enough of a businessman to know that unless he invests in David O'Leary's obvious ability his beloved Villa may miss out on their best chance in more than a decade of turning potential into a real chance of Champions League football.

MANAGERS

Ron Atkinson	1991–1994
Brian Little	1994–1998
John Gregory	1998–2002
Graham Taylor OBE	2002–2003
David O'Leary	May 2003–present

Aston Villa's Darius Vassell gets in a cross despite attention from Leicester City's Ricardo Scimecca.

Barnsley

BARNSLEY lit up the Premiership following their arrival for season 1997–98, after finishing runners-up in the First Division title race. Armed with money from a record number of season ticket sales, manager Danny Wilson invested heavily in the club's first season in the elite league and splashed out a new club record fee of £1.5 million to bring in striker Georgi Hristov from Partizan Belgrade.

With the chant 'It's just like watching Brazil' echoing around Oakwell, Barnsley got off to a flier in the opening home game against West Ham and Neil Redfearn had the honour of scoring Barnsley's first Premiership goal when he headed home after just seven minutes, although the Hammers hit back to take the points with two second-half goals. Undaunted, the 'Red Army' headed south for game number two and a first Premiership victory was achieved as, once again, Neil Redfearn scored to defeat Crystal

MANAGER

Danny Wilson	1994–1998

Palace. Two games, three points on the board and next up were Chelsea, for a televised game. Barnsley fans were loving life in the fast lane but they came down with a bump as Chelsea rattled up a 6–0 victory to remind the newcomers that the Premiership was a whole new ball game.

Confidence was shattered by that mauling but the team bounced back to win 2–1 at home to Bolton, but the victory proved a one-off as defeats followed at Derby, 1–0; at home to Aston Villa, 3–0; at Everton, 4–2; and at Wimbledon 4–1. It got worse as Leicester won 2–0 at Oakwell before Arsenal rattled up a 5–0 score at Highbury.

The rude awakening of that run forced the manager's hand and he signed Ashley Ward from Derby County. This paid off initially, as Ward opened his

account in the 2–0 win at home to Coventry that arrested a run of six consecutive league defeats. But next up were Manchester United, the reigning champions, and they delighted another capacity crowd at the Theatre of Dreams with a nightmare 7–0 thrashing for the Tykes. The 4–1 loss at Southampton meant that Barnsley had conceded 25 goals in just nine Premiership outings, so they were on a hiding to nothing when they went to Anfield in late November – but fate had something else in mind.

With new signing Peter Markste making his debut at the heart of the defence, and German 'keeper Lars Leese inspired between the sticks, Ashley Ward scrambled home the only goal for what proved to be Barnsley's best win of their campaign.

The next two fixtures were local derbies against Leeds United and Sheffield Wednesday but both were cruelly lost to last-minute goals and Barnsley remained rooted to the foot of the Premiership table in mid-December, although a run of improved form began with a 2–2 draw at home to Newcastle United. Although they then lost 3–0 at Spurs, a 1–1 draw at Bolton and a 1–0 success over Derby meant that December had yielded five points from five games. It was not earth-shattering, but enough to give Tykes' fans hope for the New Year. Unfortunately West Ham shattered that optimism with a 6–0 mauling to open 1998 with a bang. Seven days later Barnsley bounced back and completed their first league double of the season with a 1–0 win at home to Crystal Palace, but then Chel-

sea completed their double with a 2–0 win at Stamford Bridge.

February saw an improvement in form and three games yielded four points. A 2–2 draw at home to Everton was followed by a 1–0 defeat at Coventry before Wimbledon were beaten 2–1 at Oakwell, with new signing Jan Aage Fjortoft scoring both goals. Barnsley took that form into March and began the month with an impressive 1–0 win at Aston Villa; again Ashley Ward was the scorer. Three days later Barnsley delighted their home fans with a thrilling 4–3 win over Southampton in which Fjortoft scored again. Liverpool were next up at Oakwell but the game proved pivotal in the fight to avoid an immediate return to the Nationwide League.

With the score level at 1–1 the referee sent off two Barnsley players, Darren Barnard and Chris Morgan, and Liverpool went 2–1 up with Karl Heinz Riedle scoring his second goal. The referee then mysteriously left the field and after a short break returned to the game, which Barnsley levelled to 2–2. However, with nine-man Barnsley looking set for an unlikely draw, the referee then dismissed Darren Sheridan and from the resultant free-kick Steve Mc-Manaman scored for Liverpool to snatch a 3–2 victory.

That reverse effectively ended Barnsley's fight to stay in the Premiership and the team won just one of their remaining seven games, a 2–1 success at home to neighbours Sheffield Wednesday on 11 April. Seven days later Barnsley picked up their final point in the top flight with a 1–1 home draw against Spurs. Fittingly Neil Redfearn, who had scored the club's first Premiership goal back in August, was the scorer of the last one. Barnsley went on to end to a memorable first, brief, stay in the Premiership with three consecutive defeats that finished on 10 May 1998 with a 2–0 home defeat to Manchester United.

Barnsley's goalkeeper David Watson is consoled by Manager Danny Wilson as his side are relegated.

Birmingham City

				Home:				Away:				Total Goals		
Pos.	Season	P	W	D	L	F	A	W	D	L	F	A	F	A	Pts
13th	2002-03	38	8	5	6	25	23	5	4	10	16	26	41	49	48
10th	2003-04	38	8	5	6	26	24	4	9	6	17	24	43	48	50

WHEN Birmingham began their Premiership adventure with defeats by Arsenal and Blackburn you could hear the whispers around the country that they would soon be back from whence they came. But those sceptics had reckoned without the managerial nous of Steve Bruce and his mix of cast-offs, Nationwide League players and a fantastic team spirit, not to mention Steve's powers of persuasion in talking his mega-rich board into subsidising hefty wages to 'buy' another season after the first.

Bruce's boldest move was signing French World Cup-winner Christophe Dugarry from Bordeaux, halfway through the season, with the team fairly comfortable in mid-table. But, before Dugarry made his January bow, in the 4–0 thrashing at Arsenal, Blues had dropped as far as 15th and some folk questioned the Frenchman's aptitude for a relegation dog-fight. Indeed, it took a while for Dugarry to get going but once he did the wages that the manager had to prise out of his directors paid handsome dividends.

With Dugarry's flair, Robbie Savage's bolshy belligerence, and the probing of Bryan Hughes and Paul Devlin, Birmingham started to make progress. After consecutive defeats by Bolton, Manchester United and Chelsea in February 2003, the turning point came with a massive win against Liverpool, which was followed by victory at Aston Villa. But the good work was undone by defeats by Manchester City and Spurs, either side of a win against West Brom, and the team dropped to just above the relegation zone.

Then Dugarry grabbed centre stage. His first goal was the winner against Sunderland. His second goal, in successive matches, set up victory over Charlton and the second of his seven-minute brace, taking his tally to four in three games, beat Southampton. Dugarry then made it four scoring games in a row with the first goal of a 3–0 success against 'Boro and Blues were comfortably 12th in the table. So comfortable that they could lose and draw in their last two fixtures secure in the knowledge that a difficult first top-flight campaign had been successfully negotiated.

Birmingham's second season was more meritorious: they spent much of the campaign in the top 10 and even flirted with fourth place. There was a very real chance that a Champions League place could be within reach. Indeed Blues were fourth as early as October, having taken 14 points from a possible 18 before their first defeat by Manchester United. They stayed there through to November 2003 when they picked up just one point from 12, and two of their three defeats were to Arsenal and Liverpool. The turn of the year saw Bruce stabilising his side in ninth place despite the departure of Dugarry. The team improved to sixth in March, but Birmingham fell away to end April in ninth position before finishing their second Premiership campaign better than the first in 10th place.

MANAGER

Steve Bruce   December 2001–present

Christophe Dugarry, Birmingham City.

Blackburn Rovers

BLACKBURN ROVERS' RECORD IN THE PREMIERSHIP

| Pos. | Season | P | Home: | | | | | Away: | | | | | Total Goals | | Pts |
			W	D	L	F	A	W	D	L	F	A	F	A	
4th	1992-93	42	13	4	4	38	18	7	7	7	30	28	68	46	71
2nd	1993-94	42	14	5	2	31	11	11	4	6	32	25	63	36	84
1st	1994-95	42	17	2	2	54	21	10	6	5	26	18	80	39	89
7th	1995-96	38	14	2	3	44	19	4	5	10	17	28	61	47	61
13th	1996-97	38	8	4	7	28	23	1	11	7	14	20	42	43	42
6th	1997-98	38	11	4	4	40	26	5	6	8	17	26	57	52	58
19th	1998-99	38	6	5	8	21	24	1	9	9	17	28	38	52	35
10th	2001-02	38	8	6	5	33	20	4	4	11	22	31	55	51	46
6th	2002-03	38	9	7	3	24	15	7	5	7	28	28	52	43	60
15th	2003-04	38	5	4	10	25	31	7	4	8	26	28	51	59	44

IT'S A truism that one man doesn't make a team, but two do, and those two men are the main reason that Blackburn Rovers are the only club, apart from Manchester United and Arsenal, to have won the Premiership in its 12-year history. The two men in question are record signing Alan Shearer, and the man who bankrolled his £3.3 million signing, steel tycoon Jack Walker.

Blackburn's first Premiership season started well with an unbeaten start that put them top by the end of August. Rovers weren't outside the top two until December, when losing to Liverpool dropped them to third. But a bigger blow came on Boxing Day, when Blackburn went second after beating Leeds, but after scoring twice, to take his running total to 16, Alan Shearer's season was ended by injury. Any title hopes were also scuppered, as Rovers won only one of their next six games before Mike Newell's brace beat Chelsea. Another five games without winning meant that the team was in sixth place. Kevin Gallacher came in from Coventry, and although he scored five goals by the end of the season he was no Alan Shearer. But with Gallacher alongside Newell, Blackburn won seven of their last nine games to finish fourth.

Another expensive import arrived from Southampton when Tim Flowers became Britain's most expensive goalkeeper when he joined Blackburn for £2 million, but he had to wait a dozen games before displacing Bobby Mimms. Although Rovers then lost two out of four they started a great run and from December won 10 games out of 11, drawing the other one. Shearer was back, and by the turn of the year had increased his tally to 18 goals, while Rovers were in second place. The team suffered only four defeats in the second half of the campaign, but these proved decisive, two of them coming in the last four games. But the runners-up spot was a step up from the previous season's fourth place, and the next campaign would bring Rovers the ultimate prize of a

Blackburn Rovers celebrate with the FA Carling Premiership trophy in 1995.

championship win. Blackburn were a formidable team and were strengthened by the record £5 million arrival of Chris Sutton. The 'SAS', as Shearer and his co-striker were nicknamed, were, at times, impossible to play against, and with Colin Hendry supreme at the back Rovers produced consistent enough form to stay in the top three all season, bar a fortnight.

Losing at Manchester United spurred Blackburn on and they went 12 games without defeat. Seven consecutive wins had them top by December. United completed a league double over them, but Rovers stayed top. In fact only two more defeats in 15 games saw them retain pole position with three games left. But defeat at relegation-threatened West Ham made even the eight-point advantage they had over Manchester United look vulnerable.

Alan Shearer's 33rd league goal beat Newcastle to set up a dramatic last-day scenario: if United won at West Ham and Rovers lost to Liverpool the title would stay at Old Trafford. But West Ham held United and despite losing at Anfield Kenny Dalglish's Rovers were pro-claimed Premiership champions.

The summer shock was Kenny Dalglish's elevation to Football Director at Blackburn Rovers, a role that no one has ever been able to define, with his assistant Ray Harford becoming team manager. But the change had a negative affect on the field and the team failed to retain the title. Shearer continued scoring goals, another 31, more than half of Rovers' total, but got little support from elsewhere, with the second-highest scorer registering

just six! The first half of the campaign was spent in the lower half of the table though a revival and only five defeats in the second half, from 19 games, earned seventh place.

Ray Harford was given another season but it proved even worse. Alan Shearer left for his spiritual home, St James' Park, and four points from a possible 33 was an unacceptable start for Rovers, who were bottom for two months until the end of October when Ray Harford resigned and perennial caretaker manager Tony Parkes took over. Sven-Goran Eriksson was lined up for the job but then changed his mind. However, six games without defeat from February allayed relegation fears and the team limped to the end of the season, finishing 13th.

Roy Hodgson became manager in June and Rovers began the season well, leading the table by the end of August. Nine unbeaten games after losing to Leeds kept Blackburn in the top three and by the New Year they were second, but only four more games were won, from 17, and sixth was the final placing. The following season a spectacular fall saw the team relegated after a start in which only two wins were registered by December. Just three victories came in 1999 and on 12 May the club was relegated.

Two seasons were spent in Division One and when the team returned to the Premiership, finishes of 10th and sixth, in successive seasons, under Graeme Souness, were followed by a more nervous season haunted by the spectre of relegation, which loomed over the club for much of 2003–04.

MANAGERS

Kenny Dalglish	1991–1995
Ray Harford	1995–1997
Roy Hodgson	1997–1998
Brian Kidd	1998–1999
Tony Parkes	1999–2000
Graeme Souness	March 2000–present

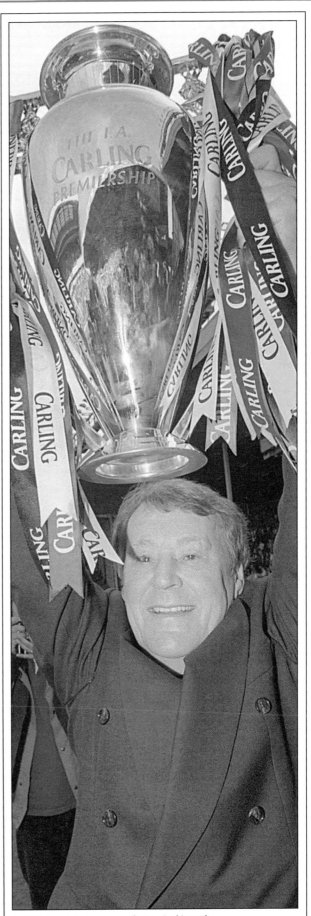

Jack Walker celebrates winning the Premiership trophy.

Bolton Wanderers

BOLTON WANDERERS' RECORD IN THE PREMIERSHIP

Pos.	Season	P	Home: W	D	L	F	A	Away: W	D	L	F	A	Total Goals F	A	Pts
20th	1995-96	38	5	4	10	16	31	3	1	15	23	40	39	71	29
18th	1997-98	38	7	8	4	25	22	2	5	12	16	39	41	61	40
16th	2001-02	38	5	7	7	20	31	4	6	9	24	31	44	62	40
17th	2002-03	38	7	8	4	27	24	3	6	10	14	27	41	51	44
8th	2003-04	38	6	8	5	24	21	8	3	8	24	35	48	56	53

BOLTON'S third consecutive Premiership season, 2003–04, saw them earn the club's highest-ever finish in the top flight, eighth. Wanderers ended the campaign with a flourish and recorded the club's best winning sequence since 1927–28 with their fifth win in a row coming with victory at Everton. Even losing the last game at home to Fulham couldn't spoil the Trotters' joy. For another inappropriately labelled 'unfashionable' club, Bolton's achievement in establishing Premiership credentials is more unique than unfashionable.

Having a sensible board of directors was a good start, as was investing in a space-age home, the magnificent Reebok Stadium. That sensible board also made, possibly, its most sensible move ever when Sam Allardyce was appointed manager in October 1999, 17 months after the club suffered its second relegation from the Premiership. Very shortly afterwards, with the security of a 10-year contract, and inside the first two years of that unprecedented mandate, Bolton were back in the Premiership via the play-offs.

Their first Premiership campaign, in 1995–96, saw Wanderers lose 25 of their fixtures and win only eight. By the halfway stage they were bottom and, with the exception of a week in March, that's where they stayed, being relegated at the end of the season. Although Bolton made an immediate return as First Division champions, the second Premiership campaign proved as fruitless as the first, although they were relegated from a higher placing than in their first season. As before, Bolton were long-term occupiers of a bottom-three berth, being stuck in the drop zone from January 1998, when the team was midway through a 12-game run without a win. Victory in the penultimate game against Crystal Palace took Bolton out of trouble but a last-day defeat by Chelsea sent them back to Division One.

Wanderers returned to the Premiership after three seasons and, despite only winning nine games in the entire campaign, they proved hard to beat, posting 13 draws. Michael Ricketts was on fire that season and his 12 goals earned him an England cap, as a substitute against Holland. Bolton actually went top of the table after three wins in a four-game unbeaten start to the campaign and stayed in the top 10 until December. In that time they registered a superb win at Old Trafford, with Ricketts scoring the winner. Unfortunately the second half of the season, with one run of 12 games without a win, saw Bolton drop into the relegation zone. But Sam Allardyce rallied his side and shrewdly recruited Youri Djorkaeff. Despite his 34 years the French World Cup-winner proved a class act and in the last 12 games he played that season Wanderers collected 12 precious points. Djorkaeff contributed four goals to help secure safety by just four points.

Djorkaeff was just one of the 'underachievers' brought to the Reebok Stadium by Sam Allardyce, whose Midas touch not only revived failing careers, but also built Bolton's survival on the quality of his imports, allied to his ability as a manager to get the best out of those he signed. And not all of his recruits were from overseas. Simon Charlton enjoyed a career resurgence after Sam rescued him from the Birmingham reserves. Kevin Davies, once a record £7 million transfer, was a revelation after joining the club and Jay-Jay Okocha was going nowhere at Paris Saint Germain until Sam signed him in 2002. He proved such a revelation that top European clubs came sniffing as he came towards the end of his contract, but Allardyce headed off any potential buyers by securing the Nigerian World Cup star on a new deal.

If a team survives a first season in the Premiership, the second campaign always proves the acid test, and for Bolton 2002–03 was a severe examination. Just two wins in the opening 12 games left Wanderers bottom until they thrashed Leeds to move up to 18th. Even then it was a struggle, as the team found it hard to stay unbeaten for more than three successive games until, critically, the last nine fixtures. Then, after three consecutive victories, and a defeat by Chelsea, nine points were gathered in five unbeaten games and Bolton secured safety.

The highlight of the third consecutive Premiership campaign, apart from reaching the Carling Cup Final, was finishing eighth, after a few hiccups following their defeat in Cardiff by Middlesbrough. But even then Sam Allardyce was trying to strengthen the side, and Rivaldo was a target, but Bolton probably had a lucky escape when the Brazilian chose to join Olympiakos instead. If Sam Allardyce can continue to pick up shrewd signings of quality players, then Bolton could enjoy life as a Premiership club for some years to come.

MANAGERS

Bruce Rioch	1992–1995
Roy McFarland	1995–1996
Colin Todd	1996–1999
Sam Allardyce	October 1999–present

The Reebok stadium, home of Bolton Wanderers.

Bradford City

THERE can have been few more dramatic escapes from relegation to Division One than that which Bradford engineered on the final day of their first Premiership campaign in May 2000. On the last day of the season, with Liverpool the visitors to City's new Bradford and Bingley Stadium, which had only been their new home for that season, Bradford had to better Wimbledon's result at Southampton in order to survive.

David Wetherall, the club's record £1.4 million signing, climbed high above the Liverpool defence to head powerfully home after just 12 minutes. But Southampton won 2-0 and Bradford held on to relish the prospect of another top-flight season, but everyone knew it was going to be even harder the following year.

Ahead of their Premiership bow Bradford's squad had been strengthened when manager Paul Jewell signed, as well as Wetherall, Lee Sharpe and Gunnar Halle from Elland Road, and Matt Clarke from Sheffield United.

With half a dozen 30-somethings in the side Bradford's start to 1999–2000 couldn't have been better and a goal from one of those 'vets', Dean Saunders, earned victory at Middlesbrough. When Peter Beagrie, another 'golden oldie', netted an 89th-minute penalty to snatch a point from Sheffield Wednesday, the Bantams were ninth in the Premiership table. But they soon plummeted into the bottom three, with four defeats in five games. By Christmas the team had only won three more games and spent most of the campaign in the relegation zone, but a Dean Windass hat-trick, Bradford's

only treble that season, earned a 4–4 draw against Derby after the Rams had led 2–0. But two successive wins gave the team and its fans hope, although defeat at Leicester dropped the team back into the relegation zone. With Liverpool heading for Bradford, things didn't look good, but David Wetherall wrote himself and his team into the record books with that dramatic last-game clincher.

Two days before the start of the following season, and their historic European bow in the Inter-Toto Cup, Bradford were rocked by a bombshell when manager Paul Jewell resigned, saying he felt he had taken the club as far as he could.

Chris Hutchings was promoted to manager and with new arrivals Peter Atherton and Ian Nolan, from Sheffield Wednesday, and new record signing David Hopkin, from Leeds, along with Stan

Collymore from Leicester City to supplement the enigmatic talents of Benito Carbone, things looked good, on paper at least. But by the fifth game the team was 15th and their one win, against Chelsea, was their last until December. After just 12 games and 137 days as manager Chris Hutchings was relieved of his duties and Stuart McCall stepped into the breach, briefly, before Jim Jefferies was appointed. But the former Hearts manager soon realised his new team wasn't good enough and they didn't persuade him otherwise.

Rock-bottom of the Premiership from 16 December, Bradford opened the New Year

by beating Leicester but then went 10 games without another victory before enjoying back-to-back Premiership wins for only the third, and last, time in their two-year stay in the top flight. The campaign petered out and the side ended their stay in the Premiership when they were relegated eight points behind 19th-placed Coventry City.

Unfortunately, the Bradford board spent huge sums of money in attempting to stave off the inevitability of relegation. If that had been the only crime it would have been bad enough, but the club couldn't sustain such huge investments in signing-on fees and salaries and when the team went into Division One administration followed, as did another relegation, and the Premiership was as far away, in 2004, as it had been 12 years earlier when the club was 16th in Division Three.

MANAGERS

Paul Jewell	1998–2000
Chris Hutchings	2000
Jim Jefferies	2000–2001

Dean Windass, scorer of Bradford City's only Premiership hat-trick, celebrates survival with goalkeeper Matt Clarke.

Charlton Athletic

CHARLTON ATHLETIC'S RECORD IN THE PREMIERSHIP

Pos.	Season	P	Home: W	D	L	F	A	Away: W	D	L	F	A	Total Goals F	A	Pts
18th	1998-99	38	4	7	8	20	20	4	5	10	21	36	41	56	36
9th	2000-01	38	11	5	3	31	19	3	5	11	19	38	50	57	52
14th	2001-02	38	5	6	8	23	30	5	8	6	15	19	38	49	44
12th	2002-03	38	8	3	8	26	30	6	4	9	19	26	45	56	49
7th	2003-04	38	7	6	6	29	29	7	5	7	22	22	51	51	53

Chris Powell became an England international as a Charlton Athletic player.

CHARLTON ATHLETIC ended their fourth consecutive Premiership season in seventh place, an achievement, in itself, that should prove a salutary lesson to every club that gets into the top flight, because of the way the Addicks established themselves in the elite after being relegated following their first campaign.

Under Alan Curbishley Charlton won promotion, via the play-offs, to take their place in the Premiership for 1998–99 and a storming start of four points from two games saw them top the table and Alan Curbishley win Manager of the Month, but after a goalless draw with Arsenal they dropped to fourth and they declined into the bottom three by Christmas.

After victory over Nottingham Forest, in the first game of October, Charlton won just one game, ironically against the manager's former club, West Ham, 4–2, before a dreadful run that yielded only three points from 13 games, including eight consecutive defeats, by February 1999. Charlton won three in a row, against Wimbledon, Liverpool and Derby, and Curbishley was again Manager of the Month, but the damage was done. From 16th Charlton won just two more games before the end of the season. The double was completed over the Hammers and Aston Villa were beaten, leaving the Addicks needing a last-day victory against Sheffield Wednesday while hoping that Southampton failed against Everton. Charlton lost and Southampton won so it was back to Division One.

That was when step one in the 'Charlton Athletic guide to becoming an established Premiership club', was taken. The club resisted the time-honoured knee-jerk reaction to relegation, sacking its manager, and keeping that continuity proved an investment that paid handsome dividends.

With the prolific Andy Hunt

netting 24 league goals, aided and abetted by Clive Mendonca on 9, John Robinson and Graham Stuart on 7 and Richard Rufus on 6, Charlton stormed to the First Division championship winning 27 of their 46 league games to take the title with 91 points, two points ahead of Manchester City. Then, as if quashing any doubts about their title-winning form, Charlton thumped City 4–0 on the opening day of the Premiership.

Charlton didn't have a prolific scorer in 2000–01 and again the goals were spread among the team. Jonatan Johansson finished top scorer with just 11 league goals, but Shaun Bartlett, Claus Jensen, Graham Stuart and Matt Svensson all hit five each. A couple of useful unbeaten runs kept Charlton floating around mid-table, although they were fifth in September after beating Newcastle. The best sequence, nine games unbeaten, came between the last game of 2000, when the league double was completed over Manchester City, 4–1, and a goalless draw with Middlesbrough that left the Addicks in eighth place. Alan Curbishley was delighted to end the campaign ninth in the table.

The following season was similar in that the team reached as high as eighth at the turn of the year, but no wins in the final eight games brought them perilously close to the drop. In the end though, three draws from the last four games ensured safety in 14th place.

Ably assisted by Keith Peacock and Mervyn Day, Alan Curbishley built a sound squad capable of holding its own in the elite league with a good balance of experience and youth, with Chris Bart-Williams, Chris Powell and Graham Stuart alongside up and coming youngsters Scott Parker and Luke Young. It looked as if the team might make a real impact and five successive wins in early 2003 elevated the side to sixth,

although defeat by Arsenal started a downward spiral of eight defeats in the last 10 games for a 12th place finish.

Charlton did so well in 2003–04 that they even threatened to claim a Champions League slot, but in the end they had to settle for the kind of final placing that 13 other Premiership clubs would have taken, not to mention £7.6 million of prize money that

would be well utilised by Alan Curbishley.

Charlton have been established in the top flight with a combination of sound judgement, good buys and the development of

quality players by Alan Curbishley, and are a lesson to clubs who think chequebooks can buy success. The biggest task ahead is retaining the manager who has presided over the minor miracle.

MANAGERS

Steve Gritt and Alan Curbishley Joint managers 1991–1995
Alan Curbishley June 1995–present

Charlton's 'Miracle Manager', Alan Curbishley.

Chelsea

CHELSEA'S RECORD IN THE PREMIERSHIP

Pos.	Season	P	Home: W	D	L	F	A	Away: W	D	L	F	A	Total Goals F	A	Pts
11th	1992-93	42	9	7	5	29	22	5	7	9	22	32	51	54	56
14th	1993-94	42	11	5	5	31	20	2	7	12	18	33	49	53	51
11th	1994-95	42	7	7	7	25	22	6	8	7	25	33	50	55	54
11th	1995-96	38	7	7	5	30	22	5	7	7	16	22	46	44	50
6th	1996-97	38	9	8	2	33	22	7	3	9	25	33	58	55	59
4th	1997-98	38	13	2	4	37	14	7	1	11	34	29	71	43	63
3rd	1998-99	38	12	6	1	29	13	8	9	2	28	17	57	30	75
5th	1999-2000	38	12	5	2	35	12	6	6	7	18	22	53	34	65
6th	2000-01	38	13	3	3	44	20	4	7	8	24	25	68	45	61
6th	2001-02	38	11	4	4	43	21	6	9	4	23	17	66	38	64
4th	2002-03	38	12	5	2	41	15	7	5	7	27	23	68	38	67
2nd	2003-04	38	12	4	3	34	13	12	3	4	33	17	67	30	79

WHEN Roman Abramovic brought his open chequebook to Stamford Bridge, the sceptics chorused 'you can't buy success'. After season 2003–04, when his expensively assembled squad proved the closest competition to Arsenal, that argument seemed to be weakening, especially in light of Leeds United's demise, with a debt roughly similar to the sum the new Chelsea owner spent on his acquisitions.

For the majority of Chelsea's continuous membership of the Premiership, the team has proved a good cup side but lacked the stamina to sustain a season-long marathon as opposed to the six or 10 game 'sprint' required to lift a cup.

Three times in the first four seasons Chelsea finished 11th but, under Ruud Gullit, that improved to sixth in 1997. Gullit was sacked midway through the following season and Gianluca Vialli became player-manager.

His influence, not to mention the 11 goals which made 'Luca' joint top scorer with Tore Andre Flo, took the team to a fourth place finish.

The following campaign there was more improvement as Chelsea finished third, behind Manchester United and Arsenal. A higher placing might have been possible – they were top on 16 January – but injuries hit hard and even though the team was unbeaten in their final 10 games they had too many draws (four) and were four points adrift of the champions. Four is a number which crops up frequently in Chelsea's Premiership life.

Any hopes of building a championship-challenging side on the foundation of that third place disappeared when Vialli's tenure was ended by Chelsea's autocratic chairman and owner, Ken Bates, in 2000, amid rumours that the manager had lost the confidence of the dressing-room. It was very bad

Chelsea celebrate winning the FA Cup in 1997.

timing, as far as the club's progress was concerned, because Chelsea, from Boxing Day 1999, strung together an impressive 16-game unbeaten run to fuel optimism for the following season, but Vialli's departure had a profound effect on the team.

Claudio Ranieri, unheard of by most football followers in England, arrived in September 2000 and his initial problems had nothing to do with dressing room unrest, and more to do with his lack of spoken English, although that probably mattered little to the multi-national Chelsea squad. The team finished Ranieri's first season fifth and dropped another rung when they finished sixth in 2000–01.

On the back of 37 league goals between Jimmy Floyd Hasselbaink, 23, and Eidur Gudjohnsen, 14, Chelsea stabilised in sixth place the following season, though they did climb as high as fourth, with four games to go. But one win in that run-in cost dear and sixth it was.

Season 2002–03 brought the first signs, even before the Roman Revolution, that Chelsea were improving as a consistent side, but they were still unable to string an impact-making run together. The best run of successive wins was four, but two of those were against relegation-threatened sides. The best unbeaten run bridged October and Boxing Day. The team briefly enjoyed second place, but defeat by Leeds, in the last game of 2002, edged them down to third. Critically Chelsea lost to the three sides who were to finish above them, Manchester United, Arsenal and Newcastle, in the space of eight games, and for the last two months of the campaign the team remained fourth.

Then along came Roman Abramovic and £100 million, plus his initial purchase costs. As Premiership runners-up, the club's highest top-flight finish since they won the championship in 1955, and after a Champions League semi-final, the club stand almost ready to challenge the domination of the championship by the teams that have won all bar one of the 12 Premiership titles, Arsenal and Manchester United. But even with their new owner's vast fortune, all was not sweet at the Bridge as the season was marred by unsavoury rumour and speculation that Ranieri was to be replaced by any number of foreign coaches, some as well-known as Sven-Goran Eriksson, and some no one had ever heard of, throughout the campaign. But Ranieri's dignified response to the almost daily speculation earned him the respect of football in general but did little to keep him in a job.

MANAGERS

Ian Portefield	1991–1993
David Webb	1993
Glenn Hoddle	1993–1996
Ruud Gullit	1996–1998
Gianluca Vialli	1998–2000
Claudio Ranieri	September 2000–present

Chelsea's John Terry, Frank Lampard, Mario Melchiot and Robert Huth celebrate Jesper Gronkjaer's first Premiership goal for a year in the 1–1 draw at Old Trafford on 8 May 2004. The scorer is far left.

Coventry City

COVENTRY CITY'S RECORD IN THE PREMIERSHIP

Pos.	Season	P	Home: W	D	L	F	A	Away: W	D	L	F	A	Total Goals F	A	Pts
15th	1992-93	42	7	4	10	29	28	6	9	6	23	29	52	57	52
11th	1993-94	42	9	7	5	23	17	5	7	9	20	28	43	45	56
16th	1994-95	42	7	7	7	23	25	5	7	9	21	37	44	62	50
16th	1995-96	38	6	7	6	21	23	2	7	10	21	37	42	60	38
17th	1996-97	38	4	8	7	19	23	5	6	8	19	31	38	54	41
11th	1997-98	38	8	9	2	26	17	4	7	8	20	27	46	44	52
15th	1998-99	38	8	6	5	26	21	3	3	13	13	30	39	51	42
14th	1999-2000	38	12	1	6	38	22	0	7	12	9	32	47	54	44
19th	2000-01	38	4	7	8	14	23	4	3	12	22	40	36	63	34

THE MOST remarkable aspect of Coventry's nine-year stay in the Premiership, from being founder members, is the very fact that they were able to survive for so long. The club's highest finish was 11th, twice, in 1994 and again four years later. But at least there was tremendous pride, in that inaugural campaign when, after opening with three successive victories, Coventry City were top of the Premiership. But it wasn't to last and two defeats followed, although Bobby Gould's team rallied and put together a seven-game unbeaten run that elevated them to third. Unfortunately three defeats in four games sent the Sky Blues down to 11th.

Coventry managed to get back up the table, to fourth by February, with Micky Quinn, a signing from Newcastle, starting to score goals, but after netting in the victory over Middlesbrough Micky didn't score for another nine games and by the time he did, in the victory over Southampton, Coventry had lost five games of the eight played. The team couldn't manage a win in any of their final five fixtures and finished a disappointing 15th when a higher placing was well within range.

The second campaign was even better than the first and the team managed the best start to a season for 56 years with an eight-game unbeaten run that saw them third in mid-September, but that couldn't be sustained and three defeats in four resulted in a drop to 13th, which was where the team was at Christmas after just two wins in eight games.

It wasn't until the latter stages of the campaign that Coventry bucked up their ideas and went on an unbeaten run to finish the season with 15 points from 21, in 11th place, but one less defeat would surely have meant a top-10 placing.

Unfortunately for the club, three seasons of mediocrity followed before that best-ever 11th place was matched, in

Coventry City's John Hartson dives to score the winning goal against Sunderland.

1997–98, by which time Gordon Strachan, still playing in his 40th year, was manager as well. With Dion Dublin and Darren Huckerby regular scorers the team should have done better than 11th. Instead of the annual joust with relegation Coventry ensured safety by the turn of the year when a win over Manchester United was seen as the turning point. The team lost only two games in the second half of the campaign but too many draws prevented an even better finishing place.

The first half of 1998–99 was spent uncomfortably close to the drop zone, but in the New Year only a defeat by Manchester United dipped the team back into the bottom three. Four wins in six followed that reverse and Coventry were 15th, where they finished, despite more than three weeks just above the relegation trio.

The next season was marginally better, and although the team went down to 17th in September, the second half of the campaign saw an improvement to 12th, in March. Four successive defeats then started a slide, and had it not been for successive victories over Everton and Bradford, the subsequent three reverses could have had a dramatic effect. But Coventry scraped two wins in their last five games to finish 11 points clear of the last relegation place.

Good luck and fortune couldn't last forever, and the following season proved to be not only the end of the club's stay in the Premiership, but also of 34 seasons in the top flight, after Jimmy Hill took them into the old First Division in 1967.

From fourth, after two wins in the opening three fixtures, Coventry won just one game before December and were 18th before beating Leicester to climb out of the drop zone.

But after a Boxing Day win over Everton a 10-game run saw the team locked in to the relegation trio. Even successive wins failed to ease Coventry out of trouble and, despite tremendous effort, by pay-as-you-play John Hartson especially, three wins and a draw in the last four games saw an end to Coventry as a top-flight club.

MANAGERS

Bobby Gould	1992–1993
Phil Neal	1993–1995
Ron Atkinson	1995–1996
Gordon Strachan	1996–2001

Coventry City manager Gordon Strachan is held back by assistant manager Gary Pendrey at the end of the match with Aston Villa, after Coventry are relegated.

Crystal Palace

CRYSTAL PALACE'S RECORD IN THE PREMIERSHIP

Pos.	Season	P	Home: W	D	L	F	A	Away: W	D	L	F	A	Total Goals F	A	Pts
20th	1992-93	42	6	9	6	27	25	5	7	9	21	36	48	61	49
19th	1994-95	42	6	6	9	16	23	5	6	10	18	26	34	49	45
20th	1997-98	38	2	5	12	15	39	6	4	9	22	32	37	71	33

Attilio Lombardo, Crystal Palace.

CRYSTAL PALACE have the unenviable record of having been relegated after each of their three seasons in the Premiership.

Palace were founder members of the Premiership, but after drawing their first four games, and being as high as 11th, they slumped following successive defeats by Manchester United, Norwich and Aston Villa, coming to rest in 20th place by 5 September. A draw against Oldham arrested the slide and took them up to 17th but the early signs were not good. Even a first victory, against Everton, with two goals from Chris Armstrong, didn't help, and losing to Southampton put Palace one place off the bottom.

A worse run followed and it was another seven games without a victory before the side clicked and reeled off five consecutive wins to end the year 15th. Unfortunately, Alan Smith's side couldn't sustain that improvement and four consecutive January defeats meant 19th place going into February. Beating Blackburn and Aston Villa didn't help and only three wins from the final 14 games meant relegation was a certainty, although beating Ipswich on May Day meant 18th place and possible survival. However, a draw at Manchester City and defeat by Arsenal on the last day meant that the Eagles dropped into Division One.

Retaining Chris Armstrong, and with Gareth Southgate scoring goals from midfield, Palace acclimatised quickly to Division One and went top just after Christmas, staying there for the rest of the campaign and winning the championship for an immediate return to the top flight. But they suffered a bad start to the new campaign and went seven games without a win until Arsenal were beaten by a couple of John Salako goals. That win elevated them from 21st to 17th but two defeats knocked them back before Palace won four in a row to climb to 11th.

Defeat at Manchester United started the downward spiral and nine games without winning saw Palace one place above the bottom three. Victory over Leicester elevated them to 16th, but inconsistency proved costly and when Arsenal beat them in February the team were 20th. April saw a bit of a revival but even two wins and two draws didn't improve matters. The team had the worst away scoring record in the Premiership, and relegation was confirmed at Newcastle on the final day of the Premiership season.

Palace spent two years back in Division One before winning back their Premiership place via the play-offs and they opened their third top-flight season with two wins and two defeats to attain a respectable fifth place, but defeats by Southampton and Blackburn saw them slump to ninth. Three wins and four draws meant mid-table security but Liverpool's victory over them, their fourth game without a win, started terminal decline and the last 20 games yielded just two victories. Indeed eight successive defeats, from January into April, virtually guaranteed another early return to Division One.

The root cause of this appalling third Premiership campaign was the worst home record in the entire English game: just two victories and a miserly 15 goals at Selhurst Park, although you had to go as high as 10th place, and Leicester, to find a club with more away goals. Palace rejoined the Premiership after winning the First Division play-offs in 2003–04.

MANAGERS

Steve Coppell	1984–1993. Technical Director 1995/1996
Alan Smith	1993–1995
Dave Bassett	1996–1997
Attilio Lombardo	1998 Head Coach
Iain Dowie	December 2003–present

Derby County

DERBY COUNTY'S RECORD IN THE PREMIERSHIP

Pos.	Season	P	Home: W	D	L	F	A	Away: W	D	L	F	A	Total Goals F	A	Pts
12th	1996-97	38	8	6	5	25	22	3	7	9	20	36	45	58	46
9th	1997-98	38	12	3	4	33	18	4	4	11	19	31	52	49	55
8th	1998-99	38	8	7	4	22	19	5	6	8	18	26	40	45	52
16th	1999-2000	38	6	3	10	22	25	3	8	8	22	32	44	57	38
17th	2000-01	38	8	7	4	23	24	2	5	12	14	35	37	59	42
19th	2001-02	38	5	4	10	20	26	3	2	14	13	37	33	63	30

JIM SMITH took Derby into the Premiership for 1996–97 and they opened with draws against Leeds and Spurs. Defeat by Aston Villa was the only reverse in the first seven games and by the end of September Derby were ninth and, apart from another very brief spell at ninth place, in November, that was to be as high as they were to get in their first Premiership season. The best sequence of the campaign, five games unbeaten, came towards the end of the year and included three consecutive wins, but from December to January Derby went nine games without a win and defeat by Liverpool dropped the team to 16th. But the 'Bald Eagle' steadied his ship and they climbed to 13th before successive away defeats, to Middlesbrough and Everton, dropped the team back a place.

The best results of the season came with successive victories over Spurs and a cracker of a result at Old Trafford, in which Paulo Wanchope bamboozled the reigning champions into only a second home defeat of the campaign. A draw with Southampton and a win against Aston Villa gave Derby their best points return sequence of the season, 10 from a possible 12, and helped avert any possibility of a quick return to Division One. The team finished a commendable 12th.

The following season Mart Poom replaced Russell Hoult in goal and Paulo Wanchope and Francesco Baiano became the main strike force, although Dean Sturridge weighed in with a nine-goal haul. A poor start ended with successive victories before Derby lost to Villa. But 11 points from a possible 15 elevated them to seventh, the spot they occupied when they ran into a rampant Liverpool, who won 4–0. But November opened with the best win of the season, against Arsenal, and Derby went sixth. They dropped to ninth at the end of November but by the first game of 1998 they were sixth after beating Blackburn and they stayed there until crushed by Leeds at the start of March. That started a decline which saw just one win in eight, but the team finished the campaign with back-to-back wins, and two clean sheets to ensure ninth place.

Derby made it three consecutive Premiership seasons of improvement when they ended 1998–99 in eighth place. Although the goal tally of 40 was among the lowest in the top flight, only five clubs had a better home record and a mere four defeats at Pride Park helped achieve that splendid position. A league double over Liverpool, with the enigmatic Wanchope scoring in both games, was the obvious highlight of the season, along with being as high as second in the Premiership table in September. Indeed this proved to be Derby's best season in the top flight, as the following campaign proved an eight-month struggle to avoid relegation.

By the last week of August 1999 Derby were 19th. A couple of wins improved the position to 14th but the writing was already on the wall. Losing at Liverpool plunged the Rams into the relegation zone and they stayed there until the first game of the New Year when beating Watford took them out of the bottom three. They stayed 17th until Watford again provided them with a lift and a draw at Vicarage Road elevated County to 16th. Although Derby lost to West Ham, four unbeaten games kept them safe enough even to lose to Chelsea in the last game. But 16th place became 17th by the end of the following season and Jim Smith was replaced by Colin Todd in October 2001. Todd was sacked and replaced by John Gregory in January, but it was too late and Derby never moved from 19th place. A staggering 24 defeats that season, including seven in a row in the final eight games, confirmed relegation, and an end to the team's six-year stint in the Premiership. A potentially lethal strike force of Malcolm Christie and the very expensive Fabrizio Ravanelli yielded just 18 goals from a total of 33 in the league and Derby used 34 players looking for the elusive winning combination that never came.

MANAGERS

Jim Smith	1995–2001
Colin Todd	2001–2002
John Gregory	2002–2003

Derby County's Lee Carsley (second left) celebrates his goal against Southampton with teammates Deon Burton (left), Paul Trollope (second right) and Chris Powell (right).

Everton

EVERTON'S RECORD IN THE PREMIERSHIP

| Pos. | Season | P | Home: | | | | | Away: | | | | | Total Goals | | Pts |
			W	D	L	F	A	W	D	L	F	A	F	A	
13th	1992-93	42	7	6	8	26	27	8	2	11	27	28	53	55	53
17th	1993-94	42	8	4	9	26	30	4	4	13	16	33	42	63	44
15th	1994-95	42	8	9	4	31	23	3	8	10	13	28	44	51	50
6th	1995-96	38	10	5	4	35	19	7	5	7	29	25	64	44	61
15th	1996-97	38	7	4	8	24	22	3	8	8	20	35	44	57	42
17th	1997-98	38	7	5	7	25	27	2	8	9	16	29	41	56	40
14th	1998-99	38	6	8	5	22	12	5	2	12	20	35	42	47	43
13th	1999-2000	38	7	9	3	36	21	5	5	9	23	28	59	49	50
16th	2000-01	38	6	8	5	29	27	5	1	13	16	32	45	59	42
15th	2001-02	38	8	4	7	26	23	3	6	10	19	34	45	57	43
7th	2002-03	38	11	5	3	28	19	6	3	10	20	30	48	49	59
17th	2003-04	38	8	5	6	27	20	1	7	11	18	37	45	57	39

EVERTON is another club that has had to operate in the shadow of a more successful city neighbour, but at least on Merseyside there are two points of view. Liverpool's last championship was in 1990, so comparisons have grown less severe, but Everton's failure to close the gap on their neighbours is more apparent now than in pre-Premiership days.

For a club of Everton's stature to record just two top 10 finishes in their 100 percent membership of the Premiership is gross underachievement and even then sixth and seventh were merely satisfactory. But when viewed alongside three 15th places, two 14th places and two 13th places, and three campaigns fighting relegation to finish 17th, a picture emerges of the frustration Everton fans have endured since 1993.

Everton's first brush with relegation came in the second Premiership campaign when the team managed one of the all-time great escapes. In the final game they were at home to Wimbledon and, with 20 minutes left, trailed 2–0. Amazingly Everton recovered to win 3–2 and with other results going their way the club avoided relegation by two points. It was a season of contradiction, which had started well with the first three games all victories. Everton were actually top of the table. But three successive defeats undid the previous good work and by the end of the year the team was 16th, after five defeats in a row.

By Easter five defeats in six games, then one point from a possible nine, and a defeat by Leeds, plunged Everton into the relegation zone until they secured safety with that dramatic last-day win over Wimbledon that aroused

Everton's Daniel Amokachi (front) leads the Everton celebrations as teammates (l-r) Gary Ablett, Barry Horne, Matt Jackson, Paul Rideout and Graham Stuart celebrate with the FA Cup.

suspicion about the performance of Dons' 'keeper Hans Segers.

Mike Walker was replaced by Joe Royle but even Goodison's prodigal son couldn't improve matters much and 15th place was a marginal improvement in the campaign after the fright before.

Royle then engineered Everton's best-ever Premiership season, 1995/96, boosted by the FA Cup win in 1995. After spending the first half of the league campaign in the lower half of the table, Everton's Russian rocket, Andrei Kanchelskis, hit the after-burners, scoring 11 of his season's tally in just 15 games, helped by Duncan Ferguson and Daniel Amokachi, and the team jostled between seventh and sixth for the remainder of the campaign. They lost just once in the final 11 games to clinch a best-ever Premiership finish of sixth.

But Everton's fortunes nose-dived, and they finished 15th a year later before the following campaign saw another struggle, culminating in salvation by goal difference, which prevented a sampling of First Division football. By November 1997 Everton were bottom with only three wins and only victory over Bolton lifted them to 18th by January. Two more wins followed and, as it turned out, probably rescued the club, because there were only two more victories in the final 15 games. Only a draw against Coventry, on the final day, and Bolton losing at Chelsea, sent Wanderers down and kept Everton up, by virtue of goal difference of minus 15 to Bolton's minus 20.

Four mediocre seasons followed with boardroom wranglings and underachieving players until the emergence of two heroes as different as chalk and cheese. 2002 saw the arrival of 'der Wunderkind' Wayne Rooney and manager David Moyes on the scene.

Unfortunately, in stark contrast to the astonishing start

Wayne Rooney, Everton.

each had to his Goodison career, neither built on that start and Everton's future still looked decidedly unclear.

Rooney became the youngest Premiership player at 16 when he made his debut, then eclipsed Tommy Lawton's record as Everton's youngest-ever scorer by netting twice in a Worthington Cup defeat of Wrexham. But that was low-key compared to his choice of the England 'keeper to beat with his sensational first Premiership goal, thus becoming the youngest-ever Premiership

scorer at 16 years 360 days.

By then David Moyes had been manager for just seven months, but he transformed the side and by November 2002 Everton sat third in the table after a record run of six

consecutive victories. But only one win in eight followed and Everton slipped to sixth until veteran Dave Watson and American loan-signing Brian McBride ensured two wins which, followed by victory over Leeds, ensured that the team climbed to fifth. Unfortunately five defeats from the last eight games meant finishing seventh, but there was Goodison glee at the emergence of a superstar striker and a good manager.

However, it was another false dawn, as Moyes had to come to terms with Everton's financial plight, which meant he could not compete in the transfer market to build on the previous season. And Rooney, raw talent though he was, failed to replicate his England form in the bread and butter games of the Premiership.

Moyes, Rooney and Everton had an indifferent 2003–04 campaign that ended one place above relegation, with one of the club's lowest-ever points hauls. The best sequence, five games unbeaten, was in the spring, before the last win was recorded on 9 April. The team lost four of the last seven games in a row, before the season was summed-up by a thrashing at fellow strugglers Manchester City on the last day.

With Manchester United and Chelsea lurking with fat cheques trying to prise Rooney away, in the summer of 2004 Everton were in a classic no-win situation. If they cashed in on the teenage sensation they would be unable to attract more quality players to Goodison. If Rooney stayed the wage ceiling at the club would prevent more quality players joining him.

MANAGERS

Howard Kendall	1990–1993
Mike Walker	1994
Joe Royle	1994–1997
Howard Kendall	1997–1998
Walter Smith	1998–2002
David Moyes	March 2002–

Fulham

FULHAM'S RECORD IN THE PREMIERSHIP

			Home:					Away:					Total Goals		
Pos.	Season	P	W	D	L	F	A	W	D	L	F	A	F	A	Pts
13th	2001-02	38	7	7	5	21	16	3	7	9	15	28	36	44	44
14th	2002-03	38	11	3	5	26	18	2	6	11	15	32	41	50	48
9th	2003-04	38	9	4	6	29	21	5	6	8	23	25	52	46	52

FULHAM have been one of the few Premiership clubs to benefit from a financial benefactor prepared to pump millions of pounds into top-flight membership and survival. But even they, as a club, have had to become self-sustaining since Mohamed Al Fayed, owner of Harrods, decided not to pump excess funds into the bottomless pit of a Premiership club.

But it wasn't all plain sailing for the Cottagers, especially as on/off plans for the development of their traditional Craven Cottage home necessitated temporary lodgings at Loftus Road.

Fulham, courtesy of a reasonable budget and Jean Tigana's coaching, only entered the Premiership as recently as 2001, as First Division champions. After nearly shocking Manchester United in the opening game they went on a three-match unbeaten run to sit 10th, but dropped back into mid-table until a seven-game run, yielding 15 points, took them to eighth.

Their neat, attacking football was a welcome addition to the Premiership and a lavishly assembled squad, including record £11.5 million signing Steve Marlet, Steed Malbranque and the exciting if inconsistent Louis Saha, impressed all, although the team did lack a consistent goalscorer and that hampered progress. The team was eventually grateful for the early season points as seven defeats in eight games saw Fulham enter April 2002 in 15th, their lowest placing of the campaign. But seven points and three consecutive clean sheets helped secure survival with a reasonable finish in 13th place.

Internal dissatisfaction between Tigana and Al Fayed, most publicly over the Marlet transfer, which cost that club record fee, not to mention the owner's lack of confidence in Tigana's tactics, marred Fulham's second season in the Premiership. Before the campaign finished, with the team safe in 14th place, Tigana left in April 2003 to be replaced by Chris Coleman, at 32 years old the youngest manager in the Premiership. The team had reached as high as fifth, although they had been third after two games, during the campaign. Managerial problems aside, four separate cup competitions added 20 games to the fixture list, although eight Inter-Toto games produced a trophy and a post-Christmas slump, in which Fulham recovered from a season low of 16th to take seven points from the last three games, allowing the team to secure 14th place.

Coleman and Fulham learnt quickly and a superb start to the third Premiership campaign was testimony to Coleman's ability as much as the confidence Al Fayed had in his manager. The team lost just one game in the first nine before the victory at Old Trafford that finally saw recognition for the Premiership force Fulham had become and they went into November fifth in the league. The inevitable glitch came that month but the team recovered and claimed a draw at Highbury that added to a growing reputation and they were as high as fourth by December.

Fulham suffered two defeats at the turn of the year which saw them enter 2004 fifth in the table, but their form was erratic and too many draws hindered recovery. Yet recover they did, and in winning half of their last six games they finished ninth.

With a return to Craven Cottage to look forward to Fulham had ridden out the usually troublesome early Premiership years and with Coleman and Al Fayed proving a more than useful combination the club's fans were very optimistic about the Premiership years ahead.

MANAGERS

Jean Tigana	2000–2003
Chris Coleman	April 2003–present

Fulham's manager Jean Tigana can not explain his side's poor performance against Everton.

Ipswich Town

IPSWICH TOWN'S RECORD IN THE PREMIERSHIP

			Home:					Away:					Total Goals		
Pos.	*Season*	*P*	*W*	*D*	*L*	*F*	*A*	*W*	*D*	*L*	*F*	*A*	*F*	*A*	*Pts*
16th	1992-93	42	8	9	4	29	22	4	7	10	21	33	50	55	52
19th	1993-94	42	5	8	8	21	32	4	8	9	14	26	35	58	43
22nd	1994-95	42	5	3	13	24	34	2	3	16	12	59	36	93	27
5th	2000-01	38	11	5	3	31	15	9	1	9	26	27	57	42	66
18th	2001-02	38	6	4	9	20	24	3	5	11	21	40	41	64	36

FOUNDER members of the Premiership, Ipswich reached as high as fourth in their first campaign, and were it not for seven draws in that opening spell, they might have made more of an impact. Though it must be said that their draws at Old Trafford and at home to Liverpool and Spurs were commendable.

With 35-year-old John Wark in his third spell at Portman Road, and Mick Stockwell in midfield, Ipswich didn't lose until their ninth game, at Oldham, but recovered to draw with Sheffield United and beat Leeds to move into eighth place. That was their highest until January, when Manchester United were beaten and suddenly people were beginning to notice the team from Suffolk, though the term 'Tractor Boys' was considered by some to be derogatory.

Matt Holland, Ipswich Town's 'Mr Consistency'.

Unfortunately that was to be the zenith for Ipswich and they fell away badly, going 13 games without a win and dropping to 17th before arresting the slide with victory over Norwich. They then lost to Palace before ending the first Premiership campaign with a win over Forest that secured 16th place in the final table.

The second season suffered badly from a dreadful scoring record, just 35 from the 42 games, which when the start to the campaign is considered is amazing. Three successive victories put Town second but eight games without a win followed before Wimbledon were beaten. Unfortunately only two points were gathered from the next four fixtures before an Eddie Youds goal beat Blackburn. Two wins and three draws lifted Ipswich to 11th, but defeat at Anfield saw them slump to 14th. Another five games produced just three draws and alarm bells started to ring. Sheffield United were beaten but then Arsenal crushed Ipswich at home and although the team won the next match, against Villa, it turned out to be the last victory of the campaign, and there were still 11 games to go. Relegation was a distinct possibility. Indeed, only a last day injury-time winner by Mark Stein put Sheffield United down, 3–2 losers to Chelsea, and saved Ipswich, who stayed up by one point.

Ipswich finally went down at the end of 1994–95 and it proved a record-breaking season for all the wrong reasons. The club was relegated with the most defeats in Premiership history, 22, the lowest-ever points total, 27, and suffered the heaviest Premiership defeat, 9–0 against Manchester United. The side only won two games in a row once, while the rest of the campaign was a catalogue of winless runs and consecutive defeats. Ipswich were in the bottom two from the end of November and bottom from 15 April. Goals were the main problem, with 93 too many at the wrong end, and only 36, one more than the previous campaign, at the right end.

Ipswich returned to the top flight in 2000 and surprised everyone with a superb season, finishing fifth. It would have been even higher had they not dropped five points in their last three matches. Two more wins and they would have been runners-up, because a six-game unbeaten run put Ipswich third by 21 April. Nevertheless a best-ever Premiership finish won George Burley Manager of the Year.

The following season again brought relegation. After just a single win in the first 17 games, leaving them bottom, Ipswich rallied with seven wins from eight to earn the relative security of 12th place by February. This was followed by yet another dismal run of 13 games and only one win, which meant relegation again for the Suffolk club.

MANAGERS

John Lyall	1990–1994
George Burley	December 1994–2002
Joe Royle	October 2002–present

Leeds United

THREE YEARS to the day after contesting the semi-final of the Champions League, Leeds United slipped out of the Premiership with a whimper, when their struggle to avoid relegation ended with another heavy defeat, 4–1 at Bolton. In fairness the rot had set in two years earlier when, in an attempt to build on success in Europe's premier competition, the club had not only spent recklessly – up to £100 million is the conservative estimate – but also mortgaged future attendances at Elland Road to subsidise the dream of conquering Europe.

Unfortunately, the players that were brought in weren't good enough to bring the success necessary to sustain their salaries and administration loomed. When that was avoided at the eleventh hour in 2002–03 Peter Ridsdale, who as chairman had sanctioned David O'Leary's spending spree, which made up the bulk of that nine-figure debt, had long gone. So too had Professor John McKenzie, and the consortium that took over at Elland Road couldn't stem the tide that was to sweep Leeds into Division One.

It was a far cry from 2001 when Leeds' odyssey, from established Premiership club to a top-six rating, began. With a fantastic blend of youth and experience under one of the game's up and coming young managers, David O'Leary, the future looked bright at Elland Road. O'Leary's tenure had started following the shock departure of George Graham for Spurs and in that first season, after picking up the reins, he guided the team to a Premiership-best finish of fourth place.

Leeds had managed a couple of fifth-place finishes under Howard Wilkinson, and another under George Graham in 1998,

The Leeds United team line up for a Champions League clash – where are they now?

but under O'Leary Leeds fans salivated at the prospect of mounting a serious challenge to Manchester United and Arsenal.

The start of season 1998/99 did not go well, and the team were unable to recover from eight draws in the first 11 games, which saw a slide down to ninth place. But five wins out of six, with Jimmy Floyd Hasselbaink scoring six goals in five matches, pushed Leeds back up to third. An erratic turn-of-the-year spell turned into seven successive victories that by April earned fourth place, but three draws prevented further progress and although only one game was lost in the last eight, four draws did the damage and fourth was the end result.

It was an exciting tussle between Leeds and Manchester United, at the head of the Premiership, from the start of 1999–2000, and up to January it was fairly even. But the Reds were without the handicap, as they saw it, of defending their FA Cup title, and thus were fresher going into the second half of the campaign. Leeds were top until the end of January when United took over. 20 February saw the critical 1–0 defeat at Old Trafford and the slow decline to a commendable third place began.

After an inconsistent first half in the following campaign Leeds suddenly clicked after the turn of the year. Four points came from two games before they lost to Newcastle, but a run of 13 unbeaten games, which included 10 wins, six of them in a row, elevated the team from 12th to third, although defeat by Arsenal then put a halt to the title surge. The last two matches were won to claim fourth place.

Leeds then managed that rarest of rare feats by carrying their form over to the start of the next season. By 16 September they were top and only a draw at Old Trafford, at the end of the month, dropped them down to second. But then off-the-field events came into

the equation and affected the players. Jonathan Woodgate, Lee Bowyer and Michael Duberry, plus the ill-timed publication of David O'Leary's book, with its 'inside-track' on the court case, took the focus away from the football.

But three successive wins saw in the New Year with the team occupying pole position, although a subsequent run of seven games without a win, including three defeats, meant sixth place and an end to title dreams, although a last-day victory over Middlesbrough edged Leeds up to fifth.

2002–03 was a pivotal season. Financial problems proved to be too heavy a burden, increased by compensation packages for David O'Leary and his successor Terry Venables, and try as he did, valiantly, Peter Reid, who was also to benefit when he was sacked, couldn't arrest an

alarming slide. The team won the opening two fixtures to go top but six defeats in 10 games plunged Leeds to 13th. A narrow win over West Ham was but a brief 'pit stop', and four consecutive defeats dropped the team to just above the relegation zone. Leeds rallied and reeled off three successive wins, but only managed another five victories from the final 16 games of the season. These proved enough to ensure the team finished safe, but only five points above the final relegation place.

Leeds 'legend' Eddie Gray struggled valiantly to maintain Premiership survival but the plain truth is that the team were not good enough to stay up. Goals were conceded too easily and leads could not be held and so relegation was confirmed, with one game to go, to end Leeds' 14-year stay in the top flight. The worry for Leeds fans was the future, because, as the club slid into Division One, that future was shrouded in financial uncertainty that threatened the very existence of Leeds United.

MANAGERS

Howard Wilkinson	1988–1996
George Graham	1996–1998
David O'Leary	1998–2002
Terry Venables	2002–2003
Peter Reid	March 2003
Eddie Gray	2003–2004

Leeds United's manager David O'Leary in happier times at Elland Road.

Leicester City

LEICESTER CITY'S RECORD IN THE PREMIERSHIP

Pos.	Season	P	Home:					Away:					Total Goals		Pts
			W	D	L	F	A	W	D	L	F	A	F	A	
21st	1994-95	42	5	6	10	28	37	1	5	15	17	43	45	80	29
9th	1996-97	38	7	5	7	22	26	5	6	8	24	28	46	54	47
10th	1997-98	38	6	10	3	21	15	7	4	8	30	26	51	41	53
10th	1998-99	38	7	6	6	25	25	5	7	7	15	21	40	46	49
8th	1999-2000	38	10	3	6	31	24	6	4	9	24	31	55	55	55
13th	2000-01	38	10	4	5	28	23	4	2	13	11	28	39	51	48
20th	2001-02	38	3	7	9	15	34	2	6	11	15	30	30	64	28
18th	2003-04	38	3	10	6	19	28	3	5	11	29	37	48	65	33

Leicester City manager Martin O'Neill celebrates with captain and two-goal hero Matt Elliott on the pitch.

THE PREMIERSHIP history of Leicester City can be roughly divided into two sections: under Martin O'Neill, and under others. The former can be deemed successful, the latter, not so.

With Martin O'Neill at the helm Leicester enjoyed a 'purple patch' in the Premiership and became an established top-flight club, with four top-10 finishes in consecutive seasons, the highest being in 1999–2000 when they finished eighth, with a goal difference of zero, and won the Worthington League Cup.

Under Mark McGhee Leicester had an awful debut season in the Premiership, in 1994–95, and never made it higher than 18th, in October, spending the bulk of the campaign in the bottom two. The Foxes only had two spells, each of three games, unbeaten all season and were relegated in 21st place.

Returning after a year, via the play-offs, with Martin O'Neill in charge and with a strike pair of youth and experience, Emile Heskey and Steve Claridge, helped fire Leicester into ninth place and with perfect timing they hit that finishing spot with victory in their last two games after spending most of the campaign in mid-table. In fact a preoccupation with the Coca-Cola Cup almost cost them their Premiership place due to a nine-game winless run after they won the trophy.

Leicester then had a couple of seasons of consolidation, with successive 10th-place finishes. The team actually went third in September 1997 but lacked a consistent run to boost chances of a top-three finish. A draw at Manchester United and victory over Everton saw Leicester second at the commencement of the following season but a poor defensive record and a mediocre scoring record meant the team had to be content with another 10th place at the end of the campaign.

As the Millennium approached the League Cup

Leicester City celebrate with the Worthington Cup.

again took centre stage and distracted the team's league focus. Before the cup started Leicester were fifth, but by the time they beat Tranmere, in February, they had dropped to 10th. Only three wins in the last four games ensured a more reasonable, and best-ever, Premiership finish in eighth.

But success has its price, and the price Leicester had to pay was to have their impressive young manager wooed by every other club looking for miracles on a tight budget. Celtic won that particular contest and O'Neill left Filbert Street for Parkhead.

With O'Neill gone Peter Taylor came in and the effect, initially, was staggering. An unbeaten eight-game start saw Leicester top the Premiership by October. A couple of defeats followed but Leicester bounced back with three wins and a draw to move back into third place and stayed in the top four until Boxing Day. Five games without a win after that saw them slide down to seventh. Three wins in four games improved their position to fifth, but eight consecutive defeats contributed to a disappointing 13th-place finish and the departure of Peter Taylor and the arrival of Dave Bassett.

Bassett brought Micky Adams to the club and after half a season Adams took over as team manager, but by then it was 'Mission Impossible', as Leicester had long since consigned themselves to relegation. Since beating Derby County, in September, the team had slumped to the bottom of the table. Seven points from 12 then lifted Leicester up to 17th before the damage was done with a 16-game run without a win, including six successive defeats, that relegated the club.

Leicester again came back up at the first attempt but it was the manner of the club's return that caused bitterness among other clubs, notably those for whom administration meant the kind of financial restraints not applied to Filbert Street. Under a new consortium, headed by Leicester's favourite son, Gary Lineker, the Foxes returned to the top flight. But it wasn't a happy homecoming, and the team quickly found life at the top, despite their brand new Walkers Stadium, not to their liking.

There was just a single victory in the opening five games and after two months Leicester were 16th. It got worse by the end of October and the team were in the bottom three, but a November improvement of three wins and a draw saw the highest position of 13th. It wasn't to last, and by the end of January they were back in the relegation zone. Leicester never escaped from the drop zone and a run of 10 games and just one win confirmed another return to Division One.

MANAGERS

Mark McGhee	1994–1995
Martin O'Neill	1995–2000
Peter Taylor	2000–2001
Dave Bassett	2001–2002
Micky Adams	April 2002–present

Liverpool

LIVERPOOL'S RECORD IN THE PREMIERSHIP

Pos.	Season	P	Home: W	D	L	F	A	Away: W	D	L	F	A	Total Goals F	A	Pts
6th	1992-93	42	13	4	4	41	18	3	7	11	21	37	62	55	59
8th	1993-94	42	12	4	5	33	23	5	5	11	26	32	59	55	60
4th	1994-95	42	13	5	3	38	13	8	6	7	27	24	65	37	74
3rd	1995-96	38	14	4	1	46	13	6	7	6	24	21	70	34	71
4th	1996-97	38	10	6	3	38	19	9	5	5	24	18	62	37	68
3rd	1997-98	38	13	2	4	42	16	5	9	5	26	26	68	42	65
7th	1998-99	38	10	5	4	44	24	5	4	10	24	25	68	49	54
4th	1999-2000	38	11	4	4	28	13	8	6	5	23	17	51	30	67
3rd	2000-01	38	13	4	2	40	14	7	5	7	31	25	71	39	69
2nd	2001-02	38	12	5	2	33	14	12	3	4	34	16	67	30	80
5th	2002-03	38	9	8	2	30	16	9	2	8	31	25	61	41	64
4th	2003-04	38	10	4	4	29	15	6	8	5	26	22	55	37	60

SUCH is the burden of expectation at Anfield, where a record 18 championships have ended up, that only two finishes outside the top six, in the first dozen years of the Premiership, is considered a failure, despite the club being third in the all-time ranking with only Manchester United and Arsenal ahead of them. It is a failure because of the team's inability to claim even a single Premiership crown, while United have been collecting titles as regularly as Liverpool did in the 1970s and 80s.

Like Chelsea, Liverpool have done very well on the cup front, especially in 2001, when Gerard Houllier's team collected five trophies in the calendar year. It would be bad enough for Liverpool fans if it were just comparison with Chelsea's record, but always lurking on the shoulder of any Liverpool manager has been the shadow of previous League Championship titles under Shankly, Paisley, Fagan and Dalglish.

Liverpool's best Premiership finish was second place in 2002.

Early in the campaign Gerard Houllier had been rushed to hospital for life-saving heart surgery but, after Phil Thompson took the reins, and after the lethal scoring potential of Michael Owen had been supplemented by Nicolas Anelka, the team looked like it could take the title. Indeed they went top for a month, having lost just two games from their first 15 fixtures. But consecutive defeats by Chelsea and Arsenal dropped Liverpool to third. Anelka came in January but the 'Incredible Sulk', as he was nicknamed in certain quarters, did little to improve the side. Indeed some felt his inclusion was detrimental, as just four goals in 20 appearances, from 13 starts, would tend to suggest, reinforced by Houllier's eventual decision not to make his move from Paris St Germain permanent.

Early 2002 was not a good time for Liverpool. Despite a fairly consistent line-up, results were anything but. Five games went without a win, until Danny

Liverpool's players celebrate with the Worthington Cup.

Liverpool's 'God', Robbie Fowler, celebrates scoring one of his 171 goals for the Anfield club.

Murphy's clincher at Old Trafford. Three more wins followed and the team were second. After a draw with Everton Liverpool reeled off seven consecutive victories. The fifth took them top with just five games to go. But a critical 1–0 defeat at Spurs proved too damaging. Even back-to-back wins over Blackburn and Ipswich couldn't rescue the situation and Liverpool fell an agonising seven points short of champions Arsenal.

The first two Premiership seasons had ended disappointingly, in sixth and eighth place respectively, but there was improvement in 1994–95. Ian Rush and Robbie Fowler proved formidable, netting 26 goals between them in 1993–94, and building on that the Sorcerer and his apprentice swapped positions at the top of the scoring charts. Fowler's 25 goals, supplemented by Rush's dozen, kept Liverpool in the top five all season. An eight-game unbeaten run saw them third at the turn of the year but three consecutive draws affected any title hopes, as did losing three of their last 15 games.

Roy Evans took over after Graeme Souness left, and it took two attempts by the Scot before the board accepted his resignation. In that first season Roy guided the team to third – they even made it to second in January – but Liverpool couldn't keep pace with Manchester United and Newcastle, despite Robbie Fowler's 28 league goals and 14 from record £8.5 million signing Stan Collymore.

Then the Anfield board brought Gerard Houllier in and set up the most bizarre dual management arrangement in Premiership history thus far. But despite another third place, in 1997, it was obvious that such an arrangement wasn't going to work and so, after more than three decades at Anfield, Evans was out and Houllier assumed sole charge in July 1998.

Seventh place for 1998–99 was explained away as 'transitional', and when that was improved to fourth and then third in 2001, a new era had arrived, or so the fans thought. That feeling became conviction when Houllier delivered runners-up spot a year later, not to mention an armful of trophies.

'Build from a position of strength' was the edict issued by Shankly but Houllier's signings, mostly from France and Africa, never gelled with the commitment and work ethic built upon the steel of Owen, Gerrard, Carragher, Murphy and McAllister. Many observers felt the manager was trying to replicate the methods of Arsene Wenger but, whereas his countryman built upon an Anglo-Saxon spine then gradually replaced it with Continental flair, Houllier's imports didn't work and flattered to deceive.

Liverpool failed to progress from second place and the following season finished fifth after starting so well. Unbeaten in the opening 12 games, they were top by 19 October, after a 1–0 win over Leeds that was a fifth consecutive victory in a run of seven. 'Boro inflicted a first defeat that not only ended the run but started one of the opposite kind and a stretch of 11 games without a win damaged

not only title hopes, but also aspirations of qualifying for a Champions League slot. Liverpool had to settle for fifth place.

Season 2003/04 may prove pivotal in Liverpool's tortuous journey towards a Premiership title. Unbeatable Arsenal was hard enough to swallow, but throwing in 'Chelski' and a hurting Manchester United, who had their worst season in the Premiership for 10 years, increased pressure on the Anfield club. Media negativity concerning Houllier's forays into the transfer market, coupled with the season-long struggle for fourth place, which seemed a valid indicator of how low Anfield standards had fallen, seemed to suggest that Monsieur Houllier's 'oliday was set to end, sooner rather than later. As the season came to a conclusion news of a possible £60 million investment by the Thai Prime Minister Thaksin Shinawatra emerged and, despite a rival bid by a Liverpool fan, businessman Steve Morgan, looked to be favoured by the club's board. Morgan eventually withdrew his offer, with the Thai deal still to be ratified. The board did, however, choose to act on Gerard Houllier's position, which still looked decidedly unsure, despite delivery of the fourth place that club chairman David Moores had designated 'a minimum requirement'. On 24 May 2004 Liverpool and their French manager parted company after six years of entente that proved less cordial than anyone connected with the club would have wanted. He was the first Liverpool manager to be sacked in almost 50 years, the last being Don Welsh, in 1956.

MANAGERS

Graeme Souness	1991–1994
Roy Evans	January 1994–1998
Roy Evans and Gerard Houllier	
Joint managers	1998
Gerard Houllier	July 1998–May 2004

Manchester City

Pos.	Season	P	Home: W	D	L	F	A	Away: W	D	L	F	A	Total Goals F	A	Pts
9th	1992-93	42	7	8	6	30	25	8	4	9	26	26	56	51	57
16th	1993-94	42	6	10	5	24	22	3	8	10	14	27	38	49	45
17th	1994-95	42	8	7	6	37	28	4	6	11	16	36	53	64	49
18th	1995-96	38	7	7	5	21	19	2	4	13	12	39	33	58	38
18th	2000-01	38	4	3	12	20	31	4	7	8	21	34	41	65	34
9th	2002-03	38	9	2	8	28	26	6	4	9	19	28	47	54	51
16th	2003-04	38	5	9	5	31	24	4	5	10	24	30	55	54	41

MANCHESTER CITY always seem to play second fiddle to United in the Premiership and the club's record is among the worst of all the clubs since the Premiership began. There have been just two top-10 finishes, ninth in 1993 and again 10 years later, two relegations, 1996 and 2001, and the other three finishes were just above relegation.

City had high hopes when they returned to the Premiership, under Kevin Keegan, in 2002, and, with a new stadium to look forward to, the future looked bright for the blue half of Manchester. However, it proved to be another false dawn. Despite investing large sums of money in the likes of the ex-Anfield quartet Nicolas Anelka, Robbie Fowler, Steve McManaman and David James, Kevin Keegan only just managed to prevent a third relegation, in 2004, after a very disappointing season which was highlighted by one disastrous run of 14 games without a win that plunged the team into trouble at the foot of the table.

With alarm bells ringing City arrested the run with victory at Bolton in late February, but the season that had started so well with three wins out of four was in danger of ending with the club having the best stadium in Division One. But, for once, Manchester United provided the crutch, however unwillingly, when the derby win at the City of Manchester Stadium became City's best for two decades. Even then the team proceeded to heap more misery on their long-suffering fans by keeping them guessing which division the club would operate in come the following campaign.

After thrashing United, and ending their chase of Arsenal for the title, which was one small crumb of comfort, City then lost two and drew four games before a goal from Paulo Wanchope ended Newcastle's Champions League aspirations and injected much-needed belief into an underachieving City side that still faced the drop. Survival hopes were then hit by defeat at Middlesbrough but, in typical enigmatic fashion, City ended the campaign with a crushing defeat of Everton, to finish eight points above the last relegated club but only two places higher in 16th.

It was an unfortunately familiar tale for City who, as a club, have never really established acceptable credentials in the Premiership and have suffered by comparison to their more successful neighbours. And yet they had a respectable first campaign, finishing 1992–93 in ninth place

The City of Manchester Stadium, home of Manchester City.

Vital penalty saves by David James ensured Premiership survival for City in 2004.

which, had they won their final game instead of getting thrashed, would have been fifth.

Ironically, fifth was the highest that the team managed during that initial season, a position they managed after losing just twice in the opening seven fixtures, but five games without a win plunged City to 14th before four wins in a row boosted them to sixth. Unfortunately, the team couldn't string together more than four unbeaten games and the 5–2 defeat at Everton, on the final day of the season, was a sign of things to come.

Under Brian Horton City fared even worse and finished 16th and then 17th before Alan Ball took over at Maine Road for 1995–96. And with City fans telling themselves 'it couldn't get any worse', it did. City were relegated, on goal difference, having conceded seven more goals than Coventry and Southampton, who survived.

After a draw City lost eight games in a row to sit very uncomfortably at the bottom of the Premiership, and to rub salt in the wound the last defeat of that run was at Old Trafford. Amazingly City then produced their best run of the season to climb to 15th. But erratic form meant that they went into the final game as one of three clubs facing the drop and when the team came back from 2–0 down to Liverpool, at half-time, Alan Ball instructed his team to retain possession because he had heard that one of the other threatened sides was losing. This turned out not to be true, and if City had gained a winner they would have been safe, but down they went. Scoring wasn't really City's strong suit in the campaign and 33 was a poor total that was a big factor in relegation by goal difference.

City then endured a 'blue' period, dropping as far as the lower reaches of Division Two before beginning their slow climb back to the top flight. It took five years, and when they recovered a Premiership place they lost it immediately and the club, in sacking Joe Royle, pettily argued that he was dismissed as a First Division manager and therefore entitled to less compensation.

Kevin Keegan took City back into the Premiership as First Division champions and in that first campaign back, with some quality players, the highest the team got was eighth in a rollercoaster season. But there was an improvement from the lower half of the table, up to Christmas, although it took an unbeaten run of three games in April to help secure a top-10 finish, just, in ninth place.

Then came that brush with relegation in 2004 that doesn't augur well for the immediate future. Once the campaign ended speculation was rife about the future of Keegan as a worried City board considered the potential disaster relegation would inflict on a club that needs Premiership football to survive.

It's one of the truisms of football that in the city of Manchester support for City is more local than those who follow United, but that is no longer enough to prosper in the top flight.

MANAGERS

Peter Reid	1990–1993
Brian Horton	1993–1995
Alan Ball	1995–1996
Frank Clark	1996–1998
Joe Royle	1998–2001
Kevin Keegan	May 2001–present

Manchester United

MANCHESTER UNITED'S RECORD IN THE PREMIERSHIP

Pos.	Season	P	W	D	L	F	A	W	D	L	F	A	F	A	Pts
					Home:						**Away:**		**Total Goals**		
1st	1992-93	42	14	5	2	39	14	10	7	4	28	17	67	31	84
1st	1993-94	42	14	6	1	39	13	13	5	3	41	25	80	38	92
2nd	1994-95	42	16	4	1	42	4	10	6	5	35	24	77	28	88
1st	1995-96	38	15	4	0	36	9	10	3	6	37	26	73	35	82
1st	1996-97	38	12	5	2	38	17	9	7	3	38	27	76	44	75
2nd	1997-98	38	13	4	2	42	9	10	4	5	31	17	73	26	77
1st	1998-99	38	14	4	1	45	18	8	9	2	35	19	80	37	79
1st	1999-2000	38	15	4	0	59	16	13	3	3	38	29	97	45	91
1st	2000-01	38	15	2	2	49	12	9	6	4	30	19	79	31	80
3rd	2001-02	38	11	2	6	40	17	13	3	3	47	28	87	45	77
1st	2002-03	38	16	2	1	42	12	9	6	4	32	22	74	34	83
3rd	2003-04	38	12	4	3	37	15	11	2	6	27	20	64	35	75

IN THE first 12 years of the Premiership Manchester United almost made the title their exclusive property. The Premiership trophy rested in the Old Trafford trophy room eight times and when the club didn't win the title, it only ever finished lower than second once, when United were third in 2002. But the team failed, miserably by their standards, in their worst Premiership campaign for 10 years, finishing outside the top two, in 2003–04, for only the second time in Premiership history, a full 15 points behind champions Arsenal and equalling their lowest-ever points total of 75.

Back in 1992 the league title had eluded Manchester United since the glory days of Matt Busby, who had taken the club to the championship in 1967. For United it became something of a 'Holy Grail', and it was with perfect timing that the inaugural Premiership season saw United lift the trophy for the first time in 26 years.

The catalyst for that first Premiership title was undoubtedly Eric Cantona. Signed from Leeds United, with whom he won the last First Division championship, Eric guided United to four Premiership titles in five years, although his fiery character and undoubted football talent were a volatile mix. After his infamous kung fu attack on a Crystal Palace fan in 1995 he was suspended for eight months.

Without Eric United were beaten to the 1995 title by Blackburn but the *enfant terrible* promised the United fans he would make up for his actions and he was true to his word. 1995–96 saw the double, which Cantona had been part of in 1994, return to Old Trafford.

United retained the league title a year later, but Cantona shook the football world by

Manchester United's Ole Gunnar Solskjaer scores the winning goal that clinches the Champions League win over Bayern Munich and the treble.

retiring to pursue fame on another stage, as an actor. But by then Eric had already helped Fergie's fledglings to bed into the Old Trafford nest.

As in the 1950s, when the FA Youth Cup provided the 'Busby Babes', it was the Youth Cup-winning side of 1992 that proved a conveyor belt of talent that allowed United to dominate the Premiership in that decade. The Neville brothers, Gary and Phil, Nicky Butt, Paul Scholes and David Beckham were half of the team that won four Premierships in the five seasons after Cantona's departure.

United's strength and resilience was a mirror of their manager and on the two occasions the club slipped to runners-up, 1995 and 1998, they bounced back to win the title the following season. And, as continuous members of the Premiership, United's 12 years to date have been scattered with records.

In 1999–2000 the team scored the most goals in a Premiership season, 97 in 38 games. That same season also saw a return of 28 wins and just three defeats, a repeat of the previous campaign, a record they shared with Arsenal until 2004. And, for good measure, United racked up a record total of 92 points, with three points for a win, in 1993–94. Not surprisingly United hold the scoring record for the highest Premiership victory, 9–0 against Ipswich on 4 March 1995, when Andy Cole scored five goals, the best individual total in one game which he shares with Alan Shearer.

In the transfer market, too, United are record breakers. The top three British transfer records involved the club. In 2002 Sir Alex Ferguson spent a record £30 million in signing Rio Ferdinand from Leeds United. A year earlier Juan Sebastian Veron had arrived from Lazio for £28.1 million and, arguably the best value for money, Ruud Van Nistelrooy moved to Old

Manchester United's Peter Schmeichel celebrates the treble.

Trafford from PSV Eindhoven for £19 million in that same year.

Ironically, the highest outgoing transfer from United was also the most controversial. In 2003 David Beckham left Old Trafford, for Real Madrid, in a £25 million deal. It was the departure of Beckham, without a suitable replacement coming in, and the absence of Rio Ferdinand, banned for eight months for missing a routine drugs test, that were the main reasons for United not proving a stronger challenge to Arsenal for the title. United led the table by four points on the day Ferdinand played his last game of 2003–04. After that defeat at Wolves, United recovered with two successive wins, but a hammer-blow came when Steve McClaren's Middlesbrough won at Old Trafford and caused a discernable gap to emerge between United and new leaders Arsenal. That gap widened as United were held to a couple of

draws before the title dream was ended by a humiliating derby defeat. Although the team bounced back with a win over Spurs, and managed a first clean sheet in eight games, the challenge to Arsenal and Chelsea was over.

As United suffered from the inference that the balance of power in the Premiership had shifted to the capital, they had a number of records to point to, as well as a few they didn't want, before being written-off as a Premiership-winning force.

True the team had suffered from a lack of goals, with too much reliance on Ruud Van Nistelrooy, who scored more than twice as many as Paul Scholes, his nearest rival, could muster. In scoring just 64 league goals United fell short of their previous worst, in 1992–93, of

67, but at least they won the title then. Nevertheless, there are still a lot more positive records on United's Premiership scoresheet than negatives.

No team has won more Premiership games: 292 to Arsenal's 244.

No club has more Premier-ship points: 983 to the Gunners' 863.

United have the fewest Premiership defeats: 69 against Arsenal's 93.

They have scored the most goals in the Premiership: 927 to Liverpool's 759.

Manchester United also have the record for the most wins in a Premiership campaign, 28, and have scored most goals in a Premiership season, 97. Accusations of a demise should be put on hold, for at least another 12 seasons.

MANAGER

Sir Alex Ferguson   November 1986–present

Middlesbrough

MIDDLESBROUGH'S RECORD IN THE PREMIERSHIP

Pos.	Season	P	Home: W	D	L	F	A	Away: W	D	L	F	A	Total Goals F	A	Pts
21st	1992-93	42	8	5	8	33	27	3	6	12	21	48	54	75	44
12th	1995-96	38	8	3	8	27	27	3	7	9	8	23	35	50	43
19th	1996-97	38	8	5	6	34	25	2	7	10	17	35	51	60	39
9th	1998-99	38	7	9	3	25	18	5	6	8	23	36	48	54	51
12th	1999-2000	38	8	5	6	23	26	6	5	8	23	26	46	52	52
14th	2000-01	38	4	7	8	18	23	5	8	6	26	21	44	44	42
12th	2001-02	38	7	5	7	23	26	5	4	10	12	21	35	47	45
11th	2002-03	38	10	7	2	36	21	3	3	13	12	23	48	44	49
11th	2003-04	38	8	4	7	25	23	5	5	9	19	29	44	52	48

MIDDLESBROUGH'S nine seasons in the Premier League have been a rollercoaster of relegation, bouncing back and just one top-10 finish, as the club tried to establish itself among the elite. 'Boro never got chance to acclimatise, as founder members, because they were relegated after the inaugural season. Yet they had a reasonable first half of that campaign and were in the top six until the end of September, after just two defeats in their first eight games.

But then came a run of just two wins in 17 and although 'Boro arrested the poor sequence with victory over Southampton, the subsequent run of five successive defeats sowed the seeds of relegation as 'Boro plunged to 21st.

The team remained in the bottom three for the rest of the season; indeed defeat by Crystal Palace in April deposited 'Boro at the bottom of the heap. The team scored three goals in each of the last three games, winning two, but it was too little, too late

and they were relegated, five points from safety.

It took three years to return to the Premiership and then the team made a promising start, with just one defeat in the first 10 games. Thanks to five successive wins spanning September and October, they climbed to fourth. But after going fifth prior to Christmas the team had an appalling run of 13 games without a win, including eight consecutive defeats. Although injuries also restricted 'Boro's impact on the

table the team's last day victory at Everton, a fifth unbeaten game in a row, ensured a 12th-place finish.

If their fans were looking for improvement the following campaign they were to be disappointed. Despite Middlesbrough reaching both domestic cup finals, and losing them, the greater concern was the relegation that a congested fixture programme, due to 15 cup matches, undoubtedly caused. Unfortunately the critical points deficit, come May, was due to 'Boro's failure to fulfil a league fixture against Blackburn, for which the club was deducted three points. Had they played and won that game, the club would have stayed in the Premiership instead of being relegated just two points adrift of 17th-placed Coventry.

'Boro's absence lasted just one season and the club retained its top-flight status from 1998–99, when that campaign brought the club its best-ever finish in the Premiership.

Flanked by Chief Executive Keith Lamb and manager Steve McClaren, Juninho signs for 'Boro for the third time.

Bryan Robson took 'Boro back to his Old Trafford stomping ground, in December, and came away with the club's first success there in 69 years, and Middlesbrough sat proudly in fourth place in the league. Unfortunately, nine games without another victory meant a slide to 13th until the team dug out a seven-game unbeaten run, but after recovering to seventh they were crushed by Arsenal and never won again that season, finishing ninth.

Two mediocre seasons followed and the board's patience with Robson, after 12th and 14th-place finishes, wore out. After being booed on the final day of 2000–01, Robbo stepped down saying that he knew his time was up after seven years. Chairman Steve Gibson brought in Steve McClaren, Manchester United's assistant manager, and gave him a five-year contract.

McClaren's start couldn't have been worse, and after losing the first four games of the season seven points from nine elevated the team out of the relegation zone, to 12th. But scoring was to prove 'Boro's biggest problem and they scored just one goal in six games before Noel Whelan netted in the defeat by Arsenal, in the final game of 2001. But McClaren, in his first managerial season, turned things around slowly, and by April Middlesbrough were in the top 10, and if they hadn't lost all of their last four games they would have finished a lot higher than 12th.

Under McClaren, highly regarded enough as a coach to be constantly linked with a return to Old Trafford, as well as having several spells as England coach, 'Boro have improved season by season. In his second campaign the team were as high as third, and in the top 10 until December, but they slipped in the second half of the season to finish one place higher than the previous season.

It's a good thing Middles-brough won their first trophy in the club's 129-year history, the Carling League Cup, because the league position was poor for most of the campaign with 10th place, at the end of November, the highest the team managed. After losing to Newcastle 'Boro went seven games without conceding a goal, but unfortunately they only scored five in that spell and by the turn of the year the team was down to 15th.

The position improved, marginally, in 2004 but the team, which still experienced problems in scoring, was unable to put together a meaningful run. Superb results, such as winning at Old Trafford and taking a point from Highbury, were interspersed with crazy results, such as the eight-goal carnival against Birmingham and the defeat by Wolves, and the season fizzled out, culminating in the last-day humiliation at Portsmouth that left 'Boro 11th.

MANAGERS

Lennie Lawrence	1991–1994
Bryan Robson	1994–2001
Steve McClaren	July 2001–present

Middlesbrough's chairman Steve Gibson lifts the Carling Cup trophy.

Newcastle United

NEWCASTLE UNITED'S RECORD IN THE PREMIERSHIP

Pos.	Season	P	Home: W	D	L	F	A	Away: W	D	L	F	A	Total Goals F	A	Pts
3rd	1993-94	42	14	4	3	51	14	9	4	8	31	27	82	41	77
6th	1994-95	42	14	6	1	46	20	6	6	9	21	27	67	47	72
2nd	1995-96	38	17	1	1	38	9	7	5	7	28	28	66	37	78
2nd	1996-97	38	13	3	3	54	20	6	8	5	19	20	73	40	68
13th	1997-98	38	8	5	6	22	20	3	6	10	13	24	35	44	44
13th	1998-99	38	7	6	6	26	25	4	7	8	22	29	48	54	46
11th	1999-2000	38	10	5	4	42	20	4	5	10	21	34	63	54	52
11th	2000-01	38	10	4	5	26	17	4	5	10	18	33	44	50	51
4th	2001-02	38	12	3	4	40	23	9	5	5	34	29	74	52	71
3rd	2002-03	38	15	2	2	36	17	6	4	9	27	31	63	48	69
5th	2003-04	38	11	5	3	33	14	2	12	5	19	26	52	40	56

NEWCASTLE'S life in the Premiership can be summed up in two words: glorious underachievement. Glorious because of being runners-up twice, in the first four seasons in the top flight, after promotion in 1993, plus another three top-six finishes. Underachievement, because in those two campaigns, which ended in second place, they never pushed on and claimed their first league championship since 1927.

The best chance of breaking that title duck came in 1995–96 when, crazily, Kevin Keegan's team threw away a January 12-point advantage over Manchester United to be overhauled by Alex Ferguson's side to finish second, four points adrift.

The following season Newcastle also finished runners-up. They spent an amazing eight months in pole position, only to blow their title hopes, big time, in the space of four games. The biggest shock was losing at West Ham, but after drawing at Maine Road, Manchester United completed the league double over Newcastle with Eric Cantona ensuring a shock first home defeat of the campaign for Keegan's men.

The Magpies got back on track by beating West Ham but losing at Liverpool, in a game dubbed the game of the century, finally ended their championship hopes. Although there was only one more defeat that season Newcastle finished runners-up. It was a bitter pill to swallow for devout Geordie fans, who had seen their heroes top the Premiership from day one.

Seen in context that season had to be viewed as progress after finishing third in their first Premiership campaign and sixth the campaign after. But Newcastle fans, drunk on a diet

The Newcastle United team line up for a pre-match photograph.

of cavalier football with Ginola and Asprilla supplying the flair and 'Sir Les' Ferdinand banging in the goals, wanted silverware, and in a brave attempt to boost title chances Kevin Keegan went out and paid a world record £15 million to bring Alan Shearer back to his native north-east.

That bold move almost paid off. After two defeats in the first three games Newcastle went top of the table, with the sixth consecutive win in a run of seven, by October and Shearer's contribution was six goals, while Sir Les weighed in with half a dozen of his own.

Newcastle's stay at the top lasted less than a month and, after losing to Arsenal, it was another five games before another victory and the 7–1 thumping of Spurs kicked off another fine run that re-ignited title hopes, but then came a massive blow in January. After beating Leeds to go fourth Kevin Keegan stunned the Magpies by resigning after five years in the job and, as at Anfield 20 years earlier, Kenny Dalglish replaced Keegan. But, despite getting back to third by the end of February, two defeats in a row effectively ended title dreams, and, in the kind of irony football throws up from time to time, it was yet another 4–3 defeat at Liverpool that proved pivotal in the chase for the Premiership crown.

Although Newcastle remained unbeaten for the rest of the campaign too many draws proved costly and their fans had to settle for another second place.

Four seasons of frustrating mediocrity followed, in which more news was made off the field, with the sensational sacking of Kenny Dalglish and his replacement Ruud Gullit taking Newcastle perilously close to the relegation zone, not to mention dropping and falling out with the Gallowgate's favourite son, Alan Shearer. Throw in scandals involving directors and Geordie fans had a pretty raw time of it, but after Ruud Gullit resigned, citing poor performances and constant scrutiny of his private life, St James' Park welcomed another messiah, and this time it was one of their own, Bobby Robson.

Despite his 66 years Robson galvanised Newcastle and with only five defeats in the first half of the year Newcastle topped the Premiership for the Christmas programme. Successive defeats were followed by six unbeaten games that took them second and back into title contention, until they were removed from the race by two consecutive March defeats. United didn't lose again until the final day, but the damage had been done. Fourth place in Robson's first season

was a success, but the championship had been there for the taking: another case of déjà vu for United.

Things got even better the following season when Newcastle, after flirting with 19th place with just four points from the first five games, began a slow but sure climb up the table, losing just four games and going top by late January. But, despite three wins and a draw Newcastle couldn't keep pace with Manchester United and Arsenal, finally giving up the chase with three successive April defeats although they rallied to finish third, the club's highest position for six years.

Geordie fans had every right to feel that they might make serious inroads into the top of the Premiership in the next campaign, but realistic predictions suggested that fourth place and another tilt at Champions League football was an achievable aim. However, a drastic re-evaluation was necessary when the team plunged to 19th by the end of September, with the first victory

not coming until game number seven. By then the number of draws was a portent of things to come: three in the first five games.

Newcastle slowly climbed the table and by February were in that all-important fourth place, but they fell back to fifth with two defeats the following month, a position they maintained in April. There were no wins in May, with three draws to end the campaign, which meant that the team were grateful to Manchester United for beating Aston Villa to hand Sir Bobby's team the consolation of fifth place and the remaining UEFA Cup slot. Too many draws, an incredible 12 away from home, and only two away wins marred what should have been a better finish.

End of season doubts about Robson's position, Shearer's forthcoming final season and what the future held for the most passionate and patient fans in the Premiership ensured that 2004–05 would be a season for watching events at St James' Park very closely.

MANAGERS

Kevin Keegan	1992–1997
Kenny Dalglish	1997–1998
Ruud Gullit	1998–1999
Sir Bobby Robson	September 1999–present

From left to right: the man who signed the cheque, Sir John Hall; Alan Shearer who cost £15 million; and the manager who paid the world record fee, Kevin Keegan.

Norwich City

NORWICH CITY'S RECORD IN THE PREMIERSHIP

Pos.	Season	P	W	D	L	F	A	W	D	L	F	A	F	A	Pts
				Home:						**Away:**			**Total Goals**		
3rd	1992-93	42	13	6	2	31	19	8	3	10	30	46	61	65	72
12th	1993-94	42	4	9	8	26	29	8	8	5	39	32	65	61	53
20th	1994-95	42	8	8	5	27	21	2	5	14	10	33	37	54	43

NORWICH CITY'S stay in the new top flight of English football lasted just three years, but their free-flowing football won them many friends in the game, friends who welcomed them back with open arms after they won the First Division championship in 2004.

Under Mike Walker Norwich made a storming start to the very first Premiership campaign, beating Arsenal on the opening day and following up with victory over Chelsea and a draw with Everton that saw the team second in the table. The Canaries then lost to Manchester City before embarking on a terrific run of five successive wins, the third of which took them top of the Premiership by September.

A record hammering at Blackburn cost them pole position and they went on to drop points in the next two games, but four consecutive victories saw Norwich top of the table, with a five-point lead over Blackburn, Aston Villa and Chelsea. The first of those wins, at Boundary Park, saw Mark Robins hit the first televised Premiership hat-trick. But it was a lack of goals that was to prove costly for the team. Despite commendably sticking to playing the game through the middle a lightweight attack weighed heavily against them and although they were still top of the table at the end of January, a five-game run, in which they only won once, dropped Norwich to third.

The team rallied with a hat-trick of victories but it was the last significant sequence and seven points from the last 18 available meant the side that had spent more than a third of the campaign top of the Premiership had to settle for third place.

After losing the opening game of the following season to Manchester United, Norwich recovered to climb to fourth after picking up 11 points out of 15. An even better sequence, 15 from 21, saw the Canaries up to second before a surprise reverse at Oldham. But the turn of the year proved pivotal in the fortunes of both club and the team.

Still handily placed, sixth, the team were beaten at home by Newcastle and soon afterwards Mike Walker resigned, amid accusations by chairman Robert Chase that the Norwich manager been poached by Everton. Shortly afterwards Walker signed a three-and-a-half-year contract to take over at Goodison Park and the effect on the team was staggering. Seven successive draws were followed by two defeats before Mike Walker brought his new team to face his old one and the Canaries registered a satisfactory win at Carrow Road. But there was to be only one more win in the remaining nine games, at Liverpool, and the Norwich side ended the campaign 12th.

Norwich began their third Premiership campaign with a defeat, but when they recovered to go four games unbeaten there was no inkling that the team were to face a battle against relegation. The side lost just three games before December and began the holiday programme in seventh place. But the cracks appeared when Norwich won just once in their next 14 games and slid to 14th. Brief respite came from victory over neighbours Ipswich, but a seven-game losing streak resulted in relegation, although they did end their Premiership stay with a draw.

In their nine seasons away from the top flight Norwich refused to surrender their principles and when TV cook Delia Smith took over and improved not only the catering at Carrow Road, but also the entire club, her new regime was rewarded with a passport back to the Premiership when they lifted the First Division championship in 2003–04.

MANAGERS

Mike Walker	1992–1994
John Deehan	1994–1995
Martin O'Neill	1995

Mike Walker and Jeremy Goss celebrate Norwich City's victory over Bayern Munich.

Nottingham Forest

NOTTINGHAM FOREST'S RECORD IN THE PREMIERSHIP

Pos.	Season	P	Home: W	D	L	F	A	Away: W	D	L	F	A	Total Goals F	A	Pts
22nd	1992-93	42	6	4	11	17	25	4	6	11	24	37	41	62	40
3rd	1994-95	42	12	6	3	36	18	10	5	6	36	25	72	43	77
9th	1995-96	38	11	6	2	29	17	4	7	8	21	37	50	54	58
20th	1996-97	38	3	9	7	15	27	3	7	9	16	32	31	59	34
20th	1998-99	38	3	7	9	18	31	4	2	13	17	38	35	69	30

NOTTINGHAM FOREST'S five seasons in the Premiership were as extreme as the nature of their most famous manager Brian Clough. The team either finished in the top half or were relegated and you can't get more extreme than that. They became known as the 'yo-yo team' for their bouncing between Division One and the Premiership.

Forest never really had time to enjoy their top-flight status after being founder members and getting off to an historic start when Teddy Sheringham scored the first Premiership goal on Sky to beat Liverpool. The season went into almost immediate terminal decline afterwards and six successive defeats deposited them bottom of the table. Selling Teddy Sheringham to Spurs, Darren Wassell to Derby and defensive rock Des Walker to Sampdoria after three games didn't help, particularly as adequate replacements weren't brought in. Moving son Nigel back to centre-half was something only dad Brian knew the reason for and the team never moved off the bottom until 30 January, when victory over Oldham, only the sixth of the season, elevated them to 21st. Three wins and a draw, the best sequence of the campaign, took Forest to their highest position, 19th, but just two wins in the rest of the season meant relegation was a certainty well before the last game.

Brian Clough's reign also ended after 18 successful years. Relegation was an entry on his CV that couldn't detract from the success he had had with the club.

The club bounced back at the first attempt and had an amazing 1994–95, enjoying an 11-match unbeaten start that had them second for the whole of October. Record £2.9 million signing Brian Roy formed a formidable scoring partnership with Stan Collymore, but after losing successive games, to Blackburn and Liverpool, a slump set in and Forest dropped to fifth before recovering with victories over Ipswich and a shock win at Old Trafford. Unfortunately, the team struggled for consistency until spring and that prevented any impact on the title race, but a run of five consecutive wins took Forest to fifth. After dropping two points to West Ham the side won their next four and were up to third, where they finished at the end of a 13-match unbeaten run.

Stan Collymore left for Liverpool in the summer and the team failed to build on their third place despite extending their unbeaten run to a Premiership record 25 games, which left the team fifth by mid-November. But that run was ended in spectacular fashion with their 7–0 drubbing by Blackburn Rovers, the club's heaviest Premiership reverse, until they shipped eight goals to Manchester United in 1999. Five more games without a win meant eighth place by Boxing Day and in the second half of the campaign inconsistency, never more than three games unbeaten, meant a disappointing finish in ninth.

1996–97 was as bad as it could get. After winning the opening game Forest's run of 16 games without a win meant they were bottom by December. Ten points over December and January improved things to 17th but Dean Saunders's winner at White Hart Lane was the last moment of joy for the team and 11 games without a win ensured another relegation.

Again Forest returned at the first time of asking, but the First Division champions again found the top flight uncompromising and after two wins in the opening three games it was a case of 'dive, dive, dive' as 19 games passed without a win. After hitting bottom, following a draw with Blackburn, Forest stayed there.

Pierre van Hooijdonk's goal beat Everton but there was only one more win before relegation was confirmed by April. With the pressure off, Forest played with a freedom that hadn't been evident since Cloughie's era and reeled off three consecutive victories to recover some pride if not status.

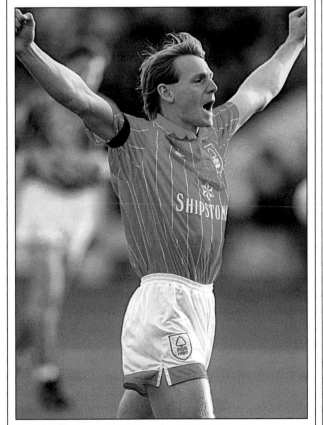

Psycho. Stuart Pearce of Nottingham Forest in typical mood.

MANAGERS

Brian Clough	1975–1993
Frank Clark	1993–1996
Stuart Pearce	1996–1997
Dave Bassett	1997–1998
Ron Atkinson	1998–1999

Oldham Athletic

OLDHAM ATHLETIC'S RECORD IN THE PREMIERSHIP

| Pos. | Season | P | Home: | | | | | Away: | | | | | Total Goals | | Pts |
			W	D	L	F	A	W	D	L	F	A	F	A	
19th	1992-93	42	10	6	5	43	30	3	4	14	20	44	63	74	49
21st	1993-94	42	5	8	8	24	33	4	5	12	18	35	42	68	40

PREMIER League founder members Oldham Athletic only had two seasons in the newly formed top-flight league and for most of that time they were in the lower half of the table, although they began the inaugural season well enough to be seventh in the rankings, after two draws and a win, over Nottingham Forest. But two defeats in the next four fixtures saw Joe Royle's team fall to 16th. Then, after beating Ipswich and victory over Royle's old team, Everton, the first bad run of the season followed.

Five defeats in six games plunged the Latics to 19th. Oldham then dropped into the bottom three, for the first time in the campaign, after two defeats in London, but then two successive victories for the first time that season elevated them to 18th.

Unfortunately consistency proved elusive and four straight defeats in January plunged Oldham to rock bottom of the table. Then Chelsea were beaten at Boundary Park before the poorest sequence of the campaign almost brought relegation.

After three successive defeats Oldham went to Everton and two goals from former Goodison star Neil Adams earned a point. Then Adams scored the only goal at home to beat Manchester United, who were Premiership leaders at the time. That win brought much needed confidence into the equation and after losing to Norwich four games unbeaten improved the league position to 20th before a thrashing at Spurs left Oldham staring at relegation.

But Oldham were down, not out, and the best sequence of the season, winning their last three games, ensured another stab at the Premiership the following season, on goal difference. They had conceded two fewer goals than Crystal Palace, but it was a close-run thing: in winning their last two games the Latics managed to concede five goals.

Unlike the first season, Oldham failed to make a decent start in the second and lost five of the first eight games, winning just one, to be 20th by mid-September. By the end of the following month they had climbed to 19th, on the back of only the team's second victory of the campaign. But the Latics were back to one place off the bottom by mid-January, after four successive defeats and a draw.

Hope of survival was renewed when a win at Southampton was followed by completion of the league double over Chelsea, although Oldham were still in the relegation zone at the end of March. The league double over Southampton was followed by victory over QPR that lifted the Latics out of trouble, two places above the bottom three, but a disastrous run of four defeats in a row and another four games without a win meant that Oldham's life at the top was over, as they were relegated in 21st place.

MANAGER

Joe Royle   1982–1994

Joe Royle wins a Manager of the Month award as Oldham boss.

Portsmouth

PORTSMOUTH defied all the prophets of doom by making a superb start to their first-ever Premiership campaign in 2003–04. Unbeaten in their opening five games, Pompey proudly topped the table after three fixtures but three consecutive defeats burst the bubble before Harry Redknapp's team responded by beating Liverpool, with a goal from former Anfield star, Patrik Berger. By the end of September Portsmouth had dropped to ninth, and in fact, after the great start, the team slid down the table for most of the season and at the end of the year were 16th. But despite successive defeats to Newcastle and Manchester United Portsmouth showed character by crushing Leeds United 6–1.

Pompey recovered early in the New Year with victory over Manchester City and a draw with Wolves but dropped down to 17th. Suddenly it was a struggle to avoid the quick return to Division One the sceptics had predicted.

Harry Redknapp, fighting with a lack of resources, not to mention injuries, managed to stabilise in 17th place, but it wasn't easy and after losing at Anfield on 17 March the team were just two points above the relegation zone. They then managed to string together a mini-run of three wins and a draw before the result that really kicked the survival surge into overdrive, a 1–0 win over Manchester United, with a Steve Stone goal.

In their last 10 games Portsmouth lost just once, against Leicester, but by then safety had been assured. In fact, by moving up to 14th Pompey were actually the Premiership's form team of April, winning three and drawing one of their four fixtures that month. The team finished eight points clear of the last relegation place, and finished the campaign in style with Ayegbani Yakuba hitting four goals in the 5–1 victory over Middlesbrough, taking his tally to 11 in that 10-game run. Yet it was stopping goals that was Portsmouth's main problem all season. They conceded 54, but another reason for their season-long struggle was a poor away record, with just two games won away from Fratton Park. Fortunately 10 home games were won and that was the foundation on which Harry Redknapp built to keep Portsmouth in the Premiership for another season.

It was sad then, that the achievement was sullied by the end of season row with Milan Mandaric, Portsmouth owner and chairman, reportedly over plans to bring in a younger, foreign coach to replace Jim Smith, Harry's right-hand man in achieving what many thought was not possible.

Redknapp must have been delighted when he received his Manager of the Month award for April, prior to kick off against 'Boro on the last day of 2003–04, with Premiership football to look forward to next season.

MANAGER

Harry Redknapp   March 2002–present

Portsmouth's manager Harry Redknapp.

Queen's Park Rangers

QUEEN'S PARK RANGERS'S RECORD IN THE PREMIERSHIP

Pos.	Season	P	Home: W	D	L	F	A	Away: W	D	L	F	A	Total Goals F	A	Pts
5th	1992-93	42	11	5	5	41	32	6	7	8	22	23	63	55	63
9th	1993-94	42	8	7	6	32	29	8	5	8	30	32	62	61	60
8th	1994-95	42	11	3	7	36	26	6	6	9	25	33	61	59	60
19th	1995-96	38	6	5	8	25	26	3	1	15	13	31	38	57	33

QPR SPENT only four seasons in the Premiership, the first four years after its inauguration, and their only finish outside the top 10 was their last, in 1995/96.

With the goal power of Les Ferdinand, on 20 goals, ably supported by the youthful exuberance of Bradley Allen, who hit 10, and the midfield probing of Ray Wilkins, QPR made an instant impact in their first Premiership season. They won three games in a row after drawing their opener with Manchester City and although they then lost to Chelsea the team stood second in the table. But four draws in the next five games caused a slide before they crushed Spurs 4–1 and lost to Norwich, then climbed to third by beating Leeds.

That was Rangers' highest placing in that first campaign as they lost too much ground by being unable to string a run together. Before such a run came, in the last quarter of the season, the best was an unbeaten run of just five games, which took QPR to fourth in mid-February.

The pivotal time came in March. Victory over Norwich again meant fourth place but defeats by Liverpool and Wimbledon then just two points from nine dropped Rangers to eighth. Then Les Ferdinand took over, scoring hat-tricks in consecutive games to beat Nottingham Forest 4–3 and Everton 5–3, elevating QPR to fifth. They might have gone even higher had they not drawn against Leeds and Arsenal, but wins over Villa and Sheffield Wednesday gave Rangers a final position of fifth and Ferdinand a place in the England team.

It was Les's fine season that affected the following campaign: rumours were rife that he was going to leave, and results very often failed to accurately reflect just how well the team played. Rangers' first two games were lost and although they beat Southampton for 15th place it soon became apparent that the team were going to struggle. By the end of September only 11 points had been gained from a possible 27 but three consecutive wins elevated Rangers to fifth.

Two wins from the next two took QPR to their highest position since the previous March, fourth. Unfortunately four games without a win followed before wins over Southampton and Oldham and a draw with Leeds claimed sixth place. QPR lacked consistency all season and four separate winless runs proved costly, the worst being in the spring when three consecutive defeats before a draw with Chelsea arrested the slide in 10th place.

Although Gerry Francis's side only lost once in their last five games, three of them were draws and they had to settle for ninth.

Les Ferdinand didn't leave QPR, and his 24 goals in 1994–95, 14 more than nearest teammate Kevin Gallen, earned eighth place, a remarkable finish considering QPR were 18th in December, after only four wins in 16 games. They were up to eighth by Easter, but three defeats and a draw in their last six games meant that was as high as they got.

When Les did eventually go, in a £6 million record move to Newcastle, the bottom fell out of the team. Mark Hateley, 'Sir Les's' £1.5 million replacement, made little impact with just two goals, and Danny Dichio, despite 10 goals, couldn't enliven the team's performances either. By November QPR were 18th. Boxing Day defeat by Arsenal started the terminal rot and six consecutive defeats followed. The team had dropped to 19th place.

There was almost an acceptance of relegation in the last portion of the campaign and four wins from the last 12 games wasn't enough. Losing to Coventry, with two games to go, ensured the end of QPR'S four-year Premiership adventure.

'Sir Les' Ferdinand proved irreplaceable at Loftus Road.

MANAGERS

Gerry Francis 1991–1994
Ray Wilkins 1994–1996

Sheffield United

SHEFFIELD UNITED'S RECORD IN THE PREMIERSHIP

Pos.	Season	P	W	D	L	F	A	W	D	L	F	A	F	A	Pts
				Home:					Away:				Total Goals		
14th	1992-93	42	10	6	5	33	19	4	4	13	21	34	54	53	52
20th	1993-94	42	6	10	5	24	23	2	8	11	18	37	42	60	42

ALTHOUGH Sheffield United were founder members of the Premiership, their stay lasted just two seasons and for most of that time they struggled. In fact the club never once featured in the top 10, spending the majority of the two years in the lower half of the table. But Sheffield United have two entries in the record books. Not only did they inflict the first Premiership defeat on the most successful club in the league's history, Manchester United, on the opening day, but Brian Deane, who scored both the Blades' goals in that win, netted the first goal in Premiership history after five minutes. Deane went on to score 15 goals in that inaugural season.

Unfortunately, after such a great start United went into immediate decline and losing five of their next six games dumped them down to 21st place, although they recovered to take eight points from the next four games and improved to 16th. Four games without losing was to prove as good a run as the Blades were to have in that first campaign and it was something they managed three times. The second and third such sequences staved off relegation.

By 6 February United were bottom of the table but within weeks three wins from five games took them out of the bottom three – until successive defeats dumped them back into the relegation zone. Then a four-game unbeaten run yielded eight points and the Blades elevated the team to 19th before they lost to Blackburn Rovers. But the side bounced back with 10 points from 12, a season's best return, to finish 14th, four points above the last relegated club.

Although the team ended August 1993 in 11th place, that was to be their highest placing of the campaign. A disastrous run of 12 games without a win saw United slide to 18th before a Steve Clarke own-goal earned victory over Chelsea, but another six games without a win saw the Blades slide even further down and by the year's end they were 21st.

United opened the year with victory over fellow strugglers Oldham Athletic but couldn't build on those three points. It wasn't that the Blades lost a lot of games – just five in the 19 games until the end of the season – but nine draws did the damage.

With four games left the team gave themselves hope with wins over Norwich and Newcastle, with Nathan Blake getting all three goals and taking them to one place short of safety. That optimism suffered when a draw at Oldham left the Blades needing a victory at Chelsea on the final day of the season and hoping that other results, involving the relegation-threatened clubs, went in their favour.

There were just 15 minutes left at Stamford Bridge and Sheffield United led 2–1, but they conceded two goals, to Mark Stein, and results elsewhere went against them. The Blades, who would have escaped by three points and four places, were relegated by a single point.

MANAGER

Dave Bassett   1988–1995

Brian Deane, scorer of the first goal on the opening day of the Premiership.

Sheffield Wednesday

Pos.	Season	P	Home: W	D	L	F	A	Away: W	D	L	F	A	Total Goals F	A	Pts
7th	1992-93	42	9	8	4	34	26	6	6	9	21	25	55	51	59
7th	1993-94	42	10	7	4	48	24	6	9	6	28	30	76	54	64
13th	1994-95	42	7	7	7	26	26	6	5	10	23	31	49	57	51
15th	1995-96	38	7	5	7	30	31	3	5	11	18	30	48	61	40
7th	1996-97	38	8	10	1	25	16	6	5	8	25	35	50	51	57
16th	1997-98	38	9	5	5	30	26	3	3	13	22	41	52	67	44
12th	1998-99	38	7	5	7	20	15	6	2	11	21	27	41	42	46
19th	1999-2000	38	6	3	10	21	23	2	4	13	17	47	38	70	31

SHEFFIELD WEDNESDAY had an unbroken spell of eight seasons in the top flight after being founder members of the Premiership. Their best-ever finish was seventh, something the club managed three times, two coming in the first two seasons. But after dropping out of the top flight in 2000, it got worse for the Owls with their relegation into Division Two in 2003.

As with a number of clubs, one of the major factors in their demise was a spending frenzy which saw millions being laid out on expensive players with huge salaries that could not be sustained by the club when success wasn't forthcoming on the field.

In the first Premiership campaign Wednesday were regarded as a decent outside bet for the championship, but not until the second half of the season. From 15th, in December, the team, with Mark Bright, David Hirst and Paul Warhurst on form, put together a 10-game unbeaten run, including seven wins in a row, to climb into fourth place by March. Unfortunately the challenge fell away after losing at Villa and the team managed just two more victories in the last 10 games to finish seventh.

Wednesday never adequately replaced Paul Warhurst, a record £2.65 million departure to Blackburn Rovers, and the loss of David Hirst to injury was another set-back that hindered any title hopes in 1993–94. In fact the team did very well to recover from an awful start, which saw Wednesday in the bottom three until they opened November with a thrashing of Ipswich Town, only the second win of the campaign. From then it was a steady climb and four consecutive April wins took Wednesday up to sixth, but they dropped six points in the last three games and again finished seventh.

The team then suffered two mediocre seasons. They finished

Wednesday keeper Kevin Pressman made more than 200 Premiership appearances.

13th, and suffered the club's heavest home defeat, 7–1 to Forest, in 1994–95, having been as low as 19th. The following campaign was even worse and Wednesday finished 15th after spending most of the season hovering around that position. It could have been bleaker, because they went into the final day as one of the clubs in danger of going down, but a point at West Ham kept them up.

Record £3 million signing Benito Carbone came in from Inter Milan after the team fell away from a four wins in a row start that saw Wednesday top of the table going into September. But Benni, like Reggie Blinker, didn't really work out at Hillsborough.

Although the team went fifth on the back of another four-game winning run, in spring, defeat by Manchester United knocked them back and they finished the season seventh after picking up a single point from the last four games.

David Pleat was sacked in November 1997, after a crushing defeat by Manchester United sent Wednesday bottom, and Ron Atkinson was lured back to the club, with strong speculation that he was on a £1 million bonus to keep them in the Premiership. He managed it, but only just, although his impact was immediate. Four consecutive wins took the team to 13th, but the eventual finish was just four points above the last relegated club.

Sheffield Wednesday's 1998–99 season was in two distinct halves, but the second part was only marginally better than the first and the major problem all season was a lack of goals, with the team managing to score in only 21 games. The highest placing, 10th, came after three February wins in a row, but five consecutive defeats undid Danny Wilson's good work and the team ended the campaign 12th.

Two wins in 20 games from August left the club facing relegation, bottom of the table. The improvement in 2000 was marginal but the team never got out of the bottom three and were relegated after the penultimate game when they let slip a 3–1 advantage over Arsenal.

MANAGERS	
Trevor Francis	1991–1995
David Pleat	1995–1997
Ron Atkinson	1997–1998
Danny Wilson	1998–2000

Des Walker.

Southampton

SOUTHAMPTON'S RECORD IN THE PREMIERSHIP

Pos.	Season	P	Home:					Away:					Total Goals		Pts
			W	D	L	F	A	W	D	L	F	A	F	A	
18th	1992-93	42	10	6	5	30	21	3	5	13	24	40	54	61	50
18th	1993-94	42	9	2	10	30	31	3	5	13	19	35	49	66	43
10th	1994-95	42	8	9	4	33	27	4	9	8	28	36	61	63	54
17th	1995-96	38	7	7	5	21	18	2	4	13	13	34	34	52	38
16th	1996-97	38	6	7	6	32	24	4	4	11	18	32	50	56	41
12th	1997-98	38	10	1	8	28	23	5	5	10	22	32	50	55	48
17th	1998-99	38	9	4	6	29	26	2	4	13	8	38	37	64	41
15th	1999-2000	38	8	4	7	26	22	4	4	11	19	40	45	62	44
10th	2000-01	38	11	2	6	27	22	3	8	8	13	26	40	48	52
11th	2001-02	38	7	5	7	23	22	5	4	10	23	32	46	54	45
8th	2002-03	38	9	8	2	25	16	4	5	10	18	30	43	46	52
12th	2003-04	38	8	6	5	24	17	4	5	10	20	28	44	45	47

O F ALL the clubs who have been hundred percenters in the Premiership, Southampton's achievement is arguably the most staggering. As what used to be termed an 'unfashionable' club, Saints defied the odds from day one with a combination of good housekeeping, excellent coaching, the occasional quality player and a whole lot of luck. Throw in attendances that rarely filled the Dell before they splashed out on the superb new St Mary's Stadium and you have the unlikely background for a club that, despite just two top-10 finishes in 12 seasons, managed to compete with the big spenders when their record fee was £4 million paid for Rory Delap.

For most football fans Southampton's survival in the Premiership was synonymous with, nay dependent on, one player: Matt Le Tissier, a one-club man, a concept rare in modern top-flight football. During his 16-year career the Channel Islander could have moved on many times, to wider fame and greater fortune, but instead he chose to devote his unique talents to keeping his club in the Premiership.

Southampton struggled for the first two Premiership seasons, finishing 18th both times, but fittingly the club's first Premiership goal was scored by Matt Le Tissier, in the team's second game, a defeat at QPR, following a drawn first game at the Dell against Spurs. After slumping to 20th the Saints improved to ninth by March but just one win in the last eight games meant finishing 18th, just one point above the last relegation place.

The team spent half of the following season in the bottom three but four wins early in 1994 lifted them out of the relegation zone. Saints diced with the drop right up to the last day, when Matt Le Tissier, who else, hit a brace, including a penalty, which was his 100th goal for the club, in the draw with West Ham that again prevented relegation by one point. Matt Le Tissier's 25 goals were a priceless contribution to that survival.

Southampton then enjoyed their best campaign, but the 10th-place finish owed much to the team equalling the

Southampton's James Beattie and All Star XI's Matthew Le Tissier.

Premiership's record number of draws, 18, of which seven came in successive matches. Although the side were still 20th in March they lost just two of the remaining 11 fixtures to finish 10th and once again Southampton's reliance on 'Le Tiss', and his goals, was immeasurable.

It was to be five more seasons of struggle before the team matched the 1995 finish. In 1996 and 1997 the club only survived on goal difference before finishing 12th in 1998, but they were still only eight points better off than the last relegated club. That finish could have been better had they not lost four of the last seven games to drop down from 10th place.

The first half of the following campaign, 1998–99, saw Southampton alternate between 19th and 20th. Survival came after the team climbed out of the drop zone with just three games to go, winning all three, a season's best sequence. Matt Le Tissier, the club's most famous No.7, was top scorer for the seventh season in a row with seven goals.

In 2000 Southampton finished 15th. With 'Le Tiss' hampered by injury, Glenn Hoddle used 29 players, but consistency eluded the Saints and the side were 15th from mid-March.

On the back of five Marian Pahars goals and a start of just one defeat in seven, Southampton climbed to eighth in 2000–01, a position they did not achieve again until the second half of the campaign, when five consecutive wins took them up from 14th. But five scoreless games proved costly, although the team recovered and beat Manchester United and Arsenal to finish 10th. The victory over the Gunners was particularly memorable as Matt Le Tissier hit the last-minute winner to end 103 years of football at the Dell before the move to St Mary's.

In 2002 Matt Le Tissier played his last game for the club, against West Ham. It was another disappointing campaign as Southampton never climbed higher than 11th, but it was seen as an achievement as the team had been bottom in November.

The following season saw Southampton's best-ever Premiership finish and the first FA Cup Final appearance since 1976. With James Beattie a regular scorer – he was only bettered by Van Nistelrooy and Henry – the team, under Gordon Strachan, proved worthy of fifth place in January. But three consecutive February defeats destroyed any hopes of European qualification via the league, although James Beattie, scoring in six successive games, tried to rescue that dream. A last-day win at Manchester City earned the team their best-ever finish, in eighth place. Even losing the FA Cup Final, to Arsenal, brought the reward of qualification for the UEFA Cup.

No one will ever know what effect Gordon Strachan's decision to leave Southampton for 'a rest away from football', had on Saints' finish the following season. But the Scot's departure, in February, came the month after the team dropped to within goal difference of the relegation zone. The campaign had started so well, with August's win over Manchester United, and after 20 games, with a defensive record bettered only by Manchester United and Arsenal, the team was eighth. The New Year arrival of Kevin Phillips provided much-needed support for James Beattie but injuries exposed the lack of depth in the squad and the team only won four of the last 13 games to finish 12th.

MANAGERS

Ian Branfoot	1991–1994
Alan Ball	1994–1995
Dave Merrington	1995–1996
Graeme Souness	1996–1997
Dave Jones	1997–2000
Glenn Hoddle	2000–2001
Stuart Gray	2001
Gordon Strachan	October 2001–February 2004
Paul Sturrock	2004–present

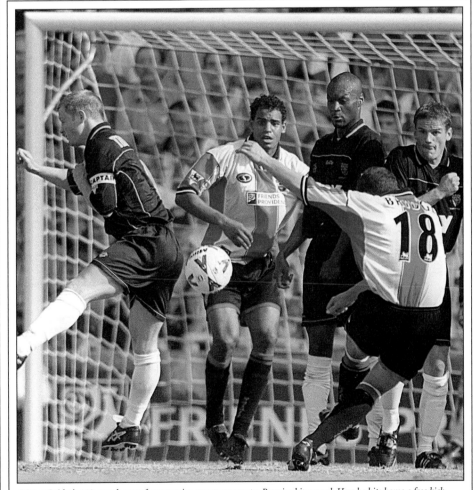

Wayne Bridge's 112-match run of consecutive appearances set a Premiership record. Here he hits home a free kick.

Sunderland

SUNDERLAND'S RECORD IN THE PREMIERSHIP

Pos.	Season	P	Home: W	D	L	F	A	Away: W	D	L	F	A	Total Goals F	A	Pts
18th	1996-97	38	7	6	6	20	18	3	4	12	15	35	35	53	40
7th	1999-2000	38	10	6	3	28	17	6	4	9	29	39	57	56	58
7th	2000-01	38	9	7	3	24	16	6	5	8	22	25	46	41	57
17th	2001-02	38	7	7	5	18	16	3	3	13	11	35	29	51	40
20th	2002-03	38	3	2	14	11	31	1	5	13	10	34	21	65	19

WITH ITS passionate support it's a mystery why Sunderland has not, as a club or team, become an established Premiership outfit. After a highest finish of seventh for two consecutive seasons, 1999–00 and 2000–01, excessive expenditure on players who didn't produce saw the club sink into Division One.

It all started so well in the first campaign, when five points in an unbeaten three-game start saw Sunderland in sixth place by September 1996, but two months later they had slipped to 17th. Goals were a continual problem as just nine were scored in the first 13 games, and two of those were penalties and four goals came against Nottingham Forest in one game. Form was erratic as the team struggled to climb to 11th by the New Year.

1997 was no kinder and after a Tony Adams own-goal gifted them victory over Arsenal, six games followed without victory until 15th-placed Sunderland scored all three goals in a shock 2–1 win over leaders Manchester United. Sunderland picked up just eight more points that campaign and slipped into Division One. Craig Russell, top scorer with just four league goals, summed up the season.

Sunderland took two seasons to return to the Premiership but after they opened with a thrashing at Chelsea there was only one more defeat before late November, and only an 89th-minute West Ham equaliser in October stopped the team topping the table. After a 2–1 reverse at Leeds, with Kevin Phillips scoring freely, the side went 10 games unbeaten and they went to Anfield in third place. Sunderland bounced back from Liverpool's defeat with three successive victories before the decisive result of the season, a heavy defeat at Everton, knocked Sunderland out of their stride and there were only five more wins in the second half of the season, three coming in succession as March turned to April. This left Sunderland seventh, where they remained for the rest of the campaign. Failure to qualify for Europe was offset by Kevin Phillips's 30 Premiership goals earning him the Carling Player of the Year award.

After beating Arsenal on the opening day of the following season, one point from the next 12 left Sunderland in the relegation zone, but a six-game unbeaten run saw them climb to ninth. Following a blip the team went fifth with victory over Middlesbrough. After losing to Leeds four wins in five games took Sunderland second, but that was as good as it got and the team dropped steadily, winning just three games in the last 15 to replicate the previous season's seventh-place finish.

Sunderland's penultimate season was punctuated by inconsistency, individually and collectively. With Niall Quinn playing his last season before retiring and Kevin Phillips only managing 11 goals by spring the team was floating just above the relegation zone and 2002 never saw more than two consecutive wins as the team survived by just four points.

Peter Reid was sacked and the appointment of managerial 'dream team' Howard Wilkinson and Steve Cotterill turned into a nightmare as the team went into free-fall. By March a run of five consecutive defeats saw the management sacked and Sunderland bottom. Five defeats became a Premiership record of 15 that was to come within one game of Darwen's 104-year-old record worst of 18 consecutive reverses. New manager Mick McCarthy couldn't stop the decline and Sunderland went down with the lowest-ever Premiership total of just four wins from a 38-game season.

Niall Quinn, Sunderland.

MANAGERS

Peter Reid	1995–2002
Howard Wilkinson	2002–2003
Mick McCarthy	2003–present

Swindon Town

SWINDON TOWN'S RECORD IN THE PREMIERSHIP

Pos.	Season	P	Home: W	D	L	F	A	Away: W	D	L	F	A	Total Goals F	A	Pts
22nd	1993-94	42	4	7	10	25	45	1	8	12	22	55	47	100	30

THE PARADOX of Swindon's glorious failure after just one taste of the Premiership is the fact that it proves that one of the small clubs can get there in the first place, but shows that financial constraints make it difficult to stay there.

With Glenn Hoddle pulling the strings in midfield Swindon won a pulsating First Division play-off final 4–3 to claim a place in the Premiership, but before the club could kick a ball in the top flight the Robins suffered a triple blow to their chances of remaining there. Unable to resist the lure of a top-flight swansong, Hoddle decamped to Chelsea as player-manager and the double whammy was losing Hoddle, the manager, and Hoddle, the player. That was compounded when defensive rock Colin Calderwood also left, for Spurs. John Gorman took over at the County Ground knowing he faced a mammoth task.

At least Swindon scored in the first game, John Moncur having the honour at Bramall Lane, but if the manager had any doubts about the difficulties ahead they were brought home by four consecutive defeats at the start of the campaign. Before Swindon managed a first Premiership point the team was bottom of the table and never moved from there.

Then came a run of 15 games without a win until they broke their duck by beating QPR, but by then it had long been apparent that scoring goals was going to be a problem for Swindon.

No one felt that more than the club's record £500,000 signing Jan Aage Fjortoft, who failed to net a single goal in that dreadful run. He was dropped for the Ipswich game and his replacement, Keith Scott, responded with a goal and retained his place against QPR and, true to script, netted the only goal to record that historic victory, despite the sending-off of Luc Nijholt.

With their confidence boosted, Swindon drew two of the next three games, and were four minutes away from beating Liverpool on their own ground before Mark Wright's equaliser. The Robins then beat Southampton but were still marooned on the bottom of the Premiership until their only back-to-back wins all season.

Jan Aage Fjortoft scored the team's only Premiership hat-trick to beat Coventry, which followed the win over Spurs in which he also scored. The Norwegian was in fine form in the second half of the season, scoring 12 times in the last 16 games, including one against Manchester United, who were fortunate to escape from the County Ground with a point. Swindon fans needed that shot in the arm after suffering the club's worst defeat in 37 years, against Newcastle, in the previous game.

There was little to shout about from there on in and the last hurrah was the team's one and only away win in the Premiership, but it was one that completed the only league double that season, against QPR.

All that was left for Swindon, long after the reality of relegation had set in, was to avoid the embarrassment of conceding 100 goals. The one they surrendered at Loftus Road sent them into the last game against Leeds with 95 in the against column and, unfortunately, it was a bitter end to the club's only Premiership campaign when the visitors scored five times, leaving relegated Swindon as the first top-flight team, since Ipswich in 1964, to concede 100 league goals, and it was a new worst defensive record for the Premiership. The other record Swindon were landed with was the lowest number of wins, five, which stood until 2003 when it was beaten by Sunderland, who managed just four.

MANAGER

John Gorman   1993–1994

Jan Aage Fjortoft enjoys a rare smile in Swindon's only Premiership campaign.

Tottenham Hotspur

TOTTENHAM HOTSPUR'S RECORD IN THE PREMIERSHIP

Pos.	Season	P	Home: W	D	L	F	A	Away: W	D	L	F	A	Total Goals F	A	Pts
8th	1992-93	42	11	5	5	40	25	5	6	10	20	41	60	66	59
15th	1993-94	42	4	8	9	29	33	7	4	10	25	26	54	59	45
7th	1994-95	42	10	5	6	32	25	6	9	6	34	33	66	58	62
8th	1995-96	38	9	5	5	26	19	7	8	4	24	19	50	38	61
10th	1996-97	38	8	4	7	19	17	5	3	11	25	34	44	51	46
14th	1997-98	38	7	8	4	23	22	4	3	12	21	34	44	56	44
11th	1998-99	38	7	7	5	28	26	4	7	8	19	24	47	50	47
10th	1999-2000	38	10	3	6	40	26	5	5	9	17	23	57	49	53
12th	2000-01	38	11	6	2	31	16	2	4	13	16	38	47	54	49
9th	2001-02	38	10	4	5	32	24	4	4	11	17	29	49	53	50
10th	2002-03	38	9	4	6	30	29	5	4	10	21	33	51	62	50
14th	2003-04	38	9	4	6	33	27	4	2	13	14	30	47	57	45

OF ALL the Premiership's founder members Spurs have had the most tempestuous 12 years. There were many in football who felt they were destined to be the next big club after Leeds to drop into Division One. Indeed the team were in the bottom three at Christmas 2003, a traditional football albatross.

Internal politics, petty rivalries and ego clashes, not to mention poor managerial appointments and even worse signings, have all caused many a Spurs fan to cast envious glances, privately anyway, towards Highbury.

Seven managers in 12 years, coupled with board takeovers, had an adverse effect on any title ambitions at White Hart Lane and for a club once considered 'top six' they were fortunate, at times, to be 'top 10'.

Spurs' highest ever Premiership finish is seventh, in 1995. They have been eighth twice, and 10th three times, so it's easy to see that Tottenham supporters, with their 'glory, glory days' legacy, haven't had much to shout about in contesting the title.

One wonders what Spurs might have achieved in their best-ever season had they not been hamstrung by the six-point penalty imposed by the Premier League for 'financial irregularities', which wasn't removed until nearly half the season had passed. With Jürgen Klinsmann scoring freely in his first Premiership campaign, ably abetted by Teddy Sheringham, the team was in the top six by New Year's Eve and stayed there until February, but a draw with Liverpool and a shock Southampton defeat hit any title aspirations. Just four more wins followed, in the last eight games, and a Premiership best of seventh was achieved. Since 1995

Tottenham Hotspur celebrate winning the Worthington League Cup, the club's only trophy as a Premiership club.

there has been a steady decline in terms of Premiership impact.

Most of the first season was spent in the lower half of the table and only nine wins, from 20 1993 fixtures, ensured eighth place. The following season the feud between Alan Sugar and Terry Venables almost cost Tottenham their top-flight status. It was during the conflict that the financial irregularities, concerning undeclared loans that were never intended to be repaid, came to light. Seven consecutive defeats meant 16th place by March and, despite a five-game unbeaten run, three more reverses dropped Spurs to 18th, although a couple of wins eased relegation worries and they finished in 15th place.

In October 1994 Ossie Ardiles was sacked and Gerry Francis engineered a remarkable transformation. The defence was turned into a unit and a tough fitness regime was instituted. The team improved from 15th to sixth inside two months. Spurs only lost five games in the second half of the campaign and might have finished higher than seventh had they not failed to win in their last five fixtures.

The team never recovered from a poor start and finished 1995–96 in eighth place, despite being in the top five until March, because of only one win in the last eight games.

An injury crisis the following season – at one stage 13 first choice players were out – contributed to mid-table mediocrity and the team was never higher than seventh. Teddy Sheringham, top scorer with seven goals, says it all as the team ended up 10th.

Tottenham were uncomfortably close to the drop zone for much of the next campaign. Gerry Francis was replaced by little-known Swiss coach Christian Gross, who swept into White Hart Lane wielding his tube ticket. Jürgen Klinsmann returned but made little impact, top scoring with nine goals. The start of January saw Spurs 19th but a five-game unbeaten run helped the side finish 14th.

Gross used the return portion of his tube ticket after the 3–0 home defeat by Sheffield Wednesday and chairman Alan Sugar made, perhaps, the most controversial managerial appointment ever when George Graham was recruited. The team finished that season 11th, so there was improvement, but only three of the campaign's 11 wins came against teams above Tottenham.

Spurs were actually second in August 1999 but soon dropped to 10th and the side were unable to match or exceed that start of three wins in a row and ended up 10th again.

2000–01 was memorable for Alan Sugar selling the club to ENIC, after 10 years in control, but the second half of the season, after being fifth in September, saw Spurs in the bottom half and they finished 12th in a season of bad will as George Graham suffered constant barracking. He didn't help himself by selling the popular David Ginola. Without the enigmatic Frenchman Spurs lacked creativity and in April, after Graham rowed with the new owners, they replaced him with Glenn Hoddle.

By the end of October 2001 eight top players were out injured and the side proved inconsistent. Three games without defeat, three times in the campaign, was the best they could manage, and ninth place was the finishing position.

An unbeaten start in 2002–03 meant top spot after four games but it was downhill afterwards. Spurs, with Robbie Keane and Sheringham combining well, were eighth at the turn of the year but could never go more than three games without losing and four defeats in the last five fixtures meant 10th place, again. White Hart Lane then lost its favourite Teddy as Sheringham left, in the summer, to join Premiership newcomers Portsmouth.

Glenn Hoddle's poor start to 2003/04 ended his reign at Tottenham and for the bulk of the campaign director of football David Pleat picked the side, which was in the bottom three at the halfway mark. Although the team rallied to finish 14th, the second half of the season was marred with uncertainty about who the manager would be for 2004–05.

After an inconspicuous first dozen years Spurs fans were left hoping that the incoming manager would be a combination of Bill Nicholson and David Blaine. They were at least owed that.

Spurs' defensive rock, Sol Campbell, left for north London rivals Arsenal.

MANAGERS

Ossie Ardiles	1993–1994
Gerry Francis	1994–1997
Christian Gross	1997–1998
George Graham	1998–2001
Glenn Hoddle	April 2001–2003
David Pleat	2003–2004

Watford

WATFORD'S short stint in the Premiership, in 1999–2000, is most remembered for the record of the fewest points in a season, just 24 from 38 games, although they did manage to avoid another unwanted record, that of most defeats, 29, which Ipswich had captured five years earlier.

It was fitting that Graham Taylor, who had masterminded the glory years as First Division runners-up and FA Cup finalists, should take Watford into the Premiership via the play-offs in his second spell at the club. However, he had to call on all his years of managerial expertise as the Hornets were stung by the gap in quality between the First Division and the Premiership.

Watford fans were still enjoying their new status, despite starting the season with defeats to Wimbledon and Sunderland, when they stunned Liverpool with a 1–0 victory at Anfield, thanks to a Tommy Mooney goal, and found themselves 15th. Imagine then their joy when Mooney repeated his feat by netting the only goal against Bradford to send the team soaring up to ninth. Six points out of six proved to be the best return of the campaign. Sadly it didn't last and three consecutive defeats sent them down to 15th. Ten Premiership games yielded just six goals and nine points but then Alan Smart's goal beat Chelsea, only for five successive defeats to follow, the worst a 4–0 thrashing at Coventry. It was a defeat by a mid-table team at best, which finally brought home the gulf in class that Watford were battling against.

The Hornets fell to 19th and it only got worse from then on. Seven games without a win followed and then Xavier Gravelaine became the first Watford player, and the last, to score more than one goal in a Premiership game when he netted twice in the 3–2 win over Southampton. The following month he left for Le Havre, the football club, not the port.

Watford remained 19th from Hallowe'en until 22 January, when Bradford got their revenge with a victory that plunged the Hornets to the foot of the table, and there they stayed. There was a lift, of sorts, for Watford fans in the form of Michel Ngonge, who had, amazingly, been signed by Graham Taylor on the strength of video evidence. After a scoring debut in the 2–2 draw at Sheffield Wednesday, Michel netted in the next two games and after a blank in the thrashing by Wimbledon, he got the only goal in the defeat by Everton. But the second half of the season saw just two victories for Watford: 1–0 over Sheffield Wednesday, – again Alan Smart was the match-winner – and a last-day 1–0 farewell success over Coventry City.

MANAGER

Graham Taylor   1997–2001

Graham Taylor, Watford manager.

West Bromwich Albion

WEST BROMWICH ALB.'S RECORD IN THE PREMIERSHIP

			Home:					Away:				Total Goals		
Pos.	Season	P	W	D	L	F	A	W	D	L	F	A	F	A	Pts
19th	2002-03	38	3	5	11	17	34	3	3	13	12	31	29	65	26

WEST BROMWICH ALBION went into their first top-flight season since 1985–86 boosted by the signing of a new three-year contract by full-back Neil Clement, who had attracted a lot of Premiership interest. Manager Gary Megson also strengthened his squad by paying a club record £2.5 million to Coventry to bring Lee Hughes back to the club he supported as a youngster, having sold him to the Sky Blues for £5 million a year earlier. Megson also signed Jason Koumas, from Tranmere, and Lee Marshall, from Leicester City.

West Brom couldn't have had a tougher start to the campaign and defeats by Manchester United, Leeds and Arsenal dumped them to the bottom of the table. Game number four provided win number one as a Darren Moore goal beat Fulham for the Baggies to end their first month by moving off the bottom. Victories over West Ham and Southampton followed to take Albion to the dizzy heights of seventh, but back-to-back defeats against Liverpool and Blackburn took them back into mid-table.

The reality of the gap between Division One and the Premiership was reinforced by October's return of just a single point, from a draw against Birmingham, and defeat to Chelsea at the end of the month dumped the side back into the bottom three.

November saw the Baggies plunge to the bottom of the table following a goalless draw with Aston Villa, but the winless streak of nine games ended with victory over Middlesbrough, with Danny Dichio coming off the bench to hit the winner that took West Brom out of the relegation zone, to 17th.

December proved the crucial month for the team and one point, from the draw with Sunderland, saw them enter 2004 in 19th place. It didn't get any better in the second half of the campaign. Albion picked up just one January point before gaining only their fifth win, against Manchester City, to end an eight-game run without a victory.

Spring didn't see any sap rising in Albion's attempts to stave off relegation. Seven consecutive defeats, by mid-April, virtually assured a quick return to Division One and by the end of the month West Brom were 11 points adrift having won just twice in 25 games. Relegation was finally confirmed, despite winning 2–1 at relegated Sunderland, because Bolton beat West Ham.

From an early stage in the campaign it was obvious that West Brom weren't good enough for the Premiership, something Gary Megson admitted, but it's to the club's credit that they didn't try to buy safety by investing vast sums in players. In accepting the inevitable, and not lumbering the club with a financial albatross, which could not be sustained on a First Division income stream, West Bromwich Albion gave themselves a realistic foundation from which they bounced back into the top flight, at the first time of asking.

MANAGER

Gary Megson   March 2000–present

West Bromwich Albion's manager Gary Megson, in typical touch-line animation, inspires Albion to victory over West Ham United.

West Ham United

WEST HAM UNITED'S RECORD IN THE PREMIERSHIP

Pos.	Season	P	Home: W	D	L	F	A	Away: W	D	L	F	A	Total Goals F	A	Pts
13th	1993-94	42	6	7	8	26	31	7	6	8	21	27	47	58	52
14th	1994-95	42	9	6	6	28	19	4	5	12	16	29	44	48	50
10th	1995-96	38	9	5	5	25	21	5	4	10	18	31	43	52	51
14th	1996-97	38	7	6	6	27	25	3	6	10	12	23	39	48	42
8th	1997-98	38	13	4	2	40	18	3	4	12	16	39	56	57	56
5th	1998-99	38	11	3	5	32	26	5	6	8	14	27	46	53	57
9th	1999-2000	38	11	5	3	32	23	4	5	10	20	30	52	53	55
15th	2000-01	38	6	6	7	24	20	4	6	9	21	30	45	50	42
7th	2001-02	38	12	4	3	32	14	3	4	12	16	43	48	57	53
18th	2002-03	38	5	7	7	21	24	5	5	9	21	35	42	59	42

WEST HAM never really made the impact on the Premiership that the quality of their players, over the years, merited. Indeed the club, under Harry Redknapp, was more a nursery club for the bigger clubs than a club capable of making its mark on the top flight, which it didn't join until 1994. In recent years Joe Cole, Frank Lampard and Rio Ferdinand have all moved on after learning their craft at Upton Park and generated huge sums of money that have left the club wealthier in monetary terms but poorer in terms of quality sold.

Dale Gordon went into the Hammers' history books with the club's first Premiership goal in the draw at Coventry, but two defeats in the first two games in the new top flight left West Ham 19th. To be fair, that was as low as the team went that season, and four November games unbeaten saw a climb to 10th. A win over Coventry, just before the Christmas programme, took the Hammers into the top 10 for the first time and things looked promising as 1994 opened with victory at Everton. But then nine games without a win plunged the team to 15th. Successive wins for only the second time in the campaign removed some of the relegation worries before the team had to settle for finishing 13th.

Before the next campaign kicked off West Ham shot themselves in the foot – not for the last time – when they discarded manager Billy Bonds, the epitome of the Hammers spirit. After 27 years at Upton Park, as player, coach and manager, Billy was asked to step down and the homely club suffered its first PR setback as incredulous fans took in the radical move. Assistant manager Harry Redknapp, a former player who was every bit as much a Hammer as Bonzo, was elevated into the hot seat but the campaign ahead proved the first of many struggles against relegation.

Just one win in the first seven left West Ham on the edge of the drop zone, and although the odd win helped that's all the team could manage and by February they were in the bottom three. Only one defeat in March took the team out of danger, but

Joe Cole, one of West Ham's starlets, was plucked from the Upton Park nursery.

194

drawing with Forest dropped them back into trouble. It wasn't that the team was losing – they suffered defeat just once in the last 11 games of the season – they just struggled to turn draws into maximum points. The team managed to rally, with five points in May, to avoid relegation by five points.

Harry Redknapp stabilised West Ham in mid-table, but trouble scoring goals and results that never truly reflected performances persisted, and two seasons of consolidation followed until the best sequence of finishes in the club's Premiership history.

With the emergence of Rio Ferdinand and Frank Lampard, the intricate skills of Eyal Berkovic and the old-fashioned centre-forward play of John Hartson as the foundation, West Ham were third by the end of August 1997 but slumped to mid-table before commencing a run of six wins in eight games that earned eighth place by January. With four games left West Ham were sixth and a European place beckoned until the defence buckled and conceded 15 goals in those last four fixtures, coming to rest eighth.

West Ham continued to improve and did even better the following campaign though goodness only knows what might have been achieved had the goals problem been sorted out. Too many conceded and not enough scored just about sums up the season. The team was only outside the top 10 for a week and the highest placing, fifth, with perfect timing, was achieved on the final day. The Hammers failed to score in 16 games and 35 of the 54 goals conceded came in just eight games.

The momentum couldn't be maintained, despite an unbeaten start to 1999–2000 that saw West Ham third by September. After floating around mid-table the Hammers were hammered by Manchester United on April

Fools' Day but, despite recovering with three consecutive wins, a poor run followed to mean finishing ninth.

Just one win in the opening 10 games of the following campaign started alarm bells ringing, but a mid-season run of successive victories took West Ham to sixth. Two wins in 13, followed by three successive defeats, left the team 15th, with only two games left. That wasn't the only worry facing the fans because, once again, West Ham's image was damaged by the abrupt departure of Harry Redknapp. With rumours circulating about disputes over money for strengthening the team, Harry walked out before the last game against Middlesbrough, which West Ham lost to finish 15th.

Glenn Roeder's first season

resulted in the second-best Premiership finish, which didn't look likely after the team slumped to 19th in October. Once again a generous defence didn't help matters, and nor did 14 draws, but by April the team was in the top 10 despite losing two of the remaining eight games and finished seventh.

West Ham's decade in the Premiership ended after a traumatic season during which Glenn Roeder was rushed to hospital, complaining of chest pains, and later underwent brain surgery. By then, April, the writing was very much on the wall for the team, which went

bottom in August and stayed there until October. Two wins the next month took them out of the drop zone but 14 games without a win followed and relegation loomed. But after superb wins over Liverpool and Leeds the survival odds improved and West Ham went unbeaten for six games. After Roeder's infirmity, with Trevor Brooking in charge, the side only lost one more game in the season, but it turned out to be a crucial one. Losing at Bolton eventually meant relegation by two points, plus goal difference, from the last safe place that was occupied by… Bolton.

MANAGERS

Billy Bonds	1990–1994
Harry Redknapp	1994–2001
Glenn Roeder	June 2001–2003

West Ham United's Paolo Di Canio walks off dejected as his side are relegated.

Wimbledon

WIMBLEDON'S RECORD IN THE PREMIERSHIP

Pos.	Season	P	W	D	L	F	A	W	D	L	F	A	F	A	Pts
			Home:					Away:					Total Goals		
12th	1992-93	42	9	4	8	32	23	5	8	8	24	32	56	55	54
6th	1993-94	42	12	5	4	35	21	6	6	9	21	32	56	53	65
9th	1994-95	42	9	5	7	26	26	6	6	9	22	39	48	65	56
14th	1995-96	38	5	6	8	27	33	5	5	9	28	37	55	70	41
8th	1996-97	38	9	6	4	28	21	6	5	8	21	25	49	46	56
15th	1997-98	38	5	6	8	18	25	5	6	8	16	21	34	46	44
16th	1998-99	38	7	7	5	22	21	3	5	11	18	42	40	63	42
18th	1999-2000	38	6	7	6	30	28	1	5	13	16	46	46	74	33

WIMBLEDON were founder members of the Premiership and although they are probably best remembered, if not fondly, for the antics that earned them their 'Crazy Gang' nickname, they nevertheless had a pretty decent team that enjoyed three top-10 finishes in the first five seasons of the new league. Just over 10 years after their first-ever game in the Football League they were FA Cup winners, and four years later they were kicking off in the Premiership. Warren Barton had the honour of scoring the Dons' first Premiership goal, on 15 August 1992, but it was game number seven before they tasted victory for the first time, and in true 'Crazy Gang' style it was Arsenal who were vanquished. The points elevated Wimbledon to 19th but most of the first campaign was spent just above the relegation zone. A run of four consecutive victories took the team up to 13th before defeats by Aston Villa and Southampton hindered further progress. But Wimbledon were learning fast and only lost three games in the last 11 to finish 12th, with a great deal of help from Dean Holdsworth's 10 goals in eight of those games.

Acclimatisation successfully completed, Wimbledon set about making their mark in the second season and only lost once in the first nine games, reaching a high of sixth following three successive wins. Erratic form into spring only saw consecutive victories once, until the team opened March with back-to-back wins. Even though two consecutive defeats followed, 11th place was a worthy slot to occupy. Then John Fashanu and Dean Holdworth hit form and nine unbeaten games, including a run of seven consecutive wins, with victories over Blackburn and Manchester United thrown in for good measure, claimed a finish in sixth place, which proved to be their best ever in the top flight.

Despite the lowest crowds in the Premiership the fervour, not to mention money, of owner Sam Hammam seemed to reflect Wimbledon's spirit, on the pitch and off it. But after the dizzy heights of the top six it was pretty much downhill from there on in. Ninth then 14th, in the two following seasons, although the team was third, twice, in 1995–96, showed how hard top-flight life had become.

For much of 1996–97 Wimbledon threatened to shake

Vinnie Jones, John Scales, Dean Holdsworth and John Fashanu of Wimbledon.

the established powers in the Premiership when, after they lost the first three games without scoring, Joe Kinnear cajoled seven consecutive victories that kicked off a superb 14-game unbeaten run that elevated the Dons to second in the table behind Arsenal. Was the unthinkable likely to happen, the title or even Europe? Even the most die-hard fan thought the only way that would happen would be if war were declared.

Unfortunately Wimbledon's form declined and by February 1997 only one win in six games saw the team down to sixth, before a Vinnie Jones goal beat Arsenal. That was Wimbledon's last win for eight games and although they lost only two of their last six matches a heavy cup involvement – they reached the semi-finals of both domestic competitions – was the main reason the Dons finished eighth.

By the start of the following season Sam Hammam had relinquished control and things began to fall apart at the seams. Carl Cort was top scorer with four goals. Level with him were Efan Ekoku, Jason Euell, Michael Hughes and Carl Leaburn. Scoring, or rather lack of it, was a major contributory factor in finishing 15th.

The following campaign saw an alarming slump in form after Joe Kinnear was taken ill with heart trouble. Wimbledon never won again that season, in 11 games, and finished 16th.

Joe Kinnear left and Egil Olsen was brought in by the club's new owners. The team started 1999/00 with a win, but the next one didn't come until October, after the team plunged to 17th. They got back to 13th by February, but after a win over Leicester the team suffered nine defeats in the last 10 games, eight of them in a row, and were relegated.

Throughout their eight-year Premiership adventure Wimbledon retained their 'Sunday league' outlook, never taking themselves too seriously, even

when they were serious contenders for a place in Europe. But all that changed when ownership of the club, and it's soul, passed from the care of Sam Hammam and Joe Kinnear to a bunch of anonymous Norwegian businessmen. So anonymous were they that few Dons' supporters could name even one just a few years after their top-flight adventure turned sour and ended up a million miles away from Plough Lane, in

Milton Keynes and Division Two.

What many afficionados tend to forget is that at times the Wimbledon team contained a number of internationals: Robbie Earle, Oyvind Leonardsen, Vinnie Jones, Hans

Segers and John Fashanu. And, on reflection, the Premiership needed Wimbledon because they reminded the entire football world that the football pyramid was something that could be climbed, to the very top.

MANAGERS

Joe Kinnear	1992–1999
Egil Olsen	1999–2000

Former Wimbledon manager Joe Kinnear.

Wolverhampton Wanderers

			Home:					Away:					Total Goals		
Pos.	Season	P	W	D	L	F	A	W	D	L	F	A	F	A	Pts
20th	2003-04	38	7	5	7	23	35	0	7	12	15	42	38	77	33

WOLVERHAMPTON WANDERERS' RECORD IN THE PREMIERSHIP

FOR A TEAM reckoned to be favourites for a quick return to Division One, Wolves had a pretty good go at proving the sceptics wrong. The fact that they eventually proved not good enough for the Premiership was due to factors well beyond the control of manager Dave Jones, although there are those who thought that dispensing with the services of coach John Ward before Wanderers had even kicked a Premiership ball was a retrograde step.

Dave Jones assembled a group of footballers who had been good enough to win the First Division play-off final to get into the Premiership, but the simple truth of the matter is that his hands were tied, financially, by a board that wouldn't let him recruit more players, experienced at playing in the top flight, to consolidate that achievement. Paul Ince and Denis Irwin, plus Mark Kennedy, were players who had plied their trade at the highest level, but those three internationals alone could not carry the weight of expectation that Wolves were burdened with.

One player linked with Wolves was Teddy Sheringham, a free agent after leaving Spurs, but it seems the board at Molineux would not sanction what they considered to be high wages for a 37-year-old. Teddy chose instead to go to Portsmouth, and helped ensure that they stayed up, as Wolves slid back into Division One after just one taste of the high life.

Dave Jones was quoted, more than once, as saying that if the club didn't pay for better players, it would prove costly. His prophetic words were very accurate, as the team spent most of the campaign marooned at the bottom, though if Mohamed Camara had actually converted a higher number of the chances that came his way, and Carl Cort had arrived at the club sooner rather than later, there might have been a better attempt at closing the points gap that eventually sent Wolves back from whence they came.

The team got off to the worst of starts and were crushed at Blackburn on the opening day, 16 August 2003, and it never got much better. Ten goals were conceded in three defeats before the first point came against Portsmouth. It was October before the first win bonus was paid out, but it did little to alter the team's plight at the foot of the table, although it did signal a mini-run of seven points from nine before they were brought back to earth by Middlesbrough.

It's likely that Wolves fans realised the inevitable when they were crushed 5–2 by fellow strugglers Spurs and went into the New Year in the relegation zone after securing just their third win of the campaign, against another relegation-threatened club, Leeds United.

In January 2004 Wolves pulled off one of the all-time great Premiership results when they beat Manchester United, with a Kenny Miller goal, in front of a season's-best attendance. Draws against Liverpool and Portsmouth followed before Arsenal brought them back to reality.

Spring wasn't kind and the team shipped 14 goals in losing four in a row before six goals were shared with Manchester City, themselves faced with a relegation fight. Wolves then beat 'Boro 2–0 and went into the final month believing a miracle was possible, but despite beating Everton and drawing at Newcastle the club were relegated.

Most observers, seeing that Wolves did not spend to survive, were left wondering whether following the example of Black Country rivals West Brom would pay off for the 'Old Gold' as it did for the Baggies.

MANAGERS

Dave Jones   January 2001–present

Dave Jones, Wolverhampton Wanderers, manager.

Section 3: Statistics

Most Appearances in the Premiership

	Full	Sub	Total	Goals
Speed, Gary	406	8	414	67
Shearer, Alan	370	11	381	243
Giggs, Ryan	337	38	375	81
Sheringham, Teddy	331	44	375	139
Southgate, Gareth	366	0	366	17
James, David	361	1	362	0
Campbell, Sol	343	11	354	15
Winterburn, Nigel	338	14	352	5
Seaman, David	344	0	344	0
Sherwood, Tim	320	21	341	37
Ferdinand, Les	305	34	339	148
Cole, Andy	293	43	336	164
Unsworth, David	303	31	334	35
Parlour, Ray	280	53	333	21
Yorke, Dwight	280	51	331	119
Keane, Roy	317	13	330	38
Irwin, Denis	316	12	328	17
Ehiogu, Ugo	316	11	327	19
Kelly, Garry	316	9	325	2
McAllister, Gary	305	20	325	49
Dodd, Jason	304	20	324	9
Keown, Martin	295	28	323	4
Martyn, Nigel	319	1	320	0
Atherton, Peter	317	1	318	9
Perry, Chris	294	22	316	6
Dublin, Dion	268	44	312	111
Walker, Ian	310	2	312	0
Fowler, Robbie	269	41	310	143
Schmeichel, Peter	310	0	310	1
Sinclair, Trevor	294	14	308	48
Ince, Paul	306	0	306	42
Dixon, Lee	288	17	305	9
Wright, Alan	292	11	303	5
Barmby, Nick	268	34	302	52
Le Saux, Graeme	289	13	302	11
Anderton, Darren	273	26	299	34
Hughes, Mark	267	31	298	63
Watson, Steve	266	30	296	25
Neville, Gary	279	14	293	5
Kenna, Jeff	282	8	290	8
Impey, Andy	268	21	289	13
Telfer, Paul	264	25	289	7
Scholes, Paul	230	58	288	78
Sinclair, Frank	273	15	288	8
Staunton, Steve	271	17	288	12
Deane, Brian	257	29	286	70
Flowers, Tim	283	3	286	0
Stuart, Graham	246	36	282	45
Flitcroft, Garry	263	17	280	24
Lee, Robert	269	11	280	34
Merson, Paul	254	26	280	46

Most Used Substitutes in the Premiership

	Full	Sub	Total	Goals
Solskjaer, Ole Gunnar	142	71	213	85
Clarke, Andy	54	70	124	11
Butt, Nicky	210	60	270	21
Flo, Tore Andre	82	59	141	38
Gillespie, Keith	148	59	207	16
Scholes, Paul	230	58	288	78
Kanu, Nwankwo	63	56	119	30
McClair, Brian	106	56	162	18
Murphy, Danny	114	56	170	25
Cadamarteri, Danny	38	55	93	13
Fenton, Graham	38	55	93	13
Joachim, Julian	101	55	156	42
Whelan, Noel	188	55	243	43
Huckerby, Darren	110	54	164	32
Parlour, Ray	280	53	333	21
Vassell, Darius	90	51	141	333
Yorke, Dwight	280	51	331	119
Holdsworth, Dean	179	50	229	63
Lua-Lua, Lumana Tresor	24	50	74	9
Quinn, Niall	200	50	250	59
Watson, Gordon	61	48	109	23
Ameobi, Shola	42	47	89	14
Dichio, Danny	46	47	93	19
Rosenthal, Ronny	71	47	118	10
Beattie, James	151	46	197	65
Neville, Phil	198	46	244	5
Burton, Deon	74	45	119	22
Dublin, Dion	268	44	312	111
Johansson, Jonatan	74	44	118	23
Konchesky, Paul	78	44	122	4
Moncur, John	172	44	216	10
Sheringham, Teddy	331	44	375	139
Smicer, Vladimir	67	44	111	10
Wilcox, Jason	229	44	273	31
Zola, Gianfranco	185	44	229	59
Cole, Andy	293	43	336	164
Gudjohnsen, Eidur	80	43	123	40
Jeffers, Francis	46	43	89	22
Morris, Jody	93	43	136	5
Tessem, Jo	67	43	110	12
Bart-Williams, Chris	169	42	211	22
Berger, Patrik	126	42	168	33
Hyde, Graham	117	42	159	11
Marshall, Ian	117	42	159	33
Poyet, Gustavo	145	42	187	54
Barlow, Stuart	21	41	62	10
Fowler, Robbie	269	41	310	143
Boa Morte, Luis	84	40	124	13
Davies, Kevin	126	40	166	29
Ricketts, Michael	51	40	91	21
Sturridge, Dean	115	40	155	38

Most Goals in the Premiership

	Full	Sub	Total	Goals
Shearer, Alan	370	11	381	243
Cole, Andy	293	43	336	164
Ferdinand, Les	305	34	339	148
Fowler, Robbie	269	41	310	143
Sheringham, Teddy	331	44	375	139
Yorke, Dwight	280	51	331	119
Owen, Michael	193	23	216	118
Wright, Ian	202	11	213	113
Henry, Thierry	158	15	173	112
Dublin, Dion	268	44	312	111
Hasselbaink, Jimmy Floyd	185	20	205	103
Le Tissier, Matthew	234	36	270	101
Solskjaer, Ole Gunnar	142	71	213	85
Giggs, Ryan	337	38	375	81
Sutton, Chris	219	18	237	81
Cottee, Tony	193	27	220	78
Scholes, Paul	230	58	288	78
Bergkamp, Dennis	225	37	262	77
Campbell, Kevin	237	37	274	76
Phillips, Kevin	167	5	172	73
Heskey, Emile	241	33	274	72
Armstrong, Chris	192	24	216	71
Cantona, Eric	154	2	156	70
Deane, Brian	257	29	286	70
Van Nistelrooy, Ruud	93	5	98	68
Speed, Gary	406	8	414	67
Di Canio, Paolo	176	14	190	66
Beattie, James	151	46	197	65
Holdsworth, Dean	179	50	229	63
Hughes, Mark	267	31	298	63
Beckham, David	237	28	265	62
Collymore, Stan	138	25	163	62
Ferguson, Duncan	173	34	207	62
Quinn, Niall	200	50	250	59
Viduka, Mark	126	4	130	59
Zola, Gianfranco	185	44	229	59
Beardsley, Peter	179	6	185	58
Anelka, Nicolas	132	23	155	57
Gallacher, Kevin	175	23	198	55
Hartson, John	141	14	155	55
Poyet, Gustavo	145	42	187	54
Euell, Jason	175	33	208	53
Barmby, Nick	268	34	302	52
Ekoku, Efan	128	32	160	52
Keane, Robbie	118	22	140	52
Kewell, Harry	205	12	217	52
Bright, Mark	118	25	143	50
Wanchope, Paulo	135	21	156	50

Most Prolific Goalscorers (scored 50 plus goals)

	Full	Sub	Total	Goals
Van Nistelrooy, Ruud	93	5	98	68
Henry, Thierry	158	15	173	112
Shearer, Alan	370	11	381	243
Owen, Michael	193	23	216	118
Wright, Ian	202	11	213	113
Hasselbaink, Jimmy Floyd	185	20	205	103
Cole, Andy	293	43	336	164
Fowler, Robbie	269	41	310	143
Viduka, Mark	126	4	130	59
Cantona, Eric	154	2	156	70
Ferdinand, Les	305	34	339	148
Phillips, Kevin	167	5	172	73
Solskjaer, Ole Gunnar	142	71	213	85
Collymore, Stan	138	25	163	62
Le Tissier, Matthew	234	36	270	101
Keane, Robbie	118	22	140	52
Sheringham, Teddy	331	44	375	139
Anelka, Nicolas	132	23	155	57
Yorke, Dwight	280	51	331	119
Dublin, Dion	268	44	312	111
Hartson, John	141	14	155	55
Cottee, Tony	193	27	220	78
Bright, Mark	118	25	143	50
Di Canio, Paolo	176	14	190	66
Sutton, Chris	219	18	237	81
Beattie, James	151	46	197	65
Armstrong, Chris	192	24	216	71
Ekoku, Efan	128	32	160	52
Wanchope, Paulo	135	21	156	50
Beardsley, Peter	179	6	185	58
Ferguson, Duncan	173	34	207	62
Bergkamp, Dennis	225	37	262	77
Poyet, Gustavo	145	42	187	54
Gallacher, Kevin	175	23	198	55
Campbell, Kevin	237	37	274	76
Holdsworth, Dean	179	50	229	63
Scholes, Paul	230	58	288	78
Heskey, Emile	241	33	274	72
Zola, Gianfranco	185	44	229	59
Euell, Jason	175	33	208	53
Deane, Brian	257	29	286	70
Kewell, Harry	205	12	217	52
Quinn, Niall	200	50	250	59
Beckham, David	237	28	265	62
Giggs, Ryan	337	38	375	81
Hughes, Mark	267	31	298	63
Barmby, Nick	268	34	302	52
Speed, Gary	406	8	414	67

Players' Premiership appearances and goal records

Player / Club	Season	Apps	Subs	Gls
Abidallah, Nabil		*Apps*	*Subs*	*Gls*
Ipswich T	2000-01	0	2	0
Ablett, Gary		*Apps*	*Subs*	*Gls*
Everton	1992-93	40	0	0
Everton	1993-94	32	0	1
Everton	1994-95	26	0	3
Everton	1995-96	13	0	0
		111	**0**	**4**
Abou, Samassi		*Apps*	*Subs*	*Gls*
West Ham U	1997-98	12	7	5
West Ham U	1998-99	2	1	0
		14	**8**	**5**
Acimovic, Milenko		*Apps*	*Subs*	*Gls*
Tottenham H	2002-03	4	13	0
Acuna, Clarence		*Apps*	*Subs*	*Gls*
Newcastle U	2000-01	23	3	3
Newcastle U	2001-02	10	6	3
Newcastle U	2002-03	2	2	0
		35	**11**	**6**
Adams, Micky		*Apps*	*Subs*	*Gls*
Southampton	1992-93	38	0	4
Southampton	1993-94	17	2	0
		55	**2**	**4**
Adams, Neil		*Apps*	*Subs*	*Gls*
Oldham Ath.	1992-93	26	6	9
Oldham Ath.	1993-94	7	6	0
Norwich C	1993-94	11	3	0
Norwich C	1994-95	23	10	3
		67	**25**	**12**
Adams, Tony		*Apps*	*Subs*	*Gls*
Arsenal	1992-93	33	2	0
Arsenal	1993-94	35	0	0
Arsenal	1994-95	27	0	3
Arsenal	1995-96	21	0	1
Arsenal	1996-97	27	1	3
Arsenal	1997-98	26	0	3
Arsenal	1998-99	26	0	1
Arsenal	1999-00	21	0	0
Arsenal	2000-01	26	0	1
Arsenal	2001-02	10	0	0
		252	**3**	**12**
Agnew, Steve		*Apps*	*Subs*	*Gls*
Leicester C	1994-95	7	4	0
Sunderland	1996-97	11	4	2
		18	**8**	**2**
Agogo, Junior		*Apps*	*Subs*	*Gls*
Sheff. Wed.	1997-98	0	1	0
Sheff. Wed.	1998-99	0	1	0
		0	**2**	**0**
Ainsworth, Gareth		*Apps*	*Subs*	*Gls*
Wimbledon	1998-99	5	3	0
Wimbledon	1999-00	0	2	2
		5	**5**	**2**
Aiston, Sam		*Apps*	*Subs*	*Gls*
Sunderland	1996-97	0	2	0
Akinbiyi, Ade		*Apps*	*Subs*	*Gls*
Norwich C	1993-94	0	2	0
Norwich C	1994-95	6	7	0
Leicester C	2000-01	33	4	9
Leicester C	2001-02	16	5	2
		55	**18**	**11**
Albert, Philippe		*Apps*	*Subs*	*Gls*
Newcastle U	1994-95	17	0	2
Newcastle U	1995-96	19	4	4
Newcastle U	1996-97	27	0	2
Newcastle U	1997-98	21	2	0
Newcastle U	1998-99	3	3	0
		87	**9**	**8**
Aleksidze, Rati		*Apps*	*Subs*	*Gls*
Chelsea	2000-01	0	2	0
Alexandersson, Niclas		*Apps*	*Subs*	*Gls*
Sheff. Wed.	1997-98	5	1	0
Sheff. Wed.	1998-99	31	1	3
Sheff. Wed.	1999-00	37	0	5
Everton	2000-01	17	3	2
Everton	2001-02	28	3	2
Everton	2002-03	4	3	0
		122	**11**	**12**
Aliadiere, Jeremie		*Apps*	*Subs*	*Gls*
Arsenal	2001-02	0	1	0
Arsenal	2002-03	0	3	1
Arsenal	2003-04	3	7	0
		3	**11**	**1**
Aljofree, Hasney		*Apps*	*Subs*	*Gls*
Bolton Wan.	1997-98	2	0	0
Allan, Derek		*Apps*	*Subs*	*Gls*
Southampton	1992-93	0	1	0
Allback, Marcus		*Apps*	*Subs*	*Gls*
Aston Villa	2002-03	9	11	5
Aston Villa	2003-04	7	8	1
		16	**19**	**6**
Allen, Bradley		*Apps*	*Subs*	*Gls*
QPR	1992-93	21	4	10
QPR	1993-94	14	7	7
QPR	1994-95	2	3	2
QPR	1995-96	5	3	1
		42	**17**	**20**
Allen, Chris		*Apps*	*Subs*	*Gls*
Nottm Forest	1995-96	1	2	1
Nottm Forest	1996-97	16	8	0
		17	**10**	**1**
Allen, Clive		*Apps*	*Subs*	*Gls*
West Ham U	1993-94	7	0	2
Allen, Graham		*Apps*	*Subs*	*Gls*
Everton	1996-97	0	1	0
Everton	1997-98	2	3	0
		2	**4**	**0**
Allen, Malcolm		*Apps*	*Subs*	*Gls*
Newcastle U	1993-94	9	0	5
Newcastle U	1994-95	0	1	0
		9	**1**	**5**
Allen, Martin		*Apps*	*Subs*	*Gls*
West Ham U	1993-94	20	6	6
West Ham U	1994-95	26	3	2
West Ham U	1995-96	3	0	1
		49	**9**	**9**
Allen, Paul		*Apps*	*Subs*	*Gls*
Tottenham H	1992-93	38	0	3
Tottenham H	1993-94	0	1	0
Southampton	1993-94	29	3	1
Southampton	1994-95	11	0	0
		78	**4**	**4**
Allen, Rory		*Apps*	*Subs*	*Gls*
Tottenham H	1996-97	9	3	2
Tottenham H	1997-98	1	3	0
Tottenham H	1998-99	0	5	0
		10	**11**	**2**
Allon, Joe		*Apps*	*Subs*	*Gls*
Chelsea	1992-93	1	2	0
Allou, Bernard		*Apps*	*Subs*	*Gls*
Nottm Forest	1998-99	0	2	0
Allsopp, Danny		*Apps*	*Subs*	*Gls*
Man. City	2000-01	0	1	0
Almeida, Marco		*Apps*	*Subs*	*Gls*
Southampton	1999-00	0	1	0
Aloisi, John		*Apps*	*Subs*	*Gls*
Coventry C	1998-99	7	9	5
Coventry C	1999-00	3	4	2
Coventry C	2000-01	8	11	3
		18	**24**	**10**
Alves, Paulo		*Apps*	*Subs*	*Gls*
West Ham U	1997-98	0	4	0
Ambrose, Darren		*Apps*	*Subs*	*Gls*
Ipswich T	2001-02	0	1	0
Newcastle U	2002-03	0	1	0
Newcastle U	2003-04	10	14	2
		10	**16**	**2**
Ambrosetti, Gabriele		*Apps*	*Subs*	*Gls*
Chelsea	1999-00	9	7	0
Ambrosio, Marco		*Apps*	*Subs*	*Gls*
Chelsea	2003-04	8	0	0
Ameobi, Shola		*Apps*	*Subs*	*Gls*
Newcastle U	2000-01	12	8	2
Newcastle U	2001-02	4	11	0
Newcastle U	2002-03	8	20	5
Newcastle U	2003-04	18	8	7
		42	**47**	**14**
Amokachi, Daniel		*Apps*	*Subs*	*Gls*
Everton	1994-95	17	1	4
Everton	1995-96	17	8	6
		34	**9**	**10**
Amoruso, Lorenzo		*Apps*	*Subs*	*Gls*
Blackburn R	2003-04	11	1	3
Andersen, Trond		*Apps*	*Subs*	*Gls*
Wimbledon	1999-00	35	1	0
Anderson, Viv		*Apps*	*Subs*	*Gls*
Sheff. Wed.	1992-93	24	2	3
Andersson, Andreas		*Apps*	*Subs*	*Gls*
Newcastle U	1997-98	10	2	2
Newcastle U	1998-99	11	4	2
		21	**6**	**4**
Andersson, Anders		*Apps*	*Subs*	*Gls*
Blackburn R	1997-98	1	3	0
Andersson, Patrik		*Apps*	*Subs*	*Gls*
Blackburn R	1992-93	6	5	0
Blackburn R	1993-94	1	0	0
		7	**5**	**0**
Anderton, Darren		*Apps*	*Subs*	*Gls*
Tottenham H	1992-93	32	2	6
Tottenham H	1993-94	35	2	6
Tottenham H	1994-95	37	0	5
Tottenham H	1995-96	6	2	2
Tottenham H	1996-97	14	2	3
Tottenham H	1997-98	7	8	0
Tottenham H	1998-99	31	1	3
Tottenham H	1999-00	22	0	3
Tottenham H	2000-01	22	1	2
Tottenham H	2001-02	33	2	3
Tottenham H	2002-03	18	2	0
Tottenham H	2003-04	16	4	1
		273	**26**	**34**
Andre, Pierre-Yves		*Apps*	*Subs*	*Gls*
Bolton Wan.	2002-03	0	9	0
Andresen, Martin		*Apps*	*Subs*	*Gls*
Wimbledon	1999-00	4	10	1
Blackburn R	2003-04	11	0	0
		15	**10**	**1**
Andrews, Ian		*Apps*	*Subs*	*Gls*
Southampton	1993-94	5	0	0
Andrews, Keith		*Apps*	*Subs*	*Gls*
Wolves	2003-04	1	0	0
Anelka, Nicolas		*Apps*	*Subs*	*Gls*
Arsenal	1996-97	0	4	0
Arsenal	1997-98	16	10	6
Arsenal	1998-99	34	1	17
Liverpool	2001-02	13	7	4
Man. City	2002-03	38	0	14
Man. City	2003-04	31	1	16
		132	**23**	**57**
Angel, Juan Pablo		*Apps*	*Subs*	*Gls*
Aston Villa	2000-01	7	2	1
Aston Villa	2001-02	26	3	12
Aston Villa	2002-03	8	7	1
Aston Villa	2003-04	33	0	16
		74	**12**	**30**
Angell, Brett		*Apps*	*Subs*	*Gls*
Everton	1993-94	13	3	1
Everton	1994-95	3	1	0
		16	**4**	**1**
Anthrobus, Steve		*Apps*	*Subs*	*Gls*
Wimbledon	1992-93	4	1	0
Appleby, Matty		*Apps*	*Subs*	*Gls*
Newcastle U	1993-94	1	0	0
Barnsley	1997-98	13	2	0
		14	**2**	**0**
Arca, Julio		*Apps*	*Subs*	*Gls*
Sunderland	2000-01	26	1	2
Sunderland	2001-02	20	2	1
Sunderland	2002-03	7	6	0
		53	**9**	**3**
Ardley, Neal		*Apps*	*Subs*	*Gls*
Wimbledon	1992-93	24	2	4
Wimbledon	1993-94	14	2	1
Wimbledon	1994-95	9	5	1
Wimbledon	1995-96	4	2	0
Wimbledon	1996-97	33	1	2
Wimbledon	1997-98	31	3	2
Wimbledon	1998-99	16	7	0
Wimbledon	1999-00	10	7	2
		141	**29**	**12**
Armstrong, Alun		*Apps*	*Subs*	*Gls*
Middlesbrough	1998-99	0	6	1
Middlesbrough	1999-00	3	9	1
Ipswich T	2000-01	15	6	7
Ipswich T	2001-02	21	11	4
		39	**32**	**13**
Armstrong, Chris		*Apps*	*Subs*	*Gls*
Crystal P	1992-93	35	0	15
Crystal P	1994-95	40	0	8
Tottenham H	1995-96	36	0	15
Tottenham H	1996-97	12	0	5
Tottenham H	1997-98	13	6	5
Tottenham H	1998-99	24	10	7
Tottenham H	1999-00	29	2	14
Tottenham H	2000-01	3	6	2
		192	**24**	**71**
Armstrong, Craig		*Apps*	*Subs*	*Gls*
Nottm Forest	1998-99	20	2	0
Arphexad, Pegguy		*Apps*	*Subs*	*Gls*
Leicester C	1997-98	6	0	0
Leicester C	1998-99	2	2	0
Leicester C	1999-00	9	2	0
Liverpool	2001-02	1	1	0
		18	**5**	**0**
Asanovic, Aljosa		*Apps*	*Subs*	*Gls*
Derby Co.	1996-97	34	0	6
Derby Co.	1997-98	3	1	1
		37	**1**	**7**
Ashton, Jon		*Apps*	*Subs*	*Gls*
Leicester C	2001-02	3	4	0
Asprilla, Faustino		*Apps*	*Subs*	*Gls*
Newcastle U	1995-96	11	3	3
Newcastle U	1996-97	17	7	4
Newcastle U	1997-98	8	2	2
		36	**12**	**9**
Atherton, Peter		*Apps*	*Subs*	*Gls*
Coventry C	1992-93	39	0	0
Coventry C	1993-94	39	1	0
Sheff. Wed.	1994-95	41	0	1
Sheff. Wed.	1995-96	36	0	0
Sheff. Wed.	1996-97	37	0	2
Sheff. Wed.	1997-98	27	0	3
Sheff. Wed.	1998-99	38	0	2
Sheff. Wed.	1999-00	35	0	1
Bradford C	2000-01	25	0	0
		317	**1**	**9**
Atkins, Mark		*Apps*	*Subs*	*Gls*
Blackburn R	1992-93	24	7	5
Blackburn R	1993-94	8	7	1
Blackburn R	1994-95	30	4	6
Blackburn R	1995-96	0	4	0
		62	**22**	**12**
Atkinson, Dalian		*Apps*	*Subs*	*Gls*
Aston Villa	1992-93	28	0	11
Aston Villa	1993-94	29	0	8
Aston Villa	1994-95	11	5	3
		68	**5**	**22**
Austin, Dean		*Apps*	*Subs*	*Gls*
Tottenham H	1992-93	33	1	0
Tottenham H	1993-94	20	3	0
Tottenham H	1994-95	23	1	0
Tottenham H	1995-96	28	0	0
Tottenham H	1996-97	13	2	0
		117	**7**	**0**
Ayegbeni, Yakubu		*Apps*	*Subs*	*Gls*
Portsmouth	2003-04	35	2	16
Ba, Ibrahim		*Apps*	*Subs*	*Gls*
Bolton Wan.	2003-04	0	9	0
Baardsen, Espen		*Apps*	*Subs*	*Gls*
Tottenham H	1996-97	1	1	0
Tottenham H	1997-98	9	0	0
Tottenham H	1998-99	12	0	0
Everton	2002-03	1	0	0
		23	**1**	**0**
Babayaro, Celestine		*Apps*	*Subs*	*Gls*
Chelsea	1997-98	8	0	0
Chelsea	1998-99	26	2	3
Chelsea	1999-00	23	2	0
Chelsea	2000-01	19	5	0
Chelsea	2001-02	18	0	0
Chelsea	2002-03	16	3	1
Chelsea	2003-04	5	1	1
		115	**13**	**5**
Babb, Phil		*Apps*	*Subs*	*Gls*
Coventry C	1992-93	27	7	0
Coventry C	1993-94	40	0	3
Coventry C	1994-95	3	0	0

Darren Anderton.

Club	Season	Apps	Subs	Gls
Liverpool	1994-95	33	1	0
Liverpool	1995-96	28	0	0
Liverpool	1996-97	21	1	1
Liverpool	1997-98	18	1	0
Liverpool	1998-99	24	1	0
Sunderland	2002-03	26	0	0
		220	**11**	**4**
Babbel, Markus		*Apps*	*Subs*	*Gls*
Liverpool	2000-01	38	0	3
Liverpool	2001-02	2	0	0
Liverpool	2002-03	2	0	0
Blackburn R	2003-04	23	2	3
		65	**2**	**6**
Badir, Walid		*Apps*	*Subs*	*Gls*
Wimbledon	1999-00	12	9	1
Baggio, Dino		*Apps*	*Subs*	*Gls*
Blackburn R	2003-04	0	9	1
Bagheri, Karim		*Apps*	*Subs*	*Gls*
Charlton Ath	2000-01	0	1	0
Baiano, Francesco		*Apps*	*Subs*	*Gls*
Derby Co.	1997-98	30	3	12
Derby Co.	1998-99	17	5	4
Derby Co.	1999-00	5	4	0
		52	**12**	**16**
Bailey, Dennis		*Apps*	*Subs*	*Gls*
QPR	1992-93	13	2	1
Baird, Chris		*Apps*	*Subs*	*Gls*
Southampton	2002-03	1	2	0
Southampton	2003-04	1	3	0
		2	**5**	**0**
Bakalli, Adrian		*Apps*	*Subs*	*Gls*
Watford	1999-00	0	2	0
Bakayoko, Ibrahima		*Apps*	*Subs*	*Gls*
Everton	1998-99	17	6	4
Baker, Clive		*Apps*	*Subs*	*Gls*
Ipswich T	1992-93	30	1	0
Ipswich T	1993-94	15	0	0
Ipswich T	1994-95	2	0	0
		47	**1**	**0**
Baker, Steve		*Apps*	*Subs*	*Gls*
Middlesbrough	1998-99	1	1	0
Bakke, Eirik		*Apps*	*Subs*	*Gls*
Leeds U	1999-00	24	5	2
Leeds U	2000-01	24	5	2
Leeds U	2001-02	20	7	2
Leeds U	2002-03	31	3	1
Leeds U	2003-04	8	2	1
		107	**22**	**8**
Balaban, Bosko		*Apps*	*Subs*	*Gls*
Aston Villa	2001-02	0	8	0
Balis, Igor		*Apps*	*Subs*	*Gls*
West Brom	2002-03	27	1	2
Ball, Kevin		*Apps*	*Subs*	*Gls*
Sunderland	1996-97	32	0	3
Sunderland	1999-00	6	5	0
		38	**5**	**3**
Ball, Michael		*Apps*	*Subs*	*Gls*
Everton	1996-97	2	3	0
Everton	1997-98	21	4	1
Everton	1998-99	36	1	3
Everton	1999-00	14	11	1
Everton	2000-01	29	0	3
		102	**19**	**8**
Ballesta, Salva		*Apps*	*Subs*	*Gls*
Bolton Wan.	2002-03	1	5	0
Banger, Nicky		*Apps*	*Subs*	*Gls*
Southampton	1992-93	10	17	6
Southampton	1993-94	4	10	0
Southampton	1994-95	4	0	2
		18	**27**	**8**
Banks, Steve		*Apps*	*Subs*	*Gls*
Bolton Wan.	2001-02	1	0	0
Bannister, Gary		*Apps*	*Subs*	*Gls*
Nottm Forest	1992-93	27	4	8
Bardsley, David		*Apps*	*Subs*	*Gls*
QPR	1992-93	40	0	3
QPR	1993-94	32	0	0
QPR	1994-95	30	0	0
QPR	1995-96	28	1	0
		130	**1**	**3**
Barker, Simon		*Apps*	*Subs*	*Gls*
QPR	1992-93	21	4	1
QPR	1993-94	35	2	5
QPR	1994-95	37	0	4
QPR	1995-96	33	0	5
		126	**6**	**15**
Barlow, Andy		*Apps*	*Subs*	*Gls*
Oldham Ath.	1992-93	6	0	0
Oldham Ath.	1993-94	3	3	0
		9	**3**	**0**
Barlow, Stuart		*Apps*	*Subs*	*Gls*
Everton	1992-93	8	18	5
Everton	1993-94	6	16	3
Everton	1994-95	7	4	2
Everton	1995-96	0	3	0
		21	**41**	**10**
Barmby, Nick		*Apps*	*Subs*	*Gls*
Tottenham H	1992-93	17	5	6
Tottenham H	1993-94	27	0	5
Tottenham H	1994-95	37	1	9
Middlesbrough	1995-96	32	0	7
Middlesbrough	1996-97	10	0	1
Everton	1996-97	22	3	4
Everton	1997-98	26	4	2
Everton	1998-99	20	4	3

Club	Season	Apps	Subs	Gls
Everton	1999-00	37	0	9
Liverpool	2000-01	21	5	2
Liverpool	2001-02	2	4	0
Leeds U	2002-03	16	3	4
Leeds U	2003-04	1	5	0
		268	**34**	**52**
Barnard, Darren		*Apps*	*Subs*	*Gls*
Chelsea	1992-93	8	5	1
Chelsea	1993-94	9	3	1
Barnsley	1997-98	33	2	2
		50	**10**	**4**
Barnes, David		*Apps*	*Subs*	*Gls*
Sheff. Utd.	1992-93	13	0	0
Sheff. Utd.	1993-94	2	0	0
		15	**0**	**0**
Barnes, John		*Apps*	*Subs*	*Gls*
Liverpool	1992-93	26	1	5
Liverpool	1993-94	24	2	3
Liverpool	1994-95	38	0	7
Liverpool	1995-96	36	0	3
Liverpool	1996-97	34	1	4
Newcastle U	1997-98	22	4	6
Newcastle U	1998-99	0	1	0
Charlton Ath	1998-99	2	10	0
		182	**19**	**28**
Barness, Anthony		*Apps*	*Subs*	*Gls*
Chelsea	1992-93	2	0	0
Chelsea	1994-95	10	2	0
Charlton Ath	1998-99	0	3	0
Bolton Wan.	2001-02	19	6	0
Bolton Wan.	2002-03	21	4	0
Bolton Wan.	2003-04	11	4	0
		63	**19**	**0**
Barnwell-Edinboro, Jamie		*Apps*	*Subs*	*Gls*
Coventry C	1995-96	0	1	0
Baros, Milan		*Apps*	*Subs*	*Gls*
Liverpool	2002-03	17	10	9
Liverpool	2003-04	6	7	1
		23	**17**	**10**
Barrett, Earl		*Apps*	*Subs*	*Gls*
Aston Villa	1992-93	42	0	1
Aston Villa	1993-94	39	0	0
Aston Villa	1994-95	24	1	0
Everton	1994-95	17	0	0
Everton	1995-96	8	0	0
Everton	1996-97	36	0	0
Everton	1997-98	12	1	0
Sheff. Wed.	1997-98	10	0	0
Sheff. Wed.	1998-99	0	5	0
		188	**7**	**1**
Barrett, Graham		*Apps*	*Subs*	*Gls*
Arsenal	1999-00	0	2	0
Barron, Mike		*Apps*	*Subs*	*Gls*
Middlesbrough	1995-96	1	0	0
Barrowman, Andrew		*Apps*	*Subs*	*Gls*
Birmingham C	2003-04	0	1	0
Barry, Gareth		*Apps*	*Subs*	*Gls*
Aston Villa	1997-98	1	1	0
Aston Villa	1998-99	27	5	2
Aston Villa	1999-00	30	0	1
Aston Villa	2000-01	29	1	0
Aston Villa	2001-02	16	4	0
Aston Villa	2002-03	35	0	3
Aston Villa	2003-04	36	0	3
		174	**11**	**9**
Bart-Williams, Chris		*Apps*	*Subs*	*Gls*
Sheff. Wed.	1992-93	21	13	6
Sheff. Wed.	1993-94	30	7	8
Sheff. Wed.	1994-95	32	6	2
Nottm Forest	1995-96	33	0	0
Nottm Forest	1996-97	16	0	1
Nottm Forest	1998-99	20	4	3
Charlton Ath	2001-02	10	6	1
Charlton Ath	2002-03	7	6	1
		169	**42**	**22**
Barthez, Fabien		*Apps*	*Subs*	*Gls*
Man. Utd.	2000-01	30	0	0
Man. Utd.	2001-02	32	0	0
Man. Utd.	2002-03	30	0	0
		92	**0**	**0**
Bartlett, Neal		*Apps*	*Subs*	*Gls*
Southampton	1992-93	0	1	0
Southampton	1993-94	4	3	0
		4	**4**	**0**
Bartlett, Shaun		*Apps*	*Subs*	*Gls*
Charlton Ath	2000-01	16	2	7
Charlton Ath	2001-02	10	4	1
Charlton Ath	2002-03	25	6	4
Charlton Ath	2003-04	13	6	5
		64	**18**	**17**
Barton, Joey		*Apps*	*Subs*	*Gls*
Man. City	2002-03	7	0	1
Man. City	2003-04	24	4	1
		31	**4**	**2**
Barton, Warren		*Apps*	*Subs*	*Gls*
Wimbledon	1992-93	23	0	2
Wimbledon	1993-94	37	2	2
Wimbledon	1994-95	39	0	2
Newcastle U	1995-96	30	1	0
Newcastle U	1996-97	14	4	1
Newcastle U	1997-98	17	6	3
Newcastle U	1998-99	17	7	0
Newcastle U	1999-00	33	1	0
Newcastle U	2000-01	27	2	0
Newcastle U	2001-02	4	1	0
Derby Co.	2001-02	14	0	0
		255	**24**	**10**

Club	Season	Apps	Subs	Gls
Bartram, Vince		*Apps*	*Subs*	*Gls*
Arsenal	1994-95	11	0	0
Basham, Steve		*Apps*	*Subs*	*Gls*
Southampton	1996-97	1	5	0
Southampton	1997-98	0	9	0
Southampton	1998-99	0	4	1
		1	**18**	**1**
Bassedas, Christian		*Apps*	*Subs*	*Gls*
Newcastle U	2000-01	17	5	1
Newcastle U	2001-02	1	1	0
		18	**6**	**1**
Bassila, Christian		*Apps*	*Subs*	*Gls*
West Ham U	2000-01	0	3	0
Batty, David		*Apps*	*Subs*	*Gls*
Leeds U	1992-93	30	0	1
Leeds U	1993-94	8	1	0
Blackburn R	1993-94	26	0	0
Blackburn R	1994-95	4	1	0
Blackburn R	1995-96	23	0	1
Newcastle U	1995-96	11	0	1
Newcastle U	1996-97	32	0	1
Newcastle U	1997-98	32	0	1
Newcastle U	1998-99	6	2	0
Leeds U	1998-99	10	0	0
Leeds U	1999-00	16	0	0
Leeds U	2000-01	13	3	0
Leeds U	2001-02	30	6	0
Leeds U	2003-04	10	2	0
		251	**15**	**5**
Beagrie, Peter		*Apps*	*Subs*	*Gls*
Everton	1992-93	11	11	3
Everton	1993-94	29	0	3
Man. City	1993-94	9	0	1
Man. City	1994-95	33	4	2
Man. City	1995-96	4	1	0
Everton	1997-98	4	2	0
Bradford C	1999-00	30	5	7
Bradford C	2000-01	9	10	1
		129	**33**	**17**
Beardsley, Peter		*Apps*	*Subs*	*Gls*
Everton	1992-93	39	0	10
Newcastle U	1993-94	35	0	21
Newcastle U	1994-95	34	0	12
Newcastle U	1995-96	35	0	8
Newcastle U	1996-97	22	3	5
Bolton Wan.	1997-98	14	3	2
		179	**6**	**58**
Beasant, Dave		*Apps*	*Subs*	*Gls*
Chelsea	1992-93	17	0	0
Southampton	1993-94	25	0	0
Southampton	1994-95	12	1	0
Southampton	1995-96	36	0	0
Southampton	1996-97	13	1	0
Nottm Forest	1998-99	26	0	0
		129	**2**	**0**
Beattie, James		*Apps*	*Subs*	*Gls*
Blackburn R	1996-97	1	0	0
Blackburn R	1997-98	0	3	0
Southampton	1998-99	22	13	5
Southampton	1999-00	8	10	0
Southampton	2000-01	29	8	11
Southampton	2001-02	24	4	12
Southampton	2002-03	35	3	23
Southampton	2003-04	32	5	14
		151	**46**	**65**
Beck, Mikkel		*Apps*	*Subs*	*Gls*
Middlesbrough	1996-97	22	3	5
Middlesbrough	1998-99	13	14	5
Derby Co.	1998-99	6	1	1
Derby Co.	1999-00	5	6	1
		46	**24**	**12**
Beckford, Darren		*Apps*	*Subs*	*Gls*
Norwich C	1992-93	7	1	1
Oldham Ath.	1992-93	6	1	3
Oldham Ath.	1993-94	13	9	6
		26	**11**	**10**
Beckham, David		*Apps*	*Subs*	*Gls*
Man. Utd.	1994-95	2	2	0
Man. Utd.	1995-96	26	7	7
Man. Utd.	1996-97	33	3	8
Man. Utd.	1997-98	34	3	9
Man. Utd.	1998-99	33	1	6
Man. Utd.	1999-00	30	1	6
Man. Utd.	2000-01	29	2	9
Man. Utd.	2001-02	23	5	11
Man. Utd.	2002-03	27	4	6
		237	**28**	**62**
Beeney, Mark		*Apps*	*Subs*	*Gls*
Leeds U	1992-93	1	0	0
Leeds U	1993-94	22	0	0
Leeds U	1995-96	10	0	0
Leeds U	1996-97	1	0	0
Leeds U	1997-98	1	0	0
		35	**0**	**0**
Beesley, Paul		*Apps*	*Subs*	*Gls*
Sheff. Utd.	1992-93	39	0	2
Sheff. Utd.	1993-94	22	3	0
Leeds U	1995-96	8	2	0
Leeds U	1996-97	11	1	0
		80	**6**	**2**
Beharall, David		*Apps*	*Subs*	*Gls*
Newcastle U	1998-99	4	0	0
Newcastle U	1999-00	0	2	0
		4	**2**	**0**
Beinlich, Stefan		*Apps*	*Subs*	*Gls*
Aston Villa	1992-93	1	6	0
Aston Villa	1993-94	6	1	1
		7	**7**	**1**

Francesco Baiano.

Club	Season	Apps	Subs	Gls
Bellamy, Craig		*Apps*	*Subs*	*Gls*
Coventry C	2000-01	33	1	6
Newcastle U	2001-02	26	1	9
Newcastle U	2002-03	27	2	7
Newcastle U	2003-04	13	3	4
		99	**7**	**26**
Bellion, David		*Apps*	*Subs*	*Gls*
Sunderland	2001-02	0	9	0
Sunderland	2002-03	5	6	1
Man. Utd.	2003-04	4	10	2
		9	**25**	**3**
Belmadi, Djemal		*Apps*	*Subs*	*Gls*
Man. City	2002-03	2	6	0
Benali, Francis		*Apps*	*Subs*	*Gls*
Southampton	1992-93	31	2	0
Southampton	1993-94	34	3	0
Southampton	1994-95	32	3	0
Southampton	1995-96	28	1	0
Southampton	1996-97	14	4	0
Southampton	1997-98	32	1	1
Southampton	1998-99	19	4	0
Southampton	1999-00	25	1	0
Southampton	2000-01	0	4	0
Southampton	2001-02	0	3	0
Southampton	2002-03	2	0	0
		217	**26**	**1**
Benarbia, Ali		*Apps*	*Subs*	*Gls*
Man. City	2002-03	21	12	3
Benjamin, Trevor		*Apps*	*Subs*	*Gls*
Leicester C	2000-01	7	14	1
Leicester C	2001-02	4	7	0
Leicester C	2003-04	2	2	0
		13	**23**	**1**
Bennett, Frankie		*Apps*	*Subs*	*Gls*
Southampton	1993-94	0	8	1
Southampton	1995-96	5	6	0
		5	**14**	**1**
Bennett, Ian		*Apps*	*Subs*	*Gls*
Birmingham C	2002-03	10	0	0
Birmingham C	2003-04	4	2	0
		14	**2**	**0**
Bent, Darren		*Apps*	*Subs*	*Gls*
Ipswich T	2001-02	2	3	1
Bent, Marcus		*Apps*	*Subs*	*Gls*
Crystal P	1997-98	10	6	5
Blackburn R	2001-02	1	8	0
Ipswich T	2001-02	22	3	9
Leicester C	2003-04	28	5	9
		61	**22**	**23**
Bentley, David		*Apps*	*Subs*	*Gls*
Arsenal	2003-04	1	0	0
Beresford, David		*Apps*	*Subs*	*Gls*
Oldham Ath.	1993-94	0	1	0
Beresford, John		*Apps*	*Subs*	*Gls*
Newcastle U	1993-94	34	0	0
Newcastle U	1994-95	33	0	0
Newcastle U	1995-96	32	1	0
Newcastle U	1996-97	18	1	0
Newcastle U	1997-98	17	1	2
Southampton	1997-98	10	0	0
Southampton	1998-99	1	3	0
Southampton	1999-00	0	3	0
		145	**9**	**2**
Beresford, Marlon		*Apps*	*Subs*	*Gls*
Middlesbrough	1998-99	4	0	0
Middlesbrough	1999-00	1	0	0
Middlesbrough	2000-01	0	1	0
Middlesbrough	2001-02	0	1	0
		5	**2**	**0**

	Season	Apps	Subs	Gls
Berg, Henning		Apps	Subs	Gls
Blackburn R	1992-93	2	2	0
Blackburn R	1993-94	38	3	1
Blackburn R	1994-95	40	0	1
Blackburn R	1995-96	38	0	0
Blackburn R	1996-97	36	0	2
Man. Utd.	1997-98	23	4	1
Man. Utd.	1998-99	10	6	0
Man. Utd.	1999-00	16	6	1
Man. Utd.	2000-01	0	1	0
Blackburn R	2001-02	34	0	1
Blackburn R	2002-03	15	1	1
		252	**23**	**8**
Berger, Patrik		Apps	Subs	Gls
Liverpool	1996-97	13	10	6
Liverpool	1997-98	6	16	3
Liverpool	1998-99	30	2	7
Liverpool	1999-00	34	0	9
Liverpool	2000-01	11	3	2
Liverpool	2001-02	12	9	1
Liverpool	2002-03	0	2	0
Portsmouth	2003-04	20	0	5
		126	**42**	**33**
Bergkamp, Dennis		Apps	Subs	Gls
Arsenal	1995-96	33	0	11
Arsenal	1996-97	28	1	12
Arsenal	1997-98	28	0	16
Arsenal	1998-99	28	1	12
Arsenal	1999-00	23	5	6
Arsenal	2000-01	19	6	3
Arsenal	2001-02	22	11	9
Arsenal	2002-03	23	6	4
Arsenal	2003-04	21	7	4
		225	**37**	**77**
Bergsson, Gudni		Apps	Subs	Gls
Tottenham H	1992-93	0	5	0
Bolton Wan.	1995-96	34	0	4
Bolton Wan.	1997-98	34	1	2
Bolton Wan.	2001-02	30	0	1
Bolton Wan.	2002-03	31	0	1
		129	**6**	**8**
Berkovic, Eyal		Apps	Subs	Gls
Southampton	1996-97	26	2	4
West Ham U	1997-98	34	1	7
West Ham U	1998-99	28	2	3
Man. City	2002-03	27	0	1
Man. City	2003-04	1	3	0
Portsmouth	2003-04	10	1	1
		126	**9**	**16**
Bernard, Olivier		Apps	Subs	Gls
Newcastle U	2001-02	4	12	3
Newcastle U	2002-03	24	6	2
Newcastle U	2003-04	35	0	1
		63	**18**	**6**
Bernard, Paul		Apps	Subs	Gls
Oldham Ath.	1992-93	32	1	4
Oldham Ath.	1993-94	32	0	5
		64	**1**	**9**
Berry, Greg		Apps	Subs	Gls
Wimbledon	1992-93	2	1	0
Wimbledon	1993-94	4	0	1
		6	**1**	**1**
Berti, Nicola		Apps	Subs	Gls
Tottenham H	1997-98	17	0	3
Tottenham H	1998-99	4	0	0
		21	**0**	**3**
Betsy, Kevin		Apps	Subs	Gls
Fulham	2001-02	0	1	0
Betts, Robert		Apps	Subs	Gls
Coventry C	1999-00	0	2	0
Coventry C	2000-01	0	1	0
		0	**3**	**0**
Bewers, Jon		Apps	Subs	Gls
Aston Villa	1999-00	0	1	0
Bilic, Slaven		Apps	Subs	Gls
West Ham U	1995-96	13	0	0
West Ham U	1996-97	35	0	2
Everton	1997-98	22	2	0
Everton	1998-99	4	0	0
		74	**2**	**2**
Billing, Peter		Apps	Subs	Gls
Coventry C	1992-93	3	0	0
Billio, Patrizio		Apps	Subs	Gls
Crystal P	1997-98	1	2	0
Biscan, Igor		Apps	Subs	Gls
Liverpool	2000-01	8	5	0
Liverpool	2001-02	4	1	0
Liverpool	2002-03	3	3	0
Liverpool	2003-04	27	2	0
		42	**11**	**0**
Bischoff, Mikkel		Apps	Subs	Gls
Man. City	2002-03	1	0	0
Bishop, Ian		Apps	Subs	Gls
West Ham U	1993-94	36	0	1
West Ham U	1994-95	31	0	1
West Ham U	1995-96	35	0	1
West Ham U	1996-97	26	3	1
West Ham U	1997-98	3	0	0
Man. City	2000-01	3	7	0
		134	**10**	**4**
Bjorklund, Joachim		Apps	Subs	Gls
Sunderland	2001-02	11	1	0
Sunderland	2002-03	19	1	0
		30	**2**	**0**
Bjornebye, Stig Inge		Apps	Subs	Gls
Liverpool	1992-93	11	0	0
Liverpool	1993-94	6	3	0
Liverpool	1994-95	31	0	0
Liverpool	1995-96	2	0	0
Liverpool	1996-97	38	0	2
Liverpool	1997-98	24	1	0
Liverpool	1998-99	20	3	0
Blackburn R	2001-02	23	0	0
		155	**7**	**2**
Black, Chris		Apps	Subs	Gls
Sunderland	2002-03	2	0	0
Black, Kingsley		Apps	Subs	Gls
Nottm Forest	1992-93	19	5	5
Nottm Forest	1994-95	5	5	2
Nottm Forest	1995-96	1	1	0
		25	**11**	**7**
Black, Tommy		Apps	Subs	Gls
Arsenal	1999-00	0	1	0
Blackmore, Clayton		Apps	Subs	Gls
Man. Utd.	1992-93	12	2	0
Middlesbrough	1995-96	4	1	0
Middlesbrough	1996-97	14	2	2
		30	**5**	**2**
Blackwell, Dean		Apps	Subs	Gls
Wimbledon	1992-93	19	5	0
Wimbledon	1993-94	16	2	0
Wimbledon	1995-96	8	0	0
Wimbledon	1996-97	22	5	0
Wimbledon	1997-98	35	0	0
Wimbledon	1998-99	27	1	0
Wimbledon	1999-00	16	1	0
		143	**14**	**0**
Blake, Mark		Apps	Subs	Gls
Aston Villa	1992-93	0	1	0
Leicester C	1994-95	26	4	3
		26	**5**	**3**
Blake, Nathan		Apps	Subs	Gls
Sheff. Utd.	1993-94	7	5	5
Bolton Wan.	1995-96	14	4	1
Bolton Wan.	1997-98	35	0	12
Blackburn R	1998-99	9	2	3
Blackburn R	2001-02	0	3	1
Wolves	2003-04	10	3	1
		75	**17**	**23**
Blake, Robbie		Apps	Subs	Gls
Bradford C	1999-00	15	13	2
Bradford C	2000-01	14	7	4
		29	**20**	**6**
Blanc, Laurent		Apps	Subs	Gls
Man. Utd.	2001-02	29	0	1
Man. Utd.	2002-03	15	4	0
		44	**4**	**1**
Blatherwick, Steve		Apps	Subs	Gls
Nottm Forest	1996-97	7	0	0
Blatsis, Con		Apps	Subs	Gls
Derby Co.	2000-01	2	0	0
Blayney, Alan		Apps	Subs	Gls
Southampton	2003-04	2	0	0
Bleidelis, Imants		Apps	Subs	Gls
Southampton	2000-01	0	1	0
Southampton	2001-02	0	1	0
		0	**2**	**0**
Blinker, Regi		Apps	Subs	Gls
Sheff. Wed.	1995-96	9	0	2
Sheff. Wed.	1996-97	15	18	1
		24	**18**	**3**
Blissett, Gary		Apps	Subs	Gls
Wimbledon	1993-94	6	12	3
Wimbledon	1994-95	4	5	0
Wimbledon	1995-96	0	4	0
		10	**21**	**3**
Blomqvist, Jesper		Apps	Subs	Gls
Man. Utd.	1998-99	20	5	1
Everton	2001-02	10	5	1
Charlton Ath	2002-03	0	3	0
		30	**13**	**2**
Blondeau, Patrick		Apps	Subs	Gls
Sheff. Wed.	1997-98	5	1	0
Blondel, Jonathan		Apps	Subs	Gls
Tottenham H	2002-03	0	1	0
Tottenham H	2003-04	0	1	0
		0	**2**	**0**
Blunt, Jason		Apps	Subs	Gls
Leeds U	1995-96	2	1	0
Leeds U	1996-97	0	1	0
		2	**2**	**0**
Boa Morte, Luis		Apps	Subs	Gls
Arsenal	1997-98	4	11	0
Arsenal	1998-99	2	6	0
Arsenal	1999-00	0	2	0
Southampton	1999-00	6	8	1
Fulham	2001-02	15	8	1
Fulham	2002-03	25	4	2
Fulham	2003-04	32	1	9
		84	**40**	**13**
Boateng, George		Apps	Subs	Gls
Coventry C	1997-98	14	0	1
Coventry C	1998-99	29	4	4
Aston Villa	1999-00	30	3	2
Aston Villa	2000-01	29	4	1
Aston Villa	2001-02	37	0	1
Middlesbrough	2002-03	28	0	0
Middlesbrough	2003-04	35	0	0
		202	**11**	**9**
Bobic, Fredi		Apps	Subs	Gls
Bolton Wan.	2001-02	14	2	4
Bocanegra, Carlos		Apps	Subs	Gls
Fulham	2003-04	15	0	0
Boden, Chris		Apps	Subs	Gls
Aston Villa	1994-95	0	1	0
Bodin, Paul		Apps	Subs	Gls
Swindon T	1993-94	28	4	7
Boere, Jeroen		Apps	Subs	Gls
West Ham U	1993-94	0	4	0
West Ham U	1994-95	15	5	6
West Ham U	1995-96	0	1	0
		15	**10**	**6**
Boertien, Paul		Apps	Subs	Gls
Derby Co.	1998-99	0	1	0
Derby Co.	1999-00	0	2	0
Derby Co.	2000-01	7	1	1
Derby Co.	2001-02	23	9	0
		30	**13**	**1**
Bogarde, Winston		Apps	Subs	Gls
Chelsea	2000-01	2	7	0
Bohinen, Lars		Apps	Subs	Gls
Nottm Forest	1994-95	30	4	6
Nottm Forest	1995-96	7	0	0
Blackburn R	1995-96	17	2	4
Blackburn R	1996-97	17	6	2
Blackburn R	1997-98	6	10	1
Derby Co.	1997-98	9	0	1
Derby Co.	1998-99	29	3	0
Derby Co.	1999-00	8	5	0
Derby Co.	2000-01	1	1	0
		124	**31**	**14**
Boksic, Alen		Apps	Subs	Gls
Middlesbrough	2000-01	26	2	12
Middlesbrough	2001-02	20	2	8
Middlesbrough	2002-03	13	5	2
		59	**9**	**22**
Boland, Willie		Apps	Subs	Gls
Coventry C	1992-93	0	1	0
Coventry C	1993-94	24	3	0
Coventry C	1994-95	9	3	0
Coventry C	1995-96	2	1	0
Coventry C	1996-97	0	1	0
Coventry C	1997-98	8	11	0
		43	**20**	**0**
Bolder, Adam		Apps	Subs	Gls
Derby Co.	2000-01	0	2	0
Derby Co.	2001-02	2	9	0
		2	**11**	**0**
Bonalair, Thierry		Apps	Subs	Gls
Nottm Forest	1998-99	24	4	1
Bonetti, Ivano		Apps	Subs	Gls
Crystal P	1997-98	0	2	0
Bonnissel, Jerome		Apps	Subs	Gls
Fulham	2003-04	16	0	0
Bonnot, Alex		Apps	Subs	Gls
Watford	1999-00	7	5	0
Boogers, Marco		Apps	Subs	Gls
West Ham U	1995-96	0	4	0
Booth, Andy		Apps	Subs	Gls
Sheff. Wed.	1996-97	32	3	10
Sheff. Wed.	1997-98	21	2	7
Sheff. Wed.	1998-99	34	0	6
Sheff. Wed.	1999-00	20	3	2
Tottenham H	2000-01	3	1	0
		110	**9**	**25**
Booty, Martyn		Apps	Subs	Gls
Coventry C	1993-94	2	0	0
Borbokis, Vassilis		Apps	Subs	Gls
Derby Co.	1998-99	3	1	0
Derby Co.	1999-00	6	6	0
		9	**7**	**0**
Borrows, Brian		Apps	Subs	Gls
Coventry C	1992-93	36	2	2
Coventry C	1993-94	29	0	0
Coventry C	1994-95	33	2	0
Coventry C	1995-96	21	0	0
Coventry C	1996-97	16	7	0
		135	**11**	**2**
Bosancic, Jovo		Apps	Subs	Gls
Barnsley	1997-98	13	4	2
Bosnich, Mark		Apps	Subs	Gls
Aston Villa	1992-93	17	0	0
Aston Villa	1993-94	28	0	0
Aston Villa	1994-95	30	0	0
Aston Villa	1995-96	38	0	0
Aston Villa	1996-97	20	0	0
Aston Villa	1997-98	30	0	0
Aston Villa	1998-99	15	0	0
Man. Utd.	1999-00	23	0	0
Chelsea	2001-02	5	0	0
		206	**0**	**0**
Bosvelt, Paul		Apps	Subs	Gls
Man. City	2003-04	22	3	0
Bothroyd, Jay		Apps	Subs	Gls
Coventry C	2000-01	3	5	0
Bould, Steve		Apps	Subs	Gls
Arsenal	1992-93	24	0	1
Arsenal	1993-94	23	2	1
Arsenal	1994-95	30	1	0
Arsenal	1995-96	19	0	0
Arsenal	1996-97	33	0	0
Arsenal	1997-98	21	3	0
Arsenal	1998-99	14	5	0
Sunderland	1999-00	19	1	0
Sunderland	2000-01	0	1	0
		183	**13**	**2**
Bound, Matthew		Apps	Subs	Gls
Southampton	1992-93	1	2	0
Southampton	1993-94	1	0	0
		2	**2**	**0**
Bowen, Jason		Apps	Subs	Gls
Southampton	1997-98	1	2	0
Bowen, Mark		Apps	Subs	Gls
Norwich C	1992-93	42	0	1
Norwich C	1993-94	41	0	5
Norwich C	1994-95	34	2	2
West Ham U	1996-97	15	2	1
Charlton Ath	1998-99	2	4	0
		134	**8**	**9**
Bowman, Rob		Apps	Subs	Gls
Leeds U	1992-93	3	1	0
Leeds U	1995-96	1	2	0
		4	**3**	**0**
Bowry, Bobby		Apps	Subs	Gls
Crystal P	1992-93	6	5	1
Crystal P	1994-95	13	5	0
		19	**10**	**1**
Bowyer, Lee		Apps	Subs	Gls
Leeds U	1996-97	32	0	4
Leeds U	1997-98	21	4	3
Leeds U	1998-99	35	0	9
Leeds U	1999-00	31	2	5
Leeds U	2000-01	38	0	9
Leeds U	2001-02	24	1	5
Leeds U	2002-03	15	0	3
West Ham U	2002-03	10	0	0
Newcastle U	2003-04	17	7	2
		223	**14**	**40**
Boxall, Danny		Apps	Subs	Gls
Crystal P	1997-98	0	1	0
Boylan, Lee		Apps	Subs	Gls
West Ham U	1996-97	0	1	0
Boyle, Wesley		Apps	Subs	Gls
Leeds U	1996-97	0	1	0
Bozinoski, Vlado		Apps	Subs	Gls
Ipswich T	1992-93	3	6	0
Bracewell, Paul		Apps	Subs	Gls
Newcastle U	1993-94	32	0	1
Newcastle U	1994-95	13	3	0
Sunderland	1996-97	38	0	0
		83	**3**	**1**
Bradley, Shayne		Apps	Subs	Gls
Southampton	1998-99	0	3	0
Southampton	1999-00	0	1	0
		0	**4**	**0**
Bradshaw, Carl		Apps	Subs	Gls
Sheff. Utd.	1992-93	24	8	1
Sheff. Utd.	1993-94	39	1	1
Norwich C	1994-95	25	1	1
		88	**10**	**3**
Brady, Garry		Apps	Subs	Gls
Tottenham H	1997-98	0	9	0
Newcastle U	1998-99	3	6	0
		3	**15**	**0**
Bragstad, Bjorn Otto		Apps	Subs	Gls
Derby Co.	2000-01	10	2	0
Bramble, Titus		Apps	Subs	Gls
Ipswich T	2000-01	23	3	1
Ipswich T	2001-02	16	2	0
Newcastle U	2002-03	13	3	0
Newcastle U	2003-04	27	2	0
		79	**10**	**1**
Branagan, Keith		Apps	Subs	Gls
Bolton Wan.	1995-96	31	0	0
Bolton Wan.	1997-98	34	0	0
Ipswich T	2000-01	2	0	0
Ipswich T	2001-02	0	1	0
		67	**1**	**0**
Branca, Marco		Apps	Subs	Gls
Middlesbrough	1998-99	0	1	0
Branch, Michael		Apps	Subs	Gls
Everton	1995-96	1	2	0
Everton	1996-97	13	12	3
Everton	1997-98	1	5	0
Everton	1998-99	1	6	0
		16	**25**	**3**
Branco, Claudio		Apps	Subs	Gls
Middlesbrough	1995-96	5	2	0
Middlesbrough	1996-97	1	1	0
		6	**3**	**0**
Bravo, Raul		Apps	Subs	Gls
Leeds U	2002-03	5	0	0
Brazier, Matt		Apps	Subs	Gls
QPR	1995-96	6	5	0
Breacker, Tim		Apps	Subs	Gls
West Ham U	1993-94	40	0	3
West Ham U	1994-95	33	0	0
West Ham U	1995-96	19	3	0
West Ham U	1996-97	22	4	0
West Ham U	1997-98	18	1	0
West Ham U	1998-99	2	1	0
		134	**9**	**3**
Breen, Gary		Apps	Subs	Gls
Coventry C	1996-97	8	1	0
Coventry C	1997-98	30	0	1
Coventry C	1998-99	21	4	0
Coventry C	1999-00	20	1	0
Coventry C	2000-01	29	2	1
West Ham U	2002-03	9	5	0
		117	**13**	**2**
Breitkreutz, Matthias		Apps	Subs	Gls
Aston Villa	1992-93	2	1	0
Aston Villa	1993-94	1	1	0
		3	**2**	**0**

Mark Bright.

Brennan, Mark		Apps	Subs	Gls
Oldham Ath.	1992-93	14	0	3
Oldham Ath.	1993-94	11	0	0
		25	**0**	**3**

Brevett, Rufus		Apps	Subs	Gls
QPR	1992-93	14	1	0
QPR	1993-94	3	4	0
QPR	1994-95	17	2	0
QPR	1995-96	27	0	1
Fulham	2001-02	34	1	0
Fulham	2002-03	20	0	0
West Ham U	2002-03	12	1	0
		127	**9**	**1**

Bridge, Wayne		Apps	Subs	Gls
Southampton	1998-99	15	8	0
Southampton	1999-00	15	4	1
Southampton	2000-01	38	0	0
Southampton	2001-02	38	0	0
Southampton	2002-03	34	0	1
Chelsea	2003-04	33	0	1
		173	**12**	**3**

Bridge-Wilkinson, Marc		Apps	Subs	Gls
Derby Co.	1998-99	0	1	0

Bridges, Michael		Apps	Subs	Gls
Sunderland	1996-97	10	15	3
Leeds U	1999-00	32	2	19
Leeds U	2000-01	6	1	0
Leeds U	2002-03	1	4	0
Leeds U	2003-04	1	9	0
Newcastle U	2003-04	0	6	0
		50	**37**	**22**

Bright, Mark		Apps	Subs	Gls
Crystal P	1992-93	5	0	1
Sheff. Wed.	1992-93	28	2	11
Sheff. Wed.	1993-94	36	4	19
Sheff. Wed.	1994-95	33	4	11
Sheff. Wed.	1995-96	15	10	7
Sheff. Wed.	1996-97	0	1	0
Charlton Ath	1998-99	1	4	1
		118	**25**	**50**

Brightwell, David		Apps	Subs	Gls
Man. City	1992-93	4	4	0
Man. City	1993-94	19	3	1
Man. City	1994-95	9	0	0
		32	**7**	**1**

Brightwell, Ian		Apps	Subs	Gls
Man. City	1992-93	21	0	1
Man. City	1993-94	6	1	0
Man. City	1994-95	29	1	0
Man. City	1995-96	26	3	0
		82	**5**	**1**

Briscoe, Lee		Apps	Subs	Gls
Sheff. Wed.	1993-94	0	1	0
Sheff. Wed.	1994-95	6	0	0
Sheff. Wed.	1995-96	22	4	0
Sheff. Wed.	1996-97	5	1	0
Sheff. Wed.	1997-98	3	4	0
Sheff. Wed.	1998-99	5	11	1
Sheff. Wed.	1999-00	7	9	0
		48	**30**	**1**

Brittain, Martin		Apps	Subs	Gls
Newcastle U	2003-04	0	1	0

Brolin, Tomas		Apps	Subs	Gls
Leeds U	1995-96	17	2	4
Crystal P	1997-98	13	0	0
		30	**2**	**4**

Brooker, Paul		Apps	Subs	Gls
Leicester C	2003-04	0	3	0

Brooker, Steve		Apps	Subs	Gls
Watford	1999-00	0	1	0

Broomes, Marlon		Apps	Subs	Gls
Blackburn R	1997-98	2	2	0
Blackburn R	1998-99	8	5	0
		10	**7**	**0**

Brown, Kenny		Apps	Subs	Gls
West Ham U	1993-94	6	3	0
West Ham U	1994-95	8	1	0
West Ham U	1995-96	3	0	0
		17	**4**	**0**

Brown, Michael		Apps	Subs	Gls
Man. City	1995-96	16	5	0
Tottenham H	2003-04	17	0	1
		33	**5**	**1**

Brown, Richard		Apps	Subs	Gls
Blackburn R	1992-93	2	0	0

Brown, Steve		Apps	Subs	Gls
Charlton Ath	1998-99	13	5	0
Charlton Ath	2000-01	15	10	0
Charlton Ath	2001-02	11	3	2
Charlton Ath	2002-03	0	3	0
		39	**21**	**2**

Brown, Wes		Apps	Subs	Gls
Man. Utd.	1997-98	1	1	0
Man. Utd.	1998-99	11	3	0
Man. Utd.	2000-01	25	3	0
Man. Utd.	2001-02	15	2	0
Man. Utd.	2002-03	22	0	0
Man. Utd.	2003-04	15	2	0
		89	**11**	**0**

Brown, Wayne		Apps	Subs	Gls
Ipswich T	2000-01	0	4	0

Browne, Paul		Apps	Subs	Gls
Aston Villa	1995-96	2	0	0

Bruce, Steve		Apps	Subs	Gls
Man. Utd.	1992-93	42	0	5
Man. Utd.	1993-94	41	0	3
Man. Utd.	1994-95	35	0	2
Man. Utd.	1995-96	30	0	1
		148	**0**	**11**

Bryson, Ian		Apps	Subs	Gls
Sheff. Utd.	1992-93	9	7	3

Buari, Malik		Apps	Subs	Gls
Fulham	2003-04	1	2	0

Bulent, Akin		Apps	Subs	Gls
Bolton Wan.	2002-03	0	1	0

Bull, Garry		Apps	Subs	Gls
Nottm Forest	1994-95	1	0	1

Bullock, Martin		Apps	Subs	Gls
Barnsley	1997-98	23	10	0

Bunjevcevic, Goran		Apps	Subs	Gls
Tottenham H	2001-02	5	1	0
Tottenham H	2002-03	31	4	0
Tottenham H	2003-04	3	4	0
		39	**9**	**0**

Burchill, Mark		Apps	Subs	Gls
Ipswich T	2000-01	2	5	1

Burley, Craig		Apps	Subs	Gls
Chelsea	1992-93	1	2	0
Chelsea	1993-94	20	3	3
Chelsea	1994-95	16	9	2
Chelsea	1995-96	16	6	0
Chelsea	1996-97	26	5	2
Derby Co.	1999-00	18	0	5
Derby Co.	2000-01	24	0	2
Derby Co.	2001-02	11	0	0
		132	**25**	**14**

Burnett, Wayne		Apps	Subs	Gls
Bolton Wan.	1995-96	0	1	0

Burns, Jacob		Apps	Subs	Gls
Leeds U	2000-01	3	1	0
Leeds U	2002-03	2	0	0
		5	**1**	**0**

Burridge, John		Apps	Subs	Gls
Man. City	1994-95	3	1	0

Burrows, David		Apps	Subs	Gls
Liverpool	1992-93	29	1	2
Liverpool	1993-94	3	1	0
West Ham U	1993-94	25	0	1
West Ham U	1994-95	4	0	0
Everton	1994-95	19	0	0
Coventry C	1994-95	11	0	0
Coventry C	1995-96	11	0	0
Coventry C	1996-97	17	1	0
Coventry C	1997-98	33	0	0
Coventry C	1998-99	23	0	0
Coventry C	1999-00	11	4	0
		186	**7**	**3**

Burton, Deon		Apps	Subs	Gls
Derby Co.	1997-98	12	17	3
Derby Co.	1998-99	14	7	9
Derby Co.	1999-00	15	4	4
Derby Co.	2000-01	25	7	5
Derby Co.	2001-02	8	9	1
Portsmouth	2003-04	0	1	0
		74	**45**	**22**

Burton, Sagi		Apps	Subs	Gls
Crystal P	1997-98	1	1	0

Busst, Dave		Apps	Subs	Gls
Coventry C	1992-93	10	0	0
Coventry C	1993-94	2	1	0
Coventry C	1994-95	20	0	2
Coventry C	1995-96	16	1	2
		48	**2**	**4**

Butler, Paul		Apps	Subs	Gls
Sunderland	1999-00	31	1	1
Sunderland	2000-01	3	0	0
Wolves	2003-04	37	0	1
		71	**1**	**2**

Butler, Peter		Apps	Subs	Gls
West Ham U	1993-94	26	0	1
West Ham U	1994-95	5	0	0
		31	**0**	**1**

Butler, Thomas		Apps	Subs	Gls
Sunderland	1999-00	0	1	0
Sunderland	2000-01	0	4	0
Sunderland	2001-02	2	5	0
Sunderland	2002-03	7	0	0
		9	**10**	**0**

Butt, Nicky		Apps	Subs	Gls
Man. Utd.	1992-93	0	1	0
Man. Utd.	1993-94	0	1	0
Man. Utd.	1994-95	11	11	1
Man. Utd.	1995-96	31	1	2
Man. Utd.	1996-97	24	2	5
Man. Utd.	1997-98	31	2	3
Man. Utd.	1998-99	22	9	2
Man. Utd.	1999-00	21	11	3
Man. Utd.	2000-01	24	4	3
Man. Utd.	2001-02	20	5	1
Man. Utd.	2002-03	14	4	0
Man. Utd.	2003-04	12	9	1
		210	**60**	**21**

Butterworth, Ian		Apps	Subs	Gls
Norwich C	1992-93	26	0	1
Norwich C	1993-94	23	2	0
		49	**2**	**1**

Byfield, Darren		Apps	Subs	Gls
Aston Villa	1997-98	1	6	0

Byrne, Shaun		Apps	Subs	Gls
West Ham U	1999-00	0	1	0
West Ham U	2001-02	0	1	0
		0	**2**	**0**

Bywater, Steve		Apps	Subs	Gls
West Ham U	1999-00	3	1	0
West Ham U	2000-01	1	0	0
		4	**1**	**0**

Caballero, Fabian		Apps	Subs	Gls
Arsenal	1998-99	0	1	0

Cadamarteri, Danny		Apps	Subs	Gls
Everton	1996-97	0	1	0
Everton	1997-98	15	11	4
Everton	1998-99	11	19	4
Everton	1999-00	3	14	1
Everton	2000-01	7	9	4
Everton	2001-02	2	1	0
		38	**55**	**13**

Cadete, Jorge		Apps	Subs	Gls
Bradford C	1999-00	2	5	0

Caig, Tony		Apps	Subs	Gls
Charlton Ath	2000-01	0	1	0

Calderwood, Colin		Apps	Subs	Gls
Tottenham H	1993-94	26	0	0
Tottenham H	1994-95	35	1	2
Tottenham H	1995-96	26	3	0
Tottenham H	1996-97	33	1	0
Tottenham H	1997-98	21	5	4
Tottenham H	1998-99	11	1	0
Aston Villa	1998-99	8	0	0
Aston Villa	1999-00	15	3	0
		175	**14**	**6**

Caldwell, Steve		Apps	Subs	Gls
Newcastle U	2000-01	5	4	0
Newcastle U	2002-03	12	2	1
Newcastle U	2003-04	3	2	0
Leeds U	2003-04	13	0	1
		33	**8**	**2**

Camara, Henri		Apps	Subs	Gls
Wolves	2003-04	29	1	7

Camara, Titi		Apps	Subs	Gls
Liverpool	1999-00	22	11	9
West Ham U	2000-01	5	1	0
West Ham U	2001-02	0	1	0
West Ham U	2002-03	0	4	0
		27	**17**	**9**

Camara, Zoumana		Apps	Subs	Gls
Leeds U	2003-04	13	0	1

Cameron, Colin		Apps	Subs	Gls
Wolves	2003-04	25	5	4

Campbell, Andy		Apps	Subs	Gls
Middlesbrough	1995-96	1	1	0
Middlesbrough	1996-97	0	3	0
Middlesbrough	1998-99	1	7	0
Middlesbrough	1999-00	16	9	4
Middlesbrough	2000-01	5	2	0
Middlesbrough	2001-02	0	4	0
		23	**26**	**4**

Campbell, Kevin		Apps	Subs	Gls
Arsenal	1992-93	32	5	4
Arsenal	1993-94	28	9	14
Arsenal	1994-95	19	4	4
Nottm Forest	1995-96	21	0	3
Nottm Forest	1996-97	16	1	6
Everton	1998-99	8	0	9
Everton	1999-00	26	0	12
Everton	2000-01	27	2	9
Everton	2001-02	21	2	4
Everton	2002-03	31	5	10
Everton	2003-04	8	9	1
		237	**37**	**76**

Campbell, Sol		Apps	Subs	Gls
Tottenham H	1992-93	0	1	1
Tottenham H	1993-94	27	7	0
Tottenham H	1994-95	29	1	0
Tottenham H	1995-96	31	0	1
Tottenham H	1996-97	38	0	0
Tottenham H	1997-98	34	0	0
Tottenham H	1998-99	37	0	6
Tottenham H	1999-00	29	0	0
Tottenham H	2000-01	21	0	2
Arsenal	2001-02	29	2	2
Arsenal	2002-03	33	0	2
Arsenal	2003-04	35	0	1
		343	**11**	**15**

Campbell, Stuart		Apps	Subs	Gls
Leicester C	1996-97	4	6	0
Leicester C	1997-98	6	5	0
Leicester C	1998-99	1	11	0
Leicester C	1999-00	1	3	0
		12	**25**	**0**

Campbell-Ryce, Jamal		Apps	Subs	Gls
Charlton Ath	2002-03	0	1	0
Charlton Ath	2003-04	0	2	0
		0	**3**	**0**

Campo, Ivan		Apps	Subs	Gls
Bolton Wan.	2002-03	28	3	2
Bolton Wan.	2003-04	37	1	4
		65	**4**	**6**

Canero, Peter		Apps	Subs	Gls
Leicester C	2003-04	2	5	0

Cantona, Eric		Apps	Subs	Gls
Leeds U	1992-93	12	1	6
Man. Utd.	1992-93	21	1	9
Man. Utd.	1993-94	34	0	18
Man. Utd.	1994-95	21	0	12
Man. Utd.	1995-96	30	0	14
Man. Utd.	1996-97	36	0	11
		154	**2**	**70**

Carbon, Matt		Apps	Subs	Gls
Derby Co.	1996-97	6	4	0
Derby Co.	1997-98	3	1	0
		9	**5**	**0**

Carbonari, Horacio		Apps	Subs	Gls
Derby Co.	1998-99	28	1	5
Derby Co.	1999-00	29	0	2
Derby Co.	2000-01	27	0	1
Derby Co.	2001-02	3	0	0
		87	**1**	**8**

Carbone, Benito		Apps	Subs	Gls
Sheff. Wed.	1996-97	24	1	6
Sheff. Wed.	1997-98	28	5	9
Sheff. Wed.	1998-99	31	0	8
Sheff. Wed.	1999-00	3	4	2
Aston Villa	1999-00	22	2	3
Bradford C	2000-01	29	2	5
Derby Co.	2001-02	13	0	1
Middlesbrough	2001-02	13	0	1
		163	**14**	**35**

Carey, Brian		Apps	Subs	Gls
Leicester C	1994-95	11	1	0

Carr, Franz		Apps	Subs	Gls
Sheff. Utd.	1992-93	8	0	3
Sheff. Utd.	1993-94	10	0	1
Leicester C	1994-95	12	1	1
Aston Villa	1994-95	0	2	0
Aston Villa	1995-96	1	0	0
Bolton Wan.	1997-98	0	5	0
		31	**8**	**5**

Carr, Steve		Apps	Subs	Gls
Tottenham H	1993-94	1	0	0
Tottenham H	1996-97	24	2	0
Tottenham H	1997-98	37	1	0
Tottenham H	1998-99	37	0	0
Tottenham H	1999-00	34	0	3
Tottenham H	2000-01	27	1	3
Tottenham H	2002-03	30	0	0
Tottenham H	2003-04	32	0	1
		222	**4**	**7**

Carragher, Jamie		Apps	Subs	Gls
Liverpool	1996-97	1	1	1
Liverpool	1997-98	17	3	0
Liverpool	1998-99	34	0	1
Liverpool	1999-00	33	3	0
Liverpool	2000-01	30	4	0
Liverpool	2001-02	33	0	0
Liverpool	2002-03	34	1	0
Liverpool	2003-04	22	0	0
		204	**12**	**2**

Carrick, Michael		Apps	Subs	Gls
West Ham U	1999-00	4	4	1
West Ham U	2000-01	32	1	1
West Ham U	2001-02	30	0	2
West Ham U	2002-03	28	2	1
		94	**7**	**5**

Carroll, Roy		Apps	Subs	Gls
Man. Utd.	2001-02	6	1	0
Man. Utd.	2002-03	8	2	0
Man. Utd.	2003-04	6	0	0
		20	**3**	**0**

Carruthers, Martin		Apps	Subs	Gls
Aston Villa	1992-93	0	1	0

Carsley, Lee		Apps	Subs	Gls
Derby Co.	1996-97	15	9	0
Derby Co.	1997-98	34	0	1
Derby Co.	1998-99	20	2	1
Blackburn R	1998-99	7	1	0
Coventry C	2000-01	21	0	2
Everton	2001-02	8	0	1

Everton	2002-03	21	3	3
Everton	2003-04	15	6	1
		141	**21**	**9**
Carson, Scott		*Apps*	*Subs*	*Gls*
Leeds U	2003-04	2	1	0
Carter, Darren		*Apps*	*Subs*	*Gls*
Birmingham C	2002-03	3	9	0
Birmingham C	2003-04	1	4	0
		4	**13**	**0**
Carter, Jimmy		*Apps*	*Subs*	*Gls*
Arsenal	1992-93	11	5	2
Arsenal	1994-95	2	1	0
		13	**6**	**2**
Carteron, Patrice		*Apps*	*Subs*	*Gls*
Sunderland	2000-01	8	0	1
Cascarino, Tony		*Apps*	*Subs*	*Gls*
Chelsea	1992-93	8	1	2
Chelsea	1993-94	16	4	4
		24	**5**	**6**
Casiraghi, Pierluigi		*Apps*	*Subs*	*Gls*
Chelsea	1998-99	10	0	1
Caskey, Darren		*Apps*	*Subs*	*Gls*
Tottenham H	1993-94	16	9	4
Tottenham H	1994-95	1	3	0
Tottenham H	1995-96	3	0	0
		20	**12**	**4**
Casper, Chris		*Apps*	*Subs*	*Gls*
Man. Utd.	1996-97	0	2	0
Castledine, Stewart		*Apps*	*Subs*	*Gls*
Wimbledon	1993-94	3	0	1
Wimbledon	1994-95	5	1	1
Wimbledon	1995-96	2	2	1
Wimbledon	1996-97	4	2	1
Wimbledon	1997-98	3	3	0
Wimbledon	1998-99	1	0	0
		18	**8**	**4**
Chadwick, Luke		*Apps*	*Subs*	*Gls*
Man. Utd.	2000-01	6	10	2
Man. Utd.	2001-02	5	3	0
Man. Utd.	2002-03	0	1	0
		11	**14**	**2**
Chadwick, Nick		*Apps*	*Subs*	*Gls*
Everton	2001-02	2	7	3
Everton	2002-03	0	1	0
Everton	2003-04	1	2	0
		3	**10**	**3**
Challis, Trevor		*Apps*	*Subs*	*Gls*
QPR	1995-96	10	1	0
Chamberlain, Alec		*Apps*	*Subs*	*Gls*
Watford	1999-00	27	0	0
Chambers, Adam		*Apps*	*Subs*	*Gls*
West Brom	2002-03	10	3	0
Chambers, James		*Apps*	*Subs*	*Gls*
West Brom	2002-03	2	6	0
Channing, Justin		*Apps*	*Subs*	*Gls*
QPR	1992-93	2	0	1
Chapman, Lee		*Apps*	*Subs*	*Gls*
Leeds U	1992-93	36	4	13
West Ham U	1993-94	26	4	7
West Ham U	1994-95	7	3	0
Ipswich T	1994-95	9	7	1
Leeds U	1995-96	2	0	0
		80	**18**	**21**
Chapuis, Cyril		*Apps*	*Subs*	*Gls*
Leeds U	2003-04	0	1	0
Charles, Gary		*Apps*	*Subs*	*Gls*
Nottm Forest	1992-93	14	0	0
Aston Villa	1994-95	14	2	0
Aston Villa	1995-96	34	0	1
Aston Villa	1997-98	14	4	1
Aston Villa	1998-99	10	1	1
West Ham U	1999-00	2	2	0
West Ham U	2000-01	0	1	0
		88	**10**	**3**

Lee Clark.

Charles, Lee		*Apps*	*Subs*	*Gls*
QPR	1995-96	0	4	0
Charlton, Simon		*Apps*	*Subs*	*Gls*
Southampton	1993-94	29	4	1
Southampton	1994-95	25	0	1
Southampton	1995-96	24	2	0
Southampton	1996-97	24	3	0
Southampton	1997-98	2	1	0
Bolton Wan.	2001-02	35	1	0
Bolton Wan.	2002-03	27	4	0
Bolton Wan.	2003-04	28	3	0
		194	**18**	**2**
Charvet, Laurent		*Apps*	*Subs*	*Gls*
Chelsea	1997-98	7	4	2
Newcastle U	1998-99	30	1	1
Newcastle U	1999-00	1	1	0
Newcastle U	2000-01	6	1	0
Man. City	2000-01	16	4	0
		60	**11**	**3**
Chettle, Steve		*Apps*	*Subs*	*Gls*
Nottm Forest	1992-93	30	0	0
Nottm Forest	1994-95	41	0	0
Nottm Forest	1995-96	37	0	0
Nottm Forest	1996-97	31	1	0
Nottm Forest	1998-99	32	2	2
		171	**3**	**2**
Cheyrou, Bruno		*Apps*	*Subs*	*Gls*
Liverpool	2002-03	8	11	0
Liverpool	2003-04	9	3	2
		17	**14**	**2**
Chippo, Youssef		*Apps*	*Subs*	*Gls*
Coventry C	1999-00	33	0	2
Coventry C	2000-01	18	14	0
		51	**14**	**2**
Chopra, Michael		*Apps*	*Subs*	*Gls*
Newcastle U	2002-03	0	1	0
Newcastle U	2003-04	1	5	0
		1	**6**	**0**
Christie, Iyseden		*Apps*	*Subs*	*Gls*
Coventry C	1995-96	0	1	0
Christie, Malcolm		*Apps*	*Subs*	*Gls*
Derby Co.	1998-99	0	2	0
Derby Co.	1999-00	10	11	6
Derby Co.	2000-01	29	5	8
Derby Co.	2001-02	27	8	9
Middlesbrough	2002-03	11	1	4
Middlesbrough	2003-04	7	3	1
		84	**30**	**28**
Cisse, Aliou		*Apps*	*Subs*	*Gls*
Birmingham C	2002-03	21	0	0
Birmingham C	2003-04	5	10	0
		26	**10**	**0**
Cisse, Edouard		*Apps*	*Subs*	*Gls*
West Ham U	2002-03	18	7	0
Clapham, Jamie		*Apps*	*Subs*	*Gls*
Tottenham H	1996-97	0	1	0
Ipswich T	2000-01	28	7	2
Ipswich T	2001-02	22	10	2
Birmingham C	2002-03	16	0	0
Birmingham C	2003-04	22	3	0
		88	**21**	**4**
Claridge, Steve		*Apps*	*Subs*	*Gls*
Leicester C	1996-97	29	3	11
Leicester C	1997-98	10	7	0
		39	**10**	**11**
Clark, Ben		*Apps*	*Subs*	*Gls*
Sunderland	2002-03	0	1	0
Clark, Lee		*Apps*	*Subs*	*Gls*
Newcastle U	1993-94	29	0	2
Newcastle U	1994-95	9	10	1
Newcastle U	1995-96	22	6	2
Newcastle U	1996-97	9	16	2
Fulham	2001-02	5	4	0
Fulham	2002-03	9	2	2
Fulham	2003-04	25	0	2
		108	**38**	**11**
Clarke, Adrian		*Apps*	*Subs*	*Gls*
Arsenal	1994-95	0	1	0
Arsenal	1995-96	4	2	0
		4	**3**	**0**
Clarke, Andy		*Apps*	*Subs*	*Gls*
Wimbledon	1992-93	23	10	5
Wimbledon	1993-94	9	14	2
Wimbledon	1994-95	8	17	1
Wimbledon	1995-96	9	9	2
Wimbledon	1996-97	4	7	1
Wimbledon	1997-98	1	13	0
		54	**70**	**11**
Clarke, Matt		*Apps*	*Subs*	*Gls*
Sheff. Wed.	1996-97	0	1	0
Sheff. Wed.	1997-98	2	1	0
Bradford C	1999-00	21	0	0
Bradford C	2000-01	17	0	0
		40	**2**	**0**
Clarke, Peter		*Apps*	*Subs*	*Gls*
Everton	2000-01	0	1	0
Everton	2001-02	5	2	0
Everton	2003-04	1	0	0
		6	**3**	**0**
Clarke, Steve		*Apps*	*Subs*	*Gls*
Chelsea	1992-93	18	2	0
Chelsea	1993-94	39	0	0
Chelsea	1994-95	29	0	0
Chelsea	1995-96	21	1	0
Chelsea	1996-97	31	0	0
Chelsea	1997-98	22	4	1
		160	**7**	**1**

Clegg, Michael		*Apps*	*Subs*	*Gls*
Man. Utd.	1996-97	3	1	0
Man. Utd.	1997-98	1	2	0
Man. Utd.	1999-00	0	2	0
		4	**5**	**0**
Cleland, Alex		*Apps*	*Subs*	*Gls*
Everton	1998-99	16	2	0
Everton	1999-00	3	6	0
Everton	2000-01	2	3	0
Everton	2001-02	0	3	0
		21	**14**	**0**
Clemence, Stephen		*Apps*	*Subs*	*Gls*
Tottenham H	1997-98	12	5	0
Tottenham H	1998-99	9	9	0
Tottenham H	1999-00	16	4	1
Tottenham H	2000-01	27	2	1
Tottenham H	2001-02	4	2	0
Birmingham C	2002-03	15	0	2
Birmingham C	2003-04	32	3	2
		115	**25**	**6**
Clement, Neil		*Apps*	*Subs*	*Gls*
Chelsea	1996-97	1	0	0
West Brom	2002-03	34	2	3
		35	**2**	**3**
Clement, Philippe		*Apps*	*Subs*	*Gls*
Coventry C	1998-99	6	6	0
Clichy, Gael		*Apps*	*Subs*	*Gls*
Arsenal	2003-04	7	5	0
Clough, Nigel		*Apps*	*Subs*	*Gls*
Nottm Forest	1992-93	42	0	10
Liverpool	1993-94	25	2	7
Liverpool	1994-95	3	7	0
Liverpool	1995-96	1	1	0
Man. City	1995-96	15	0	2
Nottm Forest	1996-97	10	3	1
Sheff. Wed.	1997-98	1	0	0
		97	**13**	**20**
Clyde, Mark		*Apps*	*Subs*	*Gls*
Wolves	2003-04	6	4	0
Cobian, Juan		*Apps*	*Subs*	*Gls*
Sheff. Wed.	1998-99	7	2	0
Cockerill, Glenn		*Apps*	*Subs*	*Gls*
Southampton	1992-93	21	2	0
Southampton	1993-94	12	2	0
		33	**4**	**0**
Cole, Andy		*Apps*	*Subs*	*Gls*
Newcastle U	1993-94	40	0	34
Newcastle U	1994-95	18	0	9
Man. Utd.	1994-95	17	1	12
Man. Utd.	1995-96	32	2	11
Man. Utd.	1996-97	10	10	6
Man. Utd.	1997-98	31	2	16
Man. Utd.	1998-99	26	6	17
Man. Utd.	1999-00	23	5	19
Man. Utd.	2000-01	15	4	9
Man. Utd.	2001-02	7	4	4
Blackburn R	2001-02	15	0	9
Blackburn R	2002-03	32	2	7
Blackburn R	2003-04	27	7	11
		293	**43**	**164**
Cole, Ashley		*Apps*	*Subs*	*Gls*
Arsenal	1999-00	1	0	0
Arsenal	2000-01	15	2	3
Arsenal	2001-02	29	0	2
Arsenal	2002-03	30	1	1
Arsenal	2003-04	32	0	0
		107	**3**	**6**
Cole, Carlton		*Apps*	*Subs*	*Gls*
Chelsea	2001-02	2	1	1
Chelsea	2002-03	2	11	3
Charlton Ath	2003-04	8	12	4
		12	**24**	**8**
Cole, Joe		*Apps*	*Subs*	*Gls*
West Ham U	1998-99	2	6	0
West Ham U	1999-00	17	5	1
West Ham U	2000-01	24	6	5
West Ham U	2001-02	29	1	0
West Ham U	2002-03	36	0	4
Chelsea	2003-04	18	17	1
		126	**35**	**11**
Coleman, Chris		*Apps*	*Subs*	*Gls*
Crystal P	1992-93	31	7	5
Crystal P	1994-95	35	0	1
Blackburn R	1995-96	19	1	0
Blackburn R	1996-97	8	0	0
		93	**8**	**6**
Coleman, Simon		*Apps*	*Subs*	*Gls*
Sheff. Wed.	1993-94	10	5	1
Sheff. Wed.	1994-95	1	0	0
Bolton Wan.	1995-96	12	0	1
		23	**5**	**2**
Colgan, Nicky		*Apps*	*Subs*	*Gls*
Chelsea	1996-97	1	0	0
Colleter, Patrick		*Apps*	*Subs*	*Gls*
Southampton	1998-99	16	0	1
Southampton	1999-00	8	0	0
		24	**0**	**1**
Collett, Andy		*Apps*	*Subs*	*Gls*
Middlesbrough	1992-93	2	0	0
Collins, John		*Apps*	*Subs*	*Gls*
Everton	1998-99	19	1	1
Everton	1999-00	33	2	2
Fulham	2001-02	29	5	0
Fulham	2002-03	0	5	0
		81	**13**	**3**
Collins, Wayne		*Apps*	*Subs*	*Gls*
Sheff. Wed.	1996-97	8	4	1

Sheff. Wed.	1997-98	8	11	5
		16	**15**	**6**
Collymore, Stan		*Apps*	*Subs*	*Gls*
Crystal P	1992-93	0	2	0
Nottm Forest	1994-95	37	0	22
Liverpool	1995-96	30	1	14
Liverpool	1996-97	25	5	12
Aston Villa	1997-98	23	2	6
Aston Villa	1998-99	11	9	1
Leicester C	1999-00	6	0	4
Leicester C	2000-01	1	4	1
Bradford C	2000-01	5	2	2
		138	**25**	**62**
Coly, Ferdinand		*Apps*	*Subs*	*Gls*
Birmingham C	2002-03	1	0	0
Cook, Paul		*Apps*	*Subs*	*Gls*
Coventry C	1994-95	33	1	3
Coventry C	1995-96	2	1	0
		35	**2**	**3**
Cooke, Stephen		*Apps*	*Subs*	*Gls*
Aston Villa	2002-03	0	3	0
Cooke, Terry		*Apps*	*Subs*	*Gls*
Man. Utd.	1995-96	1	3	0
Cooper, Colin		*Apps*	*Subs*	*Gls*
Nottm Forest	1994-95	35	0	1
Nottm Forest	1995-96	37	0	5
Nottm Forest	1996-97	36	0	2
Middlesbrough	1998-99	31	1	1
Middlesbrough	1999-00	26	0	0
Middlesbrough	2000-01	26	1	2
Middlesbrough	2001-02	14	4	2
Middlesbrough	2002-03	14	6	0
Middlesbrough	2003-04	17	2	0
		236	**14**	**13**
Cooper, Kevin		*Apps*	*Subs*	*Gls*
Wolves	2003-04	0	1	0
Coppinger, James		*Apps*	*Subs*	*Gls*
Newcastle U	2000-01	0	1	0
Cordone, Daniel		*Apps*	*Subs*	*Gls*
Newcastle U	2000-01	12	9	2
Cork, Alan		*Apps*	*Subs*	*Gls*
Sheff. Utd.	1992-93	11	16	2
Sheff. Utd.	1993-94	7	12	3
		18	**28**	**5**
Cort, Carl		*Apps*	*Subs*	*Gls*
Wimbledon	1996-97	0	1	0
Wimbledon	1997-98	16	6	4
Wimbledon	1998-99	6	10	3
Wimbledon	1999-00	32	2	9
Newcastle U	2000-01	13	0	6
Newcastle U	2001-02	6	2	1
Newcastle U	2002-03	0	1	0
Wolves	2003-04	13	3	5
		86	**25**	**28**
Costa, Jorge		*Apps*	*Subs*	*Gls*
Charlton Ath	2001-02	22	2	0
Coton, Tony		*Apps*	*Subs*	*Gls*
Man. City	1992-93	40	0	0
Man. City	1993-94	31	0	0
Man. City	1994-95	21	1	0
Sunderland	1996-97	10	0	0
		102	**1**	**0**
Cottee, Tony		*Apps*	*Subs*	*Gls*
Everton	1992-93	25	1	12
Everton	1993-94	36	3	16
Everton	1994-95	3	0	0
West Ham U	1994-95	31	0	13
West Ham U	1995-96	30	3	10
West Ham U	1996-97	2	1	0
Leicester C	1997-98	7	12	4
Leicester C	1998-99	29	2	10
Leicester C	1999-00	30	3	13
Leicester C	2000-01	0	2	0
		193	**27**	**78**
Cotterell, Leo		*Apps*	*Subs*	*Gls*
Ipswich T	1994-95	0	2	0
Cotterill, Steve		*Apps*	*Subs*	*Gls*
Wimbledon	1992-93	4	3	3
Counago, Pablo		*Apps*	*Subs*	*Gls*
Ipswich T	2001-02	1	12	0
Courtois, Laurent		*Apps*	*Subs*	*Gls*
West Ham U	2001-02	5	2	0
Couzens, Andy		*Apps*	*Subs*	*Gls*
Leeds U	1994-95	2	2	0
Leeds U	1995-96	8	6	0
Leeds U	1996-97	7	3	1
		17	**11**	**1**
Cowan, Tom		*Apps*	*Subs*	*Gls*
Sheff. Utd.	1992-93	21	0	0
Sheff. Utd.	1993-94	4	0	0
		25	**0**	**0**
Cowans, Gordon		*Apps*	*Subs*	*Gls*
Blackburn R	1992-93	23	1	1
Aston Villa	1993-94	9	2	0
		32	**3**	**1**
Cox, Ian		*Apps*	*Subs*	*Gls*
Crystal P	1994-95	1	10	0
Cox, Neil		*Apps*	*Subs*	*Gls*
Aston Villa	1992-93	6	9	1
Aston Villa	1993-94	16	4	2
Middlesbrough	1995-96	35	0	2
Middlesbrough	1996-97	29	2	0
Bolton Wan.	1997-98	20	1	1
Watford	1999-00	20	1	0
		126	**17**	**6**

Coyle, Owen		Apps	Subs	Gls
Bolton Wan.	1995-96	2	3	0
Coyne, Chris		Apps	Subs	Gls
West Ham U	1998-99	0	1	0
Coyne, Danny		Apps	Subs	Gls
Leicester C	2003-04	1	3	0
Craddock, Jody		Apps	Subs	Gls
Sunderland	1999-00	18	1	0
Sunderland	2000-01	33	1	0
Sunderland	2001-02	30	0	1
Sunderland	2002-03	25	0	1
Wolves	2003-04	31	1	1
		137	**3**	**3**
Crainey, Stephen		Apps	Subs	Gls
Southampton	2003-04	5	0	0
Crainie, Martin		Apps	Subs	Gls
Southampton	2003-04	1	0	0
Cramb, Colin		Apps	Subs	Gls
Southampton	1993-94	0	1	0
Crawford, Jimmy		Apps	Subs	Gls
Newcastle U	1996-97	0	2	0
Creaney, Gerry		Apps	Subs	Gls
Man. City	1995-96	6	9	3
Crespo, Hernan		Apps	Subs	Gls
Chelsea	2003-04	13	6	10
Cresswell, Richard		Apps	Subs	Gls
Sheff. Wed.	1998-99	1	6	1
Sheff. Wed.	1999-00	2	18	1
Leicester C	2000-01	3	5	0
		6	**29**	**2**
Crittenden, Nicky		Apps	Subs	Gls
Chelsea	1997-98	0	2	0
Croft, Gary		Apps	Subs	Gls
Blackburn R	1996-97	4	1	0
Blackburn R	1997-98	19	4	1
Blackburn R	1998-99	10	2	0
Ipswich T	2000-01	6	2	0
		39	**9**	**1**
Crook, Ian		Apps	Subs	Gls
Norwich C	1992-93	32	2	3
Norwich C	1993-94	38	0	0
Norwich C	1994-95	33	1	0
		103	**3**	**3**
Crooks, Lee		Apps	Subs	Gls
Man. City	2000-01	0	2	0
Crosby, Gary		Apps	Subs	Gls
Nottm Forest	1992-93	20	3	1
Crossley, Mark		Apps	Subs	Gls
Nottm Forest	1992-93	37	0	0
Nottm Forest	1994-95	42	0	0
Nottm Forest	1995-96	38	0	0
Nottm Forest	1996-97	33	0	0
Nottm Forest	1998-99	12	0	0
Middlesbrough	2000-01	4	1	0
Middlesbrough	2001-02	17	1	0
Fulham	2003-04	1	0	0
		184	**2**	**0**
Crouch, Peter		Apps	Subs	Gls
Aston Villa	2001-02	7	0	2
Aston Villa	2002-03	7	7	0
Aston Villa	2003-04	6	10	4
		20	**17**	**6**
Cruyff, Jordi		Apps	Subs	Gls
Man. Utd.	1996-97	11	5	3
Man. Utd.	1997-98	3	2	0
Man. Utd.	1998-99	0	5	2
Man. Utd.	1999-00	1	7	3
		15	**19**	**8**
Cudicini, Carlo		Apps	Subs	Gls
Chelsea	1999-00	1	0	0
Chelsea	2000-01	23	1	0
Chelsea	2001-02	27	1	0
Chelsea	2002-03	36	0	0
Chelsea	2003-04	26	0	0
		113	**2**	**0**
Culkin, Nick		Apps	Subs	Gls
Man. Utd.	1999-00	0	1	0
Culverhouse, Ian		Apps	Subs	Gls
Norwich C	1992-93	41	0	0
Norwich C	1993-94	42	0	1
		83	**0**	**1**
Cummins, Michael		Apps	Subs	Gls
Middlesbrough	1998-99	1	0	0
Middlesbrough	1999-00	0	1	0
		1	**1**	**0**
Cundy, Jason		Apps	Subs	Gls
Tottenham H	1992-93	13	2	1
Tottenham H	1995-96	0	1	0
		13	**3**	**1**
Cunningham, Kenny		Apps	Subs	Gls
Wimbledon	1994-95	28	0	0
Wimbledon	1995-96	32	1	0
Wimbledon	1996-97	36	0	0
Wimbledon	1997-98	32	0	0
Wimbledon	1998-99	35	0	0
Wimbledon	1999-00	37	0	0
Birmingham C	2002-03	31	0	0
Birmingham C	2003-04	36	0	0
		267	**1**	**0**
Curcic, Sasa		Apps	Subs	Gls
Bolton Wan.	1995-96	28	0	4
Aston Villa	1996-97	17	5	0
Aston Villa	1997-98	3	4	0
Crystal P	1997-98	6	2	1
		54	**11**	**5**

Cureton, Jamie		Apps	Subs	Gls
Norwich C	1994-95	9	8	4
Curle, Keith		Apps	Subs	Gls
Man. City	1992-93	39	0	3
Man. City	1993-94	29	0	1
Man. City	1994-95	31	0	2
Man. City	1995-96	32	0	0
		131	**0**	**6**
Curtis, John		Apps	Subs	Gls
Man. Utd.	1997-98	3	5	0
Man. Utd.	1998-99	1	3	0
Man. Utd.	1999-00	0	1	0
Blackburn R	2001-02	10	0	0
Blackburn R	2002-03	5	0	0
Leicester C	2003-04	14	1	0
Portsmouth	2003-04	5	1	0
		38	**11**	**0**
Cutler, Neil		Apps	Subs	Gls
Aston Villa	1999-00	0	1	0
Cygan, Pascal		Apps	Subs	Gls
Arsenal	2002-03	16	2	1
Arsenal	2003-04	10	8	0
		26	**10**	**1**
Dabizas, Nicos		Apps	Subs	Gls
Newcastle U	1997-98	10	1	1
Newcastle U	1998-99	25	5	3
Newcastle U	1999-00	29	0	4
Newcastle U	2000-01	9	0	0
Newcastle U	2001-02	33	2	3
Newcastle U	2002-03	13	3	0
Leicester C	2003-04	18	0	0
		137	**11**	**11**
Dacourt, Olivier		Apps	Subs	Gls
Everton	1998-99	28	2	2
Leeds U	2000-01	33	0	3
Leeds U	2001-02	16	1	0
Leeds U	2002-03	4	3	0
		81	**6**	**5**
Dahlin, Martin		Apps	Subs	Gls
Blackburn R	1997-98	11	10	4
Blackburn R	1998-99	2	3	0
		13	**13**	**4**
Dailly, Christian		Apps	Subs	Gls
Derby Co.	1996-97	31	5	3
Derby Co.	1997-98	30	0	1
Derby Co.	1998-99	1	0	0
Blackburn R	1998-99	14	3	0
West Ham U	2000-01	11	1	0
West Ham U	2001-02	38	0	0
West Ham U	2002-03	23	3	0
		148	**12**	**4**
Daino, Danny		Apps	Subs	Gls
Derby Co.	2001-02	2	0	0
Daish, Liam		Apps	Subs	Gls
Coventry C	1995-96	11	0	1
Coventry C	1996-97	20	0	1
		31	**0**	**2**
Daley, Tony		Apps	Subs	Gls
Aston Villa	1992-93	8	5	2
Aston Villa	1993-94	19	8	1
		27	**13**	**3**
Dalglish, Paul		Apps	Subs	Gls
Newcastle U	1998-99	6	5	1
Dalla Bona, Sam		Apps	Subs	Gls
Chelsea	1999-00	0	2	0
Chelsea	2000-01	26	3	2
Chelsea	2001-02	16	8	4
		42	**13**	**6**

Carlo Cudicini.

Dalmat, Stephane		Apps	Subs	Gls
Tottenham H	2003-04	12	10	3
Dani (Daniel Da Cruz Carvalho)		Apps	Subs	Gls
West Ham U	1995-96	3	6	2
Danilevicius, Tomas		Apps	Subs	Gls
Arsenal	2000-01	0	2	0
Danns, Neil		Apps	Subs	Gls
Blackburn R	2002-03	1	1	0
Blackburn R	2003-04	0	1	0
		1	**2**	**0**
Darby, Julian		Apps	Subs	Gls
Coventry C	1993-94	25	1	5
Coventry C	1994-95	27	2	0
		52	**3**	**5**
Darcheville, Jean-Claude		Apps	Subs	Gls
Nottm Forest	1998-99	14	2	2
Davenport, Calum		Apps	Subs	Gls
Coventry C	2000-01	0	1	0
Davidson, Callum		Apps	Subs	Gls
Blackburn R	1997-98	1	0	0
Blackburn R	1998-99	34	0	1
Leicester C	2000-01	25	3	1
Leicester C	2001-02	29	1	0
Leicester C	2003-04	8	5	0
		97	**9**	**2**
Davies, Andrew		Apps	Subs	Gls
Middlesbrough	2002-03	1	0	0
Middlesbrough	2003-04	8	2	0
		9	**2**	**0**
Davies, Gareth		Apps	Subs	Gls
Crystal P	1997-98	0	1	0
Davies, Kevin		Apps	Subs	Gls
Southampton	1997-98	20	5	9
Blackburn R	1998-99	9	12	1
Southampton	1999-00	19	4	6
Southampton	2000-01	21	6	1
Southampton	2001-02	18	5	2
Southampton	2002-03	1	8	1
Bolton Wan.	2003-04	38	0	9
		126	**40**	**29**
Davies, Simon		Apps	Subs	Gls
Tottenham H	1999-00	1	2	0
Tottenham H	2000-01	9	4	2
Tottenham H	2001-02	22	9	4
Tottenham H	2002-03	33	3	5
Tottenham H	2003-04	17	0	2
		82	**18**	**13**
Davies, Simon		Apps	Subs	Gls
Man. Utd.	1994-95	3	2	0
Man. Utd.	1995-96	1	5	0
		4	**7**	**0**
Davis, Neil		Apps	Subs	Gls
Aston Villa	1995-96	0	2	0
Davis, Paul		Apps	Subs	Gls
Arsenal	1992-93	6	0	0
Arsenal	1993-94	21	1	0
Arsenal	1994-95	3	1	1
		30	**2**	**1**
Davis, Sean		Apps	Subs	Gls
Fulham	2001-02	25	5	0
Fulham	2002-03	28	0	3
Fulham	2003-04	22	2	5
		75	**7**	**8**
Davison, Aidan		Apps	Subs	Gls
Bolton Wan.	1995-96	2	0	0
Bradford C	1999-00	5	1	0
Bradford C	2000-01	2	0	0
		9	**1**	**0**
Davison, Bobby		Apps	Subs	Gls
Sheff. Utd.	1993-94	8	1	0
Day, Chris		Apps	Subs	Gls
Watford	1999-00	11	0	0
Day, Mervyn		Apps	Subs	Gls
Leeds U	1992-93	2	0	0
De Bilde, Gilles		Apps	Subs	Gls
Sheff. Wed.	1999-00	37	1	10
Aston Villa	2000-01	4	0	0
		41	**1**	**10**
De Freitas, Fabian		Apps	Subs	Gls
Bolton Wan.	1995-96	17	10	5
De Goey, Ed		Apps	Subs	Gls
Chelsea	1997-98	28	0	0
Chelsea	1998-99	35	0	0
Chelsea	1999-00	37	0	0
Chelsea	2000-01	15	0	0
Chelsea	2001-02	6	0	0
Chelsea	2002-03	2	0	0
		123	**0**	**0**
De La Cruz, Ulises		Apps	Subs	Gls
Aston Villa	2002-03	12	8	1
Aston Villa	2003-04	20	8	0
		32	**16**	**1**
De Lucas, Enrique		Apps	Subs	Gls
Chelsea	2002-03	17	8	0
De Oliveira, Filipe		Apps	Subs	Gls
Chelsea	2002-03	0	3	0
Chelsea	2003-04	0	1	0
		0	**4**	**0**
De Zeeuw, Arjan		Apps	Subs	Gls
Barnsley	1997-98	26	0	0
Portsmouth	2003-04	36	0	1
		62	**0**	**1**
Deane, Brian		Apps	Subs	Gls
Sheff. Utd.	1992-93	41	0	14
Leeds U	1993-94	41	0	11

Leeds U	1994-95	33	2	9
Leeds U	1995-96	30	4	7
Leeds U	1996-97	27	1	5
Middlesbrough	1998-99	24	2	6
Middlesbrough	1999-00	29	0	9
Middlesbrough	2000-01	13	12	2
Middlesbrough	2001-02	6	1	1
Leicester C	2001-02	13	2	6
Leicester C	2003-04	0	5	0
		257	**29**	**70**
Dearden, Kevin		Apps	Subs	Gls
Tottenham H	1992-93	0	1	0
Debeve, Michael		Apps	Subs	Gls
Middlesbrough	2001-02	1	3	0
Defoe, Jermain		Apps	Subs	Gls
West Ham U	2000-01	0	1	0
West Ham U	2001-02	14	21	10
West Ham U	2002-03	29	9	8
Tottenham H	2003-04	14	1	7
		57	**32**	**25**
Degn, Peter		Apps	Subs	Gls
Everton	1998-99	0	4	0
Degryse, Marc		Apps	Subs	Gls
Sheff. Wed.	1995-96	30	4	8
Delaney, Damien		Apps	Subs	Gls
Leicester C	2000-01	3	2	0
Leicester C	2001-02	2	1	0
		5	**3**	**0**
Delaney, Mark		Apps	Subs	Gls
Aston Villa	1998-99	0	2	0
Aston Villa	1999-00	25	3	1
Aston Villa	2000-01	12	7	0
Aston Villa	2001-02	30	0	0
Aston Villa	2002-03	12	0	0
Aston Villa	2003-04	23	2	0
		102	**14**	**1**
Delap, Rory		Apps	Subs	Gls
Derby Co.	1997-98	10	3	0
Derby Co.	1998-99	21	2	0
Derby Co.	1999-00	34	0	8
Derby Co.	2000-01	32	1	3
Southampton	2001-02	24	4	2
Southampton	2002-03	22	2	0
Southampton	2003-04	26	1	1
		169	**13**	**14**
Delgado, Agustin		Apps	Subs	Gls
Southampton	2001-02	0	1	0
Southampton	2002-03	2	4	0
Southampton	2003-04	0	4	0
		2	**9**	**0**
Desailly, Marcel		Apps	Subs	Gls
Chelsea	1998-99	30	1	0
Chelsea	1999-00	23	0	1
Chelsea	2000-01	34	0	2
Chelsea	2001-02	24	0	1
Chelsea	2002-03	30	1	2
Chelsea	2003-04	15	0	0
		156	**2**	**6**
Deschamps, Didier		Apps	Subs	Gls
Chelsea	1999-00	24	3	0
Devlin, Paul		Apps	Subs	Gls
Birmingham C	2002-03	20	12	3
Birmingham C	2003-04	0	2	0
		20	**14**	**3**
Di Canio, Paolo		Apps	Subs	Gls
Sheff. Wed.	1997-98	34	1	12
Sheff. Wed.	1998-99	5	1	3
West Ham U	1998-99	12	1	4
West Ham U	1999-00	29	1	16
West Ham U	2000-01	31	0	9
West Ham U	2001-02	26	0	9
West Ham U	2002-03	16	2	9
Charlton Ath	2003-04	23	8	4
		176	**14**	**66**
Di Matteo, Roberto		Apps	Subs	Gls
Chelsea	1996-97	33	1	7
Chelsea	1997-98	28	2	4
Chelsea	1998-99	26	4	2
Chelsea	1999-00	14	4	2
Chelsea	2000-01	7	0	0
		108	**11**	**15**
Dia, Aly		Apps	Subs	Gls
Southampton	1996-97	0	1	0
Diao, Salif		Apps	Subs	Gls
Liverpool	2002-03	13	13	1
Liverpool	2003-04	2	1	0
		15	**14**	**1**
Diawara, Djibril		Apps	Subs	Gls
Bolton Wan.	2001-02	4	5	0
Diawara, Kaba		Apps	Subs	Gls
Arsenal	1998-99	2	10	0
West Ham U	2000-01	6	5	0
		8	**15**	**0**
Dibble, Andy		Apps	Subs	Gls
Man. City	1992-93	1	1	0
Man. City	1993-94	11	0	0
Man. City	1994-95	15	1	0
		27	**2**	**0**
Dichio, Danny		Apps	Subs	Gls
QPR	1994-95	4	5	3
QPR	1995-96	21	8	10
Sunderland	1999-00	0	12	0
Sunderland	2000-01	2	13	1
West Brom	2002-03	19	9	5
		46	**47**	**19**

Dickman, Jonjo		Apps	Subs	Gls
Sunderland	2002-03	0	1	0

Dickov, Paul		Apps	Subs	Gls
Arsenal	1992-93	1	2	2
Arsenal	1993-94	0	1	0
Arsenal	1994-95	4	5	0
Arsenal	1995-96	1	6	1
Arsenal	1996-97	0	1	0
Man. City	2000-01	15	6	4
Leicester C	2001-02	11	1	4
Leicester C	2003-04	28	7	11
		60	**29**	**22**

Dicks, Julian		Apps	Subs	Gls
Liverpool	1993-94	24	0	3
West Ham U	1993-94	7	0	0
West Ham U	1994-95	29	0	5
West Ham U	1995-96	34	0	10
West Ham U	1996-97	31	0	6
West Ham U	1998-99	9	0	0
		134	**0**	**24**

Digby, Fraser		Apps	Subs	Gls
Swindon T	1993-94	28	0	0

Dijkstra, Sieb		Apps	Subs	Gls
QPR	1994-95	11	0	0

Diomede, Bernard		Apps	Subs	Gls
Liverpool	2000-01	1	1	0

Diouf, El Hadji		Apps	Subs	Gls
Liverpool	2002-03	21	8	3
Liverpool	2003-04	20	6	0
		41	**14**	**3**

Distin, Sylvain		Apps	Subs	Gls
Newcastle U	2001-02	20	8	0
Man. City	2002-03	34	0	0
Man. City	2003-04	38	0	2
		92	**8**	**2**

Dixon, Kerry		Apps	Subs	Gls
Southampton	1992-93	8	1	2

Dixon, Lee		Apps	Subs	Gls
Arsenal	1992-93	29	0	0
Arsenal	1993-94	32	1	0
Arsenal	1994-95	39	0	1
Arsenal	1995-96	38	0	2
Arsenal	1996-97	31	1	2
Arsenal	1997-98	26	2	0
Arsenal	1998-99	36	0	0
Arsenal	1999-00	28	0	3
Arsenal	2000-01	26	3	1
Arsenal	2001-02	3	10	0
		288	**17**	**9**

Djemba-Djemba, Eric		Apps	Subs	Gls
Man. Utd.	2003-04	10	5	0

Djetou, Martin		Apps	Subs	Gls
Fulham	2002-03	22	3	1
Fulham	2003-04	19	7	0
		41	**10**	**1**

Djordjc, Bojan		Apps	Subs	Gls
Man. Utd.	2000-01	0	1	0

Djorkaeff, Youri		Apps	Subs	Gls
Bolton Wan.	2001-02	12	0	4
Bolton Wan.	2002-03	36	0	7
Bolton Wan.	2003-04	24	3	9
		72	**3**	**20**

Dobbs, Gerald		Apps	Subs	Gls
Wimbledon	1992-93	16	3	1
Wimbledon	1993-94	3	7	0
		19	**10**	**1**

Dobie, Scott		Apps	Subs	Gls
West Brom	2002-03	10	21	5

Dobson, Tony		Apps	Subs	Gls
Blackburn R	1992-93	15	4	0

Jason Dodd.

Dodd, Jason		Apps	Subs	Gls
Southampton	1992-93	27	3	1
Southampton	1993-94	5	5	0
Southampton	1994-95	24	2	2
Southampton	1995-96	37	0	2
Southampton	1996-97	23	0	1
Southampton	1997-98	36	0	1
Southampton	1998-99	27	1	1
Southampton	1999-00	30	1	0
Southampton	2000-01	29	2	1
Southampton	2001-02	26	3	0
Southampton	2002-03	13	2	0
Southampton	2003-04	27	1	0
		304	**20**	**9**

Doherty, Gary		Apps	Subs	Gls
Tottenham H	1999-00	0	2	0
Tottenham H	2000-01	18	4	3
Tottenham H	2001-02	4	3	0
Tottenham H	2002-03	7	8	1
Tottenham H	2003-04	16	1	0
		45	**18**	**4**

Doig, Chris		Apps	Subs	Gls
Nottm Forest	1998-99	1	1	0

Domi, Didier		Apps	Subs	Gls
Newcastle U	1998-99	14	0	0
Newcastle U	1999-00	19	8	3
Newcastle U	2000-01	11	3	0
Leeds U	2003-04	9	3	0
		53	**14**	**3**

Dominguez, Jose		Apps	Subs	Gls
Tottenham H	1997-98	8	10	2
Tottenham H	1998-99	2	11	2
Tottenham H	1999-00	2	10	0
Tottenham H	2000-01	0	2	0
		12	**33**	**4**

Donaghy, Mal		Apps	Subs	Gls
Chelsea	1992-93	39	1	2
Chelsea	1993-94	24	4	1
		63	**5**	**3**

Donaldson, O'Neill		Apps	Subs	Gls
Sheff. Wed.	1994-95	0	1	0
Sheff. Wed.	1995-96	1	2	1
Sheff. Wed.	1996-97	2	3	2
Sheff. Wed.	1997-98	1	4	0
		4	**10**	**3**

Donis, George		Apps	Subs	Gls
Blackburn R	1996-97	11	11	2

Donnelly, Simon		Apps	Subs	Gls
Sheff. Wed.	1999-00	3	9	1

Dorigo, Tony		Apps	Subs	Gls
Leeds U	1992-93	33	0	1
Leeds U	1993-94	37	0	0
Leeds U	1994-95	28	0	0
Leeds U	1995-96	17	0	1
Leeds U	1996-97	15	3	0
Derby Co.	1998-99	17	1	1
Derby Co.	1999-00	20	3	0
		167	**7**	**3**

Doriva, Guidoni		Apps	Subs	Gls
Middlesbrough	2002-03	3	2	0
Middlesbrough	2003-04	19	2	0
		22	**4**	**0**

Douglas, Jonathan		Apps	Subs	Gls
Blackburn R	2002-03	0	1	0
Blackburn R	2003-04	14	0	1
		14	**1**	**1**

Dow, Andy		Apps	Subs	Gls
Chelsea	1993-94	13	1	0
Chelsea	1995-96	1	0	0
		14	**1**	**0**

Dowie, Iain		Apps	Subs	Gls
Southampton	1992-93	34	2	11
Southampton	1993-94	39	0	5
Southampton	1994-95	17	0	5
Crystal P	1994-95	15	0	4
West Ham U	1995-96	33	0	8
West Ham U	1996-97	18	5	0
West Ham U	1997-98	7	5	0
		163	**12**	**33**

Downing, Stewart		Apps	Subs	Gls
Middlesbrough	2001-02	2	1	0
Middlesbrough	2002-03	0	2	0
Middlesbrough	2003-04	7	13	0
		9	**16**	**0**

Doyle, Maurice		Apps	Subs	Gls
QPR	1992-93	5	0	0
QPR	1993-94	1	0	0
		6	**0**	**0**

Dozzell, Jason		Apps	Subs	Gls
Ipswich T	1992-93	41	0	7
Tottenham H	1993-94	28	4	8
Tottenham H	1994-95	6	1	0
Tottenham H	1995-96	24	4	3
Tottenham H	1996-97	10	7	2
		109	**16**	**20**

Draper, Mark		Apps	Subs	Gls
Leicester C	1994-95	39	0	5
Aston Villa	1995-96	36	0	2
Aston Villa	1996-97	28	1	0
Aston Villa	1997-98	31	0	3
Aston Villa	1998-99	13	10	2
Aston Villa	1999-00	0	1	0
Southampton	2000-01	16	6	1
Southampton	2001-02	1	1	0
		164	**19**	**13**

Dreyer, John		Apps	Subs	Gls
Bradford C	1999-00	11	3	1

Dryden, Richard		Apps	Subs	Gls
Southampton	1996-97	28	1	1
Southampton	1997-98	11	2	0
Southampton	1998-99	4	0	0
Southampton	1999-00	1	0	0
		44	**3**	**1**

Duberry, Michael		Apps	Subs	Gls
Chelsea	1993-94	1	0	0
Chelsea	1995-96	22	0	0
Chelsea	1996-97	13	2	1
Chelsea	1997-98	23	0	0
Chelsea	1998-99	18	7	0
Leeds U	1999-00	12	1	1
Leeds U	2000-01	5	0	0
Leeds U	2001-02	3	0	0
Leeds U	2002-03	11	3	0
Leeds U	2003-04	19	0	3
		127	**13**	**5**

Dublin, Dion		Apps	Subs	Gls
Man. Utd.	1992-93	3	4	1
Man. Utd.	1993-94	1	4	1
Coventry C	1994-95	31	0	13
Coventry C	1995-96	34	0	14
Coventry C	1996-97	33	1	13
Coventry C	1997-98	36	0	18
Coventry C	1998-99	10	0	3
Aston Villa	1998-99	24	0	11
Aston Villa	1999-00	23	3	12
Aston Villa	2000-01	29	4	8
Aston Villa	2001-02	9	12	4
Aston Villa	2002-03	23	5	10
Aston Villa	2003-04	12	11	3
		268	**44**	**111**

Ducrocq, Pierre		Apps	Subs	Gls
Derby Co.	2001-02	19	0	0

Ducros, Andy		Apps	Subs	Gls
Coventry C	1996-97	1	4	0
Coventry C	1997-98	1	2	0
		2	**6**	**0**

Dudek, Jerzy		Apps	Subs	Gls
Liverpool	2001-02	35	0	0
Liverpool	2002-03	30	0	0
Liverpool	2003-04	30	0	0
		95	**0**	**0**

Dudfield, Lawrie		Apps	Subs	Gls
Leicester C	1999-00	0	2	0

Duff, Damien		Apps	Subs	Gls
Blackburn R	1996-97	1	0	0
Blackburn R	1997-98	17	9	4
Blackburn R	1998-99	18	10	1
Blackburn R	2001-02	31	1	7
Blackburn R	2002-03	26	0	9
Chelsea	2003-04	17	6	5
		110	**26**	**26**

Duffy, Richard		Apps	Subs	Gls
Portsmouth	2003-04	0	1	0

Dugarry, Christophe		Apps	Subs	Gls
Birmingham C	2002-03	16	0	5
Birmingham C	2003-04	12	2	1
		28	**2**	**6**

Dumas, Franck		Apps	Subs	Gls
Newcastle U	1999-00	6	0	0

Dumitrescu, Ilie		Apps	Subs	Gls
Tottenham H	1994-95	11	2	4
Tottenham H	1995-96	5	0	0
West Ham U	1995-96	2	1	0
West Ham U	1996-97	3	4	0
		21	**7**	**4**

Dundee, Sean		Apps	Subs	Gls
Liverpool	1998-99	0	3	0

Dunfield, Terry		Apps	Subs	Gls
Man. City	2000-01	0	1	0

Dunn, David		Apps	Subs	Gls
Blackburn R	1998-99	10	5	1
Blackburn R	2001-02	26	3	7
Blackburn R	2002-03	26	2	8
Birmingham C	2003-04	20	1	2
		82	**11**	**18**

Dunne, Richard		Apps	Subs	Gls
Everton	1996-97	6	1	0
Everton	1997-98	2	1	0
Everton	1998-99	15	1	0
Everton	1999-00	27	4	0
Everton	2000-01	3	0	0
Man. City	2000-01	24	1	0
Man. City	2002-03	24	1	0
Man. City	2003-04	28	1	0
		129	**10**	**0**

Durie, Gordon		Apps	Subs	Gls
Tottenham H	1992-93	17	0	3
Tottenham H	1993-94	10	0	1
		27	**0**	**4**

Durrant, Iain		Apps	Subs	Gls
Everton	1994-95	4	1	0

Durrant, Lee		Apps	Subs	Gls
Ipswich T	1993-94	3	4	0

Dyer, Bruce		Apps	Subs	Gls
Crystal P	1994-95	7	9	1
Crystal P	1997-98	21	3	4
		28	**12**	**5**

Dyer, Kieron		Apps	Subs	Gls
Newcastle U	1999-00	27	3	3
Newcastle U	2000-01	25	1	5
Newcastle U	2001-02	15	3	3
Newcastle U	2002-03	33	2	2
Newcastle U	2003-04	25	0	1
		125	**9**	**14**

Eaden, Nicky		Apps	Subs	Gls
Barnsley	1997-98	32	3	0

Eadie, Darren		Apps	Subs	Gls
Norwich C	1993-94	9	6	3
Norwich C	1994-95	22	4	2
Leicester C	1999-00	15	1	0
Leicester C	2000-01	16	8	2
		62	**19**	**7**

Earle, Robbie		Apps	Subs	Gls
Wimbledon	1992-93	42	0	7
Wimbledon	1993-94	42	0	9
Wimbledon	1994-95	9	0	0
Wimbledon	1995-96	37	0	11
Wimbledon	1996-97	32	0	7
Wimbledon	1997-98	20	2	3
Wimbledon	1998-99	35	0	5
Wimbledon	1999-00	23	2	3
		240	**4**	**45**

Easton, Clint		Apps	Subs	Gls
Watford	1999-00	13	4	0

Ebbrell, John		Apps	Subs	Gls
Everton	1992-93	24	0	1
Everton	1993-94	39	0	4
Everton	1994-95	26	0	0
Everton	1995-96	24	1	4
Everton	1996-97	7	0	0
		120	**1**	**9**

Edghill, Richard		Apps	Subs	Gls
Man. City	1993-94	22	0	0
Man. City	1994-95	14	0	0
Man. City	1995-96	13	0	0
Man. City	2000-01	6	0	0
		55	**0**	**0**

Edinburgh, Justin		Apps	Subs	Gls
Tottenham H	1992-93	31	1	0
Tottenham H	1993-94	24	1	0
Tottenham H	1994-95	29	2	0
Tottenham H	1995-96	15	7	0
Tottenham H	1996-97	21	3	0
Tottenham H	1997-98	13	3	0
Tottenham H	1998-99	14	2	0
Tottenham H	1999-00	7	1	0
		154	**20**	**0**

Edu (Cesar Gaspar Eduardo)		Apps	Subs	Gls
Arsenal	2000-01	2	3	0
Arsenal	2001-02	8	6	1
Arsenal	2002-03	12	6	2
Arsenal	2003-04	13	17	2
		35	**32**	**5**

Edwards, Christian		Apps	Subs	Gls
Nottm Forest	1998-99	7	5	0

Edwards, Rob		Apps	Subs	Gls
Aston Villa	2002-03	7	1	0

Edworthy, Marc		Apps	Subs	Gls
Crystal P	1997-98	33	1	0
Coventry C	1998-99	16	6	0
Coventry C	1999-00	10	0	0
Coventry C	2000-01	18	6	1
		77	**13**	**1**

Ehiogu, Ugo		Apps	Subs	Gls
Aston Villa	1992-93	1	3	0
Aston Villa	1993-94	14	3	0
Aston Villa	1994-95	38	1	3
Aston Villa	1995-96	36	0	1
Aston Villa	1996-97	38	0	3
Aston Villa	1997-98	37	0	2
Aston Villa	1998-99	23	2	2
Aston Villa	1999-00	31	0	1
Aston Villa	2000-01	1	1	0
Middlesbrough	2000-01	21	0	3
Middlesbrough	2001-02	29	0	1
Middlesbrough	2002-03	31	1	3
Middlesbrough	2003-04	16	0	0
		316	**11**	**19**

Ekelund, Ronnie		Apps	Subs	Gls
Southampton	1994-95	15	2	5
Man. City	1995-96	2	2	0
		17	**4**	**5**

Ekoku, Efan		Apps	Subs	Gls
Norwich C	1992-93	1	3	3
Norwich C	1993-94	20	7	12
Norwich C	1994-95	5	1	0
Wimbledon	1994-95	24	0	9
Wimbledon	1995-96	28	3	7
Wimbledon	1996-97	28	2	11
Wimbledon	1997-98	11	5	4
Wimbledon	1998-99	11	11	6
		128	**32**	**52**

El Karkouri, Talal		Apps	Subs	Gls
Sunderland	2002-03	8	0	0

El Khalej, Tahar		Apps	Subs	Gls
Southampton	1999-00	11	0	1
Southampton	2000-01	25	7	1
Southampton	2001-02	12	2	1
Southampton	2002-03	0	1	0
Charlton Ath	2002-03	2	1	0
		50	**11**	**3**

Elkins, Gary		Apps	Subs	Gls
Wimbledon	1992-93	17	1	0
Wimbledon	1993-94	18	0	1
Wimbledon	1994-95	33	3	1
Wimbledon	1995-96	7	3	0
		75	**7**	**2**

Ellegaard, Kevin		Apps	Subs	Gls
Man. City	2003-04	2	2	0

Elliott, Matt		Apps	Subs	Gls
Leicester C	1996-97	16	0	4

	Season	Apps	Subs	Gls
Leicester C	1997-98	37	0	7
Leicester C	1998-99	37	0	3
Leicester C	1999-00	37	0	6
Leicester C	2000-01	34	0	2
Leicester C	2001-02	31	0	0
Leicester C	2003-04	3	4	0
		195	**4**	**22**
Elliott, Paul		Apps	Subs	Gls
Chelsea	1992-93	7	0	0
Elliott, Robbie		Apps	Subs	Gls
Newcastle U	1993-94	13	2	0
Newcastle U	1994-95	10	4	2
Newcastle U	1995-96	5	1	0
Newcastle U	1996-97	29	0	7
Bolton Wan.	1997-98	4	0	0
Newcastle U	2001-02	26	1	1
Newcastle U	2002-03	0	2	0
		87	**10**	**10**
Elliott, Stephen		Apps	Subs	Gls
Man. City	2003-04	0	2	0
Elliott, Steve		Apps	Subs	Gls
Derby Co.	1997-98	3	0	0
Derby Co.	1998-99	7	4	0
Derby Co.	1999-00	18	2	0
Derby Co.	2000-01	5	1	0
Derby Co.	2001-02	2	4	0
		35	**11**	**0**
Ellis, Kevin		Apps	Subs	Gls
Ipswich T	1994-95	1	0	0
Ellison, Kevin		Apps	Subs	Gls
Leicester C	2000-01	0	1	0
Emblen, Neil		Apps	Subs	Gls
Crystal P	1997-98	8	5	0
Emerson, Moises Costa		Apps	Subs	Gls
Middlesbrough	1996-97	32	0	4
Emerton, Brett		Apps	Subs	Gls
Blackburn R	2003-04	31	6	2
Enckelman, Peter		Apps	Subs	Gls
Aston Villa	1999-00	9	1	0
Aston Villa	2001-02	9	0	0
Aston Villa	2002-03	33	0	0
Blackburn R	2003-04	2	0	0
		53	**1**	**0**
Eranio, Stefano		Apps	Subs	Gls
Derby Co.	1997-98	23	0	5
Derby Co.	1998-99	18	7	0
Derby Co.	1999-00	17	2	0
Derby Co.	2000-01	25	3	2
		83	**12**	**7**
Eriksson, Jan		Apps	Subs	Gls
Sunderland	1996-97	1	0	0
Espartero, Mario		Apps	Subs	Gls
Bolton Wan.	2001-02	0	3	0
Etherington, Matthew		Apps	Subs	Gls
Tottenham H	1999-00	1	4	0
Tottenham H	2000-01	1	5	0
Tottenham H	2001-02	3	8	0
Tottenham H	2002-03	15	8	1
		20	**25**	**1**
Euell, Jason		Apps	Subs	Gls
Wimbledon	1995-96	4	5	2
Wimbledon	1996-97	4	3	2
Wimbledon	1997-98	14	5	4
Wimbledon	1998-99	31	2	10
Wimbledon	1999-00	32	5	4
Charlton Ath	2001-02	31	5	11
Charlton Ath	2002-03	35	1	10
Charlton Ath	2003-04	24	7	10
		175	**33**	**53**
Eustace, John		Apps	Subs	Gls
Coventry C	1999-00	12	4	1
Coventry C	2000-01	22	10	2
Middlesbrough	2002-03	0	1	0
		34	**15**	**3**
Evans, Gareth		Apps	Subs	Gls
Leeds U	2000-01	0	1	0
Evans, Mickey		Apps	Subs	Gls
Southampton	1996-97	8	4	4
Southampton	1997-98	6	4	0
		14	**8**	**4**
Evatt, Ian		Apps	Subs	Gls
Derby Co.	2000-01	0	1	0
Derby Co.	2001-02	1	2	0
		1	**3**	**0**
Evtushok, Alex		Apps	Subs	Gls
Coventry C	1996-97	3	0	0
Eyre, John		Apps	Subs	Gls
Oldham Ath.	1993-94	1	1	0
Facey, Delroy		Apps	Subs	Gls
Bolton Wan.	2002-03	1	8	1
Bolton Wan.	2003-04	0	1	0
		1	**9**	**1**
Fagan, Craig		Apps	Subs	Gls
Birmingham C	2002-03	0	1	0
Fairclough, Chris		Apps	Subs	Gls
Leeds U	1992-93	29	1	3
Leeds U	1993-94	40	0	4
Leeds U	1994-95	1	4	0
Bolton Wan.	1995-96	33	0	0
Bolton Wan.	1997-98	10	1	0
		113	**6**	**7**
Falconer, Willie		Apps	Subs	Gls
Middlesbrough	1992-93	22	6	5
Sheff. Utd.	1993-94	21	2	3
		43	**8**	**8**
Farley, Adam		Apps	Subs	Gls
Everton	1998-99	0	1	0
Farrell, Dave		Apps	Subs	Gls
Aston Villa	1992-93	1	1	0
Aston Villa	1993-94	4	0	0
		5	**1**	**0**
Farrelly, Gareth		Apps	Subs	Gls
Aston Villa	1995-96	1	4	0
Aston Villa	1996-97	1	2	0
Everton	1997-98	18	8	1
Everton	1998-99	0	1	0
Bolton Wan.	2001-02	11	7	0
Bolton Wan.	2002-03	6	2	1
		37	**24**	**2**
Fashanu, John		Apps	Subs	Gls
Wimbledon	1992-93	27	2	6
Wimbledon	1993-94	35	1	11
Aston Villa	1994-95	11	2	3
		73	**5**	**20**
Faye, Amdy		Apps	Subs	Gls
Portsmouth	2003-04	27	0	0
Fear, Peter		Apps	Subs	Gls
Wimbledon	1992-93	2	2	0
Wimbledon	1993-94	23	0	1
Wimbledon	1994-95	8	6	1
Wimbledon	1995-96	4	0	0
Wimbledon	1996-97	9	9	0
Wimbledon	1997-98	5	3	2
Wimbledon	1998-99	0	2	0
		51	**22**	**4**
Feng Li Wei		Apps	Subs	Gls
Everton	2002-03	1	0	0
Fenn, Neale		Apps	Subs	Gls
Tottenham H	1996-97	0	4	0
Tottenham H	1997-98	0	4	0
		0	**8**	**0**
Fenton, Graham		Apps	Subs	Gls
Aston Villa	1993-94	9	3	1
Aston Villa	1994-95	7	10	2
Aston Villa	1995-96	0	3	0
Blackburn R	1995-96	4	10	6
Blackburn R	1996-97	5	8	1
Leicester C	1997-98	9	14	3
Leicester C	1998-99	3	6	0
Leicester C	1999-00	1	1	0
		38	**55**	**13**
Fenwick, Terry		Apps	Subs	Gls
Tottenham H	1992-93	3	2	0
Swindon T	1993-94	23	3	0
		26	**5**	**0**
Ferdinand, Les		Apps	Subs	Gls
QPR	1992-93	37	0	20
QPR	1993-94	35	1	16
QPR	1994-95	37	0	24
Newcastle U	1995-96	37	0	25
Newcastle U	1996-97	30	1	16
Tottenham H	1997-98	19	2	5
Tottenham H	1998-99	22	2	5
Tottenham H	1999-00	5	4	2
Tottenham H	2000-01	25	3	10
Tottenham H	2001-02	22	3	9
Tottenham H	2002-03	4	7	2
West Ham U	2002-03	12	2	2
Leicester C	2003-04	20	9	12
		305	**34**	**148**
Ferdinand, Rio		Apps	Subs	Gls
West Ham U	1995-96	0	1	0
West Ham U	1996-97	11	4	2
West Ham U	1997-98	35	0	0
West Ham U	1998-99	31	0	0
West Ham U	1999-00	33	0	0
West Ham U	2000-01	12	0	0
Leeds U	2000-01	23	0	2
Leeds U	2001-02	31	0	0
Man. Utd.	2002-03	27	1	0
Man. Utd.	2003-04	20	0	0
		223	**6**	**4**
Ferguson, Barry		Apps	Subs	Gls
Blackburn R	2003-04	14	1	1
Ferguson, Darren		Apps	Subs	Gls
Man. Utd.	1992-93	15	0	0
Man. Utd.	1993-94	1	2	0
		16	**2**	**0**
Ferguson, Duncan		Apps	Subs	Gls
Everton	1994-95	22	1	7
Everton	1995-96	16	2	5
Everton	1996-97	31	2	10
Everton	1997-98	28	1	11
Everton	1998-99	13	0	4
Newcastle U	1998-99	7	0	2
Newcastle U	1999-00	17	6	6
Everton	2000-01	9	3	6
Everton	2001-02	17	5	6
Everton	2002-03	0	7	0
Everton	2003-04	13	7	5
		173	**34**	**62**
Fernandes, Fabrice		Apps	Subs	Gls
Southampton	2001-02	6	5	1
Southampton	2002-03	35	2	3
Southampton	2003-04	21	6	1
		62	**13**	**5**
Fernandes, Silas		Apps	Subs	Gls
Wolves	2003-04	2	7	0
Ferrer, Albert		Apps	Subs	Gls
Chelsea	1998-99	30	0	0
Chelsea	1999-00	24	1	0
Chelsea	2000-01	12	2	0
Chelsea	2001-02	2	2	0
Chelsea	2002-03	3	0	0
		71	**5**	**0**
Ferri, Jean-Michel		Apps	Subs	Gls
Liverpool	1998-99	0	2	0
Festa, Gianluca		Apps	Subs	Gls
Middlesbrough	1996-97	13	0	1
Middlesbrough	1998-99	25	0	2
Middlesbrough	1999-00	27	2	2
Middlesbrough	2000-01	21	4	2
Middlesbrough	2001-02	8	0	1
		94	**6**	**8**
Fettis, Alan		Apps	Subs	Gls
Nottm Forest	1996-97	4	0	0
Blackburn R	1997-98	7	1	0
Blackburn R	1998-99	2	0	0
		13	**1**	**0**
Feuer, Ian		Apps	Subs	Gls
West Ham U	1999-00	3	0	0
Derby Co.	2001-02	2	0	0
		5	**0**	**0**
Figueroa, Luciano		Apps	Subs	Gls
Birmingham C	2003-04	0	1	0
Filan, John		Apps	Subs	Gls
Coventry C	1994-95	2	0	0
Coventry C	1995-96	13	0	0
Coventry C	1996-97	0	1	0
Blackburn R	1997-98	7	0	0
Blackburn R	1998-99	26	0	0
		48	**1**	**0**
Finn, Neil		Apps	Subs	Gls
West Ham U	1995-96	1	0	0
Finnan, Steve		Apps	Subs	Gls
Fulham	2001-02	38	0	0
Fulham	2002-03	32	0	0
Liverpool	2003-04	19	3	0
		89	**3**	**0**
Fish, Mark		Apps	Subs	Gls
Bolton Wan.	1997-98	22	0	2
Charlton Ath	2000-01	24	0	1
Charlton Ath	2001-02	25	0	0
Charlton Ath	2002-03	23	0	1
Charlton Ath	2003-04	23	0	0
		117	**0**	**4**
Fitzgerald, Scott		Apps	Subs	Gls
Wimbledon	1992-93	18	2	0
Wimbledon	1993-94	27	1	0
Wimbledon	1994-95	14	3	0
Wimbledon	1995-96	2	2	0
		61	**8**	**0**
Fjortoft, Jan Aage		Apps	Subs	Gls
Swindon T	1993-94	26	10	12
Middlesbrough	1995-96	27	1	6
Middlesbrough	1996-97	2	3	0
Barnsley	1997-98	12	3	6
		67	**17**	**24**
Flatts, Mark		Apps	Subs	Gls
Arsenal	1992-93	6	4	0
Arsenal	1993-94	2	1	0
Arsenal	1994-95	1	2	0
		9	**7**	**0**
Fleck, Robert		Apps	Subs	Gls
Chelsea	1992-93	28	3	2
Chelsea	1993-94	7	2	1
		35	**5**	**3**
Fleming, Craig		Apps	Subs	Gls
Oldham Ath.	1992-93	23	1	0
Oldham Ath.	1993-94	37	0	0
		60	**1**	**0**
Fleming, Curtis		Apps	Subs	Gls
Middlesbrough	1992-93	22	2	0
Middlesbrough	1995-96	13	0	1
Middlesbrough	1996-97	30	0	0
Middlesbrough	1998-99	12	2	1
Middlesbrough	1999-00	27	0	0
Middlesbrough	2000-01	29	1	0
Middlesbrough	2001-02	8	0	0
		141	**5**	**2**
Fleming, Terry		Apps	Subs	Gls
Coventry C	1992-93	8	3	0
Fletcher, Darren		Apps	Subs	Gls
Man. Utd.	2003-04	17	5	0
Flitcroft, Garry		Apps	Subs	Gls
Man. City	1992-93	28	4	5
Man. City	1993-94	19	2	3
Man. City	1994-95	37	0	5
Man. City	1995-96	25	0	0
Blackburn R	1995-96	3	0	0
Blackburn R	1996-97	27	1	3
Blackburn R	1997-98	28	5	0
Blackburn R	1998-99	8	0	2
Blackburn R	2001-02	26	3	1
Blackburn R	2002-03	33	0	2
Blackburn R	2003-04	29	2	3
		263	**17**	**24**
Flo, Jostein		Apps	Subs	Gls
Sheff. Utd.	1993-94	32	1	9
Flo, Tore Andre		Apps	Subs	Gls
Chelsea	1997-98	16	18	11
Chelsea	1998-99	18	12	10
Chelsea	1999-00	20	14	10
Chelsea	2000-01	5	9	3
Sunderland	2002-03	23	6	4
		82	**59**	**38**
Flowers, Tim		Apps	Subs	Gls
Southampton	1992-93	42	0	0
Southampton	1993-94	12	0	0
Blackburn R	1993-94	29	0	0
Blackburn R	1994-95	39	0	0
Blackburn R	1995-96	37	0	0
Blackburn R	1996-97	36	0	0
Blackburn R	1997-98	24	1	0
Blackburn R	1998-99	10	1	0
Leicester C	1999-00	29	0	0
Leicester C	2000-01	22	0	0
Leicester C	2001-02	3	1	0
		283	**3**	**0**
Flynn, Sean		Apps	Subs	Gls
Coventry C	1992-93	4	3	0
Coventry C	1993-94	33	3	3
Coventry C	1994-95	32	0	4
Derby Co.	1996-97	10	7	1
		79	**13**	**8**
Foe, Marc-Vivien		Apps	Subs	Gls
West Ham U	1998-99	13	0	0
West Ham U	1999-00	25	0	1
Man. City	2002-03	35	0	9
		73	**0**	**10**
Folan, Tony		Apps	Subs	Gls
Crystal P	1997-98	0	1	0
Foletti, Patrick		Apps	Subs	Gls
Derby Co.	2001-02	1	1	0
Foley, Dominic		Apps	Subs	Gls
Watford	1999-00	5	7	1
Folly, Yoann		Apps	Subs	Gls
Southampton	2003-04	9	0	0
Ford, Mark		Apps	Subs	Gls
Leeds U	1993-94	0	1	0
Leeds U	1995-96	12	0	0
Leeds U	1996-97	15	1	1
		27	**2**	**1**
Forlan, Diego		Apps	Subs	Gls
Man. Utd.	2001-02	6	7	0
Man. Utd.	2002-03	7	18	6
Man. Utd.	2003-04	10	14	4
		23	**39**	**10**
Forrest, Craig		Apps	Subs	Gls
Ipswich T	1992-93	11	0	0
Ipswich T	1993-94	27	0	0
Ipswich T	1994-95	36	0	0
Chelsea	1996-97	2	1	0
West Ham U	1997-98	13	0	0
West Ham U	1998-99	1	1	0
West Ham U	1999-00	9	2	0
West Ham U	2000-01	3	1	0
		102	**5**	**0**
Forrester, Jamie		Apps	Subs	Gls
Leeds U	1992-93	5	1	0
Leeds U	1993-94	2	1	0
		7	**2**	**0**
Forssell, Mikael		Apps	Subs	Gls
Chelsea	1998-99	4	6	1
Chelsea	2001-02	2	20	4
Birmingham C	2003-04	32	0	17
		38	**26**	**22**
Fortune, Jon		Apps	Subs	Gls
Charlton Ath	2001-02	14	5	0
Charlton Ath	2002-03	22	4	1
Charlton Ath	2003-04	21	7	2
		57	**16**	**3**
Fortune, Quinton		Apps	Subs	Gls
Man. Utd.	1999-00	4	2	2
Man. Utd.	2000-01	6	1	2
Man. Utd.	2001-02	8	6	1
Man. Utd.	2002-03	5	4	0
Man. Utd.	2003-04	18	5	0
		41	**18**	**5**
Foster, Colin		Apps	Subs	Gls
West Ham U	1993-94	5	0	0
Foster, John		Apps	Subs	Gls
Man. City	1993-94	1	0	0
Man. City	1994-95	9	2	0
Man. City	1995-96	4	0	0
		14	**2**	**0**
Fowler, Robbie		Apps	Subs	Gls
Liverpool	1993-94	27	1	12
Liverpool	1994-95	42	0	25
Liverpool	1995-96	36	2	28
Liverpool	1996-97	32	0	18
Liverpool	1997-98	19	1	9
Liverpool	1998-99	23	2	14
Liverpool	1999-00	8	6	3
Liverpool	2000-01	15	12	8
Liverpool	2001-02	8	2	3
Leeds U	2001-02	22	0	12
Leeds U	2002-03	2	6	2
Man. City	2002-03	12	1	2
Man. City	2003-04	23	8	7
		269	**41**	**143**
Fox, Ruel		Apps	Subs	Gls
Norwich C	1992-93	32	2	4
Norwich C	1993-94	25	0	7
Newcastle U	1993-94	14	0	2
Newcastle U	1994-95	40	0	10
Newcastle U	1995-96	2	2	0
Tottenham H	1995-96	26	0	6
Tottenham H	1996-97	19	6	1
Tottenham H	1997-98	32	0	3
Tottenham H	1998-99	17	3	3
Tottenham H	1999-00	1	2	0
		208	**15**	**36**
Foxe, Hayden		Apps	Subs	Gls
West Ham U	2000-01	3	2	0

Steve Guppy.

West Ham U	2001-02	4	2	0
Portsmouth	2003-04	8	2	1
		15	**6**	**1**
Francis, Damien		Apps	Subs	Gls
Wimbledon	1997-98	0	2	0
Wimbledon	1999-00	1	8	0
		1	**10**	**0**
Francis, Trevor		Apps	Subs	Gls
Sheff. Wed.	1992-93	1	4	0
Sheff. Wed.	1993-94	0	1	0
		1	**5**	**0**
Frandsen, Per		Apps	Subs	Gls
Bolton Wan.	1997-98	38	0	2
Bolton Wan.	2001-02	25	4	3
Bolton Wan.	2002-03	34	0	2
Bolton Wan.	2003-04	22	11	1
		119	**15**	**8**
Fredgaard, Carsten		Apps	Subs	Gls
Sunderland	1999-00	0	1	0
Freedman, Dougie		Apps	Subs	Gls
Crystal P	1997-98	2	5	0
Nottm Forest	1998-99	20	11	9
		22	**16**	**9**
Freestone, Chris		Apps	Subs	Gls
Middlesbrough	1995-96	2	1	1
Middlesbrough	1996-97	0	3	0
		2	**4**	**1**
Freund, Steffen		Apps	Subs	Gls
Tottenham H	1998-99	17	0	0
Tottenham H	1999-00	24	3	0
Tottenham H	2000-01	19	2	0
Tottenham H	2001-02	19	1	0
Tottenham H	2002-03	13	4	0
Leicester C	2003-04	13	1	0
		105	**11**	**0**
Friedel, Brad		Apps	Subs	Gls
Liverpool	1997-98	11	0	0
Liverpool	1998-99	12	0	0
Liverpool	1999-00	2	0	0
Blackburn R	2001-02	36	0	0
Blackburn R	2002-03	37	0	0
Blackburn R	2003-04	36	0	1
		134	**0**	**1**
Froggatt, Steve		Apps	Subs	Gls
Aston Villa	1992-93	16	1	1
Aston Villa	1993-94	8	1	1
Coventry C	1998-99	23	0	1
Coventry C	1999-00	21	5	1
		68	**7**	**4**
Frontzeck, Michael		Apps	Subs	Gls
Man. City	1995-96	11	1	0
Fuertes, Esteban		Apps	Subs	Gls
Derby Co.	1999-00	8	0	1
Fullarton, Jamie		Apps	Subs	Gls
Crystal P	1997-98	19	6	1
Fumaca, Jose		Apps	Subs	Gls
Newcastle U	1999-00	1	4	0
Furlong, Paul		Apps	Subs	Gls
Chelsea	1994-95	30	6	10
Chelsea	1995-96	14	14	3
		44	**20**	**13**
Futre, Paulo		Apps	Subs	Gls
West Ham U	1996-97	4	5	0
Gaardsoe, Thomas		Apps	Subs	Gls
Ipswich T	2001-02	3	1	1
Gabbiadini, Marco		Apps	Subs	Gls
Derby Co.	1996-97	5	9	0
Gage, Kevin		Apps	Subs	Gls
Sheff. Utd.	1992-93	27	0	0
Sheff. Utd.	1993-94	16	5	0
		43	**5**	**0**
Gale, Tony		Apps	Subs	Gls
West Ham U	1993-94	31	1	0
Blackburn R	1994-95	15	0	0
		46	**1**	**0**
Gallacher, Kevin		Apps	Subs	Gls
Coventry C	1992-93	19	1	6
Blackburn R	1992-93	9	0	5
Blackburn R	1993-94	27	3	7
Blackburn R	1994-95	1	0	1
Blackburn R	1995-96	14	2	2
Blackburn R	1996-97	34	0	10
Blackburn R	1997-98	31	2	16
Blackburn R	1998-99	13	3	4
Newcastle U	1999-00	15	5	2
Newcastle U	2000-01	12	7	2
		175	**23**	**55**
Gallagher, Paul		Apps	Subs	Gls
Blackburn R	2002-03	0	1	0
Blackburn R	2003-04	12	14	3
		12	**15**	**3**
Gallas, William		Apps	Subs	Gls
Chelsea	2001-02	27	3	1
Chelsea	2002-03	36	2	4
Chelsea	2003-04	23	6	0
		86	**11**	**5**
Gallen, Kevin		Apps	Subs	Gls
QPR	1994-95	31	6	10
QPR	1995-96	26	4	8
		57	**10**	**18**
Galloway, Mick		Apps	Subs	Gls
Leicester C	1994-95	4	1	0
Ganea, Vio		Apps	Subs	Gls
Wolves	2003-04	6	10	3
Gannon, John		Apps	Subs	Gls
Sheff. Utd.	1992-93	26	1	1
Sheff. Utd.	1993-94	14	0	0
		40	**1**	**1**
Garcia, Richard		Apps	Subs	Gls
West Ham U	2001-02	2	6	0
Garde, Remi		Apps	Subs	Gls
Arsenal	1996-97	7	4	0
Arsenal	1997-98	6	4	0
Arsenal	1998-99	6	4	0
		19	**12**	**0**
Gardner, Anthony		Apps	Subs	Gls
Tottenham H	2000-01	5	3	0
Tottenham H	2001-02	11	4	0
Tottenham H	2002-03	11	1	1
Tottenham H	2003-04	33	0	0
		60	**8**	**1**
Gardner, Ricardo		Apps	Subs	Gls
Bolton Wan.	2001-02	29	2	3
Bolton Wan.	2002-03	31	1	2
Bolton Wan.	2003-04	20	2	0
		80	**5**	**5**
Garry, Ryan		Apps	Subs	Gls
Arsenal	2002-03	1	0	0
Gascoigne, Paul		Apps	Subs	Gls
Middlesbrough	1998-99	25	1	3
Middlesbrough	1999-00	7	1	1
Everton	2000-01	10	4	0
Everton	2001-02	8	10	1
		50	**16**	**5**
Gaudino, Maurizio		Apps	Subs	Gls
Man. City	1994-95	17	3	3
Gavilan, Diego		Apps	Subs	Gls
Newcastle U	1999-00	2	4	1
Newcastle U	2000-01	0	1	0
		2	**5**	**1**
Gavin, Jason		Apps	Subs	Gls
Middlesbrough	1998-99	2	0	0
Middlesbrough	1999-00	2	4	0
Middlesbrough	2000-01	10	4	0
Middlesbrough	2001-02	5	4	0
		19	**12**	**0**
Gayle, Brian		Apps	Subs	Gls
Sheff. Utd.	1992-93	31	0	2
Sheff. Utd.	1993-94	13	0	3
		44	**0**	**5**
Gayle, John		Apps	Subs	Gls
Coventry C	1993-94	3	0	0
Gayle, Marcus		Apps	Subs	Gls
Wimbledon	1993-94	10	0	0
Wimbledon	1994-95	22	1	2
Wimbledon	1995-96	21	13	5
Wimbledon	1996-97	34	2	8
Wimbledon	1997-98	21	9	2
Wimbledon	1998-99	31	4	10
Wimbledon	1999-00	35	1	7
		174	**30**	**34**
Gee, Phil		Apps	Subs	Gls
Leicester C	1994-95	3	4	2
Gemmill, Scot		Apps	Subs	Gls
Nottm Forest	1992-93	33	0	1
Nottm Forest	1994-95	19	0	1
Nottm Forest	1995-96	26	5	1
Nottm Forest	1996-97	18	6	0
Nottm Forest	1998-99	18	2	0
Everton	1998-99	7	0	1
Everton	1999-00	6	8	1
Everton	2000-01	25	3	2
Everton	2001-02	31	1	1
Everton	2002-03	10	6	0
		193	**31**	**8**
Genaux, Reggie		Apps	Subs	Gls
Coventry C	1996-97	3	1	0
George, Finidi		Apps	Subs	Gls
Ipswich T	2001-02	21	4	6
Georgiadis, Georgios		Apps	Subs	Gls
Newcastle U	1998-99	7	3	0
Geremi		Apps	Subs	Gls
Middlesbrough	2002-03	33	0	7
Chelsea	2003-04	19	6	1
		52	**6**	**8**
Gerrard, Paul		Apps	Subs	Gls
Oldham Ath.	1992-93	25	0	0
Oldham Ath.	1993-94	15	1	0
Everton	1996-97	4	1	0
Everton	1997-98	4	0	0
Everton	1999-00	34	0	0
Everton	2000-01	32	0	0
Everton	2001-02	13	0	0
Everton	2002-03	2	0	0
		129	**2**	**0**
Gerrard, Steven		Apps	Subs	Gls
Liverpool	1998-99	4	8	0
Liverpool	1999-00	26	3	1
Liverpool	2000-01	29	4	7
Liverpool	2001-02	26	2	3
Liverpool	2002-03	32	2	5
Liverpool	2003-04	34	0	4
		151	**19**	**20**
Ghrayib, Naguyan		Apps	Subs	Gls
Aston Villa	1999-00	1	4	0
Giallanza, Gaetano		Apps	Subs	Gls
Bolton Wan.	1997-98	0	3	0
Giannakopoulos, Stylianos		Apps	Subs	Gls
Bolton Wan.	2003-04	17	14	2
Gibbens, Kevin		Apps	Subs	Gls
Southampton	1997-98	2	0	0
Southampton	1998-99	2	2	0
Southampton	2000-01	1	2	0
		5	**4**	**0**
Gibbs, Nigel		Apps	Subs	Gls
Watford	1999-00	11	6	0
Gibson, Terry		Apps	Subs	Gls
Wimbledon	1992-93	6	2	1
Giggs, Ryan		Apps	Subs	Gls
Man. Utd.	1992-93	40	1	9
Man. Utd.	1993-94	32	6	13
Man. Utd.	1994-95	29	0	1
Man. Utd.	1995-96	30	3	11
Man. Utd.	1996-97	25	1	3
Man. Utd.	1997-98	28	1	8
Man. Utd.	1998-99	20	4	3
Man. Utd.	1999-00	30	0	6
Man. Utd.	2000-01	24	7	5
Man. Utd.	2001-02	18	7	7
Man. Utd.	2002-03	32	4	8
Man. Utd.	2003-04	29	4	7
		337	**38**	**81**
Gilchrist, Phil		Apps	Subs	Gls
Leicester C	1999-00	17	10	1
Leicester C	2000-01	6	6	0
West Brom	2002-03	22	0	0
		45	**16**	**1**
Gillespie, Gary		Apps	Subs	Gls
Coventry C	1994-95	2	1	0
Gillespie, Keith		Apps	Subs	Gls
Man. Utd.	1994-95	3	6	1
Newcastle U	1994-95	15	2	2
Newcastle U	1995-96	26	2	4
Newcastle U	1996-97	23	9	1
Newcastle U	1997-98	25	4	4
Newcastle U	1998-99	5	2	0
Blackburn R	1998-99	13	3	2
Blackburn R	2001-02	21	11	2
Blackburn R	2002-03	10	15	0
Leicester C	2003-04	7	5	0
		148	**59**	**16**
Ginola, David		Apps	Subs	Gls
Newcastle U	1995-96	34	0	5

Shaun Goater.

Newcastle U	1996-97	20	4	1
Tottenham H	1997-98	34	0	6
Tottenham H	1998-99	30	0	3
Tottenham H	1999-00	36	0	4
Aston Villa	2000-01	14	13	3
Aston Villa	2001-02	0	5	0
Everton	2001-02	2	3	0
		170	**25**	**22**
Ginty, Rory		Apps	Subs	Gls
Crystal P	1997-98	2	3	0
Gioacchino, Stefano		Apps	Subs	Gls
Coventry C	1998-99	0	3	0
Gittens, Jon		Apps	Subs	Gls
Middlesbrough	1992-93	13	0	0
Given, Shay		Apps	Subs	Gls
Blackburn R	1996-97	2	0	0
Newcastle U	1997-98	24	0	0
Newcastle U	1998-99	31	0	0
Newcastle U	1999-00	14	0	0
Newcastle U	2000-01	34	0	0
Newcastle U	2001-02	38	0	0
Newcastle U	2002-03	38	0	0
Newcastle U	2003-04	38	0	0
		219	**0**	**0**
Glass, Stephen		Apps	Subs	Gls
Newcastle U	1998-99	18	4	3
Newcastle U	1999-00	1	6	1
Newcastle U	2000-01	5	9	3
		24	**19**	**7**
Glover, Lee		Apps	Subs	Gls
Nottm Forest	1992-93	9	5	0
Goater, Shaun		Apps	Subs	Gls
Man. City	2000-01	20	6	6
Man. City	2002-03	14	12	7
		34	**18**	**13**
Goddard, Paul		Apps	Subs	Gls
Ipswich T	1992-93	19	6	3
Ipswich T	1993-94	3	1	0
		22	**7**	**3**
Goldbaek, Bjarne		Apps	Subs	Gls
Chelsea	1998-99	13	10	5
Chelsea	1999-00	2	4	0
Fulham	2001-02	8	5	1
Fulham	2002-03	8	2	0
		31	**21**	**6**
Goma, Alain		Apps	Subs	Gls
Newcastle U	1999-00	14	0	0
Newcastle U	2000-01	18	1	1
Fulham	2001-02	32	1	0
Fulham	2002-03	29	0	0
Fulham	2003-04	23	0	0
		116	**2**	**1**
Gooden, Ty		Apps	Subs	Gls
Swindon T	1993-94	2	2	0
Goodman, Jon		Apps	Subs	Gls
Wimbledon	1994-95	13	6	4
Wimbledon	1995-96	9	18	6
Wimbledon	1996-97	6	7	1
Wimbledon	1998-99	0	1	0
		28	**32**	**11**
Goodridge, Greg		Apps	Subs	Gls
QPR	1995-96	0	7	1
Goodwin, Tommy		Apps	Subs	Gls
Leicester C	1999-00	1	0	0
Goram, Andy		Apps	Subs	Gls
Man. Utd.	2000-01	2	0	0
Gordon, Dale		Apps	Subs	Gls
West Ham U	1993-94	8	0	1
West Ham U	1995-96	0	1	0
		8	**1**	**1**
Gordon, Dean		Apps	Subs	Gls
Crystal P	1992-93	6	4	0
Crystal P	1994-95	38	3	2
Crystal P	1997-98	36	1	2
Middlesbrough	1998-99	38	0	3
Middlesbrough	1999-00	3	1	0
Middlesbrough	2000-01	12	8	2
Middlesbrough	2001-02	0	1	0
		133	**18**	**9**
Goss, Jerry		Apps	Subs	Gls
Norwich C	1992-93	25	0	1
Norwich C	1993-94	34	0	6
Norwich C	1994-95	19	6	2
		78	**6**	**9**
Gough, Richard		Apps	Subs	Gls
Nottm Forest	1998-99	7	0	0
Everton	1999-00	29	0	1
Everton	2000-01	9	0	0
		45	**0**	**1**
Gould, Jonathan		Apps	Subs	Gls
Coventry C	1992-93	9	0	0
Coventry C	1993-94	9	0	0
Coventry C	1994-95	7	0	0
		25	**0**	**0**
Grabbi, Corrado		Apps	Subs	Gls
Blackburn R	2001-02	10	4	1
Blackburn R	2002-03	1	10	1
Blackburn R	2003-04	0	5	0
		11	**19**	**2**
Graham, Richard		Apps	Subs	Gls
Oldham Ath.	1993-94	4	1	0
Grainger, Martin		Apps	Subs	Gls
Birmingham C	2002-03	8	1	0
Birmingham C	2003-04	3	1	1
		11	**2**	**1**

Grant, Gareth		Apps	Subs	Gls
Bradford C	1999-00	0	1	0
Bradford C	2000-01	0	5	0
		0	**6**	**0**
Grant, Tony		Apps	Subs	Gls
Everton	1994-95	1	4	0
Everton	1995-96	11	2	1
Everton	1996-97	11	7	0
Everton	1997-98	7	0	1
Everton	1998-99	13	3	0
Everton	1999-00	0	2	0
Man. City	2000-01	5	5	0
		48	**23**	**2**
Granville, Danny		Apps	Subs	Gls
Chelsea	1996-97	3	2	0
Chelsea	1997-98	9	4	0
Leeds U	1998-99	7	2	0
Man. City	2000-01	16	3	0
		35	**11**	**0**
Gravelaine, Xavier		Apps	Subs	Gls
Watford	1999-00	7	0	2
Gravesen, Thomas		Apps	Subs	Gls
Everton	2000-01	30	2	2
Everton	2001-02	22	3	2
Everton	2002-03	30	3	1
Everton	2003-04	29	1	2
		111	**9**	**7**
Gray, Andy		Apps	Subs	Gls
Tottenham H	1992-93	9	8	1
Tottenham H	1993-94	0	2	1
		9	**10**	**2**
Gray, Andy		Apps	Subs	Gls
Leeds U	1995-96	12	3	0
Leeds U	1996-97	1	6	0
Nottm Forest	1998-99	3	5	0
		16	**14**	**0**
Gray, Julian		Apps	Subs	Gls
Arsenal	1999-00	0	1	0
Gray, Michael		Apps	Subs	Gls
Sunderland	1996-97	31	3	3
Sunderland	1999-00	32	1	0
Sunderland	2000-01	36	0	1
Sunderland	2001-02	35	0	0
Sunderland	2002-03	32	0	1
Blackburn R	2003-04	14	0	0
		180	**4**	**5**
Gray, Wayne		Apps	Subs	Gls
Wimbledon	1999-00	0	1	0
Grayson, Simon		Apps	Subs	Gls
Leicester C	1994-95	34	0	0
Leicester C	1996-97	36	0	0
Aston Villa	1997-98	28	5	0
Aston Villa	1998-99	4	11	0
		102	**16**	**0**
Green, Adam		Apps	Subs	Gls
Fulham	2003-04	4	0	0
Green, Scott		Apps	Subs	Gls
Bolton Wan.	1995-96	26	5	3
Greening, Jonathan		Apps	Subs	Gls
Man. Utd.	1998-99	0	3	0
Man. Utd.	1999-00	1	3	0
Man. Utd.	2000-01	3	4	0
Middlesbrough	2001-02	36	0	1
Middlesbrough	2002-03	38	0	2
Middlesbrough	2003-04	17	8	1
		95	**18**	**4**
Greenman, Chris		Apps	Subs	Gls
Coventry C	1992-93	1	1	0
Gregan, Sean		Apps	Subs	Gls
West Brom	2002-03	36	0	1
Gregory, David		Apps	Subs	Gls
Ipswich T	1992-93	1	2	1
Ipswich T	1994-95	0	1	0
		1	**3**	**1**
Gregory, Neil		Apps	Subs	Gls
Ipswich T	1994-95	1	2	0
Grenet, Francois		Apps	Subs	Gls
Derby Co.	2001-02	12	3	0
Gresko, Vratislav		Apps	Subs	Gls
Blackburn R	2002-03	10	0	0
Blackburn R	2003-04	22	2	1
		32	**2**	**1**
Griffin, Andy		Apps	Subs	Gls
Newcastle U	1997-98	4	0	0
Newcastle U	1998-99	14	0	0
Newcastle U	1999-00	1	2	1
Newcastle U	2000-01	14	5	0
Newcastle U	2001-02	3	1	0
Newcastle U	2002-03	22	5	1
Newcastle U	2003-04	5	0	0
		63	**13**	**2**
Griffit, Leandre		Apps	Subs	Gls
Southampton	2003-04	2	3	2
Griffiths, Carl		Apps	Subs	Gls
Man. City	1993-94	11	5	4
Man. City	1994-95	0	2	0
		11	**7**	**4**
Grimandi, Gilles		Apps	Subs	Gls
Arsenal	1997-98	16	6	1
Arsenal	1998-99	3	5	0
Arsenal	1999-00	27	1	2
Arsenal	2000-01	28	2	1
Arsenal	2001-02	11	15	0
		85	**29**	**4**
Grobbelaar, Bruce		Apps	Subs	Gls
Liverpool	1992-93	5	0	0
Liverpool	1993-94	29	0	0
Southampton	1994-95	30	0	0
Southampton	1995-96	2	0	0
		66	**0**	**0**
Grodas, Frode		Apps	Subs	Gls
Chelsea	1996-97	20	1	0
Groenendijk, Alfons		Apps	Subs	Gls
Man. City	1993-94	9	0	0
Grondin, David		Apps	Subs	Gls
Arsenal	1998-99	1	0	0
Gronkjaer, Jesper		Apps	Subs	Gls
Chelsea	2000-01	6	8	1
Chelsea	2001-02	11	2	0
Chelsea	2002-03	20	10	4
Chelsea	2003-04	19	12	2
		56	**32**	**7**
Groves, Perry		Apps	Subs	Gls
Arsenal	1992-93	0	1	0
Southampton	1992-93	13	2	2
		13	**3**	**2**
Gudjohnsen, Eidur		Apps	Subs	Gls
Chelsea	2000-01	17	13	10
Chelsea	2001-02	26	6	14
Chelsea	2002-03	20	15	10
Chelsea	2003-04	17	9	6
		80	**43**	**40**
Gudjonsson, Joey		Apps	Subs	Gls
Aston Villa	2002-03	9	2	2
Wolves	2003-04	5	6	0
		14	**8**	**2**
Gudjonsson, Thordur		Apps	Subs	Gls
Derby Co.	2000-01	2	8	1
Gudmundsson, Johann		Apps	Subs	Gls
Watford	1999-00	1	8	0
Gudmundsson, Niklas		Apps	Subs	Gls
Blackburn R	1995-96	1	3	0
Blackburn R	1996-97	0	2	0
		1	**5**	**0**
Guentchev, Bontcho		Apps	Subs	Gls
Ipswich T	1992-93	19	2	3
Ipswich T	1993-94	9	15	2
Ipswich T	1994-95	11	5	1
		39	**22**	**6**
Guerrero, Ivan		Apps	Subs	Gls
Coventry C	2000-01	3	0	0
Guinan, Steve		Apps	Subs	Gls
Nottm Forest	1995-96	1	1	0
Nottm Forest	1996-97	0	2	0
		1	**3**	**0**
Guivarc'h, Stephane		Apps	Subs	Gls
Newcastle U	1998-99	2	2	1
Gullit, Ruud		Apps	Subs	Gls
Chelsea	1995-96	31	0	3
Chelsea	1996-97	6	6	1
Chelsea	1997-98	0	6	0
		37	**12**	**4**
Gunn, Bryan		Apps	Subs	Gls
Norwich C	1992-93	42	0	0
Norwich C	1993-94	41	0	0
Norwich C	1994-95	21	0	0
		104	**0**	**0**
Gunnlaugsson, Arnie		Apps	Subs	Gls
Bolton Wan.	1997-98	2	13	0
Leicester C	1998-99	5	4	0
Leicester C	1999-00	2	0	0
Leicester C	2000-01	3	14	3
Leicester C	2001-02	0	2	0
		12	**33**	**3**
Guppy, Steve		Apps	Subs	Gls
Leicester C	1996-97	12	1	0
Leicester C	1997-98	37	0	2
Leicester C	1998-99	38	0	4
Leicester C	1999-00	29	1	2
Leicester C	2000-01	17	11	1
Leicester C	2003-04	9	6	0
		142	**19**	**9**
Gustafsson, Tomas		Apps	Subs	Gls
Coventry C	1999-00	7	3	0
Gynn, Micky		Apps	Subs	Gls
Coventry C	1992-93	18	2	2
Haaland, Alf-Inge		Apps	Subs	Gls
Nottm Forest	1994-95	18	2	1
Nottm Forest	1995-96	12	5	0
Nottm Forest	1996-97	33	2	6
Leeds U	1997-98	26	6	7
Leeds U	1998-99	24	5	1
Leeds U	1999-00	7	6	0
Man. City	2000-01	35	0	3
		155	**26**	**18**
Haas, Bernt		Apps	Subs	Gls
Sunderland	2001-02	27	0	0
Hadji, Mustapha		Apps	Subs	Gls
Coventry C	1999-00	33	0	6
Coventry C	2000-01	28	1	6
Aston Villa	2001-02	17	6	2
Aston Villa	2002-03	7	4	0
Aston Villa	2003-04	0	1	0
		85	**12**	**14**
Hall, Fitz		Apps	Subs	Gls
Southampton	2003-04	7	4	0
Hall, Gareth		Apps	Subs	Gls
Chelsea	1992-93	36	1	2
Chelsea	1993-94	4	3	0
Chelsea	1994-95	4	2	0
Chelsea	1995-96	5	0	1
Sunderland	1996-97	32	0	0
		81	**6**	**3**
Hall, Marcus		Apps	Subs	Gls
Coventry C	1994-95	2	3	0
Coventry C	1995-96	24	1	0
Coventry C	1996-97	10	3	0
Coventry C	1997-98	20	5	1
Coventry C	1998-99	2	3	0
Coventry C	1999-00	7	2	0
Coventry C	2000-01	21	0	0
		86	**17**	**1**
Hall, Paul		Apps	Subs	Gls
Coventry C	1998-99	2	7	0
Coventry C	1999-00	0	1	0
		2	**8**	**0**
Hall, Richard		Apps	Subs	Gls
Southampton	1992-93	28	0	4
Southampton	1993-94	4	0	0
Southampton	1994-95	36	1	4
Southampton	1995-96	30	0	1
West Ham U	1996-97	7	0	0
		105	**1**	**9**
Halle, Gunnar		Apps	Subs	Gls
Oldham Ath.	1992-93	41	0	5
Oldham Ath.	1993-94	22	1	1
Leeds U	1996-97	20	0	0
Leeds U	1997-98	31	2	2
Leeds U	1998-99	14	3	2
Bradford C	1999-00	37	1	0
Bradford C	2000-01	10	3	0
		175	**10**	**10**
Hallworth, Jon		Apps	Subs	Gls
Oldham Ath.	1992-93	16	0	0
Oldham Ath.	1993-94	19	0	0
		35	**0**	**0**
Hamann, Dietmar		Apps	Subs	Gls
Newcastle U	1998-99	22	1	4
Liverpool	1999-00	27	1	1
Liverpool	2000-01	26	4	2
Liverpool	2001-02	31	0	1
Liverpool	2002-03	29	1	2
Liverpool	2003-04	25	0	2
		160	**7**	**12**
Hamilton, Des		Apps	Subs	Gls
Newcastle U	1997-98	7	5	0
Hammond, Elvis		Apps	Subs	Gls
Fulham	2002-03	3	7	0
Hammond, Nicky		Apps	Subs	Gls
Swindon T	1993-94	11	2	0
Hamon, Chris		Apps	Subs	Gls
Swindon T	1993-94	0	1	0
Hansen, Bo		Apps	Subs	Gls
Bolton Wan.	2001-02	10	7	1
Harewood, Marlon		Apps	Subs	Gls
Nottm Forest	1998-99	11	12	1
Harford, Mick		Apps	Subs	Gls
Chelsea	1992-93	27	1	9
Coventry C	1993-94	0	1	1
Wimbledon	1994-95	17	10	6
Wimbledon	1995-96	17	4	2
Wimbledon	1996-97	3	10	1
		64	**26**	**19**
Harkes, John		Apps	Subs	Gls
Sheff. Wed.	1992-93	23	6	2
West Ham U	1995-96	6	5	0
Nottm Forest	1998-99	3	0	0
		32	**11**	**2**
Harkness, Steve		Apps	Subs	Gls
Liverpool	1992-93	9	1	0
Liverpool	1993-94	10	1	0
Liverpool	1994-95	8	0	1
Liverpool	1995-96	23	1	1
Liverpool	1996-97	5	2	0
Liverpool	1997-98	24	1	0
Liverpool	1998-99	4	2	0
		83	**8**	**2**
Harley, Jon		Apps	Subs	Gls
Chelsea	1997-98	3	0	0
Chelsea	1999-00	13	4	2
Chelsea	2000-01	6	4	0
Fulham	2001-02	5	5	0
Fulham	2002-03	11	0	1
Fulham	2003-04	3	1	0
		41	**14**	**3**
Harper, Alan		Apps	Subs	Gls
Everton	1992-93	16	2	0
Harper, Kevin		Apps	Subs	Gls
Derby Co.	1998-99	6	21	1
Derby Co.	1999-00	0	5	0
Portsmouth	2003-04	0	7	0
		6	**33**	**1**
Harper, Lee		Apps	Subs	Gls
Arsenal	1996-97	1	0	0
Harper, Steve		Apps	Subs	Gls
Newcastle U	1998-99	7	1	0
Newcastle U	1999-00	18	0	0
Newcastle U	2000-01	4	1	0
		29	**2**	**0**
Harrison, Craig		Apps	Subs	Gls
Middlesbrough	1998-99	3	1	0
Harte, Ian		Apps	Subs	Gls
Leeds U	1995-96	2	2	0
Leeds U	1996-97	10	4	2
Leeds U	1997-98	12	0	0
Leeds U	1998-99	34	1	4
Leeds U	1999-00	33	0	6
Leeds U	2000-01	29	0	7
Leeds U	2001-02	34	2	5
Leeds U	2002-03	24	3	3
Leeds U	2003-04	21	2	1
		199	**14**	**28**
Hartfield, Charlie		Apps	Subs	Gls
Sheff. Utd.	1992-93	12	5	0
Sheff. Utd.	1993-94	3	2	0
		15	**7**	**0**
Hartson, John		Apps	Subs	Gls
Arsenal	1994-95	14	1	7
Arsenal	1995-96	15	4	4
Arsenal	1996-97	14	5	3
West Ham U	1996-97	11	0	5
West Ham U	1997-98	32	0	15
West Ham U	1998-99	16	1	4
Wimbledon	1998-99	12	2	2
Wimbledon	1999-00	15	1	9
Coventry C	2000-01	12	0	6
		141	**14**	**55**
Haslam, Steven		Apps	Subs	Gls
Sheff. Wed.	1998-99	2	0	0
Sheff. Wed.	1999-00	16	7	0
		18	**7**	**0**
Hasselbaink, Jimmy Floyd		Apps	Subs	Gls
Leeds U	1997-98	30	3	16
Leeds U	1998-99	36	0	18
Chelsea	2000-01	35	0	23
Chelsea	2001-02	35	0	23
Chelsea	2002-03	27	9	11
Chelsea	2003-04	22	8	12
		185	**20**	**103**
Hateley, Mark		Apps	Subs	Gls
QPR	1995-96	10	4	2
Leeds U	1996-97	5	1	0
		15	**5**	**2**
Haworth, Simon		Apps	Subs	Gls
Coventry C	1997-98	4	6	0
Coventry C	1998-99	1	0	0
		5	**6**	**0**
Hay, Danny		Apps	Subs	Gls
Leeds U	2000-01	2	2	0
Hayles, Barry		Apps	Subs	Gls
Fulham	2001-02	27	8	8
Fulham	2002-03	4	10	1
Fulham	2003-04	10	16	4
		41	**34**	**13**
Hazard, Micky		Apps	Subs	Gls
Swindon T	1993-94	7	2	0
Tottenham H	1993-94	13	4	2
Tottenham H	1994-95	2	9	0
		22	**15**	**2**
Heald, Paul		Apps	Subs	Gls
Swindon T	1993-94	1	1	0
Wimbledon	1995-96	18	0	0
Wimbledon	1996-97	2	0	0
Wimbledon	1999-00	1	0	0
		22	**1**	**0**
Healy, David		Apps	Subs	Gls
Man. Utd.	2000-01	0	1	0
Heaney, Neil		Apps	Subs	Gls
Arsenal	1992-93	3	2	0
Arsenal	1993-94	1	0	0
Southampton	1993-94	2	0	0
Southampton	1994-95	21	13	2
Southampton	1995-96	15	2	2
Southampton	1996-97	4	4	1
		46	**21**	**5**
Heath, Matt		Apps	Subs	Gls
Leicester C	2001-02	3	2	0
Leicester C	2003-04	13	0	0
		16	**2**	**0**
Hedman, Magnus		Apps	Subs	Gls
Coventry C	1997-98	14	0	0
Coventry C	1998-99	36	0	0
Coventry C	1999-00	35	0	0
Coventry C	2000-01	15	0	0
		100	**0**	**0**
Heggem, Vegard		Apps	Subs	Gls
Liverpool	1998-99	27	2	2
Liverpool	1999-00	10	12	1
Liverpool	2000-01	1	2	0
		38	**16**	**3**
Helder, Glenn		Apps	Subs	Gls
Arsenal	1994-95	12	1	0
Arsenal	1995-96	15	9	1
Arsenal	1996-97	0	2	0
		27	**12**	**1**
Helder, Rodrigues		Apps	Subs	Gls
Newcastle U	1999-00	8	0	1
Helguson, Heidar		Apps	Subs	Gls
Watford	1999-00	14	2	6
Helmer, Thomas		Apps	Subs	Gls
Sunderland	1999-00	1	1	0
Henchoz, Stephane		Apps	Subs	Gls
Blackburn R	1997-98	36	0	0
Blackburn R	1998-99	34	0	0
Liverpool	1999-00	29	0	0
Liverpool	2000-01	32	0	0
Liverpool	2001-02	37	0	0
Liverpool	2002-03	19	0	0
Liverpool	2003-04	15	3	0
		202	**3**	**0**

Hendrie, John		*Apps*	*Subs*	*Gls*
Middlesbrough	1992-93	31	1	9
Middlesbrough	1995-96	7	6	1
Barnsley	1997-98	7	13	1
		45	**20**	**11**
Hendrie, Lee		*Apps*	*Subs*	*Gls*
Aston Villa	1995-96	2	1	0
Aston Villa	1996-97	0	4	0
Aston Villa	1997-98	13	4	3
Aston Villa	1998-99	31	1	3
Aston Villa	1999-00	18	11	1
Aston Villa	2000-01	27	5	6
Aston Villa	2001-02	25	4	2
Aston Villa	2002-03	22	5	4
Aston Villa	2003-04	32	0	2
		170	**35**	**21**
Hendry, Colin		*Apps*	*Subs*	*Gls*
Blackburn R	1992-93	41	0	1
Blackburn R	1993-94	22	1	0
Blackburn R	1994-95	38	0	4
Blackburn R	1995-96	33	0	1
Blackburn R	1996-97	35	0	1
Blackburn R	1997-98	34	0	1
Coventry C	1999-00	9	0	0
Coventry C	2000-01	1	1	0
Bolton Wan.	2001-02	3	0	0
		216	**2**	**8**
Hendry, John		*Apps*	*Subs*	*Gls*
Tottenham H	1992-93	2	3	2
Tottenham H	1993-94	0	3	0
		2	**6**	**2**
Henry, Nick		*Apps*	*Subs*	*Gls*
Oldham Ath.	1992-93	32	0	6
Oldham Ath.	1993-94	22	0	0
		54	**0**	**6**
Henry, Thierry		*Apps*	*Subs*	*Gls*
Arsenal	1999-00	26	5	17
Arsenal	2000-01	27	8	17
Arsenal	2001-02	31	2	24
Arsenal	2002-03	37	0	24
Arsenal	2003-04	37	0	30
		158	**15**	**112**
Herrera, Martin		*Apps*	*Subs*	*Gls*
Fulham	2002-03	1	1	0
Heskey, Emile		*Apps*	*Subs*	*Gls*
Leicester C	1994-95	1	0	0
Leicester C	1996-97	35	0	10
Leicester C	1997-98	35	0	10
Leicester C	1998-99	29	1	6
Leicester C	1999-00	23	0	7
Liverpool	1999-00	12	0	3
Liverpool	2000-01	33	3	14
Liverpool	2001-02	26	9	9
Liverpool	2002-03	22	10	6
Liverpool	2003-04	25	10	7
		241	**33**	**72**
Hibbert, Tony		*Apps*	*Subs*	*Gls*
Everton	2000-01	1	2	0
Everton	2001-02	7	3	0
Everton	2002-03	23	1	0
Everton	2003-04	24	1	0
		55	**7**	**0**
Hiden, Martin		*Apps*	*Subs*	*Gls*
Leeds U	1997-98	11	0	0
Leeds U	1998-99	14	0	0
Leeds U	1999-00	0	1	0
		25	**1**	**0**
Higginbotham, Danny		*Apps*	*Subs*	*Gls*
Man. Utd.	1997-98	0	1	0
Man. Utd.	1999-00	2	1	0
Derby Co.	2000-01	23	3	0
Derby Co.	2001-02	37	0	1
Southampton	2002-03	3	6	0
Southampton	2003-04	24	3	0
		89	**14**	**1**
Hignett, Craig		*Apps*	*Subs*	*Gls*
Middlesbrough	1992-93	18	3	4
Middlesbrough	1995-96	17	5	5
Middlesbrough	1996-97	19	3	4
Blackburn R	2001-02	4	15	4
Blackburn R	2002-03	1	2	1
Leicester C	2003-04	3	10	1
		62	**38**	**19**
Hiley, Scott		*Apps*	*Subs*	*Gls*
Man. City	1995-96	2	4	0
Southampton	1998-99	27	2	0
Southampton	1999-00	3	0	0
		32	**6**	**0**
Hill, Andy		*Apps*	*Subs*	*Gls*
Man. City	1992-93	23	1	1
Man. City	1993-94	15	2	0
Man. City	1994-95	10	3	0
		48	**6**	**1**
Hill, Colin		*Apps*	*Subs*	*Gls*
Leicester C	1994-95	24	0	0
Leicester C	1996-97	6	1	0
		30	**1**	**0**
Hill, Danny		*Apps*	*Subs*	*Gls*
Tottenham H	1992-93	2	2	0
Tottenham H	1993-94	1	2	0
Tottenham H	1994-95	1	2	0
		4	**6**	**0**
Hill, Keith		*Apps*	*Subs*	*Gls*
Blackburn R	1992-93	0	1	0
Hillier, David		*Apps*	*Subs*	*Gls*
Arsenal	1992-93	27	3	1
Arsenal	1993-94	11	4	0
Arsenal	1994-95	5	4	0
Arsenal	1995-96	3	2	0
Arsenal	1996-97	0	2	0
		46	**15**	**1**
Hills, John		*Apps*	*Subs*	*Gls*
Everton	1996-97	1	2	0
Hinchcliffe, Andy		*Apps*	*Subs*	*Gls*
Everton	1992-93	25	0	1
Everton	1993-94	25	1	0
Everton	1994-95	28	1	2
Everton	1995-96	23	5	2
Everton	1996-97	18	0	1
Everton	1997-98	15	2	0
Sheff. Wed.	1997-98	15	0	1
Sheff. Wed.	1998-99	32	0	3
Sheff. Wed.	1999-00	29	0	1
		210	**9**	**11**
Hirst, David		*Apps*	*Subs*	*Gls*
Sheff. Wed.	1992-93	22	0	11
Sheff. Wed.	1993-94	6	1	1
Sheff. Wed.	1994-95	13	2	3
Sheff. Wed.	1995-96	29	1	13
Sheff. Wed.	1996-97	20	5	6
Sheff. Wed.	1997-98	3	3	0
Southampton	1997-98	28	0	9
Southampton	1998-99	0	2	0
		121	**14**	**43**
Hislop, Shaka		*Apps*	*Subs*	*Gls*
Newcastle U	1995-96	24	0	0
Newcastle U	1996-97	16	0	0
Newcastle U	1997-98	13	0	0
West Ham U	1998-99	37	0	0
West Ham U	1999-00	22	0	0
West Ham U	2000-01	34	0	0
West Ham U	2001-02	12	0	0
Portsmouth	2003-04	30	0	0
		188	**0**	**0**
Hitchcock, Kevin		*Apps*	*Subs*	*Gls*
Chelsea	1992-93	20	0	0
Chelsea	1993-94	2	0	0
Chelsea	1994-95	11	1	0
Chelsea	1995-96	12	0	0
Chelsea	1996-97	10	2	0
Chelsea	1998-99	2	1	0
		57	**4**	**0**
Hitzlsperger, Thomas		*Apps*	*Subs*	*Gls*
Aston Villa	2000-01	0	1	0
Aston Villa	2001-02	11	1	1
Aston Villa	2002-03	24	2	2
Aston Villa	2003-04	22	10	3
		57	**14**	**6**
Hjelde, Jon Olav		*Apps*	*Subs*	*Gls*
Nottm Forest	1998-99	16	1	1
Hoddle, Glenn		*Apps*	*Subs*	*Gls*
Chelsea	1993-94	16	3	1
Chelsea	1994-95	3	9	0
		19	**12**	**1**
Hodge, Steve		*Apps*	*Subs*	*Gls*
Leeds U	1992-93	9	14	2
Leeds U	1993-94	7	1	1
QPR	1994-95	15	0	0
		31	**15**	**3**
Hodges, Glyn		*Apps*	*Subs*	*Gls*
Sheff. Utd.	1992-93	28	3	4
Sheff. Utd.	1993-94	19	12	2
Nottm Forest	1998-99	3	2	0
		50	**17**	**6**
Hodges, Lee		*Apps*	*Subs*	*Gls*
Tottenham H	1992-93	0	4	0
Hodges, Lee		*Apps*	*Subs*	*Gls*
West Ham U	1997-98	0	2	0
West Ham U	1998-99	0	1	0
		0	**3**	**0**
Hogh, Jes		*Apps*	*Subs*	*Gls*
Chelsea	1999-00	6	3	0
Holden, Rick		*Apps*	*Subs*	*Gls*
Man. City	1992-93	40	1	3
Man. City	1993-94	9	0	0
Oldham Ath.	1993-94	28	1	6
		77	**2**	**9**
Holdsworth, Dean		*Apps*	*Subs*	*Gls*
Wimbledon	1992-93	34	2	19
Wimbledon	1993-94	42	0	17
Wimbledon	1994-95	27	1	7
Wimbledon	1995-96	31	2	10
Wimbledon	1996-97	10	15	5
Wimbledon	1997-98	4	1	0
Bolton Wan.	1997-98	17	3	3
Bolton Wan.	2001-02	9	22	2
Bolton Wan.	2002-03	5	4	0
		179	**50**	**63**
Holland, Chris		*Apps*	*Subs*	*Gls*
Newcastle U	1993-94	2	1	0
Holland, Matt		*Apps*	*Subs*	*Gls*
Ipswich T	2000-01	38	0	3
Ipswich T	2001-02	38	0	3
Charlton Ath	2003-04	38	0	6
		114	**0**	**12**
Holligan, Gavin		*Apps*	*Subs*	*Gls*
West Ham U	1998-99	0	1	0
Holloway, Darren		*Apps*	*Subs*	*Gls*
Sunderland	1999-00	8	7	0
Sunderland	2000-01	5	0	0
		13	**7**	**0**
Holloway, Ian		*Apps*	*Subs*	*Gls*
QPR	1992-93	23	1	2
QPR	1993-94	19	6	0
QPR	1994-95	28	3	1
QPR	1995-96	26	1	1
		96	**11**	**4**
Holmes, Matt		*Apps*	*Subs*	*Gls*
West Ham U	1993-94	33	1	3
West Ham U	1994-95	24	0	1
Blackburn R	1995-96	8	1	1
		65	**2**	**5**
Holmes, Paul		*Apps*	*Subs*	*Gls*
Everton	1992-93	4	0	0
Everton	1993-94	15	0	0
Everton	1994-95	1	0	0
Everton	1995-96	1	0	0
		21	**0**	**0**
Hooper, Mike		*Apps*	*Subs*	*Gls*
Liverpool	1992-93	8	1	0
Newcastle U	1993-94	19	0	0
Newcastle U	1994-95	4	2	0
		31	**3**	**0**
Hopkin, David		*Apps*	*Subs*	*Gls*
Chelsea	1992-93	2	2	0
Chelsea	1993-94	12	9	0
Chelsea	1994-95	7	8	1
Leeds U	1997-98	22	3	1
Leeds U	1998-99	32	2	4
Leeds U	1999-00	10	4	1
Bradford C	2000-01	8	3	0
		93	**31**	**7**
Horlock, Kevin		*Apps*	*Subs*	*Gls*
Swindon T	1993-94	32	6	0
Man. City	2000-01	14	0	2
Man. City	2002-03	22	8	0
		68	**14**	**2**
Horne, Barry		*Apps*	*Subs*	*Gls*
Everton	1992-93	34	0	1
Everton	1993-94	28	4	1
Everton	1994-95	31	0	0
Everton	1995-96	25	1	1
Sheff. Wed.	1999-00	7	0	0
		125	**5**	**3**
Horne, Brian		*Apps*	*Subs*	*Gls*
Middlesbrough	1992-93	3	1	0
Horsfield, Geoff		*Apps*	*Subs*	*Gls*
Birmingham C	2002-03	15	16	5
Birmingham C	2003-04	2	1	0
		17	**17**	**5**
Hottiger, Marc		*Apps*	*Subs*	*Gls*
Newcastle U	1994-95	38	0	1
Newcastle U	1995-96	0	1	0
Everton	1995-96	9	0	1
Everton	1996-97	4	4	0
		51	**5**	**2**
Houghton, Ray		*Apps*	*Subs*	*Gls*
Aston Villa	1992-93	39	0	3
Aston Villa	1993-94	25	5	2
Aston Villa	1994-95	19	7	1
Crystal P	1994-95	10	0	2
		93	**12**	**8**
Hoult, Russell		*Apps*	*Subs*	*Gls*
Derby Co.	1996-97	31	1	0
Derby Co.	1997-98	2	0	0
Derby Co.	1998-99	23	0	0
Derby Co.	1999-00	10	0	0
West Brom	2002-03	37	0	0
		103	**1**	**0**
Howard, Tim		*Apps*	*Subs*	*Gls*
Man. Utd.	2003-04	32	0	0
Howe, Bobby		*Apps*	*Subs*	*Gls*
Nottm Forest	1995-96	4	5	2
Nottm Forest	1996-97	0	1	0
		4	**6**	**2**
Howells, David		*Apps*	*Subs*	*Gls*
Tottenham H	1992-93	16	2	1
Tottenham H	1993-94	15	3	1
Tottenham H	1994-95	26	0	1
Tottenham H	1995-96	29	0	3
Tottenham H	1996-97	32	0	2
Tottenham H	1997-98	14	6	0
Southampton	1998-99	8	1	1
		140	**12**	**9**
Howey, Lee		*Apps*	*Subs*	*Gls*
Sunderland	1996-97	9	3	0
Howey, Steve		*Apps*	*Subs*	*Gls*
Newcastle U	1993-94	13	1	0
Newcastle U	1994-95	29	1	1
Newcastle U	1995-96	28	0	1
Newcastle U	1996-97	8	0	1
Newcastle U	1997-98	11	3	0
Newcastle U	1998-99	14	0	0
Newcastle U	1999-00	7	2	0
Man. City	2000-01	36	0	6
Man. City	2002-03	24	0	2
Leicester C	2003-04	13	0	1
Bolton Wan.	2003-04	2	1	0
		185	**8**	**12**
Howie, Scott		*Apps*	*Subs*	*Gls*
Norwich C	1993-94	1	1	0
Hoyland, Jamie		*Apps*	*Subs*	*Gls*
Sheff. Utd.	1992-93	15	7	2
Sheff. Utd.	1993-94	17	1	0
		32	**8**	**2**
Hoyte, Justin		*Apps*	*Subs*	*Gls*
Arsenal	2002-03	0	1	0
Arsenal	2003-04	0	1	0
		0	**2**	**0**
Hreidarsson, Hermann		*Apps*	*Subs*	*Gls*
Crystal P	1997-98	26	4	2
Wimbledon	1999-00	24	0	1
Ipswich T	2000-01	35	1	1
Ipswich T	2001-02	38	0	1
Charlton Ath	2003-04	33	0	2
		156	**5**	**7**
Hristov, Georgi		*Apps*	*Subs*	*Gls*
Barnsley	1997-98	11	12	4
Huckerby, Darren		*Apps*	*Subs*	*Gls*
Newcastle U	1995-96	0	1	0
Coventry C	1996-97	21	4	5
Coventry C	1997-98	32	2	14
Coventry C	1998-99	31	3	9
Coventry C	1999-00	1	0	0
Leeds U	1999-00	9	24	2
Leeds U	2000-01	2	5	0
Man. City	2000-01	8	5	1
Man. City	2002-03	6	10	1
		110	**54**	**32**
Hudson, Mark		*Apps*	*Subs*	*Gls*
Middlesbrough	2000-01	0	3	0
Middlesbrough	2001-02	0	2	0
		0	**5**	**0**
Hughes, Aaron		*Apps*	*Subs*	*Gls*
Newcastle U	1997-98	4	0	0
Newcastle U	1998-99	12	2	0
Newcastle U	1999-00	22	5	2
Newcastle U	2000-01	34	1	0
Newcastle U	2001-02	34	0	0
Newcastle U	2002-03	35	0	1
Newcastle U	2003-04	34	0	0
		175	**8**	**3**
Hughes, Bryan		*Apps*	*Subs*	*Gls*
Birmingham C	2002-03	10	12	2
Birmingham C	2003-04	17	9	3
		27	**21**	**5**
Hughes, Ceri		*Apps*	*Subs*	*Gls*
Wimbledon	1997-98	13	4	1
Wimbledon	1998-99	8	6	0
		21	**10**	**1**
Hughes, David		*Apps*	*Subs*	*Gls*
Southampton	1993-94	0	2	0
Southampton	1994-95	2	10	2
Southampton	1995-96	6	5	1
Southampton	1996-97	1	5	0
Southampton	1997-98	6	8	0
Southampton	1998-99	6	3	0
		21	**33**	**3**
Hughes, David		*Apps*	*Subs*	*Gls*
Aston Villa	1996-97	4	3	0
Hughes, Lee		*Apps*	*Subs*	*Gls*
West Brom	2002-03	14	9	0
Hughes, Mark		*Apps*	*Subs*	*Gls*
Man. Utd.	1992-93	41	0	15
Man. Utd.	1993-94	36	0	11
Man. Utd.	1994-95	33	1	8
Chelsea	1995-96	31	0	8
Chelsea	1996-97	32	3	8
Chelsea	1997-98	25	4	9
Southampton	1998-99	32	0	1
Everton	1999-00	9	0	1
Southampton	1999-00	18	2	1
Everton	2000-01	6	3	0
Blackburn R	2001-02	4	18	1
		267	**31**	**63**
Hughes, Michael		*Apps*	*Subs*	*Gls*
West Ham U	1994-95	15	2	2
West Ham U	1995-96	28	0	0
West Ham U	1996-97	31	2	3
West Ham U	1997-98	2	3	0
Wimbledon	1997-98	29	0	4
Wimbledon	1998-99	28	2	2
Wimbledon	1999-00	13	7	2
		146	**16**	**13**
Hughes, Paul		*Apps*	*Subs*	*Gls*
Chelsea	1996-97	8	4	2
Chelsea	1997-98	5	4	0
		13	**8**	**2**
Hughes, Richard		*Apps*	*Subs*	*Gls*
Portsmouth	2003-04	8	3	0
Hughes, Stephen		*Apps*	*Subs*	*Gls*
Arsenal	1994-95	1	0	0
Arsenal	1995-96	0	1	0
Arsenal	1996-97	9	5	1
Arsenal	1997-98	7	10	2
Arsenal	1998-99	4	10	1
Arsenal	1999-00	1	1	0
Everton	1999-00	11	0	1
Everton	2000-01	16	2	0
		49	**29**	**5**
Humphrey, John		*Apps*	*Subs*	*Gls*
Crystal P	1992-93	28	4	0
Crystal P	1994-95	19	2	0
		47	**6**	**0**
Humphreys, Richie		*Apps*	*Subs*	*Gls*
Sheff. Wed.	1995-96	1	4	0
Sheff. Wed.	1996-97	14	15	3
Sheff. Wed.	1997-98	2	5	0
Sheff. Wed.	1998-99	10	9	1
		27	**33**	**4**
Hunt, Andy		*Apps*	*Subs*	*Gls*
Charlton Ath	1998-99	32	2	6
Charlton Ath	2000-01	8	0	4
		40	**2**	**10**
Hunt, Jonathan		*Apps*	*Subs*	*Gls*
Derby Co.	1997-98	7	12	1
Derby Co.	1998-99	0	6	1
		7	**18**	**2**

Hunt, Nicky		Apps	Subs	Gls
Bolton Wan.	2003-04	28	3	1

Hurlock, Terry		Apps	Subs	Gls
Southampton	1992-93	30	0	0
Southampton	1993-94	2	0	0
		32	**0**	**0**

Hurst, Lee		Apps	Subs	Gls
Coventry C	1992-93	35	0	2

Hutchinson, Joey		Apps	Subs	Gls
Birmingham C	2002-03	1	0	0

Hutchison, Don		Apps	Subs	Gls
Liverpool	1992-93	27	4	7
Liverpool	1993-94	6	5	0
West Ham U	1994-95	22	1	9
West Ham U	1995-96	8	4	2
Everton	1997-98	11	0	1
Everton	1998-99	29	4	3
Everton	1999-00	28	3	6
Sunderland	2000-01	30	2	8
Sunderland	2001-02	2	0	0
West Ham U	2001-02	24	0	1
West Ham U	2002-03	0	10	0
		187	**33**	**37**

Huth, Robert		Apps	Subs	Gls
Chelsea	2001-02	0	1	0
Chelsea	2002-03	2	0	0
Chelsea	2003-04	8	8	0
		10	**9**	**0**

Hyde, Graham		Apps	Subs	Gls
Sheff. Wed.	1992-93	14	6	1
Sheff. Wed.	1993-94	27	9	1
Sheff. Wed.	1994-95	33	2	5
Sheff. Wed.	1995-96	14	12	1
Sheff. Wed.	1996-97	15	4	2
Sheff. Wed.	1997-98	14	8	1
Sheff. Wed.	1998-99	0	1	0
		117	**42**	**11**

Hyde, Micah		Apps	Subs	Gls
Watford	1999-00	33	1	3

Hyypia, Sami		Apps	Subs	Gls
Liverpool	1999-00	38	0	2
Liverpool	2000-01	35	0	3
Liverpool	2001-02	37	0	3
Liverpool	2002-03	36	0	3
Liverpool	2003-04	38	0	4
		184	**0**	**15**

Ilic, Sasa		Apps	Subs	Gls
Charlton Ath	1998-99	23	0	0
West Ham U	1999-00	1	0	0
Charlton Ath	2000-01	13	0	0
		37	**0**	**0**

Immel, Eike		Apps	Subs	Gls
Man. City	1995-96	38	0	0

Impey, Andy		Apps	Subs	Gls
QPR	1992-93	39	1	2
QPR	1993-94	31	2	3
QPR	1994-95	40	0	3
QPR	1995-96	28	1	3
West Ham U	1997-98	19	0	0
West Ham U	1998-99	6	2	0
Leicester C	1998-99	17	1	0
Leicester C	1999-00	28	1	2
Leicester C	2000-01	29	4	0
Leicester C	2001-02	20	7	0
Leicester C	2003-04	11	2	0
		268	**21**	**13**

Inamoto, Junichi		Apps	Subs	Gls
Fulham	2002-03	9	10	2
Fulham	2003-04	15	7	2
		24	**17**	**4**

Ince, Paul		Apps	Subs	Gls
Man. Utd.	1992-93	41	0	5
Man. Utd.	1993-94	39	0	8
Man. Utd.	1994-95	36	0	6
Liverpool	1997-98	31	0	8
Liverpool	1998-99	34	0	6
Middlesbrough	1999-00	32	0	3
Middlesbrough	2000-01	30	0	2
Middlesbrough	2001-02	31	0	2
Wolves	2003-04	32	0	2
		306	**0**	**42**

Ingebrigtsen, Kaare		Apps	Subs	Gls
Man. City	1992-93	2	5	0
Man. City	1993-94	2	6	0
		4	**11**	**0**

Ingesson, Klas		Apps	Subs	Gls
Sheff. Wed.	1994-95	9	4	2
Sheff. Wed.	1995-96	3	2	0
		12	**6**	**2**

Ingram, Rae		Apps	Subs	Gls
Man. City	1995-96	5	0	0

Ireland, Simon		Apps	Subs	Gls
Blackburn R	1992-93	0	1	0

Ironside, Ian		Apps	Subs	Gls
Middlesbrough	1992-93	11	1	0

Irving, Richard		Apps	Subs	Gls
Nottm Forest	1995-96	0	1	0

Irwin, Denis		Apps	Subs	Gls
Man. Utd.	1992-93	40	0	5
Man. Utd.	1993-94	42	0	2
Man. Utd.	1994-95	40	0	1
Man. Utd.	1995-96	31	0	1
Man. Utd.	1996-97	29	2	1
Man. Utd.	1997-98	23	2	2
Man. Utd.	1998-99	26	3	2
Man. Utd.	1999-00	25	0	3
Man. Utd.	2000-01	20	1	0
Man. Utd.	2001-02	10	2	0
Wolves	2003-04	30	2	0
		316	**12**	**17**

Isais, Marques		Apps	Subs	Gls
Coventry C	1995-96	9	2	2
Coventry C	1996-97	0	1	0
		9	**3**	**2**

Ismael, Valerien		Apps	Subs	Gls
Crystal P	1997-98	13	0	0

Iversen, Steffen		Apps	Subs	Gls
Tottenham H	1996-97	16	0	6
Tottenham H	1997-98	8	5	0
Tottenham H	1998-99	22	5	9
Tottenham H	1999-00	36	0	14
Tottenham H	2000-01	10	4	2
Tottenham H	2001-02	12	6	4
Tottenham H	2002-03	8	11	1
Wolves	2003-04	11	5	4
		123	**36**	**40**

Izzet, Muzzy		Apps	Subs	Gls
Leicester C	1996-97	34	1	3
Leicester C	1997-98	36	0	4
Leicester C	1998-99	31	0	5
Leicester C	1999-00	32	0	8
Leicester C	2000-01	27	0	7
Leicester C	2001-02	29	2	4
Leicester C	2003-04	30	0	2
		219	**3**	**33**

Jaaskelainen, Jussi		Apps	Subs	Gls
Bolton Wan.	2001-02	34	0	0
Bolton Wan.	2002-03	38	0	0
Bolton Wan.	2003-04	38	0	0
		110	**0**	**0**

Jackson, Darren		Apps	Subs	Gls
Coventry C	1998-99	0	3	0

Jackson, Johnnie		Apps	Subs	Gls
Tottenham H	2003-04	9	2	1

Jackson, Mark		Apps	Subs	Gls
Leeds U	1995-96	0	1	0
Leeds U	1996-97	11	6	0
Leeds U	1997-98	0	1	0
		11	**8**	**0**

Jackson, Mark		Apps	Subs	Gls
Everton	1992-93	25	2	3
Everton	1993-94	37	1	0
Everton	1994-95	26	3	0
Everton	1995-96	14	0	0
		102	**6**	**3**

Jackson, Richard		Apps	Subs	Gls
Derby Co.	1999-00	0	2	0
Derby Co.	2000-01	1	1	0
Derby Co.	2001-02	6	1	0
		7	**4**	**0**

Jacobs, Wayne		Apps	Subs	Gls
Bradford C	1999-00	22	2	0
Bradford C	2000-01	19	2	2
		41	**4**	**2**

James, David		Apps	Subs	Gls
Liverpool	1992-93	29	0	0
Liverpool	1993-94	13	1	0
Liverpool	1994-95	42	0	0
Liverpool	1995-96	38	0	0
Liverpool	1996-97	38	0	0
Liverpool	1997-98	27	0	0
Liverpool	1998-99	26	0	0
Aston Villa	1999-00	29	0	0
Aston Villa	2000-01	38	0	0
West Ham U	2001-02	26	0	0
West Ham U	2002-03	38	0	0
Man. City	2003-04	17	0	0
		361	**1**	**0**

Jansen, Matt		Apps	Subs	Gls
Crystal P	1997-98	5	3	3
Blackburn R	1998-99	10	1	3
Blackburn R	2001-02	34	1	10
Blackburn R	2002-03	0	7	0
Blackburn R	2003-04	9	10	2
		58	**22**	**18**

Jardel, Mario		Apps	Subs	Gls
Bolton Wan.	2003-04	0	7	0

Jeffers, Francis		Apps	Subs	Gls
Everton	1997-98	0	1	0
Everton	1998-99	11	4	6
Everton	1999-00	16	5	6
Everton	2000-01	10	2	6
Arsenal	2001-02	2	4	2
Arsenal	2002-03	2	14	2
Everton	2003-04	5	13	0
		46	**43**	**22**

Jeffrey, Mike		Apps	Subs	Gls
Newcastle U	1993-94	2	0	0

Jemson, Nigel		Apps	Subs	Gls
Sheff. Wed.	1992-93	5	8	0
Sheff. Wed.	1993-94	10	8	5
		15	**16**	**5**

Jenas, Jermaine		Apps	Subs	Gls
Newcastle U	2001-02	6	6	0
Newcastle U	2002-03	23	9	6
Newcastle U	2003-04	26	5	2
		55	**20**	**8**

Jenkins, Iain		Apps	Subs	Gls
Everton	1992-93	1	0	0

Jenkinson, Leigh		Apps	Subs	Gls
Coventry C	1992-93	2	3	0
Coventry C	1993-94	10	6	0
Coventry C	1994-95	10	1	1
		22	**10**	**1**

Jensen, Claus		Apps	Subs	Gls
Charlton Ath	2000-01	37	1	5
Charlton Ath	2001-02	16	2	1
Charlton Ath	2002-03	32	3	6
Charlton Ath	2003-04	27	4	4
		112	**10**	**16**

Jensen, John		Apps	Subs	Gls
Arsenal	1992-93	29	3	0
Arsenal	1993-94	27	0	0
Arsenal	1994-95	24	0	1
Arsenal	1995-96	13	2	0
		93	**5**	**1**

Jensen, Niclas		Apps	Subs	Gls
Man. City	2002-03	32	1	1

Jerkan, Nikola		Apps	Subs	Gls
Nottm Forest	1996-97	14	0	0

Jess, Eoin		Apps	Subs	Gls
Coventry C	1995-96	9	3	1
Coventry C	1996-97	19	8	0
Bradford C	2000-01	17	0	3
		45	**11**	**4**

Jevons, Phil		Apps	Subs	Gls
Everton	1998-99	0	1	0
Everton	1999-00	2	1	0
Everton	2000-01	0	4	0
		2	**6**	**0**

Jihai Sun		Apps	Subs	Gls
Man. City	2002-03	25	3	2
Man. City	2003-04	29	4	1
		54	**7**	**3**

Joachim, Julian		Apps	Subs	Gls
Leicester C	1994-95	11	4	3
Aston Villa	1995-96	4	7	1
Aston Villa	1996-97	3	12	3
Aston Villa	1997-98	16	10	8
Aston Villa	1998-99	29	7	14
Aston Villa	1999-00	27	6	6
Aston Villa	2000-01	11	9	7
		101	**55**	**42**

Job, Joseph-Desire		Apps	Subs	Gls
Middlesbrough	2000-01	8	4	3
Middlesbrough	2001-02	3	1	0
Middlesbrough	2002-03	22	6	4
Middlesbrough	2003-04	19	5	5
		52	**16**	**12**

Jobson, Richard		Apps	Subs	Gls
Oldham Ath.	1992-93	40	0	2
Oldham Ath.	1993-94	37	0	5
Leeds U	1995-96	12	0	1
Leeds U	1996-97	10	0	0
		99	**0**	**8**

Johansen, Stig		Apps	Subs	Gls
Southampton	1997-98	3	3	0

Johansen, Martin		Apps	Subs	Gls
Coventry C	1997-98	0	2	0

Johansen, Michael		Apps	Subs	Gls
Bolton Wan.	1997-98	4	12	1

Johansson, Jonatan		Apps	Subs	Gls
Charlton Ath	2000-01	27	4	11
Charlton Ath	2001-02	21	9	5
Charlton Ath	2002-03	10	21	3
Charlton Ath	2003-04	16	10	4
		74	**44**	**23**

Johansson, Nils-Eric		Apps	Subs	Gls
Blackburn R	2001-02	14	6	0
Blackburn R	2002-03	20	10	0
Blackburn R	2003-04	7	7	0
		41	**23**	**0**

John, Collins		Apps	Subs	Gls
Fulham	2003-04	3	5	4

John, Stern		Apps	Subs	Gls
Birmingham C	2002-03	20	10	5
Birmingham C	2003-04	7	22	4
		27	**32**	**9**

Johnsen, Erland		Apps	Subs	Gls
Chelsea	1992-93	13	0	0
Chelsea	1993-94	27	1	1
Chelsea	1994-95	33	0	0
Chelsea	1995-96	18	4	0
Chelsea	1996-97	14	4	0
		105	**9**	**1**

Johnsen, Ronny		Apps	Subs	Gls
Man. Utd.	1996-97	26	5	0
Man. Utd.	1997-98	18	4	2
Man. Utd.	1998-99	19	3	3
Man. Utd.	1999-00	2	1	0
Man. Utd.	2000-01	11	0	1
Man. Utd.	2001-02	9	1	1
Aston Villa	2002-03	25	1	0
Aston Villa	2003-04	21	2	1
		131	**17**	**8**

Johnson, Andy		Apps	Subs	Gls
Norwich C	1992-93	1	1	1
Norwich C	1993-94	0	2	0
Norwich C	1994-95	6	1	0
Nottm Forest	1998-99	25	3	0
West Brom	2002-03	30	2	1
		62	**9**	**2**

Johnson, Damien		Apps	Subs	Gls
Blackburn R	1998-99	14	7	1
Blackburn R	2001-02	6	1	1
Birmingham C	2002-03	28	2	1
Birmingham C	2003-04	35	0	1
		83	**10**	**4**

Johnson, David		Apps	Subs	Gls
Ipswich T	2000-01	6	8	0

Johnson, Gavin		Apps	Subs	Gls
Ipswich T	1992-93	39	1	5
Ipswich T	1993-94	16	0	1
Ipswich T	1994-95	14	3	0
		69	**4**	**6**

Johnson, Glen		Apps	Subs	Gls
West Ham U	2002-03	14	1	0
Chelsea	2003-04	17	2	3
		31	**3**	**3**

Johnson, Jermaine		Apps	Subs	Gls
Bolton Wan.	2001-02	4	6	0
Bolton Wan.	2002-03	0	2	0
		4	**8**	**0**

Johnson, Michael		Apps	Subs	Gls
Birmingham C	2002-03	5	1	0

Johnson, Richard		Apps	Subs	Gls
Watford	1999-00	20	3	3

Johnson, Seth		Apps	Subs	Gls
Derby Co.	1999-00	36	0	1
Derby Co.	2000-01	30	0	1
Derby Co.	2001-02	7	0	0
Leeds U	2001-02	12	2	0
Leeds U	2002-03	3	6	1
Leeds U	2003-04	24	1	2
		112	**9**	**5**

Johnson, Simon		Apps	Subs	Gls
Leeds U	2002-03	1	3	0
Leeds U	2003-04	1	4	0
		2	**7**	**0**

Johnson, Tommy		Apps	Subs	Gls
Aston Villa	1994-95	11	3	4
Aston Villa	1995-96	17	6	5
Aston Villa	1996-97	10	10	4
Everton	1999-00	0	3	0
		38	**22**	**13**

Johnston, Allan		Apps	Subs	Gls
Sunderland	1996-97	4	2	1
Middlesbrough	2001-02	13	4	1
		17	**6**	**2**

Johnston, Mo		Apps	Subs	Gls
Everton	1992-93	7	6	3

Jokanovic, Slavisa		Apps	Subs	Gls
Chelsea	2000-01	7	12	0
Chelsea	2001-02	12	8	0
		19	**20**	**0**

Jones, Bradley		Apps	Subs	Gls
Middlesbrough	2003-04	1	0	0

Jones, Cobi		Apps	Subs	Gls
Coventry C	1994-95	16	5	2

Jones, Keith		Apps	Subs	Gls
Charlton Ath	1998-99	13	10	1

Jones, Lee		Apps	Subs	Gls
Liverpool	1994-95	0	1	0
Liverpool	1996-97	0	2	0
		0	**3**	**0**

Jones, Matthew		Apps	Subs	Gls
Leeds U	1998-99	3	5	0
Leeds U	1999-00	5	6	0
Leeds U	2000-01	3	1	0
Leicester C	2000-01	10	1	0
Leicester C	2001-02	6	4	1
		27	**17**	**1**

Jones, Paul		Apps	Subs	Gls
Southampton	1997-98	38	0	0
Southampton	1998-99	31	0	0
Southampton	1999-00	31	0	0
Southampton	2000-01	35	0	0
Southampton	2001-02	36	0	0
Southampton	2002-03	13	1	0
Southampton	2003-04	8	0	0
Liverpool	2003-04	2	0	0
Wolves	2003-04	16	0	0
		210	**1**	**0**

Jones, Rob		Apps	Subs	Gls
Liverpool	1992-93	30	0	0
Liverpool	1993-94	38	0	0
Liverpool	1994-95	31	0	0
Liverpool	1995-96	33	0	0
Liverpool	1996-97	2	0	0
Liverpool	1997-98	20	1	0
		154	**1**	**0**

Jones, Ryan		Apps	Subs	Gls
Sheff. Wed.	1992-93	9	0	0
Sheff. Wed.	1993-94	24	3	6
Sheff. Wed.	1994-95	3	2	0
		36	**5**	**6**

Jones, Scott		Apps	Subs	Gls
Barnsley	1997-98	12	0	1

Jones, Steve		Apps	Subs	Gls
West Ham U	1993-94	3	5	2
West Ham U	1994-95	1	1	0
West Ham U	1996-97	5	3	0
Charlton Ath	1998-99	7	18	1
		16	**27**	**3**

Jones, Vinnie		Apps	Subs	Gls
Chelsea	1992-93	7	0	1
Wimbledon	1992-93	27	0	1
Wimbledon	1993-94	33	0	2
Wimbledon	1994-95	33	0	3
Wimbledon	1995-96	27	4	3
Wimbledon	1996-97	29	0	3
Wimbledon	1997-98	22	2	0
		178	**6**	**13**

Jonk, Wim		Apps	Subs	Gls
Sheff. Wed.	1998-99	38	0	2
Sheff. Wed.	1999-00	29	1	3
		67	**1**	**5**

Jordan, Stephen		Apps	Subs	Gls
Man. City	2002-03	0	1	0
Man. City	2003-04	0	2	0
		0	**3**	**0**

Jord, Jordao		Apps	Subs	Gls
West Brom	2002-03	0	3	0

Joseph, Roger		Apps	Subs	Gls
Wimbledon	1992-93	31	1	0
Wimbledon	1993-94	13	0	0
Wimbledon	1994-95	3	0	0
		47	**1**	**0**

Juninho, Osvaldo		Apps	Subs	Gls
Middlesbrough	1995-96	20	1	2
Middlesbrough	1996-97	34	1	12
Middlesbrough	1999-00	24	4	4
Middlesbrough	2002-03	9	1	3
Middlesbrough	2003-04	26	5	8
		113	**12**	**29**

Jupp, Duncan		Apps	Subs	Gls
Wimbledon	1996-97	6	0	0
Wimbledon	1997-98	3	0	0
Wimbledon	1998-99	3	3	0
Wimbledon	1999-00	6	3	0
		18	**6**	**0**

Kaamark, Pontus		Apps	Subs	Gls
Leicester C	1996-97	9	1	0
Leicester C	1997-98	35	0	0
Leicester C	1998-99	15	4	0
		59	**5**	**0**

Kachloul, Hassan		Apps	Subs	Gls
Southampton	1998-99	18	4	5
Southampton	1999-00	29	3	5
Southampton	2000-01	26	6	4
Aston Villa	2001-02	17	5	2
Wolves	2003-04	0	4	0
		90	**22**	**16**

Kamara, Chris		Apps	Subs	Gls
Middlesbrough	1992-93	3	2	0
Sheff. Utd.	1992-93	6	2	0
Sheff. Utd.	1993-94	15	1	0
		24	**5**	**0**

Kanchelskis, Andrei		Apps	Subs	Gls
Man. Utd.	1992-93	14	13	3
Man. Utd.	1993-94	28	3	6
Man. Utd.	1994-95	25	5	14
Everton	1995-96	32	0	16
Everton	1996-97	20	0	4
Man. City	2000-01	7	3	0
Southampton	2002-03	0	1	0
		126	**25**	**43**

Kanoute, Frederic		Apps	Subs	Gls
West Ham U	1999-00	8	0	2
West Ham U	2000-01	32	0	11
West Ham U	2001-02	27	0	11
West Ham U	2002-03	12	5	5
Tottenham H	2003-04	19	8	7
		98	**13**	**36**

Kanu, Nwankwo		Apps	Subs	Gls
Arsenal	1998-99	5	7	6
Arsenal	1999-00	24	7	12
Arsenal	2000-01	13	14	3
Arsenal	2001-02	9	14	3
Arsenal	2002-03	9	7	5
Arsenal	2003-04	3	7	1
		63	**56**	**30**

Karelse, John		Apps	Subs	Gls
Newcastle U	1999-00	3	0	0

Karembeu, Christian		Apps	Subs	Gls
Middlesbrough	2000-01	31	2	4

Karl, Steffen		Apps	Subs	Gls
Man. City	1993-94	4	2	1

Kavanagh, Graham		Apps	Subs	Gls
Middlesbrough	1992-93	6	4	0
Middlesbrough	1995-96	6	1	1
		12	**5**	**1**

Kavelashvili, Mikhail		Apps	Subs	Gls
Man. City	1995-96	3	1	1

Keane, Robbie		Apps	Subs	Gls
Coventry C	1999-00	30	1	12
Leeds U	2000-01	12	6	9
Leeds U	2001-02	16	9	3
Leeds U	2002-03	0	3	1
Tottenham H	2002-03	29	0	13
Tottenham H	2003-04	31	3	14
		118	**22**	**52**

Keane, Roy		Apps	Subs	Gls
Nottm Forest	1992-93	40	0	6
Man. Utd.	1993-94	34	3	5
Man. Utd.	1994-95	23	2	2
Man. Utd.	1995-96	29	0	6
Man. Utd.	1996-97	21	0	2
Man. Utd.	1997-98	9	0	2
Man. Utd.	1998-99	33	2	2
Man. Utd.	1999-00	28	1	5
Man. Utd.	2000-01	28	0	2
Man. Utd.	2001-02	28	0	3
Man. Utd.	2002-03	19	2	0
Man. Utd.	2003-04	25	3	3
		317	**13**	**38**

Kearton, Jason		Apps	Subs	Gls
Everton	1992-93	2	3	0
Everton	1994-95	1	0	0
		3	**3**	**0**

Keeley, John		Apps	Subs	Gls
Oldham Ath.	1992-93	1	0	0

Keenan, Joe		Apps	Subs	Gls
Chelsea	2001-02	0	1	0
Chelsea	2002-03	0	1	0
		0	**2**	**0**

Keirzerweerd, Henk		Apps	Subs	Gls
Oldham Ath.	1992-93	0	1	0

Keller, Kasey		Apps	Subs	Gls
Leicester C	1996-97	31	0	0
Leicester C	1997-98	32	0	0
Leicester C	1998-99	36	0	0
Tottenham H	2001-02	9	0	0
Tottenham H	2002-03	38	0	0
Tottenham H	2003-04	38	0	0
		184	**0**	**0**

Keller, Marc		Apps	Subs	Gls
West Ham U	1998-99	17	4	5
West Ham U	1999-00	19	4	0
		36	**8**	**5**

Kelly, Alan		Apps	Subs	Gls
Sheff. Utd.	1992-93	32	1	0
Sheff. Utd.	1993-94	29	1	0
Blackburn R	2001-02	2	0	0
Blackburn R	2002-03	1	0	0
		64	**2**	**0**

Kelly, David		Apps	Subs	Gls
Sunderland	1996-97	23	1	0

Kelly, Gary		Apps	Subs	Gls
Leeds U	1993-94	42	0	0
Leeds U	1994-95	42	0	0
Leeds U	1995-96	34	0	0
Leeds U	1996-97	34	2	2
Leeds U	1997-98	34	0	0
Leeds U	1999-00	28	3	0
Leeds U	2000-01	22	2	0
Leeds U	2001-02	19	1	0
Leeds U	2002-03	24	1	0
Leeds U	2003-04	37	0	0
		316	**9**	**2**

Kelly, Stephen		Apps	Subs	Gls
Tottenham H	2003-04	7	4	0

Kenna, Jeff		Apps	Subs	Gls
Southampton	1992-93	27	2	2
Southampton	1993-94	40	1	2
Southampton	1994-95	28	0	0
Blackburn R	1994-95	9	0	1
Blackburn R	1995-96	32	0	0
Blackburn R	1996-97	37	0	0
Blackburn R	1997-98	37	0	0
Blackburn R	1998-99	22	1	0
Birmingham C	2002-03	36	1	1
Birmingham C	2003-04	14	3	2
		282	**8**	**8**

Kennedy, Mark		Apps	Subs	Gls
Liverpool	1994-95	4	2	0
Liverpool	1995-96	1	3	0
Liverpool	1996-97	0	5	0
Liverpool	1997-98	0	1	0
Wimbledon	1997-98	4	0	0
Wimbledon	1998-99	7	10	0
Man. City	2000-01	15	10	0
Wolves	2003-04	28	3	2
		59	**34**	**2**

Kennedy, Peter		Apps	Subs	Gls
Watford	1999-00	17	1	1

Kenny, Billy		Apps	Subs	Gls
Everton	1992-93	16	1	1

Kenton, Darren		Apps	Subs	Gls
Southampton	2003-04	3	4	0

Keown, Martin		Apps	Subs	Gls
Everton	1992-93	13	0	0
Arsenal	1992-93	15	1	0
Arsenal	1993-94	23	10	0
Arsenal	1994-95	24	7	1
Arsenal	1995-96	34	0	0
Arsenal	1996-97	33	0	1
Arsenal	1997-98	18	0	0
Arsenal	1998-99	34	0	1
Arsenal	1999-00	27	0	1
Arsenal	2000-01	28	0	0
Arsenal	2001-02	21	1	0
Arsenal	2002-03	22	2	0
Arsenal	2003-04	3	7	0
		295	**28**	**4**

Kernaghan, Alan		Apps	Subs	Gls
Middlesbrough	1992-93	22	0	2
Man. City	1993-94	23	1	0
Man. City	1994-95	18	4	1
Man. City	1995-96	4	2	0
		67	**7**	**3**

Kerr, Brian		Apps	Subs	Gls
Newcastle U	2000-01	0	1	0
Newcastle U	2002-03	4	4	0
		4	**5**	**0**

Kerr, David		Apps	Subs	Gls
Man. City	1992-93	0	1	0
Man. City	1993-94	2	0	0
Man. City	1994-95	2	0	0
Man. City	1995-96	0	1	0
		4	**2**	**0**

Kerr, Dylan		Apps	Subs	Gls
Leeds U	1992-93	3	2	0

Kerr, Scott		Apps	Subs	Gls
Bradford C	2000-01	0	1	0

Kerslake, David		Apps	Subs	Gls
Leeds U	1992-93	8	0	0
Tottenham H	1993-94	16	1	0
Tottenham H	1994-95	16	2	0
Tottenham H	1995-96	2	0	0
		42	**3**	**0**

Ketsbaia, Temuri		Apps	Subs	Gls
Newcastle U	1997-98	16	15	3
Newcastle U	1998-99	14	12	5
Newcastle U	1999-00	11	10	0
		41	**37**	**8**

Kewell, Harry		Apps	Subs	Gls
Leeds U	1995-96	2	0	0
Leeds U	1996-97	0	1	0
Leeds U	1997-98	26	3	5
Leeds U	1998-99	36	2	6
Leeds U	1999-00	36	0	10
Leeds U	2000-01	12	5	2
Leeds U	2001-02	26	1	8
Leeds U	2002-03	31	0	14
Liverpool	2003-04	36	0	7
		205	**12**	**52**

Key, Lance		Apps	Subs	Gls
Oldham Ath.	1993-94	2	0	0

Kharine, Dimitri		Apps	Subs	Gls
Chelsea	1992-93	5	0	0
Chelsea	1993-94	40	0	0
Chelsea	1994-95	31	0	0
Chelsea	1995-96	26	0	0
Chelsea	1996-97	5	0	0
Chelsea	1997-98	10	0	0
Chelsea	1998-99	1	0	0
		118	**0**	**0**

Kiely, Dean		Apps	Subs	Gls
Charlton Ath	2000-01	25	0	0
Charlton Ath	2001-02	38	0	0
Charlton Ath	2002-03	38	0	0
Charlton Ath	2003-04	37	0	0
		138	**0**	**0**

Kilbane, Kevin		Apps	Subs	Gls
Sunderland	1999-00	17	3	1
Sunderland	2000-01	26	4	4
Sunderland	2001-02	24	4	2
Sunderland	2002-03	30	0	1
Everton	2003-04	26	4	3
		123	**15**	**11**

Kilcline, Brian		Apps	Subs	Gls
Newcastle U	1993-94	1	0	0
Swindon T	1993-94	10	0	0
		11	**0**	**0**

Kilgallon, Matthew		Apps	Subs	Gls
Leeds U	2002-03	0	2	0
Leeds U	2003-04	7	1	2
		7	**3**	**2**

Kilgannon, Sean		Apps	Subs	Gls
Middlesbrough	1999-00	0	1	0

Kimble, Alan		Apps	Subs	Gls
Wimbledon	1993-94	14	0	0
Wimbledon	1994-95	26	0	0
Wimbledon	1995-96	31	0	0
Wimbledon	1996-97	28	3	0
Wimbledon	1997-98	23	2	0
Wimbledon	1998-99	22	4	0
Wimbledon	1999-00	24	4	0
		168	**13**	**0**

Kinder, Vladimir		Apps	Subs	Gls
Middlesbrough	1996-97	4	2	1
Middlesbrough	1998-99	0	5	2
		4	**7**	**3**

King, Ledley		Apps	Subs	Gls
Tottenham H	1998-99	0	1	0
Tottenham H	1999-00	2	1	0
Tottenham H	2000-01	18	0	1
Tottenham H	2001-02	32	0	0
Tottenham H	2002-03	25	0	0
Tottenham H	2003-04	28	1	1
		105	**3**	**2**

King, Phil		Apps	Subs	Gls
Sheff. Wed.	1992-93	11	1	1
Sheff. Wed.	1993-94	7	3	0
Aston Villa	1994-95	13	3	0
		31	**7**	**1**

Kinkladze, Georgi		Apps	Subs	Gls
Man. City	1995-96	37	0	4
Derby Co.	1999-00	12	5	1
Derby Co.	2000-01	13	11	1
Derby Co.	2001-02	13	11	1
		75	**27**	**7**

Kinsella, Mark		Apps	Subs	Gls
Charlton Ath	1998-99	38	0	3
Charlton Ath	2000-01	27	5	2
Charlton Ath	2001-02	14	3	0
Aston Villa	2002-03	15	4	0
Aston Villa	2003-04	2	0	0
		96	**12**	**5**

Kirkland, Chris		Apps	Subs	Gls
Coventry C	2000-01	23	0	0
Liverpool	2001-02	1	0	0
Liverpool	2002-03	8	0	0
Liverpool	2003-04	6	0	0
		38	**0**	**0**

Kirovski, Jovan		Apps	Subs	Gls
Birmingham C	2002-03	5	12	2
Birmingham C	2003-04	0	6	0
		5	**18**	**2**

Kishishev, Radostin		Apps	Subs	Gls
Charlton Ath	2000-01	25	2	0
Charlton Ath	2001-02	0	3	0
Charlton Ath	2002-03	27	7	2
Charlton Ath	2003-04	30	3	0
		82	**15**	**2**

Gary Kelly.

Kitson, Paul		Apps	Subs	Gls
Newcastle U	1994-95	24	2	8
Newcastle U	1995-96	2	5	2
Newcastle U	1996-97	0	3	0
West Ham U	1996-97	14	0	8
West Ham U	1997-98	12	1	4
West Ham U	1998-99	13	4	3
West Ham U	1999-00	4	6	0
West Ham U	2000-01	0	2	0
West Ham U	2001-02	3	4	3
		72	**27**	**28**

Kiwomya, Chris		Apps	Subs	Gls
Ipswich T	1992-93	38	0	10
Ipswich T	1993-94	34	3	5
Ipswich T	1994-95	13	2	3
Arsenal	1994-95	5	9	3
		90	**14**	**21**

Kjeldbjerg, Jakob		Apps	Subs	Gls
Chelsea	1993-94	29	0	1
Chelsea	1994-95	23	0	1
		52	**0**	**2**

Kleberson, Jose		Apps	Subs	Gls
Man. Utd.	2003-04	10	2	2

Klinsmann, Jurgen		Apps	Subs	Gls
Tottenham H	1994-95	41	0	20
Tottenham H	1997-98	15	0	9
		56	**0**	**29**

Knight, Zat		Apps	Subs	Gls
Fulham	2001-02	8	2	0
Fulham	2002-03	12	5	0
Fulham	2003-04	30	1	0
		50	**8**	**0**

Konchesky, Paul		Apps	Subs	Gls
Charlton Ath	1998-99	1	1	0
Charlton Ath	2000-01	11	12	0
Charlton Ath	2001-02	22	12	1
Charlton Ath	2002-03	17	13	3
Charlton Ath	2003-04	17	4	0
Tottenham H	2003-04	10	2	0
		78	**44**	**4**

Konjic, Muhamed		Apps	Subs	Gls
Coventry C	1998-99	3	1	0
Coventry C	1999-00	3	1	0
Coventry C	2000-01	8	0	0
		14	**2**	**0**

Korsten, Willem		Apps	Subs	Gls
Leeds U	1998-99	4	3	2
Tottenham H	1999-00	4	5	0
Tottenham H	2000-01	8	6	3
		16	**14**	**5**

Kostantinidis, Kostas		Apps	Subs	Gls
Bolton Wan.	2001-02	3	0	0

Koumas, Jason		Apps	Subs	Gls
West Brom	2002-03	27	5	4

Kovacevic, Darko		Apps	Subs	Gls
Sheff. Wed.	1995-96	8	8	4

Kozluk, Robbie		Apps	Subs	Gls
Derby Co.	1997-98	6	3	0
Derby Co.	1998-99	3	4	0
		9	**7**	**0**

Kozma, Istvan		Apps	Subs	Gls
Liverpool	1992-93	0	1	0

Krizan, Ales		Apps	Subs	Gls
Barnsley	1997-98	12	0	0

Kruszynski, Detsi		Apps	Subs	Gls
Coventry C	1993-94	1	1	0

Kubicki, Dariusz		Apps	Subs	Gls
Aston Villa	1993-94	1	1	0
Sunderland	1996-97	28	1	0
		29	**2**	**0**

Kvarme, Bjorn Tore		Apps	Subs	Gls
Liverpool	1996-97	15	0	0

Liverpool	1997-98	22	1	0
Liverpool	1998-99	2	5	0
		39	**6**	**0**
Kyle, Kevin		Apps	Subs	Gls
Sunderland	2000-01	0	3	0
Sunderland	2001-02	0	6	0
Sunderland	2002-03	9	8	0
		9	**17**	**0**
Labant, Vladimir		Apps	Subs	Gls
West Ham U	2001-02	7	5	0
West Ham U	2002-03	0	1	0
		7	**6**	**0**
Lake, Mike		Apps	Subs	Gls
Sheff. Utd.	1992-93	6	0	0
Lake, Paul		Apps	Subs	Gls
Man. City	1992-93	2	0	0
Lama, Bernard		Apps	Subs	Gls
West Ham U	1997-98	12	0	0
Lambourde, Bernard		Apps	Subs	Gls
Chelsea	1997-98	5	2	0
Chelsea	1998-99	12	5	0
Chelsea	1999-00	12	3	2
Chelsea	2000-01	0	1	0
		29	**11**	**2**
Lampard, Frank		Apps	Subs	Gls
West Ham U	1995-96	0	2	0
West Ham U	1996-97	3	10	0
West Ham U	1997-98	27	4	4
West Ham U	1998-99	38	0	5
West Ham U	1999-00	34	0	7
West Ham U	2000-01	30	0	7
Chelsea	2001-02	34	3	5
Chelsea	2002-03	37	1	6
Chelsea	2003-04	38	0	10
		241	**20**	**44**
Lamptey, Nii		Apps	Subs	Gls
Aston Villa	1994-95	1	5	0
Coventry C	1995-96	3	3	0
		4	**8**	**0**
Laslandes, Lilian		Apps	Subs	Gls
Sunderland	2001-02	5	7	0
Laudrup, Brian		Apps	Subs	Gls
Chelsea	1998-99	5	2	0
Launders, Brian		Apps	Subs	Gls
Crystal P	1994-95	1	1	0
Derby Co.	1998-99	0	1	0
		1	**2**	**0**
Lauren (Bisan-Etame Mayer Laureano)		Apps	Subs	Gls
Arsenal	2000-01	15	3	2
Arsenal	2001-02	27	0	2
Arsenal	2002-03	26	1	1
Arsenal	2003-04	30	2	0
		98	**6**	**5**
Laurent, Pierre		Apps	Subs	Gls
Leeds U	1996-97	2	2	0
Laursen, Jacob		Apps	Subs	Gls
Derby Co.	1996-97	35	1	1
Derby Co.	1997-98	27	1	1
Derby Co.	1998-99	37	0	0
Derby Co.	1999-00	36	0	1
Leicester C	2001-02	10	0	0
		145	**2**	**3**
Laville, Florent		Apps	Subs	Gls
Bolton Wan.	2002-03	10	0	0
Bolton Wan.	2003-04	5	0	0
		15	**0**	**0**
Lawrence, Jamie		Apps	Subs	Gls
Leicester C	1994-95	9	8	1
Leicester C	1996-97	2	13	0
Bradford C	1999-00	19	4	3
Bradford C	2000-01	15	2	1
		45	**27**	**5**
Laws, Brian		Apps	Subs	Gls
Nottm Forest	1992-93	32	1	0
Lazaridis, Stan		Apps	Subs	Gls
West Ham U	1995-96	2	2	0
West Ham U	1996-97	13	9	1
West Ham U	1997-98	27	1	2
West Ham U	1998-99	11	4	0
Birmingham C	2002-03	17	13	2
Birmingham C	2003-04	25	5	2
		95	**34**	**7**
Le Pen, Ulrich		Apps	Subs	Gls
Ipswich T	2001-02	0	1	0
Le Saux, Graeme		Apps	Subs	Gls
Chelsea	1992-93	10	4	0
Blackburn R	1992-93	9	0	0
Blackburn R	1993-94	40	1	2
Blackburn R	1994-95	39	0	3
Blackburn R	1995-96	13	1	1
Blackburn R	1996-97	26	0	1
Chelsea	1997-98	26	0	1
Chelsea	1998-99	30	1	0
Chelsea	1999-00	6	2	0
Chelsea	2000-01	18	2	0
Chelsea	2001-02	26	1	1
Chelsea	2002-03	27	1	2
Southampton	2003-04	19	0	0
		289	**13**	**11**
Le Tallec, Anthony		Apps	Subs	Gls
Liverpool	2003-04	3	10	0
Le Tissier, Matthew		Apps	Subs	Gls
Southampton	1992-93	40	0	15
Southampton	1993-94	38	0	25
Southampton	1994-95	41	0	19
Southampton	1995-96	34	0	7
Southampton	1996-97	25	6	13
Southampton	1997-98	25	1	11
Southampton	1998-99	20	10	7
Southampton	1999-00	9	9	3
Southampton	2000-01	2	6	1
Southampton	2001-02	0	4	0
		234	**36**	**101**
Leaburn, Carl		Apps	Subs	Gls
Wimbledon	1997-98	15	1	4
Wimbledon	1998-99	14	8	0
Wimbledon	1999-00	5	13	0
		34	**22**	**4**
Leacock, Dean		Apps	Subs	Gls
Fulham	2003-04	3	1	0
Leboeuf, Frank		Apps	Subs	Gls
Chelsea	1996-97	26	0	6
Chelsea	1997-98	32	0	5
Chelsea	1998-99	33	0	4
Chelsea	1999-00	28	0	2
Chelsea	2000-01	23	2	0
		142	**2**	**17**
Lee, David		Apps	Subs	Gls
Chelsea	1992-93	23	2	2
Chelsea	1993-94	3	4	1
Chelsea	1994-95	9	5	0
Chelsea	1995-96	29	2	1
Chelsea	1996-97	1	0	1
Chelsea	1997-98	1	0	0
		66	**13**	**5**
Lee, David		Apps	Subs	Gls
Southampton	1992-93	0	1	0
Bolton Wan.	1995-96	9	9	1
		9	**10**	**1**
Lee, Jason		Apps	Subs	Gls
Nottm Forest	1994-95	5	17	3
Nottm Forest	1995-96	21	7	8
Nottm Forest	1996-97	5	8	1
		31	**32**	**12**
Lee, Robert		Apps	Subs	Gls
Newcastle U	1993-94	41	0	7
Newcastle U	1994-95	35	0	9
Newcastle U	1995-96	36	0	8
Newcastle U	1996-97	32	1	5
Newcastle U	1997-98	26	2	4
Newcastle U	1998-99	20	6	0
Newcastle U	1999-00	30	0	0
Newcastle U	2000-01	21	1	0
Newcastle U	2001-02	15	1	1
Derby Co.	2001-02	13	0	0
		269	**11**	**34**
Leese, Lars		Apps	Subs	Gls
Barnsley	1997-98	8	1	0
Legwinski, Sylvain		Apps	Subs	Gls
Fulham	2001-02	30	3	3
Fulham	2002-03	33	2	4
Fulham	2003-04	30	2	0
		93	**7**	**7**
Lehmann, Jens		Apps	Subs	Gls
Arsenal	2003-04	38	0	0
Lennon, Aaron		Apps	Subs	Gls
Leeds U	2003-04	0	11	0
Lennon, Neil		Apps	Subs	Gls
Leicester C	1996-97	35	0	1
Leicester C	1997-98	37	0	2
Leicester C	1998-99	37	0	1
Leicester C	1999-00	31	0	1
Leicester C	2000-01	15	0	0
		155	**0**	**5**
Leonhardsen, Oyvind		Apps	Subs	Gls
Wimbledon	1994-95	18	2	4
Wimbledon	1995-96	28	1	4
Wimbledon	1996-97	27	0	5
Liverpool	1997-98	27	1	6
Liverpool	1998-99	7	2	1
Tottenham H	1999-00	21	1	4
Tottenham H	2000-01	23	2	3
Tottenham H	2001-02	2	5	0
Aston Villa	2002-03	13	6	3
		166	**20**	**30**
Lewis, Eddie		Apps	Subs	Gls
Fulham	2001-02	1	0	0
Lewis, Junior		Apps	Subs	Gls
Leicester C	2000-01	15	0	0
Leicester C	2001-02	4	2	0
		19	**2**	**0**
Lewis, Neil		Apps	Subs	Gls
Leicester C	1994-95	13	3	0
Leicester C	1996-97	4	2	0
		17	**5**	**0**
Liddell, Andy		Apps	Subs	Gls
Barnsley	1997-98	13	13	1
Liddle, Craig		Apps	Subs	Gls
Middlesbrough	1995-96	12	1	0
Middlesbrough	1996-97	5	0	0
		17	**1**	**0**
Lightbourne, Kyle		Apps	Subs	Gls
Coventry C	1997-98	1	6	0
Lilley, Derek		Apps	Subs	Gls
Leeds U	1996-97	4	2	0
Leeds U	1997-98	0	13	1
Leeds U	1998-99	0	2	0
		4	**17**	**1**
Limpar, Anders		Apps	Subs	Gls
Arsenal	1992-93	12	11	2
Arsenal	1993-94	9	1	0
Everton	1993-94	9	0	0
Everton	1994-95	19	8	2
Everton	1995-96	22	6	3
Everton	1996-97	1	1	0
		72	**27**	**7**
Linderoth, Tobias		Apps	Subs	Gls
Everton	2001-02	4	4	0
Everton	2002-03	2	3	0
Everton	2003-04	23	4	0
		29	**11**	**0**
Ling, Martin		Apps	Subs	Gls
Swindon T	1993-94	29	4	1
Linighan, Andy		Apps	Subs	Gls
Arsenal	1992-93	19	2	2
Arsenal	1993-94	20	1	0
Arsenal	1994-95	13	7	2
Arsenal	1995-96	17	1	0
Arsenal	1996-97	10	1	1
Crystal P	1997-98	26	0	0
		105	**12**	**5**
Linighan, Brian		Apps	Subs	Gls
Sheff. Wed.	1993-94	1	0	0
Linighan, David		Apps	Subs	Gls
Ipswich T	1992-93	42	0	1
Ipswich T	1993-94	38	0	3
Ipswich T	1994-95	31	1	0
		111	**1**	**4**
Lisbie, Kevin		Apps	Subs	Gls
Charlton Ath	1998-99	0	1	0
Charlton Ath	2000-01	5	13	0
Charlton Ath	2001-02	10	12	5
Charlton Ath	2002-03	24	8	4
Charlton Ath	2003-04	5	4	4
		44	**38**	**13**
Litmanen, Jari		Apps	Subs	Gls
Liverpool	2000-01	4	1	1
Liverpool	2001-02	8	13	4
		12	**14**	**5**
Little, Glen		Apps	Subs	Gls
Bolton Wan.	2003-04	0	4	0
Littlejohn, Adrian		Apps	Subs	Gls
Sheff. Utd.	1992-93	18	9	8
Sheff. Utd.	1993-94	12	7	3
		30	**16**	**11**
Livesey, Danny		Apps	Subs	Gls
Bolton Wan.	2002-03	0	2	0
Livingstone, Steve		Apps	Subs	Gls
Blackburn R	1992-93	1	1	0
Chelsea	1992-93	0	1	0
		1	**2**	**0**
Ljungberg, Freddie		Apps	Subs	Gls
Arsenal	1998-99	10	6	1
Arsenal	1999-00	22	4	6
Arsenal	2000-01	25	5	6
Arsenal	2001-02	24	1	12
Arsenal	2002-03	19	1	6
Arsenal	2003-04	27	3	4
		127	**20**	**35**
Locke, Gary		Apps	Subs	Gls
Bradford C	2000-01	6	1	0
Lomas, Steve		Apps	Subs	Gls
Man. City	1993-94	17	6	0
Man. City	1994-95	18	2	2
Man. City	1995-96	32	1	3
West Ham U	1996-97	7	0	0
West Ham U	1997-98	33	0	2
West Ham U	1998-99	30	0	1
West Ham U	1999-00	25	0	1
West Ham U	2000-01	20	0	1
West Ham U	2001-02	14	1	4
West Ham U	2002-03	27	2	0
		223	**12**	**14**
Lombardo, Attilio		Apps	Subs	Gls
Crystal P	1997-98	21	3	5
Louis-Jean, Mathieu		Apps	Subs	Gls
Nottm Forest	1998-99	15	1	0
Lowe, David		Apps	Subs	Gls
Leicester C	1994-95	19	10	8
Lua-Lua, Lumana Tresor		Apps	Subs	Gls
Newcastle U	2000-01	3	18	0
Newcastle U	2001-02	4	16	3
Newcastle U	2002-03	5	6	2
Newcastle U	2003-04	2	5	0
Portsmouth	2003-04	10	5	4
		24	**50**	**9**
Lukic, John		Apps	Subs	Gls
Leeds U	1992-93	39	0	0
Leeds U	1993-94	20	0	0
Leeds U	1994-95	42	0	0
Leeds U	1995-96	28	0	0
Arsenal	1996-97	15	0	0
Arsenal	2000-01	3	0	0
		147	**0**	**0**
Lucic, Teddy		Apps	Subs	Gls
Leeds U	2002-03	16	1	1
Lumsdon, Chris		Apps	Subs	Gls
Sunderland	1999-00	1	0	0
Lund, Andreas		Apps	Subs	Gls
Wimbledon	1999-00	10	2	2
Lundekvam, Claus		Apps	Subs	Gls
Southampton	1996-97	28	1	0
Southampton	1997-98	31	0	0
Southampton	1998-99	30	3	0
Southampton	1999-00	25	2	0
Southampton	2000-01	38	0	0
Southampton	2001-02	34	0	0
Southampton	2002-03	33	0	0
Southampton	2003-04	31	0	1
		250	**6**	**1**
Luzhny, Oleg		Apps	Subs	Gls
Arsenal	1999-00	16	5	0
Arsenal	2000-01	16	3	0
Arsenal	2001-02	15	3	0
Arsenal	2002-03	11	6	0
Wolves	2003-04	4	2	0
		62	**19**	**0**
Luzi Bernardi, Patrice		Apps	Subs	Gls
Liverpool	2003-04	0	1	0
Lydersen, Pal		Apps	Subs	Gls
Arsenal	1992-93	7	1	0
Lyttle, Des		Apps	Subs	Gls
Nottm Forest	1994-95	38	0	0
Nottm Forest	1995-96	32	1	1
Nottm Forest	1996-97	30	2	1
Nottm Forest	1998-99	5	5	0
Watford	1999-00	11	0	0
West Brom	2002-03	2	2	0
		118	**10**	**2**
Mabbutt, Gary		Apps	Subs	Gls
Tottenham H	1992-93	29	0	2
Tottenham H	1993-94	29	0	0
Tottenham H	1994-95	33	3	0
Tottenham H	1995-96	32	0	0
Tottenham H	1996-97	1	0	0
Tottenham H	1997-98	8	3	0
		132	**6**	**2**
Mabizela, Mbulelo		Apps	Subs	Gls
Tottenham H	2003-04	0	6	1
McAllister, Brian		Apps	Subs	Gls
Wimbledon	1992-93	26	1	0
Wimbledon	1993-94	13	0	0
Wimbledon	1995-96	2	0	0
Wimbledon	1996-97	19	4	0
Wimbledon	1997-98	4	3	0
		64	**8**	**0**
McAllister, Gary		Apps	Subs	Gls
Leeds U	1992-93	32	0	5
Leeds U	1993-94	42	0	8
Leeds U	1994-95	41	0	6
Leeds U	1995-96	36	0	5
Coventry C	1996-97	38	0	6
Coventry C	1997-98	14	0	0
Coventry C	1998-99	29	0	3
Coventry C	1999-00	38	0	11
Liverpool	2000-01	21	9	5
Liverpool	2001-02	14	11	0
		305	**20**	**49**
McAnespie, Steve		Apps	Subs	Gls
Bolton Wan.	1995-96	7	2	0
Bolton Wan.	1997-98	1	1	0
		8	**3**	**0**
McAteer, Jason		Apps	Subs	Gls
Bolton Wan.	1995-96	4	0	0
Liverpool	1995-96	27	2	0
Liverpool	1996-97	36	1	1
Liverpool	1997-98	15	6	2
Liverpool	1998-99	6	7	0
Blackburn R	1998-99	13	0	1
Blackburn R	2001-02	1	3	0
Sunderland	2001-02	26	0	2
Sunderland	2002-03	9	0	1
		137	**19**	**7**
McAvennie, Frank		Apps	Subs	Gls
Aston Villa	1992-93	0	3	0
Swindon T	1993-94	3	4	0
		3	**7**	**0**
McBride, Brian		Apps	Subs	Gls
Everton	2002-03	7	1	4
Fulham	2003-04	5	11	4
		12	**12**	**8**
McCall, Stuart		Apps	Subs	Gls
Bradford C	1999-00	33	1	1
Bradford C	2000-01	36	1	1
		69	**2**	**2**
McCann, Gavin		Apps	Subs	Gls
Everton	1997-98	5	6	0
Sunderland	1999-00	21	3	4
Sunderland	2000-01	22	0	3
Sunderland	2001-02	29	0	0
Sunderland	2002-03	29	1	1
Aston Villa	2003-04	28	0	0
		134	**10**	**8**
McCann, Grant		Apps	Subs	Gls
West Ham U	2000-01	0	1	0
West Ham U	2001-02	0	3	0
		0	**4**	**0**
McCann, Neil		Apps	Subs	Gls
Southampton	2003-04	9	9	0
Maccarone, Massimo		Apps	Subs	Gls
Middlesbrough	2002-03	26	8	9
Middlesbrough	2003-04	13	10	6
		39	**18**	**15**
McCarthy, Alan		Apps	Subs	Gls
QPR	1993-94	4	0	0
QPR	1994-95	0	2	0
		4	**2**	**0**
McCarthy, Sean		Apps	Subs	Gls
Oldham Ath.	1993-94	19	1	4
McCartney, George		Apps	Subs	Gls
Sunderland	2000-01	1	1	0
Sunderland	2001-02	12	6	0
Sunderland	2002-03	16	8	0
		29	**15**	**0**
McClair, Brian		Apps	Subs	Gls
Man. Utd.	1992-93	41	1	9

Man. Utd.	1993-94	12	14	1
Man. Utd.	1994-95	35	5	5
Man. Utd.	1995-96	12	10	3
Man. Utd.	1996-97	4	15	0
Man. Utd.	1997-98	2	11	0
		106	**56**	**18**
McClen, Jamie		*Apps*	*Subs*	*Gls*
Newcastle U	1998-99	1	0	0
Newcastle U	1999-00	3	6	0
Newcastle U	2001-02	3	0	0
Newcastle U	2002-03	0	1	0
		7	**7**	**0**
MacDonald, Charlie		*Apps*	*Subs*	*Gls*
Charlton Ath	2000-01	1	2	0
Charlton Ath	2001-02	0	2	1
		1	**4**	**1**
McDonald, Alan		*Apps*	*Subs*	*Gls*
QPR	1992-93	39	0	0
QPR	1993-94	12	0	1
QPR	1994-95	39	0	1
QPR	1995-96	25	1	1
		115	**1**	**3**
McDonald, David		*Apps*	*Subs*	*Gls*
Tottenham H	1992-93	2	0	0
McDonald, Neil		*Apps*	*Subs*	*Gls*
Oldham Ath.	1992-93	2	2	0
Oldham Ath.	1993-94	3	0	0
		5	**2**	**0**
McDonald, Paul		*Apps*	*Subs*	*Gls*
Southampton	1994-95	0	2	0
Southampton	1995-96	0	1	0
		0	**3**	**0**
McDonald, Scott		*Apps*	*Subs*	*Gls*
Southampton	2001-02	0	2	0
McEveley, Jay		*Apps*	*Subs*	*Gls*
Blackburn R	2002-03	9	0	0
McEwen, Dave		*Apps*	*Subs*	*Gls*
Tottenham H	1999-00	0	1	0
Tottenham H	2000-01	0	3	0
		0	**4**	**0**
McFadden, James		*Apps*	*Subs*	*Gls*
Everton	2003-04	11	12	0
McGee, Paul		*Apps*	*Subs*	*Gls*
Wimbledon	1992-93	1	2	0
McGinlay, John		*Apps*	*Subs*	*Gls*
Bolton Wan.	1995-96	29	3	6
Bolton Wan.	1997-98	4	3	0
		33	**6**	**6**
McGoldrick, Eddie		*Apps*	*Subs*	*Gls*
Crystal P	1992-93	42	0	8
Arsenal	1993-94	23	3	0
Arsenal	1994-95	9	2	0
Arsenal	1995-96	0	1	0
		74	**6**	**8**
McGovern, Brian		*Apps*	*Subs*	*Gls*
Arsenal	1999-00	0	1	0
McGowan, Gavin		*Apps*	*Subs*	*Gls*
Arsenal	1992-93	0	2	0
Arsenal	1994-95	1	0	0
Arsenal	1995-96	1	0	0
Arsenal	1996-97	1	0	0
Arsenal	1997-98	0	1	0
		3	**3**	**0**
McGrath, John		*Apps*	*Subs*	*Gls*
Aston Villa	2000-01	0	3	0
McGrath, Lloyd		*Apps*	*Subs*	*Gls*
Coventry C	1992-93	20	5	0
Coventry C	1993-94	10	1	0
		30	**6**	**0**
McGrath, Paul		*Apps*	*Subs*	*Gls*
Aston Villa	1992-93	42	0	4
Aston Villa	1993-94	30	0	1
Aston Villa	1994-95	36	4	0
Aston Villa	1995-96	29	1	2
Derby Co.	1996-97	23	1	0
		160	**6**	**7**
McGreal, John		*Apps*	*Subs*	*Gls*
Ipswich T	2000-01	25	3	1
Ipswich T	2001-02	27	0	1
		52	**3**	**2**
McGregor, Paul		*Apps*	*Subs*	*Gls*
Nottm Forest	1994-95	0	11	1
Nottm Forest	1995-96	7	7	2
Nottm Forest	1996-97	0	5	0
		7	**23**	**3**
Macho, Jurgen		*Apps*	*Subs*	*Gls*
Sunderland	2000-01	4	1	0
Sunderland	2001-02	4	0	0
Sunderland	2002-03	12	1	0
		20	**2**	**0**
McInnes, Derek		*Apps*	*Subs*	*Gls*
West Brom	2002-03	28	1	2
McKee, Colin		*Apps*	*Subs*	*Gls*
Man. Utd.	1993-94	1	0	0
McKeever, Mark		*Apps*	*Subs*	*Gls*
Sheff. Wed.	1998-99	1	2	0
Sheff. Wed.	1999-00	1	1	0
		2	**3**	**0**
Macken, Jon		*Apps*	*Subs*	*Gls*
Man. City	2002-03	0	5	0
Man. City	2003-04	7	8	1
		7	**13**	**1**
McKenzie, Leon		*Apps*	*Subs*	*Gls*
Crystal P	1997-98	0	3	0
McKinlay, Billy		*Apps*	*Subs*	*Gls*
Blackburn R	1995-96	13	6	2
Blackburn R	1996-97	23	2	1
Blackburn R	1997-98	26	4	0
Blackburn R	1998-99	14	2	0
Bradford C	2000-01	10	1	0
Leicester C	2003-04	15	1	0
		101	**16**	**3**
McKinnon, Ray		*Apps*	*Subs*	*Gls*
Nottm Forest	1992-93	5	1	1
MacLaren, Ross		*Apps*	*Subs*	*Gls*
Swindon T	1993-94	10	2	0
McLeary, Alan		*Apps*	*Subs*	*Gls*
Sheff. Utd.	1992-93	3	0	0
Wimbledon	1992-93	4	0	0
		7	**0**	**0**
McLeod, Kevin		*Apps*	*Subs*	*Gls*
Everton	2000-01	0	5	0
McMahon, Gerry		*Apps*	*Subs*	*Gls*
Tottenham H	1994-95	2	0	0
Tottenham H	1995-96	7	7	0
		9	**7**	**0**
McMahon, Sam		*Apps*	*Subs*	*Gls*
Leicester C	1994-95	0	1	0
Leicester C	1997-98	0	1	0
		0	**2**	**0**
McMahon, Steve		*Apps*	*Subs*	*Gls*
Man. City	1992-93	24	3	1
Man. City	1993-94	35	0	0
Man. City	1994-95	6	1	0
		65	**4**	**1**
McManaman, Steve		*Apps*	*Subs*	*Gls*
Liverpool	1992-93	27	4	4
Liverpool	1993-94	29	1	2
Liverpool	1994-95	40	0	7
Liverpool	1995-96	38	0	6
Liverpool	1996-97	37	0	7
Liverpool	1997-98	36	0	11
Liverpool	1998-99	25	3	4
Man. City	2003-04	20	2	0
		252	**10**	**41**
McMaster, Jamie		*Apps*	*Subs*	*Gls*
Leeds U	2002-03	0	4	0
McPhail, Stephen		*Apps*	*Subs*	*Gls*
Leeds U	1997-98	0	4	0
Leeds U	1998-99	11	6	0
Leeds U	1999-00	23	1	2
Leeds U	2000-01	3	4	0
Leeds U	2001-02	0	1	0
Leeds U	2002-03	7	6	0
Leeds U	2003-04	8	4	1
		52	**26**	**3**
McSheffrey, Gary		*Apps*	*Subs*	*Gls*
Coventry C	1998-99	0	1	0
Coventry C	1999-00	0	3	0
		0	**4**	**0**
McVeigh, Paul		*Apps*	*Subs*	*Gls*
Tottenham H	1996-97	2	1	1
Madar, Mickael		*Apps*	*Subs*	*Gls*
Everton	1997-98	15	2	6
Everton	1998-99	2	0	0
		17	**2**	**6**
Maddison, Neil		*Apps*	*Subs*	*Gls*
Southampton	1992-93	33	4	4
Southampton	1993-94	41	0	7
Southampton	1994-95	35	0	3
Southampton	1995-96	13	2	1
Southampton	1996-97	14	4	1
Southampton	1997-98	5	1	1
Middlesbrough	1998-99	10	11	0
Middlesbrough	1999-00	6	7	0
		157	**29**	**17**
Maddix, Danny		*Apps*	*Subs*	*Gls*
QPR	1992-93	9	5	0
QPR	1994-95	21	6	1
QPR	1995-96	20	2	0
		50	**13**	**1**
Magilton, Jim		*Apps*	*Subs*	*Gls*
Southampton	1993-94	15	0	0
Southampton	1994-95	42	0	6
Southampton	1995-96	31	0	3
Southampton	1996-97	31	6	4
Southampton	1997-98	5	0	0
Sheff. Wed.	1997-98	13	8	1
Sheff. Wed.	1998-99	1	5	0
Ipswich T	2000-01	32	1	1
Ipswich T	2001-02	16	8	0
		186	**28**	**15**
Mahon, Alan		*Apps*	*Subs*	*Gls*
Blackburn R	2001-02	10	3	1
Blackburn R	2002-03	0	2	0
Blackburn R	2003-04	1	2	0
		11	**7**	**1**
Mahorn, Paul		*Apps*	*Subs*	*Gls*
Tottenham H	1993-94	1	0	0
Tottenham H	1997-98	2	0	0
		3	**0**	**0**
Makel, Lee		*Apps*	*Subs*	*Gls*
Blackburn R	1992-93	1	0	0
Blackburn R	1993-94	0	2	0
Blackburn R	1995-96	0	3	0
		1	**5**	**0**
Makelele, Claude		*Apps*	*Subs*	*Gls*
Chelsea	2003-04	26	4	0
Makin, Chris		*Apps*	*Subs*	*Gls*
Oldham Ath.	1993-94	26	1	1
Sunderland	1999-00	34	0	1
Sunderland	2000-01	21	2	0
Ipswich T	2000-01	10	0	0
Ipswich T	2001-02	30	0	0
		121	**3**	**2**
Malbranque, Steed		*Apps*	*Subs*	*Gls*
Fulham	2001-02	33	4	8
Fulham	2002-03	35	2	6
Fulham	2003-04	38	0	6
		106	**6**	**20**
Malz, Stefan		*Apps*	*Subs*	*Gls*
Arsenal	1999-00	2	3	1
Arsenal	2000-01	0	1	0
		2	**4**	**1**
Mancini, Roberto		*Apps*	*Subs*	*Gls*
Leicester C	2000-01	3	1	0
Manninger, Alex		*Apps*	*Subs*	*Gls*
Arsenal	1997-98	7	0	0
Arsenal	1998-99	6	0	0
Arsenal	1999-00	14	1	0
Arsenal	2000-01	11	0	0
		38	**1**	**0**
Marcelino, Marcelino		*Apps*	*Subs*	*Gls*
Newcastle U	1999-00	10	1	0
Newcastle U	2000-01	5	1	0
		15	**2**	**0**
Marcelle, Clint		*Apps*	*Subs*	*Gls*
Barnsley	1997-98	9	11	0
Marcolin, Dario		*Apps*	*Subs*	*Gls*
Blackburn R	1998-99	5	5	1
Margas, Javier		*Apps*	*Subs*	*Gls*
West Ham U	1998-99	3	0	0
West Ham U	1999-00	15	3	1
West Ham U	2000-01	3	0	0
		21	**3**	**1**
Margetson, Martyn		*Apps*	*Subs*	*Gls*
Man. City	1992-93	1	0	0
Maric, Silvio		*Apps*	*Subs*	*Gls*
Newcastle U	1998-99	9	1	0
Newcastle U	1999-00	3	10	0
		12	**11**	**0**
Marinelli, Carlos		*Apps*	*Subs*	*Gls*
Middlesbrough	1999-00	0	2	0
Middlesbrough	2000-01	2	11	0
Middlesbrough	2001-02	12	8	2
Middlesbrough	2002-03	3	4	0
Middlesbrough	2003-04	1	0	1
		18	**25**	**3**
Marker, Nicky		*Apps*	*Subs*	*Gls*
Blackburn R	1992-93	12	3	0
Blackburn R	1993-94	16	7	0
Blackburn R	1995-96	8	1	1
Blackburn R	1996-97	5	2	0
		41	**13**	**1**
Markstedt, Peter		*Apps*	*Subs*	*Gls*
Barnsley	1997-98	6	1	0
Marlet, Steve		*Apps*	*Subs*	*Gls*
Fulham	2001-02	21	5	6
Fulham	2002-03	28	0	4
Fulham	2003-04	1	0	1
		50	**5**	**11**
Marney, Dean		*Apps*	*Subs*	*Gls*
Tottenham H	2003-04	1	2	0
Marquis, Paul		*Apps*	*Subs*	*Gls*
West Ham U	1993-94	0	1	0
Marriott, Andy		*Apps*	*Subs*	*Gls*
Nottm Forest	1992-93	5	0	0
Sunderland	1999-00	1	0	0
Birmingham C	2002-03	1	0	0
		7	**0**	**0**
Marsden, Chris		*Apps*	*Subs*	*Gls*
Coventry C	1993-94	5	2	0
Southampton	1998-99	14	0	2
Southampton	1999-00	19	2	0
Southampton	2000-01	19	4	0
Southampton	2001-02	27	1	3
Southampton	2002-03	30	0	1
Southampton	2003-04	9	4	0
		123	**13**	**6**
Marsh, Mike		*Apps*	*Subs*	*Gls*
Liverpool	1992-93	22	6	1
Liverpool	1993-94	0	2	1
West Ham U	1993-94	33	0	1
West Ham U	1994-95	13	3	0
Coventry C	1994-95	15	0	2
		83	**11**	**5**
Marshall, Andy		*Apps*	*Subs*	*Gls*
Norwich C	1994-95	20	1	0
Ipswich T	2001-02	13	0	0
		33	**1**	**0**
Marshall, Dwight		*Apps*	*Subs*	*Gls*
Middlesbrough	1992-93	0	3	0
Marshall, Ian		*Apps*	*Subs*	*Gls*
Oldham Ath.	1992-93	26	1	2
Ipswich T	1993-94	28	1	10
Ipswich T	1994-95	14	4	3
Leicester C	1996-97	19	9	8
Leicester C	1997-98	22	2	7
Leicester C	1998-99	6	4	3
Leicester C	1999-00	2	19	0
Bolton Wan.	2001-02	0	2	0
		117	**42**	**33**
Marshall, Lee		*Apps*	*Subs*	*Gls*
Leicester C	2000-01	7	2	0
Leicester C	2001-02	29	6	0
West Brom	2002-03	4	5	1
		40	**13**	**1**
Marshall, Scott		*Apps*	*Subs*	*Gls*
Arsenal	1992-93	2	0	0
Arsenal	1995-96	10	1	1
Arsenal	1996-97	6	2	0
Arsenal	1997-98	1	2	0
Southampton	1998-99	2	0	0
		21	**5**	**1**
Martin, Alvin		*Apps*	*Subs*	*Gls*
West Ham U	1993-94	6	1	2
West Ham U	1994-95	24	0	0
West Ham U	1995-96	10	4	0
		40	**5**	**2**
Martin, Lilian		*Apps*	*Subs*	*Gls*
Derby Co.	2000-01	7	2	0
Martin, Lee		*Apps*	*Subs*	*Gls*
Man. Utd.	1993-94	1	0	0
Martyn, Nigel		*Apps*	*Subs*	*Gls*
Crystal P	1992-93	42	0	0
Crystal P	1994-95	37	0	0
Leeds U	1996-97	37	0	0
Leeds U	1997-98	37	0	0
Leeds U	1998-99	34	0	0
Leeds U	1999-00	38	0	0
Leeds U	2000-01	23	0	0
Leeds U	2001-02	38	0	0
Everton	2003-04	33	1	0
		319	**1**	**0**
Masinga, Phil		*Apps*	*Subs*	*Gls*
Leeds U	1994-95	15	7	5
Leeds U	1995-96	5	4	0
		20	**11**	**5**
Maskell, Craig		*Apps*	*Subs*	*Gls*
Swindon T	1993-94	8	6	3
Southampton	1993-94	6	4	1
Southampton	1994-95	2	4	0
Southampton	1995-96	0	1	0
		16	**15**	**4**
Mason, Paul		*Apps*	*Subs*	*Gls*
Ipswich T	1993-94	18	4	3
Ipswich T	1994-95	19	2	3
		37	**6**	**6**
Massey, Stuart		*Apps*	*Subs*	*Gls*
Crystal P	1992-93	0	1	0
Materazzi, Marco		*Apps*	*Subs*	*Gls*
Everton	1998-99	26	1	1
Mathie, Alex		*Apps*	*Subs*	*Gls*
Newcastle U	1993-94	0	16	3
Newcastle U	1994-95	3	6	1
Ipswich T	1994-95	13	0	2
		16	**22**	**6**
Matteo, Dominic		*Apps*	*Subs*	*Gls*
Liverpool	1993-94	11	0	0
Liverpool	1994-95	2	5	0
Liverpool	1995-96	5	0	0
Liverpool	1996-97	22	4	0
Liverpool	1997-98	24	2	0
Liverpool	1998-99	16	4	1
Liverpool	1999-00	32	0	0
Leeds U	2000-01	30	0	0
Leeds U	2001-02	32	0	0
Leeds U	2002-03	20	0	0
Leeds U	2003-04	33	0	2
		227	**15**	**3**
Matthew, Damian		*Apps*	*Subs*	*Gls*
Chelsea	1992-93	3	1	0
Crystal P	1994-95	2	2	0
		5	**3**	**0**
Matthews, Lee		*Apps*	*Subs*	*Gls*
Leeds U	1997-98	0	3	0
Mattsson, Jesper		*Apps*	*Subs*	*Gls*
Nottm Forest	1998-99	5	1	0
Mautone, Steve		*Apps*	*Subs*	*Gls*
West Ham U	1996-97	1	0	0
Mawene, Youl		*Apps*	*Subs*	*Gls*
Derby Co.	2000-01	7	1	0
Derby Co.	2001-02	17	0	1
		24	**1**	**1**
May, David		*Apps*	*Subs*	*Gls*
Blackburn R	1992-93	34	0	1
Blackburn R	1993-94	40	0	1
Man. Utd.	1994-95	15	4	2
Man. Utd.	1995-96	11	5	1
Man. Utd.	1996-97	28	1	3
Man. Utd.	1997-98	7	2	0
Man. Utd.	1998-99	4	2	0
Man. Utd.	1999-00	0	1	0
Man. Utd.	2000-01	1	1	0
Man. Utd.	2001-02	2	0	0
Man. Utd.	2002-03	0	1	0
		142	**17**	**8**
Maybury, Alan		*Apps*	*Subs*	*Gls*
Leeds U	1995-96	1	0	0
Leeds U	1997-98	9	3	0
Leeds U	2001-02	0	1	0
		10	**4**	**0**
Mayrleb, Christian		*Apps*	*Subs*	*Gls*
Sheff. Wed.	1997-98	0	3	0
Mazzarelli, Giuseppe		*Apps*	*Subs*	*Gls*
Man. City	1995-96	0	2	0
Mboma, Patrick		*Apps*	*Subs*	*Gls*
Sunderland	2001-02	5	4	1
Meaker, Michael		*Apps*	*Subs*	*Gls*
QPR	1992-93	3	0	0
QPR	1993-94	11	3	1
QPR	1994-95	7	1	0
		21	**4**	**1**

Mean, Scott		Apps	Subs	Gls
West Ham U	1997-98	0	3	0
Megson, Gary		Apps	Subs	Gls
Norwich C	1992-93	20	3	1
Norwich C	1993-94	21	1	0
Norwich C	1994-95	1	0	0
		42	**4**	**1**
Meijer, Erik		Apps	Subs	Gls
Liverpool	1999-00	7	14	0
Liverpool	2000-01	0	3	0
		7	**17**	**0**
Melchiot, Mario		Apps	Subs	Gls
Chelsea	1999-00	4	1	0
Chelsea	2000-01	27	4	0
Chelsea	2001-02	35	2	2
Chelsea	2002-03	31	3	0
Chelsea	2003-04	20	3	2
		117	**13**	**4**
Mellberg, Olof		Apps	Subs	Gls
Aston Villa	2001-02	32	0	0
Aston Villa	2002-03	38	0	1
Aston Villa	2003-04	33	0	1
		103	**0**	**2**
Mellor, Neil		Apps	Subs	Gls
Liverpool	2002-03	1	2	0
Melton, Steve		Apps	Subs	Gls
Nottm Forest	1998-99	1	0	0
Melville, Andy		Apps	Subs	Gls
Sunderland	1996-97	30	0	2
Fulham	2001-02	35	0	0
Fulham	2002-03	24	2	0
Fulham	2003-04	9	0	0
		98	**2**	**2**
Mendez, Alberto		Apps	Subs	Gls
Arsenal	1997-98	1	2	0
Arsenal	1998-99	0	1	0
		1	**3**	**0**
Mendieta, Gaizka		Apps	Subs	Gls
Middlesbrough	2003-04	30	1	2
Mendonca, Clive		Apps	Subs	Gls
Charlton Ath	1998-99	19	6	8
Mendy, Bernard		Apps	Subs	Gls
Bolton Wan.	2002-03	20	1	0
Merson, Paul		Apps	Subs	Gls
Arsenal	1992-93	32	1	6
Arsenal	1993-94	24	9	7
Arsenal	1994-95	24	0	4
Arsenal	1995-96	38	0	5
Arsenal	1996-97	32	0	6
Middlesbrough	1998-99	3	0	0
Aston Villa	1998-99	21	5	5
Aston Villa	1999-00	24	8	5
Aston Villa	2000-01	38	0	6
Aston Villa	2001-02	18	3	2
		254	**26**	**46**
Mettomo, Lucien		Apps	Subs	Gls
Man. City	2002-03	3	1	0
Middleton, Craig		Apps	Subs	Gls
Coventry C	1992-93	1	0	0
Mike, Adie		Apps	Subs	Gls
Man. City	1992-93	1	2	0
Man. City	1993-94	1	8	1
Man. City	1994-95	1	1	0
		3	**11**	**1**
Miklosko, Ludek		Apps	Subs	Gls
West Ham U	1993-94	42	0	0
West Ham U	1994-95	42	0	0
West Ham U	1995-96	36	0	0
West Ham U	1996-97	36	0	0
West Ham U	1997-98	13	0	0
		169	**0**	**0**
Miller, Alan		Apps	Subs	Gls
Arsenal	1992-93	3	1	0
Arsenal	1993-94	3	1	0
Middlesbrough	1995-96	6	0	0
Middlesbrough	1996-97	10	0	0
Coventry C	2000-01	0	1	0
		22	**3**	**0**
Miller, Charlie		Apps	Subs	Gls
Leicester C	1998-99	1	3	0
Watford	1999-00	9	5	0
		10	**8**	**0**
Miller, Kenny		Apps	Subs	Gls
Wolves	2003-04	17	8	2
Miller, Kevin		Apps	Subs	Gls
Crystal P	1997-98	38	0	0
Miller, Paul		Apps	Subs	Gls
Wimbledon	1992-93	11	8	1
Miller, Tommy		Apps	Subs	Gls
Ipswich T	2001-02	5	3	0
Milligan, Jamie		Apps	Subs	Gls
Everton	1998-99	0	3	0
Everton	1999-00	0	1	0
		0	**4**	**0**
Milligan, Mike		Apps	Subs	Gls
Oldham Ath.	1992-93	42	0	3
Oldham Ath.	1993-94	39	0	0
Norwich C	1994-95	25	1	2
		106	**1**	**5**
Mills, Danny		Apps	Subs	Gls
Charlton Ath	1998-99	36	0	2
Leeds U	1999-00	16	1	1
Leeds U	2000-01	20	3	0
Leeds U	2001-02	28	0	1
Leeds U	2002-03	32	1	1

Paul Merson.

Middlesbrough	2003-04	28	0	0
		160	**5**	**5**
Mills, Gary		Apps	Subs	Gls
Leicester C	1994-95	1	0	0
Mills, Lee		Apps	Subs	Gls
Bradford C	1999-00	19	2	5
Milner, James		Apps	Subs	Gls
Leeds U	2002-03	1	17	2
Leeds U	2003-04	27	3	3
		28	**20**	**5**
Milosevic, Savo		Apps	Subs	Gls
Aston Villa	1995-96	36	1	12
Aston Villa	1996-97	29	1	9
Aston Villa	1997-98	19	4	7
		84	**6**	**28**
Milton, Simon		Apps	Subs	Gls
Ipswich T	1992-93	7	5	2
Ipswich T	1993-94	11	4	1
Ipswich T	1994-95	19	6	2
		37	**15**	**5**
Mimms, Bobby		Apps	Subs	Gls
Blackburn R	1992-93	42	0	0
Blackburn R	1993-94	13	0	0
Blackburn R	1994-95	3	1	0
Blackburn R	1995-96	1	1	0
		59	**2**	**0**
Minett, Jason		Apps	Subs	Gls
Norwich C	1992-93	0	1	0
Minto, Scott		Apps	Subs	Gls
Chelsea	1994-95	19	0	0
Chelsea	1995-96	10	0	0
Chelsea	1996-97	24	1	4
West Ham U	1998-99	14	1	0
West Ham U	1999-00	15	3	0
West Ham U	2000-01	1	0	0
West Ham U	2001-02	5	0	0
West Ham U	2002-03	9	3	0
		97	**8**	**4**
Mitchell, Paul		Apps	Subs	Gls
West Ham U	1993-94	0	1	0
Mohan, Nicky		Apps	Subs	Gls
Middlesbrough	1992-93	18	0	2
Leicester C	1994-95	23	0	0
		41	**0**	**2**
Molby, Jan		Apps	Subs	Gls
Liverpool	1992-93	8	2	3
Liverpool	1993-94	11	0	2
Liverpool	1994-95	12	2	2
		31	**4**	**7**
Moldovan, Viorel		Apps	Subs	Gls
Coventry C	1997-98	5	5	1
Molenaar, Robert		Apps	Subs	Gls
Leeds U	1996-97	12	0	1
Leeds U	1997-98	18	4	2
Leeds U	1998-99	17	0	2
Bradford C	2000-01	21	0	1
		68	**4**	**6**
Moncur, John		Apps	Subs	Gls
Swindon T	1993-94	41	0	4
West Ham U	1994-95	30	0	2
West Ham U	1995-96	19	1	0
West Ham U	1996-97	26	1	2
West Ham U	1997-98	17	3	1
West Ham U	1998-99	6	8	0
West Ham U	1999-00	20	2	1
West Ham U	2000-01	6	10	0
West Ham U	2001-02	7	12	0
West Ham U	2002-03	0	7	0
		172	**44**	**10**
Monk, Garry		Apps	Subs	Gls
Southampton	1998-99	4	0	0
Southampton	1999-00	1	1	0
Southampton	2000-01	2	0	0
Southampton	2001-02	1	1	0
Southampton	2002-03	1	0	0
		9	**2**	**0**
Monkou, Ken		Apps	Subs	Gls
Southampton	1992-93	33	0	1
Southampton	1993-94	35	0	4
Southampton	1994-95	31	0	1
Southampton	1995-96	31	1	2
Southampton	1996-97	8	5	0
Southampton	1997-98	30	2	1
Southampton	1998-99	22	0	1
		190	**8**	**10**
Moody, Paul		Apps	Subs	Gls
Southampton	1992-93	2	1	0
Southampton	1993-94	3	2	0
		5	**3**	**0**
Mooney, Tommy		Apps	Subs	Gls
Watford	1999-00	8	4	2
Birmingham C	2002-03	0	1	0
		8	**5**	**2**
Moore, Alan		Apps	Subs	Gls
Middlesbrough	1992-93	0	2	0
Middlesbrough	1995-96	5	7	0
Middlesbrough	1996-97	10	7	0
Middlesbrough	1998-99	3	1	0
		18	**17**	**0**
Moore, Darren		Apps	Subs	Gls
West Brom	2002-03	29	0	2
Moore, Ian		Apps	Subs	Gls
Nottm Forest	1996-97	1	4	0
West Ham U	1997-98	0	1	0
		1	**5**	**0**
Moore, Joe-Max		Apps	Subs	Gls
Everton	1999-00	11	4	6
Everton	2000-01	8	13	0
Everton	2001-02	3	13	2
		22	**30**	**8**
Moore, Kevin		Apps	Subs	Gls
Southampton	1992-93	18	0	2
Southampton	1993-94	14	0	0
		32	**0**	**2**
Moore, Luke		Apps	Subs	Gls
Aston Villa	2003-04	0	7	0
Moore, Neil		Apps	Subs	Gls
Everton	1992-93	0	1	0
Everton	1993-94	4	0	0
		4	**1**	**0**
Moore, Stefan		Apps	Subs	Gls
Aston Villa	2002-03	7	6	1
Aston Villa	2003-04	2	6	1
		9	**12**	**2**
Moran, Kevin		Apps	Subs	Gls
Blackburn R	1992-93	36	0	4
Blackburn R	1993-94	19	0	1
		55	**0**	**5**
Moran, Paul		Apps	Subs	Gls
Tottenham H	1992-93	0	3	0
Tottenham H	1993-94	0	5	0
		0	**8**	**0**
Moreno, Jaime		Apps	Subs	Gls
Middlesbrough	1995-96	2	5	0
Moreno, Javi		Apps	Subs	Gls
Bolton Wan.	2003-04	1	7	0
Morgan, Chris		Apps	Subs	Gls
Barnsley	1997-98	10	1	0
Morgan, Phil		Apps	Subs	Gls
Ipswich T	1994-95	1	0	0
Morgan, Steve		Apps	Subs	Gls
Coventry C	1993-94	39	1	2
Coventry C	1994-95	26	2	0
		65	**3**	**2**
Morley, Trevor		Apps	Subs	Gls
West Ham U	1993-94	39	3	13
West Ham U	1994-95	10	4	0
		49	**7**	**13**
Mornar, Ivica		Apps	Subs	Gls
Portsmouth	2003-04	3	5	1
Morris, Chris		Apps	Subs	Gls
Middlesbrough	1992-93	22	3	1
Middlesbrough	1995-96	22	1	2
Middlesbrough	1996-97	3	1	0
		47	**5**	**3**
Morris, Jody		Apps	Subs	Gls
Chelsea	1995-96	0	1	0
Chelsea	1996-97	6	6	0
Chelsea	1997-98	9	3	1
Chelsea	1998-99	14	4	1
Chelsea	1999-00	19	11	3
Chelsea	2000-01	13	8	0
Chelsea	2001-02	2	3	0
Chelsea	2002-03	19	6	0
Leeds U	2003-04	11	1	0
		93	**43**	**5**
Morris, Lee		Apps	Subs	Gls
Derby Co.	1999-00	2	1	0
Derby Co.	2000-01	4	16	0
Derby Co.	2001-02	9	6	4
		15	**23**	**4**
Morrison, Andy		Apps	Subs	Gls
Blackburn R	1993-94	1	4	0
Man. City	2000-01	3	0	0
		4	**4**	**0**
Morrison, Clinton		Apps	Subs	Gls
Crystal P	1997-98	0	1	1
Birmingham C	2002-03	24	4	6
Birmingham C	2003-04	19	12	4
		43	**17**	**11**
Morrison, James		Apps	Subs	Gls
Middlesbrough	2003-04	0	1	0
Morrison, Owen		Apps	Subs	Gls
Sheff. Wed.	1998-99	0	1	0
Morrow, Steve		Apps	Subs	Gls
Arsenal	1992-93	13	3	0
Arsenal	1993-94	7	4	0
Arsenal	1994-95	11	4	1
Arsenal	1995-96	3	1	0
Arsenal	1996-97	5	9	0
		39	**21**	**1**
Mortimer, Paul		Apps	Subs	Gls
Crystal P	1992-93	1	0	0
Charlton Ath	1998-99	10	7	1
		11	**7**	**1**
Moses, Adie		Apps	Subs	Gls
Barnsley	1997-98	32	3	0
Moss, Neil		Apps	Subs	Gls
Southampton	1996-97	3	0	0
Southampton	1998-99	7	0	0
Southampton	1999-00	7	2	0
Southampton	2000-01	3	0	0
Southampton	2001-02	2	0	0
		22	**2**	**0**
Moulden, Paul		Apps	Subs	Gls
Oldham Ath.	1992-93	1	3	0
Mullin, John		Apps	Subs	Gls
Sunderland	1996-97	9	1	1
Mulryne, Phil		Apps	Subs	Gls
Man. Utd.	1997-98	1	0	0
Murphy, Danny		Apps	Subs	Gls
Liverpool	1997-98	6	10	0
Liverpool	1998-99	0	1	0
Liverpool	1999-00	9	14	3
Liverpool	2000-01	13	14	4
Liverpool	2001-02	31	5	6
Liverpool	2002-03	36	0	7
Liverpool	2003-04	19	12	5
		114	**56**	**25**
Murphy, David		Apps	Subs	Gls
Middlesbrough	2001-02	0	5	0
Middlesbrough	2002-03	4	4	0
		4	**9**	**0**
Murphy, Joe		Apps	Subs	Gls
West Brom	2002-03	1	1	0
Murray, Adam		Apps	Subs	Gls
Derby Co.	1998-99	0	4	0
Derby Co.	1999-00	1	7	0
Derby Co.	2000-01	4	10	0
Derby Co.	2001-02	3	3	0
		8	**24**	**0**
Murray, Matt		Apps	Subs	Gls
Wolves	2003-04	1	0	0
Murray, Paul		Apps	Subs	Gls
QPR	1995-96	1	0	0
Murray, Paul		Apps	Subs	Gls
Southampton	2001-02	0	1	0
Murray, Scott		Apps	Subs	Gls
Aston Villa	1995-96	3	0	0
Aston Villa	1996-97	1	0	0
		4	**0**	**0**
Muscat, Kevin		Apps	Subs	Gls
Crystal P	1997-98	9	0	0
Mustoe, Robbie		Apps	Subs	Gls
Middlesbrough	1992-93	21	2	1
Middlesbrough	1995-96	21	0	1
Middlesbrough	1996-97	31	0	3
Middlesbrough	1998-99	32	1	4
Middlesbrough	1999-00	18	10	0
Middlesbrough	2000-01	13	12	0
Middlesbrough	2001-02	31	5	2
Charlton Ath	2002-03	6	0	0
		173	**30**	**11**
Mutch, Andy		Apps	Subs	Gls
Swindon T	1993-94	27	3	6
Mutu, Adrian		Apps	Subs	Gls
Chelsea	2003-04	21	4	6
Myers, Andy		Apps	Subs	Gls
Chelsea	1992-93	3	0	0
Chelsea	1993-94	6	0	0
Chelsea	1994-95	9	1	0
Chelsea	1995-96	20	0	0
Chelsea	1996-97	15	3	1
Chelsea	1997-98	11	1	0
Chelsea	1998-99	1	0	0
Bradford C	1999-00	10	3	0
Bradford C	2000-01	15	5	1
		90	**13**	**2**
Myhre, Thomas		Apps	Subs	Gls
Everton	1997-98	22	0	0
Everton	1998-99	38	0	0
Everton	1999-00	4	0	0
Everton	2000-01	6	0	0
Sunderland	2002-03	1	1	0
		71	**1**	**0**
Nalis, Lilian		Apps	Subs	Gls
Leicester C	2003-04	11	9	1
Nash, Carlo		Apps	Subs	Gls
Man. City	2000-01	6	0	0
Man. City	2002-03	9	0	0
Middlesbrough	2003-04	1	0	0
		16	**0**	**0**

Nayim, Mohamed		*Apps*	*Subs*	*Gls*
Tottenham H	1992-93	15	3	3
Naylor, Lee		*Apps*	*Subs*	*Gls*
Wolves	2003-04	37	1	0
Naylor, Richard		*Apps*	*Subs*	*Gls*
Ipswich T	2000-01	5	8	1
Ipswich T	2001-02	5	9	1
		10	**17**	**2**
Naysmith, Gary		*Apps*	*Subs*	*Gls*
Everton	2000-01	17	3	2
Everton	2001-02	23	1	0
Everton	2002-03	24	4	1
Everton	2003-04	27	2	2
		91	**10**	**5**
Ndah, George		*Apps*	*Subs*	*Gls*
Crystal P	1992-93	4	9	0
Crystal P	1994-95	5	7	1
Crystal P	1997-98	2	1	0
		11	**17**	**1**
Ndlovu, Peter		*Apps*	*Subs*	*Gls*
Coventry C	1992-93	27	5	7
Coventry C	1993-94	40	0	11
Coventry C	1994-95	28	2	11
Coventry C	1995-96	27	5	5
Coventry C	1996-97	10	10	1
		132	**22**	**35**
Neill, Lucas		*Apps*	*Subs*	*Gls*
Blackburn R	2001-02	31	0	1
Blackburn R	2002-03	34	0	0
Blackburn R	2003-04	30	2	2
		95	**2**	**3**
Neilson, Alan		*Apps*	*Subs*	*Gls*
Newcastle U	1993-94	10	4	0
Newcastle U	1994-95	5	1	0
Southampton	1995-96	15	3	0
Southampton	1996-97	24	5	0
Southampton	1997-98	3	5	0
		57	**18**	**0**
Nelson, Fernando		*Apps*	*Subs*	*Gls*
Aston Villa	1996-97	33	1	0
Aston Villa	1997-98	21	4	0
		54	**5**	**0**
Nemeth, Szilard		*Apps*	*Subs*	*Gls*
Middlesbrough	2001-02	11	10	3
Middlesbrough	2002-03	15	13	7
Middlesbrough	2003-04	17	15	9
		43	**38**	**19**
Nethercott, Stuart		*Apps*	*Subs*	*Gls*
Tottenham H	1992-93	3	2	0
Tottenham H	1993-94	9	1	0
Tottenham H	1994-95	8	9	0
Tottenham H	1995-96	9	4	0
Tottenham H	1996-97	2	7	0
		31	**23**	**0**
Neville, Gary		*Apps*	*Subs*	*Gls*
Man. Utd.	1993-94	1	0	0
Man. Utd.	1994-95	16	2	0
Man. Utd.	1995-96	30	1	0
Man. Utd.	1996-97	30	1	1
Man. Utd.	1997-98	34	0	0
Man. Utd.	1998-99	34	0	1
Man. Utd.	1999-00	22	0	0
Man. Utd.	2000-01	32	0	1
Man. Utd.	2001-02	31	3	0
Man. Utd.	2002-03	19	7	0
Man. Utd.	2003-04	30	0	2
		279	**14**	**5**
Neville, Phil		*Apps*	*Subs*	*Gls*
Man. Utd.	1994-95	1	1	0
Man. Utd.	1995-96	21	3	0
Man. Utd.	1996-97	15	3	0
Man. Utd.	1997-98	24	6	1
Man. Utd.	1998-99	19	9	0
Man. Utd.	1999-00	25	4	0
Man. Utd.	2000-01	24	5	1
Man. Utd.	2001-02	21	7	2
Man. Utd.	2002-03	19	6	1
Man. Utd.	2003-04	29	2	0
		198	**46**	**5**
Nevland, Erik		*Apps*	*Subs*	*Gls*
Man. Utd.	1997-98	0	1	0
Newby, Jon		*Apps*	*Subs*	*Gls*
Liverpool	1999-00	0	1	0
Newell, Mike		*Apps*	*Subs*	*Gls*
Blackburn R	1992-93	40	0	13
Blackburn R	1993-94	27	1	6
Blackburn R	1994-95	2	10	0
Blackburn R	1995-96	26	4	3
West Ham U	1996-97	6	1	0
		101	**16**	**22**
Newhouse, Aidan		*Apps*	*Subs*	*Gls*
Wimbledon	1992-93	0	1	1
Newman, Ricky		*Apps*	*Subs*	*Gls*
Crystal P	1992-93	1	1	0
Crystal P	1994-95	32	3	3
		33	**4**	**3**
Newman, Rob		*Apps*	*Subs*	*Gls*
Norwich C	1992-93	16	2	2
Norwich C	1993-94	32	0	2
Norwich C	1994-95	23	9	1
		71	**11**	**5**
Newsome, Jon		*Apps*	*Subs*	*Gls*
Leeds U	1992-93	30	7	0
Leeds U	1993-94	25	4	1
Norwich C	1994-95	35	0	3
Sheff. Wed.	1995-96	8	0	1
Sheff. Wed.	1996-97	10	0	1
Sheff. Wed.	1997-98	25	0	2
Sheff. Wed.	1998-99	2	3	0
Sheff. Wed.	1999-00	5	1	0
		140	**15**	**8**
Newton, Adam		*Apps*	*Subs*	*Gls*
West Ham U	1999-00	0	2	0
Newton, Eddie		*Apps*	*Subs*	*Gls*
Chelsea	1992-93	32	2	5
Chelsea	1993-94	33	3	0
Chelsea	1994-95	22	8	1
Chelsea	1995-96	21	3	1
Chelsea	1996-97	13	2	0
Chelsea	1997-98	17	1	0
Chelsea	1998-99	1	6	0
		139	**25**	**7**
Newton, Shaun		*Apps*	*Subs*	*Gls*
Charlton Ath	1998-99	13	3	0
Charlton Ath	2000-01	1	9	0
Wolves	2003-04	20	8	0
		34	**20**	**0**
Ngonge, Michel		*Apps*	*Subs*	*Gls*
Watford	1999-00	16	7	5
N'Gotty, Bruno		*Apps*	*Subs*	*Gls*
Bolton Wan.	2001-02	24	2	1
Bolton Wan.	2002-03	23	0	1
Bolton Wan.	2003-04	32	1	2
		79	**3**	**4**
Nicholls, Mark		*Apps*	*Subs*	*Gls*
Chelsea	1996-97	3	5	0
Chelsea	1997-98	8	11	3
Chelsea	1998-99	0	9	0
		11	**25**	**3**
Nicol, Steve		*Apps*	*Subs*	*Gls*
Liverpool	1992-93	32	0	0
Liverpool	1993-94	27	4	1
Liverpool	1994-95	4	0	0
Sheff. Wed.	1995-96	18	1	0
Sheff. Wed.	1996-97	19	4	0
Sheff. Wed.	1997-98	4	3	0
		104	**12**	**1**
Nicolas, Alexis		*Apps*	*Subs*	*Gls*
Chelsea	2003-04	1	1	0
Nielsen, Allan		*Apps*	*Subs*	*Gls*
Tottenham H	1996-97	28	1	6
Tottenham H	1997-98	21	5	3
Tottenham H	1998-99	24	4	3
Tottenham H	1999-00	5	9	0
		78	**19**	**12**
Niemi, Antti		*Apps*	*Subs*	*Gls*
Southampton	2002-03	25	0	0
Southampton	2003-04	28	0	0
		53	**0**	**0**
Nijholt, Luc		*Apps*	*Subs*	*Gls*
Swindon T	1993-94	31	1	1
Nilis, Luc		*Apps*	*Subs*	*Gls*
Aston Villa	2000-01	3	0	1
Nilsen, Roger		*Apps*	*Subs*	*Gls*
Sheff. Utd.	1993-94	21	1	0
Tottenham H	1998-99	3	0	0
		24	**1**	**0**
Nilsson, Roland		*Apps*	*Subs*	*Gls*
Sheff. Wed.	1992-93	32	0	1
Sheff. Wed.	1993-94	38	0	0
Coventry C	1997-98	32	0	0
Coventry C	1998-99	28	0	0
		130	**0**	**1**
Nimni, Avi		*Apps*	*Subs*	*Gls*
Derby Co.	1999-00	2	2	1
Noel-Williams, Gifton		*Apps*	*Subs*	*Gls*
Watford	1999-00	1	2	0
Nolan, Ian		*Apps*	*Subs*	*Gls*
Sheff. Wed.	1994-95	42	0	3
Sheff. Wed.	1995-96	29	0	0
Sheff. Wed.	1996-97	38	0	1
Sheff. Wed.	1997-98	27	0	0
Sheff. Wed.	1999-00	28	1	0
Bradford C	2000-01	17	4	0
		181	**5**	**4**
Nolan, Kevin		*Apps*	*Subs*	*Gls*
Bolton Wan.	2001-02	34	1	8
Bolton Wan.	2002-03	15	18	1
Bolton Wan.	2003-04	37	0	9
		86	**19**	**18**
Norfolk, Lee		*Apps*	*Subs*	*Gls*
Ipswich T	1994-95	1	2	0
Normann, Runar		*Apps*	*Subs*	*Gls*
Coventry C	1999-00	1	7	0
Nunez, Milton		*Apps*	*Subs*	*Gls*
Sunderland	1999-00	0	1	0
Nyarko, Alex		*Apps*	*Subs*	*Gls*
Everton	2000-01	19	3	1
Everton	2003-04	7	4	0
		26	**7**	**1**
Oakes, Andy		*Apps*	*Subs*	*Gls*
Derby Co.	2000-01	6	0	0
Derby Co.	2001-02	20	0	0
		26	**0**	**0**
Oakes, Mike		*Apps*	*Subs*	*Gls*
Aston Villa	1996-97	18	2	0
Aston Villa	1997-98	8	0	0
Aston Villa	1998-99	23	0	0
Wolves	2003-04	21	0	0
		70	**2**	**0**
Oakes, Scott		*Apps*	*Subs*	*Gls*
Sheff. Wed.	1996-97	7	12	1

Ray Parlour.

Sheff. Wed.	1997-98	0	4	0
Sheff. Wed.	1998-99	0	1	0
		7	**17**	**1**
Oakes, Stefan		*Apps*	*Subs*	*Gls*
Leicester C	1998-99	2	1	0
Leicester C	1999-00	15	7	1
Leicester C	2000-01	5	8	0
Leicester C	2001-02	16	5	1
		38	**21**	**2**
Oakley, Matthew		*Apps*	*Subs*	*Gls*
Southampton	1994-95	0	1	0
Southampton	1995-96	5	5	0
Southampton	1996-97	23	5	3
Southampton	1997-98	32	1	1
Southampton	1998-99	21	1	2
Southampton	1999-00	26	5	3
Southampton	2000-01	35	0	1
Southampton	2001-02	26	1	1
Southampton	2002-03	28	3	0
Southampton	2003-04	7	0	0
		203	**22**	**11**
O'Brien, Andy		*Apps*	*Subs*	*Gls*
Bradford C	1999-00	36	0	1
Bradford C	2000-01	17	1	0
Newcastle U	2000-01	9	0	1
Newcastle U	2001-02	31	3	2
Newcastle U	2002-03	26	0	0
Newcastle U	2003-04	27	1	1
		146	**5**	**5**
O'Brien, Liam		*Apps*	*Subs*	*Gls*
Newcastle U	1993-94	4	2	0
O'Connor, Jon		*Apps*	*Subs*	*Gls*
Everton	1995-96	3	1	0
Everton	1997-98	0	1	0
		3	**2**	**0**
O'Donnell, Phil		*Apps*	*Subs*	*Gls*
Sheff. Wed.	1999-00	0	1	0
Ogrizovic, Steve		*Apps*	*Subs*	*Gls*
Coventry C	1992-93	33	0	0
Coventry C	1993-94	33	0	0
Coventry C	1994-95	33	0	0
Coventry C	1995-96	25	0	0
Coventry C	1996-97	38	0	0
Coventry C	1997-98	24	0	0
Coventry C	1998-99	2	0	0
Coventry C	1999-00	3	0	0
		191	**0**	**0**
O'Halloran, Keith		*Apps*	*Subs*	*Gls*
Middlesbrough	1995-96	2	1	0
O'Kane, John		*Apps*	*Subs*	*Gls*
Man. Utd.	1995-96	0	1	0
Man. Utd.	1996-97	1	0	0
Everton	1997-98	12	0	0
Everton	1998-99	2	0	0
		15	**1**	**0**
Okocha, Jay Jay		*Apps*	*Subs*	*Gls*
Bolton Wan.	2002-03	26	5	7
Bolton Wan.	2003-04	33	2	0
		59	**7**	**7**
Okon, Paul		*Apps*	*Subs*	*Gls*
Middlesbrough	2000-01	23	1	0
Middlesbrough	2001-02	1	3	0
Leeds U	2002-03	15	0	0
		39	**4**	**0**
Okoronkwo, Isaac		*Apps*	*Subs*	*Gls*
Wolves	2003-04	7	0	0
Oldfield, David		*Apps*	*Subs*	*Gls*
Leicester C	1994-95	8	6	1
O'Leary, David		*Apps*	*Subs*	*Gls*
Arsenal	1992-93	6	5	0
Leeds U	1993-94	10	0	0
		16	**5**	**0**
Olembe, Saloman		*Apps*	*Subs*	*Gls*
Leeds U	2003-04	8	4	0
Olney, Ian		*Apps*	*Subs*	*Gls*
Oldham Ath.	1992-93	32	2	12
Oldham Ath.	1993-94	10	0	1
		42	**2**	**13**
Omoyimni, Manny		*Apps*	*Subs*	*Gls*
West Ham U	1996-97	0	1	0
West Ham U	1997-98	1	4	2
West Ham U	1998-99	0	3	0
		1	**8**	**2**
O'Neil, Brian		*Apps*	*Subs*	*Gls*
Nottm Forest	1996-97	4	1	0
Derby Co.	2000-01	3	1	0
Derby Co.	2001-02	8	2	0
		15	**4**	**0**
O'Neil, Gary		*Apps*	*Subs*	*Gls*
Portsmouth	2003-04	3	0	2
O'Neill, Keith		*Apps*	*Subs*	*Gls*
Norwich C	1994-95	0	1	0
Middlesbrough	1998-99	4	2	0
Middlesbrough	1999-00	14	2	0
Middlesbrough	2000-01	14	1	0
		32	**6**	**0**
O'Neill, Michael		*Apps*	*Subs*	*Gls*
Coventry C	1996-97	1	0	0
Coventry C	1997-98	2	2	0
		3	**2**	**0**
Ord, Richard		*Apps*	*Subs*	*Gls*
Sunderland	1996-97	33	0	2
Orlygsson, Toddi		*Apps*	*Subs*	*Gls*
Nottm Forest	1992-93	15	5	1
Ormerod, Brett		*Apps*	*Subs*	*Gls*
Southampton	2001-02	8	10	1
Southampton	2002-03	22	9	5
Southampton	2003-04	14	8	5
		44	**27**	**11**
Ormerod, Anthony		*Apps*	*Subs*	*Gls*
Middlesbrough	1999-00	0	1	0
Ormondroyd, Ian		*Apps*	*Subs*	*Gls*
Leicester C	1994-95	6	0	0
Osborn, Simon		*Apps*	*Subs*	*Gls*
Crystal P	1992-93	27	4	2
QPR	1995-96	6	3	1
		33	**7**	**3**
O'Shea, John		*Apps*	*Subs*	*Gls*
Man. Utd.	2001-02	4	5	0
Man. Utd.	2002-03	26	6	0
Man. Utd.	2003-04	32	1	2
		62	**12**	**2**
Osman, Leon		*Apps*	*Subs*	*Gls*
Everton	2002-03	0	2	0
Everton	2003-04	3	1	1
		3	**3**	**1**
Ostenstad, Egil		*Apps*	*Subs*	*Gls*
Southampton	1996-97	29	1	9
Southampton	1997-98	21	8	11
Southampton	1998-99	27	7	7
Southampton	1999-00	3	0	1
Man. City	2000-01	1	3	0
Blackburn R	2001-02	2	2	0
Blackburn R	2002-03	8	9	1
		91	**30**	**29**
Oster, John		*Apps*	*Subs*	*Gls*
Everton	1997-98	16	15	1
Everton	1998-99	6	3	0
Sunderland	1999-00	4	6	0
Sunderland	2000-01	2	6	0
Sunderland	2002-03	1	2	0
		29	**32**	**1**
Otsemobor, John		*Apps*	*Subs*	*Gls*
Liverpool	2003-04	4	0	0
Bolton Wan.	2003-04	1	0	0
		5	**0**	**0**
Ouaddou, Abdeslam		*Apps*	*Subs*	*Gls*
Fulham	2001-02	4	4	0
Fulham	2002-03	9	4	0
		13	**8**	**0**
Overmars, Marc		*Apps*	*Subs*	*Gls*
Arsenal	1997-98	32	0	12
Arsenal	1998-99	37	0	6
Arsenal	1999-00	22	9	7
		91	**9**	**25**
Owen, Michael		*Apps*	*Subs*	*Gls*
Liverpool	1996-97	1	1	1
Liverpool	1997-98	34	2	18
Liverpool	1998-99	30	0	18
Liverpool	1999-00	22	5	11
Liverpool	2000-01	20	8	16
Liverpool	2001-02	25	4	19
Liverpool	2002-03	32	3	19
Liverpool	2003-04	29	0	16
		193	**23**	**118**
Ozalan, Alpay		*Apps*	*Subs*	*Gls*
Aston Villa	2000-01	33	0	0
Aston Villa	2001-02	14	0	0
Aston Villa	2002-03	5	0	0
Aston Villa	2003-04	4	2	1
		56	**2**	**1**
Paatelainen, Mixu		*Apps*	*Subs*	*Gls*
Bolton Wan.	1995-96	12	3	1
Padovano, Michele		*Apps*	*Subs*	*Gls*
Crystal P	1997-98	8	2	1
Page, Robert		*Apps*	*Subs*	*Gls*
Watford	1999-00	36	0	1

Player / Club	Season	Apps	Subs	Gls
Pahars, Marian		Apps	Subs	Gls
Southampton	1998-99	4	2	3
Southampton	1999-00	31	2	13
Southampton	2000-01	26	5	9
Southampton	2001-02	33	3	14
Southampton	2002-03	5	4	1
Southampton	2003-04	6	8	2
		105	**24**	**42**
Pallister, Gary		Apps	Subs	Gls
Man. Utd.	1992-93	42	0	1
Man. Utd.	1993-94	41	0	1
Man. Utd.	1994-95	42	0	2
Man. Utd.	1995-96	21	0	1
Man. Utd.	1996-97	27	0	3
Man. Utd.	1997-98	33	0	0
Middlesbrough	1998-99	26	0	0
Middlesbrough	1999-00	21	0	1
Middlesbrough	2000-01	8	0	0
		261	**0**	**9**
Palmer, Carlton		Apps	Subs	Gls
Sheff. Wed.	1992-93	33	1	1
Sheff. Wed.	1993-94	37	0	5
Leeds U	1994-95	39	0	3
Leeds U	1995-96	35	0	2
Leeds U	1996-97	26	2	0
Southampton	1997-98	26	0	3
Southampton	1998-99	18	1	0
Nottm Forest	1998-99	13	0	0
Coventry C	1999-00	15	0	1
Coventry C	2000-01	12	3	0
		254	**7**	**15**
Palmer, Roger		Apps	Subs	Gls
Oldham Ath.	1992-93	5	12	0
Oldham Ath.	1993-94	1	7	0
		6	**19**	**0**
Palmer, Steve		Apps	Subs	Gls
Ipswich T	1992-93	4	3	0
Ipswich T	1993-94	31	5	1
Ipswich T	1994-95	10	2	0
Watford	1999-00	38	0	0
		83	**10**	**1**
Panayi, Jimmy		Apps	Subs	Gls
Watford	1999-00	2	0	0
Panucci, Christian		Apps	Subs	Gls
Chelsea	2000-01	7	1	0
Papavasiliou, Nicky		Apps	Subs	Gls
Newcastle U	1993-94	7	0	0
Parker, Garry		Apps	Subs	Gls
Aston Villa	1992-93	37	0	9
Aston Villa	1993-94	17	2	2
Aston Villa	1994-95	12	2	1
Leicester C	1994-95	14	0	2
Leicester C	1996-97	22	9	2
Leicester C	1997-98	15	7	3
Leicester C	1998-99	2	5	0
		119	**25**	**19**
Parker, Paul		Apps	Subs	Gls
Man. Utd.	1992-93	31	0	1
Man. Utd.	1993-94	39	1	0
Man. Utd.	1994-95	1	1	0
Man. Utd.	1995-96	5	1	0
Derby Co.	1996-97	4	0	0
Chelsea	1996-97	1	3	0
		81	**6**	**1**
Parker, Scott		Apps	Subs	Gls
Charlton Ath	1998-99	0	4	0
Charlton Ath	2000-01	15	5	1
Charlton Ath	2001-02	36	2	1
Charlton Ath	2002-03	28	0	4
Charlton Ath	2003-04	20	0	2
Chelsea	2003-04	7	4	1
		106	**15**	**9**
Parkinson, Gary		Apps	Subs	Gls
Middlesbrough	1992-93	4	0	0
Parkinson, Joe		Apps	Subs	Gls
Everton	1994-95	32	2	0
Everton	1995-96	28	0	3
Everton	1996-97	28	0	0
		88	**2**	**3**
Parlour, Ray		Apps	Subs	Gls
Arsenal	1992-93	16	5	1
Arsenal	1993-94	24	3	2
Arsenal	1994-95	22	8	0
Arsenal	1995-96	20	2	0
Arsenal	1996-97	17	13	2
Arsenal	1997-98	34	0	5
Arsenal	1998-99	35	0	6
Arsenal	1999-00	29	1	1
Arsenal	2000-01	28	5	4
Arsenal	2001-02	25	2	0
Arsenal	2002-03	14	5	0
Arsenal	2003-04	16	9	0
		280	**53**	**21**
Parnaby, Stuart		Apps	Subs	Gls
Middlesbrough	2002-03	21	0	0
Middlesbrough	2003-04	8	5	0
		29	**5**	**0**
Pasanen, Petri		Apps	Subs	Gls
Portsmouth	2003-04	11	1	0
Pates, Colin		Apps	Subs	Gls
Arsenal	1992-93	2	5	0
Patterson, Darren		Apps	Subs	Gls
Crystal P	1994-95	22	0	1
Patterson, Mark		Apps	Subs	Gls
Bolton Wan.	1995-96	12	4	1
Paz, Adrian		Apps	Subs	Gls
Ipswich T	1994-95	13	4	1

Player / Club	Season	Apps	Subs	Gls
Peacock, Darren		Apps	Subs	Gls
QPR	1992-93	35	3	2
QPR	1993-94	30	0	3
Newcastle U	1993-94	9	0	0
Newcastle U	1994-95	35	0	1
Newcastle U	1995-96	33	1	0
Newcastle U	1996-97	35	0	1
Newcastle U	1997-98	19	1	0
Blackburn R	1998-99	27	3	1
		223	**8**	**8**
Peacock, Gavin		Apps	Subs	Gls
Chelsea	1993-94	37	0	8
Chelsea	1994-95	38	0	4
Chelsea	1995-96	17	11	5
Charlton Ath	2001-02	1	4	0
		93	**15**	**17**
Peake, Andy		Apps	Subs	Gls
Middlesbrough	1992-93	33	0	0
Pearce, Andy		Apps	Subs	Gls
Coventry C	1992-93	21	3	1
Sheff. Wed.	1993-94	29	3	3
Sheff. Wed.	1994-95	34	0	0
Sheff. Wed.	1995-96	3	0	0
Wimbledon	1995-96	6	1	0
		93	**7**	**4**
Pearce, Ian		Apps	Subs	Gls
Chelsea	1992-93	0	1	0
Blackburn R	1993-94	1	4	1
Blackburn R	1994-95	22	6	0
Blackburn R	1995-96	12	0	1
Blackburn R	1996-97	7	5	0
Blackburn R	1997-98	1	4	0
West Ham U	1997-98	30	0	1
West Ham U	1998-99	33	0	2
West Ham U	1999-00	1	0	0
West Ham U	2000-01	13	2	1
West Ham U	2001-02	8	1	2
West Ham U	2002-03	26	4	2
Fulham	2003-04	12	1	0
		166	**28**	**10**
Pearce, Stuart		Apps	Subs	Gls
Nottm Forest	1992-93	23	0	2
Nottm Forest	1994-95	36	0	8
Nottm Forest	1995-96	31	0	3
Nottm Forest	1996-97	33	0	5
Newcastle U	1997-98	25	0	0
Newcastle U	1998-99	12	0	0
West Ham U	1999-00	8	0	0
West Ham U	2000-01	34	0	2
		202	**0**	**20**
Pears, Steve		Apps	Subs	Gls
Middlesbrough	1992-93	26	0	0
Pearson, Nigel		Apps	Subs	Gls
Sheff. Wed.	1992-93	13	3	1
Sheff. Wed.	1993-94	4	1	0
Middlesbrough	1995-96	36	0	0
Middlesbrough	1996-97	17	1	0
		70	**5**	**1**
Pedersen, Henrik		Apps	Subs	Gls
Bolton Wan.	2001-02	5	6	0
Bolton Wan.	2002-03	31	2	7
Bolton Wan.	2003-04	19	14	7
		55	**22**	**14**
Pedersen, Per		Apps	Subs	Gls
Blackburn R	1996-97	6	5	1
Pedersen, Tore		Apps	Subs	Gls
Oldham Ath.	1993-94	7	3	0
Blackburn R	1997-98	3	2	0
Wimbledon	1999-00	6	0	0
		16	**5**	**0**
Pemberton, John		Apps	Subs	Gls
Sheff. Utd.	1992-93	19	0	0
Sheff. Utd.	1993-94	8	0	0
Leeds U	1993-94	6	3	0
Leeds U	1994-95	22	5	0
Leeds U	1995-96	16	1	0
		71	**9**	**0**
Pembridge, Mark		Apps	Subs	Gls
Sheff. Wed.	1995-96	24	1	1
Sheff. Wed.	1996-97	33	1	6
Sheff. Wed.	1997-98	31	3	4
Everton	1999-00	29	2	2
Everton	2000-01	20	1	0
Everton	2001-02	10	4	1
Everton	2002-03	19	2	1
Everton	2003-04	4	0	0
Fulham	2003-04	9	3	1
		179	**17**	**16**
Pennant, Jermaine		Apps	Subs	Gls
Arsenal	2002-03	1	4	3
Leeds U	2003-04	34	2	2
		35	**6**	**5**
Pennyfather, Glenn		Apps	Subs	Gls
Ipswich T	1992-93	2	2	0
Penrice, Gary		Apps	Subs	Gls
QPR	1992-93	10	5	6
QPR	1993-94	23	3	8
QPR	1994-95	9	10	3
QPR	1995-96	0	3	0
		42	**21**	**17**
Peralta, Sixto		Apps	Subs	Gls
Ipswich T	2001-02	16	6	3
Perez, Lionel		Apps	Subs	Gls
Sunderland	1996-97	28	1	0
Perez, Sebastien		Apps	Subs	Gls
Blackburn R	1998-99	4	1	1
Pericard, Vincent		Apps	Subs	Gls
Portsmouth	2003-04	0	6	0

Player / Club	Season	Apps	Subs	Gls
Perpetuini, David		Apps	Subs	Gls
Watford	1999-00	12	1	1
Perry, Chris		Apps	Subs	Gls
Wimbledon	1993-94	0	2	0
Wimbledon	1994-95	17	5	0
Wimbledon	1995-96	35	2	0
Wimbledon	1996-97	37	0	1
Wimbledon	1997-98	35	0	1
Wimbledon	1998-99	34	0	0
Tottenham H	1999-00	36	1	1
Tottenham H	2000-01	30	2	1
Tottenham H	2001-02	30	3	0
Tottenham H	2002-03	15	3	1
Charlton Ath	2003-04	25	4	1
		294	**22**	**6**
Petit, Emmanuel		Apps	Subs	Gls
Arsenal	1997-98	32	0	2
Arsenal	1998-99	26	1	4
Arsenal	1999-00	24	2	3
Chelsea	2001-02	26	1	1
Chelsea	2002-03	23	1	1
Chelsea	2003-04	3	1	0
		134	**6**	**11**
Petrescu, Dan		Apps	Subs	Gls
Sheff. Wed.	1994-95	20	9	3
Sheff. Wed.	1995-96	8	0	0
Chelsea	1995-96	22	2	2
Chelsea	1996-97	34	0	3
Chelsea	1997-98	31	0	5
Chelsea	1998-99	23	9	4
Chelsea	1999-00	24	5	4
Bradford C	2000-01	16	1	1
Southampton	2000-01	8	1	2
Southampton	2001-02	0	2	0
		186	**29**	**24**
Petta, Bobby		Apps	Subs	Gls
Fulham	2003-04	3	6	0
Petterson, Andy		Apps	Subs	Gls
Ipswich T	1992-93	1	0	0
Charlton Ath	1998-99	7	3	0
		8	**3**	**0**
Peyton, Gerry		Apps	Subs	Gls
Chelsea	1992-93	0	1	0
Phelan, Mike		Apps	Subs	Gls
Man. Utd.	1992-93	5	6	0
Man. Utd.	1993-94	1	1	0
		6	**7**	**0**
Phelan, Terry		Apps	Subs	Gls
Man. City	1992-93	37	0	0
Man. City	1993-94	30	0	1
Man. City	1994-95	26	1	0
Man. City	1995-96	9	0	0
Chelsea	1995-96	12	0	0
Chelsea	1996-97	1	2	0
Everton	1996-97	15	0	0
Everton	1997-98	8	1	0
Everton	1999-00	0	1	0
		138	**5**	**1**
Phillips, David		Apps	Subs	Gls
Norwich C	1992-93	42	0	9
Nottm Forest	1994-95	38	0	1
Nottm Forest	1995-96	14	4	0
Nottm Forest	1996-97	24	3	0
		118	**7**	**10**
Phillips, Jimmy		Apps	Subs	Gls
Middlesbrough	1992-93	40	0	2
Bolton Wan.	1995-96	37	0	0
Bolton Wan.	1997-98	21	1	1
		98	**1**	**3**
Phillips, Kevin		Apps	Subs	Gls
Sunderland	1999-00	36	0	30
Sunderland	2000-01	34	0	14
Sunderland	2001-02	37	0	11
Sunderland	2002-03	32	0	6
Southampton	2003-04	28	5	12
		167	**5**	**73**
Phillips, Martin		Apps	Subs	Gls
Man. City	1995-96	2	9	0
Philpott, Lee		Apps	Subs	Gls
Leicester C	1994-95	19	4	0
Pickering, Ally		Apps	Subs	Gls
Coventry C	1993-94	1	3	0
Coventry C	1994-95	27	4	0
Coventry C	1995-96	26	4	0
		54	**11**	**0**
Piechnik, Torben		Apps	Subs	Gls
Liverpool	1992-93	15	1	0
Liverpool	1993-94	1	0	0
		16	**1**	**0**
Piercy, John		Apps	Subs	Gls
Tottenham H	1999-00	1	2	0
Tottenham H	2000-01	0	5	0
		1	**7**	**0**
Pilkington, Kevin		Apps	Subs	Gls
Man. Utd.	1994-95	0	1	0
Man. Utd.	1995-96	2	1	0
Man. Utd.	1997-98	2	0	0
		4	**2**	**0**
Piper, Matt		Apps	Subs	Gls
Leicester C	2001-02	14	2	1
Sunderland	2002-03	8	5	0
		22	**7**	**1**
Pires, Robert		Apps	Subs	Gls
Arsenal	2000-01	29	4	4
Arsenal	2001-02	27	1	9
Arsenal	2002-03	21	5	14
Arsenal	2003-04	33	3	14
		110	**13**	**41**

Player / Club	Season	Apps	Subs	Gls
Pistone, Alessandro		Apps	Subs	Gls
Newcastle U	1997-98	28	0	0
Newcastle U	1998-99	2	1	0
Newcastle U	1999-00	15	0	1
Everton	2000-01	5	2	0
Everton	2001-02	25	0	1
Everton	2002-03	10	5	0
Everton	2003-04	20	1	0
		105	**9**	**2**
Pitcher, Darren		Apps	Subs	Gls
Crystal P	1994-95	21	4	0
Platt, David		Apps	Subs	Gls
Arsenal	1995-96	27	2	6
Arsenal	1996-97	27	1	4
Arsenal	1997-98	11	20	3
		65	**23**	**13**
Platts, Mark		Apps	Subs	Gls
Sheff. Wed.	1995-96	0	2	0
Plummer, Chris		Apps	Subs	Gls
QPR	1995-96	0	1	0
Poborsky, Karel		Apps	Subs	Gls
Man. Utd.	1996-97	15	7	3
Man. Utd.	1997-98	3	7	2
		18	**14**	**5**
Pointon, Neil		Apps	Subs	Gls
Oldham Ath.	1992-93	34	0	3
Oldham Ath.	1993-94	23	2	0
		57	**2**	**3**
Pollock, Jamie		Apps	Subs	Gls
Middlesbrough	1992-93	17	5	1
Middlesbrough	1995-96	31	0	1
Bolton Wan.	1997-98	25	1	1
		73	**6**	**3**
Polston, John		Apps	Subs	Gls
Norwich C	1992-93	34	0	1
Norwich C	1993-94	24	0	0
Norwich C	1994-95	38	0	0
		96	**0**	**1**
Poole, Kevin		Apps	Subs	Gls
Leicester C	1994-95	36	0	0
Leicester C	1996-97	7	0	0
Bolton Wan.	2001-02	3	0	0
		46	**0**	**0**
Poom, Mart		Apps	Subs	Gls
Derby Co.	1996-97	4	0	0
Derby Co.	1997-98	36	0	0
Derby Co.	1998-99	15	2	0
Derby Co.	1999-00	28	0	0
Derby Co.	2000-01	32	1	0
Derby Co.	2001-02	15	0	0
Sunderland	2002-03	4	0	0
		134	**3**	**0**
Popescu, Gica		Apps	Subs	Gls
Tottenham H	1994-95	23	0	3
Porfirio, Hugo		Apps	Subs	Gls
West Ham U	1996-97	15	8	2
Nottm Forest	1998-99	3	6	1
		18	**14**	**3**
Poric, Adem		Apps	Subs	Gls
Sheff. Wed.	1993-94	2	4	0
Sheff. Wed.	1994-95	1	3	0
Sheff. Wed.	1997-98	0	4	0
		3	**11**	**0**
Postiga, Helder		Apps	Subs	Gls
Tottenham H	2003-04	9	10	1
Postma, Stefan		Apps	Subs	Gls
Aston Villa	2002-03	5	1	0
Aston Villa	2003-04	0	2	0
		5	**3**	**0**
Potter, Graham		Apps	Subs	Gls
Southampton	1996-97	2	6	0
Potts, Steve		Apps	Subs	Gls
West Ham U	1993-94	41	0	0
West Ham U	1994-95	42	0	0
West Ham U	1995-96	34	0	0
West Ham U	1996-97	17	3	0
West Ham U	1997-98	14	9	0
West Ham U	1998-99	11	8	0
West Ham U	1999-00	16	1	0
West Ham U	2000-01	2	6	0
		177	**27**	**0**
Powell, Chris		Apps	Subs	Gls
Derby Co.	1996-97	35	0	0
Derby Co.	1997-98	35	2	1
Charlton Ath	1998-99	38	0	0
Charlton Ath	2000-01	31	2	0
Charlton Ath	2001-02	35	1	1
Charlton Ath	2002-03	35	2	0
Charlton Ath	2003-04	11	5	0
		220	**12**	**2**
Powell, Darryl		Apps	Subs	Gls
Derby Co.	1996-97	27	6	1
Derby Co.	1997-98	12	11	0
Derby Co.	1998-99	30	3	0
Derby Co.	1999-00	31	0	2
Derby Co.	2000-01	27	0	1
Derby Co.	2001-02	23	0	1
Birmingham C	2002-03	3	8	0
		153	**28**	**5**
Powell, Lee		Apps	Subs	Gls
Southampton	1992-93	0	2	0
Southampton	1993-94	1	0	0
		1	**2**	**0**
Power, Lee		Apps	Subs	Gls
Norwich C	1992-93	11	7	6
Norwich C	1993-94	2	3	0
		13	**10**	**6**

Poyet, Gustavo		Apps	Subs	Gls
Chelsea	1997-98	11	3	4
Chelsea	1998-99	21	7	11
Chelsea	1999-00	25	8	10
Chelsea	2000-01	22	8	11
Tottenham H	2001-02	32	2	10
Tottenham H	2002-03	22	6	5
Tottenham H	2003-04	12	8	3
		145	**42**	**54**

Pratley, Darren		Apps	Subs	Gls
Fulham	2003-04	0	1	0

Preece, Andy		Apps	Subs	Gls
Crystal P	1994-95	17	3	4

Pressley, Steven		Apps	Subs	Gls
Coventry C	1994-95	18	1	1

Pressman, Kevin		Apps	Subs	Gls
Sheff. Wed.	1992-93	3	0	0
Sheff. Wed.	1993-94	32	0	0
Sheff. Wed.	1994-95	34	0	0
Sheff. Wed.	1995-96	30	0	0
Sheff. Wed.	1996-97	38	0	0
Sheff. Wed.	1997-98	36	0	0
Sheff. Wed.	1998-99	14	1	0
Sheff. Wed.	1999-00	18	1	0
		205	**2**	**0**

Price, Chris		Apps	Subs	Gls
Blackburn R	1992-93	2	4	0

Primus, Linvoy		Apps	Subs	Gls
Portsmouth	2003-04	19	2	0

Pringle, Martin		Apps	Subs	Gls
Charlton Ath	1998-99	15	3	3
Charlton Ath	2000-01	1	7	1
		16	**10**	**4**

Prior, Spencer		Apps	Subs	Gls
Norwich C	1993-94	13	0	0
Norwich C	1994-95	12	5	0
Leicester C	1996-97	33	1	0
Leicester C	1997-98	28	2	0
Derby Co.	1998-99	33	1	1
Derby Co.	1999-00	15	5	0
Man. City	2000-01	18	3	1
		152	**17**	**2**

Proctor, Mark		Apps	Subs	Gls
Middlesbrough	1992-93	6	5	0

Proctor, Michael		Apps	Subs	Gls
Sunderland	2002-03	11	10	2

Prunier, William		Apps	Subs	Gls
Man. Utd.	1995-96	2	0	0

Prutton, David		Apps	Subs	Gls
Southampton	2002-03	9	3	0
Southampton	2003-04	22	5	1
		31	**8**	**1**

Pugh, Danny		Apps	Subs	Gls
Man. Utd.	2002-03	0	1	0

Purse, Darren		Apps	Subs	Gls
Birmingham C	2002-03	19	1	1
Birmingham C	2003-04	9	0	0
		28	**1**	**1**

Quashie, Nigel		Apps	Subs	Gls
QPR	1995-96	11	0	0
Nottm Forest	1998-99	12	4	0
Portsmouth	2003-04	17	4	1
		40	**8**	**1**

Queudrue, Franck		Apps	Subs	Gls
Middlesbrough	2001-02	28	0	2
Middlesbrough	2002-03	29	2	1
Middlesbrough	2003-04	31	0	0
		88	**2**	**3**

Quigley, Mike		Apps	Subs	Gls
Man. City	1992-93	1	4	0
Man. City	1993-94	2	0	0
		3	**4**	**0**

Quinn, Alan		Apps	Subs	Gls
Sheff. Wed.	1997-98	0	1	0
Sheff. Wed.	1998-99	1	0	0
Sheff. Wed.	1999-00	18	1	3
		19	**2**	**3**

Quinn, Barry		Apps	Subs	Gls
Coventry C	1998-99	6	1	0
Coventry C	1999-00	5	6	0
Coventry C	2000-01	25	0	0
		36	**7**	**0**

Quinn, Mick		Apps	Subs	Gls
Coventry C	1992-93	26	0	17
Coventry C	1993-94	28	4	8
Coventry C	1994-95	3	3	0
		57	**7**	**25**

Quinn, Niall		Apps	Subs	Gls
Man. City	1992-93	39	0	9
Man. City	1993-94	14	1	5
Man. City	1994-95	24	11	8
Man. City	1995-96	24	8	8
Sunderland	1996-97	8	4	2
Sunderland	1999-00	35	2	14
Sunderland	2000-01	32	2	7
Sunderland	2001-02	24	14	6
Sunderland	2002-03	0	8	0
		200	**50**	**59**

Quinn, Rob		Apps	Subs	Gls
Crystal P	1997-98	0	1	0

Quinn, Wayne		Apps	Subs	Gls
Newcastle U	2000-01	14	1	0

Rachel, Adam		Apps	Subs	Gls
Aston Villa	1998-99	0	1	0

Rachubka, Paul		Apps	Subs	Gls
Man. Utd.	2000-01	1	0	0

Radebe, Lucas		Apps	Subs	Gls
Leeds U	1994-95	9	3	0
Leeds U	1995-96	10	3	0
Leeds U	1996-97	28	4	0
Leeds U	1997-98	26	1	0
Leeds U	1998-99	29	0	0
Leeds U	1999-00	31	0	0
Leeds U	2000-01	19	1	0
Leeds U	2002-03	16	3	0
Leeds U	2003-04	11	3	0
		179	**18**	**0**

Radosavljevic, Preki		Apps	Subs	Gls
Everton	1992-93	13	10	3
Everton	1993-94	9	14	1
		22	**24**	**4**

Raducioiu, Florin		Apps	Subs	Gls
West Ham U	1996-97	6	5	2

Radzinski, Tomasz		Apps	Subs	Gls
Everton	2001-02	23	4	6
Everton	2002-03	27	3	11
Everton	2003-04	28	6	8
		78	**13**	**25**

Rae, Alex		Apps	Subs	Gls
Sunderland	1996-97	13	10	2
Sunderland	1999-00	22	4	3
Sunderland	2000-01	18	0	2
Sunderland	2001-02	1	2	0
Wolves	2003-04	27	6	5
		81	**22**	**12**

Rahmberg, Marino		Apps	Subs	Gls
Derby Co.	1996-97	0	1	0

Rankin, Isaiah		Apps	Subs	Gls
Arsenal	1997-98	0	1	0
Bradford C	1999-00	0	9	0
Bradford C	2000-01	0	1	0
		0	**11**	**0**

Ranson, Ray		Apps	Subs	Gls
Man. City	1992-93	17	0	0

Ravanelli, Fabrizio		Apps	Subs	Gls
Middlesbrough	1996-97	33	0	16
Derby Co.	2001-02	30	1	9
		63	**1**	**25**

Ready, Karl		Apps	Subs	Gls
QPR	1992-93	2	1	0
QPR	1993-94	19	3	1
QPR	1994-95	11	2	1
QPR	1995-96	16	6	1
		48	**12**	**3**

Rebrov, Sergei		Apps	Subs	Gls
Tottenham H	2000-01	28	1	9
Tottenham H	2001-02	9	21	1
		37	**22**	**10**

Reddy, Michael		Apps	Subs	Gls
Sunderland	1999-00	0	8	1
Sunderland	2000-01	0	2	0
		0	**10**	**1**

Redfearn, Neil		Apps	Subs	Gls
Barnsley	1997-98	37	0	10
Charlton Ath	1998-99	29	1	3
Bradford C	1999-00	14	3	1
		80	**4**	**14**

Redknapp, Jamie		Apps	Subs	Gls
Liverpool	1992-93	27	2	2
Liverpool	1993-94	29	6	4
Liverpool	1994-95	36	5	3
Liverpool	1995-96	19	4	3
Liverpool	1996-97	18	5	2
Liverpool	1997-98	20	0	3
Liverpool	1998-99	33	1	8
Liverpool	1999-00	18	4	3
Liverpool	2001-02	2	2	1
Tottenham H	2002-03	14	3	3
Tottenham H	2003-04	14	3	1
		230	**35**	**33**

Redmond, Steve		Apps	Subs	Gls
Oldham Ath.	1992-93	28	3	0
Oldham Ath.	1993-94	31	2	1
		59	**5**	**1**

Reeves, Alan		Apps	Subs	Gls
Wimbledon	1994-95	31	0	3
Wimbledon	1995-96	21	3	1
Wimbledon	1996-97	0	2	0
		52	**5**	**4**

Reeves, Martin		Apps	Subs	Gls
Leicester C	2001-02	1	4	0

Regis, Cyrille		Apps	Subs	Gls
Aston Villa	1992-93	7	6	1

Rehman, Zesh		Apps	Subs	Gls
Fulham	2003-04	0	1	0

Reid, Peter		Apps	Subs	Gls
Man. City	1992-93	14	6	0
Man. City	1993-94	1	3	0
Southampton	1993-94	7	0	0
		22	**9**	**0**

Reid, Steven		Apps	Subs	Gls
Blackburn R	2003-04	9	7	0

Rennie, David		Apps	Subs	Gls
Coventry C	1992-93	9	0	0
Coventry C	1993-94	34	0	1
Coventry C	1994-95	28	0	0
Coventry C	1995-96	9	2	2
		80	**2**	**3**

Repka, Tomas		Apps	Subs	Gls
West Ham U	2001-02	31	0	0
West Ham U	2002-03	32	0	0
		63	**0**	**0**

Trevor Sinclair.

Reuser, Martijn		Apps	Subs	Gls
Ipswich T	2000-01	13	13	6
Ipswich T	2001-02	18	6	1
		31	**19**	**7**

Reyes, Jose Antonio		Apps	Subs	Gls
Arsenal	2003-04	7	6	2

Reyna, Claudio		Apps	Subs	Gls
Sunderland	2001-02	17	0	3
Sunderland	2002-03	11	0	0
Man. City	2003-04	19	4	1
		47	**4**	**4**

Ribeiro, Bruno		Apps	Subs	Gls
Leeds U	1997-98	28	1	3
Leeds U	1998-99	7	6	1
		35	**7**	**4**

Ricard, Hamilton		Apps	Subs	Gls
Middlesbrough	1998-99	32	4	15
Middlesbrough	1999-00	28	6	12
Middlesbrough	2000-01	22	5	4
Middlesbrough	2001-02	6	3	0
		88	**18**	**31**

Ricar, Ricardo		Apps	Subs	Gls
Man. Utd.	2002-03	0	1	0

Richards, Dean		Apps	Subs	Gls
Southampton	1999-00	35	0	2
Southampton	2000-01	28	0	1
Southampton	2001-02	4	0	0
Tottenham H	2001-02	24	0	2
Tottenham H	2002-03	26	0	2
Tottenham H	2003-04	23	0	0
		140	**0**	**7**

Richardson, Frazer		Apps	Subs	Gls
Leeds U	2003-04	2	2	0

Richardson, Kevin		Apps	Subs	Gls
Aston Villa	1992-93	42	0	2
Aston Villa	1993-94	40	0	5
Aston Villa	1994-95	18	1	0
Coventry C	1994-95	14	0	0
Coventry C	1995-96	33	0	0
Coventry C	1996-97	25	3	0
Coventry C	1997-98	3	0	0
Southampton	1997-98	25	3	0
		200	**7**	**7**

Richardson, Kieran		Apps	Subs	Gls
Man. Utd.	2002-03	0	2	0

Richardson, Leam		Apps	Subs	Gls
Bolton Wan.	2001-02	0	1	0

Ricketts, Michael		Apps	Subs	Gls
Bolton Wan.	2001-02	26	11	12
Bolton Wan.	2002-03	13	9	6
Middlesbrough	2002-03	5	4	1
Middlesbrough	2003-04	7	16	2
		51	**40**	**21**

Ricketts, Rohan		Apps	Subs	Gls
Tottenham H	2003-04	12	12	1

Rideout, Paul		Apps	Subs	Gls
Everton	1992-93	17	7	3
Everton	1993-94	21	3	6
Everton	1994-95	25	4	14
Everton	1995-96	19	6	6
Everton	1996-97	4	6	0
		86	**26**	**29**

Ridgewell, Liam		Apps	Subs	Gls
Aston Villa	2003-04	5	6	0

Riedle, Karl-Heinz		Apps	Subs	Gls
Liverpool	1997-98	18	7	6
Liverpool	1998-99	16	18	5
Liverpool	1999-00	0	1	0
		34	**26**	**11**

Rieper, Marc		Apps	Subs	Gls
West Ham U	1994-95	17	4	1
West Ham U	1995-96	35	1	2
West Ham U	1996-97	26	2	1
West Ham U	1997-98	5	0	1
		83	**7**	**5**

Riggott, Chris		Apps	Subs	Gls
Derby Co.	1999-00	0	1	0
Derby Co.	2000-01	29	2	3
Derby Co.	2001-02	37	0	0
Middlesbrough	2002-03	4	1	2
Middlesbrough	2003-04	14	3	0
		84	**7**	**5**

Riise, John Arne		Apps	Subs	Gls
Liverpool	2001-02	34	4	7
Liverpool	2002-03	31	6	6
Liverpool	2003-04	22	6	0
		87	**16**	**13**

Ripley, Stuart		Apps	Subs	Gls
Blackburn R	1992-93	38	2	7
Blackburn R	1993-94	40	0	4
Blackburn R	1994-95	36	1	0
Blackburn R	1995-96	28	0	0
Blackburn R	1996-97	5	8	0
Blackburn R	1997-98	25	4	2
Southampton	1998-99	16	6	0
Southampton	1999-00	18	5	1
Southampton	2000-01	1	2	0
Southampton	2001-02	1	4	0
		208	**32**	**14**

Ritchie, Andy		Apps	Subs	Gls
Oldham Ath.	1992-93	10	2	3
Oldham Ath.	1993-94	13	9	1
		23	**11**	**4**

Ritchie, Paul		Apps	Subs	Gls
Man. City	2000-01	11	1	0

Rix, Graham		Apps	Subs	Gls
Chelsea	1994-95	0	1	0

Robert, Laurent		Apps	Subs	Gls
Newcastle U	2001-02	34	2	8
Newcastle U	2002-03	25	2	5
Newcastle U	2003-04	31	4	6
		90	**8**	**19**

Roberts, Andy		Apps	Subs	Gls
Crystal P	1997-98	25	0	0
Wimbledon	1997-98	12	0	1
Wimbledon	1998-99	23	5	2
Wimbledon	1999-00	14	2	0
		74	**7**	**3**

Roberts, Ben		Apps	Subs	Gls
Middlesbrough	1996-97	9	1	0
Charlton Ath	2002-03	0	1	0
		9	**2**	**0**

Roberts, Iwan		Apps	Subs	Gls
Leicester C	1994-95	32	5	9

Roberts, Jason		Apps	Subs	Gls
West Brom	2002-03	31	1	3
Portsmouth	2003-04	4	6	1
		35	**7**	**4**

Roberts, Tony		Apps	Subs	Gls
QPR	1992-93	28	0	0
QPR	1993-94	16	0	0
QPR	1994-95	31	0	0
QPR	1995-96	5	0	0
		80	**0**	**0**

Robertson, David		Apps	Subs	Gls
Leeds U	1997-98	24	2	0

Robertson, Sandy		Apps	Subs	Gls
Coventry C	1993-94	0	3	0
Coventry C	1994-95	0	1	0
		0	**4**	**0**

Robins, Mark		Apps	Subs	Gls
Norwich C	1992-93	34	3	15
Norwich C	1993-94	9	4	1
Norwich C	1994-95	14	3	4
Leicester C	1994-95	16	1	5
Leicester C	1996-97	5	3	1
		78	**14**	**26**

Robinson, Carl		Apps	Subs	Gls
Portsmouth	2003-04	0	1	0

Robinson, John		Apps	Subs	Gls
Charlton Ath	1998-99	27	3	3
Charlton Ath	2000-01	21	8	2
Charlton Ath	2001-02	16	12	1
Charlton Ath	2002-03	10	3	0
		74	**26**	**6**

Robinson, Mark		Apps	Subs	Gls
Newcastle U	1993-94	12	4	0

Robinson, Marvin		Apps	Subs	Gls
Derby Co.	1998-99	0	1	0
Derby Co.	1999-00	3	5	0
Derby Co.	2001-02	0	2	1
		3	**8**	**1**

Robinson, Matt		Apps	Subs	Gls
Southampton	1994-95	0	1	0
Southampton	1995-96	0	5	0
Southampton	1996-97	3	4	0
Southampton	1997-98	0	1	0
		3	**11**	**0**

Robinson, Paul		Apps	Subs	Gls
Newcastle U	1999-00	2	9	0

Robinson, Paul		Apps	Subs	Gls
Watford	1999-00	29	3	0

Robinson, Paul		Apps	Subs	Gls
Leeds U	1998-99	4	1	0
Leeds U	2000-01	15	1	0
Leeds U	2002-03	38	0	0
Leeds U	2003-04	36	0	0
		93	**2**	**0**

Robinson, Steve		Apps	Subs	Gls
Tottenham H	1993-94	1	1	0

Robson, Bryan		Apps	Subs	Gls
Man. Utd.	1992-93	5	9	1
Man. Utd.	1993-94	10	5	1
Middlesbrough	1995-96	1	1	0
Middlesbrough	1996-97	1	0	0
		17	**15**	**2**

Robson, Mark		Apps	Subs	Gls
West Ham U	1993-94	1	2	0

Robson, Stewart		Apps	Subs	Gls
Coventry C	1992-93	14	1	0
Coventry C	1993-94	1	0	0
		15	**1**	**0**

Rocastle, David		Apps	Subs	Gls
Leeds U	1992-93	11	7	1
Leeds U	1993-94	6	1	1
Man. City	1993-94	21	0	2
Chelsea	1994-95	26	2	0
Chelsea	1995-96	1	0	0
		65	**10**	**4**

Roche, Lee		Apps	Subs	Gls
Man. Utd.	2002-03	0	1	0

Rodger, Simon		Apps	Subs	Gls
Crystal P	1992-93	22	1	2
Crystal P	1994-95	4	0	0
Crystal P	1997-98	27	2	2
		53	**3**	**4**

Rodri, Juliano		Apps	Subs	Gls
Everton	2002-03	0	4	0

Rodrigues, Dani		Apps	Subs	Gls
Southampton	1999-00	0	2	0

Rodriguez, Bruno		Apps	Subs	Gls
Bradford C	1999-00	0	2	0

Rogers, Alan		Apps	Subs	Gls
Nottm Forest	1998-99	34	0	4
Leicester C	2001-02	9	4	0
Leicester C	2003-04	7	1	0
		50	**5**	**4**

Rogers, Paul		Apps	Subs	Gls
Sheff. Utd.	1992-93	26	1	3
Sheff. Utd.	1993-94	24	1	3
		50	**2**	**6**

Rolling, Franck		Apps	Subs	Gls
Leicester C	1996-97	1	0	0

Ronaldo, Cristiano		Apps	Subs	Gls
Man. Utd.	2003-04	15	14	4

Rooney, Wayne		Apps	Subs	Gls
Everton	2002-03	14	19	6
Everton	2003-04	26	8	9
		40	**27**	**15**

Roque Junior, Jose Victor		Apps	Subs	Gls
Leeds U	2003-04	5	0	0

Rosario, Robert		Apps	Subs	Gls
Coventry C	1992-93	28	0	4
Nottm Forest	1992-93	10	0	1
Nottm Forest	1994-95	0	1	0
		38	**1**	**5**

Rose, Matthew		Apps	Subs	Gls
Arsenal	1995-96	1	3	0
Arsenal	1996-97	1	0	0
		2	**3**	**0**

Rosenthal, Ronny		Apps	Subs	Gls
Liverpool	1992-93	16	11	6
Liverpool	1993-94	0	3	0
Tottenham H	1993-94	11	4	2
Tottenham H	1994-95	14	6	0
Tottenham H	1995-96	26	7	1
Tottenham H	1996-97	4	16	1
		71	**47**	**10**

Rosler, Uwe		Apps	Subs	Gls
Man. City	1993-94	12	0	5
Man. City	1994-95	29	2	15
Man. City	1995-96	34	2	9
Southampton	2000-01	6	14	0
Southampton	2001-02	3	1	0
		84	**19**	**29**

Roussel, Cedric		Apps	Subs	Gls
Coventry C	1999-00	18	4	6
Coventry C	2000-01	10	7	2
		28	**11**	**8**

Rowett, Gary		Apps	Subs	Gls
Everton	1993-94	0	2	0
Everton	1994-95	2	0	0
Derby Co.	1996-97	35	0	1
Derby Co.	1997-98	32	3	1
Leicester C	2000-01	38	0	2
Leicester C	2001-02	9	2	0
Charlton Ath	2002-03	12	0	1
Charlton Ath	2003-04	1	0	0
		129	**7**	**5**

Rowland, Keith		Apps	Subs	Gls
Coventry C	1992-93	0	2	0
West Ham U	1993-94	16	7	0
West Ham U	1994-95	11	1	0
West Ham U	1995-96	19	4	0
West Ham U	1996-97	11	4	1
West Ham U	1997-98	6	1	0
		63	**19**	**1**

Roy, Bryan		Apps	Subs	Gls
Nottm Forest	1994-95	37	0	13
Nottm Forest	1995-96	25	3	8
Nottm Forest	1996-97	8	12	3
		70	**15**	**24**

Roy, Eric		Apps	Subs	Gls
Sunderland	1999-00	19	5	0
Sunderland	2000-01	1	2	0
		20	**7**	**0**

Royce, Simon		Apps	Subs	Gls
Charlton Ath	1998-99	8	0	0
Leicester C	2000-01	16	3	0
Charlton Ath	2003-04	1	0	0
		25	**3**	**0**

Ruddock, Neil		Apps	Subs	Gls
Tottenham H	1992-93	38	0	3
Liverpool	1993-94	39	0	3
Liverpool	1994-95	37	0	2
Liverpool	1995-96	18	2	5
Liverpool	1996-97	15	2	1
Liverpool	1997-98	2	0	0
West Ham U	1998-99	27	0	2
West Ham U	1999-00	12	3	0
		188	**7**	**16**

Rudi, Petter		Apps	Subs	Gls
Sheff. Wed.	1997-98	19	3	0
Sheff. Wed.	1998-99	33	1	6
Sheff. Wed.	1999-00	18	2	2
		70	**6**	**8**

Rufus, Richard		Apps	Subs	Gls
Charlton Ath	1998-99	27	0	1
Charlton Ath	2000-01	32	0	2
Charlton Ath	2001-02	10	0	1
Charlton Ath	2002-03	29	1	2
		98	**1**	**6**

Rush, Ian		Apps	Subs	Gls
Liverpool	1992-93	31	1	14
Liverpool	1993-94	41	1	14
Liverpool	1994-95	36	0	12
Liverpool	1995-96	10	10	5
Leeds U	1996-97	34	2	3
Newcastle U	1997-98	6	4	0
		158	**18**	**48**

Rush, Matthew		Apps	Subs	Gls
West Ham U	1993-94	9	1	1
West Ham U	1994-95	15	8	2
		24	**9**	**3**

Russell, Craig		Apps	Subs	Gls
Sunderland	1996-97	10	19	4

Ryan, Richie		Apps	Subs	Gls
Sunderland	2002-03	0	2	0

Sadler, Matthew		Apps	Subs	Gls
Birmingham C	2002-03	2	0	0

Saha, Louis		Apps	Subs	Gls
Newcastle U	1998-99	5	6	1
Fulham	2001-02	28	8	8
Fulham	2002-03	13	4	5
Fulham	2003-04	20	1	13
Man. Utd.	2003-04	9	3	7
		75	**22**	**34**

Saib, Moussa		Apps	Subs	Gls
Tottenham H	1997-98	3	6	1
Tottenham H	1998-99	0	4	0
		3	**10**	**1**

Sakho, Lamine		Apps	Subs	Gls
Leeds U	2003-04	9	8	1

Salako, John		Apps	Subs	Gls
Crystal P	1992-93	12	1	0
Crystal P	1994-95	39	0	4
Coventry C	1995-96	34	3	3
Coventry C	1996-97	23	1	1
Coventry C	1997-98	11	0	0
Bolton Wan.	1997-98	0	7	0
Charlton Ath	2000-01	4	13	0
Charlton Ath	2001-02	2	1	0
		125	**26**	**8**

Samuel, JLloyd		Apps	Subs	Gls
Aston Villa	1999-00	5	4	0
Aston Villa	2000-01	1	2	0
Aston Villa	2001-02	17	6	0
Aston Villa	2002-03	33	5	0
Aston Villa	2003-04	38	0	2
		94	**17**	**2**

Samways, Vinny		Apps	Subs	Gls
Tottenham H	1992-93	34	0	0
Tottenham H	1993-94	39	0	3
Everton	1994-95	14	5	1
Everton	1995-96	3	1	1
		90	**6**	**5**

Sanchez, Lawrie		Apps	Subs	Gls
Wimbledon	1992-93	23	4	4
Wimbledon	1993-94	15	0	2
Swindon T	1993-94	6	2	0
		44	**6**	**6**

Sanetti, Francesco		Apps	Subs	Gls
Sheff. Wed.	1997-98	1	1	1
Sheff. Wed.	1998-99	0	3	0
		1	**4**	**1**

Sankofa, Osei		Apps	Subs	Gls
Charlton Ath	2002-03	0	1	0

Sansom, Kenny		Apps	Subs	Gls
Coventry C	1992-93	21	0	0
Everton	1992-93	6	1	1
		27	**1**	**1**

Saunders, Dean		Apps	Subs	Gls
Liverpool	1992-93	6	0	1
Aston Villa	1992-93	35	0	12
Aston Villa	1993-94	37	1	10
Aston Villa	1994-95	39	0	15
Nottm Forest	1996-97	33	1	3
Bradford C	1999-00	28	6	3
Bradford C	2000-01	4	6	0
		182	**14**	**44**

Sava, Facundo		Apps	Subs	Gls
Fulham	2002-03	13	7	5
Fulham	2003-04	0	6	1
		13	**13**	**6**

Savage, Robbie		Apps	Subs	Gls
Leicester C	1997-98	28	7	2
Leicester C	1998-99	29	5	1
Leicester C	1999-00	35	0	1
Leicester C	2000-01	33	0	4
Leicester C	2001-02	35	0	0
Birmingham C	2002-03	33	0	4
Birmingham C	2003-04	31	0	3
		224	**12**	**15**

Scales, John		Apps	Subs	Gls
Wimbledon	1992-93	32	0	1
Wimbledon	1993-94	37	0	0
Wimbledon	1994-95	3	0	0
Liverpool	1994-95	35	0	2
Liverpool	1995-96	27	0	0
Liverpool	1996-97	3	0	0
Tottenham H	1996-97	10	2	0
Tottenham H	1997-98	9	1	0
Tottenham H	1998-99	7	0	0
Tottenham H	1999-00	3	1	0
Ipswich T	2000-01	2	0	0
		168	**4**	**3**

Schemmel, Sebastien		Apps	Subs	Gls
West Ham U	2000-01	10	2	0
West Ham U	2001-02	35	0	1
West Ham U	2002-03	15	1	0
Portsmouth	2003-04	12	2	0
		72	**5**	**1**

Schmeichel, Peter		Apps	Subs	Gls
Man. Utd.	1992-93	42	0	0
Man. Utd.	1993-94	40	0	0
Man. Utd.	1994-95	32	0	0
Man. Utd.	1995-96	36	0	0
Man. Utd.	1996-97	36	0	0
Man. Utd.	1997-98	32	0	0
Man. Utd.	1998-99	34	0	0
Aston Villa	2001-02	29	0	1
Man. City	2002-03	29	0	0
		310	**0**	**1**

Schnoor, Stefan		Apps	Subs	Gls
Derby Co.	1998-99	20	3	2
Derby Co.	1999-00	22	7	0
Derby Co.	2000-01	6	2	0
		48	**12**	**2**

Scholes, Paul		Apps	Subs	Gls
Man. Utd.	1994-95	6	11	5
Man. Utd.	1995-96	16	10	10
Man. Utd.	1996-97	16	8	3
Man. Utd.	1997-98	28	3	8
Man. Utd.	1998-99	24	7	6
Man. Utd.	1999-00	27	4	9
Man. Utd.	2000-01	28	4	6
Man. Utd.	2001-02	30	5	8
Man. Utd.	2002-03	31	2	14
Man. Utd.	2003-04	24	4	9
		230	**58**	**78**

Schwarz, Stefan		Apps	Subs	Gls
Arsenal	1994-95	34	0	2
Sunderland	1999-00	27	0	1
Sunderland	2000-01	17	3	1
Sunderland	2001-02	18	2	1
		96	**5**	**5**

Schwarzer, Mark		Apps	Subs	Gls
Middlesbrough	1996-97	7	0	0
Middlesbrough	1998-99	34	0	0
Middlesbrough	1999-00	37	0	0
Middlesbrough	2000-01	31	0	0
Middlesbrough	2001-02	21	0	0
Middlesbrough	2002-03	38	0	0
Middlesbrough	2003-04	36	0	0
		204	**0**	**0**

Scimeca, Riccardo		Apps	Subs	Gls
Aston Villa	1995-96	7	10	0
Aston Villa	1996-97	11	6	0
Aston Villa	1997-98	16	5	0
Aston Villa	1998-99	16	2	2
Leicester C	2003-04	28	1	1
		78	**24**	**3**

Scott, Andy		Apps	Subs	Gls
Sheff. Utd.	1992-93	1	1	1
Sheff. Utd.	1993-94	12	3	0
		13	**4**	**1**

Scott, Keith		Apps	Subs	Gls
Swindon T	1993-94	22	5	4

Scott, Kevin		Apps	Subs	Gls
Newcastle U	1993-94	18	0	0
Tottenham H	1993-94	12	0	1
Tottenham H	1994-95	4	0	0
Tottenham H	1995-96	0	2	0
		34	**2**	**1**

Scott, Martin		Apps	Subs	Gls
Sunderland	1996-97	15	0	1

Scott, Philip		Apps	Subs	Gls
Sheff. Wed.	1998-99	0	4	1
Sheff. Wed.	1999-00	2	3	0
		2	**7**	**1**

Scowcroft, James		Apps	Subs	Gls
Ipswich T	2000-01	22	12	4
Leicester C	2001-02	21	3	5
Leicester C	2003-04	33	2	5
		76	**17**	**14**

Sealey, Les		Apps	Subs	Gls
West Ham U	1995-96	1	1	0
West Ham U	1996-97	1	1	0
		2	**2**	**0**

Seaman, David		Apps	Subs	Gls
Arsenal	1992-93	39	0	0
Arsenal	1993-94	39	0	0
Arsenal	1994-95	31	0	0
Arsenal	1995-96	38	0	0
Arsenal	1996-97	22	0	0
Arsenal	1997-98	31	0	0
Arsenal	1998-99	32	0	0
Arsenal	1999-00	24	0	0
Arsenal	2000-01	24	0	0
Arsenal	2001-02	17	0	0
Arsenal	2002-03	28	0	0
Man. City	2003-04	19	0	0
		344	**0**	**0**

Sedgley, Steve		Apps	Subs	Gls
Tottenham H	1992-93	20	2	3
Tottenham H	1993-94	42	0	5
Ipswich T	1994-95	26	0	4
		88	**2**	**12**

Sedloski, Goce		Apps	Subs	Gls
Sheff. Wed.	1997-98	3	1	0

Segers, Hans		Apps	Subs	Gls
Wimbledon	1992-93	41	0	0
Wimbledon	1993-94	41	0	0
Wimbledon	1994-95	31	1	0
Wimbledon	1995-96	3	1	0
Tottenham H	1998-99	1	0	0
		117	**2**	**0**

Sellars, Scott		Apps	Subs	Gls
Leeds U	1992-93	6	1	0
Newcastle U	1993-94	29	1	3
Newcastle U	1994-95	12	0	0
Newcastle U	1995-96	2	4	0
Bolton Wan.	1995-96	22	0	3
Bolton Wan.	1997-98	22	0	2
		93	**6**	**8**

Selley, Ian		Apps	Subs	Gls
Arsenal	1992-93	9	0	0
Arsenal	1993-94	16	2	0
Arsenal	1994-95	10	3	0
Arsenal	1996-97	0	1	0
		35	**6**	**0**

Sereni, Matteo		Apps	Subs	Gls
Ipswich T	2001-02	25	0	0

Serrant, Carl		Apps	Subs	Gls
Newcastle U	1998-99	3	1	0
Newcastle U	1999-00	2	0	0
		5	**1**	**0**

Shaaban, Rami		Apps	Subs	Gls
Arsenal	2002-03	3	0	0

Sharp, Graeme		Apps	Subs	Gls
Oldham Ath.	1992-93	20	1	7
Oldham Ath.	1993-94	31	3	9
		51	**4**	**16**

Sharp, Kevin		Apps	Subs	Gls
Leeds U	1992-93	4	0	0
Leeds U	1993-94	7	3	0
Leeds U	1994-95	0	2	0
Leeds U	1995-96	0	1	0
		11	**6**	**0**

Sharpe, Lee		Apps	Subs	Gls
Man. Utd.	1992-93	27	0	1
Man. Utd.	1993-94	26	4	9
Man. Utd.	1994-95	26	2	3
Man. Utd.	1995-96	21	10	4
Leeds U	1996-97	26	0	5
Leeds U	1998-99	2	2	0
Bradford C	1999-00	13	5	0
Bradford C	2000-01	6	5	0
		147	**28**	**22**

Shaw, Paul		Apps	Subs	Gls
Arsenal	1994-95	0	1	0
Arsenal	1995-96	0	3	0
Arsenal	1996-97	1	7	2
		1	**11**	**2**

Shaw, Richard		Apps	Subs	Gls
Crystal P	1992-93	32	1	0
Crystal P	1994-95	41	0	0
Coventry C	1995-96	21	0	0
Coventry C	1996-97	35	0	0
Coventry C	1997-98	33	0	0
Coventry C	1998-99	36	1	0
Coventry C	1999-00	27	2	0
Coventry C	2000-01	23	1	0
		248	**5**	**0**

Shearer, Alan		Apps	Subs	Gls
Blackburn R	1992-93	21	0	16
Blackburn R	1993-94	34	6	31
Blackburn R	1994-95	42	0	34
Blackburn R	1995-96	35	0	31
Newcastle U	1996-97	31	0	25
Newcastle U	1997-98	15	2	2
Newcastle U	1998-99	29	1	14
Newcastle U	1999-00	36	1	23
Newcastle U	2000-01	19	0	5
Newcastle U	2001-02	36	1	23
Newcastle U	2002-03	35	0	17
Newcastle U	2003-04	37	0	22
		370	**11**	**243**

Sheerin, Joe		Apps	Subs	Gls
Chelsea	1996-97	0	1	0

Sheffield, Jon		Apps	Subs	Gls
Swindon T	1993-94	2	0	0

Shepherd, Paul		Apps	Subs	Gls
Leeds U	1996-97	1	0	0

Sheridan, Darren		Apps	Subs	Gls
Barnsley	1997-98	20	6	0

Sheridan, John		Apps	Subs	Gls
Sheff. Wed.	1992-93	25	0	3
Sheff. Wed.	1993-94	19	1	3

Sheff. Wed.	1994-95	34	2	1
Sheff. Wed.	1995-96	13	4	0
Sheff. Wed.	1996-97	0	2	0
Bolton Wan.	1997-98	12	0	0
		103	**9**	**7**

Sheridan, Tony		Apps	Subs	Gls
Coventry C	1992-93	1	0	0
Coventry C	1993-94	4	4	0
		5	**4**	**0**

Sheringham, Teddy		Apps	Subs	Gls
Nottm Forest	1992-93	3	0	1
Tottenham H	1992-93	38	0	21
Tottenham H	1993-94	17	2	14
Tottenham H	1994-95	41	1	18
Tottenham H	1995-96	38	0	16
Tottenham H	1996-97	29	0	7
Man. Utd.	1997-98	28	3	9
Man. Utd.	1998-99	7	10	2
Man. Utd.	1999-00	15	12	5
Man. Utd.	2000-01	23	6	15
Tottenham H	2001-02	33	1	10
Tottenham H	2002-03	34	2	12
Portsmouth	2003-04	25	7	9
		331	**44**	**139**

Sheron, Mike		Apps	Subs	Gls
Man. City	1992-93	33	5	11
Man. City	1993-94	29	4	6
Norwich C	1994-95	17	4	1
		79	**13**	**18**

Sherwood, Tim		Apps	Subs	Gls
Blackburn R	1992-93	38	1	3
Blackburn R	1993-94	38	0	2
Blackburn R	1994-95	38	0	6
Blackburn R	1995-96	33	0	3
Blackburn R	1996-97	37	0	3
Blackburn R	1997-98	29	2	5
Blackburn R	1998-99	19	0	3
Tottenham H	1998-99	12	2	2
Tottenham H	1999-00	23	4	8
Tottenham H	2000-01	31	2	2
Tottenham H	2001-02	15	4	0
Portsmouth	2003-04	7	6	0
		320	**21**	**37**

Shields, Greg		Apps	Subs	Gls
Charlton Ath	2000-01	2	2	0

Shilton, Sam		Apps	Subs	Gls
Coventry C	1997-98	2	0	0
Coventry C	1998-99	1	4	0
		3	**4**	**0**

Shipperley, Neil		Apps	Subs	Gls
Chelsea	1992-93	2	1	1
Chelsea	1993-94	18	6	4
Chelsea	1994-95	6	4	2
Southampton	1994-95	19	0	4
Southampton	1995-96	37	0	7
Southampton	1996-97	9	1	1
Crystal P	1997-98	17	9	7
Nottm Forest	1998-99	12	8	1
		120	**29**	**27**

Shirtliff, Peter		Apps	Subs	Gls
Sheff. Wed.	1992-93	20	0	0
Barnsley	1997-98	4	0	0
		24	**0**	**0**

Short, Craig		Apps	Subs	Gls
Everton	1995-96	22	1	2
Everton	1996-97	19	4	2
Everton	1997-98	27	4	0
Everton	1998-99	22	0	0
Blackburn R	2001-02	21	1	0
Blackburn R	2002-03	26	1	1
Blackburn R	2003-04	19	0	1
		156	**11**	**6**

Shuker, Chris		Apps	Subs	Gls
Man. City	2002-03	1	2	0

Shutt, Carl		Apps	Subs	Gls
Leeds U	1992-93	6	8	0
Man. City	1993-94	5	1	0
		11	**9**	**0**

Sibierski, Antoine		Apps	Subs	Gls
Man. City	2003-04	18	15	5

Sibon, Gerald		Apps	Subs	Gls
Sheff. Wed.	1999-00	12	16	5

Sigurdsson, Larus		Apps	Subs	Gls
West Brom	2002-03	23	6	0

Silenzi, Andrea		Apps	Subs	Gls
Nottm Forest	1995-96	3	7	0
Nottm Forest	1996-97	1	1	0
		4	**8**	**0**

Silva, Gilberto		Apps	Subs	Gls
Arsenal	2002-03	32	3	0
Arsenal	2003-04	29	3	4
		61	**6**	**4**

Silvestre, Mickael		Apps	Subs	Gls
Man. Utd.	1999-00	30	1	0
Man. Utd.	2000-01	25	5	1
Man. Utd.	2001-02	31	4	0
Man. Utd.	2002-03	34	0	1
Man. Utd.	2003-04	33	1	0
		153	**11**	**2**

Silvinho (Silvio de Campos)		Apps	Subs	Gls
Arsenal	1999-00	23	8	1
Arsenal	2000-01	23	1	2
		46	**9**	**3**

Simonsen, Steve		Apps	Subs	Gls
Everton	1999-00	0	1	0
Everton	2000-01	0	1	0
Everton	2001-02	25	0	0
Everton	2002-03	2	0	0
Everton	2003-04	1	0	0
		28	**2**	**0**

Simpson, Fitzroy		Apps	Subs	Gls
Man. City	1992-93	27	2	1
Man. City	1993-94	12	3	0
Man. City	1994-95	10	6	2
		49	**11**	**3**

Simpson, Paul		Apps	Subs	Gls
Derby Co.	1996-97	0	19	2
Derby Co.	1997-98	1	0	0
		1	**19**	**2**

Sinama-Pongolle, Florent		Apps	Subs	Gls
Liverpool	2003-04	3	12	2

Sinclair, Frank		Apps	Subs	Gls
Chelsea	1992-93	32	0	0
Chelsea	1993-94	35	0	0
Chelsea	1994-95	35	0	3
Chelsea	1995-96	12	1	1
Chelsea	1996-97	17	3	1
Chelsea	1997-98	20	2	1
Leicester C	1998-99	30	1	1
Leicester C	1999-00	34	0	0
Leicester C	2000-01	14	3	0
Leicester C	2001-02	33	2	0
Leicester C	2003-04	11	3	1
		273	**15**	**8**

Sinclair, Trevor		Apps	Subs	Gls
QPR	1993-94	30	2	4
QPR	1994-95	32	1	4
QPR	1995-96	37	0	2
West Ham U	1997-98	14	0	7
West Ham U	1998-99	36	0	7
West Ham U	1999-00	36	0	7
West Ham U	2000-01	19	0	3
West Ham U	2001-02	34	0	5
West Ham U	2002-03	36	2	8
Man. City	2003-04	20	9	1
		294	**14**	**48**

Sinnott, Lee		Apps	Subs	Gls
Crystal P	1992-93	18	1	0

Sinton, Andy		Apps	Subs	Gls
QPR	1992-93	36	0	7
Sheff. Wed.	1993-94	25	0	3
Sheff. Wed.	1994-95	22	3	0
Sheff. Wed.	1995-96	7	3	0
Tottenham H	1995-96	8	1	0
Tottenham H	1996-97	32	1	6
Tottenham H	1997-98	14	5	0
Tottenham H	1998-99	12	10	0
		156	**23**	**16**

Skinner, Justin		Apps	Subs	Gls
Wimbledon	1992-93	1	0	0
Wimbledon	1995-96	1	0	0
		2	**0**	**0**

Slabber, Jamie		Apps	Subs	Gls
Tottenham H	2002-03	0	1	0

Slade, Steve		Apps	Subs	Gls
Tottenham H	1995-96	1	4	0

Slater, Robbie		Apps	Subs	Gls
Blackburn R	1994-95	12	6	0
West Ham U	1995-96	16	6	2
West Ham U	1996-97	2	1	0
Southampton	1996-97	22	8	2
Southampton	1997-98	3	8	0
		55	**29**	**4**

Slater, Stuart		Apps	Subs	Gls
Ipswich T	1993-94	28	0	1
Ipswich T	1994-95	22	5	1
		50	**5**	**2**

Slaven, Bernie		Apps	Subs	Gls
Middlesbrough	1992-93	13	5	4

Small, Bryan		Apps	Subs	Gls
Aston Villa	1992-93	10	4	0
Aston Villa	1993-94	8	1	0
Aston Villa	1994-95	5	0	0
Bolton Wan.	1995-96	1	0	0
		24	**5**	**0**

Smart, Allan		Apps	Subs	Gls
Watford	1999-00	13	1	5

Smertin, Alexei		Apps	Subs	Gls
Portsmouth	2003-04	23	3	0

Smicer, Vladimir		Apps	Subs	Gls
Liverpool	1999-00	13	8	1
Liverpool	2000-01	16	11	2
Liverpool	2001-02	13	9	4
Liverpool	2002-03	10	11	0
Liverpool	2003-04	15	5	3
		67	**44**	**10**

Smith, Alan		Apps	Subs	Gls
Leeds U	1998-99	15	7	7
Leeds U	1999-00	20	6	4
Leeds U	2000-01	26	7	11
Leeds U	2001-02	19	4	4
Leeds U	2002-03	33	0	3
Leeds U	2003-04	35	0	9
		148	**24**	**38**

Smith, Alan		Apps	Subs	Gls
Arsenal	1992-93	27	4	3
Arsenal	1993-94	21	4	3
Arsenal	1994-95	17	2	2
		65	**10**	**8**

Smith, Dave		Apps	Subs	Gls
Norwich C	1992-93	5	1	0
Norwich C	1993-94	5	2	0
		10	**3**	**0**

Smith, David		Apps	Subs	Gls
Coventry C	1992-93	6	0	1

Smith, Jeff		Apps	Subs	Gls
Bolton Wan.	2001-02	0	1	0

Smith, Jamie		Apps	Subs	Gls
Crystal P	1997-98	16	2	0

Smith, Martin		Apps	Subs	Gls
Sunderland	1996-97	6	5	0

Smith, Richard		Apps	Subs	Gls
Leicester C	1994-95	10	2	0

Smith, Tommy		Apps	Subs	Gls
Watford	1999-00	13	9	2

Sneekes, Richard		Apps	Subs	Gls
Bolton Wan.	1995-96	14	3	1

Snodin, Ian		Apps	Subs	Gls
Everton	1992-93	19	1	1
Everton	1993-94	28	1	0
Everton	1994-95	2	1	0
		49	**3**	**1**

Solano, Nolberto		Apps	Subs	Gls
Newcastle U	1998-99	24	5	6
Newcastle U	1999-00	29	1	3
Newcastle U	2000-01	31	2	6
Newcastle U	2001-02	37	0	7
Newcastle U	2002-03	29	2	7
Newcastle U	2003-04	8	4	0
Aston Villa	2003-04	10	0	0
		168	**14**	**29**

Solbakken, Stale		Apps	Subs	Gls
Wimbledon	1997-98	4	2	1

Solis, Mauricio		Apps	Subs	Gls
Derby Co.	1996-97	0	2	0
Derby Co.	1997-98	3	6	0
		3	**8**	**0**

Solskjaer, Ole Gunnar		Apps	Subs	Gls
Man. Utd.	1996-97	25	8	18
Man. Utd.	1997-98	15	7	6
Man. Utd.	1998-99	9	10	12
Man. Utd.	1999-00	15	13	12
Man. Utd.	2000-01	19	12	11
Man. Utd.	2001-02	23	7	17
Man. Utd.	2002-03	29	8	9
Man. Utd.	2003-04	7	6	0
		142	**71**	**85**

Soltvedt, Trond Egil		Apps	Subs	Gls
Coventry C	1997-98	26	4	1
Coventry C	1998-99	21	6	2
Southampton	1999-00	17	7	1
Southampton	2000-01	3	3	1
		67	**20**	**5**

Soma, Ragnvald		Apps	Subs	Gls
West Ham U	2000-01	2	2	0
West Ham U	2001-02	1	2	0
		3	**4**	**0**

Sommeil, David		Apps	Subs	Gls
Man. City	2002-03	14	0	1
Man. City	2003-04	18	0	1
		32	**0**	**2**

Sommer, Jurgen		Apps	Subs	Gls
QPR	1995-96	33	0	0

Song, Rigobert		Apps	Subs	Gls
Liverpool	1998-99	10	3	0
Liverpool	1999-00	14	4	0
Liverpool	2000-01	3	0	0
West Ham U	2000-01	18	1	0
West Ham U	2001-02	5	0	0
		50	**8**	**0**

Sonner, Danny		Apps	Subs	Gls
Sheff. Wed.	1998-99	24	2	3
Sheff. Wed.	1999-00	18	9	0
		42	**11**	**3**

Sorensen, Thomas		Apps	Subs	Gls
Sunderland	1999-00	37	0	0
Sunderland	2000-01	34	0	0
Sunderland	2001-02	34	0	0
Sunderland	2002-03	21	0	0
Aston Villa	2003-04	38	0	0
		164	**0**	**0**

Southall, Nicky		Apps	Subs	Gls
Bolton Wan.	2001-02	10	8	1

Southall, Neville		Apps	Subs	Gls
Everton	1992-93	40	0	0
Everton	1993-94	42	0	0
Everton	1994-95	41	0	0
Everton	1995-96	38	0	0
Everton	1996-97	34	0	0
Everton	1997-98	12	0	0
Bradford C	1999-00	1	0	0
		208	**0**	**0**

Southgate, Gareth		Apps	Subs	Gls
Crystal P	1992-93	33	0	3
Crystal P	1994-95	42	0	3
Aston Villa	1995-96	31	0	1
Aston Villa	1996-97	28	0	1
Aston Villa	1997-98	32	0	0
Aston Villa	1998-99	38	0	1
Aston Villa	1999-00	31	0	2
Aston Villa	2000-01	31	0	2
Middlesbrough	2001-02	37	0	1
Middlesbrough	2002-03	36	0	2
Middlesbrough	2003-04	27	0	1
		366	**0**	**17**

Spackman, Nigel		Apps	Subs	Gls
Chelsea	1992-93	6	0	0
Chelsea	1993-94	5	4	0
Chelsea	1994-95	36	0	0
Chelsea	1995-96	13	3	0
		60	**7**	**0**

Thomas Sorensen.

Spedding, Duncan		Apps	Subs	Gls
Southampton	1997-98	4	3	0

Speed, Gary		Apps	Subs	Gls
Leeds U	1992-93	39	0	7
Leeds U	1993-94	35	1	10
Leeds U	1994-95	39	0	3
Leeds U	1995-96	29	0	2
Everton	1996-97	37	0	9
Everton	1997-98	21	0	7
Newcastle U	1997-98	13	0	1
Newcastle U	1998-99	34	4	4
Newcastle U	1999-00	36	0	9
Newcastle U	2000-01	35	0	5
Newcastle U	2001-02	28	1	5
Newcastle U	2002-03	23	1	2
Newcastle U	2003-04	37	1	3
		406	**8**	**67**

Speedie, David		Apps	Subs	Gls
Southampton	1992-93	11	0	0

Spencer, John		Apps	Subs	Gls
Chelsea	1992-93	13	10	7
Chelsea	1993-94	13	6	5
Chelsea	1994-95	26	3	11
Chelsea	1995-96	23	5	13
Chelsea	1996-97	0	4	0
Everton	1997-98	3	3	0
Everton	1998-99	2	1	0
		80	**32**	**36**

Spink, Nigel		Apps	Subs	Gls
Aston Villa	1992-93	25	0	0
Aston Villa	1993-94	14	1	0
Aston Villa	1994-95	12	1	0
Aston Villa	1995-96	0	2	0
		51	**4**	**0**

Srnicek, Pavel		Apps	Subs	Gls
Newcastle U	1993-94	21	0	0
Newcastle U	1994-95	38	0	0
Newcastle U	1995-96	14	1	0
Newcastle U	1996-97	22	0	0
Newcastle U	1997-98	1	0	0
Sheff. Wed.	1998-99	24	0	0
Sheff. Wed.	1999-00	20	0	0
Portsmouth	2003-04	3	0	0
		143	**1**	**0**

Stam, Jaap		Apps	Subs	Gls
Man. Utd.	1998-99	30	0	1
Man. Utd.	1999-00	33	0	0
Man. Utd.	2000-01	15	0	0
Man. Utd.	2001-02	1	0	0
		79	**0**	**1**

Stamp, Phil		Apps	Subs	Gls
Middlesbrough	1995-96	11	1	2
Middlesbrough	1996-97	15	9	1
Middlesbrough	1998-99	5	11	2
Middlesbrough	1999-00	13	3	0
Middlesbrough	2000-01	11	8	1
Middlesbrough	2001-02	3	3	0
		58	**35**	**6**

Stanic, Mario		Apps	Subs	Gls
Chelsea	2000-01	8	4	2
Chelsea	2001-02	18	9	1
Chelsea	2002-03	13	5	4
Chelsea	2003-04	0	2	0
		39	**20**	**7**

Staunton, Steve		Apps	Subs	Gls
Aston Villa	1992-93	42	0	2
Aston Villa	1993-94	24	0	2
Aston Villa	1994-95	34	1	5
Aston Villa	1995-96	11	2	0
Aston Villa	1996-97	30	0	2

Aston Villa	1997-98	27	0	1
Liverpool	1998-99	31	0	0
Liverpool	1999-00	7	5	0
Liverpool	2000-01	0	1	0
Aston Villa	2000-01	13	1	0
Aston Villa	2001-02	30	3	0
Aston Villa	2002-03	22	4	0
		271	**17**	**12**

Stead, Jonathan		Apps	Subs	Gls
Blackburn R	2003-04	13	0	6

Stefanovic, Dejan		Apps	Subs	Gls
Sheff. Wed.	1995-96	5	1	0
Sheff. Wed.	1996-97	27	2	2
Sheff. Wed.	1997-98	19	1	2
Sheff. Wed.	1998-99	8	3	0
Portsmouth	2003-04	32	0	3
		91	**7**	**7**

Stein, Mark		Apps	Subs	Gls
Chelsea	1993-94	18	0	13
Chelsea	1994-95	21	3	8
Chelsea	1995-96	7	1	0
		46	**4**	**21**

Stejskal, Jan		Apps	Subs	Gls
QPR	1992-93	14	1	0
QPR	1993-94	26	0	0
		40	**1**	**0**

Stensaas, Stale		Apps	Subs	Gls
Nottm Forest	1998-99	6	1	0

Stepanovs, Igors		Apps	Subs	Gls
Arsenal	2000-01	9	0	0
Arsenal	2001-02	6	0	0
Arsenal	2002-03	2	0	0
		17	**0**	**0**

Sterland, Mel		Apps	Subs	Gls
Leeds U	1992-93	3	0	0

Stevenson, Jon		Apps	Subs	Gls
Leicester C	2001-02	0	6	1

Stewart, Jordan		Apps	Subs	Gls
Leicester C	1999-00	0	1	0
Leicester C	2001-02	9	3	0
Leicester C	2003-04	16	9	1
		25	**13**	**1**

Stewart, Marcus		Apps	Subs	Gls
Ipswich T	2000-01	33	1	19
Ipswich T	2001-02	20	8	6
Sunderland	2002-03	9	10	1
		62	**19**	**26**

Stewart, Michael		Apps	Subs	Gls
Man. Utd.	2000-01	3	0	0
Man. Utd.	2001-02	2	1	0
Man. Utd.	2002-03	0	1	0
		5	**2**	**0**

Stewart, Paul		Apps	Subs	Gls
Liverpool	1992-93	21	3	1
Liverpool	1993-94	7	1	0
Sunderland	1996-97	20	4	4
		48	**8**	**5**

Stewart, Simon		Apps	Subs	Gls
Sheff. Wed.	1992-93	6	0	0

Stimac, Igor		Apps	Subs	Gls
Derby Co.	1996-97	21	0	1
Derby Co.	1997-98	22	0	1
Derby Co.	1998-99	14	0	0
West Ham U	1999-00	24	0	1
West Ham U	2000-01	19	0	0
		100	**0**	**3**

Stockdale, Robbie		Apps	Subs	Gls
Middlesbrough	1998-99	17	2	0
Middlesbrough	1999-00	6	5	1
Middlesbrough	2001-02	26	2	1
Middlesbrough	2002-03	12	2	0
Middlesbrough	2003-04	0	2	0
		61	**13**	**2**

Stockwell, Mick		Apps	Subs	Gls
Ipswich T	1992-93	38	1	4
Ipswich T	1993-94	42	0	1
Ipswich T	1994-95	14	1	0
		94	**2**	**5**

Stolcers, Andrejs		Apps	Subs	Gls
Fulham	2001-02	0	5	0
Fulham	2002-03	0	5	0
		0	**10**	**0**

Stone, Steve		Apps	Subs	Gls
Nottm Forest	1992-93	11	1	1
Nottm Forest	1994-95	41	0	5
Nottm Forest	1995-96	34	0	7
Nottm Forest	1996-97	5	0	0
Nottm Forest	1998-99	26	0	3
Aston Villa	1998-99	9	1	0
Aston Villa	1999-00	10	14	1
Aston Villa	2000-01	33	1	2
Aston Villa	2001-02	14	8	1
Portsmouth	2003-04	29	3	2
		212	**28**	**22**

Strachan, Gavin		Apps	Subs	Gls
Coventry C	1997-98	2	7	0
Coventry C	1999-00	1	2	0
Coventry C	2000-01	2	0	0
		5	**9**	**0**

Strachan, Gordon		Apps	Subs	Gls
Leeds U	1992-93	25	6	4
Leeds U	1993-94	32	1	3
Leeds U	1994-95	5	1	0
Coventry C	1994-95	5	0	0
Coventry C	1995-96	5	7	0
Coventry C	1996-97	3	6	0
		75	**21**	**7**

Strandli, Frank		Apps	Subs	Gls
Leeds U	1992-93	5	5	2
Leeds U	1993-94	0	4	0
		5	**9**	**2**

Strong, Greg		Apps	Subs	Gls
Bolton Wan.	1995-96	0	1	0

Strupar, Branko		Apps	Subs	Gls
Derby Co.	1999-00	13	2	5
Derby Co.	2000-01	7	2	6
Derby Co.	2001-02	8	4	4
		28	**8**	**15**

Stuart, Graham		Apps	Subs	Gls
Chelsea	1992-93	31	8	9
Everton	1993-94	26	4	3
Everton	1994-95	20	8	3
Everton	1995-96	27	2	9
Everton	1996-97	29	6	5
Everton	1997-98	14	0	2
Charlton Ath	1998-99	9	0	3
Charlton Ath	2000-01	33	2	5
Charlton Ath	2001-02	31	0	3
Charlton Ath	2002-03	3	1	0
Charlton Ath	2003-04	23	5	3
		246	**36**	**45**

Stubbs, Alan		Apps	Subs	Gls
Bolton Wan.	1995-96	24	1	4
Everton	2001-02	29	2	2
Everton	2002-03	34	1	0
Everton	2003-04	25	2	0
		112	**6**	**6**

Sturridge, Dean		Apps	Subs	Gls
Derby Co.	1996-97	29	1	11
Derby Co.	1997-98	24	6	9
Derby Co.	1998-99	23	6	5
Derby Co.	1999-00	14	11	6
Derby Co.	2000-01	3	11	1
Leicester C	2000-01	12	1	3
Leicester C	2001-02	8	1	3
Wolves	2003-04	2	3	0
		115	**40**	**38**

Suker, Davor		Apps	Subs	Gls
Arsenal	1999-00	8	14	8
West Ham U	2000-01	7	4	2
		15	**18**	**10**

Sukur, Hakan		Apps	Subs	Gls
Blackburn R	2002-03	7	2	2

Sullivan, Neil		Apps	Subs	Gls
Wimbledon	1992-93	1	0	0
Wimbledon	1993-94	1	1	0
Wimbledon	1994-95	11	0	0
Wimbledon	1995-96	16	0	0
Wimbledon	1996-97	36	0	0
Wimbledon	1997-98	38	0	0
Wimbledon	1998-99	38	0	0
Wimbledon	1999-00	37	0	0
Tottenham H	2000-01	35	0	0
Tottenham H	2001-02	29	0	0
Chelsea	2003-04	4	0	0
		246	**1**	**0**

Summerbee, Nicky		Apps	Subs	Gls
Swindon T	1993-94	36	2	3
Man. City	1994-95	39	2	1
Man. City	1995-96	33	4	1
Sunderland	1999-00	29	3	1
		137	**11**	**6**

Summerbell, Mark		Apps	Subs	Gls
Middlesbrough	1995-96	0	1	0
Middlesbrough	1996-97	0	2	0
Middlesbrough	1998-99	7	4	0
Middlesbrough	1999-00	16	3	0
Middlesbrough	2000-01	5	2	1
		28	**12**	**1**

Sutch, Daryl		Apps	Subs	Gls
Norwich C	1992-93	14	8	2
Norwich C	1993-94	1	2	0
Norwich C	1994-95	20	10	1
		35	**20**	**3**

Sutton, Chris		Apps	Subs	Gls
Norwich C	1992-93	32	6	8
Norwich C	1993-94	41	0	25
Blackburn R	1994-95	40	0	15
Blackburn R	1995-96	9	4	0
Blackburn R	1996-97	24	1	11
Blackburn R	1997-98	35	0	18
Blackburn R	1998-99	17	0	3
Chelsea	1999-00	21	7	1
		219	**18**	**81**

Svensson, Anders		Apps	Subs	Gls
Southampton	2001-02	33	1	4
Southampton	2002-03	26	7	2
Southampton	2003-04	17	13	0
		76	**21**	**6**

Svensson, Mathias		Apps	Subs	Gls
Charlton Ath	2000-01	18	4	5
Charlton Ath	2001-02	6	6	0
Charlton Ath	2002-03	4	11	0
Charlton Ath	2003-04	1	2	0
		29	**23**	**5**

Svensson, Michael		Apps	Subs	Gls
Southampton	2002-03	33	1	2
Southampton	2003-04	26	0	2
		59	**1**	**4**

Swailes, Chris		Apps	Subs	Gls
Ipswich T	1994-95	4	0	0

Swierczewski, Piotr		Apps	Subs	Gls
Birmingham C	2002-03	0	1	0

Symons, Kit		Apps	Subs	Gls
Man. City	1995-96	38	0	2
Fulham	2001-02	2	2	0
		40	**2**	**2**

Taggart, Gerry		Apps	Subs	Gls
Bolton Wan.	1995-96	11	0	1
Bolton Wan.	1997-98	14	1	0
Leicester C	1998-99	9	6	0
Leicester C	1999-00	30	1	6
Leicester C	2000-01	24	0	2
Leicester C	2001-02	0	1	0
Leicester C	2003-04	9	0	0
		97	**9**	**9**

Taibi, Massimo		Apps	Subs	Gls
Man. Utd.	1999-00	4	0	0

Tal, Idan		Apps	Subs	Gls
Everton	2000-01	12	10	2
Everton	2001-02	1	6	0
		13	**16**	**2**

Talboys, Steve		Apps	Subs	Gls
Wimbledon	1992-93	3	4	0
Wimbledon	1993-94	6	1	0
Wimbledon	1994-95	7	0	1
Wimbledon	1995-96	3	2	0
		19	**7**	**1**

Tanner, Adam		Apps	Subs	Gls
Ipswich T	1994-95	9	1	2

Tanner, Nick		Apps	Subs	Gls
Liverpool	1992-93	2	2	0

Taricco, Mauricio		Apps	Subs	Gls
Tottenham H	1998-99	12	1	0
Tottenham H	1999-00	29	0	0
Tottenham H	2000-01	2	3	0
Tottenham H	2001-02	30	0	0
Tottenham H	2002-03	21	0	1
Tottenham H	2003-04	31	1	1
		125	**5**	**2**

Tarnat, Michael		Apps	Subs	Gls
Man. City	2003-04	32	0	3

Tavlaridis, Stathis		Apps	Subs	Gls
Arsenal	2002-03	0	1	0

Taylor, Ian		Apps	Subs	Gls
Sheff. Wed.	1994-95	9	5	1
Aston Villa	1994-95	22	0	1
Aston Villa	1995-96	24	1	3
Aston Villa	1996-97	29	5	2
Aston Villa	1997-98	30	2	6
Aston Villa	1998-99	31	2	4
Aston Villa	1999-00	25	4	5
Aston Villa	2000-01	25	4	4
Aston Villa	2001-02	7	9	3
Aston Villa	2002-03	9	4	0
		211	**36**	**29**

Taylor, Maik		Apps	Subs	Gls
Southampton	1996-97	18	0	0
Fulham	2001-02	1	0	0
Fulham	2002-03	18	1	0
Birmingham C	2003-04	34	0	0
		71	**1**	**0**

Taylor, Martin		Apps	Subs	Gls
Blackburn R	1998-99	1	2	0
Blackburn R	2001-02	12	7	0
Blackburn R	2002-03	29	4	2
Blackburn R	2003-04	10	1	0
Birmingham C	2003-04	11	1	1
		63	**15**	**3**

Taylor, Martin		Apps	Subs	Gls
Derby Co.	1996-97	3	0	0

Taylor, Matthew		Apps	Subs	Gls
Portsmouth	2003-04	18	12	0

Taylor, Bob		Apps	Subs	Gls
Bolton Wan.	1997-98	10	2	3
West Brom	2002-03	2	2	0
		12	**4**	**3**

Taylor, Scott		Apps	Subs	Gls
Leicester C	1996-97	20	5	0

Taylor, Scott		Apps	Subs	Gls
Bolton Wan.	1995-96	0	1	0

Taylor, Shaun		Apps	Subs	Gls
Swindon T	1993-94	42	0	4

Teale, Shaun		Apps	Subs	Gls
Aston Villa	1992-93	39	0	1
Aston Villa	1993-94	37	1	1
Aston Villa	1994-95	28	0	0
		104	**1**	**2**

Taylor, Steven		Apps	Subs	Gls
Newcastle U	2003-04	1	0	0

Taylor, Stuart		Apps	Subs	Gls
Arsenal	2001-02	9	1	0
Arsenal	2002-03	7	1	0
		16	**2**	**0**

Tebily, Olivier		Apps	Subs	Gls
Birmingham C	2002-03	12	0	0
Birmingham C	2003-04	17	10	0
		29	**10**	**0**

Telfer, Paul		Apps	Subs	Gls
Coventry C	1995-96	31	0	1
Coventry C	1996-97	31	3	0
Coventry C	1997-98	33	0	3
Coventry C	1998-99	30	2	2
Coventry C	1999-00	26	4	0
Coventry C	2000-01	27	4	0
Southampton	2001-02	27	1	1
Southampton	2002-03	26	7	0
Southampton	2003-04	33	4	0
		264	**25**	**7**

Ten Heuvel, Laurens		Apps	Subs	Gls
Barnsley	1997-98	0	2	0

Terrier, David		Apps	Subs	Gls
West Ham U	1997-98	0	1	0

Terry, John		Apps	Subs	Gls
Chelsea	1998-99	0	2	0
Chelsea	1999-00	2	2	0
Chelsea	2000-01	19	3	1
Chelsea	2001-02	32	1	1
Chelsea	2002-03	16	4	3
Chelsea	2003-04	33	0	2
		102	**12**	**7**

Tessem, Jo		Apps	Subs	Gls
Southampton	1999-00	23	2	4
Southampton	2000-01	27	6	4
Southampton	2001-02	7	15	2
Southampton	2002-03	9	18	2
Southampton	2003-04	1	2	0
		67	**43**	**12**

Thatcher, Ben		Apps	Subs	Gls
Wimbledon	1996-97	9	0	0
Wimbledon	1997-98	23	3	0
Wimbledon	1998-99	31	0	0
Wimbledon	1999-00	19	1	0
Tottenham H	2000-01	10	2	0
Tottenham H	2001-02	11	1	0
Tottenham H	2002-03	8	4	0
Leicester C	2003-04	28	1	1
		139	**12**	**1**

Thelwell, Alton		Apps	Subs	Gls
Tottenham H	2000-01	13	3	0
Tottenham H	2001-02	0	2	0
		13	**5**	**0**

Thirlwell, Paul		Apps	Subs	Gls
Sunderland	1999-00	7	1	0
Sunderland	2000-01	3	2	0
Sunderland	2001-02	11	3	0
Sunderland	2002-03	12	7	0
		33	**13**	**0**

Thomas, Tony		Apps	Subs	Gls
Everton	1997-98	6	1	0
Everton	1998-99	0	1	0
		6	**2**	**0**

Thomas, Danny		Apps	Subs	Gls
Leicester C	1999-00	0	3	0

Thomas, Geoff		Apps	Subs	Gls
Crystal P	1992-93	28	1	2
Nottm Forest	1998-99	5	0	1
		33	**1**	**3**

Thomas, Jerome		Apps	Subs	Gls
Charlton Ath	2003-04	0	1	0

Thomas, Michael		Apps	Subs	Gls
Liverpool	1992-93	6	2	1
Liverpool	1993-94	1	6	0
Liverpool	1994-95	16	7	0
Liverpool	1995-96	18	9	1
Liverpool	1996-97	29	2	3
Liverpool	1997-98	10	1	1
		80	**27**	**6**

Thomas, Scott		Apps	Subs	Gls
Man. City	1994-95	0	2	0

Thome, Emerson		Apps	Subs	Gls
Sheff. Wed.	1997-98	6	0	0
Sheff. Wed.	1998-99	38	0	1
Sheff. Wed.	1999-00	16	1	0
Chelsea	1999-00	18	2	0
Chelsea	2000-01	1	0	0
Sunderland	2000-01	30	1	1
Sunderland	2001-02	12	0	1
Sunderland	2002-03	1	0	0
Bolton Wan.	2003-04	25	1	0
		147	**5**	**3**

Thompson, Alan		Apps	Subs	Gls
Bolton Wan.	1995-96	23	3	1
Bolton Wan.	1997-98	33	0	9
Aston Villa	1998-99	20	5	2
Aston Villa	1999-00	16	5	2
		92	**13**	**14**

Thompson, David		Apps	Subs	Gls
Liverpool	1996-97	0	2	0
Liverpool	1997-98	1	4	1
Liverpool	1998-99	4	10	1
Liverpool	1999-00	19	8	3
Coventry C	2000-01	22	3	3
Blackburn R	2002-03	23	0	4
Blackburn R	2003-04	10	1	1
		79	**28**	**13**

Thompson, Garry		Apps	Subs	Gls
QPR	1992-93	0	4	0

Thompson, Neil		Apps	Subs	Gls
Ipswich T	1992-93	31	0	3
Ipswich T	1993-94	32	0	0
Ipswich T	1994-95	9	1	0
Barnsley	1997-98	3	0	0
		75	**1**	**3**

Thompson, Steve		Apps	Subs	Gls
Leicester C	1994-95	16	3	0

Thomsen, Claus		Apps	Subs	Gls
Ipswich T	1994-95	31	2	5
Everton	1996-97	15	1	0
Everton	1997-98	2	6	1
		48	**9**	**6**

Thomson, Andy		Apps	Subs	Gls
Swindon T	1993-94	1	0	0

Thorn, Andy		Apps	Subs	Gls
Crystal P	1992-93	34	0	1

Player / Club	Season	Apps	Subs	Gls
Wimbledon	1994-95	22	1	1
Wimbledon	1995-96	11	3	0
		67	**4**	**2**
Thornley, Ben		*Apps*	*Subs*	*Gls*
Man. Utd.	1993-94	0	1	0
Man. Utd.	1995-96	0	1	0
Man. Utd.	1996-97	1	1	0
Man. Utd.	1997-98	0	5	0
		1	**8**	**0**
Thornton, Sean		*Apps*	*Subs*	*Gls*
Sunderland	2002-03	11	0	1
Thorstvedt, Erik		*Apps*	*Subs*	*Gls*
Tottenham H	1992-93	25	2	0
Tottenham H	1993-94	32	0	0
Tottenham H	1994-95	1	0	0
		58	**2**	**0**
Tiatto, Danny		*Apps*	*Subs*	*Gls*
Man. City	2000-01	31	2	2
Man. City	2002-03	10	3	0
Man. City	2003-04	1	4	0
		42	**9**	**2**
Tie Li		*Apps*	*Subs*	*Gls*
Everton	2002-03	28	1	0
Everton	2003-04	4	1	0
		32	**2**	**0**
Tihinen, Hannu		*Apps*	*Subs*	*Gls*
West Ham U	2000-01	5	3	0
Tiler, Carl		*Apps*	*Subs*	*Gls*
Nottm Forest	1992-93	37	0	0
Nottm Forest	1994-95	3	0	0
Aston Villa	1995-96	1	0	0
Aston Villa	1996-97	9	2	1
Everton	1997-98	19	0	1
Everton	1998-99	2	0	0
Charlton Ath	1998-99	27	0	1
Charlton Ath	2000-01	7	0	0
		105	**2**	**3**
Tinkler, Eric		*Apps*	*Subs*	*Gls*
Barnsley	1997-98	21	4	2
Tinkler, Mark		*Apps*	*Subs*	*Gls*
Leeds U	1992-93	5	2	0
Leeds U	1993-94	0	3	0
Leeds U	1994-95	3	0	0
Leeds U	1995-96	5	4	0
Leeds U	1996-97	1	2	0
		14	**11**	**0**
Tisdale, Paul		*Apps*	*Subs*	*Gls*
Southampton	1994-95	0	7	0
Southampton	1995-96	5	4	1
		5	**11**	**1**
Toda, Kazuyuki		*Apps*	*Subs*	*Gls*
Tottenham H	2002-03	2	2	0
Todd, Andy		*Apps*	*Subs*	*Gls*
Bolton Wan.	1995-96	9	3	2
Bolton Wan.	1997-98	23	2	0
Charlton Ath	2000-01	19	4	1
Charlton Ath	2001-02	3	2	0
Blackburn R	2002-03	7	5	1
Blackburn R	2003-04	19	0	0
		80	**16**	**4**
Todd, Lee		*Apps*	*Subs*	*Gls*
Southampton	1997-98	9	1	0
Todorov, Svetoslav		*Apps*	*Subs*	*Gls*
West Ham U	2000-01	2	6	1
West Ham U	2001-02	2	4	0
Portsmouth	2003-04	1	0	0
		5	**10**	**1**
Tofting, Stig		*Apps*	*Subs*	*Gls*
Bolton Wan.	2001-02	6	0	0
Bolton Wan.	2002-03	2	6	0
		8	**6**	**0**

Mark Viduka.

Player / Club	Season	Apps	Subs	Gls
Tolson, Neil		*Apps*	*Subs*	*Gls*
Oldham Ath.	1992-93	0	3	0
Tomasson, Jon Dahl		*Apps*	*Subs*	*Gls*
Newcastle U	1997-98	17	6	3
Toure, Kolo		*Apps*	*Subs*	*Gls*
Arsenal	2002-03	9	17	2
Arsenal	2003-04	36	1	1
		45	**18**	**3**
Townsend, Andy		*Apps*	*Subs*	*Gls*
Chelsea	1992-93	41	0	4
Aston Villa	1993-94	32	0	3
Aston Villa	1994-95	32	0	1
Aston Villa	1995-96	32	1	2
Aston Villa	1996-97	34	0	2
Aston Villa	1997-98	3	0	0
Middlesbrough	1998-99	35	0	1
Middlesbrough	1999-00	3	2	0
		212	**3**	**13**
Tracey, Simon		*Apps*	*Subs*	*Gls*
Sheff. Utd.	1992-93	10	0	0
Sheff. Utd.	1993-94	13	2	0
Man. City	1994-95	3	0	0
Norwich C	1994-95	1	0	0
Wimbledon	1995-96	1	0	0
		28	**2**	**0**
Tramezzani, Paolo		*Apps*	*Subs*	*Gls*
Tottenham H	1998-99	6	0	0
Traore, Djimi		*Apps*	*Subs*	*Gls*
Liverpool	2000-01	8	0	0
Liverpool	2002-03	30	2	0
Liverpool	2003-04	7	0	0
		45	**2**	**0**
Trollope, Paul		*Apps*	*Subs*	*Gls*
Derby Co.	1996-97	13	1	1
Derby Co.	1997-98	4	6	0
		17	**7**	**1**
Trustfull, Orlando		*Apps*	*Subs*	*Gls*
Sheff. Wed.	1996-97	9	10	3
Tugay, Kerimoglu		*Apps*	*Subs*	*Gls*
Blackburn R	2001-02	32	1	3
Blackburn R	2002-03	32	5	1
Blackburn R	2003-04	30	6	1
		94	**12**	**5**
Turner, Andy		*Apps*	*Subs*	*Gls*
Tottenham H	1992-93	7	11	3
Tottenham H	1993-94	0	1	0
Tottenham H	1994-95	1	0	0
		8	**12**	**3**
Tuttle, David		*Apps*	*Subs*	*Gls*
Tottenham H	1992-93	4	1	0
Sheff. Utd.	1993-94	31	0	0
Crystal P	1997-98	8	1	0
		43	**2**	**0**
Twigg, Gary		*Apps*	*Subs*	*Gls*
Derby Co.	2001-02	0	1	0
Udeze, Iffy		*Apps*	*Subs*	*Gls*
West Brom	2002-03	7	4	0
Ullathorne, Robert		*Apps*	*Subs*	*Gls*
Norwich C	1993-94	11	5	2
Norwich C	1994-95	27	0	2
Leicester C	1997-98	3	3	1
Leicester C	1998-99	25	0	0
		66	**8**	**5**
Unsal, Hakan		*Apps*	*Subs*	*Gls*
Blackburn R	2001-02	7	1	0
Unsworth, David		*Apps*	*Subs*	*Gls*
Everton	1992-93	3	0	0
Everton	1993-94	7	1	0
Everton	1994-95	37	1	3
Everton	1995-96	28	3	2
Everton	1996-97	32	2	5
West Ham U	1997-98	32	0	2
Everton	1998-99	33	1	1
Everton	1999-00	32	1	6
Everton	2000-01	17	12	5
Everton	2001-02	28	5	3
Everton	2002-03	32	1	5
Everton	2003-04	22	4	3
		303	**31**	**35**
Upson, Matthew		*Apps*	*Subs*	*Gls*
Arsenal	1997-98	5	0	0
Arsenal	1998-99	0	5	0
Arsenal	1999-00	5	3	0
Arsenal	2000-01	0	2	0
Arsenal	2001-02	10	4	0
Birmingham C	2002-03	14	0	0
Birmingham C	2003-04	30	0	0
		64	**14**	**0**
Vaesen, Nico		*Apps*	*Subs*	*Gls*
Birmingham C	2002-03	27	0	0
Valakari, Simo		*Apps*	*Subs*	*Gls*
Derby Co.	2000-01	9	2	1
Derby Co.	2001-02	6	3	0
		15	**5**	**1**
Valery, Patrick		*Apps*	*Subs*	*Gls*
Blackburn R	1997-98	14	1	0
Van Bronckhorst, Giovanni		*Apps*	*Subs*	*Gls*
Arsenal	2001-02	13	8	1
Arsenal	2002-03	9	11	1
		22	**19**	**2**
Van Buyten, Daniel		*Apps*	*Subs*	*Gls*
Man. City	2003-04	5	0	0
Van Den Hauwe, Pat		*Apps*	*Subs*	*Gls*
Tottenham H	1992-93	13	5	0

Player / Club	Season	Apps	Subs	Gls
Van Der Gouw, Raimond		*Apps*	*Subs*	*Gls*
Man. Utd.	1996-97	2	0	0
Man. Utd.	1997-98	4	1	0
Man. Utd.	1998-99	4	1	0
Man. Utd.	1999-00	11	3	0
Man. Utd.	2000-01	5	5	0
Man. Utd.	2001-02	0	1	0
		26	**11**	**0**
Van der Laan, Robin		*Apps*	*Subs*	*Gls*
Derby Co.	1996-97	15	1	2
Derby Co.	1997-98	7	3	0
		22	**4**	**2**
Van der Sar, Edwin		*Apps*	*Subs*	*Gls*
Fulham	2001-02	37	0	0
Fulham	2002-03	19	0	0
Fulham	2003-04	37	0	0
		93	**0**	**0**
Van Gobbel, Ulrich		*Apps*	*Subs*	*Gls*
Southampton	1996-97	24	1	1
Southampton	1997-98	1	1	0
		25	**2**	**1**
Van Hooijdonk, Pierre		*Apps*	*Subs*	*Gls*
Nottm Forest	1996-97	8	0	1
Nottm Forest	1998-99	19	2	6
		27	**2**	**7**
Van Nistelrooy, Ruud		*Apps*	*Subs*	*Gls*
Man. Utd.	2001-02	29	3	23
Man. Utd.	2002-03	33	1	25
Man. Utd.	2003-04	31	1	20
		93	**5**	**68**
Varadi, Imre		*Apps*	*Subs*	*Gls*
Leeds U	1992-93	2	2	1
Varga, Stanislav		*Apps*	*Subs*	*Gls*
Sunderland	2000-01	9	3	1
Sunderland	2001-02	9	0	0
		18	**3**	**1**
Vassell, Darius		*Apps*	*Subs*	*Gls*
Aston Villa	1998-99	0	6	0
Aston Villa	1999-00	1	10	0
Aston Villa	2000-01	5	18	4
Aston Villa	2001-02	30	6	12
Aston Villa	2002-03	28	5	8
Aston Villa	2003-04	26	6	9
		90	**51**	**33**
Vaughan, Tony		*Apps*	*Subs*	*Gls*
Ipswich T	1994-95	10	0	0
Vaz Te, Ricardo		*Apps*	*Subs*	*Gls*
Bolton Wan.	2003-04	0	1	0
Veart, Carl		*Apps*	*Subs*	*Gls*
Crystal P	1997-98	1	5	0
Vega, Ramon		*Apps*	*Subs*	*Gls*
Tottenham H	1996-97	8	0	1
Tottenham H	1997-98	22	3	3
Tottenham H	1998-99	13	3	2
Tottenham H	1999-00	2	3	1
Tottenham H	2000-01	8	2	0
		53	**11**	**7**
Venison, Barry		*Apps*	*Subs*	*Gls*
Newcastle U	1993-94	36	1	0
Newcastle U	1994-95	28	0	1
Southampton	1995-96	21	1	0
Southampton	1996-97	2	0	0
		87	**2**	**1**
Venus, Mark		*Apps*	*Subs*	*Gls*
Ipswich T	2000-01	23	2	3
Ipswich T	2001-02	29	0	1
		52	**2**	**4**
Vernazza, Paolo		*Apps*	*Subs*	*Gls*
Arsenal	1997-98	1	0	0
Arsenal	1999-00	1	1	0
Arsenal	2000-01	0	2	1
		2	**3**	**1**
Veron, Juan Sebastian		*Apps*	*Subs*	*Gls*
Man. Utd.	2001-02	24	2	5
Man. Utd.	2002-03	21	4	2
Chelsea	2003-04	5	2	1
		50	**8**	**8**
Vialli, Gianluca		*Apps*	*Subs*	*Gls*
Chelsea	1996-97	23	5	9
Chelsea	1997-98	14	7	11
Chelsea	1998-99	9	0	1
		46	**12**	**21**
Viana, Hugo		*Apps*	*Subs*	*Gls*
Newcastle U	2002-03	11	12	2
Newcastle U	2003-04	5	11	0
		16	**23**	**2**
Vickers, Steve		*Apps*	*Subs*	*Gls*
Middlesbrough	1995-96	32	0	1
Middlesbrough	1996-97	26	3	0
Middlesbrough	1998-99	30	1	1
Middlesbrough	1999-00	30	2	0
Middlesbrough	2000-01	29	1	0
Middlesbrough	2001-02	2	0	0
Birmingham C	2002-03	5	0	0
		154	**7**	**2**
Vidmar, Tony		*Apps*	*Subs*	*Gls*
Middlesbrough	2002-03	9	3	0
Viduka, Mark		*Apps*	*Subs*	*Gls*
Leeds U	2000-01	34	0	17
Leeds U	2001-02	33	0	11
Leeds U	2002-03	29	4	20
Leeds U	2003-04	30	0	11
		126	**4**	**59**
Vieira, Patrick		*Apps*	*Subs*	*Gls*
Arsenal	1996-97	30	1	2
Arsenal	1997-98	31	2	2

Player / Club	Season	Apps	Subs	Gls
Arsenal	1998-99	34	0	3
Arsenal	1999-00	29	1	2
Arsenal	2000-01	28	2	5
Arsenal	2001-02	35	1	2
Arsenal	2002-03	24	0	3
Arsenal	2003-04	29	0	3
		240	**7**	**22**
Vignal, Gregory		*Apps*	*Subs*	*Gls*
Liverpool	2000-01	4	2	0
Liverpool	2001-02	3	1	0
Liverpool	2002-03	0	1	0
		7	**4**	**0**
Vivas, Nelson		*Apps*	*Subs*	*Gls*
Arsenal	1998-99	10	13	0
Arsenal	1999-00	1	4	0
Arsenal	2000-01	3	9	0
		14	**26**	**0**
Volz, Moritz		*Apps*	*Subs*	*Gls*
Fulham	2003-04	32	1	0
Vonk, Michel		*Apps*	*Subs*	*Gls*
Man. City	1992-93	26	0	2
Man. City	1993-94	34	1	1
Man. City	1994-95	19	2	0
		79	**3**	**3**
Waddle, Chris		*Apps*	*Subs*	*Gls*
Sheff. Wed.	1992-93	32	1	1
Sheff. Wed.	1993-94	19	0	3
Sheff. Wed.	1994-95	20	5	4
Sheff. Wed.	1995-96	23	9	2
Sunderland	1996-97	7	0	1
		101	**15**	**11**
Walker, Des		*Apps*	*Subs*	*Gls*
Sheff. Wed.	1993-94	42	0	0
Sheff. Wed.	1994-95	38	0	0
Sheff. Wed.	1995-96	36	0	0
Sheff. Wed.	1996-97	36	0	0
Sheff. Wed.	1997-98	38	0	0
Sheff. Wed.	1998-99	37	0	0
Sheff. Wed.	1999-00	37	0	0
		264	**0**	**0**
Walker, Ian		*Apps*	*Subs*	*Gls*
Tottenham H	1992-93	17	0	0
Tottenham H	1993-94	10	1	0
Tottenham H	1994-95	41	0	0
Tottenham H	1995-96	38	0	0
Tottenham H	1996-97	37	0	0
Tottenham H	1997-98	29	0	0
Tottenham H	1998-99	25	0	0
Tottenham H	1999-00	38	0	0
Tottenham H	2000-01	3	1	0
Leicester C	2001-02	35	0	0
Leicester C	2003-04	37	0	0
		310	**2**	**0**
Walker, Richard		*Apps*	*Subs*	*Gls*
Aston Villa	1997-98	0	1	0
Aston Villa	1999-00	2	3	2
		2	**4**	**2**
Wallace, Danny		*Apps*	*Subs*	*Gls*
Man. Utd.	1992-93	0	2	0
Wallace, Ray		*Apps*	*Subs*	*Gls*
Leeds U	1992-93	5	1	0
Leeds U	1993-94	0	1	0
		5	**2**	**0**
Wallace, Rod		*Apps*	*Subs*	*Gls*
Leeds U	1992-93	31	1	7
Leeds U	1993-94	34	3	17
Leeds U	1994-95	30	2	4
Leeds U	1995-96	12	12	1
Leeds U	1996-97	17	5	3
Leeds U	1997-98	29	2	10
Bolton Wan.	2001-02	14	5	3
		167	**30**	**45**
Wallemme, Jean-Guy		*Apps*	*Subs*	*Gls*
Coventry C	1998-99	4	2	0
Wallwork, Ronnie		*Apps*	*Subs*	*Gls*
Man. Utd.	1997-98	0	1	0
Man. Utd.	1999-00	0	5	0
Man. Utd.	2000-01	4	8	0
Man. Utd.	2001-02	0	1	0
West Brom	2002-03	23	4	0
		27	**19**	**0**
Walsh, Gary		*Apps*	*Subs*	*Gls*
Oldham Ath.	1993-94	6	0	0
Man. Utd.	1993-94	2	1	0
Man. Utd.	1994-95	10	0	0
Middlesbrough	1995-96	32	0	0
Middlesbrough	1996-97	12	0	0
Bradford C	1999-00	11	0	0
Bradford C	2000-01	19	0	0
Middlesbrough	2000-01	3	0	0
		95	**1**	**0**
Walsh, Paul		*Apps*	*Subs*	*Gls*
Man. City	1993-94	11	0	4
Man. City	1994-95	39	0	12
Man. City	1995-96	3	0	0
		53	**0**	**16**
Walsh, Steve		*Apps*	*Subs*	*Gls*
Leicester C	1994-95	5	0	0
Leicester C	1996-97	22	0	2
Leicester C	1997-98	23	3	3
Leicester C	1998-99	17	5	3
Leicester C	1999-00	5	6	0
Leicester C	2000-01	0	1	0
		72	**15**	**8**
Walters, Jonathan		*Apps*	*Subs*	*Gls*
Bolton Wan.	2002-03	0	4	0

Walters, Mark		Apps	Subs	Gls
Liverpool	1992-93	26	8	11
Liverpool	1993-94	7	10	0
Liverpool	1994-95	7	11	0
Southampton	1995-96	4	1	0
		44	**30**	**11**

Wanchope, Paulo		Apps	Subs	Gls
Derby Co.	1996-97	2	3	1
Derby Co.	1997-98	30	2	13
Derby Co.	1998-99	33	2	9
West Ham U	1999-00	33	2	12
Man. City	2000-01	25	2	9
Man. City	2003-04	12	10	6
		135	**21**	**50**

Wapenaar, Harald		Apps	Subs	Gls
Portsmouth	2003-04	5	0	0

Ward, Ashley		Apps	Subs	Gls
Norwich C	1994-95	25	0	8
Derby Co.	1996-97	25	5	8
Derby Co.	1997-98	2	1	0
Barnsley	1997-98	28	1	8
Blackburn R	1998-99	17	0	5
Bradford C	2000-01	24	9	4
		121	**16**	**33**

Ward, Darren		Apps	Subs	Gls
Watford	1999-00	7	2	1

Ward, Gavin		Apps	Subs	Gls
Leicester C	1994-95	6	0	0
Bolton Wan.	1995-96	5	0	0
Bolton Wan.	1997-98	4	2	0
		15	**2**	**0**

Ward, Mark		Apps	Subs	Gls
Everton	1992-93	19	0	1
Everton	1993-94	26	1	1
		45	**1**	**2**

Ward, Mitch		Apps	Subs	Gls
Sheff. Utd.	1992-93	22	4	0
Sheff. Utd.	1993-94	20	2	1
Everton	1997-98	8	0	0
Everton	1998-99	4	2	0
Everton	1999-00	6	4	0
		60	**12**	**1**

Warhurst, Paul		Apps	Subs	Gls
Sheff. Wed.	1992-93	25	4	6
Sheff. Wed.	1993-94	4	0	0
Blackburn R	1993-94	4	5	0
Blackburn R	1994-95	20	7	2
Blackburn R	1995-96	1	9	0
Blackburn R	1996-97	5	6	2
Crystal P	1997-98	22	0	3
Bolton Wan.	2001-02	25	0	0
Bolton Wan.	2002-03	5	2	0
		111	**33**	**13**

Wark, John		Apps	Subs	Gls
Ipswich T	1992-93	36	1	6
Ipswich T	1993-94	38	0	3
Ipswich T	1994-95	26	0	4
		100	**1**	**13**

Warner, Phil		Apps	Subs	Gls
Southampton	1997-98	0	1	0
Southampton	1998-99	5	0	0
		5	**1**	**0**

Warner, Vance		Apps	Subs	Gls
Nottm Forest	1994-95	1	0	0
Nottm Forest	1996-97	2	1	0
		3	**1**	**0**

Warren, Christer		Apps	Subs	Gls
Southampton	1995-96	1	6	0
Southampton	1996-97	0	1	0
		1	**7**	**0**

Warzycha, Robert		Apps	Subs	Gls
Everton	1992-93	15	5	1
Everton	1993-94	3	4	0
		18	**9**	**1**

Watkinson, Russ		Apps	Subs	Gls
Southampton	1996-97	0	2	0

Watson, Dave		Apps	Subs	Gls
Everton	1992-93	40	0	1
Everton	1993-94	27	1	1
Everton	1994-95	38	0	2
Everton	1995-96	34	0	1
Everton	1996-97	29	0	1
Everton	1997-98	25	1	0
Everton	1998-99	22	0	0
Everton	1999-00	5	1	0
		220	**3**	**6**

Watson, David		Apps	Subs	Gls
Barnsley	1997-98	30	0	0

Watson, Gordon		Apps	Subs	Gls
Sheff. Wed.	1992-93	4	7	1
Sheff. Wed.	1993-94	15	8	12
Sheff. Wed.	1994-95	5	18	2
Southampton	1994-95	12	0	3
Southampton	1995-96	18	7	3
Southampton	1996-97	7	8	2
		61	**48**	**23**

Watson, Kevin		Apps	Subs	Gls
Tottenham H	1992-93	4	1	0

Watson, Mark		Apps	Subs	Gls
West Ham U	1995-96	0	1	0

Watson, Steve		Apps	Subs	Gls
Newcastle U	1993-94	29	3	2
Newcastle U	1994-95	22	5	4
Newcastle U	1995-96	15	8	3
Newcastle U	1996-97	33	3	1
Newcastle U	1997-98	27	2	1
Newcastle U	1998-99	7	0	0
Aston Villa	1998-99	26	1	0
Aston Villa	1999-00	13	1	0
Everton	2000-01	34	0	0
Everton	2001-02	24	1	4
Everton	2002-03	14	4	5
Everton	2003-04	22	2	5
		266	**30**	**25**

Watts, Grant		Apps	Subs	Gls
Crystal P	1992-93	2	2	0

Watts, Julian		Apps	Subs	Gls
Sheff. Wed.	1992-93	2	2	0
Sheff. Wed.	1993-94	1	0	0
Sheff. Wed.	1995-96	9	2	1
Leicester C	1996-97	22	4	1
Leicester C	1997-98	0	3	0
		34	**11**	**2**

Weah, George		Apps	Subs	Gls
Chelsea	1999-00	9	2	3
Man. City	2000-01	5	2	1
		14	**4**	**4**

Weaver, Nicky		Apps	Subs	Gls
Man. City	2000-01	31	0	0

Webb, Neil		Apps	Subs	Gls
Man. Utd.	1992-93	0	1	0
Nottm Forest	1992-93	9	0	0
		9	**1**	**0**

Webster, Simon		Apps	Subs	Gls
West Ham U	1994-95	0	5	0

Wegerle, Roy		Apps	Subs	Gls
Blackburn R	1992-93	11	11	4
Coventry C	1992-93	5	1	0
Coventry C	1993-94	20	1	6
Coventry C	1994-95	21	5	3
		57	**18**	**13**

Weir, David		Apps	Subs	Gls
Everton	1998-99	11	3	0
Everton	1999-00	35	0	2
Everton	2000-01	37	0	1
Everton	2001-02	36	0	4
Everton	2002-03	27	4	0
Everton	2003-04	9	1	0
		155	**8**	**7**

Welsh, John		Apps	Subs	Gls
Liverpool	2003-04	0	1	0

West, Taribo		Apps	Subs	Gls
Derby Co.	2000-01	18	0	0

Westerveld, Sander		Apps	Subs	Gls
Liverpool	1999-00	36	0	0
Liverpool	2000-01	38	0	0
Liverpool	2001-02	1	0	0
		75	**0**	**0**

Weston, Rhys		Apps	Subs	Gls
Arsenal	1999-00	1	0	0

Westwood, Ashley		Apps	Subs	Gls
Bradford C	1999-00	1	4	0

Wetherall, David		Apps	Subs	Gls
Leeds U	1992-93	13	0	1
Leeds U	1993-94	31	1	1
Leeds U	1994-95	38	0	3
Leeds U	1995-96	34	0	4
Leeds U	1996-97	25	4	0
Leeds U	1997-98	33	1	3
Leeds U	1998-99	14	7	0
Bradford C	1999-00	38	0	2
Bradford C	2000-01	18	0	1
		244	**13**	**15**

Whalley, Gareth		Apps	Subs	Gls
Bradford C	1999-00	16	0	1
Bradford C	2000-01	17	2	0
		33	**2**	**1**

Whelan, Noel		Apps	Subs	Gls
Leeds U	1992-93	1	0	0
Leeds U	1993-94	6	10	0
Leeds U	1994-95	18	5	7
Leeds U	1995-96	3	5	0
Coventry C	1995-96	21	0	8
Coventry C	1996-97	34	1	6
Coventry C	1997-98	21	0	6
Coventry C	1998-99	31	0	10
Coventry C	1999-00	20	6	1
Middlesbrough	2000-01	13	14	0
Middlesbrough	2001-02	18	1	4
Middlesbrough	2002-03	2	13	1
		188	**55**	**43**

Whelan, Phil		Apps	Subs	Gls
Ipswich T	1992-93	28	4	0
Ipswich T	1993-94	28	1	0
Ipswich T	1994-95	12	1	0
Middlesbrough	1995-96	9	4	1
Middlesbrough	1996-97	9	0	0
		86	**10**	**1**

Whelan, Ronnie		Apps	Subs	Gls
Liverpool	1992-93	17	0	1
Liverpool	1993-94	23	0	1
		40	**0**	**2**

Whiston, Peter		Apps	Subs	Gls
Southampton	1994-95	0	1	0

Whitbread, Adrian		Apps	Subs	Gls
Swindon T	1993-94	34	1	1
West Ham U	1994-95	3	5	0
West Ham U	1995-96	0	2	0
		37	**8**	**1**

White, David		Apps	Subs	Gls
Man. City	1992-93	42	0	16
Man. City	1993-94	16	0	1
Leeds U	1993-94	9	6	5
Leeds U	1994-95	18	5	3
Leeds U	1995-96	1	3	1
		86	**14**	**26**

White, Devon		Apps	Subs	Gls
QPR	1992-93	3	4	2
QPR	1993-94	12	6	7
QPR	1994-95	1	0	0
		16	**10**	**9**

White, Steve		Apps	Subs	Gls
Swindon T	1993-94	2	4	0

Whitehouse, Dane		Apps	Subs	Gls
Sheff. Utd.	1992-93	14	0	5
Sheff. Utd.	1993-94	35	3	5
		49	**3**	**10**

Whitley, Jeff		Apps	Subs	Gls
Man. City	2000-01	28	3	1

Whitlow, Mike		Apps	Subs	Gls
Leicester C	1994-95	28	0	2
Leicester C	1996-97	14	3	0
Bolton Wan.	1997-98	13	0	0
Bolton Wan.	2001-02	28	1	0
Bolton Wan.	2002-03	14	3	0
		97	**7**	**2**

Whittingham, Guy		Apps	Subs	Gls
Aston Villa	1993-94	13	5	3
Aston Villa	1994-95	4	3	2
Sheff. Wed.	1994-95	16	5	9
Sheff. Wed.	1995-96	27	2	6
Sheff. Wed.	1996-97	29	4	3
Sheff. Wed.	1997-98	17	11	4
Sheff. Wed.	1998-99	1	1	0
		107	**31**	**27**

Whittingham, Pete		Apps	Subs	Gls
Aston Villa	2002-03	1	3	0
Aston Villa	2003-04	20	12	0
		21	**15**	**0**

Whitton, Steve		Apps	Subs	Gls
Ipswich T	1992-93	20	4	3
Ipswich T	1993-94	7	4	1
		27	**8**	**4**

Whyte, Chris		Apps	Subs	Gls
Leeds U	1992-93	34	0	1
Coventry C	1995-96	1	0	0
		35	**0**	**1**

Whyte, Derek		Apps	Subs	Gls
Middlesbrough	1992-93	34	1	0
Middlesbrough	1995-96	24	1	0
Middlesbrough	1996-97	20	1	0
		78	**3**	**0**

Widdrington, Tommy		Apps	Subs	Gls
Southampton	1992-93	11	1	0
Southampton	1993-94	11	0	1
Southampton	1994-95	23	5	0
Southampton	1995-96	20	1	2
		65	**7**	**3**

Wiekens, Gerard		Apps	Subs	Gls
Man. City	2000-01	29	5	2
Man. City	2002-03	5	1	0
		34	**6**	**2**

Wijnhard, Clyde		Apps	Subs	Gls
Leeds U	1998-99	11	7	3

Wilcox, Jason		Apps	Subs	Gls
Blackburn R	1992-93	31	2	4
Blackburn R	1993-94	31	2	6
Blackburn R	1994-95	27	0	5
Blackburn R	1995-96	10	0	3
Blackburn R	1996-97	26	2	2
Blackburn R	1997-98	24	7	4
Blackburn R	1998-99	28	2	3
Leeds U	1999-00	15	5	3
Leeds U	2000-01	7	10	0
Leeds U	2001-02	4	9	0
Leeds U	2002-03	23	2	1
Leeds U	2003-04	3	3	0
		229	**44**	**31**

Wilkins, Ray		Apps	Subs	Gls
QPR	1992-93	27	0	2
QPR	1993-94	39	0	1
QPR	1994-95	1	1	0
Crystal P	1994-95	1	0	0
QPR	1995-96	11	4	0
		79	**5**	**3**

Wilkinson, Paul		Apps	Subs	Gls
Middlesbrough	1992-93	41	0	13
Middlesbrough	1995-96	2	1	0
Barnsley	1997-98	3	1	0
		46	**2**	**13**

Wilkshire, Luke		Apps	Subs	Gls
Middlesbrough	2001-02	6	1	0
Middlesbrough	2002-03	7	7	0
		13	**8**	**0**

Willems, Ron		Apps	Subs	Gls
Derby Co.	1996-97	7	9	2
Derby Co.	1997-98	3	7	0
		10	**16**	**2**

Williams, Andy		Apps	Subs	Gls
Southampton	1997-98	3	17	0
Southampton	1998-99	0	1	0
		3	**18**	**0**

Williams, Brett		Apps	Subs	Gls
Nottm Forest	1992-93	9	0	0

Williams, Darren		Apps	Subs	Gls
Sunderland	1996-97	10	1	2
Sunderland	1999-00	13	12	0
Sunderland	2000-01	21	7	0
Sunderland	2001-02	23	5	0
Sunderland	2002-03	12	4	0
		79	**29**	**2**

Paul Williams.

Williams, Geraint		Apps	Subs	Gls
Ipswich T	1992-93	37	0	0
Ipswich T	1993-94	34	0	0
Ipswich T	1994-95	38	0	1
		109	**0**	**1**

Williams, John		Apps	Subs	Gls
Coventry C	1992-93	38	3	8
Coventry C	1993-94	27	5	3
Coventry C	1994-95	1	6	0
		66	**14**	**11**

Williams, Mark		Apps	Subs	Gls
Watford	1999-00	20	2	1

Williams, Mike		Apps	Subs	Gls
Sheff. Wed.	1992-93	2	1	0
Sheff. Wed.	1993-94	4	0	0
Sheff. Wed.	1994-95	8	2	1
Sheff. Wed.	1995-96	2	3	0
Sheff. Wed.	1996-97	0	1	0
		16	**7**	**1**

Williams, Paul		Apps	Subs	Gls
Coventry C	1992-93	1	1	0

Williams, Paul		Apps	Subs	Gls
Sheff. Wed.	1992-93	7	0	1
Crystal P	1992-93	15	3	0
Crystal P	1994-95	2	2	0
		24	**5**	**1**

Williams, Paul		Apps	Subs	Gls
Coventry C	1995-96	30	2	2
Coventry C	1996-97	29	3	2
Coventry C	1997-98	17	3	0
Coventry C	1998-99	20	2	0
Coventry C	1999-00	26	2	1
Coventry C	2000-01	27	3	0
Southampton	2001-02	27	1	0
Southampton	2002-03	10	1	0
		186	**17**	**5**

Williams, Paul		Apps	Subs	Gls
Coventry C	1993-94	3	6	0
Coventry C	1994-95	5	0	0
		8	**6**	**0**

Williamson, Danny		Apps	Subs	Gls
West Ham U	1993-94	2	1	1
West Ham U	1994-95	4	0	0
West Ham U	1995-96	28	1	4
West Ham U	1996-97	13	2	0
Everton	1997-98	15	0	0
		62	**4**	**5**

Williamson, Tom		Apps	Subs	Gls
Leicester C	2001-02	0	1	0

Willis, Jimmy		Apps	Subs	Gls
Leicester C	1994-95	29	0	2

Willock, Calum		Apps	Subs	Gls
Fulham	2001-02	0	2	0
Fulham	2002-03	0	2	0
		0	**4**	**0**

Wilmot, Rhys		Apps	Subs	Gls
Crystal P	1994-95	5	1	0

Wilmott, Chris		Apps	Subs	Gls
Wimbledon	1999-00	7	0	0

Wilnis, Fabian		Apps	Subs	Gls
Ipswich T	2000-01	27	2	2
Ipswich T	2001-02	6	8	0
		33	**10**	**2**

Wilson, Clive		Apps	Subs	Gls
QPR	1992-93	41	0	3
QPR	1993-94	42	0	3
QPR	1994-95	36	0	2
Tottenham H	1995-96	28	0	0
Tottenham H	1996-97	23	3	1
Tottenham H	1997-98	16	0	0
		186	**3**	**9**

Wilson, Danny
Club	Season	Apps	Subs	Gls
Sheff. Wed.	1992-93	21	5	2

Wilson, Mark
Club	Season	Apps	Subs	Gls
Man. Utd.	1999-00	1	2	0
Middlesbrough	2001-02	2	8	0
Middlesbrough	2002-03	4	2	0
		7	**12**	**0**

Wilson, Stuart
Club	Season	Apps	Subs	Gls
Leicester C	1996-97	0	2	1
Leicester C	1997-98	0	11	2
Leicester C	1998-99	1	8	0
		1	**21**	**3**

Wilson, Terry
Club	Season	Apps	Subs	Gls
Nottm Forest	1992-93	5	0	0

Wiltord, Sylvain
Club	Season	Apps	Subs	Gls
Arsenal	2000-01	20	7	8
Arsenal	2001-02	23	10	10
Arsenal	2002-03	27	7	10
Arsenal	2003-04	8	4	3
		78	**28**	**31**

Windass, Dean
Club	Season	Apps	Subs	Gls
Bradford C	1999-00	36	2	10
Bradford C	2000-01	22	2	3
Middlesbrough	2000-01	8	0	2
Middlesbrough	2001-02	8	19	1
Middlesbrough	2002-03	0	2	0
		74	**25**	**16**

Winterburn, Nigel
Club	Season	Apps	Subs	Gls
Arsenal	1992-93	29	0	1
Arsenal	1993-94	34	0	0
Arsenal	1994-95	39	0	0
Arsenal	1995-96	36	0	2
Arsenal	1996-97	38	0	0
Arsenal	1997-98	35	1	1
Arsenal	1998-99	30	0	0
Arsenal	1999-00	19	9	0
West Ham U	2000-01	33	0	1
West Ham U	2001-02	29	2	0
West Ham U	2002-03	16	2	0
		338	**14**	**5**

Wirmola, Jonas
Club	Season	Apps	Subs	Gls
Sheff. Utd.	1993-94	8	0	0

Wise, Dennis
Club	Season	Apps	Subs	Gls
Chelsea	1992-93	27	0	3
Chelsea	1993-94	35	0	4
Chelsea	1994-95	18	1	6
Chelsea	1995-96	34	1	7
Chelsea	1996-97	27	4	3
Chelsea	1997-98	26	0	3
Chelsea	1998-99	21	1	0
Chelsea	1999-00	29	1	4
Chelsea	2000-01	35	1	3
Leicester C	2001-02	15	2	1
		267	**11**	**34**

Witschge, Richard
Club	Season	Apps	Subs	Gls
Blackburn R	1994-95	1	0	0

Witter, Tony
Club	Season	Apps	Subs	Gls
QPR	1993-94	1	0	0

Woan, Ian
Club	Season	Apps	Subs	Gls
Nottm Forest	1992-93	27	1	3
Nottm Forest	1994-95	35	2	5
Nottm Forest	1995-96	33	0	8
Nottm Forest	1996-97	29	3	1
Nottm Forest	1998-99	0	2	0
		124	**8**	**17**

Wolleaston, Robert
Club	Season	Apps	Subs	Gls
Chelsea	1999-00	0	1	0

Wome, Pierre
Club	Season	Apps	Subs	Gls
Fulham	2002-03	13	1	1

Wood, Steve
Club	Season	Apps	Subs	Gls
Southampton	1992-93	4	0	0
Southampton	1993-94	27	0	0
		31	**0**	**0**

Woodgate, Jonathan
Club	Season	Apps	Subs	Gls
Leeds U	1998-99	25	0	2
Leeds U	1999-00	32	2	1
Leeds U	2000-01	14	0	1
Leeds U	2001-02	11	2	0
Leeds U	2002-03	18	0	0
Newcastle U	2002-03	10	0	0
Newcastle U	2003-04	18	0	0
		128	**4**	**4**

Woodhouse, Curtis
Club	Season	Apps	Subs	Gls
Birmingham C	2002-03	0	3	0

Woods, Chris
Club	Season	Apps	Subs	Gls
Sheff. Wed.	1992-93	39	0	0
Sheff. Wed.	1993-94	10	0	0
Sheff. Wed.	1994-95	8	1	0
Sheff. Wed.	1995-96	8	0	0
Southampton	1996-97	4	0	0
		69	**1**	**0**

Woodthorpe, Colin
Club	Season	Apps	Subs	Gls
Norwich C	1992-93	5	2	0
Norwich C	1993-94	18	2	0
		23	**4**	**0**

Wooter, Nordin
Club	Season	Apps	Subs	Gls
Watford	1999-00	16	4	1

Worthington, Nigel
Club	Season	Apps	Subs	Gls
Sheff. Wed.	1992-93	40	0	1
Sheff. Wed.	1993-94	30	1	1
Leeds U	1994-95	21	6	1
Leeds U	1995-96	12	4	0
		103	**11**	**3**

Wreh, Christopher
Club	Season	Apps	Subs	Gls
Arsenal	1997-98	7	9	3
Arsenal	1998-99	3	9	0
		10	**18**	**3**

Wright, Alan
Club	Season	Apps	Subs	Gls
Blackburn R	1992-93	24	0	0
Blackburn R	1993-94	7	5	0
Blackburn R	1994-95	4	1	0
Aston Villa	1994-95	8	0	0
Aston Villa	1995-96	38	0	2
Aston Villa	1996-97	38	0	1
Aston Villa	1997-98	35	2	0
Aston Villa	1998-99	38	0	0
Aston Villa	1999-00	31	1	1
Aston Villa	2000-01	35	1	1
Aston Villa	2001-02	23	0	0
Aston Villa	2002-03	9	1	0
Middlesbrough	2003-04	2	0	0
		292	**11**	**5**

Wright, Ian
Club	Season	Apps	Subs	Gls
Arsenal	1992-93	30	1	15
Arsenal	1993-94	39	0	23
Arsenal	1994-95	30	1	18
Arsenal	1995-96	31	0	15
Arsenal	1996-97	30	5	23
Arsenal	1997-98	22	2	10
West Ham U	1998-99	20	2	9
		202	**11**	**113**

Wright, Johnny
Club	Season	Apps	Subs	Gls
Norwich C	1994-95	1	1	0
Ipswich T	2000-01	35	2	2
Ipswich T	2001-02	24	5	1
		60	**8**	**3**

Wright, Mark
Club	Season	Apps	Subs	Gls
Liverpool	1992-93	32	1	2
Liverpool	1993-94	31	0	1
Liverpool	1994-95	5	1	0
Liverpool	1995-96	28	0	2
Liverpool	1996-97	33	0	0
Liverpool	1997-98	6	0	0
		135	**2**	**5**

Wright, Nick
Club	Season	Apps	Subs	Gls
Watford	1999-00	1	3	0

Wright, Richard
Club	Season	Apps	Subs	Gls
Ipswich T	1994-95	3	0	0
Ipswich T	2000-01	36	0	0
Arsenal	2001-02	12	0	0
Everton	2002-03	33	0	0
Everton	2003-04	4	0	0
		88	**0**	**0**

Wright, Stephen
Club	Season	Apps	Subs	Gls
Liverpool	2000-01	0	2	0
Liverpool	2001-02	10	2	0
Sunderland	2002-03	25	1	0
		35	**5**	**0**

Wright, Tommy
Club	Season	Apps	Subs	Gls
Leicester C	2001-02	0	1	0

Wright, Tommy
Club	Season	Apps	Subs	Gls
Middlesbrough	1992-93	34	2	5

Wright, Tommy
Club	Season	Apps	Subs	Gls
Newcastle U	1993-94	2	1	0
Nottm Forest	1996-97	1	0	0
Newcastle U	1999-00	3	0	0
Man. City	2000-01	1	0	0
		7	**1**	**0**

Wright-Phillips, Shaun
Club	Season	Apps	Subs	Gls
Man. City	2000-01	9	6	0
Man. City	2002-03	23	8	1
Man. City	2003-04	32	2	7
		64	**16**	**8**

Xavier, Abel
Club	Season	Apps	Subs	Gls
Everton	1999-00	18	2	0
Everton	2000-01	10	1	0
Everton	2001-02	11	1	0
Liverpool	2001-02	9	1	1
Liverpool	2002-03	4	0	0
		52	**5**	**1**

Yallop, Frank
Club	Season	Apps	Subs	Gls
Ipswich T	1992-93	5	1	2
Ipswich T	1993-94	2	5	0
Ipswich T	1994-95	41	0	1
		48	**6**	**3**

Yates, Dean
Club	Season	Apps	Subs	Gls
Derby Co.	1996-97	8	2	0
Derby Co.	1997-98	8	1	0
		16	**3**	**0**

Yates, Steve
Club	Season	Apps	Subs	Gls
QPR	1993-94	27	2	0
QPR	1994-95	22	1	1
QPR	1995-96	30	0	0
		79	**3**	**1**

Yeates, Mark
Club	Season	Apps	Subs	Gls
Tottenham H	2003-04	1	0	0

Yeboah, Tony
Club	Season	Apps	Subs	Gls
Leeds U	1994-95	16	2	12
Leeds U	1995-96	22	0	12
Leeds U	1996-97	6	1	0
		44	**3**	**24**

Yobo, Joseph
Club	Season	Apps	Subs	Gls
Everton	2002-03	22	2	0
Everton	2003-04	27	1	2
		49	**3**	**2**

Yordi (Gonzalez Diaz)
Club	Season	Apps	Subs	Gls
Blackburn R	2001-02	5	3	2

Yorke, Dwight
Club	Season	Apps	Subs	Gls
Aston Villa	1992-93	22	5	6
Aston Villa	1993-94	2	10	2
Aston Villa	1994-95	33	4	6
Aston Villa	1995-96	35	0	17
Aston Villa	1996-97	37	0	17
Aston Villa	1997-98	30	0	12
Aston Villa	1998-99	1	0	0
Man. Utd.	1998-99	32	0	18
Man. Utd.	1999-00	29	3	20
Man. Utd.	2000-01	15	7	8
Man. Utd.	2001-02	4	6	1
Blackburn R	2002-03	25	8	8
Blackburn R	2003-04	15	8	4
		280	**51**	**119**

Youds, Eddie
Club	Season	Apps	Subs	Gls
Ipswich T	1992-93	10	6	0
Ipswich T	1993-94	18	5	1
Ipswich T	1994-95	9	1	0
Charlton Ath	1998-99	21	1	2
		58	**13**	**3**

Young, Eric
Club	Season	Apps	Subs	Gls
Crystal P	1992-93	38	0	6
Crystal P	1994-95	13	0	0
		51	**0**	**6**

Young, Luke
Club	Season	Apps	Subs	Gls
Tottenham H	1998-99	14	1	0
Tottenham H	1999-00	11	9	0
Tottenham H	2000-01	19	4	0
Charlton Ath	2001-02	34	0	0
Charlton Ath	2002-03	29	3	0
Charlton Ath	2003-04	21	3	0
		128	**20**	**0**

Christian Ziege.

Zagorakis, Theo
Club	Season	Apps	Subs	Gls
Leicester C	1997-98	12	2	1
Leicester C	1998-99	16	3	1
Leicester C	1999-00	6	11	1
		34	**16**	**3**

Zamora, Bobby
Club	Season	Apps	Subs	Gls
Tottenham H	2003-04	6	10	0

Zavagno, Luciano
Club	Season	Apps	Subs	Gls
Derby Co.	2001-02	26	0	0

Zelic, Ned
Club	Season	Apps	Subs	Gls
QPR	1995-96	3	1	0

Zenden, Boudewijn
Club	Season	Apps	Subs	Gls
Chelsea	2001-02	13	9	3
Chelsea	2002-03	11	10	1
Middlesbrough	2003-04	31	0	4
		55	**19**	**8**

Ziege, Christian
Club	Season	Apps	Subs	Gls
Middlesbrough	1999-00	29	0	6
Liverpool	2000-01	11	5	1
Tottenham H	2001-02	27	0	5
Tottenham H	2002-03	10	2	2
Tottenham H	2003-04	7	1	0
		84	**8**	**14**

Zivkovic, Boris
Club	Season	Apps	Subs	Gls
Portsmouth	2003-04	17	1	0

Zohar, Itzy
Club	Season	Apps	Subs	Gls
Crystal P	1997-98	2	4	0

Zola, Gianfranco
Club	Season	Apps	Subs	Gls
Chelsea	1996-97	22	1	8
Chelsea	1997-98	23	4	8
Chelsea	1998-99	25	8	8
Chelsea	1999-00	25	8	4
Chelsea	2000-01	31	5	9
Chelsea	2001-02	19	16	3
Chelsea	2002-03	30	8	14
		185	**44**	**59**

Zuniga, Ysrael
Club	Season	Apps	Subs	Gls
Coventry C	1999-00	3	4	2
Coventry C	2000-01	7	8	1
		10	**12**	**3**